Work and Life Integration

Organizational, Cultural, and Individual Perspectives

D0888917

LEA's Organization and Management Series

Series Editors
Arthur P. Brief, *Tulane University*
James P. Walsh, *University of Michigan*

Associate Series Editors
P. Christopher Earley, *Indiana University*
Sara L. Rynes, *University of Iowa*

Ashforth (Au.) • *Role Transitions in Organizational Life: An Identity-Based Perspective*

Bartunek (Au.) • *Organizational and Educational Change: The Life and Role of a Change Agent Group*

Beach (Ed.) • *Image Theory: Theoretical and Empirical Foundations*

Brett/Drasgow (Eds.) • *The Psychology of Work: Theoretically Based Empirical Research*

Darley/Messick/Tyler (Eds.) • *Social Influences on Ethical Behavior in Organizations*

Denison (Ed.) • *Managing Organizational Change in Transition Economies*

Earley/Gibson (Aus.) • *Multinational Work Teams: A New Perspective*

Garud/Karnoe (Eds.) • *Path Dependence and Creation*

Jacoby (Au.) • *Employing Bureaucracy: Managers, Unions, and the Transformation of Work in the 20th Century, Revised Edition*

Kossek/Lambert (Eds.) • *Work and Life Integration: Organizational, Cultural, and Individual Perspectives*

Lant/Shapira (Eds.) • *Organizational Cognition: Computation and Interpretation*

Lord/Brown (Aus.) • *Leadership Processes and Follower Self-Identity*

Margolis/Walsh (Aus.) • *People and Profits? The Search Between a Company's Social and Financial Performance*

Messick/Kramer (Eds.) • *The Psychology of Leadership: Some New Approaches*

Pearce (Au.) • *Organization and Management in the Embrace of the Government*

Peterson/Mannix (Eds.) • *Leading and Managing People in the Dynamic Organization*

Riggio/Murphy/Pirozzolo (Eds.) • *Multiple Intelligences and Leadership*

Schneider/Smith (Eds.) • *Personality and Organizations*

Thompson/Levine/Messick (Eds.) • *Shared Cognition in Organizations: The Management of Knowledge*

LEA's Series in Applied Psychology

Series Editors
Edwin A. Fleishman, *George Mason University*
Jeanette N. Cleveland, *Pennsylvania State University*

WORK AND
LIFE INTEGRATION

Organizational, Cultural, and
Individual Perspectives

Edited by

Ellen Ernst Kossek
Michigan State University

Susan J. Lambert
The University of Chicago

LEA LAWRENCE ERLBAUM ASSOCIATES, PUBLISHERS
2005 Mahwah, New Jersey   London

Senior Acquisitions Editor:	Anne Duffy
Editorial Assistant:	Kristin Duch
Cover Design:	Sean Trane Sciarrone
Textbook Production Manager:	Paul Smolenski
Full-Service Compositor:	Westchester Book Services
Text and Cover Printer:	Sheridan Books, Inc.

This book was typset in 10/12 pt. Times, Italic, Bold and Bold Italic.
The heads are typeset in Americana, Americana Italic, Americana Bold,
and Americana, Bold Italic.

Lawrence Erlbaum Associates, Inc., Publishers
10 Industrial Avenue
Mahwah, New Jersey 07430
www.erlbaum.com

Library of Congress Cataloging-in-Publication Data

Work and life integration : organizational, cultural, and individual perspectives/
    edited by Ellen Ernst Kossek, Susan J. Lambert ; foreword by Linda K. Stroh.
        p. cm.—(LEA's organization and management series) (Series in applied
    psychology)
    Papers from a conference.
    Includes bibliographical references and indexes.
    ISBN 0-8058-4615-8 (alk. paper) — ISBN 0-8058-4616-6 (pbk. : alk. paper)
    1. Work and family—Congresses. 2. Organizational change—Congresses.
    3. Family policy—Congresses. I. Kossek, Ellen Ernst. II. Lambert, Susan J.
    III. Series. IV. Series: Series in applied psychology

HD4904.25.W663   2005
306.3'6—dc22   2004057709

Books published by Lawrence Erlbaum Associates are printed on acid-free paper, and
their bindings are chosen for strength and durability.

Printed in the United States of America
10   9   8   7   6   5   4   3   2

To my family, who are my blessings: my wonderful husband, Sandy; my awe-inspiring children, Andrew, Sarah, Haley, and Dylan; and my parents Ann and Dan, who raised me with love.

—Ellen Ernst Kossek
East Lansing, Michigan

To my husband, Lee, and my daughter, Eleanor, who make sure I have ample opportunity to experience personally the challenges of balancing work and family.

—Susan J. Lambert
Chicago, Illinois

We also dedicate this book to Susan C. Eaton, who was on the faculty of the Kennedy School of Government at Harvard University and who died at the end of 2003. Her scholarship exemplifies research that contributes to both theory and practice on work-life issues.

Contents

ix

Series Foreword

Arthur P. Brief
Tulane University

James P. Walsh
University of Michigan

To many, Rosebeth Moss Kanter's 1977 monograph *Work and Family in the United States* set the agenda for the study of the interplay between our family and work lives. One could view Ellen Ernst Kossek and Susan J. Lambert's provocative collection of chapters as a report card on how much we have learned in the last 25 years and as a statement of what our research agenda ought to be in the next quarter century. Particularly impressive is the degree to which the collection blurs traditional disciplinary boundaries among sociology, psychology, and economics, offering a rich account of family-work scholarship. Equally praiseworthy is that the contributors to the volume have not shied away from asserting the policy implications of their findings. Thus the book not only should enlighten our research community, but it also, appropriately so, should inform public debates on how workplaces can be made more family sensitive. We are very pleased to have Kossek and Lambert join our series.

Series Foreword

Jeanette N. Cleveland
Pennsylvania State University

Edwin A. Fleishman
George Mason University

We are excited that the book *Work and Life Integration: Organizational, Cultural, and Individual perspectives,* edited by Ellen Ernst Kossek and Susan Lambert, appears in both LEA's Series in Applied Psychology and the Organization and Management Series. It is one of the first books to be celebrated in both series and it is very aptly placed. Family and work continue to be two important domains of our lives, and the interactions of them are critically important to both psychologists and managers. Research in this area increasingly is multidisciplinary, addressing the needs and health of workers, families, and their organizations. The chapters in Kossek and Lambert examine work and family from a diversity of fields, including psychology, sociology, and economics, as well as from multiple levels of focus (individual, family, organizational, and government policy). The contributors to the volume illustrate that we have come a long way from viewing work and family issues as a woman's problem or as an individual employee issue. Rather, these contributors identify public policy implications of the research they describe and show how organizations can be pivotal partners with employees, families, the community, and government agencies in fostering the positive integration of work and life.

Foreword

Linda K. Stroh
Loyola University

Work-family researchers have had much success in encouraging both organizations and individuals to recognize the importance of achieving greater balance in our lives. We now understand how the imbalance is detrimental to the organization in terms of effectiveness and efficiency and to the individual in terms of stress, quality of life, and also our own personal effectiveness and efficiency. While we now better understand the *problems* surrounding work-life integration, we are far from providing the necessary *solutions* to create a sense of work-life equilibrium.

At the heart of the work-life problem is the increasing complexity of our modern lives. In many ways, we have unlimited work, family, and life opportunities. While these opportunities have created more choices, they have also created greater uncertainty. At the onset of the industrial revolution families were primarily male-headed households. With that predominant family form, structuring our lives and our organizations to accommodate the family form was, in comparison, reasonably simple. Fortunately, society has evolved far from that anachronistic notion of just one family form and the worker's role within this structure. Unfortunately, this progress and consequent variation in family forms and organizational structures have brought with them a plethora of options and decisions and have increased greatly the uncertainty in our lives.

Interestingly, the recent technological advances that have resulted in enormous industrial progress could have led to organizational structures that allowed greater balance, given the intrinsic flexible nature of technology. Yet, much of the current research suggests that our new technological/information society has created more, not less, complexity and, yes, even more uncertainty in our lives.

My desire to work in academia began with an interest in helping organizations and families find better ways to relocate employees and their families throughout the United States and the world. Through my own life experiences, I knew there had to be a way to help families deal with this major stress in their lives. I have seen firsthand the challenges families encounter as they attempt to build careers, build their families, and create an equilibrium in their lives between what they want for their families and what they want for their careers and the workplace; it is very evident that these two "wants" are often in conflict. Now, decades later, while the challenges and barriers that continue to have an impact on all of our lives may take different forms, it does not take a systematic research study to realize that most members of industrialized economies are still struggling with how to achieve a work-life balance while excelling in the workplace and devoting maximum attention to their families.

This volume addresses the intersect between work, life, and family in new and interesting ways, and it should convince even those steeped in work-life integration research of the importance of this volume to this field. It is clearly a must-read for both practitioners and academics interested in seeking ways to create meaningful lives. The volume addresses current-day challenges of dealing with work-life integration issues and sets the stage for future research agendas.

Acknowledgments

Writing and editing a book is a major multiyear endeavor that requires substantial resources, such as time to do the work and be creative, financing, and administrative support. The editors are grateful to Michigan State University and the University of Chicago for the resources provided to support our work on this volume. At Michigan State, Hiram Fitzgerald, the Assistant Provost for Outreach and Engagement; Jan Bokemeier and Cheryl Booth of Families and Communities Together Coalition; Richard Block, recipient of the School of Labor and Industrial Relations (SLIR) Alcoa grant; and SLIR's graduate assistantship program are all thanked for financial support of this book. Deb Bittner, Terry Curry, Becky Scott, and Helena Stovall also of SLIR are thanked for administrative support. At Chicago, the School of Social Service Administration is thanked for financial support and Elaine Waxman is thanked for her detailed note taking at the authors' conference.

We are also grateful to Marian Ruderman and the Center for Creative Leadership (CCL) for allowing us to hold a conference of contributing authors and a small cadre of leading work-life practitioners in Greensboro, North Carolina, in May 2003. CCL is designed to foster leadership development and organizational management skills for practicing managers and is also a research institution and publisher. Academics do not frequently get the opportunity to develop their thoughts and research in such a wonderful setting. We are appreciative of Marian's championing of CCL's collaboration on the conference and also of the support provided by her colleagues, John Alexander, Barbara Demarest, Marty Wilcox, Tracy Dobbins, Joan Gurvis, Gordon Patterson, and Patricia Ohlott, among many others. Bringing the contributors together midway through the writing process was extremely valuable in allowing the authors to get feedback on chapter development and content, and it fostered the culmination of what we believe is a tighter volume of higher quality.

We also thank our corporate sponsors of the conference and the volume: Candice Lange, Eli Lilly; Joan Glubczynski, S. C. Johnson; Sherise Lindsay, Dana Pulley, and Dena Papazoglou, Booz Allen Hamilton; and Kristen Camilli and Tim Reynolds, Whirlpool. We thank our LEA editor, Anne Duffy, for being so supportive, encouraging, and flexible, and Kristin Duch for timely publishing support.

About the Contributors

THE EDITORS

Ellen Ernst Kossek (Ph.D., Yale) is Professor at Michigan State University's School of Labor and Industrial Relations. She is on the National Academy of Management's Board of Governors and was chair of the Gender and Diversity in Organizations Division. She is a fellow of the American Psychological Association and the Society of Industrial Organizational Psychology. She serves on four editorial boards and has written four other books and over 30 articles in leading journals, including *Academy of Management Journal, Journal of Applied Psychology, Human Relations,* and *Personnel Psychology.* Several of her articles have been nominated for or have won Best Paper awards. Her current research examines new ways of working flexibly (e.g., reduced work load, telework) and linkages to organizational change and human resource strategies.

Susan J. Lambert is Associate Professor in the School of Social Service Administration and Co-Director of *The Project on the Public Economy of Work* at the University of Chicago. She received her doctorate from the University of Michigan in social work and organizational psychology. Lambert's research focuses on the "work side" of work-life issues. She conducts workplace-based research that examines the relationship between employer practices and policies and worker performance and well-being. Lambert's articles appear in leading journals such as *Academy of Management Journal, Annals of the American Academy of Political and Social Sciences, Human Relations,* and *Social Service Review.*

THE AUTHORS

Lotte Bailyn is the T. Wilson (1953) Professor of Management at MIT's Sloan School of Management and Co-Director of the MIT Workplace Center. In her book *Breaking the Mold: Women, Men, and Time in the New Corporate World* (1993), she argues that by challenging the assumptions in which current work practices are embedded, it is possible to meet the goals of both business productivity and employees' family and community concerns, and to do so in ways that are equitable for men and women. Bailyn's subsequent work in corporate organizations supports that basic proposition, and it is detailed in *Beyond Work-Family Balance: Advancing Gender Equity and Workplace Performance*, of which Bailyn is a co-author.

Jeanette N. Cleveland is Professor of Psychology at Pennsylvania State University. Her research interests include personal and contextual variables in performance appraisal, workforce diversity issues, sexual harassment, and work and family. She was consulting editor for *Journal of Organizational Behavior* and has served or is currently serving on the editorial boards of *Journal of Applied Psychology, Academy of Management Journal, Journal of Vocational Behavior, Human Resource Management Review, Journal of Organizational Behavior, Journal of Applied Psychology,* and *International Journal of Management Reviews.*

Cary L. Cooper, CBE, is Professor of Organizational Psychology and Health at Lancaster University Management School, Lancaster University, England. He is president of the British Academy of Management, founding editor of *Journal of Organizational Behavior,* and was made a Commander of the Excellent Order of the British Empire by Queen Elizabeth in June 2001 for his services to organizational health.

Vinit M. Desai is a doctoral student and researcher in organizational behavior and industrial relations at the Walter A. Haas School of Business, University of California at Berkeley. His research interests include organizational learning and the study of organizations in which error can have catastrophic consequences. He has worked in the private and public sectors.

James R. Detert is Assistant Professor of Management and Organization in Pennsylvania State University's Smeal College of Business. He has a Ph.D. in organizational behavior from Harvard University. His dissertation research explored the effects of leadership and formal and informal control mechanisms on employee decisions about the safety and utility of speaking up. His previous research and publications also explore leadership, cultural, and institutional influences on learning and improvement in organizations.

Pamela Lirio Dohring is a doctoral student in the Faculty of Management at McGill University. Her research interests include young women's career and family practices, cross-cultural management, and work-family issues. She has recently given presentations at the Administrative Sciences Association of Canada, the Academy of International Business, and the Gender, Work and Society conference.

Linda M. Dunn-Jensen is a doctoral candidate in the Management Department at New York University. Her current research on time explores the motivation of time allocation between work and non-work life, specifically concentrating on the motivation to be visible at work. Another area of her research interest focuses on the effect of time compression on work-family balance.

Susan C. Eaton was an assistant professor at the Kennedy School of Government at Harvard University. Dr. Eaton held a doctorate from MIT. She was a innovative scholar whose work often bridged research and practice and spanned the fields of labor relations, health care, social policy, and work-family. She died on December 30, 2003. Her insights, wisdom, and presence will be missed.

Jeffrey R. Edwards (Ph.D, Carnegie Mellon University) is the Belk Distinguished Professor of Management at the Kenan-Flagler Business School, University of North Carolina. His research examines stress, coping, and well-being, person-organization fit, work and family, and research methods. His research has appeared in the *Academy of Management Review, Academy of Management Journal, Journal of Applied Psychology, Personnel Psychology, Psychological Methods,* and *Organizational Behavior and Human Decision Processes* (*OBHDP*). He is editor of *OBHDP* and has served as associate editor and board member of other major journals. He is past chair of the Research Methods Division of the Academy of Management, fellow of the American Psychological Association and the Society of Industrial and Organizational Psychology, and has been elected to the Society of Organizational Behavior.

Amy C. Edmondson is Professor of Business Administration at Harvard University. Her research investigates learning processes in teams and organizations. Recent publications include "The Local and Variegated Nature of Learning in Organizations" (*Organization Science*, 2002), and "Disrupted Routines: Team Learning and New Technology Implementation," with Gary Pisano and Richard Bohmer (*Administrative Science Quarterly, 2001*). Edmondson received her doctorate in organizational behavior from Harvard University.

Joyce K. Fletcher is Professor of Management at the Simmons School of Management in Boston and a senior research scholar at the Jean Baker Miller Training Institute at the Wellesley College Centers for Women. She is the co-author of a widely read Harvard Business Review article entitled "A Modest Manifesto for Shattering the Glass Ceiling," and is a frequent speaker on the topic of women, power, and leadership. She is author of *Disappearing Acts: Gender, Power and Relational Practice at Work* and co-author of a book on leading change entitled *Beyond Work Family Balance: Advancing Gender Equity and Workplace Performance.*

Alyssa Friede is a doctoral student at Michigan State University. She completed her undergraduate degree in psychology at the University of Pennsylvania.

Her research interests include work-life balance and the influence of personality in the workplace.

Sabir I. Giga is currently a research fellow at the Manchester School of Management, University of Manchester Institute of Science and Technology (UMIST). Dr Giga's research interests include stress management interventions and bullying in the workplace. His publications include a number of key reports for bodies such as the UK Health and Safety Executive (on developing good practice guidelines in workplace stress prevention and management) and the UN's International Labour Office (on identifying work-related violence and stress issues concerning specific occupational sectors).

Bradley Googins is Executive Director of the Center for Corporate Citizenship and Professor in the Department of Organizational Studies at the Wallace E. Carroll School of Management at Boston College. In 1990, Dr. Googins founded, and for six years directed, The Center for Work & Family at Boston University. He has been the principal investigator on numerous research projects, including Corporate Involvement in Community and Economic Development for The Ford Foundation, Work Redesign and Work Family Research Network for the Alfred P. Sloan Foundation, and Families and Neighborhoods Cluster Evaluation for the Kellogg Foundation.

Linda Haas has a Ph.D. in sociology from the University of Wisconsin-Madison. She is Professor of Sociology and Adjunct Professor of Women's Studies at Indiana University in Indianapolis. Her research focuses on the linkages between gender, family, and work in post-industrialized societies, with an emphasis on Sweden, where she has conducted several research studies, many in collaboration with Philip Hwang. She received an Honorary Doctorate in Social Sciences from Gothenburg University in Sweden in 1997. Her publications include two books, *Equal Parenthood and Social Policy* (1992) and *Organizational Change and Gender Equity* (with P. Hwang and G. Russell, 2000), as well as many articles in edited texts and academic journals.

Karen Hopkins is Associate Professor of Management and Community Organization at the School of Social Work, University of Maryland, Baltimore. She teaches graduate courses in Program and Human Resources Management and Research in Management and Community Practice. She provides management development training and consultation to human service and other non-profit organizations. Her research and publications focus on management practices and worker outcomes, work-life issues, and supervisor intervention with troubled workers across different work settings. She received her Ph.D. from the University of Chicago in 1993.

Larry W. Hunter is Assistant Professor of Management and Human Resources at the School of Business, University of Wisconsin-Madison. He received his doctorate from the Sloan School of Management, M.I.T., where he studied human resource management and industrial relations. His research interests include the effects of firms' employment practices on both individuals and organizations, and the relationship of those practices to the use of technology, to customer segmentation strategies, and to the broader environment. He has written on the organization of work in the service sector in settings ranging from long-term nursing care to retail banking to telephone call centers. Dr. Hunter was named Outstanding Young Scholar by the Industrial Relations Research Association in 2001.

Brenda A. Lautsch is Assistant Professor in the Faculty of Business Administration at Simon Fraser University. She received her doctorate in industrial relations and human resource management from the M.I.T. Sloan School of Management. Her research focuses on new work systems and inequality, and it includes a study on the determinants of benefit provision and daycare for contingent workers, as well as projects related to alternative dispute resolution, and the effect of new flexible work arrangements (like telework) on work-life outcomes. Recent publications have appeared in *Industrial and Labor Relations Review, Industrial Relations* and *International Journal of Human Resource Management.*

Mary Dean Lee is Associate Professor in the Faculty of Management at McGill University. She received her doctorate in organizational behavior from Yale University. Her research interests include professional and managerial careers, the changing nature of work, work and family, and organizational learning. Recent publications have appeared in *Human Resource Management Journal, Academy of Management Journal,* and *Journal of Management Development.* She has previously taught at the University of New Hampshire and was a research fellow at Harvard Business School.

Suzan Lewis is Professor of Organisational and Work-Life Psychology at Manchester Metropolitan University, a director of the Work Life Research Centre, and founding editor of the international journal *Community, Work and Family.* Her research interests focus on workplace flexibility and culture and organizational change in relation to work and family. She has directed numerous national and international research projects, including a current EU study of Gender, Parenthood and the Changing European Workplace.

Shelley M. MacDermid is Professor of Child Development and Family Studies, Director of the Center for Families, and Co-Director of the Military Family Research Institute at Purdue University. She holds a Ph.D. in human development and family studies from Pennsylvania State University. Her research focuses on the links between work conditions and family life, with special attention to organizational size and to work as a context for adult development. Recent publications have appeared in *Human Resource Management Journal, Academy of Management Journal, Journal of Marriage and the Family,* and *Journal of Management Development.*

Peter Madsen is a doctoral student at the University of California Berkeley's Walter A. Haas School of Business. His research interests focus on the impact that business organizations have on people, societies, and the natural environment. His recent research examines organizational reliability, employee safety, and corporate environmental performance.

Frances J. Milliken is Professor of Management and Organizational Behavior at the Stern School of Business of New York University. One of her ongoing research interests is in understanding the processes by which diversity affects the functioning of groups and of organizations. Her most current research focuses on "time compression," a phenomenon that has been created by the pressure to speed up product and service delivery during the last decade. Dr. Milliken is currently a member of the Board of Editors of the *Academy of Management Review* and has been a member of the Board of Editors of the *Academy of Management Journal* and the *Journal of Business Research.*

Philip Moss is Professor in the Department of Regional Economic and Social Development at the University of Massachusetts at Lowell. He primarily studies the impact of structural change in the economy and within firms on the distribution of economic opportunity. Moss is particularly interested in opportunities for different race and gender groups, on the fate of low-wage workers and low-wage jobs, and on changing skill needs and skill development strategies of firms. His books (with Chris Tilly) include *Stories Employers Tell: Race, Skill, and Hiring in America.*

Raymond A. Noe is Robert and Anne Hoyt Designated Professor of Management at The Ohio State University. Professor Noe's areas of teaching and research include all areas of human resource management, including training and development, recruiting, work and family, and teams. He has published articles in the major journals in the field including *Journal of Applied Psychology, Personnel, Psychology, Journal of Organizational Behavior, Academy of Management Review,* and *Academy of Management Journal.* He is author or co-author of three books including *Fundamentals of Human Resource Management, Human Resource Management,* and *Employee Training and Development.*

Marcie Pitt-Catsouphes is Assistant Professor at the Graduate School of Social Work at Boston College. She received her doctorate in sociology and social policy from Boston University. For ten years, she has conducted research at the Center for Work & Family at Boston College, most recently as the center's director. She is also a co-principal investigator for the Sloan Work and Family Research Network and founding co-editor for the international journal *Community, Work and Family,* She currently serves as the co-editor of the peer-reviewed *Work and Family Encyclopedia* and has many publications in the area of social policy and work and family.

Steven A. Y. Poelmans is Assistant Professor in Organizational Behavior at IESE Business School in Barcelona, Spain. He holds a Ph.D. (Magna Cum Laude) in Management/Organizational Behavior (IESE Business School/University of Navarra). He has worked in a wide variety of organizations (profit and not-for-profit; government and business schools). His research, teaching, and consulting mainly focus on work-family conflict, stress management, family-friendly policies, and cognition in strategy, mostly from a cross-cultural perspective. He is founding member of the European Academy of Management, an international affiliate of the Society of Industrial and Organizational Psychology.

Winifred R. Poster is Assistant Professor of Sociology at the University of Illinois at Urbana-Champaign. Her research is in areas of globalization, work, and activism in high-tech organizations across India and the United States. Her current projects examine transnational work-family policies, the global circulation of gendered work patterns, and the outsourcing of customer service call centers. Her work has been published in *Gender & Society, International Journal of Politics, Culture and Society, Journal of Developing Societies, Social Politics,* and *American Sociological Review.*

Karlene H. Roberts is Professor at the Walter A. Haas School of Business, at the University of California at Berkeley. Roberts earned her Ph.D. in industrial psychology from the University of California at Berkeley. Since 1984, she has been investigating the design and management of organizations and systems of organizations in which error can result in catastrophic consequences. Roberts is a fellow in the American Psychological Association, the Academy of Management, and the American Psychological Society. She is a member of the Human Factors Standing Committee of the National Academy of Science and is currently on the Advisory Board for the Engineering of Complex Systems group for NASA.

Nancy P. Rothbard is Assistant Professor of Management at the University of Pennsylvania's Wharton School. She received her doctorate in organizational behavior from the University of Michigan. Professor Rothbard's research examines how people's emotional responses to one role or task affect their subsequent engagement in another role or task. She has examined these questions in the context of work and family roles and in the context of multiple tasks that people perform within the work role. Her work has been published in leading academic journals such as *Administrative Science Quarterly, Academy of Management Review,* and *Organization Behavior and Human Decision Processes.*

Marian N. Ruderman is the interim group director of Leadership in the Context of Differences at the Center for Creative Leadership in Greensboro, North Carolina. She holds a doctorate in organizational psychology from the University of Michigan. Her research focuses on the career development of women and the impact of diversity on management development processes. Ruderman is co-author of the book *Standing at the Crossroads: Next Steps for High-Achieving Women,* and co-editor of *Diversity in Work Teams: Research Paradigms for a Changing Workplace.* Her published work has been cited widely in the press and has been applied in The Women's Leadership Program offered by the Center for Creative Leadership.

Ann Marie Ryan is Professor of Industrial and Organizational Psychology at Michigan State University. She has served as president of the Society for Industrial and Organizational Psychology and is currently editor of *Personnel*

Psychology. She previously was on the faculty at Bowling Green University. Her research interests center primarily around issues of employee selection and fairness, personality testing in work settings, and recruitment.

Harold Salzman is a sociologist and Senior Research Associate at The Urban Institute, Washington, D.C. His research focuses on workplace restructuring, skill requirements, engineering, and technology design, including studies of the IT industry and the globalization of engineering work. His publications include two co-authored books, *Software by Design: Shaping Technology and the Workplace* and *Designed to Work: Production Systems and People,* and articles on issues of technology, skills, and the workplace.

Kyra L. Sutton is a doctoral student in the Department of Management and Human Resources at The Ohio State University, where she teaches classes in general HR Management and organizational behavior. She received her BA in Economics at Spelman College. Her research interests include work-family practices, recruitment, compensation, and gender.

Chris Tilly is Professor of Regional Economic and Social Development at the University of Massachusetts at Lowell. He studies low-wage work, poverty, and inequality. His books include *Stories Employers Tell: Race, Skill, and Hiring in America* (with Philip Moss, 2001) and *Work Under Capitalism* (with Charles Tilly, 1998). He has published articles in journals including *Industrial Relations, Sistema, Trabajo,* and *Work and Occupations.*

P. Monique Valcour is Assistant Professor in the Department of Organization Studies at Boston College's Carroll School of Management. She received her doctorate in organizational behavior in the School of Industrial and Labor Relations at Cornell University. Professor Valcour's research focuses on objective and subjective career success and on work-life integration among dual-career couples and among lower-skilled service workers. Recent publications have appeared in *Human Relations, Industrial Relations,* and *International Journal of Human Resource Management.*

Elaine Waxman is a doctoral candidate in the School of Social Service Administration at the University of Chicago. Her research focuses on understanding the employment experiences of women in low-skilled jobs and how employers structure opportunities for mobility and work-life balance at lower-organizational levels. She is particularly interested in informal opportunity structures that allow lower-level workers to move into jobs that are more accommodating of personal life, especially child-care responsibilities.

I

Introductory Chapters

1

"Work-Family Scholarship": Voice and Context

Ellen Ernst Kossek
Michigan State University

Susan J. Lambert
The University of Chicago

Integration of work and nonwork demands is one of the most critical challenges organizations, families, and individuals face today. Research on the integration of work and family—and work and personal life more generally—is burgeoning and crossing many disciplines. The extant psychological and management literatures, however, largely adopt an individual, psychological perspective that emanates out of role theory (Katz & Kahn, 1978), focusing particularly on perceived conflicts between work and family roles. While perspectives on role conflict are valuable and some of the contributors to this volume draw on that rich tradition, we developed this book to address a number of persistent gaps in the work-family field, with its voice focused on work and organizations.

Researchers have tended to favor the life or family side of "work-life" issues. This can be partly attributed to scholars' efforts to provide empirical evidence of what Rosabeth Moss Kanter termed the "myth of separate worlds" in her classic treatise on the relationship between work and family (Kanter, 1977). As Kanter pointed out almost 30 years ago, traditional employing organizations were designed as if typical workers did not have family or personal demands that competed for their primary identity and attention during working time. Ideal workers historically have been those who are rarely absent from or late to work and who do not let family responsibilities encumber their hours on and com-

3

mitment to the job (Williams, 1999). Of course, it is now generally accepted that growing numbers of employees have family and other life demands that influence their ability to join and contribute fully to the workplace. A critical societal problem is the structural mismatch between employers' job demands and employees' needs and responsibilities.

OBJECTIVES FOR THIS VOLUME

To Enrich Conceptualization of the Work Side of Work-Life Issues. We designed this volume with the primary objective of bringing work back into the center of the theoretical, research, and practical discussions on the interplay between employment and personal life, thus attending to the structural mismatch between job demands and worker responsibilities. Many employers have continued to treat work and personal life as separate worlds and have been slow to adapt job and career structures fully to changes in the workforce. Researchers have been slow also in reshifting their focus back to workplace influences and organizational barriers to change. As the chapters in this book demonstrate, the design of jobs and employment structures and the transmission of professional and organizational social cultures create stresses and parameters that shape the ways in which individuals are able to synthesize work and nonwork demands.

Organizational and job conditions, as well as cultural contexts, determine the extent to which employment experiences enhance economic, psychological, and physical well-being by providing an opportunity to realize the positive aspects of working and the benefits of multiple-role accumulation (cf. Barnett & Hyde, 2001). The current work-family literature has underemphasized the importance of job and organizational design in helping explain the work family nexus. Job quality; the ability to control when, where, and how one works; performing tasks that enhance skills and careers; work and societal cultures that value personal life; and opportunity structures that facilitate job security, mobility, and access to work-family supports all seem critical to workers' efforts to combine work and personal life effectively. These features of organizations and cultures are the subject of analysis in this book.

To Consider How Work-Life Issues Vary by Job, Organizational, and Cultural Factors. A significant cluster of the existing scholarly and practitioner literature on employer support for work and family has tended to take an advocacy position, suggesting that all organizations should promote the integration of work and family roles. We do not advocate a one-size model that is unlikely to fit all cultures, individuals, or organizations. Instead, we suggest that research is needed that generates understanding of the conditions under which greater employer and societal responsiveness is both warranted and possible. This volume will speak to these issues. A primary goal of this book, then, is to examine work-life integration from not only individual psychological perspectives but also from organizational, cultural, and social perspectives, using them as a critical eye to examine how employment relationships, and ultimately work-life integration, may vary between cultures and within social contexts.

To Bring an Organizational Perspective to Work-Life Integration. Greenhaus and Parasuraman (1999, p. 407) define work-life integration as occurring "when attitudes in one role positively spill over into another role, or when experiences in one role serve as resources that enrich another role in one's life." This definition is essentially grounded in a spillover perspective that views relationships between work and personal life in terms of attitudes that individuals carry from one sphere to another. Building on this good work, we argue that the study of work-life integration should also keep attuned to the conditions under which roles can be combined in ways that create psychological distress, regardless of who is in the role or whether spillover ensues. Additionally, there may be times when segmentation between work and personal life is a conscious strategy actively pursued by workers. Thus, we suggest that the study of work-life integration should measure not only integration but also the processes and strategies used to combine specific roles in specific organizational contexts.

To Build on Established Theories of Organizations. Another goal of this book is to broaden the work-life field by offering perspectives developed by writers whose focus is work and employing organizations. Many of these contributors do not define themselves primarily as work-family scholars; rather, they are organizational scholars with both strong theoretical underpinnings and knowledge of how to improve actual work practices. Although they may be new to the work-life field, they are a distinguished group at the peak of their careers in their respective disciplines.

To Integrate Organizational, Individual, and Cultural Perspectives. The book is organized around specific theoretical lenses and levels of analysis. The themes emerging from these sections are considered in a summary section that traces implications for both theory and practice. The ordering of chapters reflects an additional objective, which is to integrate multiple, sometimes disconnected, research perspectives on work and family. Organizational and social structures construct individuals' perceptions of what is possible in terms of work-life integration. Yet, individual differences beyond commonly employed measures of gender and parental status matter in explaining how workers integrate work and personal life. Moreover, the roles of the work group, and workplace social dynamics, are often ignored even though research shows us that work is defined and experienced very differently across societies and cultures. Rarely are all of these lenses brought to bear on work and family issues, as is done in this volume.

CONTEXTUAL ORIGINS: WHY THIS BOOK WAS DEVELOPED

In 1992, Sheldon Zedeck edited a seminal book in the Industrial Organizational Psychology Frontiers Series. *Work, Families, and Organizations* examined diverse perspectives on the work-family relationship. The book was published at a time when many corporations were just beginning to respond to the changing gender and family demographics of the workforce and awakening to the need for greater understanding of work-family issues. Included in Zedeck's volume, which examined both individual and organizational perspectives on the links between the workplace and the family, were contributions by a wide range of experts, from industrial-organizational (I-O) psychologists to medical experts, family therapists to organizational behaviorists, policy specialists to investment counselors, and sociologists. Zedeck called on I-O psychologists to devote greater attention to the work-family interface, which, at the time, had been largely understudied by mainstream researchers. I-O researchers were encouraged to acknowledge the influence of family and other environments on the worker and to expand their variables to recognize more explicitly that work has meaning to families and vice versa (Brief & Nord, 1990).

It has been over a decade since Zedeck's volume was published, and many important societal changes have occurred. First, research agendas have broadened from "family-friendly" to "people-friendly" issues and from "work-family initiatives" to "work-life initiatives" (cf. Kirchmeyer, 2000). The broadening of the field to encompass the work-life domain reflects the view that just because employees do not have family-care responsibilities does not necessarily insulate them from life stresses and pressures to integrate work and nonwork roles. Currently, far more research has been done on integration of parenting with work than on other life roles related to community, eldercare, personal values, leisure, and aging. We designed this volume to reflect the broadening of the field toward study of work-life integration for all employees. Our book can be distinguished by its incorporation of individual, organizational, and cultural/social perspectives focused on links to work identity and the workplace. Our book thus extends the work Zedeck began by attending to changes in society and in organizations that have occurred since that writing and by broadening the scope to include some important and sometimes critical organization and management perspectives.

A second change that has occurred is that, regardless of the motivation, many employers have begun to experiment with flextime, telecommuting, and voluntary reduced-load work arrangements to give employees more discretion and personal flexibility in how they integrate work demands with other life roles such as family, community, and leisure (Lee, MacDermid, & Buck, 2000; Scandura & Lankau, 1997). This increase in flexible work arrangements has further blurred the boundaries between work and home for many employees. Effectively switching and managing multiple work and nonwork roles has never been more complex. Findings from individual, family, and organizational perspectives are mixed in terms of the success and social acceptance of alternative work arrangements (Epstein, Seron, Oglensky, & Saute, 1998; Lee, MacDermid, & Buck, 2000). A recent review of the literature suggests that there remains much to be learned about how to make these arrangements work well (Avery & Zabel, 2001). Growing evidence shows that professionals, especially men, are often reluctant to experiment with these alternative work arrangements (Fried, 1998) and that sometimes fear keeps workers from using existing supports (chap. 18, this volume). More research is needed to examine the implications of these blurred boundaries and the ensuing social issues they raise (see chaps. 3, 4, 12, this volume). A critical eye is needed to examine the inherent conflicts that arise in employment relations by questioning organizations' motivations for providing flexible work arrangements—whether for benevolent or economic reasons (chapter 8, this volume).

Third, increasing numbers of employees now live and work in a global economy. The increases in globalization and the speed of communication have led to heightened demands to work. It also enables individuals to receive work 24 hours a day, 7 days a week. Research by the Bureau of Labor Statistics (www .bls.org, 2003) indicates that 40% of male managers and almost 20% of female managers are working 49 or more hours each week, and the number of managers working these hours is growing. The problem of "work overload" may be even more serious for wage earners in low-income families who often need to work two or three jobs to make ends meet. Research is needed on the long-term effects of working long hours on psychological and physical health and on family relations. Research also needs to address the reasons managers are working excessively long hours and whether corporations benefit when they do (Brett & Stroh, 2003; Perlow, 1998). For example, Hochschild (1997) suggests that some people choose not to take advantage of employer policies that allow more time at home because today's workplace is easier and less emotionally challenging than today's home, given increasing divorce rates, eldercare demands, troubled children, and fewer stay-at-home spouses. People escape to work in order to exchange the messy entanglements of the modern family for the less intense and less complicated workplace (Hochschild, 1997). A critical assessment of the organization's role in encouraging or discouraging overwork and the costs and benefits of this is needed (chaps. 14, 15, this volume).

Fourth, as the workforce becomes increasingly multicultural, differences in values regarding the primacy of the work role to the family and to other life roles takes on growing importance. The U.S. model of segmenting work and family roles and expecting employees to work long hours (U.S. employees now work the longest hours of workers in any Western country) is not the model followed in other parts of the world (Brett & Stroh, 2003). In Europe, for example, limits are being placed on the maximum hours employees may work per week, and rest periods and holidays are being mandated. The Working Time Directive, passed by the Social Affairs Council of the European Union (EU) in 2002, restricts employees from working more than 48 hours per week. Employees may work more hours only if they voluntarily agree to do so, and employers are not allowed to retaliate if an employee refuses to work overtime (Adnett & Handy, 2001).

Countries and cultures differ in beliefs and values about whether balancing work and family is a collective or an individual responsibility (Lewis, 1999), and whether societal, government, and employer involvement enriches a common good. The government and the community play a much less powerful role in the management of the work-life and work-family relationships in the United States, which is where the majority of I-O and management scholars work. For example, in 1998, the International Labor Organization announced that more than 120 nations provide paid maternity leave. Three prominent exceptions were Australia, New Zealand, and the United States (Wisensale, 2001). Within the United States, family is viewed as an individual responsibility with minimal intervention from the state (Lewis, 1999). Thus, employees who work for large organizations, live in wealthier communities, or have higher paying jobs are more likely to have higher quality child care and more disposable income to allocate to care. Mirroring the U.S. values of underemphasizing communal and societal responsibility for family, these issues have been understudied by I-O and management scholars, despite recent calls by researchers for the community domain to be incorporated in work-family research (Voydanoff, 2001). We included some chapters that address cross-cultural perspectives on managing work-life integration to fill this gap (chaps. 16, 17, this volume).

Fifth, more research is needed on individual differences that are linked to the organizational context (part III, this volume). For example, very little is known about how men are managing work-family responsibilities, because traditional work-family theories have relied heavily on theories of gender differences to explain work-family conflict. Recent research suggests that men who are involved in caregiving and domestic roles experience stresses similar to those experienced by women and perhaps even more severely (Schneer & Reitman, 1995; Stroh, Brett, & Reilly, 1996).

Sixth, work-family research in the organizational behavior and I-O psychology domains has largely developed separately from the human resource policy domains, fostering a gap between the application of work-family conflict theory to organizational and national policy and practice (Kossek & Ozeki, 1998). Further, the study of the climate and cultures, informal contexts, and communities in which these policies are embedded has been integrated only minimally with the study of policy (Kossek, Noe, & Colquitt, 2001). More research is needed, as well as more theory developed, measuring the informal effectiveness of organizational work-life integration policies and supervisor support (chaps. 18, 20, this volume). Most policy research has been conducted in large organizations, which are more likely than small companies to be progressive in the adoption and cultural support of work-family policies (Pitt-Catsouphes, Swanberg, Bond, & Galinsky, 2004). In short, as with much academic research, the transfer of academic models to the workplace has been met with limited success (chaps. 22, 23, this volume).

OVERVIEW OF THE CHAPTERS

We asked each author to frame his or her chapter from a particular theoretical perspective, outlining its conceptual origins, defining its key concepts, and providing an overview of how it has been and currently is used. We encouraged the authors to use examples from their own as well as others' research to illustrate how the theoretical perspective can be used in empirical investigations of issues relevant to work-life integration. We also invited authors to consider: barriers to the implementation of the practical issues they raise, suggestions for improving the usefulness of organizational theory in furthering knowledge of work-life integration, and suggestions for methodologies and research designs that would support study of the key issues raised in their chapters. In this way issues would be touched on in multiple ways but not in all chapters to avoid repetition yet the chapters would still address common gaps in the literature.

Chapter 2 by Shelley M. MacDermid (Purdue University) follows this introduction and addresses how to build and broaden theory on work-family conflict. Based on more than 20 years of study from sociological and psychological perspectives, she takes stock of the work-family conflict construct. She identifies what researchers know and what they still need to know, and how best to learn in the future. She concentrates on measurement issues, including construct validity, content validity, and construct utility.

The second part of this volume takes an *organizational perspective*. Its content ranges from time compression, technology, organizational resilience, stratification and internal labor markets, formal work-life policies to work redesign. Organizational structures are powerful because they structure how individuals experience organizations and what individuals perceive as possible for managing work-life integration. Organizational and technological design factors create demand situations that individuals need to respond to regardless of who they are.

In chapter 3 Frances J. Milliken and Linda M. Dunn-Jensen (New York University) focus on the changing time demands of managerial and professional work. They discuss how the changing nature and expectations of this work, especially in the United States are affecting people's experiences of work-life dilemmas as we enter the twenty-first century. They develop the notion of time compression and examine how the longer hours, the increased complexity of managerial and professional jobs, and the pressure to produce faster are altering the context within which individuals are making choices about how to define the boundary between the work and nonwork domains of their lives.

P. Monique Valcour (Boston College) and Larry W. Hunter (University of Wisconsin) consider in chapter 4 the relationship between technology and work-life integration. They note that new technologies—especially advances in tele-communication and information technology—enable individuals to relocate work across time and space to unprecedented degrees. But such technologies do not in themselves solve the problems of integrating work with other life interests. By considering technological advances jointly with the organizational contexts within which they are implemented, the authors describe a range of effects that technology can have on work-life integration. This ranges from the sorts of tasks to which technology is applied (routine to nonroutine activities) to how technology is associated with organizational buffers, such as whether it enables tighter as well as looser coupling of organizational activities. They conclude with four ways in which managerial choices further shape implementation, as well as how workers—users of technology—also shape the relationship between technology and work-life integration.

The issues of organizational resilience and security took on new meaning after September 11, 2001. While the attack on the Twin Towers and the Pentagon directed our attention to the need to increase organizational and individual security, it followed a large number of organizational events that piqued interest in smaller ways. The processes and oversights that contribute to catastrophic organizational events are increasingly documented in the organizational literature. One such process requests the segmentation of work and personal spheres, so that workers focus exclusively on work demands and do not allow interpersonal conflicts or nonwork obligations to break their concentration during their shifts. In chapter 5 Karlene H. Roberts, Vinit M. Desai, and Peter Madsen (University of California, Berkeley) examine what employees in "high reliability organizations" say about the normative lack of integration of work and the rest of their lives. They also explore how employees' life experiences nonetheless find ways to inform their work.

The theories and methods of stratification have long been used to develop knowledge on how organizations structure traditional employment opportunities, such as opportunities for promotion, skill development, and wage growth. Susan J. Lambert and Elaine Waxman (University of Chicago) extend this framework on the stratification of firm-level labor markets to include a broader set of opportunities essential to balancing work and personal life. They discuss in chapter 6 the ways in which organizations distribute opportunities for balancing work and personal life at lower organizational levels.

Organizational structures and restructurings are commonly neglected in the analysis of work-life balance opportunities. These factors, often in the background, interact with the more typically identified factors such as attributes of individual workers and the work-life policies and strategies adopted by a firm and its managers. Philip Moss, Hal Salzman, and Chris Tilly (University of Massachusetts—Lowell) in chapter 7 discuss research that examines the interrelationship between structural changes in industries and firms, managerial strategy, and the structure of jobs. They focus on internal labor markets and implications for the quality of jobs, particularly changes in lower-skill, lower-wage jobs in terms of opportunity or mobility and for work-life integration.

In chapter 8 Kyra L. Sutton and Raymond A. Noe (The Ohio State University) argue that employer-offered family-friendly programs may be more myth than magic. They discuss the role of the human resources (HR) department in relationship to family-friendly programs and consider three theoretical perspectives that are related to the use and consequence of family-friendly programs. These perspectives include institutional theory, boundary theory, and the degree to which the firm adopts a control or commitment perspective of HR systems. They conclude that empirical evidence supports the notion that family-friendly programs are not always effective in reducing conflict for employees.

Joyce K. Fletcher (Simmons) and Lotte Bailyn (Massachusetts Institute of Technology) argue in chapter 9 that there is an equity imperative for redesigning work for work-family integration. They believe it is critical for organizations to consider how work-family issues are linked to work design. They identify the difference between an individual-level approach to the issue of work-family integration and a systemic approach. They also highlight the barriers to this systemic, more holistic approach and suggest ways to overcome them.

In the past decade, there has been considerable research on the conflict that individuals face managing their work and family lives. It has generally focused on the negative effects of these multiple roles, lacked a strong theoretical perspective, and not considered individual differences in personality, nonwork lifestyles, and relevant outcomes. The third part of this volume examines *individual perspectives* that are lacking in the more traditional research stream. An individual perspective helps us understand that not all individuals are alike. For example, not all women or all men are alike, although sometimes the popular press makes generalizations that prompt us to forget the role of individual differences in explaining how people experience work-life integration. Some of the chapters in this part note differences in how individuals experience their environments; person-environment interactions suggest that workers experience the contexts in which they are embedded differently. Others examine dispositional factors, the evolution of individuals over their career life cycle, varying motivations for work-life decision making, the issue of redefining how individual performance and success are measured, and how individuals make decisions about managing work-life boundaries and employing flexibility.

Research on engagement in work and family roles often focuses on environmental influences (e.g., supervisor, organizational climate, social policy) on individuals' emotions, cognitions, and behaviors. Researchers have suggested that personality be given greater consideration in understanding how an individual views and experiences multiple life roles. In chapter 10 Alyssa Friede and Ann Marie Ryan (Michigan State University) discuss the ways in which personality and self-evaluations may influence how individuals feel about and react to the interface between their work and family lives. The authors' model is applicable to how disposition influences engagement in multiple life roles.

Jeffrey R. Edwards (University of North Carolina) and Nancy P. Rothbard (University of Pennsylvania) present in chapter 11 a theoretical model that applies person-environment fit theory to stress and well-being associated with work and family. They describe how "fit" can be conceptualized in parallel terms for work and family and how person and environment constructs are linked across work and family. By extending existing applications of stress theories to work-family research, they clarify how the person and environment combine to produce stress, the role of cognitive appraisal in this process, and the effects of coping and defense on stress and well-being.

In chapter 12 Ellen Ernst Kossek (Michigan State University), Brenda A. Lautsch (Simon Fraser University), and Susan C. Eaton (Harvard University) contend that the nature of flexibility and how the individual psychologically experiences flexibility matter for work and family well-being. They develop the concept of *flexibility enactment,* which is the type of use and the way flexibility is experienced psychologically, and they investigate links to key work-family outcomes such as well-being. They discuss the conditions under which the availability and use of flexibility lead to reductions in work-family conflict or increased personal effectiveness at work and home and when using work-family policies such as teleworking or flextime. The authors conclude that different people will experience varied outcomes of flexibility, even after taking into account the constraints of their families and jobs.

Steven A. Y. Poelmans (University of Navarra, Spain) argues in chapter 13 that the decision process and conservation of resources theories of work and life are useful to theorists as they shift attention away from the consequences of work-family conflict for well-being to the actions that proceed and follow a work-family dilemma. He conceptualizes work-family conflict as an ongoing decision-making process based on three different levels of motivation (extrinsic, intrinsic, altruistic) as drivers of action—relevant decision-making processes that proceed and follow interaction, based on different types of interaction (economic, social, altruistic) among multiple actors. Within this framework, work-family conflict is not treated as an external or internal stressor or a cause, as is the case in role theory, spillover theory, and self-discrepancy theory; rather it is an intermediate state.

In chapter 14 Mary Dean Lee (McGill University), Shelley M. MacDermid (Purdue University), Pamela Lirio Dohring (McGill University), and Ellen Ernst Kossek (Michigan State University) explore how the process of new identity construction and socialization into parenthood is linked to professionals' requests for reduced-load work. They suggest that professionals have different orientations or self-conceptions prior to parenthood ranging from a career defined to a career orchestrated around family. Professionals go through a process of socialization and adaptation driven by their emotional responses to their changing social situations and eventually they negotiate new identities by interlinking professional and parent roles and depending upon organizational constraints.

Adopting a well-needed critical perspective, Jeanette N. Cleveland (Pennsylvania State University) argues in chapter 15 that there has been a single stakeholder bias associated with "the criterion problem," that is, definitions of performance and success. She holds that (a) success is a much broader and encompassing construct than simply upward mobility and spills over from work to nonwork domains; (b) whoever defines success may receive undue advantage in his or her work and nonwork lives as compared to those who have little or no voice in how success is defined; and (c) the criterion problem is one avenue of diversity research that may increase our understanding and handling of workplace discrimination and work-family interfaces. Cleveland makes the case that current workplace measures of success have largely reflected the will or the judgment of a given stakeholder, when in fact there are multiple stakeholders. Drawing from the sociological literature, a discussion of pluralism, acculturation, and individual and institutional discrimination is presented to make the case for a multiple-stakeholder perspective in developing measures to assess workplace performance and also in defining the boundaries of the construct "success" itself.

The fourth part of this book examines *cultural and social perspectives* on work-life integration. Basic nature, cultural assumptions, and social values may shape how individuals manage and view work-life integration. In this part, issues addressed include variation in gender equity and work-family social policy across nations, how global corporations manage local national workforces, the importance of supervisors and workplace climate in addressing work-life issues, the development of psychosocial capital in firms, and prevailing societal views on the value of work and life in terms of the corporate bottomline.

In chapter 16 Suzan Lewis (Manchester Metropolitan University) and Linda Haas (Indiana University) propose that a greater understanding of the impact of government policy on corporate work-life practices and cultures can be achieved by applying social justice theory. They suggest ways in which social justice theory can be useful in understanding work-life integration at the family, workplace, societal, and international levels. Lewis and Haas focus particularly on how government policies can affect individuals' sense of entitlement to support for integrating work and family and hence increase institutional pressures on employers to act in ways that are perceived as just. They emphasize the socially constructed nature of justice perceptions and that ideas of what is fair and taken for granted as just in one context may be contested in another.

Winifred R. Poster (University of Illinois, Urbana-Champaign) examines in chapter 17 how a global corporation constructs diversity in its struggles with race, class, and gender issues related to employment and work-family policy. As corporate agendas have changed from family-friendly to people-friendly, the conceptions and strategies for addressing race and gender are under debate and change. She draws on case studies of a U.S. high-tech multinational corporation and its subsidiary in India. She starts by analyzing the corporation's workforce diversity policy within its work-life program at its Silicon Valley head office and then examines how this program is transferred to the Indian subsidiary. She questions why two firms that have strong diversity policies and that are owned by the same umbrella parent organization—and that are moreover situated in two countries with a strong state rhetoric of equality—articulate their discourses of diversity and work-family in very narrow and opposing ways. For a U.S. high-tech firm, gender is the lens of diversity policy (even though race is a more overt tension among employees), whereas in a similar Indian high-tech firm, race/ethnicity is the primary lens for diversity policy (even though gender is a more overt tension). The answer lies in the process of discourse formation and the role of managers and institutional contexts in shaping it.

In chapter 18, on the role of speaking up about work-life issues, Amy C. Edmondson (Harvard University) and James R. Detert (Pennsylvania State University) offer a refreshing and innovative view. Summarizing their research on speaking up in organizations ranging from huge corporations to small community hospitals, they discuss the particular challenges of speaking up about life commitments at work. Understanding how people perceive the informal, interpersonal, and cultural environment in which they work presents a critical underpinning for understanding work-life imbalances and for helping individuals and organizations create a healthy balancing process. They theorize the role of speaking up in this balancing process, with attention to three levels of analysis—organizational, group, and individual. They are especially attuned to how informal rather than formal control mechanisms affect work-life balancing and to the effects of leadership chains—a concept that captures the interplay of multiple layers of management above most employees.

Sabir I. Giga (University of Manchester Institute of Science and Technology, United Kingdom) and Cary L. Cooper (Lancaster University, United Kingdom) discuss in chapter 19 the theory behind psychological contracts and the changing nature of the implied employment relationship. They discuss the potential benefits of social capital, both at a societal level and within organizations, and they develop a framework within which organizations can create "psychosocial capital" as a long-term prerequisite of the conventional corporate aims of economic and human capital. As psychological contracts are normally interpreted in terms of individual expectations, such as for working specific hours of the day, problems can arise when firms try to encourage a cohesive or teamwork-based environment without changing the psychological contracts they have established with workers.

Adding meat to the notion of supervisor support for work-family integration, Karen Hopkins (University of Maryland) in chapter 20 discusses the key gate-keeping role that supervisors play in workers' knowledge and use of organizational benefits, resources, and programs that can facilitate workers' management of work and life responsibilities. She reviews several social-psychological theoretical perspectives for understanding supervisor support and work-life balance/integration, including bystander-equity theory, leader-member exchange theory, and social identity theory. She argues that social identity theory in particular provides a promising context for examining supportive supervisory attitudes and behaviors. She also identifies the personal and organizational factors that contribute to supervisors' supporting and helping workers with work-life integration and explores how gender and race shape workers' perceptions of supervisor support.

In chapter 21 Marcie Pitt-Catsouphes and Bradley Googins (Boston University) recast the work-family agenda as a corporate social responsibility. They suggest that work-family issues be seen not only as a HR imperative but also as a set of social issues that are relevant to sustainable business success. Once the quality of life of working families is recognized as a social issue that has strategic importance to businesses, it then becomes possible for business leaders to address these concerns from the perspective of corporate social responsibility. The authors discuss the advantages of pursuing the "corporate social responsibility argument" for business commitment to work-family. Pitt-Catsouphes and Googins also suggest that business leaders become more accountable for the progress of their work-family agendas by openly discussing these issues in social reports, which are documents prepared for businesses' stakeholder groups.

Our final section, part V, includes two chapters summarizing crosscutting themes, divergence, and future directions. In contrast to the earlier chapters in this volume, which focus on content, Marian N. Ruderman (Center for Creative Leadership) in chapter 22 looks at an issue of process—how do theories of work-life relationships connect to (or disconnect from) the real world of organizational practice? Despite the contribution of theory to building our knowledge base in a structured way, there is a disconnect between the academic world and the world of practice. This chapter examines gaps between theory and practice, suggesting ways of bridging the two.

In the final chapter to this volume, chapter 23, the editors note established assumptions and enduring challenges in the work-life field. The goal of this concluding chapter is to summarize the implications of the volume for future research frontiers. We examine where authors agree and disagree, what is unique and similar in their approaches, and how their perspectives can advance theory and practice.

The audiences for this volume include the wide range of academics who are investigating relationships between work and personal life and professionals who help workers cope with the stresses of combining work with personal responsibilities, such as psychologists and HR personnel. Managers, union leaders, and others concerned about making the workplace more "employee-friendly" may also benefit from this book. The contributors to this volume have furnished a new wealth of knowledge to the field. We hope it will inspire others to attend more fully to the nuanced relationships between conditions at work and the realities of personal life. We thank the authors for their thoughtfulness.

REFERENCES

Adnett, N., & Handy, S. (2001). Reviewing the working time directive: Rationale, implementation and case law. *Industrial Relations Journal, 32*(2), 114–125.

Avery C., & Zabel, D. (2001). *The flexible workplace: A sourcebook of information and research.* Westport, CT: Quorum.

Barnett, R. C., & Hyde, J. S. (2001). Women, men, work, and family: An expansionist theory. *American Psychologist, 56,* 781–796.

Brett, J. M., & Stroh, L. K. (2003). Working 61-plus hours a week: Why do managers do it? *Journal of Applied Psychology, 88,* 67–78.

Brief, A., & Nord, W. (1990). Work and the family. In A. Brief & W. Nord (Eds.), *Meanings of occupational work* (pp. 203–232). Lexington, MA: Lexington Books.

Bureau of Labor Statistics. (2000). Retrieved October 15, 2003, from www.bls.org

Burkett, E. (2000). *The baby boon: How family-friendly America cheats the childless.* New York: Free Press.

Epstein, C. F., Seron, C., Oglensky, B., & Saute, R. (1998). *The part-time paradox: Time norms, professional life, family, and gender.* New York: Routledge.

Fried, M. (1998). *Taking time: Parental leave policy and corporate culture.* Philadelphia: Temple University Press.

Greenhaus, J. H., & Parasuraman, S. (1999). Research on work, family, and gender: Current status and future directions. In G. N. Powell (Ed.), *Handbook of gender & work.* (pp. 391–412). Newbury Park, CA: Sage Publications.

Hochschild, A. R. (1997) *The time bind: When work becomes home and home becomes work.* New York: Metropolitan Books.

Kanter, R. M. (1977). *Work and family in the United States: A critical review and agenda for research and policy.* New York: Russell Sage Foundation.

Katz, D., & Kahn, R. L. (1978). *The social psychology of organizations* (2nd ed.) New York: Wiley.

Kirchmeyer, C. (2000). Work-life initiatives: Greed or benevolence regarding worker's time. In C. L. Cooper & D. Rousseau (Eds.), *Trends in organizational behavior* (Vol. 7, pp. 79–94). New York: Wiley.

Kossek, E. E., Noe, R. A., & Colquitt, J. (2001). Caregiving decisions, well-being, and performance: The effects of place and provider as a function of dependent type and work-family climates. *Academy of Management Journal, 44*(1), 29–44.

Kossek, E. E., & Ozeki, C. (1998). Work-family conflict, policies, and the job-life satisfaction relationship: A review and directions for organizational behavior/human resources research. *Journal of Applied Psychology, 83,* 139–149.

Lee, M. D., MacDermid, S. M., & Buck, M. L. (2000) Organizational paradigms of reduced-load work: Accommodation, elaboration, and transformation. *Academy of Management Journal, 43*(6), 1211–1226.

Lewis, S. (1999). An international perspective on work-family issues. In S. Parasuraman & J. Greenhaus (Eds.), *Integrating work and family: Challenges for a changing world* (pp. 91–103). Westport, CT: Praeger.

Pitt-Catsouphes, M., Swanberg, M., Bond, J., & Galinsky, E. (2004). Work-life policies: Comparing the responsiveness of nonprofit and for porfit organizations. *Nonprofit Management and Leadership, 14*(13), 291–312:

Perlow, L. A. (1997). *Finding time: How corporations, individuals, and families can benefit from new work practices.* Ithaca, NY: ILR Press.

Scandura, T., & Lankau, M. (1997). Relationships of gender family responsibility and flexible work hours to organization commitment and job satisfaction. *Journal of Organizational Behavior, 18*, 377–391.

Schneer, J. A., & Reitman, F. (1995). The impact of gender as managerial careers unfold. *Journal of Vocational Behavior, 47*, 290–315.

Stroh, L. K., Brett, J. M., & Reilly, A. H. (1996). Family structure, glass ceiling, and traditional explanations for the differential rate of turnover of female and male managers. *Journal of Organizational Behavior, 49*, 99–118.

Voydanoff, P. (2001). Conceptualizing community in the context of work and family. *Community, Work and Family, 4*, 133–156.

Williams, J. (1999). *Unbending gender: Why work and family conflict and what to do about it.* New York: Oxford University Press.

Wisensale, S. K. (2001). *Family leave policy: The political economy of work and family in America.* Armonk, NY: M. E. Sharpe.

Zedeck, S. (Ed.) (1992). *Work, families, and organizations.* San Francisco: Jossey-Bass.

2

(Re)Considering Conflict Between Work and Family

Shelley M. MacDermid
Purdue University

Spillover, compensation, segmentation, and accommodation are but a few of the terms that have been developed over the past few decades to describe relationships between work and family life (Lambert, 1990; Zedeck, 1992). But the construct in this domain that has received the most attention from both researchers and the popular press is work-family conflict (Greenhaus & Powell, 2003). A search in the PsycINFO database for the terms "work-family conflict" or "work-family interference" yielded 184 citations (not including dissertations), compared to 95 for studies of life satisfaction or well-being where work and family were also mentioned; 27 for work-family or negative spillover; and 25 for anxiety or depression in association with work and family. These numbers understate the case, as the citations for life satisfaction or well-being are spread over the past 76 years (a rate of 1.25 articles or chapters per year), while the citations for work-family conflict begin only 18 years ago (a rate of about 10.2 articles per year). The citations also indicate that the study of work-family conflict has spread to diverse samples including the military, expatriate workers, postpartum mothers, Presbyterian clergy, nurses, police officers, and Native Americans as well as around the globe to Australia, Canada, China, Finland, Hong Kong, Israel, Japan, Malaysia, Norway, Singapore, and Spain.

In this chapter, I take stock of theory and research about conflict between work and family. With 20 years of study completed, we should be in a good position to decide what is already known, what we still need to know, and how best to learn in the future. I address five issues. I first consider the theoretical utility of the construct in the past and in the future. Second, I assess content validity, or the degree to which existing measures cover all relevant content. Third, I look at a technical measurement issue—the degree to which respondents are able to do what measures of conflict typically ask of them. Fourth, I consider construct validity, or the degree to which measures of conflict tap that construct and not others. Finally, I reflect on whether conflict between family and work matters, and if it does, how it should be studied in the future.

I use the following conventions in the chapter. When I wish to refer to conflict without specifying a source or direction I use the terms "conflict between work and family" or "conflict between family and work." When I wish to specify a particular source or direction, I use the terms "work-to-family conflict" or "family-to-work conflict."

WHAT IS THE PAST AND FUTURE OF WORK-FAMILY CONFLICT AS A THEORETICAL CONSTRUCT?

The theoretical ancestry of conflict between work and family is rooted in the earliest days of social science, but its history as an explicit focus of scientific research is relatively short. Formal social science disciplines emerged a little over a hundred years ago, as the industrial revolution was separating economic work from the family home. The creation of assembly lines in factories institutionalized the idea that efficiency and smooth functioning would be achieved best by worker specialization—each worker performing a single task. World War II revitalized the economy following the Depression, largely through the manufacturing boom created by the need for bullets, guns, planes, and jeeps. Immediately following the war, thousands of women who had recently entered the labor force were persuaded through various means to return home, in part to make room for returning soldiers to reenter the labor force. As life returned to "normal," the birthrate boomed, the divorce rate dropped, and many families experienced a steady rise in real income (Doherty, Boss, LaRossa, Schumm, & Steinmetz, 1993).

Social institutions and their expectations of members have long figured prominently in scientific theorizing about human behavior. In the early part of the twentieth century, symbolic interactionists proposed that identities were self-meanings that were acted out in social roles (LaRossa & Reitzes, 1993). In the mid-part of the century, structural functionalists like Talcott Parsons argued that roles were where individual goals met social norms and that an allocation of specific roles based on sex would maximize the functioning of families, organizations, and societies (Kingsbury & Scanzoni, 1993). Looking back through this historical lens, it hardly seems surprising that a theory like structural-functionalism would emerge following World War II.

Structural-functionalism is built on two notions of separate spheres. First, it recognizes a separation between institutions—the most obvious example of which is workplaces—and families. Second, it proposes that families, institutions, and society all work best when men and women specialize their activities in separate spheres, women at home doing expressive work and men in the workplace performing instrumental tasks (Kingsbury & Scanzoni, 1993).

The first study I was able to locate about role conflict was a 1949 Oscar Lewis article about interpersonal conflict between husbands and wives over the women's role, documented in PsycINFO with this bluntly worded abstract: "Although wives are expected to be submissive and husbands authoritarian, in practice these roles have been altered. Women now eschew child-bearing, isolation in the home, and economic dependence. Men have been unable to curb these activities, so that suspiciousness of unfaithfulness often results in spying and wife-beating" (accession number 1950-02513-001). The earliest study I found of *intra*personal role conflict was published in 1955 by Elise Boulding, who described how participation in cooperative nursery school programs could help women relieve their internal emotional conflict about having jobs by sharing in the care of their children.

Like the study by Boulding (1955), early studies of work-family conflict (particularly among women) were motivated by concerns about the anticipated negative impact of women deviating from traditional sex roles by working outside the home for pay (Bronfenbrenner & Crouter, 1982). Although many scholars believe that structural-functionalism has faded, there is good reason to believe that it continues to influence many current studies (Kingsbury & Scanzoni, 1993). I already have described elsewhere the connection between functionalism and the theoretical foundations of conflict between work and family (Mac-Dermid, Seery, & Weiss, 2002). Today, research that focuses on the implications of wives' employment for marital stability, for example, is really asking a structural-functionalist question.

Barnett and Hyde (2001) argue, however, that the demographic landscape from which notions of specialization and separateness emerged has largely disappeared. Many businesses now seek to limit specialization, instead emphasizing "cross-functional teams" and "cross-training." Working for pay today is much less likely to involve a fixed place and a fixed schedule than it once was. Technology has made it easier for workers to do work anytime and anywhere. Globalization has stretched the boundaries of work, with competition around the world requiring more and more workplaces to run 24 hours per day. White collar workers must be ready to meet promptly the demands of clients in time zones all over the world. In the United States, workers work more hours per year on average than in any other industrialized country (although those work hours are not equally available to all workers).

The spheres of work and family, separated during the industrial revolution, are converging once again in the information age. The percentage of workers with significant caregiving responsibilities at home remains high, and the proportions of families headed by single parents and dual-earners continue to rise. Within families, the spheres of men and women also have converged in striking ways. Consider work for pay: In 1900, the labor force contained 4.5 men for every woman. By 1950, this number had fallen to 2.3. Projections indicate that by 2010 there will be only 1.1 men for every woman in the labor force (U.S. Bureau of the Census, 2003). The labor force participation rates for men and women are the closest they have ever been: By 2010, 73.2% of all men and 62.2% of all women are projected to have joined the labor force. A similar pattern is evident when considering unpaid household tasks: Women have decreased and men have increased their involvement in household work and childcare tasks such that the ratio of women's to men's time fell from almost 4:1 to 2:1 from 1965 to 1985 (Robinson & Godbey, 1997; Rogers & Amato, 2000). In many studies, men and women report similar levels of conflict between work and family (e.g., Galinsky, Bond, & Friedman, 1993).

New theories of work and family are emerging that are not built on notions of separate spheres. For example, Barnett and Hyde's (2001) expansionist theory focuses on the beneficial effects of role accumulation, including added income, the buffering effects of role combinations, social integration, and expanded personal and social opportunities. Moen and colleagues (e.g., Moen & Yu, 2000) use the image of "linked lives" to study the strategies married couples use over the course of their lives to manage work and family.

These demographic and theoretical innovations raise important questions about the likely importance of conflict between work and family in the future. On the one hand, the specialization that helped generate early interest in the construct has weakened, which might suggest low utility in the future. On the other hand, men's and women's role systems have become more complex, potentially increasing the likelihood and relevance of conflict in the future. As activities become less bounded in time and space, role boundaries may be less important than the experience of conflicting demands, whatever their source.

HAS ALL OF THE THEORETICAL CONTENT OF CONFLICT BETWEEN WORK AND FAMILY BEEN STUDIED?

The question that gives this section its title is one of content validity. Given the way the study of conflict between work and family has evolved, two questions are actually implied. First, have measures and studies adequately captured the content of the construct as originally proposed? And second, have new theoretical and empirical insights been adequately incorporated into subsequent research?

The foundation of much of today's thinking about conflict between family and work roles emerged in the 1960s. Kahn and colleagues developed a theory of roles that defined role conflict as the "simultaneous occurrence of two (or more) sets of pressures such that compliance with one would make more difficult compliance with the other" (Kahn, Wolfe, Quinn, Snoek, & Rosenthal, 1964, p. 19). Kahn and colleagues also proposed that role conflict would be more severe when the implicated roles were central to the individual's sense of self and when there was strong pressure for compliance with expectations in a role (Greenhaus & Beutell, 1985).

Another foundational contribution is Goode's theory of role strain, which he defined as "felt difficulty in fulfilling role obligations" (Goode, 1960, p. 483). Goode made several assertions that have become part of the dogma of the study of conflict between family and work. First, he assumed that the role obligations of most individuals would exceed their capacity to respond, making the experience of role strain so inevitable as to be normal. Second, he articulated the "scarcity" hypothesis, which is based on the premise that individuals have a fixed pool of resources. Thus, resources expended in one domain necessarily are deprived from another.

In 1985, Greenhaus and Beutell published what has become the second-most cited article in the work-family literature (Mason, 2002). They used Kahn et al.'s original formulation (1964) as the basis for the first explicit definition of work-family conflict: "a form of interrole conflict in which the role pressures from the work and family domains are mutually incompatible in some respect" (Kahn, et al. 1964, p. 19). In a major theoretical innovation, Greenhaus and Beutell (1985) defined three specific types of conflict: Time-based, when involvement in one role is impeded by time pressures in the other; strain-based, when performance in one role is affected by tension in the other; and behavior-based, when fulfilling the requirements of one role is made more difficult by the behavior required in the other. As the summary in the following section will show, most measures of conflict between work and family clearly cover the theoretical perspectives described so far. Most are based on the Greenhaus and Beutell (1985) definition of conflict, and most ask about multiple dimensions of conflict (e.g., time-based, behavior-based, and so on).

A more recent theoretical innovation is the proposition that research on conflict between work and family should study conflict emanating from each domain separately. Researchers have enthusiastically embraced this notion. Several measures have been developed to measure family-to-work and work-to-family conflict (Frone, Yardley, & Markel, 1997; Netemeyer, Boles, & McMurrian, 1996; Williams & Alliger, 1994), and some empirical support has been found to suggest that different antecedents produce the conflict emanating from each domain (Frone, Yardley, & Markel, 1997). Greenhaus and Powell (2003), however, recently revisited Kahn et al.'s original proposition (1964) that conflict is the result of *simultaneous* pressure from multiple domains. They continue to argue, as Greenhaus and Beutell did in 1985, that in such instances the direction of conflict is apparent only *after* an individual chooses the pressure with which he or she will comply, such as when someone must choose between a work obligation and a conflicting appointment with a teacher.

A theoretical innovation that has been less consistently embraced in measurement is what has been called the "expansion" hypothesis. Sieber (1974) and Marks (1977) questioned the hydraulic nature of the scarcity hypothesis, proposing that roles do not just use up energy and resources but also can generate them in ways that benefit performance in other roles. Barnett and colleagues (Barnett & Baruch, 1987; Baruch & Barnett, 1986) have documented empirically ways in which positive experiences in some roles can compensate for negative experiences in others; see also more recent work by Ruderman, Ohlott, Panzer, and King (2002). These ideas have led to some new items and scales, typically worded as mirror images of conflict items (e.g., In the past three months, how often have you had *more* energy to do things with your family or other important people in your life because of your job? [Bond, Galinsky, & Swanberg, 1998]). So far, this measurement strategy has had little success, but it is not at all clear that the strategy and the content are a good match. What if enhancement has a different temporal rhythm than conflict? Recently, Grzywacz and Bass have elaborated a perspective on facilitative influences between family and work that may yield new findings (Frone, 2003; Grzywacz & Bass, 2003).

The major gap in current measurement strategies vis-à-vis theoretical and empirical insights is the lack of a crisp distinction among cognitive, affective, and behavioral elements of conflict. Twenty years ago, Kopelman, Greenhaus, and Connolly (1983, p. 200), reiterating Kahn et al. (1964), asserted that "it is important to distinguish objective or sent role conflict (i.e., incompatible sets of role pressures) from experienced or psychological conflict which is based on perceptions of environmental pressures." Several recent studies make a similar distinction (e.g., Grant-Vallone & Donaldson, 2001; Wiese & Freund, 2000). Carlson and Frone (2003) draw a distinction between externally generated and internally generated interference. The external element represents behavioral interference, whereas the internal element represents internally generated psychological preoccupation with or rumination about one domain of life while operating in another. Rothbard (2001) separates cognitive engagement in and emotional response to work and family roles.

Emotion is curiously absent from most acknowledgments of received or psychological conflict (MacDermid, Seery, & Weiss, 2002; with the notable exception of Rothbard [2001] previously cited). Kossek and Ozeki (1999, p. 18) crisply express the oversight: "[N]ot being able to do two things at the same time may impact performance differently than feeling bad about it." The typical measurement strategy conflates the occurrence of the stressor (e.g., a conflicting demand) with the stress it causes (Perry-Jenkins, Repetti, & Crouter, 2000).

Better understanding of the variety of emotional experiences that can result from conflict between work and family may improve our ability to account for differences among individuals and variability within individuals over time.

Finally, coping is an element of the stress process that remains a gap in the study of conflict between work and family (Kopelman, Greenhaus, & Connolly, 1983). Rotondo, Carlson, and Kincaid (2002, p. 277) argue that coping may affect levels of stress in part by affecting perceptions of work-family conflict: "That is, the way the individual perceives his/her environment and its stressors becomes positively changed. . . . If an individual is effectively coping, his or her perceived work-family conflict should be lower because the conflict is 'under control,' so to speak. Similarly, perceived conflict should be expected to be highest (i.e., most salient) in those who are ineffectively or inefficiently managing work-family conflict." As predicted, more active forms of coping work were associated with lower family-to-work conflict but the hypothesis was not supported for work-to-family conflict.

Current Definitions and Measures of Conflict Between Work and Family

Measures of conflict between family and work have been developed by Kopelman, Greenhaus, and Connolly (1983), Gutek, Searle, and Klepa (1991), Frone, Russell, and Cooper (1992); Netemeyer, Boles, and McMurrian (1996); Stephens and Sommer (1996), and Carlson and Frone (2003), among others. Some of these measures are second-generation, meaning that they were created by selecting existing items based on their conceptual and empirical utility (e.g., Netemeyer, Boles, & McMurrian, 1996; Stephens & Sommer, 1996). Most existing measures are based on the conceptual framework laid out by Greenhaus and Beutell (1985, p. 77), and described earlier in this chapter.

Although there is considerable variation in the content of conflict measures, their form is quite consistent. The typical strategy is to ask respondents via a paper-and-pencil questionnaire to indicate the degree to which their job (or their family life) interferes with (or, occasionally, enhances) specific elements of life in the other domain. Answer options are usually in a 5- or 7-point Likert format, ranging from "strongly agree" to "strongly disagree" or "always" to "never." In most instances a reference period is not specified; when it is, the most common period is the past one to three months. Tests of internal consistency via Cronbach's alpha frequently generate acceptable values (e.g., .73 to .84 [Carlson & Frone, 2003]). Some researchers have conducted confirmatory factor analyses, which have shown reasonable separation between items measuring work-to-family and family-to-work conflict (e.g., Stephens & Sommer, 1996). Tests of construct validity usually yield moderate correlations with a variety of other variables, such as organizational commitment, job satisfaction, and life satisfaction (e.g., Netemeyer, Boles, & McMurrian, 1996). Sample items from a very recent measure by Carlson and Frone (2003) are:

How often does your job or career interfere with your home life?

How often does your job or career interfere with your responsibilities at home, such as yard work, cooking, cleaning, repairs, shopping, paying the bills, or child care?

How often does your home life interfere with your job or career?

When you are at home, how often do you think about work-related problems?

When you are at work, how often do you try to arrange, schedule, or perform family-related activities?

Existing research has established that conflict between work and family is empirically linked to a variety of other variables, including (but not limited to):

- Satisfaction with job and life (Kossek & Ozeki, 1998).
- Involvement, salience, resources, conflict, ambiguity, overload, performance, and withdrawal behaviors such as absenteeism and tardiness in the work role (Allen, Herst, Bruck, & Sutton, 2000; Carlson, 1999; Frone, 2003; Hammer, Bauer, & Grandey, 2003; Kossek & Ozeki, 1999).
- Dissatisfaction, distress, and performance in family roles (Frone, 2003).
- Conflict, quality, and warmth in marriage (Matthews, Conger, & Wickrama, 1996).
- Caregiving responsibilities (Hammer, Colton, Caubet, & Brockwood, 2002) and mothers' perceptions of their parenting (MacDermid & Williams, 1997).
- Psychological distress, perceived physical health (Frone, 2003; Grzywacz, 2000), alcohol use (Frone, 2003), chronic health problems, and obesity (Grzywacz, 2000).

CAN RESPONDENTS DO WHAT MEASURES OF WORK-FAMILY CONFLICT ASK OF THEM?

The cognitive work associated with responding to typical items indexing conflict between family and work is complex. According to Schwarz and Oyserman (2001, paraphrased from p. 129), respondents complete the following tasks to answer any question:

- Understand the question.
- Recall relevant behavior.
- Infer and estimate the data with which to answer the question.
- Map the answer onto the response format.
- Edit the answer for reasons of social desirability.

Assuming they understand the questions correctly, respondents must complete at least three assessments to assemble the data necessary to respond to work-family conflict items. They must decide whether conflict occurs at all. If it does, they must decide whether it affects the specific targets identified in the question (e.g., "home," "cooking," "cleaning"). And they must determine the degree to which their job is responsible for the effects on those targets. Research suggests that several challenges might hamper respondents in completing these assessments accurately.

One challenge relates to the specific content of the information individuals must retrieve from memory. Of course, answers to any question are vulnerable to errors of recall. But research suggests that questions that ask the respondent to identify the *source or cause* of an experience—as do most measures of work-family conflict—are especially vulnerable to memory errors (Schacter & Dodson, 2001), because it is much easier to recall that something occurred than to attribute its cause accurately (Schacter, 1999). Thus, even when respondents accurately remember interference with home responsibilities, they are at elevated risk for attributing the cause to their job when something else was actually to blame. For example, obligations to sport, church, school, or community organizations might conflict more directly with cooking or cleaning than employment because they take place during evenings and weekends.

Another challenge is the accessibility of information in memory. Since memory decreases over time, the longer the interval respondents are asked to recall, the harder it is to do so accurately. Schwarz and Oyserman (2001) cite a study where 42% of respondents failed to report a hospitalization one year later (Cannell, Fisher, & Bakker, 1965)! When recall is more difficult, respondents are more likely to estimate the data from more easily accessible sources, which often means drawing on their current mood and general disposition (Ottati & Isbell, 1996; Schwarz, 2002; Schwarz & Oyserman, 2001). Subjective assessments like that of conflict between family and work are particularly susceptible to these "contextual" influences (Schwarz & Strack, 1999). So, respondents who are unable to recall easily the information necessary to assess conflict will be more likely to report that conflict occurred if they are currently in a negative mood and have a dispositional tendency to perceive negative affect (Kelloway, Gottlieb, & Barham, 1999).

Participants' responses are shaped by the instructions they are given by researchers. For example, very different events come to mind depending on the interval of time researchers ask participants to consider. Respondents asked about conflict between work and family in the course of a day might think about the home cooked dinner they missed because they left work late. Respondents asked about a month might think about meetings that took them away from home overnight. And respondents asked to consider longer intervals might refer to promotions turned down for family reasons or important family celebrations missed or postponed due to work obligations. All of these are examples of work conflicting with family life, but existing research has focused almost exclusively on the intermediate level of specificity; there has been little discussion of the nature of the "time structure" of conflict between work and family.

Humans' perceptions are distorted in reliable ways, which presents another challenge to the measurement of conflict between work and family. Individuals display the "self-serving bias" when they selectively blame external circumstances when things go badly and credit themselves when things go well (Campbell & Sedikides, 1999). To the extent that individuals perceive high interference with family or with work, they will be predisposed to attribute it to external circumstances such as the job rather than to personal characteristics such as the tendency to take on too many commitments. Of course, most measures of work-family conflict "stack the deck" by asking respondents about only a single—and external—source of interference.

The self-serving bias is especially likely to occur when respondents perceive a threat to their self-concept (Campbell & Sedikides, 1999; Sabini, Siepmann, & Stein, 2001). To the extent that conflict between work and family makes it hard to meet the demands of important identities, it undermines individuals' abilities to maintain a positive self-image and therefore constitutes a threat (Frone, Russell, & Barnes, 1996). Thus, the measurement of conflict between work and family may be especially susceptible to the self-serving bias. Research also shows that perceptions of self-threat are especially likely to increase bias among individuals predisposed to negative affect (Jundt & Hinsz, 2002), completing a "triple whammy" for the measurement of conflict: ordinary tendencies toward bias inflated by the difficulty of retrieving information, perceptions of threats to self, and dispositional negativity.

Finally, even the answer options from which respondents are asked to choose can introduce a distortion. According to Schwarz and Oyserman (2001), respondents tend to assume that the average answer (i.e., the answer the average person would give) falls approximately in the middle of the range they are given and edit their answers accordingly. Little or no psychometric work has been done regarding the measurement of conflict between work and family to determine whether or how the use of 5- or 7-point (or 4- or 6-) answer formats matter or whether the difference between the strongly agree/strongly disagree and never/always answer options matters.

To summarize, current strategies for measuring conflict between work and family have not yet dealt satisfactorily with several possible sources of distortion in respondents' answers. It is not clear that respondents can accurately recall relevant data for the reference periods researchers ask them about. It is unclear that respondents can accurately attribute the source of whatever conflict they feel, especially when given only one source from which to choose. Although it is likely that current mood and affective tendencies shape respondents' answers, few researchers control for these factors. And the focus on conflict may interact with pre-existing personal tendencies to inflate reports of conflict from external sources.

ARE MEASURES OF CONFLICT BETWEEN WORK AND FAMILY CONSTRUCT-VALID?

As mentioned earlier, measures of conflict between work and family have demonstrated reasonable psychometric properties, including evidence of clean factor structures, reasonable convergent validity, and good internal consistency. In contrast, the evidence of discriminant validity is thin. In the two examples found (Carlson, Kacmar, & Williams, 2000; Netemeyer, Boles, & McMurrian, 1996), the assessment of this form of validity was based on the observation of low or moderate correlations among the factors measuring various indicators of conflict, as opposed to factors more conceptually distinct from conflict. As a result, three questions deserve consideration:

1. Is conflict between work and family meaningfully distinct from the outcomes of interest?
2. As a predictor does conflict between family and work tell us anything useful over and above other important variables? (Note, however, that the distinction between "predictors" and "outcomes" is mostly theoretical because virtually every test has been conducted with cross-sectional data.)
3. How confident can we be in what we think we have learned regarding conflict between work and family?

Is Conflict Meaningfully Distinct from Outcome Variables? Theoretical models of conflict between work and family have become increasingly complex. The rising number of variables provokes questions about parsimony and the clarity of the distinction among the variables, in particular the distinction between conflict and stress-related outcomes.

Based on their comprehensive review of studies connecting work-family conflict to work-related outcomes (e.g., job satisfaction, organizational commitment, job performance, absenteeism), nonwork-related outcomes (e.g., satisfaction with life, marriage, family), and stress-related outcomes (e.g., psychological strain, physical symptoms, depression, substance abuse, burnout, work- and family-related stress), Allen, Herst, Bruck, and Sutton (2000) conclude, "[O]ne of the most consistent and strongest findings in the literature was the significant relationship between work-family conflict and stress-related outcomes" (p. 301). Kelloway, Gottlieb, and Barham (1999) found that measures of stress correlated more strongly with strain-based conflict than with other forms of conflict.

Frone and colleagues (e.g., Frone, Yardley, & Markel, 1997) have made substantial contributions to the study of both work-to-family and family-to-work conflict. Their recent conceptual model proposes a network of variables that includes separate within-role indicators of distress or dissatisfaction, commitment, overload, time spent, role behaviors, supports, and conflict within work and within family. As parsimony is overtaken by complexity, how can we know when we are observing relationships between two meaningfully distinct constructs and not two facets of the same construct?

As a preliminary test of discriminant validity, I conducted a confirmatory factor analysis using data from the 1997 National Study of the Changing Workforce (Bond, Galvisky, & Swanberg, 1998). The nationally representative sample of wage and salaried workers included 1,445 married men and women with children who were included in this analysis. I tested a model with 26 variables reflecting eight constructs: global conflict between work and family (3 items); family enhancement of work (1 item); work enhancement of family (2 items), family-to-work conflict (5 items), work-to-family conflict (5 items), satisfaction with life, marriage, family, and job (4 items); job burnout (4 items), and stress (2 items). Statistical convergence required that the two enhancement factors be collapsed into one, reducing the model to seven factors. The resulting chi-square with 278 degrees of freedom was 1,709 ($p = .000$). The adjusted goodness-of-fit index was .88 and the root mean square residual was .06, both moderately acceptable values. Although the loadings of items on their respective factors all were strong, four of the factors were strongly intercorrelated: Work-to-family conflict was correlated .78 and .73, respectively, with global conflict and with job burnout, respectively. In turn, job burnout was correlated .76 with stress.

I was unable to improve substantially the fit by collapsing factors or eliminating variables. Inspection of the LaGrange multiplier test for adding parameters suggested that variables from both the work-to-family conflict and the satisfaction factors were also loading on the factors for burnout and stress. Although it is only a simple illustration, this analysis demonstrates that researchers must be very attentive to both conceptual and empirical discriminant validity when crafting and using measures of conflict between work and family.

Relative Utility.   In addition to questions about the clarity of the distinction of conflict between work and family and outcome variables, there are questions about the utility of the construct when studied as a predictor variable. Most phenomena in the social world have many causes. Practical application and parsimony demand that we try to determine which subset of causes or predictors most efficiently predicts each outcome, or the degree to which conflict between family and work is really *necessary* to predict and understand particular outcomes versus other predictors that might do the job better. In addition, theory is driven forward by progress in explaining how predictors relate to one another and why they influence the outcome. An analogy might be found in research on the predictors of risk for heart disease—it is useful to know not only that cholesterol levels are better predictors than gender, for example, but also how cholesterol levels influence risk.

Although only longitudinal data can definitively address the predictive power of conflict between work and family relative to other variables, I conducted two sets of analyses using data from the 1997 National Study of the Changing Workforce to explore the utility of work-family conflict relative to other predictors. The analysis sample included 1,139 mothers and fathers with nonmissing data on all analysis variables. I chose life satisfaction as the dependent variable because it is a key indicator of psychological well-being with an already established empirical connection to conflict between work and family (see the meta-analysis by Kossek & Ozeki, 1998). I chose to focus on work-to-family conflict because it is the most-studied indicator of conflict.

I conducted two regressions, each containing five blocks: (a) work-to-family conflict, (b) work conditions (including hours, income, supervisor support, flexibility, autonomy, learning opportunities, stimulation pressure, and benefits), (c) stress, (d) burnout, and (e) inability to cope. In the first regression I entered the work-to-family conflict first; in the second regression I entered it last.

When work-to-family conflict was entered first, it accounted for 14% of the variance in life satisfaction. When it was entered last, it accounted for only 1%. In other words, once work conditions, burnout, stress, and inability to cope were already in the model, work-to-family conflict was not needed as a predictor— in fact, work conditions and burnout at work accounted for almost all of the explained variance in life satisfaction.

The results of these analyses indicate that work-to-family conflict is certainly correlated with life satisfaction, at least in this large and representative sample. The variation in findings across analysis methods also indicates, however, that work-to-family conflict shares considerable variance with the other independent variables (job burnout being the most notable example here), and that its statistical contribution depends heavily on what variables are already in the model when it enters the equation. Of course, decisions about which variables to include should be based on theory. But eventually, it is both theoretically and practically important to determine which variables are *most* important in predicting life satisfaction and other important outcomes and when work-to-family conflict deserves to be included in that group.

Confidence.   Based on my review of existing research, I conclude that at least two major factors must be considered when assessing the level of confidence that should be attached to findings to date: the degree to which data permit causal conclusions and the degree to which findings might be affected by omitted variables.

Below are two excerpts from studies of conflict between work and family that make strong causal statements:

- "[P]arental demands and hours spent on household work were important determinants of [family-to-work] conflict . . . role conflict, role overload and hours spent on paid work influenced [work-to-family] conflict" (Fu & Shaffer, 2001, p. 502).

- "[L]ife satisfaction of Hong Kong employees is influenced primarily by work-family conflict, while that of American employees is influenced primarily by family-work conflict" (Aryee, Fields, & Luk, 1999, p. 491).

Researchers have persistently drawn causal conclusions even though virtually every study of work-family conflict is cross-sectional, making it impossible to establish the temporal sequence necessary for determining causation. Twenty years into the study of conflict between work and family, it is past the time to start thinking very carefully about what the evidence really tells us. For example, it is very likely that data from these two studies mentioned above would support the following conclusions just as well as the ones originally drawn:

- Family-to-work conflict was an important determinant of perceived parental demands and hours spent on household work . . . work-to-family conflict influenced role conflict, role overload, and hours spent on paid work.
- Work-to-family conflict of Hong Kong employees is influenced primarily by life satisfaction, while for American employees life satisfaction primarily influences family-to-work conflict.

Longitudinal studies can order variables in time and thus fulfill one of the major requirements for establishing causation. Unfortunately, only a handful of longitudinal studies of conflict between family and work have been conducted, especially those covering periods of several months or more (see Williams & Alliger, 1994, for an excellent example of a short-term longitudinal study).

Leiter and Durup (1996) conducted a study of 151 health care professionals in which work-to-family conflict (but not family-to-work conflict) significantly predicted emotional exhaustion, dysphoric mood, and marital satisfaction measured three months later. In turn, however, emotional exhaustion, family personal conflict, and personal accomplishment as measured at time 1 predicted work-to-family conflict three months later.

The finding that work-to-family conflict may be both a cause and a consequence of strain supports Kelloway, Gottlieb, and Barham's (1999, p. 338) claim that "perceptions of work and family conflict would be influenced by the individual's experience of stress." They tested the claim with a six-month longitudinal study of time- and strain-based work-to-family and family-to-work conflict. The outcome variables were perceived stress and turnover intent. Results revealed that family interference with work was more predictive of both turnover and stress than work interference with family. Both strain- and time-based family interference with work predicted stress six months later. Strain-based family interference with work and stress predicted turnover intentions six months later. Work interference with family at time 1 was not predictive of any other variable at time 2. The initial hypothesis was supported by one indicator of conflict:

strain-based work interference with family, which was predicted by stress at time 1.

Grant-Vallone and Donaldson (2001) also conducted a six-month longitudinal study, using multiple raters to avoid the limitations of self-report data. Pairs of coworkers were recruited for two waves of data collection, during which each member of the pair rated the worker's depression, positive well-being, and anxiety (correlations between workers' and coworkers' reports of well-being were $r = .37$ and .31 at time 1 and time 2, respectively). Workers rated their own work-to-family conflict; their answers were controlled for social desirability. Reports of work-to-family conflict at time 1 significantly predicted coworkers' assessments of depression, workers' assessments of anxiety, and both partners' reports of the worker's positive well-being at time 2. No analyses predicting conflict at time 2 were reported.

Matthews, Conger, and Wickrama (1996) studied the role of work-to-family conflict in marital dynamics. Marital interactions and each partner's level of distress were characterized by both partners and by a trained observer, who worked from videotaped observations. Marital quality and stability, measured one year later, were the outcomes of interest. In contrast to the abundance of raters, the measures were sparse, including very few items for each construct. Results showed that each partner's work-to-family conflict was related to his or her own and his or her partner's psychological distress, which in turn correlated with hostile and warm marital interactions, ultimately predicting both marital quality and stability a year later.

The longest study found occurred over a four-year period. Using a large random sample, Frone, Russell, and Cooper (1997) studied the predictive power of family-to-work and work-to-family conflict on an objective measure of hypertension and self-reports of depression, physical health, and alcohol use. Family-to-work conflict was a stronger predictor of the incidence of hypertension than age, race, income, body mass, education, or gender, exceeded only by family history. After baseline scores, family-to-work conflict was also the strongest predictor of depression and poor physical health (in a tie with education). Work-to-family conflict significantly predicted alcohol use four years later.

Data from the few longitudinal studies conducted so far are consistent in several ways with findings from cross-sectional research, supporting early findings that conflict between work and family is connected to a variety of indicators of well-being. In addition, longitudinal studies have provided preliminary evidence that findings hold across multiple raters and across subjective and objective measures of well-being. These studies also suggest that conflict is both a predictor and an outcome of other forms of strain and confirm suggestions from cross-sectional research that the effects of conflict reverberate between spouses. An important new insight from longitudinal research is that the influence of family-to-work conflict may become more evident with the passage of time.

Studies with more than two waves of measurement are needed to reveal exactly how conflict effects unfold over time.

Judgments about our confidence in findings about conflict between work and family must also take into account omissions from existing research. Recall the illustration in the previous section of how results vary as a function of which variables are included in (or omitted from) analyses. Drawing on Bronfenbrenner's (1988) framework, omitted variables can be considered as person, process, or context factors.

A key *person* factor that has been understudied is disposition. Carlson (1999) assessed the variance in different types of work-to-family conflict that was explained by dispositional tendencies for Type A and negativity after situational variables such as conflict and ambiguity within work and family roles were already taken into account. Even though it was entered last, the standardized regression coefficient for negative affectivity was larger than that of any other variable in equations predicting time-, behavior-, and strain-based work-to-family conflict.

Stoeva, Chiu, and Greenhaus (2002) hypothesized that trait negativity might be linked to conflict in a relationship both mediated and moderated by job and family stress. That is, negativity might affect work-family conflict by heightening individuals' perceptions of the stressfulness of their work and family roles. In a moderator role, negative affectivity may interact with job stress and family stress to predict conflict because individuals high in negativity may be more susceptible to the effects of these stressors on conflict than individuals low in negativity. Results were consistent with mediation for job stress and moderation for family stress. High negativity individuals appeared to be predisposed to perceive high levels of stress regardless of their situation.

Process factors also require greater attention in the future. Observing that studies of chronic stress tend not to reveal strong findings when samples are heterogeneous, Perry-Jenkins, Repetti, and Crouter (2000, p. 987) assert that researchers should be asking, "Under what conditions are which job stressors transferred to which families; how is stress transmitted; and what different types of outcomes are observed?" The study by Matthews, Conger, and Wickrama (1996) cited earlier offers one illustration of a model that attempts to address the "how" question so essential to understanding the processes through which work and family affect one another.

Studies of *contextual* effects sometimes lack sophistication, labeling as evidence of contextual effects, for example, simple differences between groups living or working in different contexts (Bronfenbrenner & Crouter, 1982). New hierarchical methods of analysis are permitting clearer dissection of effects into their individual and contextual components, as well as facilitating the examination of interactions among these components as processes unfold (e.g., MacDermid, Hertzog, Kensinger, & Zipp, 2001).

The bad news is that unmeasured variables do appear to be a challenge to the confidence we can have in existing findings regarding conflict between work and family. The good news is that once person, process, and context factors are more fully taken into account, it will be possible to construct explanatory models more powerful than those in use today.

DOES CONFLICT BETWEEN WORK AND FAMILY MATTER?

Since the answer to the above question likely depends on who is being asked, I consider four specific audiences: researchers, employers, workers, and workers' families. There is no question that conflict between work and family has been popular with researchers. In part, this is because it has been a productive construct to study, yielding connections to many different areas of personal and professional life. It is probably also fair to say that there is an element of self-interest in researchers' enthusiasm, given the challenges many of them face in combining their own demanding jobs with family responsibilities. In general, however, to the extent that individuals experience the needs of the institutions in which they participate as conflicting with the fulfillment of other important responsibilities, it is reasonable to ask whether distress will result and to study the phenomenon. Conceptually, conflict between family and work matters to researchers, and empirical findings so far appear to justify their interest.

Conflict between work and family also has been a very popular topic in the corporate world. Employers design 'family-friendly' programs and policies with the goal of reducing the degree to which conflicts emanating from the family can negatively impact work (Lambert, 1993), even though research evidence to date suggests that work-to-family conflict should be of far greater concern (at least in the short term). The underlying presumption is that workers who experience less conflict will be more productive. Unfortunately, there is very little evidence, experimental or otherwise, testing this claim with anything other than self-reports.

And what about workers and their families? The ease with which researchers reveal statistical connections between conflict and other variables may indicate that it really is a key indicator of their quality of life. Workers report concern about work-family conflict on national surveys, even reporting that they would change jobs or give up compensation to reduce it (Galinsky, Bond, & Friedman, 1993). Research has shown that conflict reverberates throughout families, to spouses' well-being (Matthews, Conger, & Wickrama, 1996), marital interactions (Matthews, Conger, & Wickrama, 1996), and relationships between parents and children (MacDermid & Williams, 1997).

RECOMMENDATIONS

I offer several recommendations for future research suggested by the preceding sections.

- Beware of separate spheres. Because demographic realities have shifted, a priori assumptions about the separate roles of men and women are increasingly risky as research design strategies. Untested assumptions about the implications for one role of involvement in another role are equally risky.
- Focus more on "how" and less on "how much." Analyses that explain why individuals respond differently to similar conditions are likely to be much more useful than comparisons aimed at determining which group(s) report lower or higher levels of work-family conflict. Researchers should ask when work-family conflict occurs, why it occurs, for whom it occurs, and with what results. Often, interactions are more interesting than main effects.
- Pay attention to the content of context. As in the point above, ask not just which contexts but what is it about those contexts that is important for the experience of work-family conflict. Consider "culprits" in addition to the job for interference with family life.
- Think (and act) carefully about thinking, feeling, and doing. Consider separately the cognitive, behavioral and affective aspects of relationships between work and family, including coping.
- Do not conflate stress with stressors. Make no assumptions about the impact of particular experiences on research participants—directly measure their appraisal.
- Consider the beats of different drummers. Conduct research on the time structure of different layers of work-family conflict (i.e., short-, medium-, and long-term). Further develop theoretical models of enhancing or enriching processes running between work and family, along with appropriate measurement strategies.
- Prevent unintentional obfuscation. Consider the cognitive requirements posed by the questions research participants are asked. Define terms clearly so that participants will understand questions in the same way. Reduce time intervals being asked about and/or include memory prompts to improve the accuracy of recall. Make answer choices unambiguous and design them with good information about where to position the average options to which respondents may be drawn.
- Say what is and what is not. Present evidence of both the convergent and discriminant validity of measures, especially the latter. Make sure there are meaningful distinctions—both conceptual and empirical—between the independent and dependent variables.

- Really, what difference does it make? Work to increase the rigor of measurement and research design so that causal flows can be accurately understood. Reduce reliance on cross-sectional and self-report data. Develop good measures of work-related outcomes and assess the impact of conflict at home and at work, as well as the impact of interventions. Routinely assess current mood and dispositional tendencies so their effects can be partialled or studied separately.

AUTHOR NOTE

This chapter was prepared while the author was supported by grants from the Alfred P. Sloan Foundation (with Marcie Pitt-Catsouphes and Robert Perrucci) and by cooperative agreement DASW01-00-2-0005 from the Office of Military Community and Family Policy in the Department of Defense (with Howard Weiss and Stephen Green). Thanks to Susan Lambert and Ellen Kossek for the invitation to participate in this volume; to Howard Weiss, Dan Beal, and Stephen Green for their assistance during the writing of this chapter; and to the other contributors to this volume for their supportive suggestions. Finally, I appreciate very much the sponsors who made it possible for the contributors to gather to discuss their ideas face-to-face and the comments of an anonymous reviewer. Address correspondence to shelly@purdue.edu.

REFERENCES

Allen, T. D., Herst, D.E.L., Bruck, C. S., & Sutton, M. (2000). Consequences associated with work-to-family conflict: A review and agenda for future research. *Journal of Occupational Health Psychology, 5*(2), 278–308.

Aryee, S., Fields, D., & Luk, V. (1999). A cross-cultural test of a model of the work-family interface. *Journal of Management, 25,* 491–511.

Barnett, R. C., & Baruch, G. K. (1987). Social roles, gender, and psychological distress. In R. C. Barnett, L. Biener, & G. K. Baruch (Eds.), *Gender and stress* (pp. 122–143). New York: Free Press.

Barnett, R. C., & Hyde, J. S. (2001). Women, men, work, and family: An expansionist theory. *American Psychologist, 56,* 781–796.

Baruch, G. K., & Barnett, R. C. (1986). Role quality, multiple role involvement, and psychological well-being in midlife women. *Journal of Personality and Social Psychology, 51,* 578–585.

Bond, J. T., Galinsky, E., & Swanberg, J. E. (1998). *The 1997 national study of the changing workforce.* New York: Families and Work Institute.

Boulding, E. (1955). The cooperative nursery and the young mother's role conflict. *Marriage and Family Living, 17,* 303–309.

Bronfenbrenner, U. (1988). Interacting systems in human development. Research paradigms: Present and future. In N. Bolger, A. Caspi, G. Downey, & M. Moorehouse (Eds.), *Persons in context: Developmental processes* (pp. 25–49). Cambridge, England: Cambridge University Press.

Bronfenbrenner, U., & Crouter, A. C. (1982). Work and family through time and space. In S. B. Kamerman & C. D. Hayes (Eds.), *Families that work: Children in a changing world* (pp. 39–83). Washington, DC: National Academy Press.

Campbell, W. K., & Sedikides, C. (1999). Self-threat magnifies the self-serving bias: A meta-analytic interpretation. *Review of General Psychology, 3,* 23–43.

Cannell, C. F., Fisher, G., & Bakker, T. (1965). Reporting on hospitalization in the Health Interview survey. *Vital and Health Statistics* (PHS Publication No. 1000, Series 2, No. 6). Washington, DC: U.S. Government Printing Office.

Carlson, D. S., (1999). Personality and role variables as predictors of three forms of work-family conflict. *Journal of Vocational Behavior, 55,* 236–253.

Carlson, D. S., & Frone, M. R. (2003). Relation of behavioral and psychological involvement to a new four-factor conceptualization of work-family interference. *Journal of Business and Psychology, 17,* 515–536.

Carlson, D. S., Kacmar, K. M., & Williams, L. J. (2000). Construction and initial validation of a multi-dimensional measure of work-family conflict. *Journal of Vocational Behavior, 56,* 249–276.

Doherty, W. J., Boss, P. G., LaRossa, R., Schumm, W. R., & Steinmetz, S. K. (1993). Family theories and methods: A contextual approach. In P. G. Boss, W. J. Doherty, R. LaRossa, W. R. Schumm, & S. K. Steinmetz (Eds.), *Sourcebook of family theories and methods: A contextual approach* (pp. 3–30). New York: Plenum.

Frone, M. R. (2003). Work-family balance. In J. C. Quick & L. E. Tetrick (Eds.), *Handbook of occupational health psychology* (pp. 143–162). Washington, DC: American Psychological Association.

Frone, M. R., Russell, M., & Barnes, G. M. (1996). Work-family conflict, gender, and health-related outcomes: A study of employed parents in two community samples. *Journal of Occupational Health Psychology, 1,* 57–69.

Frone, M. R., Russell, M., & Cooper, M. L. (1992). Antecedents and outcomes of work-family conflict: Testing a model of the work-family interface. *Journal of Applied Psychology, 77,* 65–78.

Frone, M. R., Russell, M., & Cooper, M. L. (1997). Relation of work-family conflict to health outcomes: A four-year longitudinal study of employed parents. *Journal of Occupational and Organizational Psychology, 70,* 325–335.

Frone, M. R., Yardley, Y. K., & Markel, K. S, (1997). Developing and testing an integrative model of the work-family interface. *Journal of Vocational Behavior, 50,* 145–167.

Fu, C. K., & Shaffer, M. A. (2001). The tug of work and family: Direct and indirect domain-specific determinants of work-family conflict. *Personnel Review, 30,* 502–522.

Galinsky, E., Bond, J. T., & Friedman, D. E. (1993). The changing workforce: Highlights of the National study. New York: Families and Work Institute.

Goode, William J. (1960). A theory of role strain. *American Sociological Review, 25,* 483–496.

Grant-Vallone, E. J., & Donaldson, S. I. (2001). Consequences of work-family conflict on employee well-being over time. *Work and Stress, 15,* 214–226.

Greenhaus, J. H., & Beutell, N. J. (1985). Sources of conflict between work and family roles. *Academy of Management Review, 10,* 76–88.

Greenhaus, J. H., & Powell, G. N. (2003). When work and family collide: Deciding between competing role demands. *Organizational Behavior and Human Decision Processes, 90*(2), 291–303.

Grzywacz, J. G. (2000). Work-family spillover and health during midlife: Is managing conflict everything? *American Journal of Health Promotion, 14,* 236–243.

Grzywacz, J. G., & Bass, B. L. (2003). Work, family, and mental health: Testing different models of work-family fit. *Journal of Marriage and Family, 65,* 248–262.

Gutek, B., Searle, S., & Klepa, L. (1991). Rational versus gender role-explanations for work-family conflict. *Journal of Applied Psychology, 76,* 560–568.

Hammer, L. B., Bauer, T. N., & Grandey, A. A. (2003). Work-family conflict and work-related withdrawal behaviors. *Journal of Business and psychology, 17,* 419–436.

Hammer, L. B., Colton, C. L., Caubet, S. L., & Brockwood, K. J. (2002). The unbalanced life: Work and family conflict. In J. C. Thomas & M. Hersen (Eds.), *Handbook of mental health in the workplace* (pp. 83–101). Thousand Oaks, CA: Sage.

Jundt, D. K. & Hinsz, V. B. (2002). Influences of positive and negative affect on decisions involving judgmental biases. *Social Behavior and Personality, 30,* 45–52.

Kahn, R. L., Wolfe, D. M., Quinn, R. P., Snoek, J. D., & Rosenthal, R. A. (1964). *Organizational stress: Studies in role conflict and ambiguity.* New York: Wiley.

Kelloway, E. K., Gottlieb, B. H., & Barham, L. (1999). The source, nature and direction of work and family conflict: A longitudinal investigation. *Journal of Occupational Health Psychology, 4,* 337–346.

Kingsbury, N., & Scanzoni, J. (1993) Structural-functionalism. In P. G. Boss, W. J. Doherty, R. LaRossa, W. R. Schumm, & S. K. Steinmetz (Eds.), *Sourcebook of family theories and methods: A contextual approach* (pp. 195–217). New York: Plenum.

Kopelman, R. E., Greenhaus, J. H., & Connolly, T. F. (1983). A model of work, family, and interrole conflict: A construct validation study. *Organizational Behavior and Human Performance, 32,* 198–215.

Kossek, E. E., & Ozeki, C. (1998). Work-family conflict, policies, and the job-life satisfaction relationship: A review and direction for organizational behavior human resources research. *Journal of Applied Psychology, 83*(2), 139–149.

Kossek, E. E., & Ozeki, C. (1999). Bridging the work-family policy and productivity gap: A literature review. *Community, Work & Family, 2,* 7–32.

Lambert, S. J. (1990). Processes linking work and family: A critical review and research agenda. *Human Relations, 43,* 239–257.

Lambert, S. J. (1993). Workplace policies as social policy. *Social Service Review, 67*(2), 237–260.

LaRossa, R., & Reitzes, D. C. (1993). Symbolic interactionism and family studies. In P. G. Boss, W. J. Doherty, R. LaRossa, W. R. Schumm, & S. K. Steinmetz (Eds.), *Sourcebook of family theories and methods: A contextual approach* (pp. 135–162). New York: Plenum.

Leiter, M. P., & Durup, M. J. (1996). Work, home, and in-between: A longitudinal study of spillover. *Journal of Applied Behavioral Science, 32,* 29–47.

Lewis, O. (1949). Husbands and wives in a Mexican village: A study of role conflict. *American Anthropologist, 51,* 602–610.

MacDermid, S. M., Hertzog, J., Kensinger, K., & Zipp, J. (2001). The role of organizational size and industry in job quality and work-family relationships. *Journal of Family and Economic Issues, 22,* 191–216.

MacDermid, S. M., & Williams, M. L. (1997). A within-industry comparison of employed mothers' experiences in small and large workplaces. *Journal of Family Issues, 18,* 545–566.

MacDermid, S. M., Seery, B. L. & Weiss, H. M. (2002). An emotional examination of the work-family interface. In R. G. Lord, R. J. Klimoski, & R. Kanfer (Eds.), *Emotions in the workplace: Understanding the structure and role of emotions in organizational behavior* (pp. 402–428). San Francisco: Jossey-Bass.

Marks, S. R. (1977). Multiple roles and role strain: Some notes on human energy, time, and commitment. *American Sociological Review, 42,* 921–936.

Mason, C. D. (2002). 100 most frequently cited articles in social sciences index: A list. *Sloan Work & Family Research Network Newsletter,* pp. 1–13. Retrieved November 2, 2003, from http://www.bc.edu/bc_org/avp/wfnetwork/loppr/top100.pdf

Matthews, L. S., Conger, R. D., & Wickrama, K.A.S. (1996). Work-family conflict and marital quality: Mediating processes. *Social Psychology Quarterly, 59,* 62–79.

Moen, P., & Yu, Y. (2000). Effective work/life strategies: Working couples, work conditions, gender, and life quality. *Social Problems, 47*(3), 291–326.

Netemeyer, R. G., Boles, J. S., & McMurrian, R. (1996). Development and validation of work-family conflict and family-work conflict scales. *Journal of Applied Psychology, 81,* 400–410.

Ottati, V. C., & Isbell, L. M. (1996). Effects of mood during exposure to target information on subsequently reported judgments: An on-line model of misattribution and correction. *Journal of Personality and Social Psychology, 71,* 39–53.

Perry-Jenkins, M., Repetti, R. L., & Crouter, A. C. (2000, November). Work and families in the 1990s. *Journal of Marriage and the Family, 62,* 981–998.

Robinson, J. P., & Godbey, G. (1997). *Time for life: The surprising ways Americans use their time.* University Park: Pennsylvania State University Press.

Rogers, S. J., & Amato, P. R. (2000). Have changes in gender relations affected marital quality? *Social Forces, 79,* 731–753.

Rothbard, N. P. (2001). Enriching or depleting? The dynamics of engagement in work and family roles. *Administrative Science Quarterly, 46,* 655–684.

Rotondo, D. M., Carlson, D. S., & Kincaid, J. F. (2002). Coping with multiple dimensions of work-family conflict. *Personnel Review, 32,* 275–296.

Ruderman, M. N., Ohlott, P. J., Panzer, K., & King, S. N. (2002). Benefits of multiple roles for managerial women. *Academy of Management Journal, 45,* 369–386.

Sabini, J., Siepmann, M., & Stein, J. (2001). The really fundamental attribution error in social psychological research. *Psychological Inquiry, 12,* 1–15.

Schacter, D. L. (1999). The seven sins of memory: Insights from psychology and cognitive neuroscience. *American Psychologist, 54,* 182–203.

Schacter, D. L., & Dodson, C. S. (2001). Misattribution, false recognition and the sins of memory. In A. Baddeley, J. P. Aggleton, & M. A. Conway (Eds.), *Episodic memory: New directions in research* (pp. 71–85). Oxford, England: Oxford University Press.

Schwarz, N. (2002). Situated cognition and the wisdom of feelings: Cognitive tuning. In L. Feldman Barrett & P. Salovey (Eds.), *The wisdom in feeling* (pp. 144–166). New York: Guilford.

Schwarz, N., & Oyserman, D. (2001). Asking questions about behavior: Cognition, communication, and questionnaire construction. *American Journal of Evaluation, 22,* 127–160.

Schwarz, N., & Strack, F. (1999). Reports of subjective well-being: Judgmental processes and their methodological implications. In D. Kahneman, E. Diener, & N. Schwarz (Eds.), *Well-being: The foundations of hedonic psychology* (pp. 61–84). New York: Russell Sage Foundation.

Sieber, S. D. (1974). Toward a theory of role accumulation. *American Sociological Review, 39,* 467–478.

Stephens, G. K., & Sommer, S. M. (1996). The measurement of work to family conflict. *Educational and Psychological Measurement, 56,* 475–486.

Stoeva, A. Z., Chiu, R. K., & Greenhaus, J. H. (2002). Negative affectivity, role stress, and work-family conflict. *Journal of Vocational Behavior, 60*(1) 1–16.

U.S. Bureau of the Census. (2003). *Statistical abstract of the United States.* Washington, DC: U.S. Government Printing Office.

Wiese, B. S., & Freund, A. M. (2000). The interplay of work and family in young and middle adulthood. In J. Heckhausen (Ed.), *Motivational psychology of human development* (pp. 233–249). New York: Elsevier.

Williams, K. J., & Alliger, G. M. (1994). Role stressors, mood spillover, and perceptions of work-family conflict in employed parents. *Academy of Management Journal, 37,* 837–888.

Zedeck, S. (1992). Exploring the domain of work and family concerns. In S. Zedeck (Ed.), *Work, families, and organizations* (pp. 1–32). San Francisco: Jossey-Bass.

II

Organizational Perspectives

3

The Changing Time Demands of Managerial and Professional Work: Implications for Managing the Work-Life Boundary

Frances J. Milliken
Linda M. Dunn-Jensen
New York University

The thief to be most wary of is the one who steals your time.

—Anonymous

INTRODUCTION

Recent data suggest that the average U.S. worker worked 175 more hours in the year 2000 than he or she worked in 1979 (Schor, 2003, citing data from the International Labor Organization).[1] In addition, there is some evidence to suggest that workers, especially professional and managerial workers in the United States, perceive that they are busier than they used to be (Milliken, Beunza, & Dunn-Jensen, 2001). Not surprisingly, according to a *Wall Street Journal* survey, "75% of those earning more than $100,000 a year . . . say managing their time is a bigger problem than managing their money" (March 8, 1996, R1). In her research on engineers at a hi-tech company, Leslie Perlow (1999) concluded that many of the workers were increasingly operating in what she called a "time famine," which she defined as "a feeling of having too much to do and not enough time to do it" (p. 57).

In this chapter, we focus on how certain technological and competitive trends have converged over the last decade, especially in the United States, to change both the nature of managerial and professional work and the expectations regarding appropriate work hours. The changes in the nature of managerial and professional work coupled with the changes in expectations about the allocation of time for work versus nonwork activities are fundamental to understanding the nature of the work-life dilemmas these workers are likely to experience as we enter the twenty-first century. In particular, we are interested in how the longer hours, the increased complexity of managerial and professional jobs, and the pressure to produce faster are altering the context within which individuals are making choices about how to define the boundary between the work and nonwork domains of their lives.

There is a good deal of evidence to suggest that the number of hours people work is related to the amount of work-family conflict they are likely to experience, especially the amount of time-based conflict (Greenhaus & Beutell, 1985), which is defined as occurring when "devoting time to the demands in one domain consumes time needed to meet the demands of the other domain" (Edwards & Rothbard, 2000, p. 182). Recent research suggests that the more hours people work, the higher the level of work interference with family and the lower their psychological well being (Major, Klein, & Erhart, 2002). In a meta-analysis of research on the relationship between work hours and health, Sparks and her colleagues (Sparks, Cooper, Fried, & Shirom, 1997) similarly found that there is also a significant relationship between hours worked and the experience of stress and other health-related outcomes. So, clearly long hours of work can have negative consequences for employees in their nonwork lives. Similarly, the feeling that one is operating under intense time pressure, or in what Perlow (1999) refers to as a time famine, can create a feeling of overwork, which can lead to stress and job dissatisfaction, possibly creating strain-based work-family conflict (Greenhaus & Beutell, 1985).

We seek to contribute to the work-life literature by enriching our understanding of how people think about and manage their work and nonwork time when faced with pressure to work fast and to work long hours. We begin our chapter with an exploration of some of the environmental trends that have altered the nature of managerial and professional work in the last 10 to 20 years. In the first section, we examine the effects that these environmental trends might have on the actual work of managerial and professional employees. We pay particular attention to the fact that work usually takes place in hierarchies, a factor that we will argue plays a big role in understanding how people conceive what is appropriate regarding work hours and work pace. In the second section, we offer some hypotheses about the factors that affect where and how people set the boundaries between activities in their work life and activities in their nonwork lives. In the final section, we discuss the implications of our thinking for understanding the work-life boundary, especially given the changes that have affected the world of managerial and professional work in the last 10 to 20 years in the United States.

THE CHANGING TIME DEMANDS ON MANAGERIAL AND PROFESSIONAL WORKERS

We argue that a number of workplace trends have combined in the last 20 years to make managerial and professional work more complex. One key factor has been the introduction of new communication technologies such as voice mail, e-mail, fax machines, and cell phones. Contrary to predictions made 25 years ago, the introduction of these allegedly efficiency-enhancing communication technologies has not reduced the number of hours that U.S. workers spend at work. Rather, the trend has been in the opposite direction. Further, "technology has created the sense that we are squeezing more and more activities into a given amount of time—giving the sense that life is moving too fast" (Gleick, 1999). But not only have we increased the number of methods available for communication between people, all of these new technologies enable us to be in communication with others about work on a constant basis. Thus, we have added channels of communication to be processed as well as added around-the-clock access to these communication methodologies.

These new technologies support the "on call" nature of work. In other words, they create a workforce that can be available, at least theoretically speaking, "24/7" from anywhere. This has had two major effects. First, the 24/7 availability of access to information from the office has increased the permeability of the boundary between work and home, causing increasing numbers of managerial and professional workers to conduct work-related activities in the time that was formerly reserved for nonwork or family activities. Many professional and managerial employees (and academics as well), for example, report that they log onto e-mail late at night from home. A second outcome of the introduction of technologies such as e-mail, voice mail, cell phones, and fax machines has been to create the expectation that communications received via these means will elicit a faster response than was expected in the past to what is now called "snail mail" (i.e., the postal system). This increased expectation for speedy replies has the effect of adding tasks that need to be accomplished to our short-term agenda.

It has also been argued that greater levels of research and development (R&D) and an increased pace of innovation in the economy have shortened the duration of the competitive advantage of industry leaders in many industries, ranging from consumer electronics to airlines to computer software and even snack foods (D'Aveni, 1994; Hamel & Pralahad, 1994). In order to sustain their rents, firms must keep up with the innovations, changes, and improvements their rivals make.

To quote a marketing letter we recently received from the *Harvard Business Review*: "Speed is power in all arenas of competition. As the pace of business increases, you need faster access to the ideas driving business." Businesses now feel intense pressure to cut their lead times on the production of products and services in order to compete successfully. This increased premium on speed is not only felt in the manufacturing sectors of the economy but also in the professional service sector of the economy as well. Consulting firms and law firms, for example, are pressured by their clients to deliver services faster and better.

Globalization also drives the perceived need for increased efficiency in order to compete with companies operating in countries with access to low-wage labor. This perceived need for enhanced efficiency led to significant downsizing in the United States in the 1990s. The effect for many workers who survived the rounds of layoffs was often the pressure to take on additional tasks and to work harder. Allen et al. (2001), for example, found that survivors of downsizing initiatives reported higher levels of role overload subsequent to the downsizing.

We believe that the aggregate effect of these trends has been to increase the work-related demands on managerial and professional workers. In particular, we believe that managerial and professional workers in the United States are experiencing three types of time pressure: the pressure to get tasks done faster; the pressure to work longer hours; and the pressure to work 24/7, or anywhere and anytime, which has been created by the widespread availability and use of cell phone, e-mail, voice mail, and fax machines.

Each of these types of time pressure has important consequences both for managing work-related tasks and for managing the boundary between work and nonwork. Consider, for example, what happens when the time given to someone to accomplish a particular job is shortened, whether that job be writing a legal brief or introducing a new product to market. In such a circumstance, it is necessarily true that more tasks have to be completed in a given time period than previously. If the number of tasks to accomplish in a given time period is increasing, then it must also be true that the amount of time to accomplish some of the subtasks must decrease or tasks must be dropped. The attempt to compress tasks to fit into smaller blocks of time creates both the sense of needing to work faster as well as a sense of being pressed for time. We refer to the effort to squeeze more tasks into a finite period of time as *time compression,* which we define as the accumulated effect of having to accomplish tasks in less time than one had to accomplish the tasks previously. If, at the same time that this demand for increased speed of task accomplishment is occurring, there is also a trend toward increased complexity of managerial and professional jobs, then one can easily understand how and why there would be upward pressure on the number of hours devoted to work versus nonwork activities.

A critical but largely unexplored aspect of the expansion of work hours is the idea that there may be social forces that contribute to this change. Whatever technological and competitive forces are involved in driving longer work hours, these forces are likely to be magnified by social forces that characterize the behavior of individuals in hierarchies. If there are limited opportunities for upward mobility in a hierarchy and more people who desire promotions than there are promotions to be had, then a worker needs to be perceived as an excellent performer in order to win a promotion. In cases in which performance is difficult to measure, this may translate into a perceived need to be seen as willing and able to work long hours, especially when one's manager and peers are doing the same. To the extent that an individual desires to move up the hierarchy and his or her peers work long hours, then it becomes as much a social imperative as a work-related imperative that an individual work long hours in order to preserve his or her status in the hierarchy. Some workers probably would argue that they have to work long hours just to keep their jobs.

In addition, the sense of urgency that an organization's clients convey about the need for fast action on a project or issue is likely to cascade down the hierarchy to affect the lives of lower-level managers and employees. Bosses who feel pressure from clients to deliver products or services faster put pressure on their employees to do tasks faster. Each successive lower level in the hierarchy pushes its sense of urgency down to the level below it, demanding greater and greater levels of dedication and speed.

When faced with deadlines or a sense of urgency, upper-level managers are also more likely to interrupt the tasks of lower-level workers to ask them to do something that is associated with the urgent task that they have on their mind at the time (Perlow, 1997). The effect of these interruptions is twofold. First, when a manager interrupts with a request, the work requested is added to the current workload, adding on tasks to the individual's job. Second, interruptions have the effect of detracting from the worker's efficiency at accomplishing the first task because there are significant costs associated with having to go back and try to remember where one was when one was interrupted (Perlow, 1997; Seshadri & Shapira, 2001). Interruptions, thus, contribute to the expansion of work hours in two ways: by adding tasks and by creating inefficiency in the accomplishment of current tasks.

CROSSING BOUNDARIES: THE IMPLICATIONS OF INCREASED TIME PRESSURES AT WORK ON EMPLOYEES AT WORK AND AT HOME

In the work-family literature, attention has recently been paid to the importance of distinguishing between work-to-family conflict and family-to-work conflict (Carlson & Kacmar, 2000; Greenhaus & Powell, 2003; Kossek & Ozeki, 1999; Netemeyer, Boles, & McMurrian, 1996). Work-to-family conflict occurs when participation in a work activity prevents an individual from participating in a family activity. Family-to-work conflict occurs when participation in a family activity prevents an individual from participating in a work activity (Frone, Yardley, & Markel, 1997). We use the term *work creep* to refer to a situation in which the work domain gradually encroaches on personal and family time. Thus, work creep is a form of work-to-family conflict. We use the word *creep* because it captures an important aspect of the phenomenon we are most interested in, which is the gradual and often unnoticed spillover of work into family time.

In this section of the chapter, we describe some of the cognitive and social processes that may affect how employees think about their allocation of time between the domain of work and the domain of home given these increased demands from the workplace on their time. Our main point is that to understand the decisions that people make when choosing between obligations at work and obligations at home, one must understand the cognitive and social phenomena that affect how people think about time and their time allocation decisions.

One explanation of why people may be working more is that they have more responsibilities than they used to have (e.g., processing various forms of communications, doing tasks that their colleagues who were let go used to do). This explanation suggests that the number of work hours an individual works is likely to be directly proportional to the amount of work to be done. Another explanation for why people may be working longer hours is that they perceive that their bosses expect them to do so. Thus, workers believe that spending time at work, even when they are not actually working (often called *face time*), is important to maximize their probability of receiving a raise or of being promoted. In this case, the explanation of long work hours rests not on an assumption of an increased workload necessarily but rather suggests an important role for organizational factors like hierarchy and norms in explaining the increase in work hours. Yet another explanation of why people are working longer hours lies in the notion that people are only boundedly rational in the way they prioritize their tasks (March & Simon, 1958). These explanations of why managerial and professional employees may be putting more time into work are, of course, not mutually exclusive. Each of these sets of factors is likely to account for at least some of the variance in the increase in hours spent on work. In this chapter, we focus particular attention on the ways in which cognitive and social factors may be influencing the expansion of work and creating work-family conflict. We start with an exploration of *bounded rationality* on individuals' thinking about the allocation of time between the work and nonwork domains of their lives.

The Bounded Rationality of Thinking About Time

When people have to prioritize tasks, they are likely to prioritize them on the basis of urgency rather than importance (Eisner & Shapira, 1999; March &

Simon, 1958). When tasks are urgent and appear to have negative consequences if the individual fails to complete them, it is likely that these tasks will be perceived to be more important than a legitimately important task without an immediate deadline or a serious consequence. Thus, one would predict that tasks without immediate deadlines would take a back seat to tasks with immediate deadlines.

Deciding between tasks on the basis of urgency is likely to lead to a situation where, all else being equal, work activities are "advantaged" in the competition for time resources over nonwork activities (especially family activities) because work-related activities have greater perceived urgency. Time with family, for example, can be postponed; finishing a report that has a deadline of tomorrow for a client appears more urgent because it has a concrete deadline. The following quote from one of our interviews with a part-time MBA student who is also a full-time employee captures the issue of how deadlines at work affect his allocation of time: "I definitely [feel more pressure] at work, because client deadlines are not flexible. Home responsibilities can be pushed off to a certain extent."

Further, the failure to finish the report on time is likely to be perceived as having serious negative consequences (e.g., if you do not finish the report, your boss will be angry and may yell at you or give you a bad performance review, and so forth). Taking the time away from family to finish the report, on the other hand, is likely to appear to have less serious negative consequences. Family members are assumed to be willing to forgive; bosses are less frequently assumed to be forgiving.

Proposition 1: In the short term, to the extent that work tasks are perceived to have deadlines and meaningful negative consequences for failing to complete them, they will be given priority in the competition for time resources over most nonwork activities.

One implication of our underlying logic is that with the increased demand for speed in organizations, there may be a concomitant increase in the number of deadlines that the average professional and managerial employee is facing. Also, the downsizing trend that took place in the United States in the last 10 to 15 years may have made the average professional and managerial worker less secure about his or her position. This sense of job insecurity may make him or her more likely to perceive that there will be serious negative consequences for the failure to meet a manager's expectations regarding deadlines and other elements of the pacing of work. Thus, both the increased emphasis on speed of product delivery and the downsizing of the workforce have the effect of making work tasks more likely to be given priority over nonwork tasks than they previously would have.

We also suspect that people are not very conscious about how they spend their time. What may seem like temporary temporal arrangements (e.g., giving work activities priority over nonwork activities) not only can continue to exist for a long period of time without much reflection, but they can also create self-perpetuating cycles, a point to which we will return later in this chapter.

The Impact of Organizational Factors on the Allocation of Time to the Work and Nonwork Domains of Life

While there are many organizational or job-related factors that may influence workers' thinking about how many hours to devote to work, we focus here on two main factors: the organization's culture and the nature of the work itself.

The Effect of Organizational Culture.   Clearly, the work-family culture of an organization will influence employee perceptions about the acceptable balance of work-family integration. Thompson, Beauvais, and Lyness (1999, p. 394) defined work-family culture as "the shared assumptions, beliefs, and values regarding the extent to which an organization supports and values the integration of employees' work and family lives." In organizations that have little to no managerial support for work-family issues or where individuals feel as though there are possible negative career consequences for balancing work-family life (Anderson, Coffey, & Byerly, 2002), employees are more likely to experience work creep. For example, a manager may schedule a breakfast meeting to address an important issue regarding an ongoing project. However, over the course of the project, the occasional breakfast meeting gradually becomes accepted as a standard meeting that the manager expects all employees to attend. Thus, the breakfast meeting has converted time that was previously family time into work time. If the employee perceives that attendance at this meeting is an expectation or norm, the employee will need to be there in order to be considered part of the team. Thus, the employee will lose family time by this meeting creeping from the work domain into family time. Perlow (1998) argues that the scheduling of activities by managers is one way that they attempt to control the employees' work-nonwork boundary by dictating expectations about expected work hours.

The gradual encroachment of the work domain into time previously set aside for nonwork activities is especially likely in individualistic organizational cultures where there is perceived to be intense competition between individuals for managerial goodwill, promotions, and monetary rewards because employees in these types of organizations will perceive that meeting managerial expectations regarding work hours is critical to the advancement of their careers. This leads to the following proposition:

Proposition 2: The more emphasis the workplace culture places on competition between individuals for promotions, raises, and bonuses, the more work creep there will be in the lives of the organization's members.

Employees' decisions about appropriate work hours for themselves are likely to be affected by what they perceive to be the expectations of appropriate work hours. Perlow (1999) argues that in the engineering culture she studied, working long hours was viewed as a measure of one's commitment to the organization. Failure to put in the hours that others do, thus, is likely to be viewed as an example of one's lack of commitment.

Proposition 3: The perceived failure of an individual to put in at least the social norm of work hours will be associated with a perceived lack of commitment to the organization.

It is likely that expectations of appropriate work hours have risen in many industries as organizations seek to cut development cycles and/or find ways to deliver products or services to clients faster. The following quote from a part-time MBA student we interviewed captures this:

Our boss seems to measure productivity by the amount of time one spends at [one's] desk, not by what [one] produces . . . Our boss keeps telling us we should work longer hours . . . I doubt he would be happy until [we worked] at least 12 hours a day.

Measurability of Performance.   In work cultures where an individual's contribution to a product or service is hard to operationalize, visible indicators such as the number of hours a person works are likely to be taken as a proxy measure of productivity (Perin, 1991; Perlow, 1998; Rutherford, 2001). This is particularly true for organizations in which speed of responsiveness to the customer is a source of potential competitive advantage.

Proposition 4: The more difficult it is to measure performance objectively, the greater the pressure on employees to work long hours.

Preventing Work Creep: The Difficulty of Managing the Work-Nonwork Boundary

Employees who have a desire to balance their work with nonwork activities face a dilemma given the strong environmental and organizational pressures that seem to be propelling forward the expansion of work hours. This is especially true when one considers that individuals may be only boundedly rational in how they make their time allocation decisions. We have argued that the pressure of dead-lines and the perceived negative consequences of failing to meet managers' ex-pectations suggest that work activities are likely to be advantaged over nonwork activities in the competition for time.

People, we argue, are generally conscious of this time-based work-family conflict but often are not sure what to do to prevent work from creeping into their nonwork lives. One possible strategy for not allowing work to drive out home tasks is to protect time at home by deliberately placing a nonpermeable boundary around family time, thereby preventing work activities from encroach-ing on blocked-off time at home. Not doing so, as we have previously argued, enables work to spill into home time, because home time is less clearly allocated and has fewer clear deadlines. This is even truer today than it was 10 to 20 years ago because e-mail, voice mail, and faxes make it much easier for people to communicate about work during nonwork hours.

This blocking out of time, however, is hard for people to do. As Perlow (1999) found, employees perceive there to be large negative consequences for them at work for insisting on rigid schedules or blocking off time with family. Judiesch and Lyness (1999) found that employees taking family-related leaves of absence were negatively affected in their performance ratings, promotions, and salary increases. In addition, Perlow (1995) argued that taking advantage of family-friendly policies hindered long-term career advancement for employ-ees who used work-family programs. Perlow (1999) also found that workers who obviously valued time at home, who left early, or who did not work week-ends tended to be perceived as not as committed to the organization as their peers.

The following quotes from part-time MBA students we interviewed as a part of our work illustrate the issue:

"Strategic face time" is important. For instance, there is someone a few offices down who spends most days telecommuting but is very visible for important meet-ings—and willing to travel or stay late when necessary. The person in the next office comes in consistently but is very rigid about working 7–2:30 because he has to go home and care for a handicapped child. The latter person is the one in the dead end job.

Absolutely [I try to block time for my personal life but] I do this at the expense of my career. If I were willing to give up, I'd have a higher position and be earning more money.

Thus, we offer the following proposition:

Proposition 5: In general, individuals in professional and managerial roles in large organizations will perceive that blocking out time for family or insisting on a particular set of hours will reduce the likelihood of rewards such as bonuses and promotions.

A Brief Consideration of the Dynamics of Work-Life Decisions

Although many employees may find it easier to balance their work and family life by choosing to work fewer hours, many individuals are unwilling to cut back their work hours in order to rid themselves of a sense of being pressed for time (Reynolds, 2003). This finding is quite intriguing since people report negative reactions to feeling so pressed for time. In her book *The Time Bind* (1997), Arlie Hochschild speculates about why people may choose such long work hours when it is obviously a source of stress for them. She argues that for some workers, work has replaced home as a safe haven because they experience less stress at work than they do at home. These individuals, she argues, choose to work long hours to avoid the stress they associate with going home. Reynolds (2003) and Brett and Stroh (2003) offer an alternative hypothesis that suggests that people are spending more time at work to support rather than escape their family life. As families grow accustomed to a higher level of income and individuals have the resources to purchase quick leisure options such as a weekend getaway or tickets to the theater, it is unlikely that individuals would be willing to reduce their hours and have a reduction of pay, thus not having the financial resources to support their current lifestyle.

Another reason people may be choosing to work long hours is that people get rewarded more for their role in the workplace than for their role in their families (Brett & Stroh, 2003; Reich, 2001). Reich (2001) discusses how exhilarating his job was and, because of this excitement in his job, how he chose to spend more time at the office and less time with his family. In these cases, not only is the role in the workplace more likely to be rewarding than the role in the family domain, but the workplace may be seen as a more exciting place to be.

Working long hours, thus, can become a positive reinforcing cycle. As individuals spend more time in their work domain, the reinforcement value of work increases and they may begin to spend less time with their family. As they spend less time with their family, transitioning into the family domain can become more stressful and less rewarding. For example, coming home from work after dinner and before bed, when the kids are working on homework and tired, can be a stressful experience. When stress is the primary experience of home life, people may be inclined to spend even less time in the family domain and more time in the work domain.

Thus, it is possible that people quite unintentionally enact Hochschild's (1997) hypothesis that people perceive work as a less stressful place to spend time than home by virtue of their prior decisions about work hours. In other words, people do not start out perceiving their time at home as stressful, but as they spend less and less time there, they come to perceive their time there as more and more stressful. This leads us to the following proposition.

> Proposition 6: Individuals who work longer hours will be less likely to perceive time spent in the family domain as rewarding/pleasurable/reinforcing/stress-reducing.

If true, this creates a self-perpetuating element to individuals' decisions about time allocation and suggests that our likely enjoyment of activities in a particular domain may be affected by how much time we have spent recently in that domain. The more time we spend at work, the less positive reinforcement we feel when we spend time at home. In part, this is because the nature of the experience is actually altered.

DISCUSSION

In this chapter, we have sought to explore the changing nature of managerial and professional work in the last 10 to 20 years and how these changes may have altered the context within which managerial and professional workers make decisions about where to place the boundary between the work and nonwork domains of their lives. In particular, we are interested in how individuals' work-life decisions are affected by the perceived need to get work accomplished faster and by the increased complexity and increased quantity of work that have characterized managerial and professional work in the last 10 to 15 years.

We have argued that there is considerable pressure on career-oriented managerial and professional workers to choose work tasks over family tasks when the two domains compete for time. Such choices need to be understood as choices made by boundedly rational individuals (March & Simon, 1958) who make these choices in a social context. A critically important aspect of choices about time is, of course, that time is a fixed resource: Time given to one activity is time taken away from another, unless one engages in multitasking, in which case the quality of one's attention to either activity is diminished. We have argued that tasks that have deadlines tend to drive out tasks that do not have clear deadlines; tasks that have clients drive out those that do not have immediate clients (i.e., strategic planning). Further, we have argued that work-related tasks are more likely to have deadlines, clients, and perceived negative consequences for failing to meet deadlines. Thus, work tasks may be advantaged in a cognitive sense over nonwork activities in the competition for time resources, all else being equal.

We have also stressed the importance of understanding that decisions about how much time to devote to work versus nonwork tasks are often made in a hierarchical work context that may penalize employees for not being seen at work or for not being available to work at home or during off hours. This fact clearly contributes to the likelihood of work creeping into time previously reserved for nonwork activities. We also believe that this tendency for work to creep into nonwork time is exacerbated by the fact that people have a rather imperfect sense of the passage of time. It is easy to believe that there is always another Little League game and that you will have more time next season to coach the soccer team.

The picture we have painted is one that suggests that work may expand almost without individuals noticing it. In other words, it may require quite conscious attention to the choices we make to keep work from expanding and creeping into time that we might have, at one time, sought to allocate to nonwork activities. Further, we have argued that, due to social pressure and managerial expectations, insisting on set schedules or insisting on blocking out time for nonwork activities generally will not be viewed positively.

One implication of our theorizing in this chapter is that we, as management scholars interested in work-life issues, need to spend more time examining how individuals make temporal allocation choices between the demands of work and nonwork life (Greenhaus & Powell, 2003). In terms of future research, we have offered a number of propositions in this chapter that could provide a foundation for guiding empirical research in this area. While each of these propositions is stated in very general terms for the purposes of this chapter, it seems likely that there are important moderating or contingency factors that need to be considered. For example, there are likely to be important individual differences in how people react to the perceived pressures to work longer hours and to work 24/7. Greenhaus and Powell (2003) find some support for the idea that self-esteem may be an important moderator of the degree of work-to-family spillover. Individuals with high self-esteem may be more willing to attempt to protect their time for nonwork activities than individuals with low self-esteem. Another difference that may matter is the degree to which the individual segments his or her work and nonwork identities versus trying to integrate them (Nippert-Eng, 1996). People who are high segmentors may be more capable of blocking out time for their nonwork activities than people who are integrators. Yet another variable that may influence time allocation decisions is the centrality of the work identity in an individual's identity set. The more central an individual's work identity is to his or her sense of self, the less likely it is that the individual will be able to resist the pressures that cause the expansion of work hours.

We also have hypothesized in this chapter that there would be significant differences across organizations in the time demands being placed on managerial and professional workers. In particular, the work-family culture of the organization is an important organizational characteristic that is likely to affect how professional and managerial workers define work-life boundaries. We have speculated that the nature of the work matters. The harder it is to measure job performance using objective criteria, the stronger the pressures to work long hours. In order to examine this proposition, one would need to compare the hours worked in managerial or professional roles in different organizational contexts. One would expect, for example, that managers and professionals working in consulting firms might experience more pressure to work long hours than salespeople, whose performance is easy to measure. Similarly, one might hypothesize that professionals who work in back-office jobs would experience more pressure to put in face time than those who are on the front line delivering services to clients. The trend in the United States toward more employment in knowledge-intensive jobs where performance is difficult to measure suggests that this is a sector of the economy where expected work hours may continue to expand.

Another interesting area for future research lies in looking at differences in the pace of activities between the work and nonwork domains of life. Work, for example, is likely to be fast-paced, creating the expectation that tasks will be accomplished quickly. Research suggests that people who want to operate at a faster pace find dealing with people who want to operate at a slower pace frustrating (Blount & Janicik, 2002). When career-oriented employees with children go home after a long day in the office, they may find it hard to change their pace to adapt to the slowness of a child's pace, and they may find the experience rather frustrating. It would be interesting to explore whether there were differences across occupations in the stress and frustration levels that workers experience when they go home. One would expect that people who work in faster paced jobs or settings (e.g., equity trading) would have a more difficult time in transitioning to the pace of children and the home setting.

CONCLUSION

The manner in which we choose to spend our time is critical to shaping the texture of our lives. We have told a story in this chapter of how the boundaries between work and nonwork are becoming more permeable for managerial and professional workers who do not punch time clocks. Further, we have argued that it is work that is likely to creep into nonwork time rather than the other way around, especially for professional and managerial employees in the United States.

While high-powered professional and managerial jobs offer many rewards, they also may inadvertently take time that we never really intended to give to work if we are not conscious of our choices. Because of the power of hierarchy, the insidious way that work may creep into the time we have allocated previously to nonwork activities, and because of the positive feedback feature that can make home look less and less attractive as we spend less and less time there, a powerful countervailing force may be required to push back the expansion of work. One striking observation is that while work hours have increased in the United States in the last 25 years, this has not been the case in many European countries, especially those where labor and/or government have been active in attempting to create a social force that legitimizes the value of time spent by parents with family and thus legitimizes the restriction of work hours.

AUTHOR NOTE

We thank Peter Balsam, Ellen Kossek, Susan Lambert, an anonymous reviewer, and the participants in the Managing Work-Life Integration in Organizations Conference for their helpful comments and suggestions.

NOTE

1. Although the number of hours spent at work has increased enormously in the United States in the last 20 years, this has not necessarily been the case in other countries.

REFERENCES

Allen, T. D., Freeman, D. M., Russell, J., Reizenstein, R. C., & Rentz, J. O. (2001). Survivor reactions to organizational downsizing: Does time ease the pain? *Journal of Occupational and Organizational Psychology, 74,* 145–164.

Anderson, S. E., Coffey, B. S., & Byerly, R. T. (2002). Formal organizational initiatives and informal workplace practices: Links to work-family conflict and job-related outcomes. *Journal of Management, 28,* 787–810.

Blount, S., & Janicik, G. A. (2002). Getting and staying in-pace: The "in-synch" preference and its implications for work groups. In E. A. Mannix, M. A. Neale, & H. Sondak (Eds.), *Research on managing groups and teams* (Vol. 4, pp. 235–266). New York: Elsevier Science.

Brett, J. M., & Stroh, L. K. (2003). Working 61-plus hours a week: Why do managers do it? *Journal of Applied Psychology, 88,* 67–78.

Carlson, D. S., & Kacmar, K. M. (2000). Work-family conflict in the organization: Do life role values make a difference? *Journal of Management, 26*(5), 1031–1054.

D'Aveni, (1994). *Hypercompetition: Managing the dynamics of strategic maneuvering.* New York: Free Press.

Edwards, J. R., & Rothbard, N. P. (2000). Mechanisms linking work and family: Clarifying the relationship between work and family constructs. *Academy of Management Review, 25,* 178–199.

Eisner, A., & Shapira, Z. (1999). Attention allocation and managerial decision-making. Working paper, New York University.

Frone, M. R., Yardley, J. K., & Markel, K. S. (1997). Developing and testing an integrative model of the work-family interface. *Journal of Vocational Behavior, 50,* 145–167.

Gleick, J. (1999). *Faster: The acceleration of just about everything*. New York: Pantheon.

Graham, E., & Crossen, C. (1996, March 8). American opinion (A special report): A quarterly survey of politics, economics, and values—The overloaded American: Too many things to do, too little time to do them. *Wall Street Journal*.

Greenhaus, J. H., & Beutell, N. J. (1985). Sources of conflict between work and family roles. *Academy of Management Review, 10*, 76–88.

Greenhaus, J. H., & Powell, G. N. (2003). When work and family collide: Deciding between competing role demands. *Organizational Behavior and Human Decision Processes, 90*(2), 291–303.

Hamel, G., & Pralahad, C. K. (1994). *Competing for the future*. Boston: Harvard Business School Press.

Hochschild, A. R. (1997). *The time bind: When work becomes home and home becomes work*. New York: Metropolitan Books.

Judiesch, M. K., & Lyness, K. S. (1999). Left behind? The impact of leaves of absences on managers' career success. *Academy of Management Journal, 47*, 641–651.

Kossek, E. E., & Ozeki, C. (1998). Work-family conflict, policies, and the job-life satisfaction relationship. A review and directions for organizational behavior-human resources research. *Journal of Applied Psychology, 83*, 139–149.

Major, V. S., Klein, K. J., & Erhart, M. G. (2002). Work time, work interference with family, and psychological distress. *Journal of Applied Psychology, 87*, 427–436,

March, J. G., & Simon, H. A. (1958). *Organizations*. New York: Wiley.

Milliken, F. J., Beunza, D., & Dunn-Jensen, L. M. (2001). *The experience of time compression: Causes and consequences*. Paper presented at the Academy of Management Meetings. Washington, DC.

Netemeyer, R. G., Boles, J. S., & McMurrian, R. (1996). Development and validation of work-family conflict and family-work conflict scales. *Journal of Applied Psychology, 81*, 400–410.

Nippert-Eng, C. E. (1996). *Home and work: Negotiating boundaries through everyday life*. Chicago: University of Chicago Press.

Perin, C. (1991). The moral fabric of the office: Panopticon discourse and schedule flexibilities. *Research in the Sociology of Organizations, 8*, 241–268.

Perlow, L. A. (1995). Putting the work back into work/family. *Group & Organization Management, 20*, 227–239.

Perlow, L. A. (1997). *Finding time: How corporations, individuals, and families can benefit from new work practices*. Ithaca, NY: ILR Press.

Perlow, L. A. (1998). Boundary control: The social ordering of work and family time in a high-tech corporation. *Administrative Science Quarterly, 43*, 328–357.

Perlow, L. A. (1999). The time famine: Toward a sociology of work time. *Administrative Science Quarterly, 44*, 57–81.

Reich, R. B. (2001). *The future of success*. New York: Knopf.

Reynolds, J. (2003). You can't always get the hours you want: Mismatches between actual and preferred work hours in the U.S. *Social Forces, 81*, 1171–1199.

Rutherford, S. (2001). "Are you going home already?" The long hours culture, women managers and patriarchal closure. *Time & Society, 10*, 259–276.

Schor, J. (2003). The (even more) overworked American. In J. De Graaf (Ed.), *Take back your time: Fighting overwork and time poverty in America* (pp. 6–11). San Francisco: Barrett-Koehler Publishers.

Seshadri, S., & Shapira, Z. (2001). Managerial allocation of time and effort: The effects of interruptions. *Management Science, 47*, 647–662.

Solomon, C. M. (1994). Work/family's failing grade: Why today's initiatives aren't enough. *Personnel Journal, 73*, 72–87.

Sparks, K., Cooper, C., Fried, Y., & Shirom, A. (1997). The effects of hours of work on health: A meta-analytic review. *Journal of Occupational and Organizational Psychology, 70*, 391–408.

Thomas, L. T., & Ganster, D. C. (1995). Impact of family-supportive work variables on work-family conflict and strain: A control perspective. *Journal of Applied Psychology, 80,* 6–15.

Thompson, C. A., Beauvais, L. L., & Lyness, K. S. (1999). When work-family benefits are not enough: The influence of work-family culture on benefit utilization, organizational attachment, and work-family conflict. *Journal of Vocational Behavior, 54*(3), 392–415.

4

Technology, Organizations, and Work-Life Integration

P. Monique Valcour
Boston College

Larry W. Hunter
University of Wisconsin—Madison

INTRODUCTION

How does technology influence work-life integration? New technologies—especially advances in telecommunication and information technology—have had profound impacts on the mix of jobs in the economies of the United States and other industrialized nations, on how work is organized, and on people's experience at work. In this chapter we offer a framework for considering the relationship between technology and work-life integration. We draw from a *contextualist* perspective on technology (Adler, 1992) to advance a theory that offers few generalizations and instead emphasizes the microdynamics through which technology affects the balance between work and life outside of work.

Technology is sometimes portrayed as a force enabling the successful integration of multiple life roles (Earls, 2002; Jackson, 2002). According to this line of reasoning, technology can provide opportunities for people to balance their responsibilities at work with family duties and other interests. A recent AT&T television commercial epitomized this optimistic vision of technology's effects of work-life integration: A working mother phoned into a conference call via cell phone from the beach while her children stage-whispered, "Shh! Mommy is in a meeting."

To other observers, technology is viewed as a vehicle for enslavement to work and subjugation of the nonwork domain to the job (Foegen, 1993). In this vision, workplace technology has the potential to invade workers' lives. Employers apply advances in communication and information technology to monitor employees incessantly, render them ever-available for work, and reduce their latitude to balance the realms of work and nonwork. As Jill Andresky Fraser, the author of *White Collar Sweatshop*, observed in an interview:

> Although we thought technology would make our work lives easier and more creative, the real impact of our laptops, our Palm Pilots, our e-mail and our cellphones is that we can't ever *not* work. There's no justification (cited in Mieszkowski, 2001).

In fact, empirical examinations of the relationship between technology and work-life integration have offered few consistent findings. In this chapter, we argue that this is because meaningful examination of this relationship must take into account the many contextual factors that lie between technology and the integration of work and life. Our claim is by no means unique to work-life phenomena; we draw explicitly on the perspective that notes that technology considered devoid of context tends to explain little of the variance in other phenomena to which it may conceivably be connected, such as workers' attitudes or workplace skill structures (Adler & Borys, 1995). Our contextualist perspective suggests that technology per se has few implications for work-life integration. Rather, configurations of technology in economic, organizational, individual, and family contexts may exacerbate work-life conflict or, in contrast, provide people with opportunity to balance their work and nonwork lives successfully.

The term *technology* evokes a number of images. Its most general definition refers to know-how that is objectified independently of specific actors (Cyert & March, 1963). In this chapter, we explicitly focus on technology as embodied in machines and, to a lesser extent, work processes (we consider organizational practices as separate from this "hard" definition). We give much of our attention to recent advances, focusing largely on information technology (IT)—hardware, software, and telecommunication. Our framework also allows us to consider technology in historical perspective and thus to frame our claims more generally.

We focus on ways in which technology affects work-life integration, "a perceptual phenomenon characterized by a sense of having achieved a satisfactory resolution of the multiple demands" of work and nonwork domains (Higgins, Duxbury, & Johnson, 2000). People whose work and nonwork (especially family) lives are well integrated function effectively at work and at home, feel a sense of satisfaction with both domains, and experience minimal levels of conflict between work and family. As this definition suggests, work-life integration is a multifaceted construct. Researchers interested in work-life integration have modeled multiple outcomes under the conceptual umbrella of work-life or work-family integration or balance, including: job satisfaction; family satisfaction; work interference with family; family interference with work; work-family conflict that is time-based, strain-based or behavior-based; role overload; and psychological distress or well-being (e.g., Carlson & Perrewé, 1999; Clark, 2001; Frone, Russell, & Cooper, 1992; Gareis & Barnett, 2002; Higgins et al., 2000; Marks, Huston, Johnson, & MacDermid, 2001; Milkie & Peltola, 1999; Thomas & Ganster, 1995).

Research has shown that technology can have differential effects on different components of work-life integration. For instance, higher use of IT increases people's autonomy and work functioning while simultaneously increasing their felt conflict between work and family (Batt & Valcour, 2003; Valcour & Batt, 2003b). Technology use is associated also with both reported spillover from work to family and workers' sense of personal mastery (Chesley, Moen, & Shore, 2003). In this chapter, we employ our contextual approach to illuminate the mixed and sometimes contradictory nature of these relationships.

A MODEL OF THE EFFECTS OF TECHNOLOGY ON WORK-LIFE INTEGRATION

We organize our discussion by presenting a model illustrating the connections between technology and the work-life interface. The model begins with a discussion of mediating paths: the links in the causal chain from technology to work-life integration. Central to these paths is the idea that technology shapes jobs in a number of ways. It then presents a set of moderating influences on these links: factors that influence the extent to which technology affects work-life integration.

Three linking paths are conceptually distinguishable though related to one another. First, technology affects the mix of jobs and occupations in the economy. Because different kinds of work have different implications for work-life integration, this macrolevel view, displayed in Fig. 4.1, helps demonstrate the broad effects of technology on the work-life interface. The macrolevel trajectory

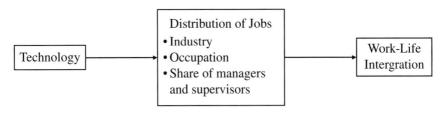

FIG. 4.1.   Macroeffects of technology on work-life integration.

of technological development, however, is linked only loosely to the level of work-life integration. A service or production context rarely invokes a single dominant technology; similar "hard" technologies can be deployed to quite varied effect, and even dominant technologies may only emerge over time.

Thus our more elaborate model, illustrated in Fig. 4.2, highlights the importance of the second and third mediating paths with implications for work-life integration: the effects of technology on the distribution of work over time and space, and the ways in which technology shapes work tasks in particular jobs. Examination of these paths helps illuminate the importance of choices made by managers in the deployment of technologies, how the responses of workers to those choices matter, and the factors that shape those choices and responses. In describing these paths, we draw heavily on the contextualist view of technology, which holds that explanations of the effects of technology on important workplace outcomes must consider the dynamics of the workplace set in broader perspective: managerial goals and strategies, workforce bargaining power and responses, the broader institutional environment.[1] Different organizations, for example, might end up with quite different configurations of technology (and thus deploy the technology to different effects) despite evident similarities in industry or institutional environments. Such differences might be understood with reference to organizational culture, the business goals of the organization and its managers, or differences in human resource practices.

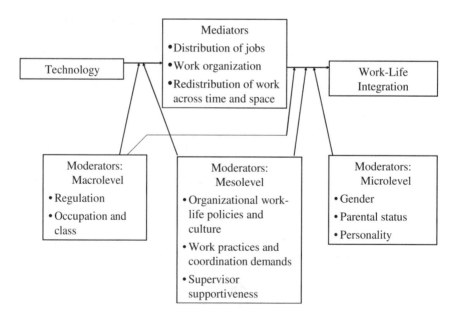

FIG. 4.2.   A model of the effects of technology on work-life integration.

We further elaborate on the effects of technologies in context by discussing influences on the strength of the relationship between particular deployments of technologies in jobs and work-life integration. Multiple factors influence, or moderate, these relationships. Fig. 7.2 illustrates these effects and provides examples of these moderating variables, which fall into three sets: microlevel moderators (characteristics of the individual and his or her family environment); mesolevel (organizational influences); and macrolevel (markets, institutions, and occupations, considered broadly). Factors at the macro- and mesolevel affect the ways in which technology is deployed, as well as influencing how technology as deployed affects workers' experiences. The effects of microlevel factors are concentrated on workers' experiences.

HOW TECHNOLOGY SHAPES WORKERS' EXPERIENCES: MEDIATING PATHS

Technology and the Mix of Jobs

As economies develop, the mix of jobs in which people are employed changes. For example, about 38% of the U.S. labor force worked in agriculture at the turn of the twentieth century. In 2001, agriculture employed about 2% of the labor force. Similarly, manufacturing employed over one third of U.S. workers in 1950; half a century later, fewer than 15% of workers were employed in manufacturing (Herzenberg, Alic, & Wial, 1998). This trajectory of development, driven by technological advances, underlies the relationship between work and the rest of life.

Concerns over the effects of development on work-life conflict have a long history.[2] Prior to the advent of the factories that emerged with the industrial revolution, work and other aspects of life were relatively tightly integrated. In contrast to their agrarian and artisanal predecessors, industrial jobs uprooted workers from their homes and families and subjected them to extensive, rigid, and closely monitored working hours. With the advent of factory employment, work no longer responded to the dictates of family and home life; instead, life outside the workplace came to be something that was fitted around work (Thompson, 1966). The assembly line and the factory floor of the industrial age became the exemplars of the split between work and the rest of life. Marx, for example, famously observed of the worker under industrial capitalism that "life begins for him where [work] ceases" (1849/1978b, p. 205).

Some see, in a post–industrial age, promise for reversing this trend, suggesting that as the march of technology automates work and eliminates lower-skilled jobs, societal problems might stem not from inability to integrate work with other aspects of life but from dealing with displaced workers and from attempts to fill hours that were once spent working (Bell, 1973; Rifkin, 1995).

There is little evidence, especially in the United States, to support this view. In the second half of the twentieth century, even as technology advanced rapidly, the American economy found jobs for millions of new workers (participation by women in the labor force, for example, increased from about 33% in 1950 to over 60% by 2000). Instead of a reduction in working hours, the period from 1976 and 1993 saw an increase in the average weekly work hours for both men and women between the ages of 25 and 54 (Rones, Gardner, & Ilg, 2001). At the beginning of the twenty-first century, the "end of work" (Rifkin, 1995) is less a concern than the "overworked American" (Schor, 1991) or the "time bind" (Hochschild, 1997). Technological advances, rather than reducing employment to a sideshow, seem to have been associated with an intensification of work.

Though we have not seen the end of work, the decline in the share of workers employed in manufacturing and concomitant increases in service-sector employment suggest that workers have moved into jobs that—in some instances— permit more freedom of movement and communication outside the workplace, allow more flexible scheduling, and provide other opportunities to achieve effective integration between work and the rest of life. For example, U.S. service-sector employers are more than half again more likely than manufacturing establishments to offer flextime and job sharing to their employees (Hunter, 2000).

More finely grained industry distinctions are also instructive, as differences in the nature of production technology across industries are associated with differences in the ability of individuals in various jobs to integrate work and family. For instance, in some industries work may be tied to machinery that is not portable and that may need to be operated on an inflexible schedule, with the result that work schedules are determined by the location and scheduling of the technology itself rather than by workers' needs. Other industries that rely more on flexible, portable forms of information technology (e.g., the use of laptop computers and cell phones among sales professionals or consultants) offer greater opportunities for the integration of work and family demands, because workers have more ability to control how, where, and when they deploy the technology (Valcour & Batt, 2003b). These differences and trends merit more study. For example, employment in fixed locations with rigid work schedules associated with heavy manufacturing may be in decline, but we also see growth in employment in industries such as health services and retail trade, which have similar constraints rooted in quite different technological bases.

Another important shift driven by technological advances is the increasing share of people employed as managers and professionals. In 1940, fewer than 15% of American workers outside the agricultural sector were managers and professionals; by 2003, this category encompassed nearly a third of U.S. workers. The increase in the share of workers with supervisory responsibility or professional standing suggests a concomitant increase in the autonomy and discretion enjoyed by workers, and research has established that job autonomy is associated with increased opportunity to exercise control over the relationship between work and nonwork and with lower work-family conflict (Barnett, 1998; Batt & Valcour, 2003; Duxbury, Higgins, & Lee, 1994; Thomas & Ganster, 1995; Williams & Alliger, 1994).

This is not to say that successful work-life integration is easily achieved by white-collar, managerial, or professional workers. In fact, much of the scholarly attention given to the challenges associated with work-life integration is directed at managers and professionals. Even as technological progress has led to increases in the share of jobs in which individuals ostensibly direct and control their own schedules and working hours, concerns have focused on the fact that people in these groups seem to be working, on average, more than ever and are having a great deal of difficulty in balancing their responsibilities at work with the rest of their interests (Bailyn, 1993; Friedman & Greenhaus, 2000; Thompson, Beauvais, & Lyness, 1999).

To summarize, technology influences the overall mix of jobs, and because jobs in themselves differ in the ways in which they influence the relationships between work and life outside of work, technology affects work-life conflict. As Fig. 4.1 suggests, technological change matters in the aggregate level. As it creates some kinds of jobs and destroys others, the overall state of the relationship between work and life outside work also changes.

Technology and the Organization of Work

The characterization of the macrolevel relationship between technology and work-life integration has important limitations. It does not account well for variation of the effects of technology within jobs or occupations. It provides only sparse guidance to understanding why variance occurs across these jobs. Moreover, the model implies a deterministic view of the effects of technology that is actually inconsistent with what we know about how technology affects work.

In particular jobs, technology influences work-family-integration by shaping the tasks workers perform. An assembly line under mass production, for example, permits workers little control over the content of their work, its pace, or the order in which they do particular tasks (Edwards, 1979). Technology deployed in this fashion has long been held to have invidious effects on workers, underlying, for example, the upward-sloping portion of Blauner's (1964) famous "inverted-U" relationship between technology and workplace alienation.

Automation may raise obstacles to effective work-life integration. Such effects are not limited to manufacturing assembly lines. Service environments such as telephone call centers can feature never-ending queues of customers and relentless pressure to handle calls (Batt, Hunter, & Wilk, 2003). To the extent that technology controls the pace of work and is combined with discretion-reducing managerial practices, it can diminish workers' ability to engage, both physically and psychologically, in other life activities (Barnett, 1998). To take a simple example, automation-governed work can limit access to spur-of-the-moment telephone calls to or from baby-sitters, teachers, or family members and restricts workers' discretion in scheduling times to take or make such calls.

In addition to reducing autonomy, technology can also place workers under closer managerial scrutiny by facilitating extensive monitoring of employees' work. Sophisticated computer systems are replacing mechanical time clocks and are extending managers' ability to track when employees start and stop—a capacity previously applied primarily to nonmanagerial employees but that now can be applied to more highly skilled workers. For example, lawyers and members of other occupational groups who are responsible for billable hours may be required to have software on their computers that tracks exactly when they log on and log off, as well as the number and length of periods of inactivity (Epstein, Seron, Oglensky, & Saute, 1999). Instant messaging can serve the same purpose; when employees log off, or even fail to respond promptly, it is apparent to others that they are not at their desks. Many companies have installed monitoring software that tracks their employees' usage of the Internet and records all keystrokes made by employees.

Telephone call center workers are subject to some of the most sophisticated electronic monitoring technology currently in use. Monitoring systems record the number of calls taken by each worker, the length of each call, the amount of time callers are placed on hold, the number of rings before the call is answered, and so on. The systems allow managers to monitor the extent to which workers comply with specified work procedures, as in the case of operators who are required to limit the number of keystrokes they use when searching the database for telephone numbers. The monitoring system identifies those operators who are entering more keystrokes than the number specified for optimal productivity. Research suggests that electronic monitoring is a source of stress for those workers who are subject to it (Holman, Chissick, & Totterdell, 2002) and that it can have deleterious consequences for work-life integration. Electronic monitoring has been identified as a predictor of emotional exhaustion (Deery, Iverson, & Walsh, 2002), an aversive state that is likely to spill over into the nonwork domain. Evidence from a study of call center workers shows that the intensity of monitoring is positively related to work exhaustion and negatively related to satisfaction with work-life balance (Valcour & Batt, 2003a). It is likely that these negative effects are most pronounced when monitoring technology is used in such a way as to reduce workers' discretion and to make them feel as if they are being constantly scrutinized.

Not all advanced technology, however, has these kinds of effects. A key distinction in the literature addressing the effects of automation on job content is between equipment that is designed with the goal of minimizing errors and reducing reliance on workers' discretion and equipment that is aimed at enhancing and leveraging workers' skills and abilities (Adler & Borys, 1995). Blauner's (1964) inverted-U stemmed from the observation that jobs under continuous process technologies (e.g., chemical plants or oil refineries) require higher levels of skill and engagement, offer workers a greater variety of tasks, and return to workers some control over the pace of work. Zuboff (1988) and Kelley (1990) draw similar attention to IT's potential for varied effects on workplaces. Modern technology does more than automate tasks: It also provides supporting tools for nonroutine activities that require high levels of skill and worker engagement (Hunter & Lafkas, 2003; Zuboff, 1988). Software applications such as spreadsheets, word processing, and sales-support technologies automate sets of tasks ranging from the routine to the very complex, providing workers with the means to do higher-level activities more efficiently.

On the one hand, to the extent that such technologies provide tools for workers to do their jobs more effectively, effects on work-life balance come from possible increases in the discretion that workers enjoy. Alternatives to command-and-control technologies, on the other hand, also create new threats to work-life integration, particularly where processes have been designed to be tightly coupled (Perrow, 1984) and to minimize buffers (MacDuffie, 1995). The elimination of redundancy in processes means that every worker's role may be vital; the leaner the process, the more tightly linked its steps, the more difficult it is for workers to exercise the sorts of discretion that would take them away from focus on their work tasks.

Contextualist views suggest that the effects of technology are not simply determined by the arc of development or the characteristics inherent in technological advances. Rather, choices among alternative strategies for deployment have lasting effects on workers' experiences. For example, alternatives to mass production technologies in manufacturing such as "flexible specialization" (Piore & Sabel, 1984) and "lean production" (MacDuffie, 1995) rely more heavily on teamwork, worker skills, and decision making than on traditional assembly lines. In services, too, firms may organize work more or less restrictively. Call centers, for example, have been alternatively characterized as the "dark Satanic mills" of the New Economy and as a setting for a variety of approaches to the organization of work (Taylor & Bain, 1999). In either case, the point is that the organizing logic of the workplace is neither dictated by the environment nor fixed by design; rather, technologies are deployed by managers (and this deployment may be contested by workers).

The contextualist perspective on the organization of work raises two important issues for work-life integration. The first is the extent to which different configurations of technology in use actually influence workers' abilities to balance their work responsibilities with their lives outside of work. Our review suggests that effects may be associated with the extent to which workers enjoy task discretion, that technology is used to facilitate flexible rather than constraining work schedules and that monitoring is used to limit workers' behaviors.

A second issue is the extent to which work-life integration is a consideration, explicitly or implicitly, in managerial decisions about technological implementation or in workers' responses to these decisions. The literature describing the contested terrain over the deployment of technology tends to focus on managerial interests in efficiency and control and on managerial assumptions about what technology can and should do, particularly with respect to enhancing productivity (e.g., Thomas, 1994). Research on workforce responses tends to focus on workers' attempts to exercise and to preserve control over their domain and skill bases (e.g., Edwards, 1979), with little attention to their interests in work-life integration.

The absence of evidence on this latter question is consistent with a number of possibilities. For example, it may be that considerations of work-life integration are less important than other issues such as productivity, quality improvement, or control over the work process. Or, even if such considerations are relatively important, the parties may not perceive them as being so at the time of implementation. Effects on work-life balance may become clear only over time. It may even be that such effects are both important and understood by the parties, but have not received research attention.

Technology and the Distribution of Work Across Time and Space

In terms of its contemporary impact on work-life integration, the most fundamental and prevalent change brought on by advances in information technology is arguably the redistribution of work across time and space. Such redistribution is not entirely distinct from changes in the mix of industries and in workplace technologies described earlier: New technologies allowed firms to gather workers together in factories in the nineteenth century; today, the latest advances allow firms to disperse workers to do jobs such as consulting that barely existed half a century ago. For example, telecommuting is today pervasive across work organizations, with 37% of all employers and the majority of the *Fortune* 1,000 firms currently offering telecommuting to their employees (Wells, 2001). The occupational penetration of telecommuting is wide as well, with telecommuters currently represented throughout the spectrum of jobs performed by information workers (Hill, Hawkins, & Miller, 1996).

Some of today's most notable effects on work-life balance occur through teleworking, in which workers use information technologies including computers, e-mail, telephones, pagers, fax machines, modems, and other networking devices—combined with servers that allow files to be accessed from and transmitted to remote locations—to perform some or all of their work at home (or in another location away from the main office). Related advances include policies such as flexible scheduling, which have been facilitated through the implementation of technology that frees workers from a fixed, standardized schedule for the completion of their work tasks. Additionally, even when employees do not work from home for some portion of their regular work hours, the increasingly pervasive use of communication and information technologies often brings work into the home domain, particularly for information workers.

Although estimates of the number of telecommuters in the United States vary due to definitional differences, the numbers are clearly substantial, ranging from 10 million to nearly 30 million. According to the International Telework Association & Council (2002), 28 million Americans reported teleworking at least part time in 2001. This figure includes people who work at home, at a telework center or satellite office, on the road, or some combination of the aforementioned. Approximately one fifth of working Americans report working some portion of their working hours at home (International Telework Association & Council, 2002). Under a more restrictive definition of telecommuters as "employees who engage in work at home on a regular basis two or more days per week for an outside company," the Institute for the Study of Distributed Work provides the current low-end estimate of 10.4 million telecommuters (Wells, 2001). Compared to nonteleworkers, teleworkers are significantly more likely to be from the Northeast and West, are male, have higher education and income, work in professional or managerial occupations, and be employed in smaller or larger organizations (International Telework Association & Council, 2002).

Teleworking is clearly associated with increased permeability of the boundary between work and nonwork domains. The spatial, temporal, social, and psychological aspects of the work-nonwork boundary are all affected by the movement of work into the home (Standen, Daniels, & Lamond, 1999). Physically, work and nonwork activities now take place in the same location. Temporally, telecommuters often report interweaving work and family activities, for instance, by occasionally performing housework or child care during the workday (Mirchandani, 1999). Whereas the social roles that people occupy at work and at home had been generally separated in industrial societies, telecommuting causes these roles to overlap. Finally, the movement from home to work and vice versa involves crossing a psychological boundary; this aspect is also changed when people work at home (Ashforth, Kreiner, & Fugate, 2000). Indeed, telecommuters often develop rituals to facilitate crossing the role boundary from family to work, including such actions as putting on work clothes, reading the business section of the newspaper, saying good-bye to the family before entering the home office, and taking files and work implements out of cabinets (Ashforth et al., 2000; Mirchandani, 1999). Nonetheless, work and family life are both more susceptible to intrusions when they are carried out in the same location.

Evidence on the impact of technology and telecommuting on aspects of work-life integration is equivocal. Generally, research suggests that use of portable information and communication technologies is associated with increased negative spillover from work to family, even when controlling for occupation, work hours, and commuting time (Chesley et al., 2003). In a series of studies of IBM employees in professional occupations, however, Hill and colleagues found that telecommuters reported higher levels of work-life balance and success at personal/family life than did employees who worked in a traditional office setting (Hill, Ferris, & Martinson, 2003; Hill, Hawkins, Ferris, & Weitzman, 2001; Hill,

Miller, Weiner, & Colihan, 1998). Other studies indicate that work intrudes on and interferes with the family and personal lives of telecommuters (Epstein et al., 1999; Kurland & Bailey, 1999; Mirchandani, 1999). Says one respondent in Mirchandani's (1999) study, "I was feeling very keenly a sense of intrusion into my house . . . couriers showing up, a telephone line ringing, a fax machine going in the middle of the night. . . . [T]his was not a pristine environment; I had sullied it." The net effect of bringing more work into the home may be to help individuals integrate across different spheres while creating a work environment in the home that intrudes on family life (Epstein et al., 1999). This paradox is epitomized by the work of Batt and Valcour (2003), who found that more extensive use of information technologies was associated with more perceived control over managing work and family but also with *higher* levels of work-family conflict.

Processes of establishing teleworking options for workers, and other forms of redistributing work outside the workplace and beyond the traditional working day, may strongly resemble other kinds of choices made in the deployment of workplace technology. In one respect, however, they are unique: Unlike other workplace technologies, these innovations have on occasion been implemented by managers and workers who have as primary goals influence over the balance between work and family life. With regard to teleworking, for example, early views (Kraut, 1989) suggested it as a way to help women hold down jobs while managing their family responsibilities effectively, and teleworkers were stereotyped as women with young children. Indeed, although telecommuting was initially conceived as a strategy to make firms less vulnerable to fuel shortages during the OPEC oil crisis in the early to mid-1970s, most telework arrangements prior to the 1990s were established to accommodate the family needs of individual employees (Hill et al., 1996).

The search for a technological solution to enhance work-life integration is not, however, the only force underlying implementation of teleworking technology. By the 1990s, more kinds of teleworkers emerged and a number of organizational rationales for teleworking were offered, including reduction of real estate and labor costs, efforts to increase productivity, customer proximity, complementarity with the required mobility of many client-focused workers, compliance with regulations such as the Clean Air Act and the Americans with Disabilities Act, and the desire to contract out activities to workers who are not employees (Bailey & Kurland, 2002; Kurland & Bailey, 1999). Individuals, too, have a variety of reasons for telecommuting, including increasing their productivity, gaining greater control over the environment in which they work, reducing the amount of time spent commuting, and avoiding office politics, as well as more effectively integrating the demands of work and family (Bailey & Kurland, 2002; Kurland & Bailey, 1999; Mirchandani, 1999). In general, the relative importance of work-life integration in implementation of telework remains somewhat unclear. Among other things, it can be difficult to distinguish between those who work remotely by choice and those who do so involuntarily (Goldstein, 2003), as many companies have systematically moved certain groups of workers into telecommuting programs.

FACTORS INFLUENCING THE RELATIONSHIP BETWEEN TECHNOLOGY AND WORK-LIFE INTEGRATION

We have described the main mediating mechanisms through which work technology affects the work-family interface. We now turn to a review and discussion of factors that further influence the relationship between implemented technology and workers' work-life integration experiences. Our earlier discussion considered the main effects of technology on work-life balance. The factors to which we now turn, as illustrated in Fig. 7.2, have the potential to amplify or dampen these main effects in particular jobs.

We consider these moderating variables at three levels: micro-, meso-, and macrolevel forces. Our discussion is not intended to be exhaustive. Where possible, we draw on empirical evidence to describe what is known about these effects. We also hope to frame subsequent inquiry by sketching moderators that deserve further research attention.

Microlevel

Many individual- and family-level differences have direct effects on work-life integration. A number of these kinds of differences may also influence the extent and manner of the effects of technology on this integration. As examples, we consider explicitly gender, parental status, and personality.

Gender. It has long been argued that there are gender differences in the ways in which work and family roles intersect and affect each other. For instance, Pleck (1977) proposed that traditional gender role expectations lead to opposite patterns between men and women in the experience of work-family conflict. According to this argument, women are more family-identified and take primary responsibility for home and caregiving at the same time that men are more work-involved. Subsequent research has found that teleworking women intersperse their paid work activities with nonwork activities more often than do men and are more likely to interrupt their work in order to respond to family-related demands (Mirchandani, 1999). Rothbard (2001) studied the dynamics of engagement in work and family roles (attention to and absorption in each role, as well as emotional responses to work and family roles) and found that work and family are more tightly linked for women than for men and that women experience depletion from work to family roles while men do not. To the extent that technology increases the permeability of the boundary between work and family roles, it is possible that work-life integration may be more strongly affected by technology for women than for men. Consistent with this argument, Batt and Valcour (2003) found that technology use is associated with work-family conflict for women but not for men.

Parental Status.   A recent study of technology use among dual-earner couples indicates that parents are significantly more likely to use cell phones and pagers in order to communicate with family members than are nonparents (Chesley et al., 2003). While communication technologies are highly valued by parents for their capacity to facilitate work-life integration (Jackson, 2002), extant research suggests that technology can be also the means for excessive interaction between work and home life. For example, the presence of preschool-aged children is negatively associated with work-life balance for telecommuters (Hill et al., 2003). Telecommuters who have primary-care responsibilities tend to experience higher levels of work-family conflict than those who are not primary caregivers (Mirchandani, 1999; Standen et al., 1999). Within the home, technology has the potential to affect negatively family interaction and functioning (Watt & White, 1999). For instance, the introduction of a computer is associated with decreases in family interaction and time spent sleeping, as well as an increase in time spent alone (Venkatesh & Vitalari, 1987).

Personality.   Among personality characteristics, research has found that self-efficacy is predictive of individuals' satisfactory adjustment to virtual work and also to the extent that they use structuring behaviors to plan and proactively organize their workday (Raghuram, Wiesenfeld, & Garud, 2003). The effect of self-efficacy on telecommuter adjustment is even stronger for employees who spend a larger proportion of their time telecommuting (Raghuram et al., 2003). The results of this study suggest that individuals with high self-efficacy are more likely to be able to employ strategies to meet the challenges associated with the distribution of work across time and space and thereby achieve more satisfactory work-life integration.

The relative salience of work versus family role identities may also moderate the relationship between technology and work-life integration. Technology-based job stressors such as pervasive electronic monitoring are associated with higher levels of job burnout and work exhaustion, which is in turn related to lowered satisfaction with work-life integration (Valcour & Batt, 2003a). High work role salience should serve to buffer employees against the negative effects of electronic monitoring and other aversive technologies both by motivating them to commit more psychological and emotional resources to the role and also by increasing positive and decreasing negative evaluations of work role experiences (Baumeister, 1982; Lobel & St. Clair, 1992). Hence, people who are more work-identified may be able to tolerate higher levels of stressors at work without experiencing negative consequences such as increased negative spillover from work to family (Valcour & Batt, 2003a). However, with respect to telecommuting, people whose family identities are more salient may fare better in terms of work-life integration both because they may find family-related interruptions during home-based work less stressful and also because they may be less likely to miss the visibility and social rewards associated with work in the office environment (Standen et al., 1999).

Mesolevel

Mesolevel factors have effects at the levels at which individuals interact with one another. These include both organizational and suborganizational (e.g., division, work unit) considerations. As exemplars of these factors, we consider the roles that may be played by organizational policies and culture regarding work and family, the effects of supervisor support, and the demands that workplace practices and strategies place on coordination.

Organizational Work-Life Policies and Culture.   Technology is implemented in the context of a set of organizational practices governing work-life balance. Organizational culture and values also shape this relationship. The most effective organizational responses to the challenge of work-life integration are those that combine the deployment of flexible information technology with work designed to give employees discretion and autonomy, work-life benefits and flexibility policies, adequate compensation and human resource incentives, and a workplace culture that values and supports the integration of employees' work and nonwork lives (Batt & Valcour, 2003; Valcour & Batt, 2003b).

Flexibility is a key element of the family-supportive workplace (Pleck, Staines, & Lang, 1980). Most organizational initiatives heralded under the banner of work-life (e.g., flextime, job sharing, part-time work, family leaves, dependent-care time, time off for volunteering, compressed work weeks, flexplace/telecommuting) have been developed in order to increase the schedule flexibility afforded to employees (Kingston, 1990). For many workers—particularly white-collar employees—flexible communication technologies (such as portable computers, cell phones, faxes, and e-mail) are associated with work design characteristics that have the potential to enable flexibility in the place and timing of work. However, technology is likely to have a positive effect on employees' work-life integration only if the employer also has other flexible work policies and practices in place. Thus, it follows that work-life policies and culture moderate the relationship between technology and work-life integration such that technology contributes to successful work-life integration when family-supportive policies and culture are well established but undermines effective integration when these elements are absent.

Work Practices and Coordination Demands. In practice, information technologies can be deployed in such a manner as to render workers independent from or interdependent with one another and to enhance or decrease autonomy. When workers are organized into self-managing groups and overlap in task assignments, they may be able to take at least temporary responsibility for one another's work when needed, thereby allowing individual workers to accommodate needs arising from the family domain. For example, a recent study of some 4,000 manufacturing workers found that membership in a self-directed work team is associated with greater work-family balance (Berg, Kalleberg, & Appelbaum, 2003).

The sorts of coordination required also can have important effects on the relationship between technology used to distribute work and workers' experiences with that technology. Standen et al. (1999, p. 369), for example, argue that researchers should view telework as a multidimensional variable rather than as a dichotomous one. They identify five dimensions of telework: (a) the degree to which information and communication technologies connect workers to the office, (b) the distribution of time between the office and the home, (c) the extent to which the job requires communication with other employees, (d) the amount of communication with clients or other external parties, and (e) the degree of knowledge intensity, indicating among other things the different levels of autonomy experienced by professional and routine teleworkers. Note that only the degree of connection is a characteristic of the technology itself; the other factors represent organizational variables. The nature of the connection between telecommuters and their organizations, supervisors, coworkers, and clients affects the degree to which these workers are able to capitalize on the flexibility that is a core potentiality of telecommuting. When the demands for coordination with others are quite high, integrating work and family roles becomes more challenging, and work-family conflict may increase (Batt & Valcour, 2003). To the extent that technology keeps the telecommuter tightly linked and continuously available for communication, particularly in jobs that have high demands for communication, telecommuters are likely to report lower levels of work-life integration (Epstein et al., 1999). Several researchers have suggested that the greater the proportion of time spent telecommuting, the higher the level of threat to work-life integration and the greater the need for strategies to manage effectively the boundary between work and nonwork (Mirchandani, 1999; Raghuram et al., 2003; Standen et al., 1999).

Supervisor Supportiveness. Supervisors play an important role in setting the overall tone and expectations regarding the extent to which family demands will be permitted to influence work for the employees who report to them. Therefore, their support is particularly important. In many cases, supervisors also have the authority to approve or deny their employees' requests to make use of technology in the most flexible ways possible, as well as to take advantage of a range of flexible work policies. Supportive supervisors can provide their employees with more flexibility than is granted by the written policies of the organization; unsupportive supervisors can subvert the employer's family-friendly policies (Eaton, 2003; Raabe & Gessner, 1988).

The overall effect is that organizational practices, culture, and supervisor behavior moderate the extent to which technology is a force for conflict or integration. For example, where a performance management system and organizational norms combine to legitimate discussion over the conditions under which accessibility to supervisors or coworkers is deemed unreasonable, cell phones and home computers can be relatively liberating for individuals; where expectations for performance and availability are non-negotiable, in contrast, the same technologies exacerbate work-life conflict.

Macrolevel

In our earlier discussion of workplace technology we argued that, although macrolevel forces did not determine outcomes, factors at this level would surely bound the range of possibilities and influence their deployment. Many of the same macrolevel considerations are also likely to influence the relationship between configurations of workplace technology and work-life integration. As examples we consider regulation and occupational and class differences.

Regulation. Discussions about the regulation of overtime pay and compensatory work for time off often relate to the use of new technologies in the workplace. Current American standards require that most workers be paid for hours worked in excess of 40 per week. In March 2003 the U.S. Department of Labor proposed changes in these rules to redefine the range of workers qualifying for overtime pay, so that a greater share of workers would be defined as managerial or executive workers, and therefore exempt. Similarly, proposed legislation in the U.S. Congress (U.S. Department of Labor, 2003), billed by its supporters as family-friendly, would allow employers to pay overtime only after 80 hours in 2 weeks (workers who worked 50 hours in one week, for example, could receive "compensatory" time off the following week).

While clearly having the potential for direct impact on work-life integration, such regulatory changes could also influence the extent to which technology facilitated or inhibited work-life balance. Workers in jobs not qualifying for overtime pay, for example, might become more attractive candidates for employers interested in implementing technologies that would enable flexible work or extended hours outside the workplace. These workers might begin to experience more of the pressures on work-life integration that the research has associated with professional workers, as well as more of the opportunities associated with such technologies.

Occupation and Class. Managerial and professional employees tend to have a higher level of psychological involvement with their jobs than do working-class employees (Li et al., 2002), which places them at higher risk for work-family conflict. Frone and colleagues (1992) found that job involvement is positively related to work-to-family conflict among white-collar workers, whereas these two variables are unrelated among blue-collar workers. In addition to reflecting occupational differences in job involvement, this finding may signal the greater tendency of white-collar work to spill over into the family domain, an effect that has been intensified by the increasing use of a variety of communication technologies (e.g., cell phones, laptop computers, and Internet connections) among white-collar workers (Chesley et al., 2003).

Occupational norms and standards may also moderate the relationship between technology and the work-life interface. In certain occupations, technological advances may be accompanied by expectations of increased speed and productive capacity. Members of professional and other highly skilled occupations often enjoy significantly more work autonomy than do workers with less human capital and labor market power, and autonomy is consistently associated with better work-life integration. However, these same occupational groups tend to have long work hours and high job involvement, characteristics that are likely to interact with technology in such a way as to increase the difficulty of achieving a satisfactory balance between work and nonwork.

Consider the case of social scientists. While the pace of work was influenced formerly by computing speed for statistical analysis and library access for research, social scientists and other academics now typically have home computers with fast processing speed, sophisticated statistical software, and other tools that far outpace the tools available just 10 to 20 years ago. Additionally, Internet access to research databases and electronic full-text document delivery services allows for much greater research productivity. Occupational expectations for research productivity have risen hand-in-hand with the technological advances that make the greater productivity possible, and these expectations have been incorporated into commonly accepted job standards. A similar process of technology-induced work intensification has been documented in the legal profession (Epstein et al., 1999).

IMPLICATIONS

Our analysis suggests that applications of technology per se have unpredictable implications for the balance between work and home life. It is naïve to view technology as a liberating counterweight to work practices and workplaces that might otherwise destroy work-life integration. It is just as misleading to depict technological advances as the villains responsible for increasing pressures that work places on family life. Rather, configurations of technology in organizational context may exacerbate work-life conflict or, in contrast, provide workers with more opportunity to balance these spheres successfully.

If we are to continue to develop our understanding of how technological change is likely to affect work-life integration, as a start it would be helpful to know more about how differences in occupations and industries influence work-life integration and balance. We have some of the basic data in place: We know that there are significant interindustry and interoccupational differences in hours worked (Rones et al., 2001) and the provision of work-family benefits (Glass & Fujimoto, 1995; Osterman, 1995). We also know that managerial practices including scheduling policies and the use of aspects of "high-performance work systems" differ systematically across industries (Hunter, 2000) and that these practices are associated with positive work-family outcomes (Berg et al., 2003).

Other differences, however, are less well documented, with the bulk of the research being conducted on white-collar workers (Eaton, 2003). Further, we have relatively little knowledge of within-industry differences of the deployment of technology or the effects of these differences on workers' lives outside work. Our analysis also suggests that research organized around jobs and industries will lead us to only a partial understanding of the effects that technology is likely to have on the work-family interface. We need to have a more nuanced understanding of the microdynamics of technology implementation. Such understanding is likely to shed light on how contextual factors shape workers' experiences with technology.

Despite extensive speculation on the effects of technology implementation on work-life integration, we noted that there is very little research on the extent to which these effects actually are considered by those parties involved with this implementation. We therefore urge greater interaction between the research community and the managers who are responsible for the implementation of technology in organizations. Organization-based case studies would be a useful first step in gaining awareness of how organizational decision makers perceive linkages between technology and work-life integration. Additionally, case studies would help to round out our understanding of the relevant variables that should be included in subsequent research to test the effects of technology on various aspects of work-life integration in a variety of organizational contexts.

Our discussion of moderating variables that affect the strength and direction of the relationship between technology and work-life integration is not intended to be exhaustive, and we urge further attention to empirical research and theorizing on this question. For example, we have suggested that the extent to which jobs are configured so as to provide workers with autonomy will influence the level and character of work-life integration; more research on this subject and on potential moderators of this effect would be extremely helpful.

We also encourage more attention to the family side of the equation. As we noted at the outset, work-life integration is a multifaceted phenomenon, and technology can have contradictory effects on various dimensions of work-life integration. Researchers could study the effects of technology on a variety of work-family outcomes, include multiple types and directions of work-family conflict (i.e., time-based, behavior-based, strain-based), satisfaction at work and at home, effectiveness and good functioning at work and at home, and so on. Researchers also should investigate the prevalence of technology in the nonwork domain so that we can learn more about how and to what extent people are using technology and how this use is affecting them and their families. This line of inquiry should consider people not just as individuals in and of themselves, but also within the context of their family units. Researchers should take into account the patterns of technology use among couples, as well as the family resources and demands that may moderate the relationship between work and nonwork. Of particular interest, given the contradictory findings highlighted in this chapter, is the extent to which technology is a positive force for the integration of work and nonwork life versus the extent to which technology drives unwelcome crossdomain intrusions and negative spillover effects.

We call special attention to two implications for practice. We have argued that technologies explicitly aimed at work-family issues (e.g., teleworking) as well as those that have no such intent (e.g., office automation, performance monitoring) may have effects on work-life integration. Yet it is not always the case that these effects are considered fully in advance of implementation (or, in fact, even after implementation). Technologies may have a number of side effects, and some of these effects may have ramifications for the ability of adopters to achieve their goals. For example, where technologies aimed at enhancing efficiency have negative spillover on work-life integration, any effects of such spillovers on efficiency ought to be considered as part of the package. To the extent that the inability to balance conflicting demands leads to poor performance or employee turnover, such costs need to be weighed against efficiency gains. For workers, too, responses to technologies need to be considered in this light.

A second implication for practice is that it may be misleading to forecast or to analyze the effects of technologies without a good sense of the surrounding context. Technology in practice may stray far from what managers intend once it is implemented in the context of broader institutional and market forces and is shaped by a range of organizational policies, with its use contested by various parties to implementation. Even where deployment comes close to matching intention, a host of potential influences on the relationship between technology and work-life integration may intervene to alter the hoped-for effects.

NOTES

1. For a more extended discussion of the emergence of the contextualist argument and the relationship of this perspective to other views of technology, see Adler (1992).

2. Marx's account of alienation and Durkheim's (1933/1997) notion of anomie, to take two examples; each drew contrasts between the capitalist era and its predecessors.

REFERENCES

Adler, P. S. (1992). Introduction. In P. S. Adler (Ed.), *Technology and the future of work* (pp. 3–14). New York: Oxford University Press.

Adler, P. S., & Borys, B. (1995). A portrait of the relationship between mechanization and work in the U.S. economy. *The International Journal of Human Factors in Manufacturing, 5*(4), 345–375.

Ashforth, B. E., Kreiner, G. E., & Fugate, M. (2000). All in a day's work: Boundaries and micro role transitions. *Academy of Management Review, 25*(3), 472–491.

Bailey, D. E., & Kurland, N. B. (2002). A review of telework research: Findings, new directions, and lessons for the study of modern work. *Journal of Organizational Behavior, 23*(4), 383–400.

Bailyn, L. (1993). *Breaking the mold: Women, men, and time in the new corporate world.* New York: Free Press.

Barnett, R. C. (1998). Toward a review and reconceptualization of the work/family literature. *Genetic, Social, and General Psychology Monographs, 124*(2), 125–182.

Batt, R., Hunter, L. W., & Wilk, S. (2003). How and when does management matter? Job quality and career opportunities for call center workers. In E. Appelbaum, A. Bernhardt, and R. J. Murnane (Eds.), *Low-wage America: How employers are reshaping opportunity in the workplace* (pp. 270–315). New York: Russell Sage Foundation.

Batt, R., & Valcour, P. M. (2003). Human resource practices as predictors of work-family outcomes and employee turnover. *Industrial Relations, 42*(2), 189–220.

Baumeister, R. R. (1982). A self-presentational view of social phenomena. *Psychological Bulletin, 91*(1), 3–25.

Bell, D. A. (1973). *The coming of post-industrial society: A venture in social forecasting.* New York: Basic Books.

Berg, P., Kalleberg, A. L., & Appelbaum, E. (2003). Balancing work and family: The role of high-commitment environments. *Industrial Relations, 42*(2), 168–188.

Blauner, R. (1964). *Alienation and freedom: The factory worker and his industry.* Chicago: University of Chicago Press.

Carlson, D. S., & Perrewé, P. L. (1999). The role of social support in the stressor-strain relationship: An examination of work-family conflict. *Journal of Management, 25*(4), 513–540.

Chesley, N., Moen, P., & Shore, R. P. (2003). The new technology climate. In P. Moen (Ed.), *It's about time: Couples and careers* (pp. 220–241). Ithaca, NY: Cornell University Press.

Clark, S. C. (2001). Work cultures and work/family balance. *Journal of Vocational Behavior, 58*(3), 348–365.

Cyert, R. M., & March, J. G. (1963). *A behavioral theory of the firm.* Englewood Cliffs, NJ: Prentice-Hall.

Deery, S., Iverson, R., & Walsh, J. (2002). Work relationships in telephone call centers: Understanding emotional exhaustion and employee withdrawal. *Journal of Management Studies, 39*(4), 471–496.

Durkheim, E. (1997). *The division of labor in society.* W. D. Halls, trans. New York: Free Press. (Original work published 1933, New York: MacMillan)

Duxbury, L. E., Higgins, C. A., & Lee, C. (1994). Work-family conflict: A comparison by gender, family type, and perceived control. *Journal of Family Issues, 15*(3), 449–466.

Earls, A. (2002, June 30). Managing on the run in a virtual world: Technology helps executives whose work and family life connect at airports. *Boston Globe,* p. 1.

Eaton, S. C. (2003). If you can use them: Flexibility policies, organizational commitment, and perceived performance. *Industrial Relations, 42*(2), 145–167.

Edwards, R. (1979). *Contested terrain: The transformation of the workplace in the twentieth century.* New York: Basic Books.

Epstein, C. F., Seron, C., Oglensky, B., & Saute, R. (1999). *The part-time paradox: Time norms, professional life, family, and gender.* New York: Routledge.

Foegen, J. H. (1993). Telexploitation. *Labor Law Journal, 44*(5), 318–321.

Friedman, S. D., & Greenhaus, J. H. (2000). *Work and family—Allies or enemies?* New York: Oxford University Press.

Frone, M. R., Russell, M., & Cooper, M. L. (1992). Antecedents and outcomes of work-family conflict: Testing a model of the work-family interface. *Journal of Applied Psychology, 77,* 65–78.

Gareis, K. C., & Barnett, R. C. (2002). Under what conditions do long work hours affect psychological distress? A study of full-time and reduced-hours female doctors. *Work and Occupations, 29*(4), 483–497.

Glass, J., & Fujimoto, T. (1995). Employer characteristics and the provision of family policies. *Work and Occupations, 22*(4), 380–411.

Goldstein, N. (2003). *IT at work: Information technologies and remote working in the United States.* Manuscript, SRI International.

Herzenberg, S., Alic, J. A., & Wial, H. (1998). *New rules for a new economy: employment and opportunity in postindustrial America.* Ithaca, NY: ILR Press.

Higgins, C. A., Duxbury, L. E., & Johnson, K. L. (2000). Part-time work for women: Does it really help balance work and family? *Human Resource Management, 39*(1), 17–32.

Hill, E. J., Ferris, M., & Martinson, V. (2003). Does it matter where you work? A comparison of how three work venues (traditional office, virtual office, and home office) influence aspects of work and personal/family life. *Journal of Vocational Behavior, 63*(2), 220–241.

Hill, E. J., Hawkins, A. J., Ferris, M., & Weitzman, M. (2001). Finding an extra day a week: The positive influence of perceived job flexibility on work and family life balance. *Family Relations, 50*(1), 49–58.

Hill, E. J., Hawkins, A. J., & Miller, B. C. (1996). Work and family in the virtual office: Perceived influences of mobile telework. *Family Relations, 45*(3), 293–301.

Hill, E. J., Miller, B. C., Weiner, S. P., & Colihan, J. (1998). Influences of the virtual office on aspects of work and work/life balance. *Personnel Psychology, 51,* 667–683.

Hochschild, A. R. (1997). *The time bind: When work becomes home and home becomes work.* New York: Metropolitan Books.

Holman, D., Chissick, C., & Totterdell, P. (2002). The effects of performance monitoring on emotional labor and well-being in call centers. *Motivation and Emotion, 26*(1), 57–81.

Hunter, L. W. (2000). The adoption of innovative work practices in service establishments. *International Journal of Human Resource Management, 11*(3), 477–496.

Hunter, L. W., & Lafkas, J. J. (2003). Opening the box: Information technology, work practices, and wages. *Industrial & Labor Relations Review, 56*(2), 224–244.

International Telework Association & Council. (2002). *Telework America 2001.* Silver Spring, MD: ITAC.

Jackson, M. (2002, October 22). Using technology to add new dimensions to the nightly call home. *New York Times,* p. 8.

Kelley, M. (1990). New process technology, job design, and work organization: A contingency model. *American Sociological Review, 55,* 191–208.

Kingston, P. W. (1990). Illusions and ignorance about the family-responsive workplace. *Journal of Family Issues, 11*(4), 438–454.

Kraut, R. (1989). Telecommuting: The trade-offs of home work. *Journal of Communication, 39*(3), 19–47.

Kurland, N. B., & Bailey, D. E. (1999). Telework: The advantages and challenges of working here, there anywhere, and anytime. *Organizational Dynamics, 28*(2), 53–68.

Li, Y. J., Bechhofer, F., Stewart, R., McCrone, D., Anderson, M., & Jamieson, L. (2002). A divided working class? Planning and career perception in the service and working classes. *Work, Employment and Society, 16*(4), 617–636.

Lobel, S. A., & St. Clair, L. (1992). Effects of family responsibilities, gender, and career identity salience on performance outcomes. *Academy of Management Journal, 35*(5), 1057–1069.

MacDuffie, J. P. (1995). Human resource bundles and manufacturing performance: Organizational logic and flexible production systems in the world auto industry. *Industrial and Labor Relations Review, 48*(2), 197–221.

Marks, S. R., Huston, T. L., Johnson, E. M., & MacDermid, S. M. (2001). Role balance among white married couples. *Journal of Marriage and the Family, 63*(4), 1083–1098.

Marx, K. (1978a). The Gundrisse (Foundations of the Critique of Political Economy). In R. C. Tucker (Ed.), The Marx-Engels reader (pp. 221–293). New York: W. W. Norton. (Original work published 1939–1941 by the Institute of Marx-Engels-Lenin, Moscow)

Marx, K. (1978b). *Wage labour and capital.* In R. C. Tucker (Ed.), *The Marx-Engels reader* (pp. 203–217). New York: W. W. Norton. (Original work published 1849)

Mieszkowski, K. (2001, March 1). The age of overwork. *Salon.* Retrieved June 15, 2004, from http://archive.salon.com/tech/feature/2001/03/01/white_collar_sweatshop/print.html

Milkie, M. A., & Peltola, P. (1999). Playing all the roles: Gender and the work-family balancing act. *Journal of Marriage and the Family, 61*(2), 476–490.

Mirchandani, K. (1999). Legitimizing work: Telework and the gendered reification of the work-nonwork dichotomy. *The Canadian Review of Sociology and Anthropology, 36*(1), 87–107.

Osterman, P. (1995). Work family programs and the employment relationship. *Administrative Science Quarterly, 40*(4), 681–700.

Perrow, C. (1984). *Normal accidents: Living with high-risk technologies.* New York: Basic Books.

Piore, M. J., & Sabel, C. F. (1984). *The second industrial divide: Possibilities for prosperity.* New York: Basic Books.

Pleck, J. H. (1977). The work-family role system. *Social Problems, 24*(4), 17–27.

Pleck, J. H., Staines, G. L., & Lang, L. (1980). Conflict between work and family life. *Monthly Labor Review, 3,* 29–32.

Raabe, P. H., & Gessner, J. C. (1988). Employer family-supportive policies: Diverse variations on a theme. *Family Relations, 37,* 196–202.

Raghuram, S., Wiesenfeld, B., & Garud, R. (2003). Technology enabled work: The role of self-efficacy in determining telecommuter adjustment and structuring behavior. *Journal of Vocational Behavior, 63*(2), 180–198.

Rifkin, J. (1995). The end of work: The decline of the global labor force and the dawn of the post-market era. New York: G. P. Putnam's Sons.

Rones, P. L., Gardner, J. M., & Ilg, R. E. (2001). Trends in hours of work in the United States. In G. Wong and G. Picot (Eds.), *Working time in comparative perspective, Vol. 1: Patterns, trends, and the policy implications of earnings inequality and unemployment* (pp. 45–70). Kalamazoo, MI: W. E. Upjohn Institute for Employment Research.

Rothbard, N. P. (2001). Enriching or depleting? The dynamics of engagement in work and family roles. *Administrative Science Quarterly, 46*(4), 655–684.

Schor, J. B. (1991). *The overworked American: The unexpected decline of leisure.* New York: Basic Books.

Standen, P., Daniels, K., & Lamond, D. (1999). The home as a workplace: Work-family interaction and psychological well-being in telework. *Journal of Occupational Health Psychology, 4*(4), 368–381.

Taylor, P., & Bain, P. (1999). "An assembly line in the head": Work and employee relations in the call centre. *Industrial Relations Journal, 30*(2), 101–115.

Thomas, L. T., & Ganster, D. C. (1995). Impact of family-supportive work variables on work-family conflict and strain: A control perspective. *Journal of Applied Psychology, 80*(1), 6–15.

Thomas, R. J. (1994). *What machines can't do: Politics and technology in the industrial enterprise.* Berkeley: University of California Press.

Thompson, C. A., Beauvais, L. L., & Lyness, K. S. (1999). When work-family benefits are not enough: The influence of work-family culture on benefit utilization, organizational attachment, and work-family conflict. *Journal of Vocational Behavior, 54*(3), 392–415.

Thompson, E. P. (1966). *The making of the English working class.* New York: Vintage.

U.S. Department of Labor. (2003, March 27). U.S. Department of Labor will secure overtime for 1.3 million more low-wage workers: Department seeks to modernize 50-year-old wage regulations. Press release, Washington DC.

Valcour, P. M., & Batt, R. (2003a). *Work exhaustion, organizational commitment and work-life integration: The moderating effects of work-family identity salience.* Working paper #03–07. Ithaca, NY: Bronfenbrenner Life Course Center.

Valcour, P. M., & Batt, R. (2003b). Work-life integration: Challenges and organizational responses. In P. Moen (Ed.), *It's about time: Couples and careers* (pp. 310–331). Ithaca, NY: Cornell University Press.

Venkatesh, A., & Vitalari, N. (1987). A post-adoption analysis of computing in the home. *Journal of Economic Psychology, 8*(2), 161–180.

Watt, D., & White, J. M. (1999). Computers and the family life: A family development perspective. *Journal of Comparative Family Studies, 30*(1), 1–15.

Wells, S. J. (2001). Making telecommuting work. *HR Magazine, 46*(10), 34–46.

Williams, K. J., & Alliger, G. M. (1994). Role stressors, mood spillover, and perceptions of work-family conflict in employed parents. *Academy of Management Journal, 37*(4), 837–868.

Zuboff, S. (1988). *In the age of the smart machine: The future of work and power.* New York: Basic Books.

5

Organizational Reliability, Flexibility, and Security

Karlene H. Roberts
Vinit M. Desai
Peter Madsen
University of California, Berkeley

The issues of organizational resilience and security took on new meaning after September 11, 2001. While the attack on the Twin Towers and the Pentagon directed our attention to the need to increase organizational and individual security, it followed a large number of organizational events that piqued interest in smaller ways. The purpose of this chapter is to describe one organization in which errors can lead to catastrophic outcomes and to describe how this organization and others like it encourage work-life segmentation and how people and policies in these organizations address this process.

In the last 20 years alone we have experienced the largest industrial accident in the world (Union Carbide's chemical plant at Bhopal), the demise of two space shuttles (*Challenger* and *Columbia*), the failure of two Mars probes, the sinking of a Japanese fishing boat by a U.S. Navy submarine (*U.S.S. Greeneville*), environmental ruin at the hands of the oil industry (Piper Alpha, *Exxon Valdez,* Petrobras), and the demise of Barings Bank. The list goes on and on. A recent *Wall Street Journal* article stated, "Nearly 20 years after an environmental disaster at a Union Carbide plant in Bhopal, India, the tragedy remains a thorn in the side of Dow Chemical Co. . . . Union Carbide's environmental legacy has begun to appear on Dow's bottom line" (cited in Carlton & Herrick, 2003).

The point is that in a technologically complex world we continue to develop organizations that have ever increasing capabilities to do massive damage to someone, somewhere. As Robert Pool writes:

> In a generation or two, the world will likely need thousands of high-reliability organizations running not just nuclear power plants, space flight [control], and air traffic control, but also chemical plants, electrical grids, computer and telecommunication networks, financial networks, genetic engineering, nuclear-waste storage, and many other complex, hazardous technologies. Our ability to manage a technology, rather than our ability to conceive and build it, may be the limiting factor in many cases. (1997, p. 276)

All of the aforementioned catastrophes share in common a number of human and organizational oversights that led to demise. The processes and oversights that contribute to catastrophic organizational events increasingly are documented in the organizational literature. Whereas there has long been a social science literature on crisis and crisis management, until 1978 it focused more on response and community rebuilding than on cause. In 1978 Turner published his seminal work on organizational causes of catastrophe (see also Turner & Pidgeon, 1997). Soon after, sociologist Charles Perrow published *Normal Accidents: Living with High Risk Technologies* (1999), which identified organizational complexity and tight coupling as culprits of major misfortunes.

Several other sociologists devoted their energies to uncovering sources of errors in organizations (e.g., Clarke, 1999; Clarke & Short, 1993; Heimer, 1988; Short & Clarke, 1992). A major research effort in this area initiated at the University of California at Berkeley labeled as "high reliability organizations" examines organizations that engage in behaviors exposing them to the potential of catastrophic outcomes but seem to avoid these kinds of outcomes (e.g., La Porte, 1996; Roberts, Stout, & Halpern, 1994; Rochlin, 1997). This was followed by similar research activities at the University of Michigan (e.g., Weick, 1987; Weick & Sutcliffe, 2001), MIT (e.g., Carroll, 1998), Stanford (e.g., Gaba, 1989; Sagan, 1993), and other research institutions (e.g., Bierly & Spender, 1995; Helmreich & Foushee, 1993; Lagadec, 1993; Reason, 1997; Vaughan, 1996).

Even prior to 9/11, which many think of as a watershed disaster, some organizations addressed issues of how to mitigate risk. A few of these organizations developed risk mitigation strategies. Among these organizations are commercial airlines, health care settings, a chemical production company, a financial institution, the U.S. Coast Guard, and U.S. Navy/Marine Corps aviation. Unfortunately, when the champions of such programs leave their organizations, the programs tend to deteriorate.

The population, at least in the United States, perceives itself to be at greater risk today than it used to be. This perception may motivate researchers and organizational members to pay attention to issues that should have concerned them previously.

TODAY'S ORGANIZATIONS AND RESILIENCY

Many organizations address safety, often through developing strategies that foster resilience. Various community organizations exist largely to protect citizen safety. Some other organizations, like health care organizations (e.g., Kohn, Corrigan, & Donaldson, 1999), should largely function around issues of safety. Units of the military (e.g., safety officers aboard naval ships) and other organizations (e.g., flight crews and in-flight crews aboard commercial airliners) are primarily concerned with safety. High reliability organizations research suggests that increased resilience increases reliability and, thus, safety.

Resiliency means "1. The ability to recover quickly from illness, change or misfortune; buoyancy. 2. The property of a material that enables it to resume its original shape or position after being bent, stretched, or compressed; elasticity" (*American Heritage Dictionary*, 1991, p. 1051). Organizations today are largely information processors, and information processing and decision making are precursors to resilience. Information processing and decision making take place in structures that either contribute to or detract from resiliency.

Often organizations in which reliability maintenance is a key feature are characterized also by task time compression, and certainly responding to mischief directed toward discombobulating an organization or its members requires time-compressed activities. One way HROs deal with time compression is through redundancy (e.g., Roberts, Stout, & Halpern, 1993), which contributes to resiliency.

Increasingly we have come to recognize that organizations must somehow integrate tasks. This is particularly critical in large-scale complex organizations that by definition can do more harm than small organizations with low-level technologies. In the 9/11 situation, a few people backed by a larger, more complex organization were the frontline contributors to a disaster in which they harnessed complex organizations and technology (commercial airliners) to destroy other complex systems.

Weick and Roberts (1993) developed the concept of *collective mind* to explain organizational performance in situations requiring nearly continuous operational reliability. Collective mind is a pattern of heedful interrelations of actions and actors in a social system. The actors understand their actions are connected and construct actions with this understanding. Variance in heed influences comprehension of unfolding events and the commission of errors. In other words, actors must size up their situations correctly in concert and make heedful contributions to their situations to avoid contributing to error. "As heedful interrelating and mindful comprehension increases organizational errors decrease" (Weick & Roberts, 1993, p. 357). Collective mind and heedful interrelating contribute to elasticity.

Consistent with this approach is research done by coordination scholars. These researchers emphasize the exploration of relationships and interactions within and among groups as important, and they examine the interrelated, interdependent, and intersubjective nature of social-organizational forces (Bradbury & Liechtenstein, 2000). This perspective places the locus of human organization within the space of interaction among members. The complexity facing organizations emerges prominently at these intersections within and across groups causing ripple effects that move through a complex maze of interactions, sometimes leading to unintended consequences. As organizations become more complex and nonlinear, greater numbers of interdependent agents involve themselves in exponentially increasing interactions (Jervis, 1997).

In these interactions, coordination fails and coordination neglect takes root when organizational participants focus on partitioning tasks and concentrate on their individual components but fail to pay attention to reintegrating the tasks (Heath & Staudenmeyer, 2000), thus reducing buoyancy and elasticity. This has deleterious consequences when failure can result in catastrophic outcomes.

In these complex systems with multiple interactions, coordination is confounded by behavioral uncertainties. Each human component of a complex system is a unique individual and behaves in a way that, however slightly, resists perfect prediction. Humans enter and leave organizations, belong to multiple organizations simultaneously, and occupy multiple roles in their organizations. When role conflicts arise, humans become difficult to motivate in a predictable fashion. Determining the impact of people's multiple roles on performance in high reliability settings, and the success of various policies designed to direct performance around cognitive conflicts, becomes as central to coordination as coordination itself.

Literature on work and family seeks to explore interactions among the multiple roles and responsibilities of modern workers, concentrating on the interplay between their family and work obligations and behaviors. This research has been prompted largely by changes in the substance of the workforce, trends toward dual-earning couples and more women entering the workforce, as well as by institutional advances in the use of flextime policies, paid leave, and other incentives addressing the workforce's family and life responsibilities. This research casts doubt on the myth that family and work are independent (Blood & Wolfe, 1960; Dubin, 1973) and instead identifies numerous mechanisms linking work and family (Burke & Greenglass, 1987; Lambert, 1990; Zedeck, 1992).

Research suggests at least three mechanisms describing the relationship between work and life activities (Edwards & Rothbard, 2000; Sumer & Knight, 2001). According to the *segmentation* model, work and life are different and noninteracting spheres. The *compensation* model suggests that life activities are purposely different than work activities, as one compensates for the other by providing satisfaction not realized in the other domain. Finally, the *spillover* model holds that one's choice of life or work activities may be affected by interests and attitudes in the other domain (Edwards & Rothbard, 2000; Sumer & Knight, 2001).

In sum, today we are faced with a situation in which organizations and the people in them wish to increase safe operations for themselves and their con- stituencies. Safety is increased through reliable operations that are characterized, in part, by resilience. These processes occur in an organizational framework offering more relaxed organizational structures, to ensure that employees engage in flexible and resilient behaviors that utilize various skills and tie them together to obtain successful outcomes. These mechanisms are contributed to by infor- mation processing in the organization. To function in this vigilant capacity smoothly, organizations often seek to reduce uncertainty by placing demands on their workers. One such cost entails requesting that employees leave the rest of life at the organization's door. Disputes or tension at home should not infiltrate working behavior. However, as research demonstrates (e.g., Burke & Greenglass, 1987; Dubin, 1973), this is easier said than done, because employees inadver- tently bring their life experiences to work and take work experiences home.

The remainder of this chapter explores one organization with a goal to protect citizen safety. We spotlight one part of the organization and discuss the processes that seem to contribute to this goal. One such process requests the segmentation of work and personal spheres, such that workers focus on work rather than on interpersonal conflicts or nonwork obligations during their shift. We examine what employees say about the normative lack of integration of work and the rest of their lives and also explore how the employees' life experiences none- theless find ways to inform their work.

BIG CITY POLICE DEPARTMENT

By mandate, police departments are in business to protect citizen safety and to detain criminals. Big City Police Department (BCPD) serves an urban popula- tion of approximately 380,000 people. In 2000 each of this department's 911 operators answered an average of 17,000 calls. This was the highest level of activity of any comparable U.S. city surveyed. In large communication centers such as BCPD's, the same personnel do not simultaneously answer 911 calls and dispatch police units in the field. Complaint operators answer the emergency and nonemergency phone lines. Dispatchers broadcast assignments and maintain radio communications with officers in the field.

BCPD and its constituencies' interrelations are diagrammed in Fig. 5.1. A police officer may see a transgression of the law or a civil problem, advise the

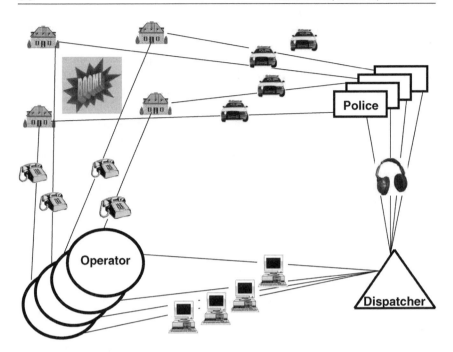

FIG. 5.1. BCPD's 911 network.

communications division, and take immediate action. Citizens report crimes or problems in person or, more frequently, through the 911 telephone system. The communications division may receive several reports of any one crime or incident.

In this system, dispatchers rotate across three jobs in any one shift. These jobs are complaint operator, dispatcher, and service operator. Complaint operators answer and evaluate citizen calls. If they determine that a call requires police response, they record pertinent details in the communications computer and electronically transmit information about who, what, when, where, and why to dispatchers. Dispatchers assign available street units to handle calls. Dispatchers use the primary police radio channels to make assignments and to monitor the disposition of the calls for service. Police officers and dispatchers remain in contact throughout the duration of the event. Service operators use administrative radio channels to communicate additional information such as outstanding warrants, driver's license and vehicle registration data, and so forth.

Two important goals at BCPD are citizen and police safety. Activities across various parts of the organization are designed to ensure safety. Many safety-related activities establish institutional resiliency, which is critical to BCPD. Eighty to 85% of the 911 calls received by BCPD are mundane or nonacute. Our focus is on the remaining 15% of calls that are inherently difficult to interpret and significantly related to safety concerns. In run of the mill operations the organization needs less resiliency than it does during more hectic emergencies. One BCPD dispatcher said to us:

> Dispatchers are now the core of everything that's going wrong. As soon as something happens, everyone picks up 911 and they want us to save [them], they want us to fix it.

ORGANIZATIONAL STRUCTURE
FOR RESILIENCY AND THE OPERATION
OF COLLECTIVE MIND

BCPD is a paramilitary organization and, as such, structures itself along bureaucratic military lines. However, if we examine the small slice of the organization represented by the police on the street and by the communication center, we notice several characteristics of high reliability organizations designed to increase safety through organizational interdependence, flexibility, and resilience.

Figure 5.1 illustrates how redundancy and resiliency are built into the system. Each person in Fig. 5.1 tries to make sense of a particular incident based on the facts they have and their perspective of the incident. They are redundant in their ability to do this, and the redundancy helps people in the system make appropriate interpretations of what is going on in the community. The police department employees must recognize their interdependence with one another and relate to one another heedfully. That is, they must not fail to integrate the partitioning of activities. The way the system is organized helps employees feel like an important part of it. They each understand that reported information is incomplete, not entirely accurate, and sometimes deliberately deceptive. They understand that by ensuring redundancy and communicating their respective understandings, they will validate information and provide one another with a more complete understanding of each incident as it unfolds.

Figure 5.1 shows also that important activities occur at the interstices among interacting and interdependent people, necessitating attention to issues of *coordination*. As an example of how this happens we focus on a homicide incident.

In this incident a female citizen places a 911 call. She tells the complaint operator that the man in her apartment is bleeding. He takes the phone, says they do not want service, and hangs up. The complaint operator calls back (complaint operators always call back people who hang up). This time the caller hesitates about whether they need service, but the complaint operator has determined that she does and starts transmitting data to the dispatcher. The complaint operator can change the interpretation of the complaint or its seriousness at any time during the incident. The dispatcher also can change either the status of the call or its interpretation. Calls labeled *A priority* require immediate officer dispatch while *B* and *C priority* callers may wait minutes or hours for an officer.

The dispatcher radios a police car on patrol in the area of the call with the address of the caller and other pertinent information, including the fact that the complaint operator has labeled the call A priority. Neither the complaint operator nor the dispatcher has labeled this call a homicide. But the police officer radios back that he has visited the address several times in the past and he suspects this is an issue of passion gone terribly wrong. He is correct. The system makes an accurate interpretation because one person can add information no one else has. It is organized so any one of the three people involved may be the first to make a correct interpretation. This is done through *collective mind* and *heedful interaction* that result in system elasticity. The three police department representatives are interdependent with one another, which helps them feel connected to the system, and each is searching for clues. Clues help people recognize that the current incident is similar to an incident they encountered some time previously and enable them to piece together things that now make sense to them. This spillover of experience gained through prior individual and team activity increases group cohesion and the probability of effectively *coordinating* with one another. This in turn serves as a component of organizational resiliency.

THE DIVIDE: WHEN SEGMENTATION WORKS

The previous example illustrates some of the trade-offs that must be made if an organization like BCPD is to operate effectively. On the one hand, BCPD personnel often are able to coordinate more effectively on difficult and ambiguous calls when they draw on their previous histories of working as a team and on their own life experiences. On the other hand, shared history with coworkers is not always positive, and personal experiences are often more distracting than relevant. Consequently, emergency operators are called on to manage their personal lives, work relationships, and emotions in such a way that these elements do not interfere with the work at hand but are available to be drawn from when doing so enhances performance.

The work-life literature refers to this separation of personal life from work life and of personal feelings for coworkers from interactions with them at work as *segmentation* (e.g., Greenhaus & Singh, 2003; Sumer & Knight, 2001). As will be seen, segmentation is standard operating procedure at BCPD and in most instances this is optimal. Segmentation increases efficiency on most 911 calls because it allows emergency operators to deal with information effectively. However, segmentation can be counterproductive when an emergency operator re-

ceives an especially difficult call. Highly effective emergency operators and dispatchers manage to segment their emotions during most calls but draw on them
when needed.

Inherent in the culture of the Communications Center at BCPD is the norm
that once you walk through the door you leave everything else behind. And if
you happen to dislike a fellow worker, you leave that behind too. This norm is
not unique to BCPD. Rather it is common in organizations that require error-
free performance. Research on high-reliability organizations finds that fighter
pilots are taught to leave everything behind as they begin a mission and sailors
on aircraft carriers are instructed to put the safety of their shipmates above
everything else, including their personal feelings. Similarly, the Blue Angels
(U.S. Navy precision flight team) practice their routines together cognitively
before they depart on missions. In the thick of things the organization cannot
be concerned about lack of concentration. This culture of segmentation is well
understood and even endorsed by BCPD operators and dispatchers. The following quotes are representative.

> The other thing to me is that [you can be] going through a divorce or going through
> a death in the family. Once you walked through that door, you leave everything
> behind and you give 100% as soon as you come in.

> There are some that can't do that and it interferes with their work up on the
> channel, because they're thinking, or even on calls because they are thinking.

> An effecive dispatcher to me has to leave everything at the door and give 100%
> to the people she works with. . . . And that's on the phone also and on the radio.
> So, we have three areas and they can all work together when you can leave it all
> behind. It's like I can be having a bad day. You're going to have bad days.

Segmentation of personal life from work life prevents distraction, increasing
performance. Segmentation further increases efficiency by preventing emergency
operators and dispatchers from becoming personally involved in the calls they
receive. Many requests for service from BCPD must be left unanswered because
the department has limited resources. BCPD policy explicitly forbids dispatchers
from sending officers to certain categories of crime. For instance, BCPD policy
requires that officers are not sent in response to calls regarding drug dealing.
Over many years of responding to such calls, the BCPD leadership has learned
that suspects are usually gone by the time officers arrive and that finding evidence of the deal is difficult. However, it becomes very difficult for dispatchers
to tell citizens calling about drug deals occurring in their neighborhoods that
BCPD resources are better spent elsewhere. On a personal level dispatchers
empathize with these citizens and want to help them. Segmentation allows them
to put aside these personal feelings and make decisions that best serve the city
as a whole.

When an organization's culture is strong and when it requires almost fully involving its employees in sensing their environments and then deciding on courses of action, it often cannot afford to have the employees distracted by other aspects of their lives. One thing people do in such a system is take care of each other. As one operator/dispatcher said:

> To be a team player [is] to help out your fellow workers in a situation like a fire or a plane crash, something like that. Somebody takes the initiative to help everybody on the crew get the job done.

Another operator/dispatcher noted how important it is to help fellow workers even if they are not particularly likeable:

> But then we are on the radio and I'm on the main channel and she's on the service channel—which provides backup for the main channel—and we hate one another, and we don't speak, we don't speak at all. . . . [S]omething happens, and I need something from service or vice versa. When it comes to that and I say, Diane[1] I need you to run this plate or I need you to call the helicopter or whatever, she'll do it. She'll do it because that's our job and you have to do it, 'cause like Tom said, you'll get in trouble, and you just forget about the fact [that you do not like her]. And when you're done and the critical incident and the help is over, then you go back to not speaking if that's what you want to do. That's how it works.

Segmentation prevents personal conflicts at work from interfering with the proper execution of the job. In high-stress work environments, personal conflicts are inevitable. The culture of segmentation allows BCPD employees to overcome these conflicts.

BCPD Employee: Can we take that a step further? Because I think one of the factors is that we do the same thing with each other all the time. We always run into conflicts with each other, all the time. We always run into conflict with each other, not on a huge basis, but on a regular basis. We have situations where we're just coming up and something's got to be done. All the matters get left outside and we focus on getting the job done. And sometimes there's something I think in a normal job environment would be, I think, some really bad feelings and long-term problems. But with us, we do it, we get it over with.
Interviewer: How do you do it?
BCPD Employee: You don't take it personally. When an emergency arises, you take off that soft-skinned stuff and you just do what has to be done.
Interviewer: How do you learn something like that?

BCPD Employee: They've worked here so long that, in the words of one former supervisor, they've learned to hate each other in detail. But what Sue identified and [what] you are elaborating on is an ability, you could either call it focus or the ability to divorce yourself from the argument you were just having, stop in mid-sentence and, for the job, work together.

The vast majority of 911 calls received at the Communication Center require little sense-making effort to understand. They are straightforward and operators and dispatchers are able to make correct decisions by simply following established department policy. In dealing with these calls, segmentation increases the efficiency and performance of the BCPD Communications Center staff. Segmentation is the operationalization of coordination neglect across work and life domains.

BEYOND THE DIVIDE: BYPASSING THE SEGMENTATION OF LIFE AND WORK

Resilience at BCPD and other organizations concerned with reliability depends on the heedful integration of multiple minds in team actions when necessitated by the complexity of the situation. As shown, coworker disputes are often abandoned and family stresses repressed, if only temporarily. Response to common calls for service gains efficiency when complex and unrelated life issues are discounted.

Calls to the 911 center, however, are not always so simple. Callers witnessing stressful events may unintentionally (or deliberately) mislead the fact-finder, become evasive or hysterical, and even may be in danger themselves. For instance, in some domestic violence situations callers fear reprisal and consequently may not be able to respond freely. Further complications arise when seemingly routine calls escalate into complex, high-priority emergencies. Before police arrive on a scene, the only connection BCPD usually has with an unfolding event is through the telephone. Skillful interrogation can uncover informational cues, sometimes ones as subtle as a gut feeling about the caller's tone of voice, which prompt the complaint operator to upgrade a call's priority. We reviewed over 30 adjudicated homicide cases; not one of them began as a homicide. Although not a representative sample, this finding is not unique. In general, the heedful interpretation of facts and the coordination of information that flow through the organization become critical not only in complex situations but also in some seemingly routine instances.

Operators and dispatchers need to be skilled in assessing which situations require which behavior. In quickly shifting and dynamic engagements, with considerable environmental uncertainty, elaborated policies and formal training cannot delineate a systematic organizational plan of action for every imaginable scenario. Responders must become flexibly adapted, with the burden on organizational members to make sense of particular situations, determine an appropriate response, and coordinate with others to implement the response. Buoyancy, elasticity, resilience, coordination, and collective mind are all at work. Nonwork experiences and learning may at times play a central role in this process.

Life experiences may routinely infuse role obligations at work. A worker desiring to exclude his or her personal distractions and perhaps even guiding emotions from a work situation likely engages in an active cognitive process to this end, since galvanized links between nonwork and job factors have been established (Edwards & Rothbard, 2000; Lambert, 1990; Zedeck, 1992). That members of BCPD and other organizations experience some level of integration between work and nonwork experiences is perhaps an inconsequential statement. After all, individuals may select to join and remain employed by BCPD or other organizations because of congruence between organizational and individual or family values.

When BCPD complaint operators interpret ambiguous and often incomplete information from calls to make sense of complex situations, however, the incorporation of nonwork experience at times plays a central role in decision making. Furthermore, as complaint operators, dispatchers, and police officers involved in any given situation add their own interpretations and information to the collectively perceived situation and work together to develop an organizational response, individual differences in life experience carry group-level implications for coordination. When it occurs, the bypassing of segmentation between life and work may either improve or detract from performance. That life experiences, emotions, and attitudes are not always strictly segmented from work behavior is central to an understanding of organizational resilience at BCPD.

To illustrate, a dispatcher recounts listening in on a call during her training. A female caller claimed her husband had beaten her and absconded with their daughter, who was ill and needed medication. The risk level at the scene initially appeared low because the alleged abuser was no longer present, important information for the responding police officer. Through the conversation, aided by an interpreter as the caller spoke limited English, details began to emerge regarding the nature and extent of the caller's victimization. The observing dispatcher's own experience in a similar situation led her to assess the situation differently as the call progressed.

Dispatcher in training: Then, well, the ending part is he's actually had her locked in. She couldn't leave the house at all. He had the phones tapped, I mean there [were] just so many pieces coming out, coming, coming, coming. He had the phones tapped. . . . He had threatened to kill her, kill the family if she ever left, kill the daughter. So, it was a really big mess.

> **Interviewer:** What was your sense of things, that he might . . . that there was a good chance that he might do something like that?

> **Dispatcher:** Yeah.

> **Interviewer:** Why? People say that all the time.

> **Dispatcher:** No, and . . . yeah, people say that all the time. And I think it's just for me, I think that it was more of a personal issue for me. This was a 24-year-old . . . no, no, no, wait a minute. She was younger than 24. She had . . . this man took her from Mexico at the age of 14, he was a 48-year-old man. He had her really under his control. And the likes of him to do it. . . . I don't know, I think probably he would. He threatened all her family in Mexico. . . .

> **Interviewer:** You mentioned it was a personal issue for you.

> **Dispatcher:** Just I've been in that boat of being under the control of someone who stated they're going to beat you if you do something and then actually receiving the beating the day that you decide that you are ready to go.

> **Interviewer:** So it was very credible to you. . . . It's almost the sort of thing, objectively any of us in, looking at it, could say that it's controlling behavior, which raises the risk level. But also because of your personal experiences, you really attached some real significance to what was going on. And that's what happens. And you'll find people will react to some calls very differently because you have personal experience.

The responding police officer was merely to query the woman about where her husband and daughter possibly had gone. Despite the absence of imminent threat at the scene, information gathered from the call and an interpretation enhanced by the almost certainly stressful similarity of a recounted personal experience led the complaint operator and dispatcher in training to make a different recommendation. Police evacuated the woman to a shelter. The complaint operator went as far as calling the shelter in advance to find out if there would be room for her.

When the initial link between BCPD and an unfolding emergency occurs over the telephone, sense is made about situations based on often ambiguous and, at times, incorrect information from callers. As nonverbal cues and visual pictures of the scene are absent, complaint operators listen for subtleties such as a caller's tone of voice, pace of speech and pauses, and background noises to improve their situational awareness. At times, organizational members report drawing on life events, stressful nonwork situations, and other external influences to inform their sense of situations and to coordinate activities. Although job-related and external roles may be segmented at times, during certain complex

events the life experiences and nonwork roles of employees are inextricable from
their job performance and from the organization's resilience and reliability.

Complaint operators routinely report drawing from life experiences especially
when making the distinction between mundane calls and complex emergencies.
Gut reactions and instincts derived from callers' speech patterns supplement or
replace formal work policies in motivating behavior. The recognition of subtle
distinctions in speech pattern and tone comes with the diligent application of
experience, broadly accessing and blending work experience on prior calls with
personal learning gained from interactions in prior situations. Complaint operators become forthcoming when discussing such experience-based rule breaking.

> **Operator:** I was just going to say that I had a call similar to Sue's
> where, based on what the person was saying, it would have been a
> medium priority call. It was a gal who said, "My boyfriend is out front,
> they broke into the car and he's going out there to check." And then
> something in her voice, she said, "Oh, now the people are coming
> back." And this was a long time ago and something in her voice, the
> sound of her voice made me want to send the officers with the lights
> and sirens on, so I indicated that on the call. Because ordinarily for
> this type of call we wouldn't have [done that].
>
> **Interviewer:** What did you indicate on the call?
>
> **Operator:** To send the officers with the lights and sirens on, you know,
> a code three response. Just because I had a feeling like Sue was saying,
> something about her voice. And sure enough, her boyfriend, when he
> rounded the corner, there [were] like ten guys waiting for him and he
> got killed. Unfortunately the officers didn't get there fast enough. But
> it's true what Sue and Diane are saying that a lot of this job is common
> sense. I mean they can teach you to memorize codes and they can teach
> you to make this a this priority and this a this priority because it's
> written, but if you don't use common sense you're not a good effective
> dispatcher. You're just not.

Alternatively, life experiences and instincts may lead to potentially dangerous
misjudgments when truly complex emergencies are dismissed as hoaxes. To
enhance resilience and reliability, BCPD policies design around this by mandating callbacks to callers who hang up and also by stipulating the presumption
of severity when in doubt. The following instance illustrates such an integration
of conflicting personal instincts and policy in which policy was favored. A complaint operator took a 911 call with heavy background music, through which
she spoke with a man reporting that nine people had been shot. His tone of
voice was extremely calm and smooth, not indicative of typical callers from
such emergency scenes. The complaint operator reported deliberating whether
to dismiss the call as a hoax, because incorrectly dispatching an ambulance and

police would be costly. The complaint operator decided to put personal instinct on hold and follow policy, dispatching an ambulance.

> That's generally true that whenever our senses hear one thing and words are telling us another thing, we always believe our senses. And that's true in any industry. That's true of human beings generally. We trust our senses more than we trust [what we hear]. Somebody can objectively tell you nine people have been shot, but you didn't trust them. "No, that's not true," because you were trusting your senses. You were reading that body language [through verbal cues over the phone]. And body language wasn't consistent with nine people being shot.
>
> But then I fell back on policy, and policy said that you had to send an ambulance.
>
> Discretion is very important.
>
> Discretion, because up to a point you had discretion. You could not send anybody. You could deny service to that person. Nine people have just been shot, and you deny service. But because nine people being shot, I mean that's a powerful word, or set of powerful words, you fall back on policy. Are you telling me that usually policy doesn't really [matter?].
>
> Policy says that you treat it like a real call, and thank God I did, because I truly did not want to send an ambulance, because I absolutely did not believe that guy, and nines times out of. . . . Because he was saying things like [that and] there was music blasting in the background, and I said, "Sir, can you turn down the music? I can't hear you." And he goes, "No, the DJ's dead, the DJ's dead." Well, the DJ was dead.

The ultimate behavioral outcome of the incident is consistent with a segmentation mind-set. Policy suggests an ambulance be dispatched, and an ambulance was sent. However, one cannot suggest that life experience and gut feelings were strictly left out of the determination. Resiliency includes the ability to decide when and how to apply external experiences and bypass segmentation. In this instance, the complaint operator decided to temporarily suppress her instincts and err on the side of sending service. In other cases in which formal work rules and personal instinct come into conflict, determinations favoring personal experience and circumventing policy may be made. Even when segmentation between work and life appears to occur in workplaces, workers may nonetheless be mentally accessing personal experiences and judgments even if they are ultimately disregarded. To bypass segmentation is a consequence of humans' integrative mental complexity. To integrate life and work may be natural.

CONCLUSION

We see here that the separation and integration of work and life issues is tricky at BCPD. The organization requires this separation but also requires resilience in responding to 911 calls. For an important percentage of received calls an appropriate response is a judgment call. Operators/dispatchers first have to make sense of the call through heedful interrelating across the people involved. That is why the priority of calls can change as an incident progresses. They also have to decide when to segment their life and work experiences, that is, when to pay attention to partitioning of life and work without reintegrating the two.

At other times, integration of the two is important so that operators/dispatchers can make better sense of what they confront. The world of the 911 responder is a complicated world in which the responder has to merge heedfulness with resiliency while simultaneously paying attention to the partitioning-integrating issue. This chapter highlights a number of issues usually not seen in the work-life literature. These issues are important in the day-to-day management of reliability-enhancing organizations; heedful interrelating, resiliency, and partitioning and coordination in the sense that Heath and Staudenmayer (2000) discuss the issue.

AUTHOR NOTE

The research for this chapter was supported by the National Science Foundation Grant SeS-0105402.

NOTE

1. Names have been changed to protect informant anonymity.

REFERENCES

American heritage dictionary (2nd ed.). (1991). Boston: Houghton Mifflin.

Bierly, P. E., & Spender, J. C. (1995). Culture and high reliability organizations: The case of the nuclear submarine. *Journal of Management, 21,* 636–656.

Blood, R. O., & Wolfe, D. M. (1960). *Husbands and wives.* New York: Macmillan.

Bradbury, H., & Lichtenstein, B.M.B. (2000). Relationality in organizational research: The space between. *Organization Science, 11,* 551–564.

Burke, R. J., & Greenglass, E. (1987). Work and family. In C. L. Cooper & I. T. Robertson (Eds.), *International review of industrial and organizational psychology* (pp. 273–320). New York: Wiley.

Carlton, J., & Herrick, T. (2003, May 8). Bhopal haunts Dow Chemical—Disaster survivors to speak at shareholders meeting. *Wall Street Journal,* section B3.

Carroll, J. S. (1998). Organizational learning activities in high-hazard industries: The logics underlying self-analysis. *Journal of Management Studies, 35,* 699–717.

Clarke, L. (1999). *Mission improbable: Using fantasy documents to tame disaster.* Chicago: University of Chicago Press.

Clarke, L., & Short, J. F. (1993). Social organization and risk: Some current controversies. *Annual Review of Sociology, 19,* 375–399.

Dubin, R. (1973). Work and non-work: Institutional perspectives. In M. D. Dunnette (Ed.), *Work and non-work in the year 2001* (pp. 53–68). Monterey, CA: Brooks/Cole.

Edwards, J. R., & Rothbard, N. P. (2000). Mechanisms linking work and family: Clarifying the relationship between work and family constructs. *Academy of Management Review, 25,* 178–199.

Gaba, D. (1989). Human error in anesthetic mishaps. *International Anesthesiology Clinics, 27,* 137–147.

Greenhaus, J. H., & Singh, R. (2003). Work-family linkages. In M. Pitts-Catsouphes & E. E. Kossek (Eds.) *Work-family encyclopedia.* Retrieved July 1, 2003, from www.bc.edu/wfnetwork

Heath, C., & Staudenmayer, N. (2000). Coordination neglect: How lay theories of organizing complicate coordination in organizations. *Research in Organizational Behavior, 22,* 153–191.

Heimer, C. A. (1988). Social structure, psychology, and the estimation of risk. *Annual Review of Sociology, 14,* 491–519.

Helmreich, R. L., & Foushee, C. (1993). Why crew resource management? Empirical and theoretical bases of human factors training in aviation. In E. L. Wiener, B. G. Kanki, & R. L. Helmreich (Eds.), *Cockpit resource management* (pp. 3–46). New York: Academic Press.

Jervis, R. (1997). *System effects: Complexity in political and social life.* Princeton, NJ: Princeton University Press.

Kohn, L. T., Corrigan, J. M., & Donaldson, M. S. (1999). *To err is human: Building a safer health system.* Washington, DC: National Academy Press.

Lagadec, P. (1993). *Preventing chaos in a crisis.* London: McGraw-Hill International.

Lambert, S. J. (1990). Processes linking work and family: A critical review and research agenda. *Human Relations, 43,* 239–257.

La Porte, T. R. (1996). High reliability organizations: Unlikely, demanding, and at risk. *Journal of Contingencies and Crisis Management, 4,* 60–71.

Perrow, C. (1999). *Normal accidents: Living with high-risk-technologies.* New York: Basic Books. (Original work published in 1984).

Pool, R. (1997). *Beyond engineering: How society shapes technology.* New York: Oxford University Press.

Reason, J. (1997). *Managing the risks of organizational accidents.* Aldershot, England: Ashgate.

Roberts, K. H., Stout, S. K., & Halpern, J. J. (1993). Decision dynamics in two high reliability military organizations. *Management Science, 40,* 614–624.

Rochlin, G. I. (1997). *Trapped in the net: The unanticipated consequences of computerization.* Princeton, NJ: Princeton University Press.

Sagan, S. (1993). *The limits of safety: Organizations, accidents, and nuclear weapons.* Princeton, NJ: Princeton University Press.

Short, J. F., & Clarke, L. (Eds.). (1992). *Organizations, uncertainties, and risk.* San Francisco: Westview.

Sumer, H. C., & Knight, P. A. (2001). How do people with different attachment styles balance work and family? A personality perspective on work-family linkage. *Journal of Applied Psychology, 86,* 653–663.

Turner, B. M. (1978). *Man-made disasters.* London: Wykeham.

Turner, B. M., & Pidgeon, N. (1997). *Man-made disasters* (2nd ed.). Oxford, England: Butterworth-Heinemann.

Vaughan, D. (1996). *The* Challenger *launch decision: Risky technology, culture, and deviance at NASA.* Chicago: University of Chicago Press.

Weick, K. E. (1987). Organizational culture as a source of high reliability. *California Management Review, 29,* 116–136.

Weick, K. E., & Roberts, K. H. (1993). Collective mind in organizations: Heedful interrelating on flight decks. *Administrative Science Quarterly, 38,* 357–381.

Weick, K. E., & Sutcliffe, K. M. (2001). *Managing the unexpected: Assuring high performance in an age of complexity.* San Francisco: Jossey-Bass.

Zedeck, S. (Ed.). (1992). *Work, families, and organizations.* San Francisco: Jossey-Bass.

6

Organizational Stratification: Distributing Opportunities for Balancing Work and Personal Life

Susan J. Lambert
Elaine Waxman
The University of Chicago

Casual and fun place to work . . . family friendly . . .
great benefits and flexible schedule for the right person!

A quick scan of the help wanted ads on any given day signals that employers routinely promote employment conditions outside of the traditional "good pay" and "rapid advancement!" As employers have struggled to compete for workers using an evolving array of strategies loosely bundled as *work-life policies*, academics have made significant contributions to our understanding of why employers vary in their adoption of these policies and why employees vary in their use of them.

On the one end, studies investigate how environmental factors, such as industry norms, can help explain firms' adoption of formal work-life supports, documenting the slow uptake of supports in some industries (cf. Goodstein, 1994; Ingram & Simons, 1995). At the other end, studies examine how workers' personal and occupational characteristics can help explain their use of available supports, generating concern that many formal supports are underutilized by workers (Blair-Loy & Wharton, 2002; Kossek, Barber, & Winters, 1999; Lambert, 1998). What is missing is the middle piece, that is, an understanding of how organizational structures and processes serve as gatekeepers to work-life supports and, more broadly, to opportunities for balancing work and personal life.

Building knowledge on the gatekeeping role of organizations requires both a conceptual framework and data to support a systematic assessment of how organizations structure access to policies, programs, and relationships that influence workers' ability to manage work and personal life. As we explain later, social scientists have considerable experience in using the theories of social stratification to investigate how organizations structure traditional employment opportunities, such as wage growth, promotion, and skill development. Extending this framework to include a broader set of opportunities essential to balancing work and personal life opens up the possibility of building on, and ultimately extending, knowledge about the processes and mechanisms of stratification.

Notably, the theories and methods of stratification can be used to identify the role formal and informal organizational structures and processes play in creating differential access to opportunity, whether intended or not. Thus, stratification perspectives have the potential to take us beyond superficial discussion of "who gets more" to an in-depth understanding of *how* inequality happens. This refined knowledge can be useful to practitioners interested in developing strategies that more effectively distribute work-life opportunities across organizational levels and jobs.

We begin this chapter with a brief overview of organizational perspectives on stratification to illustrate how past research and thinking about labor markets within firms can illuminate issues in the work-life field. We then describe a project we have undertaken with major corporations in the Chicago area in which we are employing a stratification lens. We summarize what we are learning about the ways in which firms distribute opportunities for balancing work and personal life among workers, with particular attention to workers in lower-level jobs. We suggest ways in which a stratification lens can further both research and practice in the work-life field.

PERSPECTIVES ON STRATIFICATION

Stratification is basically the way rewards and opportunities are divvied up among individuals, jobs, organizations, or even countries. What is central to the study of stratification is the way in which inequalities of both opportunity and outcome become institutionalized by groups, organizations, or states. Within employing organizations, inequalities may be based on employment status, job classification, level in organizational hierarchy, and geographic locations, among other factors.

Understanding the structures and processes that define opportunities for different individuals or groups does not immediately determine whether resulting inequalities are fair. Constructing notions of fairness depends on the principle being applied. *Fairness* may be defined in terms of the process by which rewards are allocated (procedural justice) or in terms of the end result (distributional justice). It may be measured in terms of equality (all given same rewards), equity (rewards given in proportion to contributions), or need (rewards given in proportion to need) (Deutsch, 1985; Greenberg, 1990; Schappe, 1996). As Lewis and Haas (chap. 10, this volume) explain, perceptions of justice and fairness are socially constructed, "usually by processes of social comparison, within specific contexts, and therefore differ across time and place, in families, workplaces, and societies." Regardless of the principle selected, however, a first step in addressing issues of fairness is to understand the nature and extent of inequality, that is, how opportunities are currently distributed.

In this chapter, we employ theories of stratification with the goal of advancing knowledge of the nature and extent of inequality in opportunities for balancing work and personal life. Although the scope of the literature on stratification is too vast to review here in detail, we highlight some of the key perspectives on stratification in order to give the reader a sense of how we believe our approach fits into this larger stream of inquiry.

The literature on status attainment and human capital may be most familiar to readers. A rich body of research has investigated how personal characteristics (e.g., age, gender) and human capital factors (e.g., education and skills) combine to explain variations in the distribution of individual and family income. In recent years, work in such areas as occupational stratification by gender (cf. Blau, Ferber, & Winkler, 2002; Petersen & Morgan, 1995; Reskin & McBrier, 2000) has enhanced our understanding of how human capital alone cannot fully account for variations in the distribution of income. As Reskin (2003) laments, the use of individual-level data tends to pin the causes for observed inequalities in outcomes (such as income) on individual characteristics rather than on the constraints imposed by organizational and social structures. In the practical world of employment, this bias creates a focus on changing people to fit jobs rather than on changing jobs to fit people.

Some areas of stratification have pushed past the individual level to examine the way labor markets institutionalize inequality in both opportunities and rewards. The notion of firm-level labor markets has provided a useful framework for thinking about the ways in which employers structure opportunities. The literature has evolved to look at how jobs within the same workplace vary in terms of how well they position workers to access existing opportunities (Appelbaum, Berg, Frost, & Preuss, 2003; Bills, 1987; Jacobs, 1994; Ospina, 1996; Osterman 1999). Some scholars (cf. Jacobs, 1994; Lambert, 2003) propose that jobs within the same employing company may be lodged in very different labor markets—some in internal labor markets designed to maximize worker retention and others in spot labor markets designed to maximize flexibility in labor costs.

Expanding Definitions of *Opportunity*

While the prospect of bringing such a rich body of theory and empirical knowledge to the work-life field is enticing, the ways in which scholars have typically defined *opportunity* limit its usefulness to work-life scholars and practitioners. Research has tended to center on advancement within a hierarchy, relying on data depicting the height of job ladders and the breadth of legal protections. Although other scholars have noted the drawbacks of defining success in terms of promotion, given a world of flattening organizations, new definitions of opportunity tend to remain job-centered. For example, added dimensions may include professional development and nonwage compensation (Haley-Lock, 2002; Milliman, 1992; Ospina, 1996) but the broader definition of success often implicit in work-life perspectives is still neglected in research on firm-level labor markets.

A work-life perspective necessitates a definition of success that recognizes workers' need for and appreciation of the opportunity to meet personal responsibilities and, ultimately, to develop a fulfilling personal life. The work-life field has taught us that there are multiple occupational conditions known to enhance one's chances of a high quality of life—conditions that are appreciated, and increasingly demanded, by today's workforce. Our recommended definition of *work-life opportunities* includes, at a minimum (Lambert & Haley-Lock, 2004):

- Job security, the backbone of sustainable family well-being.
- Skill development, to help ensure job security in a changing labor market.
- Mobility into jobs that facilitate work-life balance—this may not mean moving up.
- Income stability and growth, resulting in a stable, above-poverty income.
- Scheduling flexibility and predictability.
- Benefits that support families as well as individual workers.

Opportunity in Policy, in Practice, and as Experienced

We also suggest a modification in how data on firm-level labor markets are gathered. Usually, information is gathered for the firm overall—the number of jobs on ladders or with multiple titles, the types of worker protections offered (e.g., grievance procedures), firm turnover rate, and so forth.[1] Information on the organization's overall policies is clearly essential to understanding how an organization structures the distribution of opportunities to workers. But one key point of the literature on the use of formal workplace policies is that what is put down on paper does not always happen in practice, what Lewis and Haas (chap. 12, this volume) refer to as an "implementation gap." For example, a company may have a formal flextime program that in policy is available to all professionals but in practice may be targeted to a select group of "high performers" (Kossek, Barber, & Winters, 1999). Conversely, workers may have greater access to flexibility through informal practices than through formal programs (Kossek, Lautsch, & Eaton, chap. 12, this volume). Drawing on 1997 CPS data, Golden (2001) highlights disparities in the distribution of flexibility in daily scheduling, detailing variations by gender and race as well as occupation. Thus, in addition to assessing how organizations structure access to work-life opportunities through formal policies, it is useful to examine how organizations *practice* these opportunities at different organizational levels, in different types of jobs, and with different workers.

An additional, third layer of opportunity is, of course, workers' experiences of opportunities. Only individuals can provide information on what it takes, and what it means, to access meaningful opportunities for balancing work and personal demands. In sum, understanding how employers distribute opportunities for work-life balance may be best achieved by assessing the policy, practice, and experience of opportunity in distinct workplace settings.

Breaking Open Variation in Opportunity Within Organizational Levels

Current conceptualizations of organizational stratification focus on variations in rewards and opportunities across levels—at different points in the hierarchy or across different job classifications (white vs. blue collar, for example). But not all jobs are equal, even at the same level. In the following section, we provide an example from our own research in which we are investigating variations in how opportunities for work-life balance are distributed at lower organizational levels. Our results suggest that lower-level jobs vary a great deal in terms of the policy, practice, and experience of opportunities for balancing work and personal life.

A METHODOLOGY FOR INVESTIGATING OPPORTUNITIES FOR BALANCING WORK AND PERSONAL LIFE

In this section, we briefly describe our ongoing research project that employs an organizational stratification perspective to examine variations in how firms structure lower-level jobs in terms of the opportunities for work-life balance defined earlier. The study is part of the Project on the Public Economy of Work at the University of Chicago, a multiyear investigation of the institutions (public welfare offices, labor market intermediaries, and private employers) central to implementing changes in welfare legislation.[2] The study is designed to address the limitations of theory and methods on firm-level labor markets discussed in the previous section. That is, the study gathers data on an expanded set of opportunities, explores variations in how employers structure seemingly similar lower-level jobs, and examines opportunities in policy, in practice and—drawing on data from a complementary study of workers—as experienced.

Research Design

The research approach employed is comparative organizational analysis that combines multiple sources of data (administrative, interview, observation) to develop an understanding of *variations* (across jobs, workplaces, and industries) in daily employer practices. The sampling design began with the selection of three welfare agencies in Chicago for in-depth case study, purposely chosen to provide variation on client characteristics and access to jobs; the initial employers selected had hired someone who is/was a public aid client of one of the three welfare offices. We have expanded our data collection to include additional retailers in order to link our organizational-level analysis with data from workers and their child-care providers collected through the Study of Work–Child Care Fit, described later.

Overall, our selection of workplaces has been purposeful. We have targeted industries with large numbers of lower-skilled jobs: hospitality (hotels and catering, n = 7), transportation (airlines and package delivery services, n = 3), retail (stores and distribution centers, n = 10), and financial services (banks, n = 2). We have combined information from interviews and public sources to identify firms' local competitors, constructing matched comparisons within each industry. All of the employers are what one would call major employers. We have detailed data on approximately 80 lower-skilled jobs housed in 22 workplaces in the Chicago area. Of all firms approached, two declined to participate.

A Three-Step Approach to Studying Opportunity

In this section, we summarize a three-step approach to the study of opportunity that is designed to assess the distribution of different types of work-life opportunities throughout the organization. Table 6.1 provides examples of the data we have collected in each of these steps. Although our approach is unique in terms of its attention to work-life opportunities, it builds on the work of others who have investigated the disjuncture between opportunity as put down on paper and opportunity as experienced by workers (cf. Lewis, 2003; Ospina, 1996; Riemer, 2001; Tilly, 1996).

TABLE 6.1

Examples of Data Used to Capture Opportunities for Balancing Work and Personal Life in Policy, as Practiced and as Experienced

Dimensions of Opportunity	Opportunity in Policy (in overall organization and in target job)	Opportunity in Practice (broken out by target job)	Opportunity as Experienced (by workers in target jobs)
Job Security	Policies on formal layoffs, job status categories used in the organization and in target jobs (part-time, full-time, seasonal/temporary).	Employer reports of formal and informal layoffs, percentage of incumbents in target jobs with full-time/part-time/temporary status, turn-over rates per job.	Employee reports of layoffs or reductions in hours.
Skill Development	Description of job training programs and requirements, formal mentoring programs.	Percentage of employees in target jobs who actually receive training and/or mentoring.	Reports by employees of training experience and expansion of job/skill requirements (with or without training).
Mobility	Description of jobs and job ladders, promotion and job change policies.	Percentage of employees in target jobs who complete probation, percentage who actually move into another position or are promoted.	Reports by employees of opportunities offered/not offered by employer, and accepted/refused by employee.
Income Stability and Growth	Wage scales, salary grades, commission scales, raise and bonus guidelines.	Percentage of employees in target jobs in different grades or pay bands, range of wages in target jobs.	Actual take-home pay, factoring in both wage rate and hours worked.
Flexibility/ Predictability	Scheduling guidelines, policies on advance notice of scheduling.	Typical scheduling practices reported by employer for target jobs.	Fluctuations in scheduling experienced by employees, fit between job status and work hours.
Benefits	Benefits available in the company, eligibility by job category, tenure.	Percentage of employees who are eligible for and who actually receive benefits, practices that affect actual access to benefits (e.g., accrual).	Reports by employees of ability to afford and use benefits.

Step 1: Opportunity in Policy. In the first step, we follow the traditional approach of collecting detailed information on the firm's overall labor market, gathering additional data relevant to our definition of *opportunities for work-life balance.* For example, we gather data on firm policies related to job categories and ladders, training and education, benefits, scheduling, conventions, and flextime. Our primary source of information is a semistructured interview conducted with upper-level human resource (HR) professionals. These data allow us to see what potential opportunities are available in the company overall and how the firm uses formal policy to limit or extend opportunities to workers in different types of jobs and at different organizational levels.

Step 2: Opportunity in Practice. In this particular study, our goal is to break open variation at the lower level of organizations by assessing how opportunities for work-life balance are provided to different types of lower-level jobs. Specifically, we collect information on four particular lower-level jobs (requiring at most a high school diploma or equivalent): (a) a lower-skilled, entry-level job viewed by the employer as critical to the firm's success (a *core job*); (b) a lower-skilled, entry-level job viewed as relatively unimportant to firm success (a *noncore job*); (c) a *comparison*, lower-skilled job found in all the organizations studied (i.e., an entry-level clerical job); and (d) a job filled by a person on public aid, in order to assess the relative quality of the jobs into which welfare recipients are channeled.

From corporate representatives closest to relevant organizational practices, we gather information on the proportion of workers in each job who have realized the different types of opportunities for work-life balance that should be available to them, at least in policy. For example, we gather data on the proportion of workers in each job who have received the different kinds of training that the firm makes available to workers in their type of job, the proportion currently eligible for and actually covered by health insurance that is available in policy to workers in their type of job, and the proportion of workers in each job who complete any probation period and who move into a different job within the company. We also ask about employment status (full-time vs. part-time), scheduling practices, and turnover rates for each job. Information from the interview protocol is supplemented with data gathered from organizational records, observations of job sites, and, in some workplaces, participant observation. This information allows us to assess the extent to which opportunities for work-life balance make it down to the lower levels of a company and, if so, for which kinds of jobs.

Step 3: Opportunity as Experienced. Information on workers' experiences with opportunities for work-life balance is being collected as part of a complementary study (Study of Work–Child Care Fit[3] [SWCCF]) examining the child-care strategies of low-income mothers working in the retail sector

(Henly & Lambert, in press). As part of SWCCF, interviews were conducted with mothers (n = 55) with children age five or younger working at seven retail sites that we have assessed via steps 1 and 2. Most relevant to our analysis is the information collected from women (n = 50) on their experiences of opportunities for balancing work and personal life in retail jobs.

EXAMPLES OF STRATIFICATION OF OPPORTUNITIES FOR WORK-LIFE BALANCE

In this section, we draw on data from our research on lower-level jobs to examine how opportunities for work-life balance are structured in policy, implemented in practice, and experienced by workers. Because of chapter-length limitations, we limit our examination to three opportunities for work-life balance outlined earlier: opportunities for job security, scheduling flexibility and predictability, and benefits that support families as well as individuals. These examples are used to highlight the relative strengths and weaknesses of our approach to furthering knowledge about the role firms play in shaping workers' prospects for balancing work and personal life. In our analysis, we emphasize variations in how firms structure and practice opportunities for work-life balance, making comparisons, as appropriate, within organizations as well as across organizations housing seemingly similar jobs.

Job Security

The importance of employment security to family well being is well documented by studies investigating the effects of both employment and unemployment on individual and family physical and mental health (cf. Lewis, Kagan, & Heaton, 1999; Price, Friedland, Choi, & Caplan, 1998). The popular view is that jobs are becoming increasingly tenuous and insecure; today's workers are fairly pessimistic about their prospects for job security (Schmidt, 2000). Recent studies, however, provide mixed support for declines in job stability overall, with some studies reporting little evidence of decreasing job stability during the 1980s and 1990s (Gottschalk & Moffitt, 2000) but others finding declines in long-term retention rates (Jaeger & Stevens, 2000; Neumark, Polsky, & Hansen, 2000). In the case of lower-level jobs, there is less disagreement. Studies show how such employer practices as outsourcing and the hiring of temporary labor are creating new sources of insecurity for workers at the bottom of today's workplaces (Houseman & Polivka, 2000; Osterman, 1999; Tilly, 1996).

Policy. We examine two employer policies that have implications for the ability of workers to realize job security: the use of temporary workers to fill job positions and formal lay-offs. Employers in our study varied somewhat in their formal policies on each of these employment strategies. Several of the corporations we studied reported that they did not hire temporary workers for regular jobs; these included companies in hospitality (hotels and airline catering), retail, transportation, and financial services (a bank). The companies that hired temporary workers, either directly or through an agency, used them to fill positions predominately in entry-level jobs, such as seasonal sales associates in retail stores and differentiated temp workers from consultants who were hired for projects rather than for jobs. The most dramatic example of ongoing use of temporary labor was found at one retail distribution center, where about 100 regular company employees with full benefits and regular schedules worked alongside about 50 workers from a temporary agency doing the same work but with no benefits or steady work hours.

There was less variation among firms in terms of their policy on formal layoffs. Given the relatively good economic conditions during which the majority of the data were conducted (1999–2003), it is not surprising that the majority of the firms studied reported that they had not laid off any workers during the past two years, even though they reported previously implementing formal layoffs in poorer economic times. Several companies reported that they had an explicit policy of trying to avoid formal layoffs because of the effect layoffs have on employee and stockholder morale and because of increased costs for unemployment insurance. One well-known transportation company pointed with pride to the fact that it had never laid off an employee in the company's history. In policy, then, firms appear to structure lower-level jobs in a way that promote job security, although the use of temporary workers as a labor strategy varies somewhat.

Practice.   An examination of employer practice reveals a less positive portrait of job security. One indicator of this is the turnover rates associated with many lower-level jobs. Although firmwide turnover rates typically ranged from 5 to 35%, with most averaging between 15 and 25%, turnover rates for lower-level jobs were often much higher and varied widely by job type. Half of the lower-level jobs we studied had an annual turnover rate exceeding 50% (half became vacant during the year) and a third over 80% (80% became vacant during the year).

The range was also quite striking. Of the 60 jobs for which we have specific turnover data, annual turnover rates range from 0 to 500%. We found the highest annual turnover rates in the transportation industry among package-handlers (500%), where the average length of time in this core job was reported to be, at longest, 16 weeks for one employer and only five to six weeks for another. In contrast, the average tenure of sales associates in retail was reported to be six months to one year, with little variation among the employers we studied. Housekeepers in the hospitality industry had the longest average job tenure, ranging from one and a half years to seven years across employers. Entry-level clerical jobs had the lowest rates of annual turnover across industries and employers, typically ranging from 0 to 10% in the previous year.

The substantial variation in turnover rates among lower-skilled jobs *within* workplaces highlights the stratification in opportunities for job security among different lower-level jobs. For example, in a hotel with a 44% turnover rate in housekeeping jobs, there was a much lower turnover rate in food preparation jobs—about 10%. In the same company where there was a 500% turnover rate for the package-handling position, there was at most a 10% turnover rate for entry-level administrative jobs. Although it can be argued that such variation is partly driven by the differing nature of the work to be performed, such enormous disparity raises the specter that employer practices beyond the actual tasks performed play a role in determining the stability of positions. In either case, the prospects for secure employment may be largely predetermined before a worker sets foot in the workplace—a job with very high turnover does not offer a new worker much in the way of prospects for stability or success.

One might be tempted to conclude that variations in firms' practices of job security can be accounted for by differences in their formal policies. Our data suggest, however, that formal policies related to temporary workers and formal layoffs are, at best, only loosely related to how job security is distributed within and between firms. In fact, companies that actively avoided hiring temporary workers for regular jobs reported very high rates of turnover in some lower-level jobs. For example, the transportation company reporting a 500% turnover rate in package-handling jobs did not fill these positions with temporary workers. Yet, it is hard to conclude that employment in this job should be considered anything but temporary. As one representative from an airline catering company that had a union contract restricting the hiring of temporary workers remarked, "Temp workers? We don't need them. Wait a day."

In general, many of the lower-level jobs studied look more secure on paper than in practice. HR representatives reported that they were "always hiring" for some jobs, such as package handling, housekeeping, food preparation, and lock box (jobs in banks that process payments to corporate clients) jobs. This might lead one to conclude that these jobs could provide long-term employment because workers' labor is always in demand, and they did—but for a very small percentage of workers. Our interviews and observations suggest that the pressure for constant hiring was created primarily by the high turnover rates in these jobs and not by company expansion or employee mobility into new positions.

Employers' practices of layoffs also offer an interesting contrast to their formal policies. Among the workplaces reporting that they had not laid off workers during the past two years, all reported practicing informal layoffs termed *workloading* or *workload adjustments* in at least one lower-level job (e.g., housekeepers in the hospitality industry, food preparation workers in airline catering, and bank tellers in financial services). During times of workloading, employees continue to be included on personnel rolls at their usual status but have their hours reduced, sometimes dramatically. In some cases, employees are not scheduled to work at all, sometimes for weeks or even months at a time. Our data suggest that the burden of furloughs often falls on either newer workers or those in part-time jobs, creating further stratification of opportunities for job security within job classifications. Thus, employer *practices* of job security are not always consistent with their *policies* and serve to stratify the workplace by means of the unequal distribution of opportunities for job security.

Experience.   As explained earlier, our examples of experienced opportunity come from interviews with workers in the retail industry. Our information on workers' experiences of job security obviously is censored because all the women held a job at the time of study recruitment. Nonetheless, some had left their positions by the time they were scheduled for an in-person interview, and the perceptions of others about the probability of continued employment helps to shed light on the implications of job security for balancing work and family responsibilities.

One warehouse worker we interviewed had been officially laid off but had been "called in" to work twice in the few weeks after the announcement. Although she technically had no job, the call-ins gave her hope that she might be rehired, and thus, she was hesitant to look for a new job, which would almost certainly be farther away from her home. As a mother of young children, she valued having a short commute and seemed willing to risk future layoffs if she could regain her job. A more veteran worker had experienced past layoffs at the same workplace and had managed to return but expressed concern that whole segments of the workforce within the company were being phased out. She was grateful that she had secured a clerical position that seemed less affected by fluctuations in product demand; she placed a high priority on stability in order to provide financially for her young children. Yet another worker at the same distribution center reported choosing to accept a layoff rather than take another position that lacked guaranteed hours—she viewed the potential instability of income as a worse alternative than looking for another job.

An employee at a different retail distribution center recounted her experiences as a temporary worker doing the same job she eventually was able to get on a permanent basis. Although she did the same type of work as the regular employees (in fact, she contended that temps were often asked to do the heaviest and dirtiest physical labor), she was paid less per hour and received no benefits. Moreover, her hours fluctuated dramatically, ranging from 20 to 55 hours per week, while her permanent coworkers experienced a relatively stable schedule. As a temporary worker, she was forced to find a second job in a fast-food establishment in order to make ends meet. She reported that her unpredictable schedule and long hours during this period had created significant family stress; her main goal when she assumed a permanent position was to do "whatever it took" to spend more time with her daughter.

Not all workers were as concerned about job security. Many felt that the prospects within retail were fairly good. Indeed, forecasts about the fastest-growing jobs between 1996 and 2006 identified sales clerks and cashiers as two of the top 10 growth areas (U.S. Department of Labor, 2001). The major concern for many workers was not whether their job would disappear, but whether they would be able to weather the requirements for time availability that were often demanded in the industry. These are discussed in the next section.

Summary. Workers' prospects of balancing work and personal life are in no small measure affected by employer policies and practices related to job security. In analyzing the distribution of opportunities for job security across industries, firms appear to differ more on paper than in practice. Although most firms had not practiced formal layoffs in the two years prior to the study, they regularly had practiced informal layoffs in at least some lower-level jobs. And all housed lower-level jobs with annual turnover rates so high that workers might be foolish to put much faith in continuous employment. Moreover, all the firms we have studied evidenced marked stratification in terms of opportunities for job security; as reported, prospects for job security varied across and within firms as well as among jobs at lower organizational levels.

Scheduling Flexibility and Predictability

Flexibility in scheduling of work effort is central to workers' ability to combine work with family responsibilities, although as Kossek, Lautsch, and Eaton (chap. 12, this volume) point out, it may not always decrease work-family conflict. Flexibility can range from formal flextime programs that allow workers to select from a menu of prescribed start and end times to almost total flexibility in which workers are held accountable for performance but not hours (Rapoport, Bailyn, Fletcher, & Pruitt, 2001). Falling in between these extremes are policies that set core work hours or days around which employees construct their own schedules.

These forms of flexibility vary in the extent to which they provide workers with control over the days and hours they work. Without control, variations in work hours are better characterized as introducing instability rather than flexibility into workers' lives (Lambert, Waxman, & Haley-Lock, 2002). In jobs with variable schedules, sufficient advance notice of one's work schedule can help temper the effects of a lack of control by allowing workers to plan for child care, transportation, and other personal responsibilities. In this section, we compare and contrast corporations' formal policies on scheduling flexibility and predictability with actual workplace practices at lower organizational levels.

Policy. The absence of a policy guaranteeing nonexempt workers a minimum number of hours per week best reveals employers' approaches to scheduling in the companies we studied. All indicated that hours could be, and often were, adjusted to fit changing business conditions. Several companies (all retail sites and three out of five hotels) have policies that give priority to maintaining full hours for full-time jobs, often using part-time jobs to absorb fluctuations in demand. But even so, company representatives in all of the workplaces studied reported that workers in nonexempt full-time jobs could be and were shorted hours. Perhaps ironically, all but two workplaces also reported that workers in some part-time jobs worked beyond part-time limits for at least some parts of the year.

Companies' policies relevant to scheduling predictability varied to a greater extent. Some jobs were organized according to shifts, with set start and end times, such as warehouse jobs in distribution centers, food preparation jobs in airline caterers, and housekeeping jobs in all hotels. Some companies (airline caterers, some hotels) limited shift changes to twice a year. Thus, even if shift work began at a time that did not line up well with family life (e.g., 3 A.M., 10 P.M.), these schedules were at least predictable both on a daily basis and over the course of a year—at least in policy. But other companies, such as an airline we studied, had a policy of moving workers into new jobs with differing shifts throughout the year, with little if any lead time for workers to adjust.

Companies had few policies granting flexibility to workers in lower-level jobs. Several of the companies reported formal flextime programs at their corporate headquarters, perhaps benefiting lower-level administrative assistants in these settings. Most of the lower-level jobs we studied, however, were not covered by formal policies that granted workers control over the timing of work hours. One industry with greater apparent flexibility was retail. In all but one of the retail stores we studied, policies specified that workers could "claim availability" at the time of hiring, suggesting the potential for employees to exert some control over their schedule.

Practice. Practices related to both flexibility and predictability of scheduling varied a great deal within and across employers and jobs. While the practice of claiming availability in retail means that many workers can indicate the hours and days for which they are available, this apparent flexibility comes at a price. If workers' claimed availability does not match the scheduling priorities for their department, they may get few, if any, hours. What looks, then, like the opportunity to exert control over working hours in reality puts a worker at risk of not working at all.

For most of the lower-level jobs we have studied, scheduling practices not only provided limited control over work effort but also limited predictability. All but one of the retailers we studied stated that they posted schedules for sales associates at most one week in advance. Although associate schedules were slated for posting three weeks in advance at the other company, representatives admitted that this did not always happen in each department. Moreover, even jobs with regular starting times could be unpredictable, as workers in some jobs were regularly sent home early (food preparation jobs in airline catering companies) or pressed to accept overtime (housekeeping jobs). At one bank, lock box jobs with a standard start time required workers to stay until all transactions were processed, which could take six to ten hours depending on the volume of mail received that day. In almost all jobs, some percentage of workers had their hours change as workload adjustments were made across days, weeks, and seasons.

Our data suggest that the proportion of workers experiencing fluctuating work hours on a weekly or seasonal basis varied more by job than by employer, with sales associate jobs fluctuating the most and housekeeping jobs the least—on a weekly basis. Employers varied, however, in how they practiced scheduling for similar jobs. For example, two hotels asked for volunteers for overtime and furloughs before basing scheduling decisions on seniority; other unionized hotels based scheduling almost exclusively on seniority. One retailer we studied reported hiring workers only for full-time jobs with stable schedules for all but the holiday season, in contrast to the variable scheduling strategies pursued by its competitors. Because not every worker in a given job experiences a varying schedule, data on the proportion who work fluctuating hours could provide a useful indicator of a job's potential for providing its workers with a predictable, if not a flexible, work schedule, information we hope to secure in future research.

Experience. Fluctuating work schedules are the rule rather than the exception in sales associate jobs. Women who had been able to maintain a stable schedule at some point during their employment reported how important it was to their ability to combine work with child care. One long-time retail employee recounted how she had jumped repeatedly from one entry-grade job to another in order to hang onto her stable daytime hour schedule. She continued to avoid promotions to the next grade level, opting to restrict her pay rather than having to face coordinating a fluctuating schedule with her husband, who had a nonstandard schedule. A supervisor in another retail chain initially was able to coordinate her schedule with her husband, who also worked at the same site, through the help of a sympathetic manager. When she was transferred to a new store, however, she was forced to take a part-time job because she was unable to declare *full availability*—the ability to work any combination of hours that the store was open, which was required for full-time work. An employee in a retail distribution center said she felt unable to take a supervisory job because it would reduce her control over the hours she would work and, as a single mother, she depended on a predictable schedule in order to share child-care responsibilities with her mother, who also worked. In fact, the downside of promotions—specifically in terms of losing control over scheduling—was a persistent theme across employee interviews.

Summary. Firms are increasingly passing fluctuations in consumer demand directly onto workers to absorb (Lambert, 2003). In the firms we have studied, the goal of tightly linking consumer demand to labor costs resulted in "just-in-time" scheduling practices, last minute changes to schedules, and workload adjustments that, at their extreme, amount to informal layoffs (Henly & Lambert, in press). Because of these practices, the opportunity for flexibility and predictability in scheduling of work is especially scarce for workers in the lower-level jobs we have studied.

Particularly troublesome are the long-term implications for employees who avoid promotions in order to preserve their ability to meet personal responsibilities. Initially, these workers lose out on opportunities to improve their short-term economic prospects by increasing their earnings or by achieving full-time status, which heightens workers' prospects of accessing benefits and stable work hours. In the long run, employees who make such decisions may be frozen out of mobility chains that, ultimately, may have delivered greater flexibility and a higher-quality job. Moss and his colleagues (chap. 7, this volume) find similar cause for concern in their study of opportunity structures in call centers.

Benefits That Support Families as Well as Individual Workers

In this section, we focus on two main types of benefits of critical interest to working families: the availability of health insurance and of paid leave. Health insurance facilitates access to medical care and provides some buffer for employees from the high cost of care. Time off from work allows individuals to recover from illness, care for sick children or a new baby, handle other family responsibilities, or simply enjoy free time.

Policy. All of the employers in our study offered health insurance to workers in at least some lower-level jobs. Eligibility waiting periods typically were in effect for new employees, and these periods could range from 30 days to one year. For example, entry-level employees at one national retailer had to wait a year to be eligible for the company's regular health insurance, although after three months, workers could opt to purchase a "bridge plan" that covered emergencies and accidents. Workers in part-time jobs were excluded frequently from coverage (a threshold of 30 weekly hours was common, although at least one employer required a 40-hour week for eligibility). At one national transportation company, workers in part-time jobs were eligible for health insurance after 40 working days, but a 36-month waiting period was necessary before dependent coverage was available.

Regardless of the number of hours worked, employees may have different access to benefits based on job-grade classification or exempt (salaried) and nonexempt (hourly) status. Exempt workers may have little or no waiting period for health insurance eligibility, while nonexempt workers may wait as long as one year before coverage is effective (at least 60 days was typical). For example, at one catering firm, hourly employees (who were unionized) had a waiting period of six months, while nonunion exempt employees were covered on the first day of employment. In a national transportation firm workers in part-time, hourly package-handling jobs were not eligible for health insurance benefits at all, but staff in part-time clerical jobs were eligible after 60 days.

Most companies required employee contributions to premium costs, although two workplaces—both unionized—provided paid health insurance benefits to workers in certain categories of jobs. Contribution amounts were typically established according to health plan type, rather than wage levels or employment category.

In terms of paid time-off benefits, employers were more likely to offer planned paid time off (e.g., vacation or personal holidays) rather than unplanned time (sick leave) and to make it available sooner. For example, at one catering firm, employees could earn vacation days after six months but had to work at least one year before getting 24 hours of paid sick time. A national retailer offered vacation on an accrual basis after six months but no sick pay to its entry-level workers. Workers hired at higher-grade levels in the same company could elect a short-term disability plan that provided partial payment after three to six days of illness but had to forgo electing health insurance if they wanted to enroll in this protection. An exception to the trend toward differentiating planned and unplanned time off was a national hotel chain, which offered flexible paid time off to both full-time and part-time employees after six months. In several firms, however, workers holding part-time jobs were excluded from receiving any type of paid time off.

All of the firms studied offered unpaid family and medical leave (because of their size, the firms were all subject to federal law in this area). Only one company offered paid family leave to employees (one week at full pay for each year of service), but workers in part-time jobs—a large percentage of the workforce—were excluded.

Practice. It is difficult to obtain accurate statistics on just what proportion of eligible employees in different jobs are covered by health insurance, because few companies track participation rates in this way. Employer representatives at several companies, however, pointed out how only a small percentage of employees in some of the jobs we targeted for detailed data collection were actually covered by available insurance; for example, cashiers at a retail store, lock box workers at a bank, package handlers at a transportation company. Our data reveal a number of employer practices that are likely to reduce the likelihood of coverage for many employees, even when their company offers health insurance "on the books." Specifically, high turnover rates, coupled with benefit–waiting periods, mean that few employees in some jobs ever qualify for health insurance. At one national transportation firm, the average tenure for new package handlers was less than six weeks—slightly shorter than the waiting period for major medical coverage.

Practices around scheduling of hours can create barriers to benefits as well. In a major retail firm, employees had to work a minimum number of hours each pay period to retain insurance eligibility. If an employee fell below the minimum in two consecutive pay periods, the benefits were at risk of suspension, even when the reduction in hours was solely at the employer's discretion.

Employee contribution levels can also serve as a practical deterrent to health insurance, especially for lower-wage workers, as others have shown (Glied, Lambrew, & Little, 2003; Medoff et al., 2001). In one company, employees who chose either an HMO or the highest deductible PPO plan paid $75 to $82 per week for 2003 family coverage. Entry-level employees who were fortunate enough to work full-time hours (37.5) earned approximately $300 per week in pretax wages. Therefore, about one-quarter of a worker's weekly income would be required to maintain family coverage.

Whether or not the companies allowed workers to accrue vacation and sick days, the actual ability of workers to take time off with pay was shaped by employer rules that attempted to minimize employee absenteeism. For example, in one retailer, when employees took unscheduled time off (paid or unpaid), they were assigned points, which, when accumulated, could lead to probationary status, even if medical documentation of an illness was presented. In most firms, employees could be written up for taking either vacation or sick days during high volume business seasons, and in several workplaces, workers had to wait at least six months before they could use accrued sick or vacation days. In one hospitality workplace, time-banking policies required all employees to wait until the January after their first anniversary date to access vacation time; this meant that workers hired during the year could not use the vacation pay they had accrued to soften the financial blow of seasonal reductions in work hours.

Experience.   Many employees interviewed in the retail sector reported that health insurance costs were out of reach. Even some of the full-time retail employees we interviewed, including supervisors, said they relied on access to Medicaid or other state health insurance programs. This was especially true for dependent coverage; while employees may have been willing to go without their own health benefits, they were more vigilant about seeking alternative coverage for their children.

Policies around paid time off were also a frequent source of reported stress for employees. Working parents struggled with unpaid time off and penalties accumulated when they or their children became ill. In one flagship department store division, a manager reported that 80% of the department's employees (many the parents of young children) were on probation because they had hit the maximum threshold for taking unscheduled days off (three) before the benefit year ended. One employee bemoaned the fact that she could be subject to termination if she had to miss another day caring for her preschool-aged daughter, noting that she herself still had to make it through an entire flu season on probation. This employee's experience reflects the reality faced by many parents. The National Center for Health Statistics (NCHS) reported in 2003 that almost half of all children aged 5 to 17 missed three or more school days in an average year due to illness (NCHS, 2003). Those families with very young children often experience illness in even greater frequency. Given that parents also get sick—sometimes following a child's illness—employer policies and practices governing unscheduled time off are not created with the average family's experience in mind.

Summary. Our examination of organizational practices reveals that, among the firms studied, health insurance and paid time off looked much better on paper than in practice at lower organizational levels. The realities of informal layoffs, fluctuating work hours, penalties for taking accrued time off, and low incomes all created hazards to accessing benefits that companies provided at least in policy. Employees' experiences of these hazards suggest that they were not easily navigated and often led workers to difficult trade-offs between being a good worker and being a good parent.

Stratification Within Lower Organizational Levels, Across Work-Life Opportunities

Looking across the areas of work-life opportunity we chose to examine in this chapter (job security, scheduling flexibility and predictability, and benefits), our analyses highlight the types of inequality in the distribution of opportunities for work-life balance that can occur both within and across workplaces. Some of this stratification can be traced to formal organizational policies; for example, firms varied in terms of the munificence of their benefit plans for lower-level workers and in terms of their use of employment status (full-time vs. part-time) to define eligibility. Our research suggests, however, that much of the inequality in opportunities we observed within lower organizational levels can be traced to how employers practice their policies.

Our data suggest that employers may be, in fact, more similar in terms of their practices than their policies. Those employers who appeared on paper to be more supportive and inclusive than others, in practice looked strikingly similar to their counterparts, at least in terms of the range of opportunities they presented to workers in lower-level jobs. For example, although the firms varied a great deal in terms of their benefit plans for lower-level workers and their recent history of formal layoffs, they were fairly similar when it came to related practices. All firms reported a lack of company-sponsored health insurance for a large proportion of lower-level workers, and all reported implementing forced reductions in work hours in some lower-level jobs.

In general, even when available in policy, lower-level workers' access to op-portunities for balancing work and personal life is limited when it is linked to employment status (full-time vs. part-time) or to job tenure (benefit–waiting periods, seniority-based preferences). Note that these eligibility criteria are not normally applied to jobs lodged higher in an organization's hierarchy. For ex-ample, in most of the companies we studied, health insurance takes effect on the first day of work for exempt employees. Also, we found that some companies categorized professionals working less than full time as "reduced compensation *professionals*" because it allowed them to extend benefits to these workers while simultaneously excluding less-educated workers in part-time jobs from benefits (Lambert et al., 2002). Thus, our research suggests that linking opportunities to tenure and to employment status disproportionately limits lower-level workers' ability to access available opportunities.

Perhaps the most consistent theme in our research is the importance of sched-uling stability and predictability, in and of themselves and as precursors to ac-cessing other types of opportunity. Without a predictable schedule and source of income, the retail workers interviewed found it challenging to just hold onto a job lodged at the lower rung, making it difficult for them to take advantage of other opportunities (such as for benefits and mobility) that could result from sustained employment. Employers' efforts to manage employee behavior (e.g., by discouraging absences through a point system or requiring total flexibility in scheduling) may further degrade the quality of existing opportunities by disad-vantaging those employees with significant personal responsibilities—whether these take the form of dependent children, elderly parents, or other caregiving roles. In the long run, those employees who find themselves shut out of impor-tant work-life opportunities may be precluded from transferring into other po-sitions that might better suit their personal needs and enable them to have greater success in the workplace and in their personal life.

IMPLICATIONS FOR RESEARCH
AND PRACTICE

We propose two directions for future research examining inequalities in the distribution of opportunities for balancing work and personal life. First is re-search that identifies the forces leading to variations in employer practices that distribute work-life opportunities differently to different jobs. Understanding the basis of inequality has been a central interest of scholars of ascriptive inequal-ity—too much so, according to Reskin (2003). As she points out, often the reasons employers, and social scientists, give for inequality are inferred rather than directly observed. For example, the longer tenure of men than women in the same job may be used to explain gender differences in average wages, even when employers' active favoring of work experience is not directly assessed.

Thus, as Reskin argues, explanations of observed inequality often appear rational (based on differences discovered in workers' human capital) but can just as easily be interpreted as post hoc rationales for practices that serve to advantage some at the expense of others. When men do not have longer tenure, for example, then wage differentials are explained in terms of other criteria that continue to advantage men, such as years of schooling or physical size and strength.

The literature on firm-level labor markets makes clear how a firm's labor strategy often develops out of practice rather than vice versa and occurs in a context of limited information and competing incentives (cf. Batt, Hunter, & Wilk, 2003; Lane, Moss, Salzman, & Tilly, 2003). Thus, in developing knowledge on the reasons that opportunities for balancing work and personal life are distributed unequally within organizations, employer explanations should not be the sole source of information. Systematic attention must be given to assessing rather than just assuming the reasons work-life opportunities are unequally distributed in the workplace.

Reskin (2003), in fact, recommends that less time be given to figuring out the causes of inequality (*why*) and more effort be given to identifying the mechanisms of inequality (*how*). Our second suggestion for future research is consistent with this recommendation. Although our current research sheds light on some of the mechanisms by which organizations ration opportunities for balancing work and personal life among lower-level jobs (job status and scheduling practices), much remains to be learned. Additional research is needed that investigates possible mechanisms of inequality at other organizational levels, because the specific mechanisms employers use to structure opportunities for balancing work and personal life are likely to vary by level. For example, formal scheduling practices may not be important mechanisms for rationing flexibility and predictability to workers in professional jobs; instead, the extent to which project schedules are realistic may be key to determining which professional workers will face pressures for increased work hours and, in turn, diminished opportunities for flexibility and predictability (Rapoport et al., 2001).

Moreover, a stratification perspective draws attention to the fact that advantage often comes at the expense of others. Thus, research encompassing multiple organizational levels is needed to ensure that interventions focused on decreasing instability in some jobs does not, for example, result in increased instability in other jobs. Without better management practices, fluctuations in consumer demand may be simply passed from one group to another to absorb.

Differentiating opportunities for balancing work and personal life in policy, in practice, and as experienced can suggest avenues for practice as well. For example, different intervention strategies may be needed if working with a corporation that already has good opportunities on the books but problems with distributing them to certain types of jobs, as compared to a corporation that has few opportunities for anyone. In the former case, the target would be to extend existing opportunities to a broader set of workers. This might require analyzing obstacles to access—such as job status, scheduling instability, low pay—but at least the basic business-case for providing the supports is likely to have been made. In the latter case, making the business-case for developing a high-quality work environment may be the first, if not the primary, task.

In conclusion, ensuring complete equality is not necessarily the reason one seeks to understand the processes and outcomes of stratification. What we, and many others, seek is an equitable distribution of opportunities and outcomes that results in enough equality to ensure an adequate quality of life for all. The greater the inequality in outcomes, however, the more difficult it is to make the case that opportunities have been distributed equitably. Given the widening gap in well-being between citizens lodged at the top and the bottom of America's income distribution (Heymann, 2000), it seems important to develop insights into how workplaces might play a role in diminishing inequality in those opportunities essential to balancing work and family life and, ultimately, to the well-being of workers, their families, and communities. An organizational stratification perspective is useful for understanding the nature and extent of workplace inequality and for uncovering the mechanisms by which inequality is established and maintained.

NOTES

1. Notable exceptions of research on internal labor markets that also gather information at the job level can be found in this volume (Valcour & Hunter [chap. 4] and Moss, Salzman, & Tilly [chap. 7]).

2. The Project on the Public Economy of Work is supported by grants from the Ford Foundation, the National Science Foundation, and the Open Society Institute. Codirectors: Evelyn Z. Brodkin and Susan J. Lambert.

3. The Study on Work–Child Care Fit is supported by a research grant from U.S. Health and Human Services in collaboration with the Joint Center for Poverty Research and by additional funds from the McCormick-Tribune Center for Early Childhood Research and the Louise R. Bowler Faculty Research Award, School of Social Service Administration. Principal Investigator: Julia Henly.

REFERENCES

Appelbaum, E., Berg, P., Frost, A., & Preuss, G. (2003). The effects of work restructuring on low-wage, low-skilled workers in U.S. hospitals. In E. Appelbaum, A. Bernhardt, & R. J. Murnane (Eds.), *Low-wage America: How employers are reshaping opportunity in the workplace* (pp. 77–117). New York: Russell Sage Foundation.

Batt, R., Hunter, L. W., & Wilk, S. (2003). How and when does management matter? Job quality and career opportunities for call center workers. In E. Appelbaum, A. Bernhardt, & R. J. Murnane (Eds.), *Low-wage America: How employers are reshaping opportunity in the workplace* (pp. 270–313). New York: Russell Sage Foundation.

Bills, D. B. (1987). Costs, commitment, and rewards: Factors influencing the design and implementation of internal labor markets. *Administrative Science Quarterly, 32,* 202–221.

Blair-Loy, M., & Wharton, A. (2002). Employee's use of work-family policies and workplace social context. *Social Forces, 80,* 813–845.

Blau, F. D., Ferber, M. A., & Winkler, A. E. (2002). *The economics of women, men and work* (4th ed.). Upper Saddle River, NJ: Prentice Hall.

Deutsch, M. (1985). Equity, equality, and need: What determines which value will be used as the basis for distributive justice? *Journal of Social Issues, 31,* 137–149.

Glied, S., Lambrew, J., & Little, S. (2003). *The growing share of uninsured workers employed by large firms.* New York: The Commonwealth Fund.

Golden, L. (2001). Flexible work time: Correlates and consequences of work scheduling. *American Behavioral Scientist, 44,* 1157–1178.

Goodstein, J. D. (1994). Institutional pressures and strategic responsiveness: Employer involvement in work-family issues. *Academy of Management Journal, 37,* 350–382.

Gottschalk, P., & Moffitt, R. (2000). Job instability and insecurity of males and females in the 1980s and 1990s. In D. Neumark (Ed.), *On the job: Is long-term employment a thing of the past?* (pp. 142–190). New York: Russell Sage Foundation.

Greenberg, J. H. (1990). Organizational justice: Yesterday, today, and tomorrow. *Journal of Management, 16,* 399–432.

Haley-Lock, A. (2002). Social networks and career orientation in human services employee development. Paper presented to the annual meeting of the Association of Nonprofit Organizations and Voluntary Associations, Montreal November 15.

Henly, J. R., & Lambert, S. J. (in press). Nonstandard work and child care needs of low-income parents. In S. M. Bianchi, L. M. Casper, K. E. Christensen, & R. B. King (Eds.), *Workforce/workplace mismatch? Work, family, health, & well-being.* Mahwah, NJ: Erlbaum.

Heymann, J. (2000). *The widening gap.* New York: Basic Books.

Houseman, S., & Polivka, A. (2000). The implications of flexible staffing arrangements for job stability. In D. Neumark (Ed.), *On the job: Is long-term employment a thing of the past?* (pp. 427–462). New York: Russell Sage Foundation.

Ingram, P., & Simons, T. (1995). Institutional and resource dependence determinants of responsiveness to work-family issues. *Academy of Management Journal, 38,* 1466–1482.

Jacobs, D. (1994). Organizational theory and dualism: Some sociological determinants of spot and internal labor markets. *Research in Social Stratification and Mobility, 13,* 203–235.

Jaeger, A., & Stevens, A. (2000). Is job stability in the United States falling? Reconciling trends in the Current Population Survey and the Panel Study of Income Dynamics. In D. Neumark (Ed.), *On the job: Is long-term Employment a thing of the past?* (pp. 31–69). New York: Russell Sage Foundation.

Kossek, E. E., Barber, A., & Winters, D. (1999). Using flexible schedules in the managerial world: The power of peers. *Human Resource Management, 38,* 33–46.

Lambert, S. J. (1998). Workers' use of supportive workplace policies: Variations by race and class-related characteristics. In A. Daly (Ed.), *Workforce diversity: Issues and perspectives* (pp. 297–313). Washington, DC: NASW Press.

Lambert S. J. (2003). *Managing work flows: How firms transform fluctuations in demand into instability for workers.* Working paper for the Project on the Public Economy of Work, School of Social Service Administration, University of Chicago.

Lambert, S. J., & Haley-Lock, A. (2004). The organizational stratification of opportunities for work-life balance: Addressing issues of equality and social justice in the workplace. *Community, Work, and Family, 7*(2), 181–197.

Lambert, S. J., Waxman, E., & Haley-Lock, A. (2002). *Against the odds: A study of sources of instability in lower-skilled jobs.* Working Paper for the Project on the Public Economy of Work, University of Chicago.

Lane, J., Moss, P., Salzman, H., & Tilly, C. (2003). Too many cooks? Tracking internal labor market dynamics in food service with case studies and quantitative data. In E. Appelbaum, A. Bernhardt,

& R. Murnane (Eds.), *Low-wage America: How employers are reshaping opportunity in the workplace* (pp. 229–269). New York: Russell Sage Foundation.

Lewis, S. (2003). Flexible working arrangements: Implementation, outcomes, and management. In C. Cooper & I. Robertson (Eds.), *Annual review of industrial and organisational psychology* (pp. 1–28). New York: Wiley.

Lewis, S., Kagan, C., & Heaton, P. (1999). Economic and psychological benefits from employment. *Disability and Society, 14,* 561–575.

Medoff, J., Shapiro, H., Calabrese, M., & Harless, A. (2001). *How the new labor market is squeezing workforce health benefits.* New York: The Commonwealth Fund.

Milliman, J. F. (1992). *Causes, consequences, and moderating factors of career plateauing.* Unpublished doctoral dissertation, University of Southern California.

National Center for Health Statistics. (2003). *Summary health statistics for U.S. Children: National Health Interview survey, 2000.* Hyattsville, MD: NCHS.

Neumark, D., Polsky, D., & Hansen, D. (2000). Has job stability declined yet? New evidence for the 1990s. In D. Neumark (Ed.), *On the job: Is long-term employment a thing of the past?* (pp. 70–110) New York: Russell Sage Foundation.

Ospina, S. (1996). *Illusions of opportunity: Employee expectations and workplace inequality.* Ithaca, NY: ILR Press.

Osterman, P. (1999). *Securing prosperity: The American labor market: How it has changed and what to do about it.* Princeton, NJ: Princeton University Press.

Petersen, T., & Morgan, L. A. (1995). Separate and unequal: Occupation-establishment sex segregation and the gender wage gap. *American Journal of Sociology, 101*(2), 329–365).

Price, R. H., Friedland, D. S., Choi, J. N., & Caplan, R. D. (1998). Job loss and work transitions in a time of global economic change. In X. B. Arriaga & S. Oskamp (Eds.), *Addressing community problems: Research and intervention* (pp. 195–222). Thousand Oaks, CA: Sage.

Rapoport, R., Bailyn, L., Fletcher, J., & Pruitt, B. (2001). *Beyond work-family balance.* San Francisco: Jossey-Bass.

Reskin, B. (2003). Including mechanisms in our models of ascriptive inequality. *American Sociological Review, 68,* 1–21.

Reskin, B., & McBrier, D. (2000). Why not ascription? Organizations' employment of male and female managers. *American Sociological Review, 65,* 210–233.

Riemer, F. J. (2001). *Working at the margins: Moving off welfare in America.* Albany: State University of New York Press.

Schappe, S. (1996). Bridging the gap between procedural knowledge and positive employee attitudes: Procedural justice as keystone. *Group and Organizational Management, 21,* 337–364.

Schmidt, S. (2000). Job security beliefs in the General Social survey: Evidence on long-run trends and comparability with other surveys. In D. Neumark (Ed.), *On the job: Is long-term employment a thing of the past?* (pp. 300–331). New York: Russell Sage Foundation.

Tilly, C. (1996). *Half a job: Bad and good part-time jobs in a changing labor market.* Philadelphia: Temple University Press.

U.S. Department of Labor. (2001). *Report on the American workforce.* Washington, DC: U.S. Government Printing Office.

7

When Firms Restructure: Understanding Work-Life Outcomes

Philip Moss
University of Massachusetts Lowell

Harold Salzman
The Urban Institute

Chris Tilly
University of Massachusetts Lowell

INTRODUCTION

Organizational structures are commonly neglected in the analysis of work-life balance opportunities (with important exceptions, such as Lambert, Waxman, & Haley-Lock, 2002). These factors, often in the background, interact with the more typically identified factors such as attributes of individual workers and the work-life policies and strategies adopted by a firm and its managers. Our on-going research examines the interrelationship among structural changes in industries and firms, managerial strategy, and jobs. We focus on internal labor markets and implications for the quality of jobs, particularly the changes in lower-skill and lower-wage jobs, and for opportunity or mobility. In this chapter, we extend that framework to consider implications for work-life integration opportunities as well.

Our Analytical Framework

A key element in the structure of "work-life opportunities," as Lambert and Haley-Lock (2004) put it, is workplace flexibility. We consider two elements of flexibility: schedule flexibility and career flexibility. Flexibility can be *employer-*

driven or *employee-driven.* In the arena of schedule flexibility, for instance, employers who are capricious in their flexibility requests of employees mark the extreme of employer-driven flexibility; Lambert, Waxman, and Haley-Lock (2002) suggest the term *instability* rather than flexibility to describe this situation. At the other extreme are employees who come and go without making an effort to notify supervisors or to try to cover their shifts. It is certainly possible to combine employer- and employee-driven flexibility, as in the case of employees who need flexibility to respond to their life events and family and who will work cooperatively with supervisors and other workers to maintain staffing, and employers who have work practices that allow flexibility within the constraints of maintaining needed-staffing levels. Similarly, where career tracks are concerned, in some cases the employee must do all the adapting: Companies demand geographic relocation and total devotion to the company as a condition of upward mobility, or they simply offer no avenues for promotion within the company, requiring the employee to rely on his or her own devices to move up. But in other cases, businesses accommodate employees' needs for stability and/ or flexibility.

Our study tracks how the organizational structure of opportunities and constraints shapes these aspects of flexibility in case studies of 36 firms in four industries: electronics manufacturing, food service, financial services, and retail sales. Our theoretical perspective is that work-life outcomes emerge through a recursive process among various factors including organizational structure, trends in the broader industry and the economy as a whole, managerial strategy, and worker preferences. Contrary to frequent argument, a single factor such as technology or managerial dictates does not determine work-life outcomes, nor are work-life outcomes fixed at a single point. We focus not only on the managerial strategy as originally conceptualized but also on how it evolves during and following implementation (interacting recursively with the environment, often yielding unintended consequences). Our perspective challenges a rational-choice view that policies and practices are the outcome of planned, strategic initiatives that reflect corporate decision making in a straightforward or deterministic manner. Akin to bounded rationality theories (Simon, 1976), we propose that decision makers do not consider all possible options, and furthermore, we propose that even the bounded rational choices that are made in constructing strategy will be transformed through the process of implementation (Weick, 1995; Ortmann & Salzman, 2002). Moreover, there is variation in outcome, within and between firms. Firms, and even sites within firms, can pursue disparate strategies for long periods of time, even when operating under similar environmental conditions (e.g., in the same markets). Practice may diverge from official policy.

From at least the 1930s, most large U.S. businesses have organized work in internal labor markets: long-term jobs with predictable wage progressions and opportunities for upward mobility. During the 1990s, much analysis of corporate restructuring depicted the dissolution of such internal labor markets and of work-place commitment in general (Cappelli, 2001). The outcome was thought to be a nomadic workforce that moved from firm to firm, changing career, skills, and employment conditions every few years. In this scenario, accommodation of work-life issues is mediated by the market and presumable outcomes depend on whether it is a seller's or buyer's market at any given time. In earlier work based on case studies that overlap with the ones reported on here, we questioned these commonplace sweeping assertions of the decline of internal labor markets (Moss, Salzman, & Tilly, 2000, 2002). We found, consistent with our theoretical suppositions, that corporate restructuring is highly iterative, consisting of a long series of large reorganizations and small adjustments rather than a small number of decisive changes. Moreover, although businesses did replace long-standing internal labor markets with more market-mediated relationships, they subse-quently rebuilt internal labor markets in a variety of ways. We replicate these findings, based on a larger sample of firms, in this chapter.

The implications for work-life integration are mixed. Given the current bal-ance of forces between businesses and workers in the United States, it is not surprising that we find *employer*-driven flexibility predominated in the 1990s, at the expense of *employee*-driven flexibility. Consonant with this business dom-ination of the terrain of flexibility, we also find that shifts in either kind of flexibility are, for the most part, incidental to firms' pursuit of other goals. However, in our sample, businesses are about as likely to move in the direction of flexibility that benefits workers as in the opposite direction. Recent restruc-turing has neither broadly expanded nor radically narrowed workers' degree of choice or control over flexibility. In a more global view, it could be argued that by providing service outside of standard work hours, firms require some workers to sacrifice standard or predictable work schedules to provide flexibility, or at least convenience, to other workers in their lives as consumers.

Focus and Outline of the Chapter

Out of the many possible directions of restructuring, we focus on two: outsourc-ing of functions from the firm and the creation of remote facilities—in particular, call centers. Most of our case studies center on large, leading-edge firms. We supplement these core firm case studies with studies of suppliers to selected core firms and, in a few cases, to smaller competitors. Our sample may not represent the full spectrum of current corporate practice but it represents both emerging trends in core firms that are likely to be emulated and some of the variation within our chosen industries.

Our research focus is on *re*structuring and, in particular, on the path and process of restructuring over time. In our discussion, however, we have embed-ded business restructuring strategy as one element in a broader analytical frame-work. In this framework, we look at the impact of two more static structural factors: industry and occupation. We also examine labor supply, which in reality interacts with business strategy in fairly elaborate ways, but we largely limit our attention to the point-in-time effects of differences in labor supply. The idea of the broader framework is both to verify and to begin to explore the importance of these other structural dimensions and to peel them back or control for them in order to demonstrate that restructuring has an independent effect on work-life balance.

In what follows, we start by presenting our methods and sample. We then report first on schedule flexibility outcomes and then on career flexibility; in each case we march through differences by industry and occupation, labor supply effects, and finally the iterative pathways of corporate and managerial strategy. Our goal is to contribute to work-life integration research by examining the changing nature of the stage (organizational structure and strategy) on which specific, firm-level policies and practices about work-life integration are developed and by examining the new job structures as they affect work-life integration.

METHODS AND INDUSTRY BACKGROUND

Our research consists of case studies of 36 companies, not all of which are discussed in this chapter. We have gained varying degrees of access to companies, but our goal—successfully realized in the majority of cases—is to speak to top managers, human resource (HR) officials, and frontline managers (as well as in some cases workers) at each site we visit. We learned about the trajectory of change in internal labor markets primarily by asking retrospective questions. In addition, the unintended benefit of the long time it takes to complete the cases (often due to the logistics) is that we are able to observe the changes in real time. Data gathering extended from 1996 to 2003.

Our interviews were open-ended and in-depth. We emphasized the gathering of detailed qualitative information. The interviewees at comparable levels in the organization were administered essentially the same interview protocol, but with particular added questions and follow-up prompts tailored to the particular industry or specific changes that had recently occurred in the individual company. Our data give us a useful window for understanding how industry and organizational restructuring have affected work-life questions as our standard interview protocol begins with a request for a detailed career biography of our interviewee.

Our sample of cases includes:

- 6 companies in financial services.
- 6 in retail.
- 2 third-party call centers.

- 14 in food, including food servers, wholesalers, and manufacturers.
- 8 in electronics manufacturing.

At the time we studied them, these companies employed a total of 1,136,00 people. All company and employee names in this paper are pseudonyms.

Retail and financial services have disproportionately female workforces (in 2002, 50% in the case of retail and 61% for financial services, compared to 47% for all private nonfarm employment; the retail percentage is much higher in particular retail subsectors, such as department stores with 67% women in 2000) (U.S. Bureau of Labor Statistics, 2003; U.S. Census Bureau, 2003). In recent decades these sectors have grown and have attracted large numbers of women managers.

In contrast, food service and electronics have few women managers. In electronics manufacturing this tracks the demographics of the industry's overall workforce (which is only 36% female, based on the Computer and Electronic Products manufacturing category). In food service, the reasons are less transparent. Staff at food and accommodation establishments is 53% women. Looking further back on the supply chain to include food distribution (26% women) and food manufacturing (37% women) changes the picture significantly but still results in a cumulative female percentage of 49% (U.S. Census Bureau, 2003a). Yet, perhaps because of the enduring influence of the male-dominated chef system, men occupy the lion's share of managerial jobs in the food service industry.

We studied retail and financial firms' creation of remote sites (in particular, call centers) to pursue new channels of service delivery, and electronics and food manufacturers' expansion of outsourcing to reap lower costs and the advantages of specialization. In each industry these processes, which we term the *de-integration* of particular functions, have taken place within the context of other changes, which we describe in more detail elsewhere (Lane, Moss, Salzman, & Tilly 2003; Moss, Salzman, & Tilly, 2000, 2003). Our task, then, is to explain variations and changes in work-life flexibility within these turbulent contexts.

FINDINGS

Hours Flexibility

In terms of hours worked, we found little employee-driven flexibility and much employer-driven flexibility. Our data suggest several important factors that shape how changes in firm and industry structure have altered the hours flexibility available to—or, more often, imposed on—entry-level workers.

Industry Matters for Hours Flexibility.   The key distinction across industries that influences hours staffing is that between goods-producing industries and service-producing industries. Goods-producing industries such as food manufacturing and electronics manufacturing can inventory goods and can run production shifts that do not vary greatly during the day or among days of the week or of the month. This is not true for service—producing sectors such as food service, retail sales, and much of financial services, which respond to the daily, weekly, and monthly demand schedules of consumers, in a clear-cut case of employer-driven flexibility. In fact, much of the demand for consumer services such as those provided in retail and financial call centers falls outside of normal work times. Ironically, work's demands on retail and call center *customers* dictate that these sector's *workers* must serve the customers at times traditionally devoted to rest or to household work. Call centers are typically open very early in the morning to very late at night and on weekends, if they are not open 24 hours per day, 7 days per week.

Recent technological changes allow retail and financial customer service tasks to be inventoried to an extent, lessening somewhat the need to respond immediately to consumer demands. Self-service through the Internet and telephone voice response units (VRUs) is the most important of these developments, and many firms in our study made efforts to increase the proportion of transactions that customers could handle themselves over the phone or through the Internet. E-mail correspondence also allows customer service representatives to schedule responses independently of the customer inquiry. However, we found in our most recent interviews that many companies are now striving to integrate sales pitches into customer-initiated service calls (in part because of limits imposed by the Do Not Call list) and therefore are trying to drive some business back to phone representatives.

At the food manufacturers and electronics manufacturers with whom we spoke, not all workers are permanent—several firms hire from temp agencies or assign entry workers to temporary status for a period of time—but all workers are full time, and hours generally are fixed for permanent workers. In contrast, food service operations are dictated by the rhythm of mealtimes, and cafeterias and restaurants are much more likely to employ part-timers and to change work schedules with little warning. At the Picnic Basket restaurant chain, work schedules are posted only four days before the work week starts, and a district manager told us that on slow days restaurant managers are expected to send workers home, which makes their pay unpredictable and flexible as well.

Industry differences *among* call centers also affect scheduling patterns. Jobs in finance call centers are more likely to be full-time jobs with steady schedules. For many types of financial transactions, industry standards require that customer service representatives (CSRs) pass licensing tests in order to make financial transactions over the phone, and companies typically provide the necessary training. Thus, managers of financial call centers expressed particular concern with recouping their training investments and retaining talented workers. Employees with more education and training have, on average, higher career expectations and are less likely to be satisfied with part-time or unstable employment.

But not all financial service call center jobs are full time. Call center jobs in banks, most of which do not require licensure, may adopt a more flexible method of staffing. For example, the customer service director at MultiBank described employer-driven hours flexibility at its call centers:

Respondent: We hire all of our employees in typically 30-hour flex positions. That means that they're guaranteed 30 hours but that we may schedule them anywhere between 30 and 40 hours. They give us 6 days a week availability, 9 hours within those days. Then they may be scheduled anywhere within that 9-hour window, usually 4 or 5 days a week. So that helps workforce management in filling in the holes.

Interviewer: And at what point do people move from flex . . . into full time or part time?

Respondent: They first schedule a change request. We have like a 5-month waiting period, I guess, after you're hired that we won't look at a schedule change request until 5 months, unless it's an emergency schedule change, which comes to like day-care or medical reasons, that type of thing. So [the employee] put[s] it in and when it meets the business need, then it would be approved at that point.

Lambert, Waxman, and Haley-Lock (2002) describe similar flexible scheduling arrangements.

Job Level Matters for Hours Flexibility. Employer-driven hours flexibility varies by the level of the job. Entry-level workers in retail call centers are more likely to be part time than full time, to be assigned the least desirable hours, and to have unstable schedules. At retail cataloger Just for Her, where call centers run 7 days, 22 hours, new employees start on night and evening shifts and typically seek to move to days as quickly as possible. The client services manager lamented, "The problem is not so much that we don't get good people, but that people hope to move quickly from evening or night to day. They say, 'My baby-sitting arrangement broke down,' and they expect to move to days."

Hours flexibility does not vary along the job ladder in a simple fashion, however. At the upper end, managers may have more discretion about when to arrive at and leave from the workplace but are often called on to work longer hours and fill in for others as needed. A manager at MultiBank described one of the bank's top sales managers as "selling 24 hours a day," whether at work or not. And while low-level workers can swap shifts at many companies, including MultiBank, Just for Her, and Picnic Basket, managers do not have this option.

Labor Supply Matters for Hours Flexibility.   The pull toward trimming costs encourages firms to staff their call centers with part-time employees with fewer benefits, lower pay, and scheduling matched to demand, while the objective of higher quality service leads firms to create full-time jobs with better-trained and motivated employees. Where firms end up on this continuum depends not only on the firm's strategy but also on the labor market conditions the firm faces. The more abundant, and the more capable the available labor supply, the more latitude the firm has to maintain employer-driven flexibility and to deny employee-driven flexibility. The cyclical and seasonal state of the economy, the location of the firm in relation to competing firms, and the demographic composition of available employees all affect the supply of labor.

The exceptionally low unemployment during 1998–2000 affected the hiring and staffing strategy at several firms we studied. In such tight labor markets, prospective employees gain a bargaining advantage, as do current employees who can implicitly or explicitly threaten to quit. Alicia, the codirector of call center operations at the Clarendon retail chain, indicated that the tight labor market conditions had shifted the balance toward employee-driven scheduling.

> We have tried to keep as much of a flexible workforce as requested and I think that is what has given us our competitive advantage over the years . . . [W]e could hire someone [who] would be working in the 15–20 hour range throughout the year and then be able to get up to 40 and beyond during our peak season. That whole situation has changed. The people either want more hours or fewer hours and there are more limitations, so our ability to stretch during that peak time has been reduced significantly. So we either have to hire more people with lesser availabilities and/or full-time people.

The demographic composition of the available labor force influenced several of our firms' staffing decisions, and in turn that demographic composition was partly a result of company location decisions. Moreover, in addition to reflecting the available supply, the demography of a particular firm's workforce also reflects the part-time versus full-time strategy the firm has adopted and what groups of workers best fit that strategy (Tilly, 1996). Women make up the majority of financial services call center representatives and a sizable majority of retail call center representatives. Clarendon's Alicia reported 90% of her employees are women; at Treats, a gift cataloger, the figure is 70%. Housewives appear to be particularly desirable employees, but they have become less available. For example, Alicia explained:

> We've had a tremendous change in the labor market in that when we started the call centers we were primarily getting housewives [who] had kids in school, or

[who said], "I'll come in and work, I can work from eight in the morning until three, then I need to be home because the kids will be home from school," and then you had the other housewife [who] would say, you know, "I don't want to work during the day, I'd like to be there when my kindergartener gets home, but as soon as my husband gets home and I get dinner on the table then I can be in at six or seven."

So we got a lot, and that's how we first started [in the early 1980s]. I mean, it was a wonderful workforce. They were reliable, they knew how to measure curtains, they knew how to measure jeans, they knew all about taking care of a family, so they were very good customer service reps. Now, that labor market has dramatically changed, as you know. Everyone has two people in the family working these days. . . .

So what we get now is we still have a lot of the old-timers [who] have been with us for years. . . . But we're getting second-jobbers now. They work a full-time job and they want to supplement. And/or we still get a few women [who] want to be home during the day when the kids get home from school and stuff, but they'll come in and work in the evening when their spouse is home. . . . We get students in most of our cities; we do have colleges.

The demographics of the available labor force are determined by location as well. One of the call center locations of Treats is a university town. Sandy, Treats's operations manager, told us, "The workforce there is younger, students. We can give them a very flexible schedule. They can go to class, come back and work for 2 hours, go back to class, come back and work for 2 hours."

Of course, the location decision itself is a strategic decision by firms. A business may locate a call center to tap a labor force of housewives interested in part-time employment. But if both pursue a zero-sum objective, one firm's strategy may negate another firm following a similar strategy (e.g., both moving to the same location for low-cost labor supply or to be able to recruit the highest quality workers). This situation faced Marketplace Stores in its CenterWest call center location, where a variety of other companies' call centers also had chosen to locate. Facing the loss of employees to higher-wage call centers, managers at this call center indicated that they were offering more schedule flexibility as one strategy for attracting and retaining workers.

Corporate Strategy and Managerial Discretion Matter for Hours Flexibility.   Market pressure and competition constrain much of what a firm does, but competition does not dictate a unique competitive strategy. Many firms have sufficient discretion to adopt varying strategies to respond to market competition. In addition to the location decision, which we have already touched on, the strategic decisions on which we focus in this study are: first, *whether* and *how much* of the firms' operations to outsource or shift to remote sites; and second, *how to do* the outsourcing or de-integration, specifically, how to balance the frequently competing objectives of lowering costs in the short run and boosting quality and service. One key strategic decision in retail and financial services is the decision to transform the vehicle for delivery of services from stores or local offices to call centers. This generally extends work to nontraditional night and weekend times, in practice heightening employer-driven flexibility. In a typical description of retail call center staffing, the HR manager at Clarendon's Southwestern center reported that it usually recruits workers as part time and has people starting every quarter hour, with shifts ranging from four to seven hours in half-hour increments. Sandy, the Treats call center manager, indicated, "It'd be nice if you could just hire 240 seats, 8–4:30. But that's not how the calls come—there are a lot more at certain times of day."

The choice to staff the retail call center with flexible part-time workers in response to consumer demand is not without problems for management. We asked HR and operations managers about the biggest challenges in running call centers. Even in 2002–2003, long after the 1990s hiring boom had cooled, we got answers such as "Making sure you have enough people who are qualified [and] who will be here during the hours you want them" (Treats) and "The challenge of staffing for the variability in call volume" (Style Associates, another cataloger). The manager of Clarendon's Southland call center reported that the most common complaint among employees is not enough hours.

Outsourcing has also had an impact on the degree of hours flexibility available to entry-level workers in the industries we have studied. For instance, food servers such as cafeterias and restaurants prepare less and less food on site, preferring to purchase the items from food manufacturers (Lane, Moss, Salzman, & Tilly, 2003). Food service jobs, which are consumer-demand scheduled, are frequently part time; food manufacturing jobs, which are machine-scheduled, rarely are. On net, this outsourcing has shifted jobs from part-time to full-time status. Although food manufacturing jobs undergo seasonal fluctuations, they have more stable schedules than those in food service. In electronics, the outsourcing of functions and jobs from final manufacturers probably has had little effect on the degree of part-time work, the shifts available to production workers, or the degree of schedule predictability.

In addition to creation of remote sites and outsourcing, a third strategic shift we observed was the professionalization of call center jobs—a step that itself in some cases involved outsourcing of peak-load call traffic to third-party call centers in order to stabilize the hours of the core call center workforce. Particularly in financial services, but also in retail sales, companies have been shifting the view of call centers from a cost center primarily concerned with order taking to a value-adding center within the company that increases repeat sales through better customer service and "cross-selling" or "up-selling" by selling the customer more or more costly merchandise when he or she calls to place an order. In some places, this involved an effort to train order-taking call center workers into skilled sales people similar to those who work in upscale retail stores. One of the steps in this professionalization process has been to transform part-time customer service representative jobs into full-time jobs.

While the professionalization of call center jobs can be seen as a step up for call center employees—better training, more upward mobility, more opportunity for full-time status—there may be some costs in the loss of a wider range of schedule choices. In particular, some women who preferred to work "mother's hours," 9:00 to 2:00, for example, may now have less opportunity to do so. The replacement option may be the full-time mother's shift, in which mothers leave the house when the father gets home and can watch the children. At MultiBank, for example, tellers worked part-time schedules, including mother's hours shifts, 10 or 20 years ago. Today, MultiBank has moved to make most tellers full-time, and mothers of young children are more likely to work a late afternoon or evening mother's shift in the call centers. The mother's shift imposes significant stresses on the family, because it makes it difficult for a mother to see her children or her husband.

To recap, we have identified three major changes in our industries that affect the hours scheduling confronting employees. First, in retail, transactions are shifting from stores to call centers. Retail stores are backing off from expanded hours, while call centers are expanding hours toward 24/7 coverage. Overall, then, demands for employer-driven flexibility are increasing in retail. Second, the increase in outsourcing of food preparation by food service firms to food manufacturers is increasing the relative amount of full-time work and predictable schedules in food service. Finally, within call centers in both retail and financial services, call center work is being professionalized, which has the effect of curtailing the proportion of jobs that are part time and of increasing the proportion that are full time. These last two developments increase the career possibilities and pay and benefit conditions of call center jobs to some extent but reduce certain hours arrangements that benefit some families. The professionalization of call center work has also affected career mobility, to which we now turn.

Career Flexibility

The second dimension of work-life flexibility we examine is *career flexibility*. Again, flexibility can have two meanings: the degree to which an employee must adapt his or her life—particularly by relocating—in order to pursue a career and/or the degree to which a company will adjust its career ladder to accommodate employees' life needs. As in the case of work hours, we found (consistent with Moen, 2003) that the employer rather than the workers typically drives patterns of career flexibility over the life course. However, we also found more examples of employees who were able to limit these employer demands and, in some cases, obtain flexibility on their own terms. Once more, we focus on four job characteristics that shape the nature of flexibility: the industry, the level of the job, the balance between labor supply and labor demand in a particular place and time, and strategic choices by corporations. We discuss each in turn.

Industry Matters for Career Flexibility. The striking industrial divide in career flexibility cuts between retail and financial services, on the one hand, and food service and electronics manufacturing, on the other. In the former two sectors, we found a managerial "mommy track" that allowed women to undertake childrearing and still pursue a managerial career (whether simultaneously or sequentially). In food service and electronics manufacturing, however, this type of flexibility was far scarcer.

For instance, Gladys started as a clerical worker in At Your Service (AYS), a subcontractor providing telephone customer service for Marketplace Stores, and climbed the ranks as Marketplace absorbed AYS; ten years later she was occupying the position of HR director of a call center with over 1,000 employees—the whole time in a single southwestern metropolitan area. Consolidation of companies through mergers and acquisitions—a common pattern in all four industries we study—often brings with it expanded mobility opportunities such as the ones Gladys enjoyed.

Sally of MultiBank at first appears to be a counterexample: She charted an upwardly mobile course that involved frequent branch-to-branch moves—"probably ten" branches in eight years. But in fact, all her moves took place within a geographically compact area that did not require relocation. Sally's background before coming to MultiBank reinforces the career flexibility available in retail and financial services—and indeed the possibility of mobility between these two industries. After high school (she did not attend college), she worked as an insurance underwriter, then left paid work for a few years "to take care of my kids." She then went to work as a front-end (cashier) manager in retail on a part-time basis and shifted to MultiBank at first in a part-time teller job. Today she manages the largest branch in her region. Sally's boss, Laura, who oversees 14 MultiBank branches, followed a similar path: She started out 24 years earlier as a part-time teller who worked opposite shifts with her husband and went on to work in half a dozen locations, but all in the same bank (give or take a few mergers and acquisitions) and the same area.

Contrast these geographically localized upward trajectories with stories from electronics manufacturing and food service. Perhaps the most extreme example is Helmut, head of a high technology product division within Monarch Electronics. After Helmut had worked as an engineer and engineering manager for a European company for 15 years, Monarch acquired the company and he moved to the midwestern United States to work with Monarch engineers. Achieving success in one division, he was made head of a second, more troubled division that at the time was viewed as a "meat grinder," in his words. Not long after, in 1993, "I took the job to globalize the division," and when we spoke to him in 1996 he had for years literally spent two weeks of each month in the Midwest and two weeks in Europe.

We did not find other cases of managers whose careers required them to be in two places at once, but examples of managers who jumped from location to location to get ahead were common in electronics and food. Mike, a manager at Great Meals (a large institutional food service contractor), advanced from running coffee services at a university to serving as a regional manager. In the process he hopscotched from the mid-Atlantic to Florida, back to the mid-Atlantic, and finally to New England. His job has been based in New England since the late 1980s but requires him to range across the New England states visiting food service sites. Mike, like Helmut, clearly has paid a price in terms of opportunities to spend time with family, as well as over raising a family in a stable location.

In the four industries, the availability of managerial career paths that incorporate childrearing is linked to broader demographic patterns in each industry's workforce. It is not coincidental that our managerial examples from retail and finance are women, whereas the examples from electronics and food are men. This mirrors the composition of managerial ranks in the four industries.

Job-Level Matters for Career Flexibility. Despite the opportunities for women to rise to management in retail and financial services, the mommy track in these industries should not be confused with the "fast track." As we scan up the hierarchy from supervisors and managers overseeing a dozen employees to those managing hundreds or thousands, we still find women in many cases, but their work histories often look quite different: Employers are dictating their career paths rather than accommodating employee-driven flexibility. At MultiBank, we profiled Sally and Laura, who rose from part-time tellers to branch manager and area manager—but the staffs they manage amount to 10 people for Sally and 121 in Laura's case. Kathleen, on the other hand, heads MultiBank's call center operations, with 900 employees. She commenced her education in Ohio then continued it in the mid-Atlantic, earning two master's degrees (unlike Sally and Laura, who never attended college). Her banking career began in with an Ohio-based bank that promoted her from project work to management, but she then hopped to another bank in Minnesota, only to hop again to MultiBank in another Midwestern state. Kathleen rose far, but only by adopting a stereotypical corporate model of geographic mobility in pursuit of career opportunities.

In the catalog call centers of broad-line retailer Clarendon, a similar contrast can be drawn between Bea, a shift manager over 300 employees at the Southland call center, and Alicia, one of two top managers responsible for all 7,000 call center employees. Bea was teaching preschool, and "my middle son went to live with his father in Colorado and I decided I needed a part-time job to keep up, to occupy my time." She started part-time at the Clarendon call center while continuing to teach preschool, but soon became a trainer and then manager of a small part of the operation and finally shift manager—over a 15-year period based at the same call center. Alicia's career had a similarly modest beginning— she never attended college and worked as the catalog desk manager at a Clarendon's store in the Northeast. But Alicia moved to a regional training position, then to a distribution center in the Midwest, and at that point her career took off. She was involved in setting up Clarendon's first call center, based at this distribution center, bounced between three other locations in the Northeast and Midwest as she started additional call centers, and finally—17 years after starting at Clarendon—settled in the Southwest where call center operations are now headquartered. We saw similar contrasts between the biographies of store managers and those of their subordinate managers.

Even at the very male, hard-charging environment of engineering at Monarch Electronics, where we saw Helmut's bicontinental job, lower-level jobs permit more family-friendly trajectories than the top positions. Lance, a veteran Monarch HR official, commented on the situation of Helmut and other global managers:

> At the human level, how long can you be a global warrior? . . . [Helmut] is worn out. . . . The scariest thing about my career if I look ahead and say, I'm 45 years old. I'm at [Monarch]. I travel 30% of the time now globally. If I continue on a path like this, why wouldn't it be 80%? How could I . . . I cannot imagine it being like that. How much can you take?

And in fact, Monarch provided an implicit "daddy track" for *individual contributors*, engineers who prefer stability to a management career. Frank, a Monarch software engineering manager, commented on the location of Monarch's main U.S. engineering facility: "[City name] is a good place to raise a family, so, I swear, 80% of the people we hired have kids between the ages of two and six. So people who won't work in California, won't work in Boston, won't work in Texas are glad to work here because they have California technology and get to do it in a place that's family-friendly." Shortly after we spoke to Frank, he left the company. His interim replacement, Art, explained, "[Frank] grew up in Sioux Falls, and he had an opportunity to go back there for a job. I'm the same way—if a job came up in Green Bay." He added, in words that were particularly striking coming from a man. "We *have* a software culture here. It's our own software culture, not a California [Silicon Valley] culture. . . . I shoot people if they're here weekends. . . . My kids are seven, four, and two. I work for two companies. One is Monarch, and the other is [Art's last name], Incorporated— the CEO's my wife!"

Labor Supply Matters for Career Flexibility.   Monarch's appeal to software engineers seeking a family-friendly area illustrates how companies respond to labor supply in striking the balance between employer and employee flexibility needs. As Frank remarked, "Instead of trying to say, 'Well, we have a dinner theater and we have rock concerts,' we say, 'We have good schools and we have 5-minute drives to work.' . . . So instead of trying to compete with Silicon Valley technology and culture, we play into families, [a shorter] commute drive." Given that the company must rely on this market niche to attract software designers, Monarch tolerates managers like Art—even though these managers go against the predominant company culture, summed up by management in the principle of *push*, which means running "in the red zone on the tachometer," in the words of Monarch HR's Lance.

We observed an analogous adaptive process, though one with a completely different outcome, at the CenterWest Marketplace call center where Gladys handles HR duties. The call center relocated and found itself close to call centers of two major financial service providers and a mail order computer sales company. According to Gladys and other managers, Marketplace simply could not match the $12–13 starting wage of these other call centers (pay started at $8.40–11.85 at the Marketplace center, depending on the job). As a result, Gladys said, the company had developed "a system that supports churn"—to the tune of 88% turnover in the previous year. The Marketplace call center did its best to retain employees by offering schedule flexibility, less rigid work rules, and innovative benefits, but managers were resigned to replacing a substantial chunk of their workforce each year.

At Treats, the gift mail order company, the labor supply available in its rural Midwestern location facilitates yet another career pattern. Treats has a core workforce of 260 but this number increases to 4,000–5,000 during the holiday giving season, necessitating a huge seasonal workforce, including large numbers of seasonal supervisors. But interestingly, about half the seasonal workforce— and up to 59% in the largest Treats call center—consists of workers who are returning from the previous year. Some seasonal employees have worked yearly for 40 years. According to Treats' operations director:

> A lot of them are stay-at-home moms or retired—or this is their only job—they like summers off and being able to create their own schedules. . . . Company wide, a good share of our returning employees . . . are retired [and] enjoy working at [Treats] both for the socialization and outlet as well as [for the] additional holiday income.

The combination of a highly rooted rural population plus Treats' position as the largest employer in several small towns allows the company to fashion stable careers out of the most unstable of jobs. Although employer-driven, this pattern meets employee needs as well.

In short, the nature of available labor supply—including what other companies are offering to the relevant labor pool—shapes the career patterns each company creates, even after taking into account cross-industry and job-level differences. Moreover, as the Marketplace example illustrates, the labor pool changes, based on strategic decisions by a company and by its competitors in the labor market. Labor supply and corporate strategy respond to each other.

Company Strategy and Managerial Discretion Matter for Career Flexibility. Company strategy and managerial discretion might appear, at first, to have entirely opposite types of implications. One might expect company strategies to vary systematically, with systematic implications for career patterns. Contrariwise, one might expect managerial discretion to lead to a wide range of fairly unpredictable outcomes.

In our company case studies, neither expectation is completely borne out. On one hand, company strategies include a large component of experimentation driven by fairly speculative beliefs about the state of the world. On the other hand, managerial discretion often follows stable, deeply embedded social and economic patterns. In both cases, however, the implications involve variation in *employer*-driven flexibility rather than openings for *employee*-driven flexibility.

First, briefly consider two examples of managerial discretion. Monarch's Art, as described earlier, used his managerial power to discourage engineers from working weekends. This flouted the principle of push touted by top managers. Yet it reflected the reality that Monarch's strongest appeal to software engineers lay in a family-friendly lifestyle—a lifestyle not consistent with the thoroughgoing implementation of push in the workplace.

At Clarendon, Alicia recounted how, about 10 years before we spoke to her in 2000, top executives issued a directive to "get some more outside blood in"— bring in more managers from outside the company, altering career trajectories. "And we did really work hard at that," she continued, "and we ended up with a few good people. The truth is, they didn't stay with us." In many cases the outside hires quickly left for more money. In other cases, "when I did hire a college grad, the person was not reliable. They thought they were still in college, I guess. They tend to have attendance problems; they would do stupid things." Alicia soon reverted to promoting from within at the same rate as before, ignoring the corporate mandate. In addition to Alicia, we spoke to managers at the Southwestern and Southland Clarendon call centers who had been in management at the time of the outside blood directive—but none of them even remembered the policy. The point is not simply that it is difficult for top executives to drive a policy down through the ranks of middle management, but that Alicia and her team of call center managers had worked out a successful HR management model that clashed with increased reliance on outside blood. They had good reasons for sticking with their model.

What about company strategy? Our study focuses on two particular strategic initiatives: the creation of remote sites and outsourcing. Following these two, we examine the strategy of professionalizing jobs, which we already considered in the context of schedule flexibility.

It seems self-evident that relocating activity to remote sites such as call centers disrupts job ladders, making upward mobility more difficult and often adding a requirement of geographic relocation for promotion. The reality, however, is somewhat more complex. The case of Clarendon is instructive. In the early 1980s, when Clarendon first created call centers, they had three job layers from bottom to top: CSR, shift manager, and call center manager. Opportunities to rise were far more limited than in Clarendon stores, which boasted eight layers in the selling organization, from clerk to store manager. But in the ensuing 20 years, three things changed to alter this comparison. First, within eight years Clarendon call centers added three more layers: senior CSR, team leader, and operations manager, bringing the number of layers to six. Their stated goals were to motivate and retain workers and to increase supervisory capacity. Second, more recently Clarendon stores removed two layers, bringing their total down to six. Third, over time Clarendon call centers grew to a typical size of 500 employees, whereas stores remained at 150 to 200, with the uppermost end around 300.

The result is that, far from being a gulag shut off from promotion possibilities, Clarendon call centers offer more such possibilities than the stores do. We recount above Bea's ascent to shift manager. At the same Southland call center, we interviewed four team leaders in the Internet section of the center. Although one was a student working part time who had been at the center only three or four years and did not plan to stay, the others described careers at the center spanning 12 to 16 years. In each case they started out as a CSR, then moved into a variety of more responsible jobs (senior CSR, administrative assistant, customer inquiries, special services), on the way to a lead job. The shift of call centers from very flat organizations to elaborate hierarchies was not limited to Clarendon. We saw it repeated in company after company (Moss, Salzman, & Tilly, 2003).

Above a certain level, of course, upward mobility in the call center worlds of Clarendon and other companies requires geographic relocation—much as it does in the world of Clarendon's stores. The biography of Alicia, Clarendon's codirector of call center operations, illustrates this pattern. In fact, Clarendon's first few call centers (set up by Alicia in the early 1980s) proved a seedbed for top call center leadership: The top two managers in the Southland call center earned their stripes at the original call center in the Midwest; Clarendon's second call center (in an Eastern city) launched the career of the current manager of the Southwestern center and one of his shift managers.

As with the creation of remote facilities, the self-evident notion that outsourcing functions must snap promotion chains is complicated by the evolution of actual business practices. Monarch's outsourcing history documents the twists this evolution can take. Monarch escalated its outsourcing in the late 1980s. At the outset of this wave of outsourcing, many of Monarch's suppliers looked like Expert Machining. Expert, a family-owned business, in 1980 employed only 12 and annual sales totaled $630,000. But Monarch soon discovered that small companies in the Expert Machining mold lacked the capacity to design and assemble complex components, and thus it made a series of adjustments to its outsourcing strategy. The electronics manufacturer re-insourced some components and helped companies like Expert to integrate vertically and expand their management and design capabilities. Expert ballooned from 12 employees in 1980 to 130 in 1997, with sales of $25 million. Growth expanded career possibilities at Expert Machining. Expert hired assemblers at $8–11 per hour, machinists at rates ranging from $8 for an apprentice to $22 for a master machinist, and engineers—one third of whom were nondegreed designers who had "learned from the school of hard knocks," according to the CEO. From a small shop consisting of machinists and one owner/manager, Expert grew to include some basic job ladders.

But even more important, Monarch shifted to purchasing from larger companies. One purchasing manager said, "I went from looking for a $2 million [per year in sales] company to produce subassemblies to $5 million, $10 million, $15 million—now I think it takes more like a $50 million company." As Monarch sought larger suppliers, it increasingly shifted business from job shops to contract manufacturers. Contract manufacturers are, in general, large employers: Average employment in a printed circuit assembly plant (which describes a large proportion of electronic contract manufacturers) was 148 in 2001, compared to 95 in computer and electronic product manufacturing as a whole and 46 in machinery manufacturing, the category that includes Expert (U.S. Census Bureau, 2003b).

Of the two contract manufacturers we visited, Spectrum had 2,400 employees in two locations in 1998 (it has since grown to 16 locations on three continents); the much smaller Galaxy Electronics (not a Monarch supplier) had 130 employees divided between two plants in 2003. (By comparison, Monarch had 14,000 when we began studying the company in 1996.) But even in Galaxy's small plants, there are well-defined job ladders. Employees can move from hand assembly to machine operation, and from there either to a management track extending up to production manager or to manufacturing support jobs such as purchasing, quoting (estimating jobs for customers), or even engineering. "Well over half our positions are filled internally," reported Galaxy's HR director. He continued:

> Everyone who's in the [engineering] department as an engineering assistant [80% of the engineering staff] started on the shop floor. . . . The general manager came to the facility as a test technician. He moved up to manufacturing engineer, plant manager, and finally general manager. Except for the accounting manager, there's

not a single person in a management position in [the larger of the two plants] [who] didn't come in through [Galaxy].

In short, over time Monarch shifted its sourcing to larger subcontractors with more developed internal career ladders, expanding the possibility for upward mobility at a single location. However, it is only fair to add that shortly after we ended our Monarch case study in 1998, news media reported that Monarch was pushing its suppliers to relocate to Mexico or Asia. Another wave of corporate strategy threatened to undo the opportunities for mobility in a fixed location that the previous wave had created.

Alternatively, outsourcing in food service unambiguously expanded opportunities to move up the career ladder (Lane, Moss, Salzman, & Tilly, 2003). Two outsourcing trends predominated. First, institutional food service—cafeterias at companies, schools, and other institutions—was subcontracted to food service contractors. Second, food preparation was shifted increasingly out of restaurants and cafeterias into food manufacturing settings that provided more and more processed food for final service.

The subcontracting of institutional food service did not change the size of each individual facility—cafeterias still only averaged 16 employees in 2001 (U.S. Census Bureau, 2003b)—but it linked the jobs in each facility to far more extensive local, regional, and national job ladders. These links became denser as three giant businesses—Compass, Aramark, and Sodexho—came to dominate food service contracting. As we saw with the example of Mike, the regional manager for Great Meals, high-ranking jobs in such food service contractors require geographic mobility. But the same is not true at lower levels of management. Rocky, a Great Meals facility manager, achieved his position by moving among Great Meals locations within a metropolitan area: from chef at a small facility to executive chef at a bank to executive chef at a campus where he subsequently ascended two more steps to become general manager.

Outsourcing food preparation from the restaurant to the factory *does* shift employment to larger units. The average eating place employs 17, whereas employment in the average food manufacturing plant was measured at 73 in 1997 and 55 in 2001 (the drop is due to a change in the definitions of industrial categories); either way, the manufacturing units are several times as large (U.S. Census Bureau, 2003b). To see the implications, compare career trajectories of employees at Bellavista, an upscale restaurant, with those at Salads Supreme, a manufacturer of salads and prepared dinners. At Bellavista, which has 14 kitchen jobs, we spoke to a line cook and two chefs. All had worked at a variety of restaurants, jumping from job to job in order to advance in the industry. But at Salads Supreme, a one-plant operation with a core production workforce of 100 (spiking up to 200 during the summer peak season), Meg, the vice president of operations, told us, "Cooks and mixers come up through the ranks. . . . The plant manager has been here since the beginning of time. One supervisor [of the four], the same thing." (Moreover, Meg, her boss, and two of her supervisors had all moved to Salads Supreme together after working at another food manufacturer in the same metropolitan area.) We heard similar stories at other food manufacturers: a supervisor who started as a production worker 27 years earlier at Deluxe Meats, a plant manager who was shoveling seafood 23 years earlier at Ocean Fresh, and so on.

Thus, outsourcing in food service expanded possibilities for career mobility within a single company and even a single city; outsourcing in electronics and the creation of call centers in finance and retail fractured career ladders but then unexpectedly rebuilt them. But one other strategic shift by companies created new hurdles for upward mobility: the professionalization of management positions. The trend toward professionalization can be seen by comparisons of some of the same managers we have described already. For example, Alicia started at Clarendon in 1972, set up the company's first call center in the early 1980s, and went on to colead the company's call center organization. She rose based on talent and pluck despite not having a college degree, reflecting the "back office" status of call centers in the retail chain for most of these years. In contrast, MultiBank's Kathleen, who entered banking in 1988 and rose to head call center operations in 2003, acquired an MBA and a master's of banking as her entrée to the field. And Alicia's recently hired counterpart in codirecting Clarendon call center operations is himself a younger, MBA-educated manager. We observed similar patterns in banking, food manufacturing, and electronic components.

Over time, this process of professionalization is closing off some of the internal paths to upward mobility we have described in such detail. In these examples and others, three factors affect the degree to which jobs require professional credentials. First, there has been an overall trend toward professionalization. Second, not surprisingly, higher level jobs have professionalized more rapidly. Third, the transition has been most dramatic in rapidly growing sectors such as call centers. In such sectors, the early days offered nearly boundless opportunities for talented individuals like Alicia to rise through on-the-job learning; but as the sectors have matured, companies increasingly have sought to bring scientific knowledge into management.

In summary, many forces shape the nature of career flexibility in the companies we study. Cross-industry disparities, job level differences, and labor market pressures all condition the degree to which a person must move from place to place in order to climb the corporate ladder. But even after taking into account industry, job level, and labor market, variations in corporate strategy also determine career requirements. Corporate strategy giveth, sometimes in surprising ways: Outsourcing and the creation of call centers ended up rebuilding internal labor markets rather than wiping them out. But corporate strategy taketh away as well: Monarch's drive to shift sourcing offshore and the multi-industry drive toward professionalization have limited the family-friendly mobility opportunities that characterize the histories of so many of today's managers.

CONCLUSION

In this chapter, we have made three main claims. First, we argue that a business's organizational structure, and changes in that structure, have critical implications for work-life balance. Second, we posit that firm restructuring is not a linear process but an iterative, exploratory one and that, contrary to many accounts of restructuring by U.S. businesses over the last 20 years, restructuring has in many cases either preserved internal labor markets or knocked them down only to rebuild them, though usually in new forms. Finally, we claim that although employer-driven restructuring predominates, and changes in flexibility are usually collateral consequences rather than goals of restructuring, the restructuring we observe sometimes has increased employee-friendly flexibility, sometimes decreased it—making it difficult to generalize about the impact of restructuring.

Our results come under the four headings of industry, occupation, labor supply, and corporate strategy. We find that industry distinctions cut differently on schedule flexibility than on career flexibility. For *schedule* flexibility, the key distinction is between manufacturing industries (electronics, food manufacturing) that can inventory products and service industries (retail, financial services, food service) that must provide service directly to a consumer. Manufacturing industries more typically adopt standard, full-time shifts and predictable schedules, whereas service industries more often run shifts on nights, weekends, and nonstandard or unstable schedules keyed to fluctuations in customer demand and often in inverse relationship to consumers' work schedules. In financial services, foreshadowing the labor supply issue, this tendency toward nonstandard schedules is moderated to some extent by the need to attract and retain skilled workers. For *career* flexibility, one side of the divide is marked by industries in which large female workforces have led to a significant presence of women in the managerial ranks (in our sample, retail and financial services). In these feminized industries, we find, on one side, career tracks into management that accommodate upward mobility in a fixed geographic location and offer more flexibility around family needs. On the other side, electronics manufacturing (with an overwhelmingly male workforce) and food service (with a disproportionately female workforce but continuing male dominance at the management level), management career tracks more often require geographic relocation, potentially placing stresses on families.

Job level, again, plays out differently for schedule flexibility than for career flexibility. Junior employees are particularly likely to be assigned nonstandard shifts, though supervisors are typically responsible for problem solving and coverage that may involve unexpectedly long or irregular hours. Schedule demands are thus usually most extreme for lower-level workers, even if such demands do not disappear after rising to management. To the contrary, requirements to relocate become *more* common the higher in management one ascends.

The basic facts about the impact of labor supply on flexibility are unsurprising. One such fact is that in times when and places where qualified labor becomes more scarce, businesses tend to decrease their demands for employer-driven flexibility (both career and schedule) and increase their concessions to worker needs. The other fundamental fact is that businesses such as call centers or stores searching for workers to fill nonstandard (part-time, night, weekend) schedules draw on populations who themselves seek nonstandard schedules due to other life activities: mothers of young children, students, moonlighters. Of course, the messy reality is that labor supply, a given company's strategies for tapping it, and other companies' strategies with respect to the same pool of labor, are all moving targets. Rarely do we see major workplace changes due to pure labor supply shifts. Rather, workers' needs and aspirations, and those of the companies that employ or seek to employ them, interact in complex ways.

Finally, then, we turn to the impact of strategic restructuring. In our case studies, we find two kinds of restructuring trajectories. On the one hand, some restructuring essentially carries out compositional shifts of employment, shifting work from one industry or setting to another without radically changing activities in either setting. Thus, for instance, food preparation shifts from restaurants and cafeterias (where nonstandard and fluctuating schedules are common and career tracks are limited) to food factories (where standard, stable shifts predominate and mobility paths are well developed). Similarly, retailing moves from stores to call centers, where schedules, already extended and variable in the case of stores, are even more extended and variable.

On the other hand, restructuring can involve evolution of organizational structures as initial managerial strategies are implemented and found wanting. In the most dramatic example in our findings, retailers and financial institutions created call centers as very flat organizations in line with then-current managerial predilections for eliminating hierarchies and minute job distinctions. These provided little upward mobility or sometimes offered pay increases but little visible mobility in job titles. In response to workers' preferences for mobility and recognition, firms added levels and career paths. Along the same lines, Monarch and other electronics manufacturers originally outsourced to tiny shops but then grew those shops or, more often, shifted to much larger suppliers—truncating mobility paths but then rebuilding them. And across many industries, businesses professionalized jobs—coupling expanded opportunities for mobility with heightened credential requirements and, in many cases, reduced employee-driven flexibility. Finally, we have seen that managerial discretion can channel, supplement, or subvert companies' strategic restructuring initiatives.

Let us return to our three central claims. All of these findings point to the implications of organizational structure for work-life balance. In this chapter, the evidence for iterative rather than linear restructuring is limited to the evolutionary vignettes summarized in the previous paragraph, but we believe the examples cited are sufficient to make a case for the meandering nature of much restructuring. (In other work [Lane, Moss, Salzman, & Tilly, 2003; Moss, Salzman, & Tilly, 2003], we have detailed additional examples of this exploratory process from our data.) And, both compositional change (in the case of outsourcing of food preparation) and evolutionary restructuring (in the case of call center creation and electronics outsourcing) do appear to often strengthen or rebuild internal labor markets—although there is nothing automatic about this, and we have also observed continuing trends (offshore outsourcing, professionalization) that close off avenues of upward mobility.

Employer-driven patterns, and changes in those patterns, certainly dominate our narratives of schedule and career flexibility. Nonetheless, we found cases of expanded work-life opportunities (as when on-site job ladders reemerged), others where they contracted (as when call centers absorbed functions formerly based in stores, banks, and offices), and still others with mixed effects (as when professionalization offered added full-time opportunities but foreclosed part-time options and more often required relocation for career mobility). Employees were more likely to achieve flexibility on their own terms when and where labor was scarce or when they possessed valuable skills. Our finding of iterative restructuring counsels caution regarding the finality of particular flexibility outcomes.

Having illustrated the usefulness of exploring the work-life consequences of restructuring that is pursued for reasons unrelated to work-life, we would propose extending this line of research in two directions. First, it would be worthwhile to replicate this type of process-focused case study research in several ways. It would be instructive to look at a wider range of work-life outcomes, not simply two rather narrowly defined arenas of flexibility. Studying additional industries would be fruitful, as would searches for cases in which work-life objectives actually have motivated restructuring. We did not find such instances, but that may be unsurprising because our chief research focus is the restructuring process itself, rather than work-life issues. Perhaps most important, we urge research on the work-life impacts of a wider range of types of business restructuring. Second, for purposes of generalization, it would be valuable to trace these sorts of changes in large, representative data sets—particularly longitudinal data sets allowing researchers to track schedule changes and career and life course progressions. We hope that continuing exploration of the links between organizational structure—and restructuring—and work-life balance will inform both organizational theory and the work-life interface, strengthening the much-needed bridge between these two areas of inquiry.

AUTHOR NOTE

We thank the Rockefeller, Russell Sage, and Sloan Foundations and the University of Massachusetts Lowell for financial support. We thank Radha Biswas for outstanding research assistance and Julia Lane for essential input into co-authored work on which this chapter draws. Thanks also to the editors of this volume and an anonymous reviewer for very constructive feedback on an earlier draft.

REFERENCES

Cappelli, P. (2001). Assessing the decline of internal labor markets. In I. Berg & A. Kalleberg (Eds.), *Sourcebook of labor markets: Evolving structures and processes* (pp. 207–245). New York: Plenum.

Lambert, S. J., & Haley-Lock, A. (2004, August). Theories of organizational stratification: Addressing issues of equity and social justice in work-life research. *Journal of Community, Work, and Family, 7*(2), pp. 181–197.

Lambert, S., Waxman, E., & Haley-Lock, A. (2002). *Against the odds: A study of instability in lower-skilled jobs.* Working paper for the Project on the Public Economy of Work, University of Chicago.

Lane, J., Moss, P., Salzman, H., & Tilly, C. (2003). Too many cooks? Tracking internal labor market dynamics in food service with case studies and quantitative data. In E. Appelbaum, A. Bernhardt, & R. J. Murnane, (Eds.), *Low-wage America: How employers are reshaping opportunity in the workplace* (pp. 229–269). New York: Russell Sage Foundation.

Moen, P. (2003). *It's about time: Couples and careers.* Ithaca: Cornell University Press.

Moss, P., Salzman, H., & Tilly, C. (2000). Limits to market-mediated employment: From deconstruction to reconstruction of internal labor markets. In F. Carré, M. A. Ferber, L. Golden, & S. A. Herzenberg (Eds.) *Nonstandard work: The nature and challenges of changing employment relationships* (pp. 95–121). Champaign, IL: Industrial Relations Research Association.

Moss, P., Salzman, H., & Tilly, C. (2002). *Tracking internal labor market shifts in four industries.* Paper presented at the Proceedings of the Industrial Relations Research Association Annual Meeting.

Moss, P., Salzman, H., & Tilly, C. (2003). *Under construction: The continuing evolution of job structures in call centers.* Working paper for the Center for Industrial Competitiveness, University of Massachusetts Lowell.

Ortmann, G., & Salzman, H. (2002). Stumbling giants: The emptiness, fullness, and recursiveness of strategic management. *Soziale Systeme: Zeitschrift für Soziologische Theorie, 8*(2), 205–230

Simon, H. (1976). *Administrative behavior: A study of decision-making processes in administrative organizations.* New York: Free Press. (Original work published in 1945)

Tilly, C. (1996). *Half a job: Bad and good part-time jobs in a changing labor market.* Philadelphia: Temple University Press.

U.S. Bureau of Labor Statistics. (2003). Employment statistics for various years. *Current employment statistics.* Retrieved in September 2003, from http://stats.bls.gov/ces/home.htm

U.S. Bureau of the Census. (2003a). Table PCT85, Sex by industry for the employed civilian population 16 years and over. Census Summary File 4. Retrieved in September 2003, from http://factfinder.census.gov

U.S. Bureau of the Census. (2003b). *County business patterns.* Retrieved in September 2003, from http://censtats.census.gov/cbpnaic/cbpnaic.shtml

Weick, K. E. (1995). *Sensemaking in organizations.* Thousand Oaks, CA: Sage.

8

Family-Friendly Programs and Work-Life Integration: More Myth Than Magic?

Kyra L. Sutton
Raymond A. Noe
The Ohio State University

INTRODUCTION

The importance of work and family programs is increasing due to an influx in the number of female workers, in addition to a rise in the number of dual-earner families, single-parent households, and employees managing the care of both elder members and children. As a result, individuals are expressing growing concerns about responsibilities at home, which still require their attention and time. For example, recent reports have indicated that 90% of working adults expressed a concern about not spending enough time with their family (Lockwood, 2003). Furthermore, while many workers are facing constraints on their family time, the total numbers of hours worked by employees have increased continuously over the last 20 years (Saltzstein, Ting, & Saltzstein, 2001). In addition, a recent study found that if organizations maintain comparable or heavier workloads, organizational policies will do little to relieve pressure for employees and productivity may not increase; thus family-friendly human resource (HR) policies will be effective only if organizations can help employees manage overall work demand (Fredriksen-Goldsen & Scharlach, 2001).

In an effort to help employees manage their time between work and home, many organizations have implemented family-friendly programs. Broadly defined, *family-friendly programs* are programs designed to alleviate individual conflict between work and family (Arthur & Cook, 2003). Some examples of family-friendly programs include job sharing, flexible scheduling, on-site day care, elder/child-care provisions, and condensed work weeks.

As noted in many articles written about family-friendly conflict, there are two types of conflict individuals face: work-to-family and family-to-work. Work-to-family conflict occurs when involvement in a work-related activity interferes with participation in a competing family activity (Greenhaus & Powell, 2002). Some of the workplace characteristics that may impact work-to-family conflict include lack of support from management and coworkers, limited job autonomy, increased job demand and overload, inflexible working schedules, and increased number of hours worked (Fredriksen-Goldsen & Scharlach, 2001).

Alternatively, family-to-work conflict occurs when involvement in a family activity interferes with participating in a work activity (Greenhaus & Powell, 2002). This type of pressure is common to many working partners. It may be something as clear as one partner being required to travel often, or it may be a scenario in which the employee is responsible for taking the children to after-school programs. Other factors thought to impact family-to-work conflict include: spousal support, equity in the division of labor at home, adequacy of child-care or eldercare provision (and facilities), gender and martial status of the person working (who is experiencing family-work conflict), impairment level of adult-care recipients, and ages of dependent children (Fredriksen-Goldsen & Scharlach, 2001).

Generally speaking, there are two areas of research related to family-friendly programs. One area of research is interested in the conflict individuals face as a result of involvement in multiple roles. The other area is specifically concerned with the examination of family-friendly programs and their impact on the individual (Arthur & Cook, 2003). The purpose of this chapter is to integrate the findings from these two research areas to understand why family-friendly programs intended to eliminate work-life conflict are not always effective in reducing conflict. There appears to be at least two key reasons why organizations are not effective in reducing work-life conflict. First, organizations adopt family-friendly programs with little regard for operational efficiencies (i.e., Who will administer the family-friendly programs? Does the organizational climate support family-friendly programs?), and second, existing programs do not always meet the needs of employees. Continuing, although family-friendly programs provide employees with more options, there are risks and challenges faced by employees that are often unaddressed. Middle management is usually responsible for implementing programs, which often allows managers to implement family-friendly programs selectively. Also, employees participating in family-friendly programs often miss out on *face time*, or a physical presence within their organization. Face time is usually understood by organizations as a sign of commitment to and loyalty for the organization (Bailyn, Fletcher, & Kolb, 1997). Furthermore, some organizations buy into the more traditional myth that any compensable hours worked by an employee "belong to the organization," and some managers (and organizations) are very concerned with monitoring the performance of their employees (Bailyn et al., 1997).

The chapter begins with a discussion of the role of the human resources (HR) department in relationship to family-friendly programs. Next, the chapter discusses three theoretical perspectives that are related to the use and consequence of family-friendly programs. These perspectives include institutional theory, boundary theory, and a "control versus commitment" perspective of human resources systems. Following the discussion of these theoretical perspectives, empirical evidence supporting the notion that family-friendly programs are not always effective in reducing conflict for employees is presented. The chapter concludes with suggestions for future research related to the effectiveness of family-friendly programs.

FAMILY-FRIENDLY PROGRAMS AND THE ROLE OF THE HR DEPARTMENT

Within organizations, the role of the HR department is to identify and implement programs (i.e., family-friendly programs) that best address the needs of employees and facilitate the development of a healthy work-life balance. Previous research suggests that employees who have difficulties managing their work and nonwork lives may experience productivity losses including increased absences, turnover, and reduced output among other adverse effects (Comfort, Johnson, & Wallace, 2003). Furthermore, HR departments are concerned about retaining valuable employees whom they have recruited and trained as well as reducing employee withdrawal behaviors such as decreased work effort, lateness, and absenteeism (Konrad & Mangel, 2000). Given that not all organizations offer family-friendly programs, those organizations that do offer these programs are thought to have a competitive advantage thereby giving employees incentives to perform well on the job.

Upon acceptance of family-friendly programs by the organization, the HR department typically uses the programs to address the following business needs: attracting new employees, retaining employees, reducing employee stress, and increasing employee productivity. The assumption underlying employee attraction is that job applicants desiring family-friendly programs will be more attracted to firms that offer these options, thereby increasing the size of the applicant pool (Arthur & Cook, 2003). Family-friendly programs also may help enhance the organization's image for prospective applicants (Lee et al., 2002). The underlying assumption regarding family-friendly programs with the reduction in employee stress is that these programs will benefit employees therefore resulting in increased job satisfaction and a better work-life balance (Arthur & Cook, 2003). Furthermore, organizations that employ individuals with generalizable skills are concerned about employee retention, because employees with generalizable skills can move easily to other organizations (Coff, 1997; Konrad & Mangel, 2000). In addition, there seems to be a trend among employees, especially those with higher education, to delay the start of their families until their thirties or forties; research suggests that often employees are at their highest productivity level when they begin their families, hence organizations must develop programs to respond to family needs or risk losing highly productive employees (Konrad & Mangel, 2000).

An *efficiency-based perspective* of HR departments is a useful way to consider why family-friendly programs are offered. That is, the benefits of family-friendly programs outweigh all associated costs (Arthur & Cook, 2003). If HR departments help employees balance their work and family needs, the employees will be more productive while on the job, thereby positively contributing to organizational efficiency and profits (Arthur & Cook, 2003). Furthermore, HR departments will be able to achieve two important objectives; attracting better candidates and reducing employee turnover. Both of these objectives are key concerns because HR departments need to help organizations retain talented employees to meet competitive pressures (i.e., cost containment, more efficient production schedule) and customer demands.

Researchers have begun to question the usefulness of family-friendly programs. Christensen (1998) suggests that programs are "glitter without substance or application" that "desensitize" the organization's leaders to the concerns involved with the implementation of family-friendly programs. Hochschild (1997) argues that companies may be interested in promoting family-friendly programs to attract the best new workers and shine brightly before the corporate world by offering family-friendly programs; however, they are unwilling to suffer the nuisance of implementing them. Others argue that family-friendly programs appear to be operating in a closed system (Parasuraman & Greenhaus, 2002). The 40-hour workweek and usual 8-hour workday have remained unchanged; thus, HR departments have not yet reduced their expectations of an employee's time commitment for work, despite the implementation of family-friendly programs designed to help employees improve productivity and reduce stress (Hochschild, 1997; Parasuraman & Greenhaus, 2002). Finally, human resource departments are often the first area to reduce or eliminate family-friendly programs if the return on investment is not immediate and measurable (Christensen, 1998). Consistent with concerns presented by previous researchers, we also question the effectiveness of family-friendly programs. Many programs are designed without consideration of the individual needs of employees and are operationally inefficient.

THEORETICAL PERSPECTIVES RELATED TO USE AND CONSEQUENCES OF FAMILY-FRIENDLY PROGRAMS

Institutional Theory

Despite the efficiency perspective assumed by HR departments and organizations, there are trade-offs (i.e., operational inefficiencies) experienced by both individuals and organizations when these family-friendly programs are implemented. Some organizations have attempted to create a "one-stop shopping" solution to family-friendly programs, thereby implementing programs that have worked well at other organizations. The most common family-friendly programs that have been implemented across organizations are flexible work arrangements (i.e., flextime) and reduction of hours (i.e., part-time work) (Gottlieb, Kelloway, & Barham, 1998). However, despite the number of organizations that have adopted these programs, the programs are not implemented without several operational efficiency risks and disadvantages. In Table 8.1 the advantages, disadvantages, and risks related to typical family-friendly programs are presented. As shown in Table 8.1 the major risks include both organizational and individual concerns. Organizational concerns include a lack of support from management, fewer employees available for customers, low employee participation rates, and difficulty in coordinating work schedules (i.e., setting meeting times, coordinating training classes). Individual concerns include increases in work hours and reductions in employee face time.

Institutional theory suggests that organizations adopt family-friendly programs to gain legitimacy, but adoption of programs occurs with little consideration to how programs should be operated (Arthur & Cook, 2003). As a result organizations may implement various programs, including flextime, without taking into account the risks inherit in operating those programs. There are at least three pressures organizations experience that are consistent with institutional theory. These include normative pressure, mimetic pressure, and coercive pressure (Arthur & Cook, 2003; DiMaggio & Powell, 1983). Normative pressures suggest internal groups insist the organization adopt a specific family-friendly program in order to make the organization legitimate. For example, as reported in the *Chicago Tribune* (Kleiman, 2003), a group of female employees at Bank One in Chicago attended workshops in which work-life issues were discussed. The workshops were offered by the Women's Forum, which is organized by a group of executive and senior management female employees who meet to discuss career development, financial empowerment, and networking. The Women's Forum allows female employees an opportunity to discuss and learn about programs that will improve work-life balance. Based on their experience in the

TABLE 8.1

Overview of Family-Friendly Programs Commonly Utilized by Organizations: Advantages, Disadvantages, and Risks

Alternative Work Arrangement (DEF.)	Advantages	Disadvantages	Reasons Programs May Not Be Implemented: Risks (Gottlieb et al. 1998)
Flexible Work Arrangements (Flextime and Telecommuting)			
Purpose: Enable employees to participate in flexible work arrangements and meet responsibilities/priorities in their lives (e.g., family demands) in ways that conventional full-time work arrangements do not permit. Flexible work arrangements allow employees to design a working pattern that allows them the most efficient use of their time. They help reduce work-family conflict because they enable employees to have discretion over scheduling their work. Furthermore, these programs should help organizations attract new employees, retain existing employees, and reduce employee stress if programs are implemented well and if employees receive support from management.			
Flextime Start/end the workday earlier (or later) than usual.	(1) Allows employees to coordinate work hours with other obligations.	(1) Some flexible schedules allow for very little flexibility. (2) Work time requires employees to be on-site. (3) Number of hours worked may increase.	(1) Does not fit well with strategic mission/plan. (2) May cause difficulties in ensuring office coverage. (3) Lack of management support.
Telecommuting Work from home for all or part of the workweek.	(1) Enables employees to assist a dependent for limited periods of time throughout the day. (2) Commuters can reduce their travel to/from work.	(1) Reduces the employee's visibility and social integration at work.	(1) Customers may be concerned about availability of employees. (2) May cause difficulty in ensuring office coverage. (3) May cause problems with scheduling meetings.

156

Alternative Work Arrangement (DEF.)	Advantages	Disadvantages	Reasons Programs May Not Be Implemented: Risks (Gottlieb et al. 1998)

Reduction of Hours (Compressed Hours, Part Time, and Job Sharing)

Purpose: Enable employees to reduce the total number of hours worked at their workplace. Reduction of hours worked will reduce time pressures for employees as well reduce fatigue that full-time employees often experience. Enables employees to have a voice in deciding the amount of time they spend on work versus the amount of time they spend on other commitments. Furthermore, these programs should help organizations retain existing employees, reduce employee stress, and increase productivity and service levels if programs are implemented well and if employees receive support from management.

Flexible Work Arrangements (Flextime and Telecommuting)

Alternative Work Arrangement (DEF.)	Advantages	Disadvantages	Reasons Programs May Not Be Implemented: Risks (Gottlieb et al. 1998)
Compressed Hours Work fewer (or no) hours some days and longer hours on other days (i.e., work 37.5 hours in 4 days with 1 day off).	(1) Blocks of time off work, at times when services can be accessed.	(1) Difficult to schedule caregiving arrangements for the extra portion of their working days. (2) Employees may suffer from fatigue at the end of long work hours.	(1) May cause difficulties in ensuring office coverage. (2) Concerns with scheduling meetings. (3) May cause customer complaints regarding availability.
Part Time Working less than 30 hours/week.	(1) Enables those with time-consuming domestic or community responsibilities to be employed.	(1) Part-time positions may be vulnerable to lower pay, lower job security, or fringe benefits.	(1) No employee interest expressed in the program. (2) Lack of management support. (3) May cause difficulties in ensuring office coverage.
Job Sharing Share the responsibility and benefits of one full-time position with another employee.	(1) Allows higher-level employees to work part-time hours.	(1) Job performance of each employee may not be distinguished; problematic if employees make unequal contributions.	(1) No employee interest expressed in the program. (2) Lack of management support. (3) Benefits do not outweigh cost of program.

Source: Based on Gottlieb et al. (1998). *Flexible work arrangements: Managing the family-friendly boundary.* Chichester: John Wiley & Sons; *Agency responses to 1998 Family-Friendly Programs survey.* (2003). Washington, DC: United States Office of Personnel Management.

forum, employees share strategies with other colleagues on returning to their workgroup. This exchange results in a more productive workforce throughout the bank and puts pressure on the management team to respond to work-family concerns discussed during the forum.

Mimetic pressures cause organizations to change as a result of imitating a competitor, and the organization seeks legitimacy by "mimicking successful competitors" (Arthur & Cook, p. 233). For example, several organizations have adopted flexible schedules, a family-friendly program that allows employees to choose their start and end times. However, organizations may have adopted this program in response to other competitors, without assessing the value of the programs within their particular organization. In another example research found that employees who utilize flexible scheduling experience significantly higher levels of role strain than those who work normal schedules, and flexible schedules have been found to decrease absenteeism and tardiness by very slight amounts, if at all (Fredriksen-Goldsen & Scarlach, 2001; McGuire & Liro, 1987). Hence, flextime may not always be a beneficial family-friendly program, despite its widespread usage among organizations.

Coercive pressures are usually government-mandated rules, which force organizations to change family-friendly programs. For example, the Family Medical Leave Act requires employers to offer unpaid leave. Thus, organizations are forced to develop programs to comply with the law. Although organizations respond to normative, mimetic, and coercive pressures, the danger is that organizations take very little time to consider how the various family-friendly programs should be operated and administered. As a result, organizations are challenged by operational concerns such as difficulties in ensuring that employees are physically present in the office to respond to customer needs. In addition, there may be a lack of management support for employees to participate in family-friendly programs. Employees are impacted also by operational inefficiencies, as they are likely to work longer hours should they participate in family-friendly programs (Hochschild, 1997).

Boundary Theory

Boundary theory is useful for understanding how individuals move between their work and family roles and for understanding the potential impact of family-responsive HR policies on the transition between roles. From a conceptual perspective, we argue that family-friendly programs may not meet the needs of employees because the current programs do not enable employees to make a clear transition between their role at work and their role at home. Boundary theory suggests that meeting individual preferences to integrate or segment work and family roles is a key determinant of role conflict. Family-friendly programs may not result in positive individual and organizational outcomes due to the failure to meet employee preferences.

The purposes of boundary theory are to understand how individuals engage in daily role transitions and to understand the psychological movement between roles, from role exit to role entry (e.g., leaving work and going home to the parenting role). Boundaries are physical and temporal limits that help individuals conceptualize two entities, work and family, as separate from one another. Role boundaries specifically describe how individuals make the distinction between various roles in which they are engaged (i.e., employee, parent). Finally, role identity seems to describe a social construction wherein individuals use various cues (i.e., goals, values, beliefs) to identify their occupancy in a particular role.

Ashforth, Kreiner & Fugate (2000) make four key assumptions regarding their model of role transition. The first assumption is that assumed roles are relatively stable. Second, there is variance among individuals in terms of the actual number of roles they prefer to enact. Third, individuals vary in their preference for role segmentation or role integration. Finally, people seek to minimize the difficulty associated with role transitions.

Role segmentation suggests that there are large differences in the roles experienced by individuals at work and at home. Furthermore, given the large discrepancies in roles, it is unlikely that the various roles will influence one another; a "mental fence is drawn around each identity" (Ashforth et al., 2000; Clark, 2000). Under the condition of segmented roles, the roles are not only highly differentiated but they are tied to specific settings and permit few interruptions across roles. For example, an individual who prefers his or her work and family roles segmented will utilize and react positively to employee-sponsored summer programs or afterschool programs. The benefits of high role segmentation include an overall reduction in blurring between two roles. Specifically, each role is associated with specific settings, there are few cross-role interruptions, and individuals feel psychologically different in each role.

Examples of family-friendly programs that seem to help individuals segment roles include condensed workweeks and part-time and job-sharing arrangements. In general, those programs that help employees segment roles are programs that also reduce the total number of hours the employee works. Condensed workweeks allow employees to work fewer hours on some days and longer hours on other days. Part-time work allows employees to maintain their job but the employees work less than 30 hours per week, allowing the rest of their time to be allocated to family obligations. Similarly, job-sharing arrangements enable employees to split their full-time job responsibilities with another employee, such that both employees have essentially the same set of responsibilities but they come to work on different days (i.e., one employee works Monday through Wednesday and the other job-sharing employee works Thursday and Friday).

However, employees may experience some dissatisfaction with work arrangements that allow for high segmentation of their work and family roles. Some of the costs associated with role segmentation are the difficulty individuals face when they try to cross role boundaries and the difficulty faced when transitioning between their role at work to their role at home. In other words, if an employee works only part-time (e.g., job sharing or a condensed workweek), he or she may be less efficient on the days when he or she comes to work. It may take him or her longer than a regular employee to get up to speed in terms of job obligations, as a result of their working only part-time.

In comparison, role integration is described as roles that are weakly differentiated (low contrast), are not tied to specific times and places, and are often subject to interrole interruptions (Ashforth et al., 2000; Clark, 2000; Edwards & Rothbard, 2000). In integrated roles, there is hardly any difference between the roles of individuals at home and in their workplace. An individual who enjoys having his or her work and family roles integrated will likely enjoy working from home. In general, those programs that help employees integrate roles are programs that allow employees to design a working pattern that allows them the most efficient use of their time and an opportunity to fulfill both work and family obligations simultaneously.

Some examples of family-friendly programs that seem to help individuals integrate roles include on-site day care, telecommuting options, and flextime. On-site day care provides employees with the opportunity to have their children close to their job site, which allows them to check on their children throughout the workday. Telecommuting allows employees to work from home, giving them the opportunity to care for children or elders while also completing their work responsibilities. Finally, flextime allows employees to schedule the start and end of their workdays, which helps them take care of family obligations and still be physically present in the office.

The concern or cost with high role integration is a severe blurring within the work and family roles of an individual. Stated differently, role blurring "may cause confusions and interruptions" that may impact the individuals' motivation and/or productivity (Ashforth et al., 2000). An example of an interruption associated with high role integration may be a case when the parent is working from home and a child requires the attention of his or her parent during a teleconference.

Finally, Ashforth et al. (2000), also describe the individual and contextual factors that determine the ease of role transition. The three conditions hypothesized to explain role transitions of individuals include role identification, situational strength, and culture. Role identification suggests an individual's desire for roles that are extrinsically and intrinsically rewarding. In terms of role transition, if an individual identifies strongly with a particular role (e.g., employee), he or she is more eager to enter the role. The caveat is that strong role identification makes it difficult to exit the role. Individuals with a strong identity to their role as an employee may benefit little from family-friendly programs that are designed to help them create a better balance between work and family. For example, for individuals who strongly identify with their employee role, the opportunity to work a compressed workweek may not have any influence on helping them balance work and family, as they may have a challenge transitioning between their work and family roles. Situational strength refers to situations in which individuals are exposed to prescribed norms, or a "right and a wrong way to behave" (Ashforth et al., 2000). Under conditions of situational strength, it is likely the influence of individual preferences for a segmented (e.g., childcare provisions) or integrated family-friendly program (e.g., telecommuting) would be weak. Rather employees have little voice in identifying programs that would best meet their work-family need, and they have an option limited to participating in an available program or not participating at all. An implication for family-friendly programs is that if an employee is working in an environment where he or she perceives he or she has little support from coworkers or managers, he or she may be less likely to utilize various family-friendly programs. Therefore, the employee may experience stress as a result of knowing that various family-friendly programs are available in the organizations, yet he or she may have little opportunity to use them.

Our discussion illustrates that individuals vary in their preference and need for highly integrated or segmented roles. Simply providing a menu of family-friendly programs may not help employees meet these needs (Ashforth et al., 2000). Assessment of employee needs for integration and segmentation is necessary to ensure the success of family-friendly programs. Providing family-friendly polices due to normative, mimetic, and coercive pressure is not likely to meet employee needs, and therefore expected organizational outcomes such as increased productivity and reduced turnover rates will not be realized.

Control or Commitment HR Department Policies

HR policies can be characterized as focused on "control" or "commitment" initiatives (Arthur, 1994). HR policies, including family-friendly programs, are designed to improve the quality of an employee's work experience, thereby making him or her a more productive and efficient worker. A *control* set of HR policies is designed to reduce direct labor costs or improve efficiency by enforcing employee compliance with specified rules (Arthur, 1994). In comparison, a *commitment* HR policy is designed to shape employee behaviors and attitudes by forging a psychological link between organization and employee goals (Arthur, 1994).

Typically, family-friendly programs are designed by organizations to mimic the commitment perspective, such that family-friendly programs help employees reduce conflict, thereby encouraging employee retention and higher productivity. However, commitment programs usually allow employees to have greater involvement in managerial decisions and higher average wage rates (Arthur, 1994). Interestingly, most organizations measure the effectiveness of family-friendly programs based on reduction in employee tardiness and/or absenteeism, improvements in employee production, and retention. The measures currently used to assess the effectiveness of family-friendly programs are measures traditionally used by organizations that utilize a control HR system, not a commitment HR system. The goals of a control HR system are a reduction in direct labor costs and an improvement in efficiency (in which employees must comply with specific rules or guidelines). If organizations are interested in developing a more committed workforce through their HR system, why are organizations using measures associated with a control HR system to assess the effectiveness their family-friendly programs? If organizations want to develop a more committed workforce, they could measure the success of their programs in the following ways: assess the amount of employee involvement with the development of programs, measure employee satisfaction with programs, and analyze links between the employee's psychological contract and utilization of available family-friendly programs.

Consistent with this view, Siegel et al. (2003) found procedural fairness moderated the relationship between work-life conflict and organizational commitment. In other words, employees want a voice or an opportunity to be involved with the planning and implementation of organization decisions related to family-friendly programs. For example, employees want their managers to provide adequate information about program offerings and to listen closely to their concerns impacting their work-life balance (Siegel et al., 2003). It appears that employees have a preference for a commitment HR system that will allow them to create an understanding with the HR department regarding their family needs and subsequent family-friendly programs.

RESEARCH REVIEW

Table 8.2 presents an overview of organizational goals of family-friendly programs and research results. Organizational goals of family-friendly programs include attracting new employees, improving employee retention, reducing employee stress, and increasing productivity. The research results suggest that the effectiveness of family-friendly programs is not unequivocal. In the studies presented in Table 8.2 there either is no relationship between family-friendly programs and individual or organizational outcomes or the effect was negative. For example, Shamir and Salomon (1985) found that working from home increased (rather than decreased) role conflict.

FUTURE RESEARCH DIRECTIONS

To understand better the relationship between family-friendly HR policies and work-family conflict, employee satisfaction, employee turnover, and productiv-

TABLE 8.2
Are Family-Friendly Programs Really Working? Overview of Common Goals
of Organizations and Family-Friendly Programs

Organizational Goals	Results
Attract New Employees	Applicants who have high w-f (work-family) or f-w (family-work) conflict reported the same level of attraction to organizations. Findings suggest that teleworking blurs roles between work and family, which is undesirable for individuals already experiencing high levels of role conflict (and teleworking is thus a less attractive option) (Rau & Hyland, 2002).
Improve Employee Retention	Employees may not benefit from the family-friendly program offered and may be required to leave current job. For example, one study (Roehling et al.) examines the impact of various child-care programs on employee loyalty or commitment. Results from the study indicate that employees with school-age children benefit from child-care programs and have higher levels of loyalty to their employer. Of note, employee loyalty is operationalized as a three-item scale that measures how loyal respondents feel about their employer, current position, and supervisor. In comparison to the employees with school-age children, there is no relationship found between child-care programs and employee loyalty for employees with preschool-age children.
	Dalton and Mesch (1990) find no evidence that the introduction of flexible scheduling, a family-friendly program that allows employees to self-select the start and end times, has any effect on subsequent levels of employee turnover.
	Perceptions of a family-supported work environment are found to mediate the relationship between family-friendly program availability and turnover intentions. Allen (2001) finds that employees who perceive their organization as less family-supportive experience more work-family conflict, less job satisfaction, and greater turnover intentions, despite the availability of family-friendly programs. Thus the availability of family-friendly programs alone has a small effect on job attitude and job experience (Allen, 2001).
Reduce Employee Stress	Previous findings indicate that working from home is more stressful for employees with young children due to negative effects of children's interruptions on both work productivity and the relationship with children (Christensen, 1998; Hall, 1990; Metzger and Von Glinow, 1988).
	Shamir and Salomon (1985) find working from home actually exacerbates role conflict, as a result of removing the physical barriers between work and family settings.
	Another factor that may result from an employee's use of family-friendly programs, and subsequently increase employee stress, is an increase in work hours. A recent study (Comfort et al., 2003) finds employees who take advantage of flextime, a work arrangement wherein employees work a certain set of core hours and vary start and stop times, also report an insubstantial increase in work hours. In fact, the percentage of employees working 50+ hours (where the standard workweek is 40 hrs/wk) doubles or triples in the presence of a flextime arrangement (Comfort et al., 2003).
Increase Employee Productivity	For example, Kossek and Nichol (1992) demonstrate that there is no correlation between work performance and an on-site day-care center. However, the employees who use the services report higher tenure and more positive attitudes than those who do not have access to the services (i.e., those employees who are waitlisted). The employer must consider what happens to the productivity of the both individual and the workgroup.
	Productivity of members of an extended workgroup may be impacted by the absence of an employee who is participating in family-friendly program (i.e., needing pertinent information to generate reports) (Bailey & Kurland, 2000).

ity, research needs to address methodological concerns and new questions, and it needs to develop further existing theories used to understand work-family conflict and the influence of family-friendly programs. (See Table 8.3.)

First, there are several methodological concerns researchers must address to evaluate the effectiveness of family-friendly programs. These concerns include: (1) few studies have used multiple organizations; (2) given that typically one organization is utilized, the sample sizes of studies are often small; (3) more often than not most family-friendly programs are grouped together during the analyses thereby confounding the effectiveness of any individual family-friendly policy; (4) studies capture employees' responses to family-friendly programs in questionnaires thereby relying on the employees' memory and their perception of family-friendly programs; (5) very few studies actually observe the behaviors of employees; (6) most data measures collected are perceptual; (7) most of the studies conducted do not include both a control and a comparison group within their sample; (8) most studies measure satisfaction with benefits instead of measuring overall job satisfaction (overall job satisfaction is a better predictor of turnover intentions and absenteeism); (9) most studies focus solely on the individual who participates in the family-friendly programs, and many do not measure other members of work group who are also impacted when their team member participates in programs (e.g., an increase in stress of team members due to work overload); (10) most studies are not longitudinal in nature, and some employees participate in family-friendly programs for a specific time period—usually when their children reach school age—and thus participation in family-friendly programs may or may not be permanent; (11) studies need to measure impact of family-friendly programs on interpersonal processes (e.g., management of team projects in consulting companies); and (12) family-friendly conflict can be influenced by variables not currently being captured in studies (e.g., marital problems, child behavior problems).

In addition to various methodological concerns, there are at least four areas related to the studies of the effectiveness of family-friendly programs that should be addressed in future research.

These areas include; individual differences among employees; social support in organizations; job/organizational characteristics; and uses of additional organizational level outcomes. First, HR departments must recognize that employees differ in their preferences for family-friendly programs. These differences may be dependent on personality traits such as consciousness, career orientation, age, or gender. Future research must identify how personality traits impact the employee's ability to balance work and family demands and determine which family-friendly programs best meet his or her needs. Second, the perceived utility of family-friendly programs is impacted by both the social support employees receive and the job environment in which they work. Kossek et al. (2001) found that a supportive work climate positively affects job performance. One factor that may contribute to a supportive work environment is the development of a

TABLE 8.3
Future Research Directions

Area of Concern	Research Questions	Sources of Research Questions
Personality Traits/Individual Differences **Suggestion:** Move beyond measuring situational determinants of family-friendly conflict; explore situational and dispositional variable and their interactions. **Relevance:** Perhaps various personality traits or dispositions impact the employees' ability to effectively balance work responsibilities and family-friendly programs that are provided by organizations. Individual differences may impact employee's ability and desire to have highly integrated or highly segregated family-friendly roles.	*What is the relationship between various personality traits and family-friendly conflict (i.e., self-monitoring)? *Can dispositional factors predict work and family conflict (i.e., conscientiousness)? *To what extent do individuals prefer and seek segmentation of work and family roles? *Research designs are needed to identify when, why, and for whom family-friendly programs should be targeted.	**Bruck, et al. (2002)** **Stoeva et al. (2002)** **Ashforth et al. (2000)**
Social Support **Suggestions:** Study the influence of social support mechanisms on work-family conflict. **Relevance:** Lack of both family and workplace social support negatively impacts the employee's ability to utilize family-friendly programs established by organizations.	*How does mentoring influence role stressors (role conflict, role ambiguity) investigated in work and family conflict? *What is the relationship between being a mentor and reduction of work and family conflict?	**Nielson et al. (2001)** **Martins et al. (2002)**
Job and Organizational Characteristics **Suggestions:** Study the influence of various organizational and workplace characteristics on the employee's ability to effectively utilize family-friendly programs. **Relevance:** Various characteristics may enable employee's ability to utilize family-friendly programs (e.g., job autonomy, temporal flexibility).	*Do family-friendly programs relate to other organizational constructs such as perceived organizational support and perceptions of fairness? *How can firms create environments where it is acceptable to use flexible schedules? *What business needs motivate establishments to provide family-friendly programs? Is innovation, time to market, or improved customer service a priority?	**Allen (2001)** **Parker & Allen (2001)** **Kossek et al. (1999)** **Comfort et al. (2003)**

(Continued)

TABLE 8.3

(Continued)

Area of Concern	Research Questions	Sources of Research Questions
	*How is the availability of family-friendly programs related to other high commitment HR practices? Do establishments that offer family-friendly benefits also tend to invest in training?	
Use of Additional Organizational Outcomes **Suggestions:** Study the relationship between family-friendly programs and interaction with other organizational outcomes (e.g., career satisfaction, participation in training programs). In addition, the employee's satisfaction with various family-friendly programs should also be studied. **Relevance:** Employee participation in various family-friendly polices may negatively impact the employee's desire to partake in various family-friendly programs (e.g., career development programs, training).	*Research on the impact of family-friendly programs have on career satisfaction and career development opportunities is needed. *Research on the impact of utilization of family-friendly programs and the desirability to participate in training programs is needed.	**Ruderman et al. (2002) Comfort et al. (2003)**

mentoring program for employees participating in family-friendly programs. Employees could meet with their mentor and gain suggestions regarding how to best manage their work and family challenges and determine which family-friendly program would meet their needs. Research on the influence of job and organizational characteristics should focus on the relationship between family-friendly programs and organizational strategy and on how the use and satisfaction with family-friendly programs is related to organizational support. The study of work environment characteristics needs to be expanded to include perceptions of fairness and trust. Finally, the relationship between using family-friendly programs and other HR systems, such as training and development, needs further investigation. For example, Web-based training may not be an effective training strategy for employees who take advantage of flexible schedules to care for children or elders. Further, organizations do not always provide middle level managers the training necessary to administer family-friendly programs.

Research on use of family-friendly programs needs further theoretical and empirical development. For example, there needs to be further development of measures/scales used to assess family-friendly programs. Measures should include both individual and family perceptions related to the efficiency of family-friendly programs. Furthermore, researchers need to understand the extent to which individuals prefer high integration and high segregation of their work and family roles and what causes individuals to select segmented or integrated roles. Although role transitions, role integration, and role separation are intriguing concepts for understanding work-family conflict, use of family-friendly programs, and the consequences of their use, research needs to develop measures of these concepts.

Although organizations offer family-friendly programs, it is unclear if these programs are actually meeting the objective of improving the employee's quality of work environment or helping them to reduce work or family conflict. Research also suggests that organizations do not change their family-friendly programs in order to meet the changing needs of their employees. In fact, there has been little or no change in the types of family-friendly programs offered between 1992 and 1998, with the exception of the availability of eldercare services (Saltzstein et al., 2001). Because organizations are implementing family-friendly programs that primarily focus on addressing business/organizational needs, (e.g., lower absenteeism, increase productivity, improve organizational attraction), the effectiveness of the family-friendly programs in addressing the needs of employees (e.g., career satisfaction, ability to participate in training, satisfaction with child or eldercare) should be investigated.

REFERENCES

Allen, T. D. (2001). Family-supportive work environments: The role of organizational perspectives. *Journal of Vocational Behavior, 58,* 414–435.

Arthur, J. B. (1994). Effects of human resource systems on manufacturing performance and turnover. *Academy of Management Journal, 37,* 670–687.

Arthur, M., & Cook, A. (2003). The relationships between work-family human resource practices and firm profitability: A multitheoretical perspective. *Research in Personnel and Human Resources Management, 22,* 219–252.

Ashforth, B. E., Kreiner, G. E., & Fugate, M. (2000). All in a day's work: Boundaries and micro role transitions. *Academy of Management Review, 25,* 472–491.

Bailey, D. E., & Kurland, N. B. (2002). A review of telework research: findings, new directions, and lessons for the study of modern work. *Journal of Organizational Behavior, 23,* 383–400.

Bailyn, L., Fletcher, J. K., & Kolb, D. M. (1997). Unexpected connections: Considering employees' personal lives can revitalize your business. *Sloan Management Review, 38*(4), 11–19.

Bruck, C. S., Allen, T. D., & Spector, P. E. (2002). The relation between family-friendly conflict and job satisfaction: A finer-grained analysis. *Journal of Vocational Behavior, 60,* 336–353.

Christensen, K. (1998). *Women and home-based work: The unspoken contract.* New York: Henry Holt.

Clark, S. C. (2000). Work/family border theory: A new theory of work/family balance. *Human Relations, 53,* 747–770.

Coff, R. W. (1997). Human assets and management dilemmas: Coping with hazards on the road to resources-based theory. *Academy of Management Review, 22,* 374–403.

Comfort, D., Johnson, K., & Wallace, D. (2003). Part-time work and family-friendly practices in Canadian workplaces. *Human Resources Development Canada, 6,* 1–78.

Dalton, D., & Mesch, D. (1990). The impact of flexible scheduling on employee attendance and turnover. *Administrative Science Quarterly, 35,* 370–387.

DiMaggio, P., & Powell, W. (1983). The iron cage revisited: Institutional isomorphism and collective rationality in organizational fields. *American Sociological Review, 23,* 111–136.

Edwards, J. R., & Rothbard, N. P. (2000). Mechanisms linking work and family: Clarifying the relationship between work and family constructs. *Academy of Management Review, 25,* 178–199.

Fredriksen-Goldsen, K. I., & Scharlach, A. E. (2001). *Families and work: New directions in the twenty-first century.* New York: Oxford University Press.

Gottlieb, B. H., Kelloway, E. K., & Barham, E. J. (1998). *Flexible work arrangements: Managing the family-friendly boundary.* Chichester, England: John Wiley & Sons.

Greenhaus, J. H., & Powell, G. N. (2003). When work and family collide: Deciding between competing role demands. *Organizational Behavior and Human Decision Processes, 90*(2), 291–303.

Hall, D. T. (1990) Promoting work/family balance: An organization-change approach. *Organizational Dynamics, 18,* 4–18.

Hochschild, A. R. (1997). *The time bind: When work becomes home and home becomes work.* New York: Metropolitan Books.

Kleiman, C. (2003, November 25). Network in comfort at in-house forums. *Chicago Tribune.*

Konrad, A. M., & Mangel, R. (2000). The impact of work-life programs on firm productivity. *Strategic Management Journal, 21,* 1225–1237.

Kossek, E., Barber, A., & Winters, D. (1999). Using flexible schedules in the managerial world: The power of peers. *Human Resource Management, 38,* 33–46.

Kossek, E., & Nichol, V. (1992). The effects of on-site child care on employee attitudes and performance. *Personnel Psychology, 45,* 485–509.

Kossek, E. E., Colquitt, J. A., & Noe, R. A. (2001). Caregiving decisions, well-being, and performance: The effects of place and provider as a function of dependent type and work-family climates. *Academy of Management Journal, 44*(1), 29–44.

Lee, M. D., MacDermid, S. M., Williams, M. L., Buck, M. L., & Leiba-O'Sullivan S. (2002). Contextual factors in the success of reduced-load work arrangements among managers and Professionals. *Human Resources Management, 41,* 209–223.

Lockwood, N. R. (2003). Work/life balance: Challenges and solutions. *HR Magazine, 48,* 2–10.

Martins, L. L., Eddleston, K. A., & Veiga, J. F. (2002). Moderators of the relationships between family-friendly conflict and career satisfaction. *Academy of Management Journal, 45,* 399–409.

McGuire, J., & Lore, J. (1987). Absenteeism and flexible work schedules. *Public Personnel Management, 16,* 47–59.

Metzger, R. O., & Von Glinow, M. (1988). Off-site workers: At home and abroad. *California Management Review, 30,* 101–111.

Nielson, T. R., Carlson, D. S., & Lankau, M. J. (2001). The supportive mentor as a means of reducing family-friendly conflict. *Journal of Vocational Behavior, 59,* 364–381.

Parasuraman, S., & Greenhaus, J. H. (2002). Toward reducing some critical gaps in work-family research. *Human Resource Management Review, 12,* 299–312.

Parker, L., & Allen, T. (2001). Work/family benefits: Variables related to employees' fairness perceptions. *Journal of Vocational Behavior, 58,* 453–468.

Rau, B., & Hyland, M. M. (2002). Role conflict and flexible work arrangements: The effects on applicant attraction. *Personnel Psychology, 55,* 111–136.

Roehling, P. U., Roehling, M. U., & Moen, P. (2001). The relationship between work-life polices and practices and employee loyalty: A life course perspective. *Journal of Family and Economic Issues, 22,* 141–170.

Ruderman, M. N., Ohlott, P. J., Panzer, K., & King, S. N. (2002). Benefits of multiple roles for managerial women. *Academy of Management Journal, 45,* 369–386.

Saltzstein, A. L., Ting, Y., & Saltzstein, G. H. (2001). Family-friendly balance and job satisfaction: The impact of family-friendly policies on attitudes of federal government employees. *Public Administration Review, 4,* 452–467.

Shamir, B., & Salomon, I. (1985). Work-at-home and the quality of working life. *Academy of Management Review, 10,* 455–464.

Siegel, P., Post, C., Brockner, J., Fishman, A., & Graden, C. (under review). The moderating influence of procedural fairness on the relationship between work-life conflict and organizational commitment. Available from author.

Stoeva, A. Z., Chiu, R. K., & Greenhaus, J. H. (2002). Negative affectivity, role stress, and work-family conflict. *Journal of Vocational Behavior, 60*(1), 1–16.

9

The Equity Imperative: Redesigning Work for Work-Family Integration

Joyce K. Fletcher
Simmons

Lotte Bailyn
Massachusetts Institute of Technology

In a recent class with international midlevel executives, the discussion centered on work time. It was pointed out that the United States now has the longest work hours of any industrialized nation. Participants from Europe could not understand why Americans do not take vacations. Americans were concerned about the effect of these long hours on their families. And so it seemed as if a consensus were building that American work hours are too long. But then a voice from China entered the discussion: The United States, he said, is the most productive nation in the world—might it not be related to the long work hours?

Yet the United States is also the country that has the most unequal income and benefit distribution in the industrial world. There is a significant part of the population that cannot find work and another segment that reaches long working hours only by multiplying jobs. There are also workers who are not protected by labor legislation, who are not eligible for employer-provided benefits and cannot get the medical care they need. Perhaps more than long hours, this one-sided emphasis on competition and production at the expense of many other goals and many people creates and reinforces the global superiority of this country. But can such a situation last? And what consequences does it have for the care of children, elders, and communities—for work-family integration?

It is the argument of this chapter that without coupling equity with effect-iveness—the equity imperative—there will not only be a crisis of care but also the very effectiveness that is sought will be undermined. Furthermore, only a reconceptualization of work, competence, commitment, and time—a radical re-design—can achieve the double goals of equity and effectiveness. Finally, we argue that work-family integration requires more than family-friendly policies (as important as they are) superimposed on the status quo. It requires, rather, that work design be looked at through an equity lens in order to make changes in the structure, culture, and practice of work that reflect the reality of people's lives.

First, however, what do we mean by *equity*? Our emphasis is on gender equity, even though we know there are many other kinds, and in particular we link gender equity to families because of the continuing greater responsibility of women for care and the stereotyped expectations that this is where their skills lie and their main work should be. Our sense of equity, therefore, is a workplace where it is assumed that everyone has some form of private life that needs attention and that this must be taken into account when exploring systemic issues such as work design, norms, and practices.

Our chapter starts with recent work that has begun to explore how work-family issues are linked to work design. It then proceeds to a theoretical expla-nation of why taking this link seriously is so difficult, despite the fact that we all live in both worlds and must link them in some way to our own experience. We then detail the difference between an individual level approach to the issue of work-family integration and a systemic approach. Then, after a case example, we highlight the barriers to this systemic, more holistic approach and suggest ways to overcome them. Finally, we present the implications of this perspective for research and practice.

LINKING WORK AND FAMILY

A number of surveys in recent years have shown the close connection between work-family integration and characteristics of work. These include the national survey of the Families and Work Institute (Bond, Galinsky, & Swanberg, 1998), the work of Appelbaum, Berg, and Kalleberg (2000), and that of Batt and Val-cour (2003; also Valcour & Batt, 2003). They show that participation, autonomy, challenge, and control over the conditions of work, including time, all have important effects on employees' ability to integrate their work with their family lives.

Lately there have also been some experimental efforts to redesign work to enhance effectiveness by placing the employee's personal life *at the center* rather than at the margins of the effort. These experimental efforts, based in large part on the findings of a landmark study funded by the Ford Foundation,[1] which linked equity and effectiveness, start from the premise that efforts to make work practices more equitable in their effects (i.e., not penalizing people who have family and community commitments) can lead to greater effectiveness (Rapoport, Bailyn, Fletcher, & Pruitt, 2002). The goal of these experiments was to improve both effectiveness and equity—a dual agenda. They included work practice changes in processes such as planning, operations review procedures, information flow, and project scheduling (see also Casner-Lotto, 2000; Costello, with Kolb, & Johnson, 2002; Merrill-Sands, Fletcher, & Acosta, 1999; Rayman, Bailyn, Dickert, & Carre, 1999). Experiments in work practice change are also being carried out in a number of European countries.[2] They differ from traditional approaches to work redesign in their explicit inclusion of workers' personal lives when assessing work practices. What is seen as dysfunctional and in need of change is based, therefore, on equity (the assumption that all employees have personal lives) as well as effectiveness. We argue that workers' personal lives are a valid and necessary source of diagnostic data in the work redesign process and can yield new insights on the issues of long work hours, productivity, and work-family integration.

Though we have been part of many of these experimental initiatives and applaud the effort to incorporate this approach more broadly, we also recognize that the link between equity and effectiveness is a link that remains counterintuitive (Bailyn, Fletcher, & Kolb, 1997) and therefore is not easy to institutionalize. The argument we offer in this chapter is that the reason this link remains counterintuitive is that it defies one of the bedrock assumptions on which organizational life in the Western world has been based: Private life and employment are separate spheres and employers need only concern themselves with one.

Many have noted that the societal belief in the separation of spheres, with its accompanying notions of the ideal worker and ideal caretaker (Acker, 1990; Bailyn, 1993; Fletcher, 1999; Harrington, 1999; Kanter, 1977; Williams, 2000), accounts for current work norms and practices in the industrial world. We argue that while theorists and practitioners have adequately commented on the impact on work design of separate sphere images of an "ideal" worker, these same theorists and practitioners have not adequately explored other dimensions of separate spheres thinking and their impact on work redesign. We argue that understanding how these unexplored dimensions of separate spheres thinking inform work redesign efforts is necessary to achieve work-family integration. Furthermore, this exploration provides a theoretical framework for why linking equity and effectiveness is in an organization's best interest and also why making this link remains counterintuitive and difficult to institutionalize.

THE THEORY OF THE SEPARATION
OF SPHERES

While the separation of the two spheres of life has never reflected the actual
life situation or experience of most of the population, the belief in it as an ideal
is quite powerful and exerts significant, albeit often unacknowledged, influence.
Indeed, seeing the world in terms of separate spheres seems so natural that we
rarely think of it or question its influence. But if we do look more closely, there
are a number of assumptions embedded in this image that have implications for
the task of work redesign to achieve equity and effectiveness. We will focus on
three such characteristics. First, the spheres are constructed in the discourse as
a dichotomy; second, they are gendered; and third, there is a body of knowledge
underlying each sphere about what it means to do good work in that sphere.[3]

Dichotomy.   The first characteristic relevant to a discussion of work redesign is that the spheres are constructed as a dichotomy. That is, the spheres
are socially constructed as separate and discrete, are set in adversarial relationship to each other, and are differentially valued (Calás & Smircich, 1991; Diamond & Quinby, 1988; Flax, 1990). These features interact and reinforce each
other to produce several corollary assumptions about the primary actor in each
sphere. As has been indicated already, the separation and adversarial relationship
of the spheres leads to a view of an ideal worker (Acker 1990; Bailyn, 1993;
Fletcher, 1999; Kanter, 1977; Williams, 2000) in each sphere whose life situation
affords the luxury of being involved primarily in that one sphere. Thus, ideal
workers in the occupational arena are assumed to have a partner in the domestic
sphere who handles family and community responsibilities. And, although this
is not often made explicit, the reverse is also true. In the domestic realm it is
assumed that the ideal caregiver—the one who would get the best outcomes—
is a person who focuses exclusively on that task and has a partner in the paid
sphere who supports the family enterprise. The result is that work practices in
each sphere are designed with this ideal worker in mind: The best business
practices and the best parenting practices both reflect the assumption that the
actors have unlimited time and energy to devote to their sphere's activity. These
ideal images, of course, reflect an outdated, white, Western, middle- and upper-
class understanding of the world. Not only do they no longer fit the life situation
of even that small subset of the population, they are also even more problematic
for others who cannot afford to live on one salary or who are single parents.
Nonetheless, despite the contradictions embedded in it,[4] this ideal exerts powerful influence on the way society understands the issues of work and personal
life.

The fact that the spheres are assumed to be at odds means that the skills and
attributes associated with each are set in opposition and deemed inappropriate

when practiced in the opposing sphere. Thus not only are skills valued in one devalued in the other, but also conventional wisdom holds that having skills in one sphere almost disqualifies you from being good at the other. For example, if you are a caring sensitive person, we assume you will have a hard time succeeding in the workplace; if you are a hard-driving, bottom-line thinker, you might not be the best at parenting. What it takes to be good in one sphere is different from—or even opposite to—what it takes to be good in the other.

The last feature of dichotomies—that entities in a dichotomous relationship to each other are unequally valued—places the issue in a larger societal context of power and privilege and reminds us that while the phenomenon of separate spheres might seem like a power-neutral concept, it is not. As a society we place more importance on work in the public sphere than in the private. Skills associated with public sphere work are seen as signs of competence and value to society, and as an important part of one's identity. Skills associated with private life, in contrast, are seen as just "natural" and are undervalued, whether paid or not paid.

Gendered. The second and perhaps most obvious characteristic of the spheres is that they are gendered. In our mind's eye, we tend to associate men with producing things and women with growing people. But it is not just the ideal workers who are gendered; the notion of ideal work itself is also gendered. That is, doing good work in the occupational realm—producing things—is associated with traditionally masculine characteristics (Yancey Martin & Collinson, 1998). Both men and women can display these characteristics but the characteristics themselves—such as linear thinking, rationality, assertiveness, and competitiveness—typically are thought of as masculine. Of course, the opposite is also true: Doing good work in the domestic sphere—being effective at growing people—is associated with traditionally feminine characteristics such as empathy, listening, and sensitivity (Bellah, 1985; Welter, 1966). Again, both men and women could display these characteristics but the characteristics themselves traditionally are thought of as feminine.

Bodies of Knowledge. The third distinctive characteristic of the discourse of separate spheres is the one most relevant for a discussion of the link between equity and effectiveness. Each sphere has its own definition and set of beliefs about what it means to be effective and these, too, are set in a dichotomous relationship to each other—that is, they are constructed as separate, at odds, and unequally valued. We have a body of knowledge about how to produce things and a separate body of knowledge about how to grow people. Because the two spheres are assumed to be at odds, these bodies of knowledge rarely inform each other. In fact, using the rules of one in the other typically is seen as inappropriate. Thus, parents do not usually pit children against each other in competitive battles where the bottom 10% are let go in the name of continuous improvement (Greenwald, 2001). Likewise, it is assumed that good managers do not use family rules about fairness and equality to determine pay increases or merit bonuses.

Implications of These Characteristics

These characteristics of the two spheres help us see that the metaphor of work-family *balance* leads to a focus on individual choice about where one wants to excel. People, especially women, are often told "you can't have it all." The implicit goal of balance is to make accommodations in the workplace for people with problems (Fletcher & Bailyn, 1996)—that is, people who need and want time and energy to care for family. Work for them might indeed change (e.g., flextime) but work for everyone else, in this model, remains the same. In other words, visioning balance as our goal leads to a situation where we tacitly accept work as it is and family as it is, and see our task as helping (some) individuals keep them separate and cope with the demands of each.

Integration is quite different. It looks at the issue as a systemic problem, not an individual one. Gendered work practices (those that are inappropriately linked to an idealized vision of masculinity and an idealized, middle- and upper-class masculine life situation) are seen as problematic not only for women but also for men and, importantly, for the quality of the work. The image of integration defines a different task: Relaxing the separation of the two spheres in a way that allows everyone to be involved in both and that expects that both spheres will change—and both will be improved—by the connection.

This image is not entirely utopian. There is an emerging recognition, for example, that everyone has a personal life and whether we acknowledge it or not, it has an effect on our work. And there is mounting evidence that people with multiple roles benefit, as do the organizations that employ them. Rosalind Barnett and Caryl Rivers in *She Works/He Works* (1996) note that people who are active in both spheres are happier and healthier. It is better not only for their own mental health but also the mental health and well-being of their children and their marriage. Marian Ruderman and Patricia Ohlott in *Standing at the Crossroads* (2002) document that people with multiple responsibilities are the highest performers in organizations. Based on performance data on people from their leadership programs, they found that those with multiple roles did the best. Furthermore, many of the strategic initiatives in large companies—a focus on teamwork, collaboration, delighting customers, Six Sigma quality initiatives, Kaizen process improvements—tacitly acknowledge that private sphere, historically undervalued skills in "growing people," are exactly what organizations need to compete in today's knowledge-intensive world.

It appears, therefore, that the world may be ready for an integration of the spheres that captures the potential synergies between them and encourages a sharing of knowledge and a more equal valuing of the skills and competencies in each. This, we believe, is why the experimental interventions based on linking equity and effectiveness have had such positive results (Rapoport et al., 2002). However, it is also true that despite these positive results, making this kind of work-practice change remains difficult. We argue that it is the gendered, dichotomous relationship embedded in separate spheres thinking that accounts for much of this difficulty. Moreover, we argue that an understanding of these dynamics must be present in the change methodology itself, taking into account the history of adversarial thinking, its connection to gender identity, and the reality that these dynamics lie hidden in organizational assumptions about what constitutes good work, good workers, and good work practices. Thus, change methodologies must include ways to surface these assumptions and make them discussible and actionable, as the following case illustrates.

A CASE EXAMPLE

Our work in one organization highlights some of these points. It consisted of initial interviews followed by a context-specific survey and more detailed interviews and group sessions, all geared to understanding the underlying assumptions that were guiding the practices in this organization. The goal was to consider changes in work practices and ways of thinking about them that would have the double purpose of increasing the ability of employees to integrate their work with their personal lives as well as enhancing the effectiveness of the organization.

The work of the organization we studied is project-based and involves much travel to different parts of the world. Workers are well trained and highly skilled, and we quickly learned that they very much enjoy their work and are strongly committed to the mission of the organization. Despite this, however, they experienced heavy workloads and reported numerous symptoms of stress. Furthermore, we heard from employee spouses and from some of the women employees that the work-family link is very difficult for these workers, though most (particularly the men) did not talk much about this issue—an indication of the impact of separate spheres thinking.

The organization is dependent on creativity and innovation to keep its competitive position, and the survey showed that experienced workload and stress were negatively associated with the conditions necessary for innovation (Kellogg, 2002). Interestingly, though, work-family integration was positively correlated with innovation potential (Kellogg, personal communication). Hence the conditions were ripe for a reconsideration of work practices that were undermining both effectiveness and the ability of employees to integrate work with family responsibilities, which had a differentially negative impact on the women employees.

In analyzing all these data we asked ourselves questions like: What work gets rewarded in this place? What is considered the real work? What people are seen as the most committed and competent? We discovered that certain people were seen as the core of what was most valued in the organization: those who developed new projects, did the most traveling, did "whatever it takes," and never said "no." Though all of these characteristics contributed to the work of the organization, they also greatly increased the workload of most employees and left important tasks of implementation and synthesis undone.

In trying to understand what lay beneath these beliefs and practices, we identified a series of underlying assumptions that constrained work-personal life integration and impeded gender equity without seeming to be necessary for effectiveness. One of these we labeled *Competence is new ideas*. The activities associated with this assumption included priority always given to new ideas and new projects; much travel to distant sites in order to introduce new ideas and to work closely with overseas partners; and highest valuation given to knowledge generation skills. All of this fit the mission of the organization, which sees itself as being very innovative and hands-on. But there also were unintended negative consequences.

From the point of view of work-personal life integration and gender equity, travel is hard for anybody with caring responsibilities, and that includes mainly women. Certain critical skills like synthesizing, supporting, and following through were undervalued because they do not produce new ideas. And often these very tasks were done by women, which means they were not as likely to be promoted. When we looked further, there were also negative consequences for work effectiveness. The frequent travel that was supported by this assumption subtly undermined the learning of overseas partners by having organization employees there so much of the time. Also, the lack of synthesis and reflection on ongoing projects impeded the organization's learning from what it is doing. The work practices that stem from this assumption also increased workloads, because the organization was always adding things and nothing was ever dropped, which obviously made the work-personal life situation even worse.

Once these connections were made, it was possible to rethink some of these practices. For example, the organization evolved a team structure that included people with these "secondary skills." They also renamed these teams to indicate the importance of the work of all participants, and they began to rethink the need for continuous travel and to consider alternative ways of collaborating across borders. All of this led to better models of learning and knowledge management, both in the home office and in relation to their partners overseas.

UNDERLYING ASSUMPTIONS

This case example shows how separate spheres thinking creates assumptions around commitment and competence that impede not only work-family integration but also work effectiveness. Indeed, our work has shown that commitment, competence, and time are key areas to consider when looking for leverage points of change.

Commitment. Commitment, like competence, is a critical attribute expected of top performers, those who are worthy of fast track status. But how is it to be gauged? What separate spheres thinking leads to are indicators that involve time (discussed in a later section), as well as being able to display those masculine characteristics previously associated with doing good work:

- Doing whatever it takes—demonstrating that work comes *first*, going to extraordinary lengths, and never questioning the wisdom or effectiveness of what you are asked to do.
- Rewarding acts of heroic individualism—jumping in at the last minute to save the project, even if it was your poor planning that created the emergency in the first place; hoarding information rather than sharing it; creating competition by pitting people against each other (e.g., sales teams).

Though such norms seem as if they exist for the sake of the work, often there are other things holding them in place.

We saw this in the case example just given where taking on anything, especially travel, was seen as the highest form of commitment to the mission of the organization. Another example comes from a unit we worked with where one way of demonstrating commitment was always to have the answer to anything that comes up, to never show you might not know something. This led to dysfunctional norms about not asking questions, even clarifying questions. So if someone, especially a higher-up, asked for financial projections, people often worked up multiple scenarios when only one or two were actually needed or they created reports with sophisticated charts when only "back of the envelope" preliminary ideas were called for. Asking questions that would establish boundaries—like what do you really want here—was almost taboo and might mark you as unwilling or unable to go the extra mile, as not being sufficiently committed. From the equity point of view, extra time spent doing things that are not needed or even used adds stress and informal overtime. But this also clearly is not an effective way of doing work, because it results in so-called *re-do's*—scenarios that do not quite fit the bill and hence have to be done over.

Similarly, the engineering manager who said he identifies his best workers as those who "never know enough to go home" shares this definition of commitment. In other words, employees must give their first and only priority to their paid work in order to be seen as committed. Indeed, one classic text on commitment includes in its definition the "willingness to make personal sacrifices" (Kinlaw, 1989, p. 5).

Work practices that have sprung up based on this construction of commitment often lead to overwork, long hours, and a lack of support and collaboration, all of which have clear implications for personal life. And they interestingly contravene many strategic initiatives about process and quality improvement that try to get people thinking outside the box and working smart and efficiently.

Competence. Two issues underlie the dysfunctional assumptions about competence: issues of control and the narrow definition of *real work*. The latter was particularly evident in the example given above, where the most important work was narrowly defined as the creation of new projects at the expense of implementation and follow through. Not only did this emphasis on travel and on creating new projects work against the life needs of those with outside responsibilities (mainly women), it also devalued the jobs in which women tended to cluster—those in synthesizing and following through. This narrow definition of real work undermined the effectiveness of the overall project as well as the ability of all to work up to their true potential. And, of course, it created stress and work overload for everyone as well.

Our work shows that this narrow construction of competence is quite common in organizations and, as in the case example above, often has negative business as well as work-family and gender equity consequences. A separate spheres lens helps us understand why. Because the spheres are constructed as *dichotomous* (separate, at odds, and unequally valued), the stereotypical masculine attributes and behaviors associated with the public sphere are more highly prized than those associated with the feminine gendered domestic sphere. Thus, behaviors not in line with idealized images of masculinity are often devalued or even invisible in what is counted as real work, even when this invisible work is critical to success.

For example, in other organizations we have found assumptions about competence and real work that overemphasize technical capability and individual achievement, while deemphasizing equally important skills such as facilitating collective achievement, team building, or the ability to relate effectively to peers and external customers. While most managers would say that both sets of skills are important to success, we find that when push comes to shove, the technical skills are given precedence. The fact that people who have overly developed technical skills may be *deficient* in relational skills is often overlooked. Indeed, the lack of relational skills—especially in men—is rarely seen as a problem. Instead, it is often assumed that these skills will somehow be gained on the job.

The equity problem is that people who have skills developed from their personal lives are not necessarily at an advantage (Fletcher, 1999), because these skills are seen as feminine, "nice" things to have but their link to effectiveness is not made. Thus, the potential link and synergy between the two spheres—for example, how having multiple responsibilities is linked to high performance—is not made. Instead, people who get burnt out because of the stress of the job are seen as not competent enough, and it is seen as their problem, not necessarily a problem for the unit and its work.

Such constructions of competence also reflect one of the most deeply held assumptions about how to *produce things*—that is, that work is best done when people in charge are good at giving directions and others are good at taking directions. Though the new rhetoric in business is that command and control need to shift to empowerment and self-management, we found that deeply embedded beliefs about hierarchy and control show up in many work practices that have equity and effectiveness implications.

For example, in one clerical group there was a strong belief that supervisors must be there when their people are. This meant that despite progressive flextime policies, schedules were rigid and there was very little flexibility beyond one hour before and one hour later, because that was all the supervisors could handle. Or in another example in an engineering site, supervisors were continually checking on the engineers and asking them for status reports to pass on to their managers—clearly a waste of time for all involved. Such patterns of belief are thrown into relief when the lens of separate spheres thinking is applied, because they emerge from the notion of the ideal worker whose only priority is to his employment and his (or her) responsibilities in the private sphere can safely be ignored (Kanter, 1977).

Time. As is clear from previous discussion, time creates problems when it is used as an indicator to judge commitment and competence. It means that work practices—particularly those surrounding evaluation—are based on the assumption that the best workers are those who are willing and able to devote as much time to work as it seems to demand; in other words, that "time is cheap." There are countless examples, like the marketing team in a high-tech company that was so crisis-driven that it continually had to pull all-nighters to deliver a proposal to a client on time. Lack of planning and coordination is so rampant in places like this that some even talk about the 24-hour rule: If it is not due in the next 24 hours, don't talk to me about it because I can't focus on it. Separate spheres thinking allows such patterns to emerge and contributes to the dynamics that have been identified as leading to the "firefighting" mode of operation (Repenning, 2001).

Not only the use of time but the politics of time is embedded in separate spheres thinking. One team we worked with had so-called voluntary early morning meetings (at 7 A.M.) before the start of the workday to discuss problems and work flow. In another team decisions that were made by the group during the day were often reversed in after-hours discussions between the boss and those who hung around late. Such patterns clearly disempower workers with responsibilities of care.

Work practices like pulling all-nighters seem to be based on the needs of the work and therefore unchangeable. But when people are given an opportunity to talk about the costs of these practices—costs not only to personal life but to the quality of the work—the possibility for change emerges. For example, when the people on the marketing team discussed the all-nighter norm, it became apparent that although the people who pull all-nighters are seen as heroes that morning, they often crash during the afternoon and go home for the day. The rest of the team now has to put on hold other projects that required input from those who are gone, which leads to scheduling backups and situations that will require future all-nighters. While these costs are probably obvious to everyone on the team, there is great reluctance to bring them up, because to raise them as an issue risks being labeled a whiner or someone who is not committed or not willing to do what it takes.

The equity and effectiveness implications in situations such as these are easy to see once this integrative lens is used. Unnecessary time at work makes it hard for people to be active contributing members of family and community. And using time as a proxy for high performance is more likely to lead to presentism and inefficiencies than to effectiveness. Common to all these sets of assumptions is that they concern work practices that are in place for reasons other than that they are good for the work, despite the fact that that is usually their stated goal. In most cases, such work practices are rooted in separate spheres thinking and have evolved as opportunities to demonstrate some aspect of ideal work in the occupational sphere.

In summary, the theoretical perspective of the separation of spheres highlights organization processes, practices, and structures that are deeply embedded in assumptions around commitment, competence, and time. As such, they point to potential leverage points for change that could enhance both equity and effectiveness in organizations and would thus enable a competitive society to exist without undermining its care of children, elders, and communities.

MAKING CHANGE

While the theory supporting this approach to change might be straightforward, the change process itself is neither simple nor straightforward. We posit that one reason is because making change of this type is so tightly linked to gendered assumptions about appropriate behavior in the workplace that it engages deeply ingrained issues of gender identity. But if these issues are acknowledged and discussed, as in the examples above, change can and does work. For example, in the finance department where it was not okay to ask clarifying questions, the group came up with a simple solution: They designed an information form with several simple parameters that had to accompany all requests. Since this took the onus off individuals to ask questions, the career consequences of getting proper requirements for a job were diminished. We worked with them to come up with two sets of metrics: one about personal life where they expect benefits in terms of less unpredictability and less overtime or late-night work; and one about work, where there would be fewer re-do's and better quality in the scenarios that were required.

Similarly, the group in which the managers believed they always had to be there if their people were, came up with an experiment that was a self-managed process for scheduling and meeting customer requirements. Finally, a group that was in crisis mode and constantly interrupting each other to get data they needed came up with an experiment they called *quiet time*, where they had time at the beginning or end of the day when no meetings were scheduled and you could not interrupt anyone unless it was life or death for the project (Perlow, 1997). There were double benefits in all these cases. The work of the group is enhanced in some way and the lives of the people doing the work are made easier.

One of the less visible but most effective vehicles for making change is helping people come up with new narratives to discuss their work culture and norms (Ely & Meyerson, 2000; Kolb & Merrill-Sands, 1999). The notion of invisible work, for example—typically done by women—needs to be named in order to be recognized and evaluated in terms of *competence* rather than *niceness* (Fletcher, 1999). Giving voice to hidden processes such as this is a way of surfacing and making discussible the differential impact of seemingly gender-neutral norms, like devaluing certain types of work and overvaluing others. Once people have a language to talk about these things, it is easier not only to suggest changes but also to note times when old norms reassert themselves or when seemingly benign actions are unwittingly undermining the change effort.

In general, we found that a number of conditions must be present to make these kind of changes in work culture and its resulting structures and practices. First, it is important that people at the top understand the business reason for changing the culture and have made the link to the strategic goals of the organization. Second, and at the same time, it needs to be understood that the process itself is highly context-specific and must be based on small wins in particular units (Meyerson & Fletcher, 2000) rather than top-down edicts demanding change. Third, it is important to provide opportunities for reflection, when people can consider what they are learning, and to create occasions for conversations across the hierarchy about what is working and what is not. In organizations pressed for time, this may seem a contradictory expectation. But our experience has been that taking time out for reflection and analysis actually saves time in the end. Furthermore, such mutual inquiry produces the insights necessary to expand the theory of gender's impact on both research and practice. Finally, it is critically important to keep the connection between equity and effectiveness. We found that it is easy to drop one or the other. So, when designing a pilot experiment, it is crucial to have the group work on two kinds of metrics: one related to personal life gains and one to work-improvement gains.

VISIONING INTEGRATION

Our argument for integrating work and personal life, therefore, is not on the *individual level*—the level of lived realities that has been studied both ethnographically (Nippert-Eng 1996) and in all the research surrounding the debate of compensatory versus spillover effects (e.g., Barnett, 1994; Kirchmeyer,

1993)—but on a more abstracted, conceptual *societal level*. What this means, primarily, is legitimating a diverse range of relationships to work: Paid work would no longer be expected to be primary; career choices and opportunities of individuals who seek fulfillment through commitments in both work and personal life would no longer be automatically limited. It would also mean redefining implicit notions of commitment and competence and encouraging and rewarding a more diverse set of skills and contributions.

Such a world would be based on the assumption that everyone—men, women, parents, nonparents—has a personal life. It would bestow legitimacy on this aspect of people's lives and recognize how such legitimacy could actually benefit the effectiveness of the work. Obviously, it would not be a world based on strict equality but on fairness, recognizing that equal opportunity superimposed on unequal constraints is not an equitable arrangement (Bailyn, 1993).

Moving in this direction, we argue, requires understanding how the assumption of separate spheres affects both equity—fairness—and effectiveness. It necessitates a systemic approach that *challenges* gendered concepts of commitment, competence, and time rather than accepting them as gender-neutral standards that individuals can "choose" to accept.

IMPLICATIONS FOR RESEARCH AND PRACTICE

We believe that understanding the effects of separate spheres thinking offers a theoretical perspective that can inform future research and practice in several important ways. First, it highlights the need to engage in research and action that fosters increased *integration* between the spheres, focusing on systemic issues of changing work practices and work cultures more than on individual issues of helping people cope with things the way they are. More specifically, it highlights the need to diminish the separation between these two spheres of life in ways that will *change* both rather than merely reallocating—or balancing—time between them as they currently exist. In practical terms we believe this means that research and practice in the field must take gender—not just sex—seriously; it is not enough merely to divide data by men and women. Taking gender seriously means probing the gendered nature—and differential impact on men and women—of seemingly gender-neutral practices in both the public and private spheres of life. We believe that taking gender seriously requires a specific kind of action research. The details of this approach, something we call Collaborative, Interactive, Action Research (CIAR), are available in *Beyond Work-Family Balance* (Rapoport et al., 2002). While specific methods others use may vary, we believe an intentionally collaborative approach is a key principle in all efforts to link equity to effectiveness. Action researchers cannot understand the dynamics of these links without working closely with their organizational partners. And practitioners need the research skills necessary to surface underlying assumptions if they are to be successful in making change. Moreover, important issues are contextually situated, which requires methods that are participative and particular, not distant and generic.

The second research implication this theoretical framing highlights is the issue of social identity. Historically, the field of work and family research—including our work—has focused primarily on one aspect of social identity: gender. But once we unpack the assumptions underlying the separation of the spheres—and the way these assumptions reflect an outdated ideal life situation based on white, Western, middle-and upper-class norms—we can see that there may be many unexplored implications for other aspects of an ideal worker's social identity such as race, class, and sexual orientation. While the separation of spheres is a myth for almost everyone, only a privileged subset of the population can live *as if* it were true. Thus, professional couples who can live on one salary or afford full-time, live-in nannies have an easier time meeting the implicit definitions of commitment and competence embedded in organizational life. Single parents or people whose career advancement is limited by racism, homophobia, or other institutionalized prejudices will experience the constraints of separate spheres thinking differently. In other words, the negative effects of separate spheres thinking may be ubiquitous but they are not uniform. Taking action to foster integration, therefore, is likely to have a differential impact on the material circumstances of people's lives depending on the way aspects of their social identities interact (e.g., gender *and* race; sexual orientation *and* class). Thus, in thinking about solutions, policies, and practices that would enhance equity between those who have family and community responsibilities and those who can hide or otherwise absolve their responsibilities in these areas, we believe it is important to include social identity as a multidimensional concept. One approach might be to include a multitude of voices in the data collection process, not only to understand the issues but also to devise solutions and remedies.[5]

Finally, we believe that understanding the inner workings of separate spheres thinking and the resulting images of good work, competence, and commitment can serve as a guide for future action research focused on work-culture change. Rather than a single-minded focus on time and flexibility, we believe that a separate spheres lens uncovers other work norms, such as how to demonstrate competence, that are critical leverage points for change. Our work has surfaced some of the relevant norms, but this typology is only a beginning. Additional action research that uses a separate spheres lens is needed to expand the typology and enhance our understanding of how to institutionalize this kind of change. As we noted in an earlier section, changing work cultures by focusing on concrete work practices is a burgeoning area in the field. We argue that because work norms linked to separate spheres thinking might, at first glance, appear to have little to do with work-personal life integration, they may not become evident in initiatives focused only on time and flexibility. Moreover, we believe that the impact of separate spheres thinking on the change process (i.e., the way these work practices are linked to gender identity and a dichotomous view of the world) needs to be made more explicit. Without an understanding and awareness on the part of change agents of how deeply embedded the image of separate spheres is in the psyche of organizational life, its impact on the change process is likely to be underestimated. Our method of dealing with these deeply embedded images is to create many opportunities for people to discuss and reflect and to experiment with and revise the way they work. Our hope is that additional research using this theoretical frame will expand this method.

CONCLUSION

We started this chapter with a new American dilemma: a crisis of care and equity in the richest and most productive nation of the world. Our argument is that we must include equity considerations in the pursuit of effectiveness and competitive strength, and our theoretical perspective explains this necessary link between equity and effectiveness.

The reason they are linked has to do with the consequences of separate spheres thinking and the images it evokes. In terms of equity, it is easy to see that conflating idealized masculinity with work in the public sphere is going to create equity issues for women. Not only might they have more difficulty in pretending they do not have a personal life or family responsibilities, but they might also have more difficulty displaying stereotypically masculine characteristics without negative consequences.[6]

The effectiveness issue has to do with how conflating idealized masculinity with doing this work is problematic for the work itself. In today's knowledge-intensive world where the importance of teamwork and collaboration is increasing, wisdom about people is critical to business success. Work practices that are constrained by gendered images of competence may not be accessing this wisdom and may, in fact, be undermining an organization's ability to meet its goals. Thus, it is easy to see that relaxing the separation and integrating the two spheres of knowledge would have potential benefits for the work itself. This is the basic premise of our book *Beyond Work-Family Balance* (Rapoport et al., 2002): It is possible to challenge conventional wisdom about ideal workers (equity) *and* ideal work (effectiveness) and make changes that benefit both.

In general, linking equity and effectiveness helps one identify dysfunctional work practices in organizations that are rooted in separate spheres thinking. While many of these work practices seem to be driven by the needs of the work, we found that when we use a separate spheres frame to understand them, they are often held in place because they serve another, even more powerful purpose. They give people an opportunity to demonstrate their fit with a traditional image of occupational success: either as an ideal worker for whom time at work is no object or as performing ideal work by displaying stereotypical masculine attributes. In the presence of such powerful images, it is not surprising that creating a truly family-friendly workplace is so difficult. Only with awareness of these gendered dynamics—and their interaction with other aspects of social identity—can we hope to reach a productive and equitable workplace. Hence the equity imperative.

NOTES

1. This project, one of three funded in the early 1990s by the Ford Foundation, had as its goal to use work-personal life as a "catalyst for change" to help organizations change work cultures to make them more family-friendly. Unexpectedly, the findings indicate that changing work cultures to make them more family-friendly also made them more effective. The original members of the research team were Lotte Bailyn, Susan C. Eaton, Joyce K. Fletcher, Maureen Harvey, Robin Johnson, Deborah M. Kolb, Leslie Perlow, and Rhona Rapoport. The report to the Ford Foundation (R. Rapoport, L. Bailyn, D. M. Kolb, J. K. Fletcher, D. E. Friedman, S. C. Eaton, M. Harvey, & B. Miller. [1996.] *Relinking life and work: Toward a better future.* New York: Ford Foundation) describes all three projects.

2. For example, Ragnhild Sohlberg in Norway, Shirley Dex and Suzan Lewis in England, Louise Boelens in the Netherlands. See Rapoport et al., 2002, p. 194, for a brief description of this work.

3. This framing is adapted from Bailyn and Fletcher (2002) and is developed further in Fletcher (forthcoming).

4. It is ironic, for example, that with welfare reform, ideal poor mothers are expected to function effectively in both the paid work and care domains. Nonetheless, organizational practices, norms, and expectations are anchored in these assumptions, and these are the focus of our concern.

5. For one model of how to incorporate a multidimensional concept of social identity into action research, see Holvino (2001).

6. As an aside, the opposite equity issue would be true for men in the domestic sphere. Although we do not focus on this here, it is the flip side of the work-personal life issue at work and is only beginning to be explored.

REFERENCES

Acker, J. (1990). Hierarchies, jobs, bodies: A theory of gendered organizations. *Gender & Society, 4,* 139–158.

Applebaum, E., Berg, P., & Kalleberg, A. L. (2000). Balancing work and family: Effects of high performance work systems and high commitment workplaces. In E. Applebaum (Ed.), *Balancing acts: Easing the burdens and improving the options for working families* (pp. 115–124). Washington, DC: Economic Policy Institute.

Bailyn, L. (1993). *Breaking the mold: Women, men, and time in the new corporate world.* New York: Free Press.

Bailyn, L., & Fletcher, J. K. (2002). *Work redesign: Theory, practice, and possibility.* MIT Workplace Center working paper #4. Cambridge: MIT.

Bailyn, L., Fletcher, J. K., & Kolb, D. M. (1997). Unexpected connections: Considering employees' personal lives can revitalize your business. *Sloan Management Review, 38*(4), 11–19.

Barnett, R. C. (1994). Home-to-work spillover revisited: A study of full-time employed women in dual-earner couples. *Journal of Marriage and the Family, 56,* 647–656.

Barnett, R. C., & Rivers, C. (1996). *She works/he works: How two-income families are happier, healthier, and better off.* San Francisco: HarperCollins.

Batt, R., & Valcour, P. M. (2003). Human resource practices as predictors of work-family outcomes and employee turnover. *Industrial Relations, 42*(2), 189–220.

Bellah, R. N. (1985). *Habits of the heart: Individualism and commitment in American life.* Berkeley: University of California Press.

Bond, J. T., Galinsky, E., & Swanberg, J. E. (1998). *The 1997 National Study of the Changing Workforce.* New York: Families and Work Institute.

Calás, M. B., & Smircich, L. (1991). Using the "f" word: Feminist theories and the social consequences of organizational research. In A. J. Mills & P. Tancred (Eds.), *Gendering organizational analysis* (pp. 222–234). London: Sage Publications.

Casner-Lotto, J. (2000). *Holding a job, having a life: Strategies for change.* Scarsdale, NY: Work in American Institute.

Costello, C., with S. C. Kolb, & W. N. Johnson (2002). *Designing work for life: A report on three work redesign projects in the U.S. Department of Health & Human Services.* Washington, DC: U.S. Department of Health & Human Services.

Diamond, I., & Quinby, L. (1988). *Feminism and Foucault.* Boston: Northeastern University Press.

Ely, R. J., & Meyerson, D. E. (2000). Theories of gender in organizations: A new approach to organizational analysis and change. In B. M. Staw & R. L. Sutton (Eds.), *Research in Organizational Behavior* (pp. 103–151). New York: JAI Press.

Flax, J. (1990). *Thinking fragments.* Berkeley: University of California Press.

Fletcher, J. K. (1999). *Disappearing acts: Gender, power and relational practice at work.* Cambridge: MIT Press.

Fletcher, J. K. (forthcoming). Gender perspectives on work and personal life research. In S. M. Bianchi, L. M. Casper, K. E. Christensen, & R. B. King (Eds.), *Workforce/workplace mismatch? Work, family, health, and well-being.* Washington, DC: National Institutes of Health.

Fletcher, J. K., & Bailyn, L. (1996). Challenging the last boundary: Reconnecting work and family. In M. B. Arthur & D. M. Rousseau (Eds.), *The boundaryless career: A new employment principle for a new organizational era.* (pp. 256–267). Oxford, England: Oxford University Press.

Greenwald, J. (2001, June 18). Rank and fire. *Time, 157,* 38–40.

Harrington, M. (1999). *Care and equality: Inventing a new family politics.* New York: Knopf.

Holvino, E. (2001). *Complicating gender: The simultaneity of race, gender and class in organization change(ing).* CGO Insight #14. Boston: Center for Gender in Organizations.

Kanter, R. M. (1977). *Work and family in the United States: A critical review and agenda for research and policy.* New York: Russell Sage Foundation.

Kellogg, K. (2002). *When less is more: Exploring the relationship between employee workload and innovation potential.* CGO Insight #11. Boston: Center for Gender and Organizations.

Kinlaw, D. C. (1989). *Coaching for commitment: Managerial strategies for obtaining superior performance.* San Diego: University Associates.

Kirchmeyer, C. (1993). Nonwork-to-work spillover: A more balanced view of the experiences and coping of professional women and men. *Sex Roles, 28*(9/10), 531–552.

Kolb, D. M., & Merrill-Sands, D. (1999). Waiting for outcomes: Anchoring a dual agenda for change to cultural assumptions. *Women in Management Review, 14*(5), 194–202.

Merrill-Sands, D., Fletcher, J. K., & Acosta, A. (1999). Engendering organizational change: A case study of strengthening gender-equity and organizational effectiveness in an international agricultural research institute. In A. Rao, R. Stuart & D. Kelleher (Eds.), *Gender at work: Organizational change for equality* (pp. 77–128). West Hartford, CT: Kumarian Press.

Meyerson, D., & Fletcher, J. K. (2000, January–February). A modest manifesto for shattering the glass ceiling. *Harvard Business Review, 78,* 127–136.

Nippert-Eng, C. E. (1996). *Home and work: Negotiating boundaries through everyday life.* Chicago: University of Chicago Press.

Perlow, L. A. (1997). *Finding time: How corporations, individuals, and families can benefit from new work practices.* Ithaca, NY: ILR Press.

Rapoport, R., Bailyn, L., Fletcher, J. K., & Pruitt, B. H. (2002). *Beyond work-family balance: Advancing gender equity and workplace performance.* San Francisco: Jossey-Bass.

Rapoport, R., Bailyn, L., Kolb, D. M., Fletcher, J. K., Friedman, S. C., Eaton, S. C., Harvey, M., & Miller, B. (1996). Rethinking life and work: Toward a better future. Report. New York: Ford Foundation.

Rayman, P. M., Bailyn, L., Dickert, J., & Carre, F. (1999). Designing organizational solutions to integrate work and life. *Women in Management Review, 14,* 164–176.

Repenning, N. P. (2001). Understanding fire fighting in new product development. *Journal of Product Innovation Management, 18,* 285–300.

Ruderman, M. N., & Ohlott, P. J. (2002). *Standing at the crossroads: Next steps for high-achieving women.* San Francisco: Jossey-Bass.

Valcour, P. M., & Batt, R. (2003). Work-life integration: Challenges and organizational responses. In P. Moen (Ed.), *It's about time: Couples and careers* (pp. 310–33). Ithaca, NY: Cornell University Press.

Welter, B. (1966). The cult of true womanhood: 1820–1860. *American Quarterly, 18*(2), 151–174.

Williams, J. (1999). *Unbending gender: Why family and work conflict and what to do about it.* New York: Oxford University Press.

Yancey Martin, P., & Collinson, D. L. (1998). Gender and sexuality in organizations. In M. M. Ferree, J. Lorder, & B. Hess (Eds.), *Revisioning gender* (pp. 285–310) London: Sage Publications.

III

Individual Perspectives

10

The Importance of the Individual: How Self-Evaluations Influence the Work-Family Interface

Alyssa Friede
Ann Marie Ryan
Michigan State University

Research on engagement in work and family roles often focuses on environmental influences (e.g., supervisor, organizational climate, social policy) on individual's emotions, cognitions, and behaviors. Several researchers (e.g., Carlson, 1999; Lockwood, Casper, Eby, & Bordeaux, 2002; Sumer & Knight, 2001; Wayne, Musisca, & Fleeson, 2004) have suggested that personality be given greater consideration in understanding how an individual views and experiences multiple life roles. This chapter outlines the ways in which personality may influence how individuals feel about and react to the interface between their work and family lives. While we believe our model can be applicable to how disposition influences engagement in multiple life roles, we focus our discussion on work and family roles due to a more abundant literature to draw upon in illustrating influences.

In order to develop a descriptive model, we have adopted a theory from the stress literature and integrated work-family research on multiple role engagement into that framework. Bolger and Zuckerman (1995) propose a model that describes the differential pathways by which personality can influence stress. They use a stressor-strain model in which stressors exist as environmental realities, whereas strain is the emotional experiences that result from the stressors (Bolger & Zuckerman, 1995). First, they suggest that personality can influence what they call "differential exposure" to stressors. That is, personality may influence the actual number or type of events that a person experiences that can cause stress. Second, personality may lead to "differential reactivity," or individual differences in the felt intensity or reaction to stressors (Bolger & Zuckerman, 1995). Two subcomponents of differential reactivity, according to Bolger and Zuckerman (1995), are "differential coping choice," in which individuals with different personality types may select different means of coping with stressors, and "differential coping effectiveness," in which certain coping strategies may be more effective for people with certain personality traits or people with certain dispositions may be more skilled at using certain coping strategies.

This stressor-strain model will serve as the foundation for this chapter on the influence of personality on the work-family interface. First, we describe and elaborate on the model as it applies to engaging in work and family roles. Next, we provide illustrations to delineate the possible ways in which personality can influence an individual's experience of and reaction to work and family roles. Our goal is to show how personality can affect both the depleting and enriching processes that arise from engaging in multiple roles. Finally, we take a step back to discuss broader issues with operationalizing some of the elements of the model.

THE EFFECTS OF ENGAGEMENT IN WORK AND FAMILY ROLES: POSITIVE AND NEGATIVE?

Traditional research on the work-family interface has tended to focus on the negative outcomes associated with work and family roles (Hanson, Colton, & Hammer, 2003; Wayne et al., 2004). That is, most researchers have focused on the *conflict* associated with the management of these two roles (e.g., Frone, Russell, & Cooper, 1992). The widely accepted and used term *work-family conflict* focuses on the fact that engaging in one role makes participation in the other role more difficult (Greenhaus & Beutell, 1985). It is defined as a type of interrole conflict in which the competing demands of work and family roles are incompatible (Greenhaus & Beutell, 1985). Recently, however, researchers have begun to address the fact that the potential benefits of engaging in work and family roles have largely been overlooked (Brockwood, Hammer, & Neal, 2003; Hanson et al., 2003). Researchers who have studied the positive side of the work-family interface have called the positive correlate of work-family conflict "enrichment" (Rothbard, 2001), "facilitation" (Grzywacz & Bass, 2003), and "positive spillover" (Brockwood et al., 2003). In contrast to the difficulties associated with work-family conflict, enrichment occurs when having multiple roles provides benefits to the individual (Rothbard, 2001). We feel that it is important to address both the positive and negative outcomes that can be associated with managing work and family roles and will use the term *conflict* to address the negative aspects of the work-family interface and the term *enrichment* to address the positive ones. It is important to note that there is limited research on the enriching potential of multiple roles (Rothbard, 2001). Thus, while we reference more research related to work-family conflict in this chapter, we do not argue that work-family conflict is any more likely or influential than work-family enrichment.

MODEL OF PERSONALITY'S EFFECT ON WORK AND FAMILY ROLE ENGAGEMENT

As Fig. 10.1 illustrates, there are a number of ways in which personality can influence the relationship between work and family role requirements and reactions to them:

1. Personality may affect the actual type and amount of work and family role requirements that an individual experiences. Individuals may self-select into more challenging or supportive environments based on their personality, thus making work-family management easier or more challenging.
2. Personality may influence the perceptions of work and family role requirements in the environment. Even under the same conditions, individuals with different personality types may perceive situations as involving work-family conflict or as enriching or may differ in the magnitude of their perceptions.
3. Personality may influence the strategies selected to approach the work-family interface, which may influence the amount of felt emotional strain

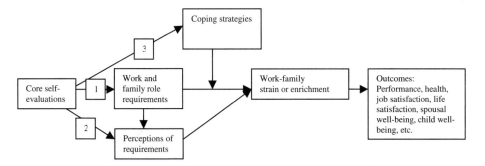

FIG. 10.1.   Personality's influence on work and family role engagement.

or enrichment. This can be through the choice of coping strategy or the effectiveness of the coping strategy chosen.

While we expect that this model can be applied to assess the influence of any number of personality traits, theory and research on work-family conflict, multiple role engagement, stress, and personality can be used to inform which dispositional tendencies are likely to have the greatest influence. In the past, research on disposition and work-family conflict has examined traits such as the Big Five and negative affectivity (see Bruck & Allen, 2003; Carlson, 1999, for examples). Based on our review of these literatures, we focus the remainder of this chapter on the traits thought to comprise the overarching concept of core self-evaluations (Judge, Locke, & Durham, 1997). Core self-evaluations are described as the fundamental premises individuals hold about themselves or the extent to which individuals possess a positive self-concept (Judge, Erez, & Bono, 1998). The four traits that make up this higher level construct are self-esteem, generalized self-efficacy, locus of control, and emotional stability. In this chapter we provide a new angle on both Bolger and Zuckerman's (1995) model and Judge, Erez, and Bono's (1998) core self-evaluations by discussing them in the context of the work-family interface. We feel that a focus on core self-evaluations provides the best illustration of personality's influence on the work-family interface because they reflect overall perceptions that individuals have of themselves. While the model can be applied to other personality traits, it is not within the scope of this chapter to posit all possible influences. Our goal is to illustrate the paths in the model with the traits we believe to be highly influential, the core self-evaluations.

CORE SELF-EVALUATIONS

Core self-evaluations are a latent, multivariate construct or a compound personality variable in that it comprises four more specific traits (Judge, Erez, & Bono, 1998). Judge, Erez, and Bono (1998) define the core self-evaluations as follows. *Self-esteem* is the overall value one places on oneself as a person. *Generalized self-efficacy* is a judgment of how well one can perform across a variety of situations. *Locus of control* is the perceived degree of control in life. Individuals with internal loci of control see themselves as in charge of what happens to them. Individuals with external loci of control see factors external to themselves (such as powerful others or luck) as responsible for what happens to them (Rotter, 1966). *Emotional stability/neuroticism* is the tendency to experience negative or positive affective states. Note that Judge and Bono (2001) argue that meta-analytic evidence indicates that negative affectivity is simply a measure of neuroticism, and Judge, Locke, Durham, and Kluger (1998) note that negative affectivity loads on the same factor as core self-evaluations; thus, we discuss findings regarding negative affectivity as part of the core self-evaluation of neuroticism.

In a meta-analysis Judge, Erez, and Bono (1998) found fairly substantial true correlations between the four traits (.36 to .86 in magnitude; see also Judge & Bono, 2001), and a principal components analysis of the meta-analyzed correlations indicated one factor. Erez and Judge (2001) also found a higher order factor and found that the traits predicted motivation and performance better as a set. They note that although each trait has a unique component that may lead to differential relations with outcomes, considering the set of traits together may improve prediction and understanding. Thus, whereas one can expect these traits to have relationships of differing magnitudes with various outcomes of interest, overall similar predictions can be made for the set (Judge, Erez, & Bono, 1998; Judge, Locke, et al., 1998).

We now turn to placing the core self-evaluations within our model to illustrate how personality might influence multiple role engagement.

Pathway 1: Differential Work and Family Environments

Diener, Larson, and Emmons (1984) note that individuals seek out situations based on their personality, such that positively disposed individuals experience more positive events in life (Magnus, Diener, Fujita, & Payot, 1993). Judge, Erez, and Bono (1998) have noted how self-consistency theory (Korman, 1970) suggests that individuals will seek out and be satisfied with roles that maximize cognitive consistency; those with more positive self-evaluations will choose situations in which they can be competent and avoid those in which they cannot. Thus, individuals low in core self-evaluations may actually experience more negative home and work events (i.e., more stressors). Those high in core self-evaluations may seek out enriching rather than depleting situations.

With regard to the work role, Judge, Bono, and Locke (2000) showed that those with more positive core self-evaluations held more complex jobs (i.e., more challenging and more intrinsically satisfying) and therefore had greater job satisfaction. In 1995, Spector, Jex, and Chen found that individuals high in optimism tend to be in jobs with higher autonomy, skill variety, and task identity. Additionally, Burke, Brief, and George (1993) suggest that individuals with high negative affectivity may influence coworkers to respond to them in certain ways (e.g., being unsupportive), creating an environment that is more stressful than the environment of individuals with supportive coworkers. For example, an individual who often laments how much he or she has to do will receive less offers of help in a crunch than the coworker who seldom moans. Spector (1982) also suggests that cognitive consistency explains why individuals with high internal loci of control tend to be more satisfied with their jobs—they believe they can choose to leave or stay in a job situation. Individuals who do not feel that they are in control of their environment may not actively seek out work or home environments that allow them flexibility and control over their work or family schedules. Further, research shows that individuals with an internal locus of control have more sources of social support available to them (Hansson, Jones, & Carpenter, 1984; Jones, 1982).

In terms of the family role, evidence exists that core self-evaluations may influence characteristics of one's family environment, thus influencing the challenges or benefits associated with managing multiple roles. Van Os, Park, and Jones (2001) demonstrate that neuroticism assessed in adolescence predicted the occurrence of stressful life events among adults in their thirties and forties. Researchers have also found relationships between the components of core self-evaluations and marital and family outcomes (e.g., Larson, Anderson, Holman, & Niemann, 1998; Shackelford, 2001; Voss, Markiewicz, & Doyle, 1999). However, it is difficult to tell from these studies the pathway by which these personality traits influence the stressful and enriching qualities of the family environment. That is, the authors do not address the process by which certain personality styles lead to certain family outcomes. However, some research does indicate that the core self-evaluations of an individual may influence objective characteristics of the family environment that they live in. In terms of parent-child relationships, Aunola, Nurmi, Onatsu-Arvilommi, and Pulkkinen (1999) found that parental self-esteem is related to authoritarian parenting styles. It is, therefore, possible that personality (through its influence on parenting style) alters the family environment that an individual must deal with (e.g., whether children are more or less obedient) thus influencing how difficult it is for individuals to balance the responsibilities of their work and family lives. Larson et al. (1998) found that the self-esteem of a wife is the best premarital predictor of a husband's marital sexual satisfaction. The personality of a spouse may directly influence the quality of a marriage and the ease with which individuals can manage both work and family simultaneously.

In sum, individuals with less positive core self-evaluations may *self-select* into work and family environments that are more stress laden and not supportive of obligations in the other domain. Furthermore, negative core self-evaluations may lead to the *creation* of greater stress because of how others respond to the individual. In contrast, those with positive core self-evaluations may self-select into work and family situations that are enriching.

Pathway 2: Perceptions of Work and Family Roles

Judge, Locke, Durham, and Kluger (1998) note that the positive frame of those with more positive self-concepts influences how they appraise situations. Thus, not only do those with more positive core self-evaluations have more positive work situations as noted earlier, they also perceive characteristics of the same job (or family life) more positively than those with more negative self-evaluations. For example, neuroticism affects whether one's role requirements are seen as stressful. Fogarty, Machin, Albion, Sutherland, Lalor, and Revitt (1999) discuss the possibility that one reason for the relationship between negative affectivity and self-reports of environmental stressors is that individuals with high negative affectivity may be more likely to interpret stimuli negatively. Larsen (1992) found that people high in negative affectivity tend to encode more negative information about themselves and situations (see also Moyle, 1995).

There is considerable evidence that those with more positive dispositions rate tasks or jobs as more enriched than those with less positive outlooks (James & Jones, 1980; Judge, Locke et al., 1998; Necowitz & Roznowski, 1994). Levin and Stokes (1989) found that individuals high in negative affectivity perceive their jobs as containing fewer desirable characteristics than do low negative affectivity individuals and that those individuals high in negative affectivity may attend more selectively to the negative aspects of their jobs. In an experimental manipulation, the authors found that subjects high in negative affectivity reported less task satisfaction than subjects low in negative affectivity, even when controlling for task type (Levin & Stokes, 1989). For locus of control, researchers have found that externals report more job stressors and a lack of professional latitude as compared to individuals with an internal locus of control (Hahn, 2000).

Core self-evaluations may also be related to perceptions of stressors in the family domain. For example, Narayanan and Venkatachalam (1980) found that females who are neurotic tend to perceive more problems with family interactions than do non-neurotic females. Camp and Ganong (1997) also found that couples in which both partners had an internal locus of control report more satisfaction with their marriage than do other couples. Of course, these results may be related to pathway 1 (environmental self-selection), but it is also plausible that these self-reports of family problems, marital satisfaction, and so forth, are related to a tendency of an individual to view situations in a positive light and perceive control within him- or herself (based on personality) rather than solely as a result of the actual environments. For example, a commuter marriage (where one spouse lives away for work for some period of time) can be seen as enriching, leading to renewed appreciation for family time, boosting the independence and self-confidence of family members, and facilitating the redefining of work and family boundaries in a positive way (Jackson, 2003). Perceptions by individuals with positive core self-evaluations of both the work and family domains as less stressful may lead to a decreased perception of conflicts between the two and an increased belief in the enhancing qualities of the interaction between the two roles.

In general, core self-evaluations may be related to how interactions between work and family are perceived. For example, an individual who views the world negatively and believes that he or she has little control may see a situation in which a child's doctor appointment is at the same time as an important meeting as a stressor because he or she perceives that he or she cannot control the environment and that this time conflict is unavoidable and problematic. However, a more positive, self-efficacious person may perceive control in this situation (like the ability to reschedule the meeting or ask a friend or relative to take the child to the doctor appointment) and see it as another example of the way in which he or she has control over work and family lives and can successfully meet obligations in both roles.

There is, thus, some research to suggest that even when controlling for actual aspects of the environment, individuals with less positive core self-evaluations may perceive the environment more negatively. Indeed, core self-evaluations may influence whether one perceives engagement in multiple roles as depleting or enriching (Rothbard, 2001). That is, whether one views oneself as having limited resources and engaging in multiple roles as requiring trade-offs or whether one sees a greater number of role commitments as leading to a benefit may relate to one's core self-evaluations.

Pathway 3: Use of Coping Strategies

Coping is defined as efforts, both cognitive and behavioral, used to deal with events that are appraised as stressful (Lazarus & Folkman, 1984). Coping strategies are typically divided into those that are problem-focused (attempting to identify the problem and act in ways to eliminate it or thwart it, thus reducing strain) and those that are emotion-focused (reducing strain through altering emotions regarding the stressor, such as avoidance and distancing) (Aryee, Luk, Leung, & Lo, 1999). The type of coping strategy selected has been shown to be related to the experience of work-family strain and overall well-being. For example, Aryee et al. (1999) found that individuals who use more problem-focused coping experience less work-family conflict.

As noted earlier, core self-evaluations can affect both the choice of coping strategy and effectiveness in deploying a strategy. Researchers have found locus of control and self-efficacy to link to the effectiveness of coping (Anderson, 1977; Bandura, 1997). Furthermore, poor self-concept has been related to a number of negative coping strategies, such as substance abuse, binge eating, and suicide attempts (Baumeister, 1997). Additionally, individuals with low core self-evaluations may be less effective at implementing certain coping strategies to alleviate strain. Cimbolic Gunthert, Cohen, and Armeli (1999) found that even when more neurotic individuals employed the same coping strategies as less neurotic individuals, they were still less effective.

Judge, Erez, and Bono (1998) note that control theory research shows that individuals with high self-esteem, high self-efficacy, and an internal locus of control tend to increase their efforts when performance does not meet standards, whereas those with negative self-concepts either lower standards or withdraw from a task when given negative feedback. In the case of multiple role engagement, individuals with positive self-concepts will respond to information that they are not fulfilling their role obligations to their standard by increasing their efforts to do so; those with negative self-evaluations will be more likely to shift their standards (e.g., being home for dinner with the family each night or obtaining a promotion are not goals anymore) or to withdraw from the situation. As another example, low self-esteem individuals have been shown to overgeneralize the negative implications of failure (Brown & Dutton, 1995). After a failure to negotiate successfully a work and family role conflict, low self-esteem individuals may tend to generalize that failure experience to future attempts to negotiate these roles.

Judge, Erez, and Bono (1998) suggest that locus of control and self-efficacy have strong influences on whether individuals adopt an optimistic or a pessimistic coping style (Seligman & Schulman, 1986). That is, learned helplessness researchers have indicated that individuals with more pessimistic evaluation styles are more likely to display helplessness deficits (e.g., lower their effort, withdraw from task) when faced with a bad event than individuals with more optimistic evaluation styles (Seligman, Abramson, Semmel, & von Baeyer, 1979). Judge, Erez, and Bono (1998) suggest that those with an internal locus of control will perceive bad events as less stable and will possess a more optimistic evaluation style, and those with high generalized self-efficacy will believe in their ability to change bad situations. Thus, when work and family role demands conflict, those with a more optimistic evaluation style will believe it is a fixable situation, whereas those with a lower self-evaluation will make a more pessimistic evaluation and be more likely to engage in helplessness types of behaviors.

However, it is important to consider the complexities associated with trying to use coping strategies that attempt to fix or control the situation. In reality, some situations are more controllable than others. Researchers such as Miller and Kirsch (1987) and Mak and Mueller (2000) have suggested that the ability to control the situation may influence the effectiveness of certain coping strategies. That is, problem-focused, action-oriented coping strategies (which are more likely to be used by individuals with an internal locus of control) may be less effective when the situation is less controllable (Parkes, 1990). Krause and Stryker (1984) found that, when faced with uncontrollable stressors, having an extremely internal locus of control is no better than having a moderate external locus of control. Noor (2002) similarly found that for women in situations outside of their control, having an internal orientation is not helpful. Furthermore, work and family domains may be differentially controllable and using strategies that are effective in one domain but not the other may intensify the difficulties associated with the work-family interface. Mak and Mueller (2000) write that certain coping strategies effective in the personal domain may be less effective in the work domain because of a decreased ability to control the environment.

Parkes (1990) also states that "some research suggests that coping strategies that are effective in domestic and marital settings may fail to alleviate distress in occupation settings or may alleviate stress only to a limited extent" (p. 399).

The use of ineffective coping strategies by individuals with low core self-evaluations might be especially important in engagement in work and family roles. Because individuals have to manage the interface between both their work and home lives and interact with numerous others in these situations (bosses, coworkers, spouses, and children), managing the boundary between work and family may provide a particularly intense and complicated situation where the selection of coping strategies is important. For example, coping with the stressor of an unexpected increase in workload may be challenging, but attempting to manage this increased workload while meeting family obligations is even more challenging. Judge, Erez, and Bono (1998) note that core self-evaluations give people the ability to cope better with change, and the authors cite several studies indicating that those with a positive self-concept cope more effectively with organizational transformations. Ormel and Wohlfarth (1991) found that life situation changes were much more strongly related to distress for individuals high on neuroticism than for individuals low on neuroticism. This suggests an increased sensitivity to life changes on the part of individuals high on neuroticism that may be due, at least in part, to difficulties in coping with these changes (Ormel & Wohlfarth, 1991). Johnson and Sarason (1978) found that the relationship between life changes and depression is significant only for individuals with an external locus of control. The implication is that as changes occur in one's work or family roles (e.g., a promotion, the birth of a child, an elderly parent moving in), those with more positive self-evaluations would be able to cope better with such changes. We would also speculate that the ability to enhance one's life via change may be connected to self-evaluations.

In sum, research has shown that there are many ways in which core self-evaluations influence stress and enhancement. Differences in environments, differences in reactivity to stressors, differences in coping choice, and differences in coping effectiveness are all ways in which core self-evaluations may influence the experience of work-family conflict and work-family enrichment. However, this is not to say that individuals with positive core self-evaluations will always experience less conflict and more enrichment than will individuals with low core self-evaluations. Remember that having an internal locus of control in an uncontrollable situation can lead to frustration and adverse outcomes (Krause & Stryker, 1984; Noor, 2002). Furthermore, being overly positive about one's self and one's environment may lead to unrealistic expectations and unrealistic perceptions of the environment. It is possible that this optimism may negatively impact the work-family interface by causing people to perceive that everything is going well when, in fact, it is not. For example, Peterson (2000) writes that individuals who are overly optimistic may neglect their health and health maintenance activities. Oettingen (1996) argues that people may not make concrete plans as to how to attain their goals if they engage in wishful thinking. Thus, while the literature suggests that the benefits of positive core self-evaluations outweigh the negatives, highly positive core self-evaluations may not be ideal in all situations, including those related to managing the work-family interface.

IMPLICATIONS FOR THEORY, RESEARCH, AND PRACTICE

Next, we turn our attention to how the model and reasoning described in this chapter might affect work-life theory, research, and practice.

Implications for Theory

Work-family research has been studied using numerous theoretical frameworks. We chose to focus on a framework from the stress literature to examine the pathways by which personality may relate to the perceptions that the work and family domains are conflicting with each other or enriching each other. This framework should be related also to some of the more commonly used operationalizations of work-family conflict.

One traditional way of conceptualizing work-family conflict is to categorize conflict as family interfering with work or work interfering with family (see Duxbury, Higgins, & Lee, 1994; Perrewe, Hochwarter, & Kiewitz, 1999; Stoeva, Chiu, & Greenhaus, 2002, for examples). Sometimes conflicts exist as a choice between the priorities of the two domains. However, the perceptions of a situation as family interfering with work or work interfering with family may be related to personality. For example, an individual with an internal locus of control may perceive a less controllable home environment to be interfering with a more controllable work environment because of his or her inability to use preferred coping strategies in the home environment and his or her ability to use them in the work domain. Researchers who choose to study work-family conflict within the framework of domain interference should acknowledge that perceptions of family interfering with work (FIW) or work interfering with family (WIF) do not necessarily stem from objective realities of the work and family situations. That is, personality may directly influence whether a work-related appointment that conflicts with a child's school play is viewed as WIF or FIW. Furthermore, job or family characteristics may interact with personality characteristics to influence perceptions regarding the direction of interference. For example, self-efficacy may interact with characteristics of the job or family environment such as competence in parenting or on the job to influence the perceived direction of the conflict. Locus of control may interact with actual job or family controllability, as well. Researchers should examine personality for its direct influences on the perceptions of the direction of interference as well as interactions between personality and job characteristics when attempting to explain WIF or FIW.

Work-family conflict is also frequently conceptualized and operationalized in terms of time-, behavior-, and strain-based conflict. Greenhaus and Beutell (1985) define time-based conflict as conflict that arises because time pressures in one domain interfere with the fulfillment of obligations in the other domain. They define strain-based conflict as conflict that arises because strain (or fatigue) in one role affects the ability to meet the demands of the other role. Behavior-based conflict is when behaviors in one role are incompatible with the behaviors necessary in the other role (Greenhaus & Beutell, 1985). Researchers have found little empirical support for behavior-based conflict, though (Greenhaus, Parasuraman, Granrose, Rabinowitz, & Beutell, 1989). As this is a commonly utilized framework, researchers ought to take into account the ways in which personality may differentially affect experiences of these different types of conflict. For example, it is possible that individuals with positive core self-evaluations may be less likely to experience strain-based conflict due to their positivity and internal locus of control. However, these individuals may be equally likely to experience time-based conflict as individuals with low core self-evaluations because their personalities may not affect how much time they have to or want to dedicate to their responsibilities in each domain. Although this is simply hypothesizing, these relationships are worth examining.

At a broader level this chapter highlights the need for a greater recognition of individual differences in work-life theorizing. That is, most theoretical perspectives look at structural or situational influences (e.g., organizational policy, demographic composition of the workforce) on an individual's experience without directly considering how the individual creates his or her own experience. While contextual influences are certainly important to understanding the challenges faced at the work life interface, theories often ignore the individual as an actor. Some may ignore this because of a concern that focusing on individual differences, such as personality, as a key influence on work-family conflict and work-life enhancement may lead to viewing problems in work-life balancing as individual responsibilities, with little or no accountability on the part of the firm or of societal institutions. Another concern may be that including a focus on how personality affects perceptions of role engagement may lead to a conclusion that "work-family conflict is all in how you perceive things." Theoretical perspectives should consider an individual's actions and perceptions in conjunction with structural and contextual influences on experienced roles. Theories should recognize that the individual is a key influence on his or her experience of role conflict or enrichment through role choice, role enactment, and role perceptions, while not ignoring or underplaying the influence of firm, job, society, and so forth on role experiences.

Research Implications

This chapter has implications for the way that research on the work-family interface is conducted. Recently, researchers have called for the incorporation of individual differences in the study of the work-family interface (Sumer & Knight, 2001). Researchers should not be content simply to correlate personality factors with work-family conflict or enrichment but should take the step further to examine the causal pathways that are responsible for the observed relationships.

To this end, we suggest that researchers measure objective job and family characteristics when at all possible. As discussed earlier, personality can color self-reports of work and family characteristics. The ramifications of understanding whether perceived rather than objective job or family characteristics are responsible for reported work-family conflict or enrichment are quite large. For example, reporting that supervisor supportiveness is related to work-family conflict may be interesting, but it is important to note whether this is objective (or other-reported) supervisor supportiveness or merely a result of the tendency of an individual to perceive others in a negative light. The assumptions made from this finding and the practical implications associated with it are vastly different depending on whether the observed relationship is due to objective or to perceptual factors.

Researchers may want to examine the interactive effects of multiple individual differences, including personality traits and demographic differences. For example, the effects of personality on environment self-selection may be greater for those belonging to privileged groups that have a greater ability to select or change their life circumstances. Another example would be considering interactions between personality traits and demographics in coping: Given that women and men differ in choices of coping mechanisms, how does personality interact with gender to affect choices?

Furthermore, researchers should continue to examine coping strategies in the study of work-family conflict. The evidence provided here suggests that this pathway between personality and work-family conflict is likely an important factor in the observed relationships. Importantly, researchers should investigate what strategies are used by individuals to allow them to thrive in the management of their work and family roles. Rather than merely coping, are there thought-processes or actions that individuals take to buffer themselves against the challenges associated with these multiple roles and actually allow them to feel like the two roles enhance each other? Additionally, what role does personality play in the ability to identify, select, and implement these various thriving strategies?

Practical Implications

Whereas practical implications would have to follow from rigorous research examining the multiple pathways by which personality can influence the work-family interface, one can imagine certain steps that organizations and individuals may want to take to create positive outcomes. For example, individuals may want to attend to what job and family arrangements will best foster environments in which they can successfully cope with the difficulties of managing work and nonwork lives and potentially even thrive in these domains. Employees could be offered training to help them identify stressors or enhancers in the environment and then could select the appropriate coping or thriving strategies to deal with them. As we have seen, individuals with certain personality types may have tendencies toward selecting coping strategies that may be differentially effective. Training could be offered to help people select more objectively effective coping strategies. Alternatively, research may find that certain coping strategies work best for individuals with certain personality types. Individuals could be trained to select those coping or thriving strategies that work best with their personality type. Furthermore, research may show that the flexible use of coping strategies, the skill to use different coping strategies in different situations (e.g., at home vs. at work), may be important for handling the pressures of both domains. Adaptability training and sensitivity to social cues may be important skills that can be taught to employees.

CONCLUSIONS

This chapter has attempted to show that there may be multiple ways in which personality may influence how individuals handle and feel about the interaction between their home and work lives. Research on the differential pathways discussed can be enlightening for theory, research, and practice, as it reflects an issue that is both personally relevant to individuals and practically relevant to organizations.

REFERENCES

Anderson, C. R. (1977). Locus of control, coping behaviors, and performance in a stress setting: A longitudinal study. *Journal of Applied Psychology, 62,* 446–451.

Aryee, S., Luk, V., Leung, A., & Lo, S. (1999). Role stressors, interrole conflict, and well-being: The moderating influence of spousal support and coping behaviors among employed parents in Hong Kong. *Journal of Vocational Behavior, 54,* 259–278.

Aunola, K., Nurmi, J., Onatsu-Arvilommi, T., & Pulkkinen, L. (1999). The role of parents' self-esteem, mastery-orientation and social background in their parenting styles. *Scandinavian Journal of Psychology, 40,* 307–317.

Bandura, A. (1997). *Self-efficacy: The exercise of control*. New York: W. H. Freeman.

Baumeister, R. F. (1997). Identity, self-concept, and self-esteem. In R. Hogan & J. A. Johnson (Eds.), *Handbook of personality psychology* (pp. 681–710). San Diego: Academic Press.

Bolger, N., & Zuckerman, A. (1995). A framework for studying personality in the stress process. *Journal of Personality and Social Psychology, 69,* 890–902.

Brockwood, K. J., Hammer, L. B., & Neal, M. B. (2003, April). *An examination of positive work-family spillover among dual-earner couples in the sandwiched generation.* Presented at the annual meeting of the Society for Industrial and Organizational Psychology, Orlando, FL.

Brown, J. D., & Dutton, K. A. (1995). The thrill of victory, the complexity of defeat: Self-esteem and people's emotional reactions to success and failure. *Journal of Personality and Social Psychology, 68,* 712–722.

Bruck, C. S., & Allen, T. D. (2003). The relationship between big five personality traits, negative affectivity, type A behavior, and work-family conflict. *Journal of Vocational Behavior, 63,* 457–472.

Burke, M. J., Brief, A. P., & George, J. M. (1993). The role of negative affectivity in understanding relations between self-reports of stressors and strains: A comment on the applied psychology literature. *Journal of Applied Psychology, 78,* 402–412.

Camp, P. L., & Ganong, L. H. (1997). Locus of control and marital satisfaction in long-term marriages. *Families in Society, 78,* 624–631.

Carlson, D. S. (1999). Personality and role variables as predictors of three forms of work-family conflict. *Journal of Vocational Behavior, 55,* 236–253.

Cimbolic Gunthert, K., Cohen, L., & Armeli, S. (1999). The role of neuroticism in daily stress and coping. *Journal of Personality and Social Psychology, 77,* 1087–1100.

Diener, E., Larsen, R. J., & Emmons, R. A. (1984). Person-situation interactions: Choice of situations and congruence of coping models. *Journal of Personality and Social Psychology, 47,* 580–592.

Duxbury, L. E., Higgins, C. A., & Lee, C. (1994). Work-family conflict: A comparison by gender, family type, and perceived control. *Journal of Family Issues, 15*(3), 449–466.

Erez, A., & Judge, T. A. (2001). Relationship of core self-evaluations to goal setting, motivation, and performance. *Journal of Applied Psychology, 86,* 1270–1279.

Fogarty, G. J., Machin, M. A., Albion, M. J., Sutherland, L. F., Lalor, G. I., & Revitt, S. (1999). Predicting occupational strain and job satisfaction: The role of stress, coping, personality, and affectivity variables. *Journal of Vocational Behavior, 54,* 429–452.

Frone, M. R., Russell, M., & Cooper, M. L. (1992). Antecedents and outcomes of work-family conflict: testing a model of the work-family interface. *Journal of Applied Psychology, 77,* 65–78.

Greenhaus, J. H., & Beutell, N. J. (1985). Sources of conflict between work and family roles. *Academy of Management Review, 10,* 76–88.

Greenhaus, J. H., Parasuraman, S., Granrose, C. S., Rabinowitz, S., & Beutell, N. J. (1989). Sources of work-family conflict among two-career couples. *Journal of Vocational Behavior, 34,* 133–153.

Grzywacz, J. G., & Bass, B. L. (2003). Work, family, and mental health: Testing different models of work-family fit. *Journal of Marriage and Family, 65,* 248–262.

Hahn, S. E. (2000). The effects of locus of control on daily exposure, coping and reactivity to work interpersonal stressors: A diary study. *Personality and Individual Differences, 29,* 729–748.

Hanson, G. C., Colton, C. L., & Hammer, L. B. (2003, April). *Develoment and validation of a multidimensional scale of work-family positive spillover.* Paper presented at the annual meeting of the Society for Industrial and Organizational Psychology, Orlando, FL.

Hansson, R. O., Jones, W. H., & Carpenter, B. N. (1984). Relational competence and social support. *Review of Personality and Social Psychology, 5,* 265–284.

Jackson, M. (2003, September). Global nomads. *Working Mother,* 52–56, 90.

James, L. R., & Jones, A. P. (1980). Perceived job characteristics and job satisfaction: An examination of reciprocal causation. *Personnel Psychology, 33,* 97–135.

Johnson, J. H., & Sarason, I. G. (1978). Life stress, depression, and anxiety: Internal-external control as a moderator variable. *Journal of Psychosomatic Research, 22,* 205–208.

Jones, W. (1982). Loneliness and social behavior. In A. Peplau, & D. Perlman, (Eds.), *Loneliness: A sourcebook of current theory, research and therapy* (pp. 238–254). New York: Wiley.

Judge, T. A., & Bono, J. E. (2001). A rose by any other name: Are self-esteem, generalized self-efficacy, neuroticism and locus of control indicators of a common construct? In B. W. Roberts & R. Hogan (Eds.), *Personality psychology in the workplace* (pp. 93–120). Washington, DC: American Psychological Association.

Judge, T. A., Bono, J. E., & Locke, E. A. (2000). Personality and job satisfaction: The mediating role of job characteristics. *Journal of Applied Psychology, 85,* 237–249.

Judge, T. A., Erez, A., & Bono, J. E. (1998). The power of being positive: The relation between positive self-concept and job performance. *Human Performance, 11,* 167–188.

Judge, T. A., Locke, E. A., & Durham, C. C. (1997). The dispositional causes of job satisfaction: A core evaluations approach. *Research in Organizational Behavior, 19,* 151–188.

Judge, T. A., Locke, E. A., Durham, C. C., & Kluger, A. N. (1998). Dispositional effects on job and life satisfaction: The role of core evaluations. *Journal of Applied Psychology, 83,* 17–34.

Korman, A. K. (1970). Toward an hypothesis of work behavior. *Journal of Applied Psychology, 54,* 31–41.

Krause, N., & Stryker, S. (1984). Stress and well-being: The buffering role of locus of control beliefs. *Social Science and Medicine, 18,* 783–790.

Larsen, R. J. (1992). Neuroticism and selective encoding and recall of symptoms: Evidence from a combined concurrent-retrospective study. *Journal of Personality and Social Psychology, 62,* 480–488.

Larson, J. H., Anderson, S. M., Holman, T. B., & Niemann, B. K. (1998). A longitudinal study of the effects of premarital communication, relationship stability, and self-esteem on sexual satisfaction in the first year of marriage. *Journal of Sex and Marital Therapy, 24,* 193–206.

Lazarus, R. S., & Folkman, S. (1984). *Stress, appraisal, and coping.* New York: Springer Publishing Company.

Levin, I., & Stokes, J. P. (1989). Dispositional approach to job satisfaction: Role of negative affectivity. *Journal of Applied Psychology, 74,* 752–758.

Lockwood, A. L., Casper, W. J., Eby, L. T., & Bordeaux, C. (2002). *A review of work-family literature: Where we've been and where we need to go.* Paper presented in W. J. Casper (chair) and J. Barling (discussant) symposium, Emerging Directions in Work and Family Research, at the annual American Psychological Association Conference, Chicago, IL.

Magnus, K., Diener, E., Fujita, F., & Payot, W. (1993). Extraversion and neuroticism as predictors of objective life events: A longitudinal analysis. *Journal of Personality and Social Psychology, 65,* 1046–1053.

Mak, A. S., & Mueller, J. (2000). Job insecurity, coping resources and personality dispositions in occupational strain. *Work and Stress, 14,* 312–328.

Miller, S. M., & Kirsch, N. (1987). Sex differences in cognitive coping with stress. In R. C. Barnett, L. Biener, & G. K. Baruch (Eds.), *Gender and stress* (pp. 278–307). New York: Free Press.

Moyle, P. (1995). The role of negative affectivity in the stress process: Tests of alternative models. *Journal of Organizational Behavior, 16,* 647–668.

Narayanan, S., & Venkatachalam, R. (1980). Perceived problems of interaction in family in relation to sex and neuroticism. *Journal of Psychological Researches, 24,* 16–20.

Necowitz, L. B., & Roznowski, M. (1994). Negative affectivity and job satisfaction: Cognitive processes underlying the relationship and effects on employee behaviors. *Journal of Vocational Behavior, 45,* 270–294.

Noor, N. (2002). Work-family conflict, locus of control, and women's well-being: Tests of alternative pathways. *Journal of Social Psychology, 142,* 645–662.

Oettingen, G. (1996). Positive fantasy and motivation. In M. Gollwitzer & J. A. Bargh (Eds.), *The psychology of action: Linking cognition and motivation to behavior* (pp. 236–259). New York: Guilford Press.

Ormel, J., & Wohlfarth, T. (1991). How neuroticism, long-term difficulties, and life situation change influence psychological distress: A longitudinal model. *Journal of Personality and Social Psychology, 60,* 744–755.

Parkes, K. R. (1990). Coping, negative affectivity, and the work environment: Additive and interactive predictors of mental health. *Journal of Applied Psychology, 75,* 399–409.

Perrewé, P. L., Hochwarter, W. A., & Kiewitz, C. (1999). Value attainment: An explanation for the negative effects of work-family conflict on job and life satisfaction. *Journal of Occupational Health Psychology, 4,* 318–326.

Peterson, C. (2000). The future of optimism. *American Psychologist, 55,* 44–55.

Rothbard, N. P. (2001). Enriching or depleting? The dynamics of engagement in work and family roles. *Administrative Science Quarterly, 46,* 655–684.

Rotter, J. B. (1966). Generalized expectations for internal versus external control of reinforcement. *Psychological Monograms: General and Applied, 80,* 1–28.

Seligman, M. E., Abramson, L. Y., Semmel, A., & von Baeyer, C. (1979). Depressive attributional style. *Journal of Abnormal Psychology, 88,* 242–247.

Seligman, M. E., & Schulman, P. (1986). Explanatory style as a predictor of productivity and quitting among life insurance sales agents. *Journal of Personality and Social Psychology, 50,* 832–838.

Shackelford, T. K. (2001). Self-esteem in marriage. *Personality and Individual Differences, 30,* 371–390.

Spector, P. E. (1982). Behavior in organizations as a function of employee's locus of control. *Psychological Bulletin, 91,* 482–497.

Spector, P. E., Jex, S. M., & Chen, P. (1995). Relations of incumbent affect-related personality traits with incumbent and objective measures of characteristics of jobs. *Journal of Organizational Behavior, 16,* 59–65.

Stoeva, A. Z., Chiu, R. K., & Greenhaus, J. H. (2002). Negative affectivity, role stress, and work-family conflict. *Journal of Vocational Behavior, 60*(1), 1–16.

Sumer, H. C., & Knight, P. A. (2001). How do people with different attachment styles balance work and family? A personality perspective on work-family linkage. *Journal of Applied Psychology, 86,* 653–663.

Van Os, J., Park, B. G., & Jones, P. B. (2001). Neuroticism, life events and mental health: Evidence for person-environment correlation. *British Journal of Psychiatry, 178* (suppl. 40), 72–77.

Voss, K., Markiewicz, D., & Doyle, A. (1999). Friendship, marriage, and self-esteem. *Journal of Social and Personal Relationships, 16,* 103–122.

Wayne, J. H., Musisca, N., & Fleeson, W. (2004). Considering the role of personality in the work-family experience: Relationships of the big five to work-family conflict and facilitation. *Journal of Vocational Behavior, 64,* 108–130.

11

Work and Family Stress and Well-Being: An Integrative Model of Person-Environment Fit Within and Between the Work and Family Domains

Jeffrey R. Edwards
University of North Carolina

Nancy P. Rothbard
University of Pennsylvania

PERSON-ENVIRONMENT FIT IN WORK AND FAMILY

In recent years, a growing body of research has examined the interconnections between work and family (Burke & Greenglass, 1987; Eckenrode & Gore, 1990; Edwards & Rothbard, 2000; Zedeck, 1992). This research has been stimulated by contemporary societal changes that have an impact on work and family roles, such as the influx of women into the workforce, the increased prevalence of dual-earner couples, movement away from traditional gender-based family roles, and evidence debunking the myth that work and family are separate (Burke & Greenglass, 1987; Lambert, 1990; Voydanoff, 1987). The research has shed light on how structural and social aspects of work and family are related to perceived conflict between those two domains; how perceived conflict is related to satisfaction, well-being, and functioning in both domains; and how work and family relationships are influenced by individual differences, coping resources, and the availability of social support (Burke & Greenglass, 1987; Eckenrode & Gore, 1990; Greenhaus & Beutell, 1985; Voydanoff, 1987).

The growing body of empirical work-family research has generated the need to develop theories to organize existing evidence and to guide further inquiry

(Burke & Greenglass, 1987; Greenhaus, 1989; Near, Rice, & Hunt, 1980; Voydanoff, 1989). Several investigators have brought theoretical rigor to work-family research by drawing from theories in other areas, such as stress research (Eckenrode & Gore, 1990; Frone, Russell, & Cooper, 1992; Grandey & Cropanzano, 1999; Greenhaus & Parasuraman, 1986; Higgins, Duxbury, & Irving, 1992; Kopelman, Greenhaus, & Connolly, 1983; Martin & Schermerhorn, 1983). As noted by Greenhaus (1989), viewing work-family research from a stress perspective is useful because it allows researchers to draw from an established paradigm. The stress paradigm is particularly appropriate for work-family research, given that many constructs (e.g., situational stressors, conflict, well-being, coping, social support) are common to both areas of inquiry.

Theories of stress may also benefit from incorporating concepts developed in work-family research. For example, studies of work and family have identified various mechanisms that link the two domains, such as spillover, compensation, and segmentation (Burke & Greenglass, 1987; Edwards & Rothbard, 2000; Kabanoff, 1980; Lambert, 1990; Staines, 1980; Voydanoff, 1989). In contrast, stress research has focused on experiences within the work or nonwork domains, devoting little attention to mechanisms that link work and family experiences or how these experiences combine to influence health and well-being (Bhagat, 1983; Cooper & Marshall, 1976; Greenhaus & Parasuraman, 1986). Incorporating these mechanisms into stress research is important, given that experiences in one life domain may create stress in other domains (Greenhaus & Beutell, 1985), and many outcomes of interest in stress research, such as mental and physical health, are the culmination of stressful experiences across domains.

One potentially useful framework for integrating stress and work-family research is person-environment (P-E) fit theory (Edwards, Caplan, & Harrison, 1998; French, Caplan, & Harrison, 1982; French, Rodgers, & Cobb, 1974). P-E fit theory states that stress arises not from the person or environment separately but rather from misfit between the person and environment. This basic premise underlies numerous theories of stress and well-being in the organizational and psychological literatures (Diener, 1984; Edwards, 1992; Lazarus & Folkman, 1984; McGrath, 1976; Rice, McFarlin, Hunt, & Near; 1985; Schuler, 1980). The primary contribution of P-E fit theory is that it provides an explicit and systematic framework for understanding how person and environment factors combine to produce stress. P-E fit theory also underscores the notion that stress not only influences well-being but also stimulates efforts to resolve misfit or dampen its effects (Edwards et al., 1998; French et al., 1982). Despite its value and central position in stress research, the concept of P-E fit has not been applied to stress and well-being in work-family research.

The purpose of this chapter is to present a theoretical model that applies P-E fit to stress and well-being associated with work and family. The model builds on P-E fit theory (Edwards et al., 1998; French et al., 1982) by describing how fit can be conceptualized in parallel terms for work and family and how person and environment constructs can be linked across work and family. The model also extends existing models of stress in work-family research by using principles of P-E fit to clarify how the person and environment combine to produce stress, the role of cognitive appraisal in this process, and the effects of coping on stress and well-being.

This chapter is organized as follows. First, we summarize and evaluate models of stress in work-family research. Next, we discuss principles of P-E fit theory to establish a foundation for applying the theory to work and family. We then outline the proposed model, which explains how P-E fit processes can operate concurrently in work and family; how these processes relate to stress and well-being associated with work, family, and life as a whole; and how conceptualizing P-E fit theory in terms of work and family can explain mechanisms that link these two domains, such as spillover, compensation, and work-family conflict.

MODELS OF STRESS IN WORK-FAMILY RESEARCH

As previously noted, many constructs in work-family research are prominent in theories of stress. Several investigators have proposed models that bridge the stress and work-family literatures. For example, Kopelman et al. (1983) applied role stress theory (Kahn, Wolfe, Quinn, Snoek, & Rosenthal, 1964) to develop a model relating work conflict, family conflict, and interrole conflict to satisfaction with work, family, and life as a whole. This model was elaborated by Higgins et al. (1992), who added work expectations and job involvement as predictors of work conflict and family expectations and family involvement as predictors of family conflict. Frone et al. (1992; Frone, Yardley, & Markel, 1997) extended this work by distinguishing two forms of work-family conflict, one in which work interferes with family and another in which family interferes with work. Greenhaus and Parasuraman (1986) developed a work-nonwork interactive model that adopted a definition of stress as a psychological state in which a person is faced with demands, constraints, or opportunities with important but uncertain outcomes (Beehr & Bhagat, 1985; Schuler, 1980). Eckenrode and Gore (1990) presented a model that relates role stressors, role functioning, and coping resources to well-being within work and family and connects these concepts between work and family. These models typify the treatment of stress in work-family research and incorporate key features of other models in the literature (e.g., Adams, King, & King, 1996; Aryee, Luk, Leung, & Lo, 1999; Bacharach, Bamberger, & Conley, 1991; Bedeian, Burke, & Moffett, 1988; Bhagat, McQuaid, Lindholm, & Segovis, 1985; Burke, 1986; Cooke & Rousseau, 1984; Grandey & Cropanzano, 1999; Kline & Cowan, 1989; Martin & Schermerhorn, 1983; Rice, Frone, & McFarlin, 1992).

Models of work and family stress have established important connections between the work-family and stress literatures and have spawned a growing body of research. Nonetheless, a critical examination of these models reveals several issues that merit attention. One such issue is the definition of stress itself. The meaning of stress has generated considerable debate in the stress literature (Edwards, 1992; Lazarus & Folkman, 1984; McGrath, 1970; Parker & DeCotiis, 1983; Schuler, 1980; Shirom, 1982). This debate has not been engaged by models of work and family stress. Rather, these models typically omit a definition of stress (e.g., Eckenrode & Gore, 1990; Frone et al., 1992; Higgins et al., 1992; Kopelman et al., 1983) or adopt a definition without evaluating it against alternative definitions (e.g., Grandey & Cropanzano, 1999; Greenhaus & Parasuraman, 1986). The definition of stress is critical, as it positions a model of stress within the broader stress literature, provides the basis for explaining how stress relates to its causes and consequences, and determines how stress should be operationalized.

A second issue is the role of cognitive appraisal in the stress process. Cognitive appraisal refers to the evaluation of the environment relative to salient personal standards (e.g., values, goals, commitments) to determine whether the environment is harmful or beneficial to the person (Lazarus & Folkman, 1984). Cognitive appraisal is prominent in theories of stress (Edwards, 1992; French et al., 1982; Lazarus & Folkman, 1984; Schuler, 1980) but has received little attention in models of stress in work-family research. Some of these models indicate that individual differences, such as demographics, personality, or role involvement, influence the stress process (e.g., Eckenrode & Gore, 1990; Frone et al., 1992; Grandey & Cropanzano, 1999; Greenhaus & Parasuraman, 1986; Higgins et al., 1992). Although individual differences may influence cognitive appraisal, they do not capture cognitive appraisal itself. Cognitive appraisal is implied by person-role conflict (Kopelman et al., 1983) and perceived stress (Greenhaus & Parasuraman, 1986), but the models that contain these concepts do not include the variables involved in the cognitive appraisals that these concepts imply. For example, the Greenhaus and Parasuraman (1986) model includes perceived stress but not the variables ostensibly involved in the cognitive appraisal of stress (i.e., demands, constraints, opportunities, importance, uncertainty). Models of work and family stress would benefit from including variables that underlie the cognitive appraisal of stress, because doing so would allow researchers to examine the underlying causes of stress and how they relate to coping, well-being, and other variables involved in the stress process.

A third issue concerns the role of coping in the stress process. Few models of work-family stress address coping, and those that do indicate that coping influences strain directly or by moderating the effects of stressors on strain (e.g., Aryee et al., 1999; Burke, 1993; Eckenrode & Gore, 1990; Greenhaus & Parasuraman, 1986). Notably missing from these models are linkages from coping to the root causes of stress (Edwards, 1988). These linkages are evident in coping research, which distinguishes between coping efforts directed toward the situation (i.e., problem-focused coping) or the person (i.e., emotion-focused coping), with the latter including efforts to reappraise the situation and manage emotional reactions (Edwards, 1988; Kahn et al., 1964; Lazarus & Folkman, 1984; Pearlin & Schooler, 1978). Although models of work-family stress sometimes include linkages from coping to emotional reactions (Greenhaus & Parasuraman, 1986), they omit linkages from coping to the situational and personal sources of stress.

A final issue is how models of work-family stress incorporate mechanisms that link work and family (Edwards & Rothbard, 2000). The linkage most prevalent in these models is work-family conflict (Bacharach et al., 1991; Bedeian et al., 1988; Cooke & Rousseau, 1984; Higgins et al., 1992; Kopelman et al., 1983; Rice et al., 1992), which is sometimes separated into work interfering with family and family interfering with work (Adams et al., 1996; Aryee et al., 1999; Frone et al., 1992; Frone et al., 1997; Grandey & Cropanzano, 1999). Some models also include paths that connect stressors or coping resources between work and family (Eckenrode & Gore, 1990; Greenhaus & Parasuraman, 1986). Although these linkages are important, they represent a limited subset of the linking mechanisms discussed in the work-family literature (Burke & Greenglass, 1987; Edwards & Rothbard, 2002; Lambert, 1990). For example, spillover may transmit stress between work and family, and compensation may represent efforts to cope with stress in one domain by seeking fulfillment in the other domain (Edwards & Rothbard, 2000). Thus, models of work and family stress may be strengthened by including a broader array of work-family linking mechanisms, many of which have clear implications for stress, coping, and well-being.

In sum, models of stress in work-family research have made important contributions by integrating the stress and work-family literatures and by advancing our understanding of work and family stress and well-being. These models provide a useful platform for theory development that draws further from stress research and addresses the issues summarized above. The P-E fit model outlined in this chapter builds on existing models of work-family stress by incorporating their key strengths and addressing issues concerning the meaning of stress, the operation of cognitive appraisal and coping, and work-family linking mechanisms relevant to the stress process.

P-E FIT THEORY OF STRESS

To establish a foundation for the model we develop, we first summarize the principles of P-E fit theory. The origins of P-E fit theory can be traced to Murray (1938) and Lewin (1951), and formal statements of the theory have been presented by French et al. (1974), French et al. (1982), Harrison (1978, 1985), Caplan (1983, 1987), and Edwards et al. (1998). These sources provide the basis for the following summary.

Principles of P-E Fit Theory

As stated earlier, P-E fit theory indicates that stress arises from misfit between the person and environment. The core elements of P-E fit theory are shown in Fig. 11.1, which captures three key distinctions in P-E fit theory. The first distinction is between the person and environment, as depicted in the lower and upper portions, respectively, of Fig.11.1. The second distinction is between the objective and subjective person and environment. The *objective person* refers to attributes of the person as he or she actually exists, whereas the *subjective person* is how these attributes are perceived by the person. Likewise, the *objective environment* refers to situations and events as they exist in reality, and the *subjective environment* is the person's perception of situations and events. As shown in Fig. 11.1, the objective person affects the subjective person and, likewise, the objective environment influences the subjective environment. The subjective person and environment are imperfect representations of their objective counterparts due to selective attention, perceptual distortion, and barriers to information access and processing (Harrison, 1978).

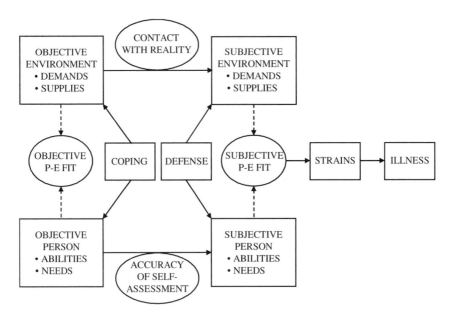

FIG. 11.1. Person-environment (P-E) fit theory of stress. *Sources*: French et al., 1982; Harrison, 1978.

The distinctions between the objective and subjective person and environment combine to yield four types of fit between person and environment constructs: *objective P-E fit*, which is the fit between the objective person and environment; *subjective P-E fit*, or the fit between the subjective person and environment; *contact with reality*, meaning the correspondence between the objective and subjective environment; and *accuracy of self-assessment*, representing the match between the objective and subjective person (Caplan, 1983; French et al., 1974; Harrison, 1978).

As indicated by Fig. 11.1, P-E fit theory proposes that subjective P-E fit is the proximal cause of strains and illness. Hence, these outcomes should not be affected by objective P-E fit unless it is perceived by the person and thus translated into subjective P-E fit (French et al., 1982; Harrison, 1985). This proposition does not disregard the relevance of the objective person and environment or the importance of contact with reality and accurate self-assessment (French et al., 1974; Harrison, 1978; Hobfoll, 1998). For instance, if an individual accurately perceives the objective person and environment, he or she can take appropriate action to enhance objective P-E fit and, by doing so, improve subjective P-E fit. On the other hand, when an individual is confronted with overwhelming stressors, he or she might benefit from some disengagement from the objective situation, given that distancing or denial can dampen initial anxiety and ultimately facilitate adaptation (Caplan, 1983; Lazarus, 1983). Hence, all four types of fit shown in Fig. 11.1 are relevant to health and illness, but subjective P-E fit is the critical pathway through which the person and environment combine to influence strain and illness.

A third and final distinction in Fig. 11.1 entails two types of P-E fit. The first type involves the demands of the environment and the abilities of the person. *Demands* are quantitative and qualitative requirements, expectations, and social norms experienced by the person, and *abilities* are skills, competencies, time, and energy of the person that pertain to these demands. The second type of P-E fit concerns the needs of the person and the supplies in the environment relevant to the person's needs. *Needs* include innate biological and psychological drives, values acquired through learning and socialization, and motives to achieve desired states, ends, or goals. *Supplies* are extrinsic and intrinsic resources and rewards that pertain to the person's needs, such as food, shelter, money, status, companionship, variety, and so forth. According to P-E fit theory, the person and environment constructs involved in needs-supplies fit and demands-abilities fit must be commensurate, meaning that they refer to the same content dimension (French et al., 1982; Harrison, 1978). For instance, demands-abilities fit involving family responsibilities is gauged by comparing the responsibilities imposed by the family to the person's ability to meet those responsibilities. Analogously, needs-supplies fit for job security involves comparing the amount of job security the person wants to the amount of security offered by the person's job. Commensurate dimensions are essential because the degree of

P-E fit can be determined only if the person and environment refer to the same concept and are assessed on the same scale. For example, demands-abilities fit for family responsibilities can be expressed in terms of required and available hours, and needs-supplies fit for job security can refer to desired and actual stability of employment. Thus, commensurate dimensions establish a common conceptual metric for the person and environment and allow meaningful assessment of their degree of fit.

Outcomes of P-E Fit

According to P-E fit theory, subjective P-E misfit leads to two sets of outcomes. One set of outcomes includes strains and illness, which were previously highlighted as consequences of subjective P-E fit. *Strains* are deviations from normal psychological, physical, and behavioral functioning (French et al., 1982; Harrison, 1978). *Psychological* strains include dissatisfaction, anxiety, dysphoria, and other forms of negative affect. *Physiological* strains include high blood pressure, elevated serum cholesterol, compromised immune system functioning, and other symptoms of poor physical health. Behavioral strains include smoking, overeating, absenteeism, and frequent utilization of health care services. The cumulative experience of strains over time can lead to mental and physical *illnesses* such as chronic depression, hypertension, coronary heart disease, peptic ulcers, and cancer. Conversely, sustained good P-E fit can produce positive mental and physical health outcomes (Edwards & Cooper, 1988; Harrison, 1978, 1985).

A second set of outcomes involves efforts to resolve P-E misfit, which are labeled coping and defense in Fig. 11.1 *Coping* signifies efforts to improve objective P-E fit by changing the objective environment (i.e., environmental mastery) or the objective person (i.e., adaptation). For example, a person experiencing excess work demands may seek training to improve his or her ability to meet work demands or seek reassignment to a job with more manageable demands (Harrison, 1978). *Defense* involves efforts to enhance subjective P-E fit by changing the perceived person and environment without affecting their objective counterparts. Defense includes various forms of cognitive distortion (e.g., selective perception, repression, denial) and attempts to reprioritize dimensions that are sources of misfit, as when an individual decides that an unattainable goal is not worth pursing (Klinger, 1975). For instance, in response to excess work demands, a person may inflate perceptions of his or her abilities, reinterpret or ignore work demands, or decide that fulfilling work demands is less important than other life pursuits, such as nurturing a positive family life. The choice between different methods of coping and defense is influenced by person and environment factors such as individual traits, styles, and preferences and by situational opportunities, resources, and constraints.

Although the term *stress* does not appear in Fig. 11.1, it is explicitly defined by P-E fit theory (Edwards et al., 1998; Harrison, 1978). According to P-E fit theory, stress occurs when the environment does not provide adequate supplies to meet the person's needs or when the abilities of the person fall short of demands that are instrumental to receiving supplies. Hence, stress results from P-E misfit when supplies fall short of needs or when demands exceed abilities, provided that meeting demands would help fulfill the needs of the person. Stress arises from subjective rather than objective P-E misfit, given that subjective P-E misfit is the link from the person and environment to strain, illness, coping, and defense (French et al., 1982; Harrison, 1985). Contrary to some conceptualizations of stress (McGrath, 1976; Shirom, 1982), P-E fit theory asserts that excess demands produce stress only when meeting demands yields valued supplies or when demands have been internalized as desires or goals, as when a person adopts role expectations as a guideline for his or her own behavior. Thus, P-E fit theory defines *stress* as *a subjective appraisal indicating that supplies are insufficient to fulfill the person's needs*, with the provision that insufficient supplies may result from unmet demands (Edwards et al., 1998). Defining stress in terms of needs-supplies fit avoids problems with definitions that frame stress as stressors in the environment (Cooper & Marshall, 1976) or as strain experienced by the person (Parker & DeCotiis, 1983), both of which have important conceptual shortcomings (Edwards, 1992; Lazarus & Folkman, 1984; McGrath, 1970).

Relationships Between P-E Fit and Outcomes

Initial presentations of P-E fit theory framed the effects of fit in two dimensions, with the horizontal axis representing P-E misfit and the vertical axis signifying strain (French et al., 1974; French et al., 1982; Harrison, 1978). These effects are illustrated in Fig. 11.2, which depicts the effects of needs-supplies fit on strain. Graph a shows a *monotonic* function in which strain decreases as supplies increase toward needs and continues to decrease as supplies exceed needs. Graph b shows an *asymptotic* function where strain decreases as supplies increase toward needs but levels off as supplies exceed needs. Finally, Graph c depicts a *parabolic* function in which strain increases as supplies deviate from needs in either direction. Each of these functions indicates that deficient supplies increase strain, but they differ regarding the effects of excess supplies, such that strain decreases, levels off, or increases for the monotonic, asymptotic, and parabolic functions, respectively. P-E fit theory describes an analogous set of functions for demands-abilities fit in which strain increases as demands exceed abilities but decreases, levels off, or increases as demands fall short of abilities (Edwards et al., 1998; Harrison, 1978). For reasons stated earlier, these effects of demands-

a. Monotonic function relating needs-supplies fit to strain.

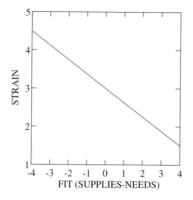

b. Asymptotic function relating needs-supplies fit to strain.

c. Parabolic function relating needs-supplies fit to strain.

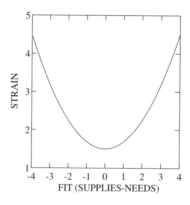

FIG. 11.2.   Two-dimensional functions relating needs-supplies fit to strain.

abilities fit on strain should occur only when meeting demands yields valued supplies or demands have been internalized as desires or goals.

Although the functions in Fig. 11.2 represent an intuitive approach to conceptualizing the effects of P-E misfit, they reduce the inherently three-dimensional relationship among the person, the environment, and strain to two dimensions. This point is demonstrated by Fig. 11.3, which shows three-dimensional surfaces that correspond to the two-dimensional functions in Figure 11.2. Underneath each surface is a grid that depicts various combinations of needs and supplies. The solid line running diagonally from the front to the back of the grid is the *fit line*, which comprises all values where needs and supplies are equal. The dashed line that runs diagonally from left to right across the grid is the *misfit line*, which captures the discrepancy between needs and supplies.[1]

Comparing Figs. 11.2 and 11.3 shows that conceptualizing P-E fit in two dimensions entails several key assumptions. First, it is assumed that the person and environment have equal but opposite effects on strain. This assumption is evident in the scale for needs-supplies fit in Fig. 11.3, which represents the algebraic difference between supplies and needs. When a concept is conceived as an algebraic difference between two constructs, it disregards the possibility that the effects of the constructs differ in magnitude. Likewise, when an algebraic difference is used as a predictor, the variables that constitute the difference are forced to have equal but opposite effects on outcomes (Edwards, 1994). Studies testing this assumption have shown that the effects of supplies usually outweigh those of needs (Edwards, 1994, 1996; Edwards & Harrison, 1993; Edwards & Rothbard, 1999; Hesketh & Gardner, 1993; Livingstone, Nelson, & Barr, 1997; Rice, Peirce, Moyer, & McFarlin, 1991; Taris & Feij, 2001).

Second, the two-dimensional view incorporates the assumption that the level of strain is unaffected by the absolute levels of the person and environment, given that fit takes into account only the person relative to the environment. This assumption is depicted by the surfaces in Fig. 11.3, each of which indicates the same amount of strain along the fit line regardless of the absolute levels of needs and supplies. From a conceptual standpoint, this assumption disregards the possibility that strain may be lower when needs and supplies are both high than when both are low, as when a person wants and obtains a job rich in rewards. Empirically, this assumption has been rejected by studies showing that, along the fit line, strain often decreases as needs and supplies both increase (Edwards, 1996; Edwards & Harrison, 1993; Edwards & Rothbard, 1999).

A third and related assumption is that the shape of the relationship between misfit and strain is unaffected by the absolute levels of the person and environment. This assumption is evident in Fig. 11.3, graph c, which shows that the minimum of the parabolic function is centered along the fit line regardless of the absolute levels of needs and supplies. Theoretically, this assumption disregards the possibility that the optimal degree of P-E fit may depend on whether the person and environment are both high or low. For instance, when demands

a. Monotonic surface relating needs-supplies fit to strain.

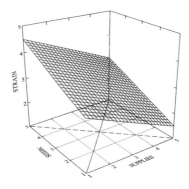

b. Asymptotic surface relating needs-supplies fit to strain.

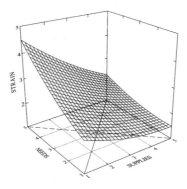

c. Parabolic surface relating needs-supplies fit to strain.

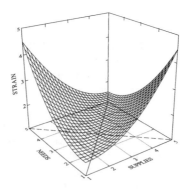

FIG. 11.3.   Three-dimensional surfaces relating needs-supplies fit to strain.

and abilities are low, excess demands may be optimal because they provide opportunities for growth and skill development. Conversely, when demands and abilities are high, deficient demands may be optimal because they allow respite from striving to fulfill taxing demands. Studies have challenged this assumption by showing that at low levels of needs and supplies, strain is minimized when supplies exceed needs; whereas at high levels of needs and supplies, strain is minimized when supplies are less than needs (Edwards, 1996; Edwards & Harrison, 1993).

Complexities that can be accommodated by conceptualizing the effects of P-E fit in three dimensions were anticipated during the development of P-E fit theory (Caplan, 1983; Harrison, 1978), and attempts to assess these complexities were undertaken in unpublished work (Caplan & Harrison, 1993). Nonetheless, these complexities were concealed by methods available at the time P-E fit theory was developed, which relied on difference scores that reduced the effects of P-E fit on strain to two dimensions (Caplan, Cobb, French, Harrison, & Pinneau, 1980; French et al., 1982). The three-dimensional view relaxes the assumptions of the two-dimensional approach and better captures the complexity of P-E fit theory. Empirical research that incorporates the three-dimensional view has been facilitated by recent methodological developments that replace difference scores with polynomial regression and response surface methodology, which can be used to test hypotheses regarding the shapes of surfaces such as those in Fig. 11.3 (Edwards, 1994, 2002; Edwards & Parry, 1993).

The transition to the three-dimensional view of P-E fit has been accompanied by the development and refinement of conceptual principles to predict the shape of the relationship between P-E fit and strain. Most research within the general paradigm of P-E fit is based on the premise that fit is beneficial and misfit is harmful (Edwards, 1991; Kristof, 1996; Spokane, Meir, & Catalano, 2000). This premise is captured by Fig. 11.3, graph c, which shows that strain is minimized when needs and supplies are equal and increases as needs and supplies differ in either direction. Some theories describe other relationships between P-E fit and outcomes (Locke, 1976; Rice et al., 1985), such as the monotonic, asymptotic, and parabolic relationships identified by P-E fit theory (French et al., 1974; French et al., 1982; Harrison, 1978). However, these theories treat the alternative relationships between P-E fit and outcomes not as hypotheses but instead as possibilities. Consequently, results can be declared consistent with P-E fit theory regardless of which relationship is found. This situation is undesirable, as it effectively treats the relationship between P-E fit and outcomes as exploratory, which means that P-E fit theory is not subjected to formal testing and falsification.

Hypotheses regarding the relationship between P-E fit and outcomes can be developed using principles organized around four mechanisms that explain the monotonic, asymptotic, and parabolic functions (Edwards, 1996; Edwards et al., 1998; Edwards & Rothbard, 1999). To illustrate, consider the functions relating needs-supplies fit and strain in Fig 11.3. For all three functions, strain is predicted to decrease as supplies increase toward needs. This prediction is based on the premise that deficient supplies create tension, negative affect, and other forms of strain, and these strains are ameliorated when supplies increase to fulfill needs (Diener, 1984; Murray, 1938). The functions differ for the effects of excess supplies, with the monotonic, asymptotic, and parabolic functions predicting negative, null, and positive relationships with strain, respectively. The monotonic function can be explained by two principles. The first is termed *carryover,* which means that excess supplies on one dimension can be used to achieve needs-supplies fit on other dimensions. For example, if a person's basic need for control is fulfilled, excess supplies for control may used to modify the environment to achieve needs-supplies fit on other dimensions. The second principle is *conservation,* where excess supplies on a dimension can be saved to achieve needs-supplies fit on the same dimension in the future. For instance, income that exceeds a person's basic material needs can be saved to ensure monetary needs-supplies fit at a later time. Carryover and conservation both predict that excess supplies will decrease strain, resulting in the monotonic function shown in Fig. 11.3, graph a.

Two complementary principles can be used to explain the parabolic function in Fig. 11.3, graph c. One principle is *interference,* whereby excess supplies on one dimension interfere with needs-supplies fit on another dimension. Harrison (1978) illustrates this principle using contact with coworkers, whereby supplies that exceed a person's need for affiliation can interfere with his or her need for privacy. Another principle is *depletion,* in which excess supplies on a dimension reduce the availability of supplies on that dimension in the future. For example, an employee who solicits excess support from a supervisor can reduce the willingness of the supervisor to provide needed support at a later date. Interference and depletion predict that excess supplies will increase strain, producing the parabolic function in Fig. 11.3 graph c. When excess supplies are not subject to carryover, conservation, interference, or depletion, then the asymptotic function in Fig. 11.3, graph b is predicted, which results when excess supplies do not increase or decrease needs-supplies fit on other dimensions and do not promote or inhibit future needs-supplies fit on the same dimension.

The principles of carryover, conservation, interference, and depletion can also be applied to demands-abilities fit to explain the effects of deficient demands (Edwards, 1996). As noted earlier, P-E fit theory predicts that strain increases as demands exceed abilities but may decrease, level off, or increase as abilities exceed demands, which respectively yield monotonic, asymptotic, or parabolic relationships between demands-abilities fit and strain (French et al., 1982; Harrison, 1978). Excess abilities can decrease strain due to carryover, as when abilities that exceed a particular demand can be used to fulfill other demands. For example, a person who is able to fulfill role demands in less time than required can apply the remaining time to other demands. Excess abilities can also decrease strain when they can be conserved, as exemplified by reserving energy that exceeds a current demand to meet that demand in the future. Carryover and conservation both indicate that excess abilities reduce strain, indicating a monotonic function between demands-abilities fit and strain. Conversely, abilities that exceed one demand may interfere with the fulfillment of other demands, as when developing and maintaining skills beyond current job demands prevents the attainment of skills needed to meet other demands. Excess abilities may also create depletion, as when abilities that are untapped by demands atrophy, making it more difficult to meet future demands (McGrath, 1970). Interference and depletion increase strain, producing a parabolic relationship between demands-abilities fit and strain. If excess abilities are not subject to carryover, conservation, interference, or depletion, then excess abilities would be unrelated to strain, yielding an asymptotic relationship between demands-abilities fit and strain. Again, this reasoning is based on the premise that meeting demands will bring valued supplies or that demands are internalized as desires or goals.

Carryover, conservation, interference, and depletion entail the shape of the surface along the misfit line. P-E fit research based on the three-dimensional view also addresses the shape of the surface along the fit line (Edwards, 1996; Edwards & Harrison, 1993; Edwards & Rothbard, 1999; Livingstone et al., 1997). For instance, Edwards and Rothbard (1999) reasoned that strain would be lower when needs and supplies are both high than when both are low, based on the notion that high needs coupled with high supplies signifies the attainment of ambitious goals. Meeting such goals yields a sense of accomplishment that itself can fulfill needs regarding growth, mastery, and self-actualization (Harrison, 1978; White, 1959). Analogously, when high demands are coupled with high abilities, the person is able to meet extreme role requirements, which can also produce feelings of accomplishment as well as rewards and approval from role senders. This reasoning rests on the premise of *metafit*, whereby attaining needs-supplies fit or demands-abilities fit on one dimension constitutes a supply for needs on other dimensions.

USING P-E FIT THEORY TO EXPLAIN WORK AND FAMILY STRESS

Because P-E fit theory is expressed in general terms, it can be used to study stress in a wide range of situations. In this section, we describe how P-E fit theory can be used to examine stress associated with work and family. To this end, we show how constructs from P-E fit theory can be characterized in terms of work and family, discuss how P-E fit theory can explain stress within work and family, and demonstrate how parallel conceptions of P-E fit in work and family provide a platform for understanding work-family linkages that shed light on work stress, family stress, and their combined effects on strain and illness.

The following discussion is organized around the model in Fig. 11.4. This model depicts parallel versions of the general P-E fit model shown in Fig. 11.1 for work and family. For the purposes of this model, we treat work and family in a broad sense, such that work entails instrumental activity intended to provide goods and services to support life and family comprises persons related by biological ties, marriage, social custom, or adoption (Edwards & Rothbard, 2000; Piotrkowski, Rapoport, & Rapoport, 1987). The boundary between the work and family versions of the model contains work-family linking mechanisms, which represent a range of processes that connect constructs in the work and family domains. After presenting the model, we discuss linking mechanisms that are particularly relevant to work and family stress.

Applying Constructs from P-E Fit Theory to Work and Family

The constructs that constitute P-E fit theory can be conceptualized in terms of work and family, as indicated by the model in Fig. 11.4. Work demands may refer to task requirements, managing subordinates, and other expectations entailed by the work role. Likewise, family demands may include household chores, caring for children, and other family role expectations. Work and family abilities are conceptualized as commensurate with these demands, such that demands-abilities fit would entail the comparison between demands and abilities for work or family on a single content dimension (e.g., demands and abilities for work task requirements or household chores). At a general level, some demands and abilities may be conceptualized as commensurate across work and family. For instance, work task requirements and household chores can be framed as quantitative or qualitative work load, and managing subordinates and child care can be framed as responsibility for others. At this level, the effects of demands-abilities fit can be compared across work and family. This general approach can be complemented by a more fine-grained approach that captures qualitative differences between work and family demands and the abilities required to meet these demands.

Needs and supplies can also be distinguished between work and family. Work needs include intrinsic job characteristics, extrinsic rewards, and relationships with peers, coworkers, and supervisors. Family needs include companionship, intimacy, emotional support, and the desire to raise children. These needs are compared to commensurate supplies to determine the degree of needs-supplies fit (e.g., whether extrinsic rewards from work or emotional support from the family exceed or fall short of their corresponding needs). Like demands and abilities, some needs and supplies can be conceived in general terms such that they are commensurate across work and family. Examples of such needs and supplies include autonomy, security, and relationships with others, each of which

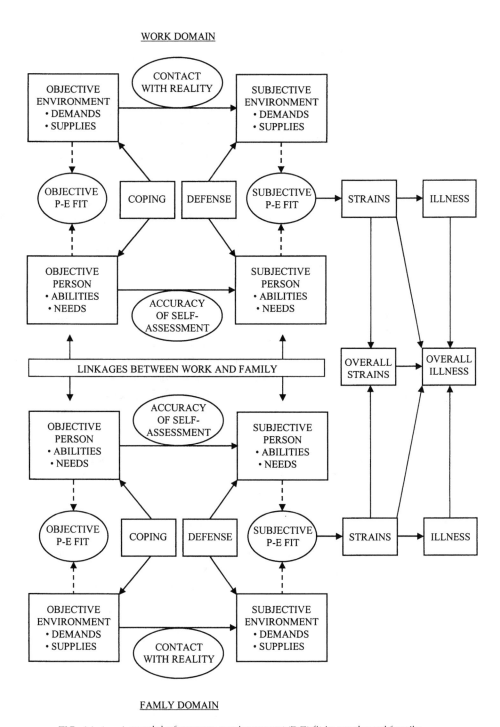

FIG. 11.4.   A model of person-environment (P-E) fit in work and family.

227

can refer to work or family. When the same need and supply dimensions are used for work and family, the effects of needs-supplies fit for work and family can be compared (Edwards & Rothbard, 1999). Again, this general approach can be accompanied usefully by research that delves into specific needs and supplies that are unique to work and family, thereby capturing similarities and differences in the effects of needs-supplies fit for the two domains.

Other constructs that constitute P-E fit theory can also be conceptualized in parallel terms for work and family. For instance, some forms of psychological strain, such as dissatisfaction and negative affect, can refer to either work or family. Likewise, certain behavioral strains, such as smoking and absenteeism, can be exhibited in either the work domain or family domain. Other psychological and behavioral strains, such as anxiety and using health care services, are usually conceived as general outcomes that are not specific to a particular life domain. Likewise, most physiological strains and health outcomes are not specific to work or family but instead reflect the cumulative effects of misfit across life domains, including work and family. Thus, high blood pressure, elevated serum cholesterol, coronary heart disease, and cancer refer to the whole person and cannot be differentiated into work and family counterparts.

Coping and defense can be distinguished for work and family, given that efforts to change the objective or subjective person or environment can focus on either work or family versions of these constructs. For example, coping with demands-abilities misfit at work can involve reducing job demands or increasing job-related skills, and coping with demands-abilities misfit associated with family can entail reducing parenting demands by using child-care services or increasing parenting skills by reading books or seeking advice on childrearing. Likewise, defense may involve downplaying the demands of work or parenting, exaggerating one's skills and abilities regarding these demands, or creating some combination of these strategies. Similar distinctions between work and family also apply to coping and defense directed toward needs-supplies misfit. Although most forms of coping and defense are likely to be domain-specific, some forms can target the person or environment as a whole, transcending the work and family domains. For example, a person may acquire general skills in conflict resolution that help meet interpersonal demands for both work and family. Likewise, a person may reprioritize his or her life values to place less emphasis on material wealth, thereby reducing the perceived need for a high salary at work and a luxurious lifestyle for the family.

Effects of Work and Family P-E Fit on Outcomes

The effects of work and family P-E fit may be considered separately for each domain and in combination for both domains. We predict that the separate effects of P-E fit in each domain will follow the logic of P-E fit theory articulated earlier, given that this logic should apply to the effects of P-E fit in any life domain. Thus, for both work and family, strain should increase as supplies fall short of needs and may increase, remain constant, or decrease as supplies exceed needs. Likewise, strain should increase as demands exceed abilities and may increase, remain constant, or decrease as abilities exceed demands, assuming that meeting demands brings valued supplies or that demands are internalized as desires or goals. The effects of excess supplies and excess abilities on strain depend on carryover, conservation, interference, and depletion, as articulated earlier. Moreover, for both work and family, strain should decrease as supplies and needs increase or as demands and abilities increase, given that achieving high aspirations or meeting high demands can create feelings of growth, mastery, and self-actualization.

We predict that the combined effects of work and family P-E fit on strain are additive, such that increased misfit in either domain will increase strain. This premise is consistent with existing models of work and family stress as well as with models that treat total life stress as a function of stress associated with multiple life domains (Bhagat et al., 1985). We further argue that the effects of work and family P-E fit on strain depend on the centrality, or importance, of work and family to the person's overall concept (Gecas & Seff, 1990). Centrality should increase the effects of P-E fit on strain because, as the centrality of a domain increases, misfit regarding that domain should pose a greater threat to the person's overall self-concept (Gecas & Seff, 1990; Locke, 1976; Rice et al., 1985). In this sense, centrality serves as a moderator of the effects of P-E misfit on strain. Moderating effects for domain centrality were observed by Edwards and Rothbard (1999), who studied needs-supplies fit on commensurate work and family dimensions with a sample of employees who rated family centrality substantially higher than work centrality. As expected, strain was more strongly related to needs-supplies fit for family than for work. This difference is illustrated in Fig. 11.5, which shows surfaces relating needs and supplies for autonomy to dissatisfaction for work and family.[2] Both surfaces show asymptotic relationships between needs-supplies fit and dissatisfaction, such that dissatisfaction increases as supplies fall short of needs but remains essentially constant as supplies exceed needs. However, the overall slope of the surface is steeper for family than for work, consistent with the notion that the effects of needs-supplies fit on strain is stronger when domain centrality is higher. Edwards and Rothbard (1999) also tested the moderating effects of centrality within the work and family domains, using polynomial regression with domain centrality as a moderator variable. Some support was found for the moderating effects of domain centrality within the family domain, although these effects were less pronounced than those for centrality between the work and family domains.

a. Surface relating autonomy needs and supplies to dissatisfaction for work.

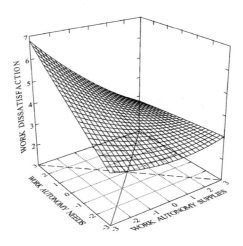

b. Surface relating autonomy needs and supplies to dissatisfaction for family.

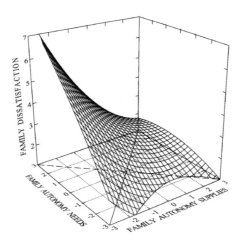

FIG. 11.5.   Surfaces relating autonomy needs and supplies to dissatisfaction for work and family.

Linkages Between the Work and Family Domains

As noted earlier, models of work and family stress typically include linkages between work and family. These linkages distinguish models of work and family stress from general models of stress, which occasionally discuss the combined effects of stress from different life domains but rarely address linkages between domains (e.g., Bhagat et al., 1985; Rice et al., 1985). The parallel conceptions of P-E fit in work and family described here provide a useful platform for identifying linkages between work and family relevant to the stress process. These linkages can be identified using the framework presented by Edwards and Rothbard (2000), who isolated three basic features of linkages between work and family constructs: *sign,* or whether an increase in one construct is associated with an increase or decrease in the other construct; *causal structure,* which casts the relationship between work and family constructs as a direct effect, an indirect effect, or a spurious association due to a common cause; and *intent,* or whether a work-family linkage is purposely created, modified, or eliminated by the person.

In principle, it is possible to consider linkages between work and family for each construct of P-E fit theory. The model in Fig. 11.4 contains 12 constructs each in the work and family domains (i.e., strain, illness, coping, defense, and objective and subjective demands, abilities, needs, and supplies), and connecting these constructs across the two domains would yield 144 possible linkages. Addressing each of these linkages is well beyond the scope of this chapter and would produce a model that lacks any semblance of parsimony that makes theories useful (Popper, 1959; Weick, 1979). Instead, we focus on linkages that are relevant to the stress process, build on previous models of work and family stress, and are prominent in work-family research (Burke & Greenglass, 1987; Edwards & Rothbard, 2000; Lambert, 1990; Zedeck, 1992).

Work-Family Conflict.   As noted previously, models of work and family stress often incorporate work-family conflict as a central feature (Adams et al., 1996; Aryee et al., 1999; Bacharach et al., 1991; Bedeian et al., 1988; Frone et al., 1992; Frone et al., 1997; Grandey & Cropanzano, 1999; Higgins et al., 1992; Kopelman et al., 1983). Work-family conflict is a form of interrole conflict in which work and family role demands are incompatible, such that meeting demands in one domain makes it difficult to meet demands in the other domain (Burke & Greenglass, 1987; Cooke & Rousseau, 1984; Greenhaus & Beutell, 1985). Greenhaus and Beutell (1985) identify three forms of work-family conflict, each of which can be explained using linkages between parallel constructs from P-E fit theory in work and family. *Time-based conflict* occurs when devoting time to the demands of one domain leaves insufficient time to meet the demands of the other domain. In P-E fit theory, time is an ability people can use to fulfill demands. Therefore, time-based conflict implies a negative relationship between work and family abilities, whereby an increase in work time decreases family time and vice versa. The negative relationship between work and family time is direct and intentional, driven by time allocation decisions of the person (Edwards & Rothbard, 2000). Time-based conflict further stipulates that drawing time from a domain leaves the demands of that domain unmet. This condition signifies demands-abilities misfit in which environmental demands exceed the abilities of the person. Hence, time-based conflict results from demands-abilities misfit in work and family whereby demands in a domain are unmet because time is shifted from that domain to the other domain.

A second form of work-family conflict described by Greenhaus and Beutell (1985) is *strain-based conflict,* which occurs when strain generated in one domain makes it difficult to meet demands in the other domain. Greenhaus and Beutell (1985) characterize strain as fatigue, tension, anxiety, depression, and irritability, each of which can reduce the ability of the person to meet role requirements. Hence, strain-based conflict implies that increased strain in one domain reduces abilities in the other domain. The effect of strain on abilities may be direct or indirect, mediated by general forms of strain such as overall physical exhaustion (Edwards & Rothbard, 2000). Drawing from P-E fit theory, strain-based conflict would occur only when abilities fall below demands. Thus, strain-based conflict arises when strain in one domain reduces abilities in the other domain to the point that demands in that domain are unmet.

The third type of work-family conflict discussed by Greenhaus and Beutell (1985) is *behavior-based conflict,* which occurs when behaviors exhibited in one domain are incompatible with demands in the other domain and the person does not adapt his or her behavior when moving between domains. The behaviors described by Greenhaus and Beutell (1985) are manifestations of skills used by the person to fulfill role expectations. For instance, the work role may require skills that promote self-reliance, aggressiveness, and objectivity, whereas the family role may require skills that foster nurturing, warmth, and emotional expression (Eckenrode & Gore, 1990; Greenhaus & Beutell, 1985). In terms of P-E fit theory, behavior-based conflict implies a negative relationship between work and family abilities, such that abilities developed in one domain are inappropriately transferred to the other domain, reducing abilities to meet demands in that domain. This relationship can be direct or indirect, as when domain-specific skills become part of the person's general skill set before being applied to the other domain. The relationship can also be intentional, reflecting errant attempts to transfer skills, or unintentional, as when skills become ingrained as habits that inadvertently influence behavior across domains.

Viewing work-family conflict in terms of demands-abilities fit underscores three key points not captured by existing models of work and family stress. First, existing models depict work-family conflict as an outcome of role demands (or stressors, depending on the terminology of the model) (Frone et al., 1992; Grandey & Cropanzano, 1999; Higgins et al., 1992). P-E fit theory emphasizes that role demands do not produce work-family conflict unless demands exceed the abilities of the person. Thus, abilities must be considered along with demands to explain work-family conflict. Second, P-E fit theory shows that the three forms of work-family conflict identified by Greenhaus and Beutell (1985) can be attributed to the effects of time, strain, and skills in one domain on abilities in the other domain. Thus, abilities are the primary channel through which work-family conflict occurs, which reinforces the importance of incorporating abilities into models that explain work-family conflict. Third, P-E fit theory states that misfit between demands and abilities will generate stress only when unmet demands create a deficit of supplies relative to needs. Because work-family conflict is rooted in demands-abilities misfit, it follows that work-family conflict will not produce stress unless failure to resolve conflict prevents the person from satisfying his or her needs. This point is suggested by discussions of work-family conflict (Greenhaus & Beutell, 1985) but is not incorporated into models of work and family stress, which depict direct paths from work-family conflict to strain.

Spillover.   Work-family research has examined various forms of spillover between work and family. One is *mood spillover,* in which moods experienced in one domain are related to moods in the other domain (Burke & Greenglass, 1987; Lambert, 1990; Staines, 1980; Zedeck, 1992). In P-E fit theory, moods are captured by strain, which includes affective consequences of P-E misfit. Drawing from P-E fit theory, mood in one domain can influence mood in the other domain when mood in the former domain affects the fit between needs and supplies in the latter domain. One explanation for this effect is that negative moods in one domain interfere with the person's ability to fulfill role demands in the other domain (Barling & Macewen, 1992; Nolen-Hoeksema, Parker, & Larson, 1994). This process may occur because negative moods inhibit problem-solving and reduce self-efficacy (Staw, Sutton, & Pelled, 1994) and because work and family role demands often proscribe the exhibition of negative moods (Ashforth & Humphrey, 1993; Rafaeli & Sutton, 1987). Thus, the effects of mood spillover can be captured by a negative relationship between strain in one domain and abilities in the other domain. This relationship is largely unintentional because it operates through cognitive and motivational processes that do not require intent (Edwards & Rothbard, 2000).

Another form of spillover examined in work-family research is *values spillover,* where values in one domain influence values in another domain. In terms of P-E fit theory, values spillover signifies a causal relationship between psychological needs associated with work and family, given that values are represented by psychological needs in P-E fit theory. Drawing from Edwards and Rothbard (2000), the effects of work and family needs on one another can be direct or indirect. Direct effects are illustrated by research indicating that employees in organizations that value authority and control place a high priority on obedience in their children (Payton-Miyazaki & Brayfield, 1976; Pearlin & Kohn, 1966). Indirect effects are evident when needs developed and reinforced in one domain influence the person's overall life values, which then affect needs expressed in other domains. This process recognizes work and family as important socializing forces that influence what people consider valuable and desirable (Payton-Miyazaki & Brayfield, 1976; Piotrkowski, 1979; Repetti, 1987). Following Edwards and Rothbard (2000), the effects relating work and family needs can represent intentional strivings for value consistency between work and family (Cialdini, Trost, & Newsom, 1995) or unintentional transmissions of ingrained values between domains (Lord & Maher, 1991).

Work-family research also addresses spillover of skills and behavior between work and family (Champoux, 1978; Edwards & Rothbard, 2000; Repetti, 1987; Staines, 1980; Zedeck, 1992). These two forms of spillover underlie behavior-based conflict, in which skills and their associated behaviors are inappropriately transferred from one domain to the other (Greenhaus & Beutell, 1985). Although behavior-based conflict frames this transfer as dysfunctional, skills and behaviors developed in one domain can also enhance the person's ability to meet demands in other domains. For instance, employees who learn participative management skills at work can transfer these skills to family situations (Crouter, 1984). Likewise, teachers develop interaction patterns with students that shape their parenting behavior (Ispa, Gray, & Thornburg, 1984). The linkages between work and family skills and behavior can be direct or indirect, as when skills and behaviors become generalized knowledge structures or behavioral scripts. These linkages can also reflect intentional applications of skills and behaviors across domains or unintentional displays of schemas and scripts (Edwards & Rothbard, 2000; Lord & Kernan, 1987; Lord & Maher, 1991).

Compensation.   Compensation refers to efforts to offset dissatisfaction in one domain by seeking satisfaction in another domain (Burke & Greenglass, 1987; Lambert, 1990; Zedeck, 1992). One form of compensation occurs when the person decreases involvement in the dissatisfying domain and increases involvement in another domain, where involvement refers to the perceived importance of a domain or the time devoted to a domain (Lambert, 1990; Staines, 1980; Zedeck, 1992). For P-E fit theory, domain importance is captured by the intensity of work and family needs, and time is part of the abilities the person can devote to work and family demands. Because compensation is a response to dissatisfaction, it signifies coping and defense efforts to reduce strain by managing objective and subjective P-E fit, respectively. Given that domain importance is subjective (Lambert, 1990; Lobel, 1991), altering domain importance represents defensive efforts directed toward work and family needs. On the other hand, time is objective, which means that reallocating time between domains reflects coping targeted at work and family abilities. Hence, compensation by shifting involvement between work and family is captured by positive direct effects between strain in one domain and coping and defense in the other domain, which influence abilities and needs in the latter domain, respectively. These linkages represent conscious efforts to manage strain and are therefore intentional (Edwards & Rothbard, 2000).

Another form of compensation occurs when the person responds to dissatisfaction in one domain by seeking rewards in another domain (Kando & Summers, 1971; Zedeck, 1992). Rewards correspond to supplies in P-E fit theory, which the person can seek through coping efforts. For example, a person who is dissatisfied with the amount of emotional support from family members may seek supportive relationships with supervisors and coworkers. A person can also pursue supplies in an alternative domain by increasing efforts to meet demands in that domain that are instrumental to supplies. For instance, a manager whose work role performance is insufficient to fulfill his or her need for achievement may invest additional time and energy in family role performance. This type of compensation entails coping efforts that increase abilities applied to the alternative domain. Compensation by seeking alternative rewards again implies a positive intentional direct effect between strain in one domain and coping in another domain, where coping is targeted at supplies and abilities in the form of effort dedicated to role demands.

Additional Linkages. Compensation, spillover, and work-family conflict are three types of work-family linkages that are particularly relevant to understanding work and family stress. However, P-E fit theory provides a platform to study additional linkages between work and family. For instance, *segmentation* refers to the active separation of work and family (Burke & Greenglass, 1987; Lambert, 1990; Zedeck, 1992), which can be viewed as intentional efforts to reduce or eliminate linkages between work and family constructs highlighted by P-E fit theory (Edwards & Rothbard, 2000). *Resource drain* is the transfer of personal resources such as time and energy between domains (Eckenrode & Gore, 1990; Small & Riley, 1990; Staines, 1980), which is captured by the relationship between work and family abilities underlying time-based conflict. *Congruence* refers to similarity between work and family due to a third variable that serves as a common cause (Morf, 1989; Zedeck, 1992). In P-E fit theory, congruence can be incorporated as general aptitudes that influence work and family abilities, overarching life values that influence work and family needs, and psychological and physical predispositions that affect strain and health in work and family. These and other linkages between work and family can be conceptualized as relationships between P-E fit constructs in the work and family domains, using the model in Fig. 11.4 and the framework developed by Edwards and Rothbard (2000).

Reframing linkages between work and family in terms of relationships between constructs in P-E fit theory offers several contributions. First, it resolves basic ambiguities regarding the sign, causal structure, and source of the relationships that work-family linkages represent. These ambiguities have prompted researchers to characterize work-family linkages as "pretheoretical metaphors" (Rice, Near, & Hunt, 1980, p. 61) and were a major motivation for the Edwards and Rothbard (2000) framework. Here we show how the Edwards and Rothbard (2000) framework can be applied using our model of P-E fit within and between work and family. Second, specifying work-family linking mechanisms as relationships between constructs in our model of work and family P-E fit reveals the theoretical processes underling these mechanisms. By making these processes explicit, the nature and causes of the linking mechanisms can be understood and empirically tested. Third, our mechanisms linking work and family P-E fit constructs substantially expand the range of linking mechanisms addressed by models of work and family stress, which focus primarily work-family conflict. Our model incorporates additional linking mechanisms prevalent in work-family research and shows how these mechanisms are relevant to stress, coping, and health.

CONCLUSIONS AND DIRECTIONS FOR FUTURE RESEARCH

The model of work and family P-E fit presented here offers several advantages over existing models of work and family stress. First, the model explicitly defines stress as subjective needs-supplies misfit. This definition avoids problems with other conceptualizations of stress (Lazarus & Folkman, 1984; McGrath, 1970) and is well anchored in the stress literature (Edwards, 1992; French et al., 1982; Harrison, 1978; Schuler, 1980). Second, the model incorporates cognitive appraisal by distinguishing between objective and subjective person and environment constructs and by emphasizing the cognitive comparison of subjective needs and supplies as the essence of psychological stress. Third, the model captures the effects of coping and defense on the objective and subjective person and environment constructs that serve as the root causes of stress. Finally, we demonstrated how the model can incorporate linkages between work and family that are relevant to the stress process.

The P-E fit model of work and family stress offers several promising avenues for future research. One avenue concerns the relationship between P-E fit and strain within work and family. As noted previously, this relationship can be conceived as a three-dimensional surface oriented around the fit and misfit lines, and hypotheses can be developed regarding the shape of the surface along these lines. A growing body of research has tested three-dimensional relationships between P-E fit and strain (Edwards, 1996; Edwards & Harrison, 1993; Livingstone et al., 1997; Taris & Feij, 2001), some of which focus on P-E fit for work and family (Edwards & Rothbard, 1999). Additional research along these lines is clearly warranted. Rather than adopting an exploratory approach, studies should develop and test *a priori* hypotheses regarding the shapes of surfaces relating P-E fit to strain, which can be facilitated by applying the concepts of carryover, conservation, interference, and depletion.

Another promising avenue of research involves linkages between work and family and their implications for stress. To date, work-family conflict has received the majority of attention, but few studies have examined the interplay between work and family demands and abilities that theoretically underlie work-family conflict. In addition, some studies have separated conflict in terms of whether work interferes with family or family interferes with work (Adams et al., 1996; Aryee et al., 1999; Frone et al., 1992; Frone et al., 1997; Grandey & Cropanzano, 1999), but few studies have distinguished time-based, strain-based, and behavior-based conflict (Greenhaus & Beutell, 1985). As shown by our model, these three forms of conflict are captured by different linkages among parallel work and family constructs indicated by P-E fit theory. The three forms of conflict can also be separated in terms of work interfering with family or family interfering with work by reversing the causal flow of the linkages that describe conflict. Other linkages, such as spillover and compensation, are relevant to the stress process but have received little attention in research on work and family stress. The model presented here provides a useful starting point for investigating these and other linkages between work and family and how they relate to stress.

The P-E fit model developed here also has several implications for practice. Specifically, by emphasizing person-environment misfit as the root cause of stress, the model highlights multiple levers for intervention. For example, coping with demands-abilities misfit at work may involve decreasing job demands such as work load or responsibility, increasing job-related skills, or both. Likewise, coping with demands-abilities misfit associated with family might entail reducing parenting demands by using child-care services, increasing parenting skills through training or workshops, or both. Moreover, because of linkages between work and family, interventions that target one domain can reduce stress in that domain as well as the other domain. For example, flextime at work can provide people with resources to meet family demands. Likewise, developing conflict management skills in the family setting can help resolve conflicts among employees in the work setting (cf. Crouter, 1984). Finally, the model also emphasizes the importance of perception, where the perceived person and environment are the critical linkages between the objective person and environment and stress. Thus, communication of policies is critical in ensuring that organizational interventions are seen and understood by employees.

The model presented here is an initial attempt to integrate P-E fit theory with work and family stress research. Further theoretical development is clearly warranted. For instance, we considered only a subset of the possible linkages between work and family that the model can accommodate. It would be useful to consider the conceptual, empirical, and practical value of examining the full set of linkages offered by the model. In addition, the model could be further expanded into parallel versions for different roles within work and family (e.g., boss, coworker, subordinate, parent, spouse) and additional life domains (e.g., leisure). Expanding the model in this manner would increase its complexity, but this complexity mirrors the multifaceted nature of the stress process across different aspects of life. We hope the model presented here stimulates research that increases our understanding of this process.

NOTES

1. Strictly speaking, any line running perpendicular to the fit line represents variation in the difference between needs and supplies. However, the misfit line depicted in Fig. 11.3 captures the maximum differences between needs and supplies, as indicated when needs reach their maximum and supplies reach their minimum or vice versa (as indicated by the end points of the misfit line).

2. Edwards and Rothbard (1999) used satisfaction rather than dissatisfaction as the outcome of needs and supplies. Therefore, to construct the surfaces in Fig. 11.5, the scaling of the vertical axis was reversed. Other than this modification, the surfaces in Fig. 11.5 are identical to those reported by Edwards and Rothbard (1999).

REFERENCES

Adams, G. A., King, L. A., & King, D. W. (1996). Relationship of job and family involvement, family social support, and work-family conflict with job and life satisfaction. *Journal of Applied Psychology, 81,* 411–420.

Aryee, S., Luk, V., Leung, A., & Lo, S. (1999). Role stressors, interrole conflict, and well-being: The moderating influence of spousal support and coping behaviors among employed parents in Hong Kong. *Journal of Vocational Behavior, 54,* 259–278.

Ashforth, B. E., & Humphrey, R. H. (1993). Emotional labor in service roles: The influence of identity. *Academy of Management Review, 18,* 88–115.

Bacharach, S. B., Bamberger, P., & Conley, S. (1991). Work-home conflict among nurses and engineers: Mediating the impact of role stress on burnout and satisfaction at work. *Journal of Organizational Behavior, 12,* 39–53.

Barling, J., & Macewen, K. E. (1992). Linking work experiences to facets of marital functioning. *Journal of Organizational Behavior, 13,* 573–583.

Bedeian, A. G., Burke, B. G., & Moffett, R. G. (1988). Outcomes of work-family conflict among married male and female professionals. *Journal of Management, 14,* 475–491.

Beehr, T. A., & Bhagat, R. S. (1985). Introduction to human stress and cognition in organizations. In T. A. Beehr & R. S. Bhagat (Eds.), *Human stress and cognition in organizations* (pp. 3–19). New York: Wiley.

Bhagat, R. S. (1983). Effects of stressful life events on individual performance effectiveness and work adjustment processes within organizational settings: A research model. *Academy of Management Review, 8,* 660–671.

Bhagat, R. S., McQuaid, S. J., Lindholm, H., & Segovis, J. (1985). Total life stress: A multimethod validation of the construct and its effects on organizationally valued outcomes and withdrawal behaviors. *Journal of Applied Psychology, 70,* 202–214.

Burke, R. J. (1986). Occupational and life stress and the family: Conceptual frameworks and research findings. *International Review of Applied Psychology, 35,* 347–369.

Burke, R. J. (1993). Work-family stress, conflict, coping, and burnout in police officers. *Stress Medicine, 9,* 171–180.

Burke, R. J., & Greenglass, E. (1987). Work and family. In C. L. Cooper & I. T. Robertson (Eds.), *International review of industrial and organizational psychology* (pp. 273–320). New York: Wiley.

Caplan, R. D. (1983). Person-environment fit: Past, present, and future. In C. L. Cooper (Ed.), *Stress research* (pp. 35–78). New York: Wiley.

Caplan, R. D. (1987). Person-environment fit theory and organizations: Commensurate dimensions, time perspectives, and mechanisms. *Journal of Vocational Behavior, 31,* 248–267.

Caplan, R. D., Cobb, S., French, J.R.P., Jr., Harrison, R. V., & Pinneau, S. R. (1980). *Job demands and worker health: Main effects and occupational differences.* Ann Arbor, MI: Institute for Social Research.

Caplan, R. D., & Harrison, R. V. (1993). Person-environment fit theory: Some history, recent developments, and future directions. *Journal of Social Issues, 49,* 253–275.

Champoux, J. E. (1978). Perceptions of work and nonwork: A reexamination of the compensatory and spillover models. *Sociology of Work and Occupations, 5,* 402–422.

Cialdini, R. B., Trost, M. R., & Newsom, J. T. (1995). Preference for consistency: The development of a valid measure and the discovery of surprising behavioral implications. *Journal of Personality and Social Psychology, 69,* 318–328.

Cooke, R. A., & Rousseau, D. M. (1984). Stress and strain from family roles and work role expectations. *Journal of Applied Psychology, 69,* 252–260.

Cooper, C. L., & Marshall, J. (1976). Occupational sources of stress: Review of literature relating to coronary heart disease and mental ill health. *Journal of Occupational Psychology, 49,* 11–28.

Crouter, A. C. (1984). Participative work as an influence on human development. *Journal of Applied Developmental Psychology, 5,* 71–90.

Diener, E. (1984). Subjective well-being. *Psychological Bulletin, 95,* 542–575.

Eckenrode, J., & Gore, S. (1990). Stress and coping at the boundary of work and family. In J. Eckenrode & S. Gore (Eds.), *Stress between work and family* (pp. 1–16). New York: Plenum.

Edwards, J. R. (1988). The determinants and consequences of coping with stress. In C. L. Cooper & R. Payne (Eds.), *Causes, coping, and consequences of stress at work* (pp. 233–263). New York: Wiley.

Edwards, J. R. (1991). Person-job fit: A conceptual integration, literature review, and methodological critique. In C. L. Cooper & I. T. Robertson (Eds.), *International review of industrial and organizational psychology* (Vol. 6, pp. 283–357). New York: Wiley.

Edwards, J. R. (1992). A cybernetic theory of stress, coping, and well-being in organizations. *Academy of Management Review, 17,* 238–274.

Edwards, J. R. (1994). The study of congruence in organizational behavior research: Critique and a proposed alternative. *Organizational Behavior and Human Decision Processes, 58,* 51–100 (*erratum, 58,* 323–325).

Edwards, J. R. (1996). An examination of competing versions of the person-environment fit approach to stress. *Academy of Management Journal, 39,* 292–339.

Edwards, J. R. (2002). Alternatives to difference scores: Polynomial regression analysis and response surface methodology. In F. Drasgow & N. W. Schmitt (Eds.), *Advances in measurement and data analysis* (pp. 350–400). San Francisco: Jossey-Bass.

Edwards, J. R., Caplan, R. D., & Harrison, R. V. (1998). Person-environment fit theory: Conceptual foundations, empirical evidence, and directions for future research. In C. L. Cooper (Ed.), *Theories of organizational stress* (pp. 28–67). Oxford, England: Oxford University Press.

Edwards, J. R., & Cooper, C. L. (1988). The impacts of positive psychological states on physical health: A review and theoretical framework. *Social Science and Medicine, 27,* 1447–1459.

Edwards, J. R., & Harrison, R. V. (1993). Job demands and worker health: Three-dimensional re-examination of the relationship between person-environment fit and strain. *Journal of Applied Psychology, 78,* 628–648.

Edwards, J. R., & Parry, M. E. (1993). On the use of polynomial regression equations as an alternative to difference scores in organizational research. *Academy of Management Journal, 36,* 1577–1613.

Edwards, J. R., & Rothbard, N. P. (1999). Work and family stress and well-being: An examination of person-environment fit in the work and family domains. *Organizational Behavior and Human Decision Processes, 77,* 85–129.

Edwards, J. R., & Rothbard, N. P. (2000). Mechanisms linking work and family: Clarifying the relationship between work and family constructs. *Academy of Management Review, 25,* 178–199.

French, J.R.P., Jr., Caplan, R. D., & Harrison, R. V. (1982). *The mechanisms of job stress and strain.* London: Wiley.

French, J.R.P., Jr., Rodgers, W. L., & Cobb, S. (1974). Adjustment as person-environment fit. In G. Coelho, D. Hamburg, & J. Adams (Eds.), *Coping and adaptation* (pp. 316–333). New York: Basic Books.

Frone, M. R., Russell, M., & Cooper, M. L. (1992). Antecedents and outcomes of work-family conflict: Testing a model of the work-family interface. *Journal of Applied Psychology, 77,* 65–78.

Frone, M. R., Yardley, J. K., & Markel, K. S. (1997). Developing and testing an integrative model of the work-family interface. *Journal of Vocational Behavior, 50,* 145–167.

Gecas, V., & Seff, M. A. (1990). Social class and self-esteem: Psychological centrality, compensation, and the relative effects of work and home. *Social Psychology Quarterly, 53,* 165–173.

Grandey, A. A., & Cropanzano, R. (1999). The Conservation of Resources model applied to work-family conflict and strain. *Journal of Vocational Behavior, 54,* 350–370.

Greenhaus, J. H. (1989). The intersection of work and family roles: Individual, interpersonal, and organizational issues. In E. B. Goldsmith (Ed.), *Work and family: Theory, research, and applications* (pp. 23–44). Newbury Park, CA: Sage.

Greenhaus, J. H., & Beutell, N. J. (1985). Sources of conflict between work and family roles. *Academy of Management Review, 10,* 76–88.

Greenhaus, J. H., & Parasuraman, S. (1986). A work-nonwork interactive perspective of stress and its consequences. *Journal of Organizational Behavior Management, 8,* 37–60.

Harrison, R. V. (1978). Person-environment fit and job stress. In C. L. Cooper & R. Payne (Eds.), *Stress at work* (pp. 175–205). New York: Wiley.

Harrison, R. V. (1985). The person-environment fit model and the study of job stress. In T. A. Beehr & R. S. Bhagat (Eds.), *Human stress and cognition in organizations* (pp. 23–55). New York: Wiley.

Hesketh, B., & Gardner, D. (1993). Person-environment fit models: A reconceptualization and empirical test. *Journal of Vocational Behavior, 42,* 315–332.

Higgins, C. A., Duxbury, L. E., & Irving, R. H. (1992). Work-family conflict in the dual-career family. *Organizational Behavior and Human Decision Process, 51,* 51–75.

Hobfoll, S. E. (1998). *Stress, culture, and community: The psychology and philosophy of stress.* New York: Plenum.

Ispa, J. M., Gray, M. M., & Thornburg, K. R. (1984). Childrearing attitudes of parents in person-oriented and thing-oriented occupations: A comparison. *Journal of Psychology, 117,* 245–250.

Kabanoff, B. (1980). Work and nonwork: A review of models, methods, and findings. *Psychological Bulletin, 88,* 60–77.

Kahn, R. L., Wolfe, D. M., Quinn, R. P., Snoek, J. D., & Rosenthal, R. A. (1964). *Organizational stress: Studies in role conflict and ambiguity.* New York: Wiley.

Kando, T. M., & Summers, W. C. (1971). The impact of work on leisure: Toward a paradigm and research strategy. *Pacific Sociological Review, 14,* 310–327.

Kline, M., & Cowan, P. A. (1989). Re-thinking the connections among work and family well-being: A model for investigating employment and family work contexts. In E. B. Goldsmith (Ed.), *Work and family: Theory, research, and applications* (pp. 61–90). Newbury Park, CA: Sage.

Klinger, E. (1975). Consequences of commitment to and disengagement from incentives. *Psychological Review, 82,* 1–25.

Kopelman, R. E., Greenhaus, J. H. & Connolly, T. F. (1983). A model of work, family, and interrole conflict: A construct validation study. *Organizational Behavior and Human Performance, 32,* 198–215.

Kristof, A. L. (1996). Person-organization fit: An integrative review of its conceptualization, measurement, and implications. *Personnel Psychology, 49,* 1–49.

Lambert, S. J. (1990). Processes linking work and family: A critical review and research agenda. *Human Relations, 43,* 239–257.

Lazarus, R. S. (1983). The costs and benefits of denial. In S. Breznitz (Ed.), *Denial of stress* (pp. 1–30). New York: International Universities Press.

Lazarus, R. S., & Folkman, S. (1984). *Stress, appraisal, and coping.* New York: Springer.

Lewin, K. (1951). *Field theory in social science.* New York: Harper.

Livingstone, L. P., Nelson, D. L., & Barr, S. H. (1997). Person-environment fit and creativity: An examination of supply-value and demand-ability versions of fit. *Journal of Management, 23,* 119–146.

Lobel, S. A. (1991). Allocation of investment in work and family roles: Alternative theories and implications for research. *Academy of Management Review, 16,* 507–521.

Locke, E. A. (1976). The nature and causes of job satisfaction. In M. Dunnette (Ed.), *Handbook of industrial and organizational psychology* (pp. 1297–1350). Chicago: Rand McNally.

Lord, R. G., & Kernan, M. C. (1987). Scripts as determinants of purposeful behavior in organizations. *Academy of Management Review, 12,* 265–277.

Lord, R. G., & Maher, K. J. (1991). Cognitive theory in industrial and organizational psychology. In M. D. Dunnette & L. M. Hough (Eds.), *Handbook of industrial and organizational psychology* (2nd ed., Vol. 2, pp. 1–62). Palo Alto, CA: Consulting Psychologists Press.

Martin, T. N., & Schermerhorn, J. R., Jr. (1983). Work and nonwork influences on health: A research agenda using inability to leave as a critical variable. *Academy of Management Review, 8,* 650–659.

McGrath, J. E. (1970). A conceptual formulation for research on stress. In J. E. McGrath (Ed.), *Social and psychological factors in stress* (pp. 10–21). New York: Holt, Rinehart, and Winston.

McGrath, J. E. (1976). Stress and behavior in organizations. In M. Dunnette (Ed.), *Handbook of industrial and organizational psychology* (pp. 1351–1395). Chicago: Rand McNally.

Morf, M. (1989). *The work/life dichotomy.* Westport, CT: Quorum Books.

Murray, H. A. (1938). *Explorations in personality.* Boston: Houghton Mifflin.

Near, J., Rice, R., & Hunt, R. (1980). The relationship between work and nonwork domains: A review of empirical research. *Academy of Management Review, 5,* 415–429.

Nolen-Hoeksema, S., Parker, L. E., & Larson, J. (1994). Ruminative coping with depressed mood following loss. *Journal of Personality & Social Psychology, 67,* 92–104.

Parker, D. F., & DeCotiis, T. A. (1983). Organizational determinants of job stress. *Organizational Behavior and Human Performance, 32,* 160–177.

Payton-Miyazaki, M., & Brayfield, A. H. (1976). The good job and the good life: Relationship of characteristics of employment to general well being. In A. D. Biderman & T. F. Drury (Eds.), *Measuring work quality for social reporting* (pp. 105–150). New York: Sage.

Pearlin, L. I., & Kohn, M. (1966). Social class, occupational, and parental values: A cross-national study. *American Sociological Review, 31,* 466–479.

Pearlin, L. I., & Schooler, C. (1978). The structure of coping. *Journal of Health and Social Behavior, 19*, 2–21.

Piotrkowski, C. S. (1979). *Work and the family system.* New York: Free Press.

Piotrkowski, C. S., Rapoport, R. N., & Rapoport, R. (1987). Families and work. In M. Sussman & S. Steinmetz (Eds.), *Handbook of marriage and the family* (pp. 251–283). New York: Plenum.

Popper, K. R. (1959). *The logic of scientific discovery.* New York: Basic Books.

Rafaeli, A., & Sutton, R. I. (1987). Expression of emotion as part of the work role. *Academy of Management Review, 12*, 23–37.

Repetti, R. L. (1987). Linkages between work and family roles. *Applied Social Psychology Annual, 7*, 98–127.

Rice, R. W., Frone, M. R., & McFarlin, D. B. (1992). Work-nonwork conflict and the perceived quality of life. *Journal of Organizational Behavior, 13*, 155–168.

Rice, R. W., McFarlin, D. B., Hunt, R. G., & Near, J. P. (1985). Organizational work and the perceived quality of life: Toward a conceptual model. *Academy of Management Review, 10*, 296–310.

Rice, R. W., Near, J. P., & Hunt, R. G. (1980). The job-satisfaction/life-satisfaction relationship: A review of empirical research. *Basic and Applied Social Psychology, 1*, 37–64.

Rice, R. W., Peirce, R. S., Moyer, R. P., & McFarlin, D. B. (1991). Using discrepancies to predict the perceived quality of work life. *Journal of Business and Psychology, 6*, 39–55.

Schuler, R. S. (1980). Definition and conceptualization of stress in organizations. *Organizational Behavior and Human Performance, 25*, 184–215.

Shirom, A. (1982). What is organizational stress? A facet analytic conceptualization. *Journal of Occupational Behavior, 3*, 21–37.

Small, S. A., & Riley, D. (1990). Toward a multidimensional assessment of work spillover. *Journal of Marriage and the Family, 52*, 51–61.

Spokane, A. R., Meir, E. I., & Catalano, M. (2000). Person-environment congruence and Holland's theory: A review and reconsideration. *Journal of Vocational Behavior, 57*, 137–187.

Staines, G. L. (1980). Spillover versus compensation: A review of the literature on the relationship between work and nonwork. *Human Relations, 33*, 111–129.

Staw, B. M., Sutton, R. I., & Pelled, L. H. (1994). Employee positive emotion and favorable outcomes at the workplace. *Organization Science, 5*, 51–71.

Taris, R., & Feij, J. A. (2001). Longitudinal examination of the relationship between supplies-values fit and work outcomes. *Applied Psychology: An International Review, 50*, 52–80.

Voydanoff, P. (1987). *Work and family life.* Newbury Park, CA: Sage.

Voydanoff, P. (1989). Work and family: A review and expanded conceptualization. In E. B. Goldsmith (Ed.), *Work and family: Theory, research, and applications* (pp. 1–22). Newbury Park, CA: Sage.

Weick, K. E. (1979). *The social psychology of organizing.* New York: McGraw Hill.

White, R. W. (1959). Motivation reconsidered: The concept of competence. *Psychological Review, 66*, 297–333.

Zedeck, S. (1992). Exploring the domain of work and family concerns. In S. Zedeck (Ed.), *Work, families, and organizations* (pp. 1–32). San Francisco: Jossey-Bass.

12

Flexibility Enactment Theory: Implications of Flexibility Type, Control, and Boundary Management for Work-Family Effectiveness

Ellen Ernst Kossek
Michigan State University

Brenda A. Lautsch
Simon Fraser University

Susan C. Eaton
Harvard University

I don't really have . . . walls around either of them [work and family]. If something big is going on, one tends to bleed over into the other.
—"Sarah," Infocom employee who often teleworks

A general tenet of the work-family scholarship is that individuals who are employed in workplaces that are designed as if work and family were separate spheres will experience higher work-family role conflict unless employers adopt policies to provide greater flexibility to support integration between work and home (Friedman, Christensen, & DeGroot, 1998; Kanter, 1977). Flextime, telecommuting, and other flexibility policies are proliferating to help employees blend work and family roles to reduce conflicts (Golden, 2001). National surveys show that 84% of major employers have adopted flexible schedules and nearly two thirds (64%) offer telecommuting (Alliance for Work-Life Progress, 2001) with these policies most available to professionals (Bureau of Labor Statistics, 2000).

Yet as the opening quotation suggests, even with access to flexible work arrangements, managing boundaries between work and home remains a significant challenge for many individuals (Ashforth, Kreiner, & Fugate, 2000). The purpose of this chapter is to theoretically unpack a widely used construct in the work-family field: flexibility. Our main arguments are that there may be "good" and "bad" forms of flexibility and that the type of flexibility enacted and how individuals manage and experience boundaries matter for positive outcomes.

Our assumption is that work-family research would be enhanced if more studies shift focus away from viewing use of and formal access to flexibility as a panacea. Nor should scholars frame flexibility as a dichotomous variable (i.e., one either has it or does not) that is usually always positive and underdifferentiate the effects of different types of flexibility. Research on alternative work arrangements has underexamined the way in which access to flexibility is a necessary but insufficient condition for reducing work-family conflict and enhancing well being. We contend that what matters most for effectiveness in the synthesis of work and family roles are the conditions under which flexibility is enacted. This perspective is consistent with Rapoport and colleagues' (2002) argument that research should shift from a focus on formal policy to focus on informal and change processes.

FLEXIBILITY ENACTMENT

We develop the concept of *flexibility enactment*, which is the type of use and the way boundaries are psychologically managed, and identify the conditions under which flexibility promotes positive work-life outcomes. Our main thesis is that the type of flexibility used and how the individual psychologically experiences flexibility matters most for work and family well-being. A focus on flexibility enactment acknowledges that variation exists in the way that flexibility is employed, the degree to which access and use of flexibility practices promote individual autonomy and job control, and in how individuals' psychologically experience managing boundaries between work and home. Our chapter argues that different individuals will experience varied outcomes of flexibility, even after taking into account the constraints of their families and jobs. Although conventional wisdom might strongly suggest that some people are well-suited to working in a highly flexible environment and others are not (MacDermid, 2004), the parameters of our chapter are to focus our discussion on flexibility types and boundary management. This focus is due to space limitations and our belief that certain structuring of flexibility and boundaries between work and family may create strong situations that are more likely to lead to positive or negative outcomes than to individual differences.

In this chapter, we draw on insights gleaned from an empirical study we conducted involving interviews with over 300 professional knowledge workers from two Fortune 500 firms who had varying access to flexibility in the location (e.g., teleworking, telecommuting), personal autonomy, and timing and regularity of work and from a subset of their supervisors (Eaton, Lautsch, & Kossek, 2003; Kossek, Lautsch, & Eaton, 2002; Kossek, Lautsch, Eaton, & Van Vanden Bosch, 2004).

Figure 12.1 depicts aspects of the constructs capturing flexibility enactment we develop. It refers to the type of flexibility used (i.e., formality, individual job control/autonomy, irregularity, mobility, and portability volume) and one's boundary management strategy. An individual's boundary management strategy does not involve a dichotomy between segmentation and integration as some of the work-family literature to date has implied, but rather combinations of various

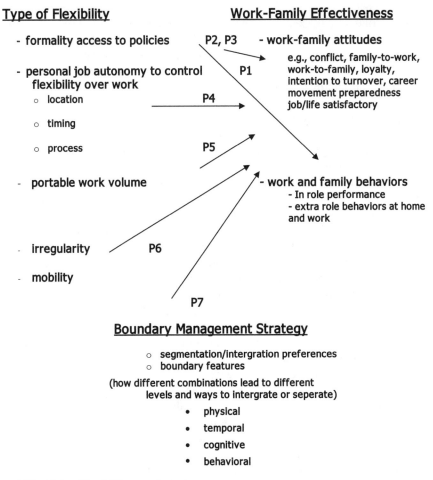

FIG. 12.1. Flexibility enactment

types of boundaries (e.g., temporal, mental, physical, behavioral). We identify predictors and outcomes of the different ways in which individuals manage the boundaries and borders between work and home.

Figure 15.1 also notes the importance of considering positive and well as negative effects from flexibility use for various work and family attitudes and behaviors. In other words, in the short run, some kinds of boundaries and flexibility such as high mobility and high integration may be beneficial for work outcomes because one has greater accessibility to work but over the long run may negatively affect personal well being or family outcomes by resulting in increased work-to-family conflict. We hope our chapter will encourage more research that is derived from assumptions of mixed effects from flexibility.

This chapter is derived from the identification of several gaps in the literature. First, variation may exist in the extent and nature of flexibility used such as in the formality, location, control, volume, or regularity of flexible work that could have differing implications for work and family outcomes. We believe work-family research generally underexamines the reality that employees often use different and multiple forms and amounts of flexibility; that employees usually do not experience flexibility in the same way or as an all-or-nothing phenomenon; and that employees' having access to flexibility does not necessarily capture its use. More research to date has examined the availability of formal flexible work arrangement policies (e.g., telecommuting, flextime) than the consequences of use or the way that flexibility is practiced on the job. We believe that the work-family literature has underconsidered informal flexibility and that job design measures need to be updated to account for this job characteristic.

An understudied recent change is the increase in many professionals' access to informal flexibility in terms of how their jobs are designed instead or in addition to a formal human resource (HR) policy. Greater numbers of employees are taking their work home or are working while traveling on planes, visiting the customer, or commuting in cars or trains, and they may not all (or mostly) be formally teleworking or using other formal flexibility policies. Some may be working flexibly different hours each week, while others work at flexible hours at the same time each week. We develop constructs to conceptualize variation in the nature and degree in which flexibility is practiced as well as implications for work-family outcomes.

Additionally, more research is needed on how employees enact boundaries as linking mechanism between work and family. In recent years, there has been considerable study of the conflicts that individuals face in managing their work and family lives, but limited research has examined how people differ in their preferences for managing work and family boundaries or in their feelings of control over job flexibility. While some theoretical and qualitative work has been conducted on the blending of work and family boundaries (cf. Ashforth et al., 2000; Nippert-Eng, 1996), more theory is needed on the correlates of an individual's boundary management strategy defined as the principles one uses to organize and separate role demands and expectations into specific realms of home (i.e., dependent caregiving) and work (i.e., doing one's job) (Kossek, Noe, & DeMarr, 1999). Given our movement toward a virtual workplace where increasing numbers of individuals have access to work at any hour of the day, we theorize correlates of an individual's boundary management strategy and examine linkages between perceptions of control over flexibility and work-family outcomes.

A recent review of the telework literature notes that "how people telework" has been overlooked with most employees working away from the office part-time rather than full-time (Bailey & Kurland, 2002). We believe there is considerable variability in the enactment of flexibility policies as the preferences of individual supervisors regarding how to best manage changes associated with policy use differ (Eaton, 2003; Glass & Fujimoto, 1995). For example, one manager may state that teleworkers must be in the office on set days, while another allows more flexibility, and another may offer only policies that allow for lower role commitment on the job if one takes advantage of the policies. A study of three types of flexible work schedules including flextime found that supervisors are more likely to provide more work-life flexibility to top performers and only if not too many workers in the same work group use the policy at the same time (Kossek, Barber, & Winters, 1999). Using a sample of MBA students, Rau and Hyland (2002) note differences in hypothesized influences on conflict and turnover intentions between vignettes of telecommuting and flextime arrangements. These results indicate that not all types of flexibility may relate to work-family outcomes similarly. We theorize differing effects of various flexibility types: formality, personal job autonomy, volume, regularity, and mobility.

Formality: Divergence Between Supervisors' Performance Ratings and Users' Self-Reported Attitudes. Formality is defined as the degree to which permission to use flexibility is formalized by established organizational practices or procedures. The more that an individual uses formal flexibility policies that publicly acknowledge the asking of permission from supervisors or the HR department to work flexibly, and/or establishes ritualized use of nonstandard work times or locations, the higher one's use of formal flexibility. It well documented that conventional stereotypes of workers on alternative schedules are that they are less committed (Williams, 2000). It is perfectly reasonable to assume supervisors might share these biases and to assume that workers who formally acknowledge that they need to use flexibility policies are not ideal workers who can work anywhere or anytime at the beck and call of their firms. Studies also show that supervisors have resistance to flexibility programs, as there is a prevailing belief that they create more work for them and they make their job of managing and coordinating more difficult (Eaton, Lautsch, & Kossek, 2003; Kossek, Barber, & Winters, 1999). It can be burdensome for supervisors to keep track of all the different arrangements when the number of workers in flexible arrangements starts to rise. There also may be a supervisory fear that higher formal access to flexibility will make flexibility be viewed as an entitlement, and individuals will be unwilling to work certain times when unexpected demands arise.

> Proposition 1: Due to stereotypes regarding the negative effects of flexibility on the organization, supervisors are more likely to rate the performance of individuals who are users of formal flexibility lower on performance ratings than other employees who do not formally use flexibility policies.

We were surprised to find that our pessimistic views of supervisors attitudes toward users would be disproved, after controlling for many individual differences such as gender, family demographics, and job characteristics. Our hierarchical regression analysis shows that formal users of flexibility had significantly higher supervisor performance ratings. This counter-intuitive finding is because of the way that the supervisors had implemented flexibility at the companies we studied. They tended to be more likely to grant formal access to flexibility to their better performers.

Much of the published literature on teleworking relies only on self-report data from users of the policies, which tends to have a positive bias supporting general use for all workers, as employees have a vested interest in not losing access to flexibility (Bailey & Kurland, 2002). Our findings may have been strengthened by the fact that we measured actual formal access to teleworking based on personnel records confirming the granting of organizational permission to telework and the provision of technical capability to regularly work offsite, which was in contrast to most of the published research on teleworking. Although we measured formal use as a dichotomous variable, because that is how the companies in our study measure use, we note that it may be that the effects of flexibility cannot be fully captured dichotomously but rather as a continuous variable. There may be a sensitivity level (likely a curvilinear relationship) where the amount of flexibility matters in shaping positive individual productivity and well-being (Baltes, Briggs, Huff, Wright, & Newman, 1999). In addition, individual differences in caregiving and job demands and high personal capability to excel on and off those as well as motivational influences such as good supervision and clear performance standards may moderate the effects of flexibility. Mere access to formal programs may not tap into these other influences. Certainly, we are not suggesting that theories consider formal access unimportant. If policies are not available, most individuals will not be able to access flexibility at all. What we are suggesting is that theories need to not assume that formal access or use is necessarily sufficient to ensure positive work and family outcomes.

We theorize that greater access to formal work-life supports will affect organizational membership behaviors such as retention and career stability. Kossek and Nichol (1992) found that nurses are much less prone to turnover if they have formal employer support for family such as on-site child care. Furthermore, there is an established literature on the existence of positive relationships between the availability or use of formal organizational supports for family and employee attitudes (Ozeki, 2003) such as loyalty and organizational commitment (Allen, 2001; Grover & Crooker, 1995; Roehling, Roehling, & Moen, 2001). Indeed, research consistently shows a positive relationship between the existence or use of flexibility policies and a lower intention to turnover and the preparedness to move to a new job (Rau & Hyland, 2002; Scandura & Lankau, 1997).

> Proposition 2: Formal access to flexibility (e.g. telework) will relate positively to favorable *employee work retention attitudes* such as lower intention to turnover or prepare for career mobility.

Although not significant at the .05 level, we indeed did find in our study (Kossek et al., 2004) that formal access to flexibility (e.g., telework) is related positively to favorable employee work retention attitudes such as lower intention to turnover or preparation for a career change. We surmise that although employees are motivated to perform basic job requirements by a host of factors that may not necessarily be related to employer support of work and family, the availability and use of formal flexibility may be an attractive job characteristic that enables a company or profession to retain individuals. It is a way of differentiating a job or career from others in the marketplace.

Research on whether there is a positive relationship between formal access to telework and lower work-family conflict is inconclusive. While some research is positive (Duxbury, Higgins & Neufeld, 1998; Hill, Hawkins, Ferris, & Weitzman, 2001), other studies are not. Hill, Miller, Weiner, and Colihan (1998) find no difference in levels of work-family conflict experienced by professionals who were required to work under a virtual office plan that reduced office space while giving them electronic supports to work from anywhere (often at home) compared to those who worked in company offices. Allen (2001) finds that greater *use* of work-family policies providing flexibility such as telecommuting, flextime, and compressed weeks is related to less work-family conflict, while mere *availability* is not. Eaton (2003) also finds that usability of work-family policies—that employees feel free to use actually them—is what is critical for positive outcomes not mere availability. Notwithstanding some notable exceptions (e.g., Eaton, 2003; Grover & Crooker, 1995; Lambert, 2000), some work-family studies confound access and use. Given the mixed results on work-family conflict, we theorized and found:

> Proposition 3: Formal access to telework is insufficient in and of itself to affect work to family and family to work conflict.

After considering the effects of individual differences such as gender and job characteristics, and using a control group of users and nonusers, we found that formal access to telework does not significantly reduce work-to-family and family-to-work conflict. It is a null effect. We advise researchers to try to not only rely on self-report data of use or only measure access to policies. Our research suggests that formal access has more symbolic than tangible effects or some other unmeasured variables such as job design, workload, personal control over flexibility and family caregiving demands, supportive supervision and work cultures may matter more for the reduction of work-family conflict than access alone. More research is needed that not only documents the public relations benefits of flexibility access but also measures how well these policies actually are working to benefit employees and their families.

Job Autonomy/Control: Personal Control over Where, When, and How One Works May Be the Most Critical Flexibility Construct for Assessing Employee Well-Being. Parker, Wall, and Cordery (2001) note that developments in work and job design theory have not kept pace with changes in organizational practices related to the variation in the experience of autonomy while teleworking. For example, telework professionals such as information technology consultants who work from home might have high autonomy, whereas other teleworkers such as telemarketers might have jobs that are designed to be quite tightly controlled, even though both employees have access to telework (Feldman & Gainey, 1997). Research has long demonstrated the importance of personal autonomy for well being (Parker et al., 2001).

Some literature reviews have noted that one problem with early work-family conflict research is that few studies measure whether the use of policies such as flexibility actually reduce conflict or improve personal effectiveness (cf. Kossek & Ozeki, 1998, 1999). Given the changing nature of work in which technological changes have made it easier for professionals to be accessible to work around the clock, we believe that an underinvestigated variable is the degree to which individuals can control their flexibility: the degree to which they have personal autonomy over where, when, and how they work.

Previous research on telework has focused more on formal access to telework than on the degree of autonomy one has over his or her flexibility. For example, a company may offer formal work-family policies, but despite the organizational rhetoric regarding HR management progressivism, these policies may not necessarily benefit employees in the way they are stated on paper (Still & Strang, 2003). The rhetoric of family-friendly flexibility policies may not always match their reality (Avery & Zabel, 2001): They may not necessarily give employees greater autonomy over their flexibility.

When we looked at traditional measures of autonomy in job design, we did not see measures of control over the location and flexible scheduling of work being fully captured as basic elements of job design in widely used measures such as the Job Diagnostic Survey (Hackman & Oldham, 1980), that measure personal job autonomy in how the work is done at the workplace and some degrees of interdependence. We theorize that individual autonomy over where and when one works is a key aspect of job autonomy that should be assessed to update measures of autonomy within work environments in which the job can increasingly be done portably or away from the main workplace at different times of the day. We propose this construct, personal job flexibility autonomy, and believe it positively relates to work and family outcomes. We believe that the more individuals perceive they have control over flexibility, the more they will experience lower work-family conflict and lower intention to turnover or change careers.

Preposition 4: Personal job flexibility autonomy, defined as control over where, when, and how one works is positively related to lower work-family conflict, intention to turnover, and career movement preparedness.

Of all of the flexibility enactment measures in our study, personal job autonomy, is the strongest predictor of good flexibility outcomes. Those who have higher personal job flexibility control have lower work-family conflict, better work attitudes such as lower intention to turnover, and low career movement preparation. What was surprising is they do not necessarily get higher performance ratings, suggesting some supervisor resistance to personal autonomy or that this is not what matters for good ratings—other factors are more important, such as how one manages boundaries that matter.

Portable Work Volume: Are There Any Downsides to Being Able to Carry Around Our Work? Most previous research has not measured the volume or proportion of work done portably or away from the office. Some studies on teleworking have assumed a full-time at-home arrangement, although recent research suggests that this is more the exception than the rule (Bailey & Kurland, 2002). We believe the richness in the variation in the nature of place flexibility has not been fully captured in most previous studies. *Telework* and *telecommuting* are too constricting terms, as they do not fully portray all aspects of the job that employees might do away from the main work location.

We suggest the term *portable work*, which we define as "work you can take with you," might better capture all the work employees might be doing in enacting their flexibility in time and place. Portable work includes not only telework, which has been defined as working outside of the workplace and communicating by means of communications or computer-based technology (Bailey & Kurland, 2002), but also any other job-related work the employee conducts away from the office such as phone calls, writing, doing analytic work without telecommunications, face-to-face meetings, and so on. These later tasks are still clearly work, but they often do not rely on wired technology. We believe that the act of working away from the office location is what needs to be captured in theory regardless of whether one is using telecommunications. Portable work extends to any kind of work an individual can conduct away from a workplace setting (although it may also be conducted in groups) and without large-scale capital investment. Tasks like grading term papers for a university professor are portable, for example, as are manual tasks such as sewing, clerical tasks such as word processing, service tasks such as phone answering, and creative tasks such as writing or computer programming. Work that is dependent on being in a particular place at a particular time, such as direct patient care in nursing, or active firefighting, is by definition not portable.

We believe that individuals who engage in higher volumes of portable work will be more likely to develop positive work retention attitudes such as lower intention to turnover (Allen, Shore, & Griffith, 2003) or change careers. This may be due to a perceived greater implementation of new ways of working to accommodate the changing composition of the workforce, higher perceived organizational support for family, and more signaling from the firm that it trusts its workers. Furthermore, because employees will be able to work at home when needed for family demands, they may experience lower work-to-family or family-to-work conflict.

> Proposition 5: High volume of portable work will result in positive work retention attitudes and lower work-family conflict.

In our study, we found that higher volume of portable work does significantly reduce preparedness to make career changes, but does not affect significantly turnover intentions. Future research should examine different effects of the amount of work done away from the office on job turnover as well as career turnover. We found few studies that examine these differential predictors, yet we believe they are important for future research. Professionals like the career freedom to work away from the office but may be less loyal to a particular job regardless of flexibility volume.

While the employer might reap more favorable employee attitudes from permitting high volumes of portable work, as in the case of formal access, future research needs to continue to investigate less positive outcomes related to work-family conflict. Although we found no positive effects on conflict from higher volumes of portable work in and of itself (as we will share later in this chapter, it was the type of boundary management strategy used that mattered, not volume per se), some scholars go as far as to suggest that those in jobs with higher volumes of portable tasks will encounter higher work-family conflict. These individuals will find it more difficult to set limits between work and family demands and may experience joint role overload. They may be seen as more available to interruptions from *both* work and family demands (Mirchandani,

1998). Rau (2003) notes that while a goal of flexible working arrangements is to make time less scarce and reduce work-family conflict, it is not clear whether or under what circumstances increased flexibility in job spatial and temporal boundaries increases or decreases conflict and well being. She observes that while higher flexibility can improve the ability to manage work and family demands, it could also result in increased role-blurring, which in turn could create confusion about which demands (work or family) should be attended to at any given time and actually could increase role conflict.

Schedule Irregularity and Place Mobility: Is Flux in Time and Place Generally a "Good Thing" for Employees? We conceptualize two other variables future research should use to capture flux in flexibility enactment and how it relates to work and family outcomes: schedule irregularity (i.e., frequent changes in daily working hours) and place mobility (e.g., working at multiple locations, such as at home, the office, a client's office, or on the road).

> Proposition 6: Due to increased process losses and switching costs, individuals with high use of "bad types of flexibility" such as high place mobility and high schedule irregularity, will have higher intention to turnover and higher work to family conflict.

Given the higher likely number of process losses and transaction costs (cf. Ashforth et al., 2000) resulting from shifting between varying work schedules and/or multiple places, we argue that, contrary to the positive bias most literature on flexibility posits, flux aspects of flexibility negatively affect work and family outcomes. We found that those with more schedule irregularity have higher work-family conflict. These adverse outcomes can be attributed to increased cognitive complexity and demands (Crooker, Smith, & Tabak, 2002), more stress from the increased transaction and switching cost, and also the fact that increased schedule irregularity can make it harder to arrange child care or form consistent family plans. In one study examining factors that inhibited work and family well-being in dual career couples, irregular schedules are cited as the most significant negative influence (Moen & Yu, 1999). Higher irregularity can make it more difficult to set aside places that are solely for family and personal space and not work, thereby also increasing the potential for role conflict. Building on our research, future studies need to further investigate how the type and degree of flexibility enacted on the job results in mixed relationships to work and family outcomes. We found that individuals in jobs with higher schedule irregularity have higher work-family conflict. Building on our study, future research should examine how place mobility and schedule irregularity driven by professional work affects turnover and conflict and relates to other flexibility forms such as place mobility.

Boundary Management Strategy: Is Integration Really Always Better? We believe theory and research on employee outcomes from flexibility will be enhanced if studies examine not only access to and use of flexibility but also the psychological experience of flexibility pertaining to one's boundary management strategy. Little research has been conducted on the construct and correlates of boundary management strategies, in part because the concept is relatively new in the literature. We argue people psychologically enact a particular type of boundary management strategy that is partly shaped as a result of the structure of the job they are in and partly by individual differences. We did not examine individual predictors (e.g., gender, age) of one's boundary management strategy here because the focus of this chapter is on linkages between different types of flexibility and work and family outcomes, However, given the likely asymmetric permeability of boundaries between work and family for men and women, it is critical that future studies examine individual differences in boundary management strategies.

Theoretical perspectives on how work and family roles can intersect range on a continuum from segmentation (work and family are highly distinct) to integration (work and family are highly mixed) (Nippert-Eng, 1996). The segmentation view holds that work and family roles are completely independent and that individuals can participate in one role without any influence on the other (Blood & Wolfe, 1960). This perspective emanates from traditional work and family structures that reflect eras when it was common to create boundaries to clearly separate work and family and also from blue-collar work experiences (Kanter, 1977; Nippert-Eng, 1996). Usually, there was one breadwinning parent focused on the workplace (often the male) and one caregiving parent (often the female) focused on domestic life. Jobs were designed so there was no option to even attempt flexibility in the timing and location of work.

Today, job and family structures have evolved so that it is more common to blur work and family borders, especially in white-collar and "knowledge" work that involves computer and communications technology (Apgar, 1998). A major factor is the changing nature of today's workforce, in which dual-earner families are the typical American family (Barnett, 2001). Fathers are increasingly involved in caregiving (Coltrane, 1996), and eldercare demands are rising dramatically (Musselwhite, 1994). Given this shift in the contemporary nature of work and family structures, segmentation has been viewed more recently as an intentional separation of work and family roles such that the thoughts, feelings, and behaviors of one role are actively suppressed from affecting the individual's performance in the other role (Greenhaus & Singh, 2003). In this sense, it is more of a personal preference, an effort to be truly "at home" when one is not working.

We believe there is some social choice in how individuals define boundaries, as do Ashforth and colleagues (2001). Kossek, Noe, and DeMarr (1999) hold that a *boundary management strategy* is part of one's preferred approach to work-life role synthesis. Everyone has a preferred, even if implicit, approach for meshing work and family roles that reflects his or her values and the realities of his or her lives for organizing and separating role demands and expectations in the specific realms of home and work. This view is consistent with what Zedeck (1992) argues is at the heart of the issue of work-family balance: the way individuals shape the scope and parameters of work and family activities, create personal meaning, and manage the relationships between families and employees in organizations. Nippert-Eng (1996) suggests that in order to organize their varying work and family roles, individuals construct mental and sometimes physical fences as a means of ordering their social, work, and family environments. Through ethnographic interviews, she found that some of us are mainly integrators. We like to blend work and family roles, switching between baking cookies with the kids and downloading e-mail. Also, some of us are separators—we prefer to keep work and nonwork separate, rarely working from home or on the weekends.

The access to flexibility over where and when one works provides a robust possibility for people to develop preferences for boundary management from segmentation to integration. Ilgen and Hollenbeck (1990) note that creating a position (establishing a role) in an organization is a starting point and not an ending point. Similarly, allowing individuals to self-manage the flexibility enactment is a starting point for the negotiation of role expectations and meanings, not an ending point. Many employers have moved professional work into the home and to other places and have allowed greater schedule flexibility without clearly negotiating role expectations. Most of this work-family role synthesis or figuring out how to combine and structure multiple roles is left up the employee (Kossek, Noe, & DeMarr, 1999).

Noting that it is difficult today for growing numbers of employees to perform their jobs without interaction with the caregiving role and vice versa, many work-family theorists argue that greater integration between work and family roles is a way to balance work and family life and even to use one to catalyze positive effects in the other (Friedman et al., 1998; Rapoport, Bailyn, Fletcher, & Pruitt, 2002). Yet recent theory runs counter to the prevailing belief that integration is generally a good thing for individuals. The increased process losses, role transitions, and transactions costs associated with role switching may not necessarily lead to less conflict (Ashforth et al., 2000).

Proposition 7: Individuals with a boundary management strategy higher on integration will experience higher family-to-work and work-to-family conflict.

Our surprising results showed that having a boundary management strategy favoring integration is related only to significant negative effects for family-to-work conflict *but not* work-to-family. These findings suggest that integration strategies may more negatively affect family than work. Consistent with our formal access findings, we also predicted and found positive performance effects for those favoring an integration strategy. Although many supervisors do not see preferences for integration favorably, as many corporate cultures still value face time and segmentation (Major, Klein, & Ehrhart, 2002), they make exceptions for better performers.

FUTURE RESEARCH

Future empirical research is needed that draws on the flexibility enactment concepts developed here to improve research on flexible working arrangements (e.g., telecommuting, flextime), which to date shows mixed results in terms of productivity, work-family conflict, and other outcomes (Avery & Zabel, 2001; Bailey & Kurland, 2002). Such study would simultaneously examine the mixed effects of flexible work arrangements in the *same* study. More research is needed on whether flexible arrangements decrease (Mokhtarian, Bagley, & Saloman, 1998) or actually increase work-family conflict (Hill et al., 1998) and on the effects of flexibility on employees' home lives (Ezra, 1996). There may also be additional dimensions to identify measures for in future research such as flexibility in how tasks are carried out (i.e., methodology), what tasks are carried out (i.e., content), and the speed and sequence in which tasks are carried out. What is clear from this chapter is that personal job autonomy is a powerful flexibility attribute that has highly beneficial effects for work and family outcomes.

It's the Job Stupid: Flexibility Is Not a Countervailing Panacea for Poor Job Characteristics   More work-family research is needed that does not examine the effect of flexibility use and access in isolation but looks at it jointly with the effects of other key job characteristics, such as long hours and access to regular job performance feedback. It is well researched that long work hours relate to higher work-family conflict and worse work attitudes (cf. Major, Klein, & Ehrhart, 2002), whereas results for performance effects are mixed. Some scholars see negative effects for performance due to role overload and burnout (Ozeki, 2003), while others find long work hours associated both with higher work-family conflict and higher performance (Brett & Stroh, 2003). Individuals who get little feedback on their performance will also have more adverse outcomes, due both to the greater ambiguity over how they are doing and lower morale (cf. Parker, Wall, & Cordery, 2001).

Improved methodologies are needed as reviews suggest that empirical studies sometimes lack methodological rigor by overrelying on same source or anecdotal data rather than on statistical analysis or control groups, making it difficult to overcome a positive bias toward the effects of using formal flexibility in work-family programs (Gottlieb, Kelloway, & Barham, 1998). Studies should be designed with control groups, and non-same-source data for assessing outcomes. Time diaries and beepers are needed that get better data than just self-report Likert scales or recounts of schedules.

We also believe that more research is needed on the extent to which some of the flexibility enactment variables we propose—such as what tasks are portable—and how much of work is portable are to some extent socially constructed (Berger & Luckmann, 1966) so that different people may view the same task as differentially portable. This can create conflicts both at home and work and is a fundamental yet underexamined issue embedded in the enactment of portable work arrangements. Family members may wonder why a person is bringing work home or checking e-mail at night. A supervisor may believe that most tasks of a particular job have to be conducted in the office while an employee believes differently.

Future research should build on our research on the construct of boundary management strategy to further examine how people may shift rhythms over daily, weekly, and life-span changes and how they are associated with different formal flexibility policies and forms of flexibility enactment. As noted, the work-family literature places boundary management on a continuum from segmentation to integration, and there may be more complexity to this issue to investigate in future work. For example, if an employee is working at home with the door closed while his or her child is watching television, some could say he or she is physically integrating roles; he or she is working at home and is physically there but is mentally segmenting as he or she is not interacting with his or her family. People cannot move work into the home without changing their social relationships. Future research should develop additional measures of the various aspects of boundaries noted in Fig. 15.1 that are being integrated or separated— physical, mental, behavioral, temporal. This research should examine the implications of integrating on some parts of the boundary but not others and the waxing and waning of the process of boundary management. Research is needed on how different aspects of integration may also allow for greater permeability between roles. We need to increase our understanding of how, when something good or bad is happening in one domain, it may be more difficult to buffer good or bad things entering the other life space.

Supervisors clearly need additional training on how to better manage and provide more effective support to employees in these transformational work arrangements. What we need is more research on the factors that influence the degree to which new ways of working and flexibility are accepted by supervisors, clients, and in corporate cultures. Our findings suggest that flexible work in time and place is still not fully embedded in work cultures for the management of professional work. In general, separating work and family issues is still preferred by supervisors in assessing work performance. Although employers have formally adopted policies to support new ways of working, such as teleworking and working portably or away from the office, there is a cultural lag between adoption and cultural integration. Many firms have organizational cultures that value face time as an indicator of employee effectiveness (Rapoport et al., 2002) and may hold ambivalent or even negative attitudes toward teleworking (Eaton et al., 2003). More research is needed on why employers are not reciprocating the social exchange of better worker attitudes in return for flexibility access.

Another limitation is that we measured flexibility enactment and boundary management at one period of the employee's life. These phenomena may wax and wane over the course of one's life span, job demands, and career and family stages. Future research could follow a group of individuals longitudinally over changes in family and career structures. It is also difficult to unequivocally show causality between the positive relationship between a boundary management strategy higher on integration and family-to-work conflict, and future research should measure both of these variables at two points in time. Yet what is clear from our data is they are linked; we just do not know if individuals with more family-to-work conflict are likely to adopt a boundary management strategy toward higher integration or whether such a strategy induces higher family-to-work conflict. Our sample is solely professional with similar kinds of work—future researchers would surely want to broaden the lens to look at more kinds of employees in a wider variety of jobs at all levels of organizations. We hope this chapter will prompt future empirical scholarly work on flexibility enactment to better understand the individual, family, and organizational conditions that lead to their effectiveness.

AUTHOR NOTE

Susan Eaton died December 30, 2003. We are grateful for her excellent contributions to the research reported here and other scholarly works from this multi-year research project.

REFERENCES

Allen, D., Shore, L., & Griffith, R. (2003). The role of perceived organizational support and supportive human resources practices in the turnover process. *Journal of Management, 29,* 99–118.

Allen, T. D. (2001). Family-supportive work environments: The role of organizational perceptions. *Journal of Vocational Behavior, 58,* 414–435.

Alliance for Work-Life Progress. (2001). Survey report. Retrieved April 15, 2003, from http://www.awlp.org/Surveyreport.pdf

Apgar, M. (1998). The alternative workplace: Changing where and how people work. *Harvard Business Review, 76*(3), pp. 121–136.

Ashforth, B. E., Kreiner, G. E., & Fugate, M. (2000). All in a day's work: Boundaries and micro-role transitions. *Academy of Management Review, 25,* 472–491.

Avery, C., & Zabel, D. (2001). *The flexible workplace: A sourcebook of information and research.* Westport, CT: Quorum.

Bailey, D. E., & Kurland, N. B. (2002). Review of telework research: Findings, new directions, and lessons for the study of modern work. *Journal of Organizational Behavior, 23,* 383–400.

Baltes, B. B., Briggs, T. E., Huff, J. W., Wright, J. A., & Neuman, G. A. (1999). Flexible and compressed workweek schedules: A meta-analysis of their effects on work-related criteria. *Journal of Applied Psychology, 84,* 496–513.

Barnett, R. C., & Hyde, J. S. (2001). Women, men, work and family: An expansionist theory. *American Psychologist, 56,* 781–796.

Berger, P., & Luckmann, T. (1966). *The social construction of reality: A treatise: It's the sociology of knowledge.* Garden City, NY: Anchor Books.

Blood, R., & Wolfe, D. (1960). *Husbands and wives.* Glencoe, IL: Free Press.

Brett, J. M., & Stroh, L. K. (2003). Working 61-plus hours a week: Why do managers do it? *Journal of Applied Psychology, 88,* 67–78.

Bureau of Labor Statistics. (2000). National Compensation survey, Survey of Employee Benefits. Retrieved April 15, 2003, from www.bls.org

Coltrane, S. (1996). *Family man: Fatherhood, housework and gender equity.* New York: Oxford University Press.

Crooker, K., Smith, F., & Tabak, F. (2002). Creating work-life balance: A model of pluralism across life domains. *Human Resource Development Review, 1,* 387–419.

Duxbury, L. E., Higgins, C. A., & Neufeld, D. (1998). Telework and the balance between work and family: Is telework part of the problem or part of the solution? In M. Igbaria & M. Tan (Eds.), *The virtual workplace* (pp. 218–255). Hershey, PA: Idea Group Publishing.

Eaton, S. C. (2003). If you can use them: Flexibility policies, organizational commitment, and perceived performance. *Industrial Relations, 42*(2), 145–167.

Eaton, S. C., Lautsch, B., & Kossek, E. E. (2003). *Managerial support of portable work.* Paper presented at the annual meeting of the National Academy of Management, Seattle.

Ezra, M. (1996). Balancing work and family responsibilities: Flextime and child care in the federal government. *Public Administration Review, 56,* 174–179.

Feldman, D., & Gainey, T. (1997). Patterns of telecommuting and their consequences: Framing the research agenda. *Human Resource Management Review, 7,* 369–388.

Friedman, S. D., Christensen, P., & DeGroot, J. (1998, November–December). Work and life: The end of the zero-sum game. *Harvard Business Review,* 119–129.

Glass, J. L., & Fujimoto, T. (1995). Employer characteristics and the provision of family responsive policies. *Work and Occupations, 22,* 380–411.

Golden, L. (2001). Flexible work schedules: What are we trading to get them? *American Behavioral Scientist, 44,* 1157–1178.

Gottlieb, B., Kelloway, E., & Barham, E. (1988). *Flexible work arrangements: Managing the work-family boundary.* Chichester, England: John Wiley & Sons.

Greenhaus, J. H., & Singh, R. (2003). Work-family linkages. In M. Pitt-Catsouphes & E. E. Kossek (Eds.), *Work-family encyclopedia.* Retrieved February 15, 2003, from www.bc.edu/wfnetwork

Grover, S., & Crocker, K. (1995). Who appreciates family-responsive human resource policies: The impact of family-friendly policies on the organizational attachment of parents and non-parents. *Personnel Psychology, 48,* 271–288.

Hackman, R., & Oldham, G. (1980). *Work redesign.* Reading, MA.: Addison-Wesley.

Hill, E. J., Miller, B. C., Weiner, S. P., & Colihan, J. (1998). Influences of the virtual office on aspects of work and work/life balance. *Personnel Psychology, 51,* 667–683.

Hill, E. J., Hawkins, A. J., Ferris, M., & Weitzman, M. (2001). Finding an extra day a week: The positive influence of perceived job flexibility on work and family balance. *Family Relations, 50*(1), 49–58.

Ilgen, D., & Hollenback, J. R. (1990). The structure of work: Job design and roles. In M. D. Dunnette & L. M. Hugh (Eds.), *Handbook of industrial and organizational psychology* (2nd ed., Vol. 2, pp. 165–207). Palo Alto, CA: Consulting Psychology Press.

Kanter, R. M. (1977). *Work and family in the United States: A critical review and agenda for research and policy.* New York: Russell Sage Foundation.

Kossek, E. E., Barber, A., & Winters, D. (1999). Using flexible work schedules in the Managerial World: The power of peers. *Human Resource Management Journal, 38,* 33–46.

Kossek, E., Lautsch, B., & Eaton, S. J. (2002). *Bargaining with the baby.* Paper presented at the annual meeting of the National Academy of Management Annual, Denver, Colorado.

Kossek, E. E., Lautsch, B., Eaton, S. C., & Van Vanden Bosch, K. (2004, April 13). *Managing work—home boundaries, performance and well-being: The effects of formal access to telework and flexibility enactment.* Paper presented in the symposium Holding Multiple Roles and Using Family Policies: Benefits and Costs (Chairs: B. L. Cordeiro & A. A. Grandey) at the annual meetings of the Society of Industrial Organizational Psychology, Chicago, Illinois.

Kossek, E., & Nichol, V. (1992). The effects of employer-sponsored child care on employee attitudes and performance. *Personal Psychology, 45,* 885–509.

Kossek, E. E., Noe, R. A., & DeMarr, B. J. (1999). Work-family role synthesis: Individual, family and organizational determinants. *International Journal of Conflict Resolution, 10,* 102–129.

Kossek, E. E., & Ozeki, C. (1999). Bridging the work-family policy and productivity gap. Inter-national *Journal of Community Work, and Family, 2*(1), 7–32.

Kossek. E., & Ozeki, C. (1998). Work-family conflict, policies, and the job-life satisfaction rela-tionship: A review and directions for organizational behavior/human resources research. *Journal of Applied Psychology, 83,* 139–149.

Lambert, S. J. (2000). Added benefits: The link between work-life benefits and organizational citi-zenship behavior. *Academy of Management Journal, 43*(5), 801–815.

MacDermid, S. (2004). Reviewer comments to E. E. Kossek.

Major, V., Klein, K., & Ehrhart, M. (2002). Work time, work interference with family, and psycho-logical distress. *Journal of Applied Psychology, 87,* 427–436.

Mirchandani, K. (1998). Protecting the boundary: Teleworker insights on the expansive concept of work. *Gender and Society, 12,* 168–187.

Mokhtarian, P., Bagley, M., & Saloman, I. (1998). The impact of gender, occupation, and presence of children on telecommuting motivations and constraints. *Journal of the American Society for Information Science, 49,* 115–134.

Moen, P., & Yu, Y. (1999). Having it all: Overall work/life success in two earner families. In T. Parcel (Ed.), *Research in the sociology of work* (Vol. 7, pp. 129–139). Greenwich, CT: JAI Press.

Musselwhite, J. (1994). *Long term care: Private sector elder care could yield multiple benefits.* Washington, DC: General Accounting Office.

Nippert-Eng, C. E. (1996). *Home and work: Negotiating boundaries through everyday life.* Chicago: University of Chicago Press.

Ozeki, C. (2003). *The effects of a family supportive work environment on work-to-family conflict, family-to-work conflict, and emotional exhaustion: Does income level matter?* Unpublished doc-toral dissertation, East Lansing, Michigan State University.

Parker, S., Wall, T., & Cordery, J. L. (2001). Future work design research and practice: Towards an elaborated model of work design. *Journal of Occupational and Organizational Psychology, 74,* 413–440.

Rapoport, R., Bailyn, L, Fletcher, J. K., & Pruitt, B. H. (2002). *Beyond work-family balance: Ad-vancing gender equity and workplace performance.* San Francisco: Jossey-Bass.

Rau, B. (2003). Alternative work arrangements. In M. Pitts-Catsouphes & E. E. Kossek (Eds.), *Work-family encyclopedia.* Retrieved October 15, 2003, from www.bc.edu/wfnetwork

Rau, B. L., & Hyland, M. (2002). Role conflict and flexible work arrangements: The effects on applicant attraction. *Personnel Psychology, 55,* 111–136.

Roehling, P. V., Roehling, M. V., & Moen, P. (2001). The relationship between work-life policies and practices and employee loyalty: A life course perspective. *Journal of Family and Economic Issues, 22,* 141–170.

Scandura, T., & Lankau, M. 1997. Relationship of gender, family responsibility and flexible work hours to organizational commitment and job satisfaction. *Journal of Organizational Behavior, 18,* 377–391.

Still, M., & Strang, D. (2003). Institutionalizing family-friendly policies. In P. Moen (Ed.), *It's about time: Couples and careers* (pp. 288–309). Ithaca, NY: Cornell University Press.

Williams, J. (1999). *Unbending gender: Why family and work conflict and what to do about it.* New York: Oxford Press.

Zedeck, S. (1992). Exploring the domain of work and family concerns. In S. Zedeck (Ed.), *Work, families, and organizations* (pp. 1–32). San Francisco: Jossey-Bass.

13

The Decision Process
Theory of Work and Family

Steven A. Y. Poelmans
University of Navarra, Spain

INTRODUCTION

Since its early development, theoretical discourse in the field of work-family conflict has been confined to a few dominant theories, such as role theory (Kahn, Wolfe, Quinn, Snoek, & Rosenthal, 1964; Katz & Kahn, 1978) and spillover theory (Piotrkowski, 1979; Staines, 1980; Zedeck & Mosier, 1990). Since Zedeck's (1992) call for the refinement and development of theory in the work-family field, a series of alternative theories have been suggested as a conceptual basis for explaining work-family conflict, such as Hobfoll's (1989) conservation of resources theory (Grandey & Cropanzano, 1999; Rosenbaum & Cohen, 1999), self-discrepancy theory (Higgins, Bond, Klein, & Strauman, 1986; Polasky & Holahan, 1998), social identity theory (Lobel, 1991; Tajfel & Turner, 1985), expansionist theory of gender, work, and family (Barnett & Hyde, 2001), boundary theory (Nippert-Eng, 1996), and work/family border theory (Clark, 2000).

This chapter seeks to contribute an alternative paradigm to the field, one that tackles several of the gaps Parasuraman and Greenhaus (2002) recently identified in the work-family literature. It encompasses positive connections between work and family, puts more emphasis on individual differences and psychological characteristics (decision making), and breaks open the unit of analysis to include couple interactions and crossover effects (Westman & Etzion, 1995). As pointed out by Greenhaus and Powell (2003) we know very little about the decision process that determines whether work interferes with family or family interferes with work. Still, it has been recognized by work-family scholars that workers limit their involvement in work or in family life so that they can better accommodate the demands of the other (Lambert, 1990), that individuals make intentional allocation decisions of time or attention between work and family demands (Edwards & Rothbard, 2000), and that individuals consciously use strategies to manage the enactment of work and caregiving roles (Kossek, Noe, & DeMarr, 1999). The decision process theory of work and family shifts the attention away from the consequences of work-family conflict for well-being to the immanent actions of deliberation, decision making, and learning that precede and follow a work-family dilemma. As suggested by Zedeck (1992) and Carlson and Kacmar (2000) this chapter conceptualizes work-family conflict as a process and, more specifically, as an intermediate result in an ongoing decision-making process.

The focus on decision making may become increasingly important as companies create more flexible workplaces and boundariless careers. Initiatives like flextime and telework have blurred considerably the existing boundaries between work and family. As a consequence, the responsibility for "drawing the line" between work and family has been shifted even further toward the individual employee. Armed with devices like cell phones and portable computers, employees now can work anywhere and anytime. In addition, these employees work in an increasingly global workplace, which means they collaborate with colleagues in different parts of the world and in different time zones. Although they may not always be conscious of their choices, employees today are confronted constantly with the question of whether to connect or disconnect from work, physically or virtually, in the office or at home, day or night.

The decision process theory has not been created in a vacuum. The theory of human action developed by Pérez-López (1991) has provided the theoretical basis. Although Pérez-López' work has not yet been translated into English, it offers an almost infinite source of inspiration for research and practice in organizational behavior. The theory analyzes decision making as an interaction between an active agent and reactive agent. As such, it could be considered a social cognitive theory. Basic to all models of social cognition are structural constructs that order and influence information processing (Ilgen & Klein, 1989). The intention of this chapter is to offer a complementary view to the work-family theories introduced above, shifting the focus away from individuals enacting their social roles or identity and toward individuals making decisions in a social context, and modeling individuals as active processors of information derived from their environments and respondents to their construals of that information (Ilgen & Klein, 1989).[1] I will refer to the person as an active agent, actor, or decision maker.

At the same time, the decision process theory is based on previous empirical research (Greenhaus & Powell, 2003) that emphasizes decision making in the experience of work-family conflict. In parallel with Greenhaus and Powell's research, I conducted qualitative research among dual-earner couples and analyzed many real-life case studies derived from this research. Respondents were interviewed at home or at work, during one and a half to two hours, generally together with their partner, using semistructured interviews. The topics that were addressed generally were description of the family, description of work, career track, work attitudes, chronological description of a typical day, conflicts between work and family, how the respondent copes with these conflicts, company policies concerning family, and suggestions/advice for other couples. A first series of interviews were done in 1999 among 14 respondents, all members of managerial couples, that is, couples of which at least one member has a managerial responsibility. Detailed results are reported elsewhere (Poelmans, 2001). A second series of interviews were done in 2002–2003 among 15 members of dual-income couples. In summary these studies have revealed some promising new lines of inquiry for the field of work-family conflict.

The data suggest that by overemphasizing quantitative methods, scholars in the field are overlooking some fundamental phenomena, especially tacit, time-related, intrapersonal, and interpersonal processes that are difficult to capture with cross-sectional studies. Examples are personal values and priorities, decision making and choices in situations of work-family conflict, the quality of the relationship of the couple, time people actually spend with their children, job characteristics, and learning. In this chapter I present just one example of the many case studies that have nourished the theory. From these interviews and case studies I distilled many examples of how individuals make decisions when confronted with work-family dilemmas and what information and criteria they use to make decisions. Pérez-López' (1991) theory allowed me to model these decision processes as ongoing interactions between decision makers or "active agents," and their environment, symbolically represented by "reactive agents."

First, I will briefly present the basic concepts of the theory. Second, I will make the assumptions of the theory explicit. Then I will develop the theory distinguishing between two fundamentally different contexts within which a work-family dilemma can take place: economic exchange and social exchange. In these sections I will formulate the propositions of the theory, which when combined, will constitute the decision process theory of work and family. Finally, I will point out strengths and weaknesses of the theory and make recommendations for future research.

DEVELOPMENT OF THE THEORY

Basic Concepts

As the name suggests, the decision process theory of work and family concentrates on decisions actors make. Within this framework work-family conflict can still be seen as an external or internal stressor, as is the case in role theory, spillover theory, and self-discrepancy theory, but the decision process theory fundamentally conceives *work-family conflict as the intermediate result of decisions made in the course of time.* It centers on decisions preceding and following conflict rather than on the consequences of work-family conflict.

The decision process theory is complementary to existing theory in the sense that other theories may offer explanations for behavior in situations where individuals are constrained by their environment and role expectations, whereas decision process theory focuses on situations in which individuals do have some minimum degree of liberty and decision discretion. Existing theory can explain work-family conflict as a consequence of a lack of choice. In the decision process theory attention shifts to conflicting situations between work and family where the individual can deliberate alternative actions, however brief, badly informed, or irrational this decision process may be. It focuses on the many instances when actors can make small day-to-day choices and major life and career cycle choices between work and family. For instance, one can choose to have a career, giving more weight to work, or to dedicate more time to family. In the course of life, individuals can make career choices that can change fundamentally the nature and intensity of the conflicts between work and family. It can be a choice to discontinue work temporarily or definitively, build beyond a career plateau, or shift gears to reduce, maintain, or intensify levels of responsibility. Even in daily situations individuals are regularly confronted with choices between work and family, for instance when choosing to work one hour more or less, giving priority to work or family, respectively. And even within the time constraints depicted earlier, an individual can choose to concentrate on the quality of the time spent with others or to mentally disconnect, to the advantage of work or family.

In the tradition of cognitive theories like decision theory (Cyert & March, 1963; March & Simon, 1958; Simon, 1947) and problem-solving theory (Nisbett & Wilson, 1977), I assume that the anticipation and appreciation of a future reward is central in the explanation of behavior. I follow behavioral decision-making theory,[2] according to which decision makers turn to less than rationally optimal strategies such as satisfizing (Simon, 1976) and incrementalism (Janis & Mann, 1977). As in March (1994) I follow a general framework distinguishing *alternatives, expectations, preferences,* and *decision rules.* Underlying choices is a set of decision criteria with different weights, reflecting the preferences and values of an individual. Previous research has pointed out the importance of values individuals place on various life roles (Carlson & Kacmar, 2000; Lobel, 1992). Here, values are reflected in decision criteria and weights that are used to evaluate alternatives and the associated rewards. For instance, applying this to the case study in box 13.1, the husband implicitly uses a set of decision criteria (e.g., wage, long-term career development opportunities). He gives them a certain weight (e.g., he places more weight on his own future wage than on

BOX 13.1.
A Case of Work-Family Conflict: Expatriation to Mexico

This is a fragment of the transcript of an interview with one couple. The female respondent works as an owner/manager in a small lawyer's office, subsidiary of a larger office owned by her father in another major city.

He: I got a proposal to go to Mexico to start up a company. At that time, I was assistant commercial director at the company. I went there during one month to get things started. When I came back I got the proposal to actually go and become general director of the company in Mexico. It was a very attractive offer, which implicated a serious step in my professional career.

She: This was a completely unexpected offer. My first reaction was negative.

He: I told her, think about it [on Friday] because Tuesday I have to give an answer.

She: I passed the weekend crying a lot, experiencing enormous pressure.

He: The truth was that the company did not want an answer that quickly. It was me who was impatient and anxious to make a decision. I was impressed by her reaction. I was aware that she had to give up a job in which, at that moment, she was earning a lot more than me. They were going to pay me very well in Mexico, and although I was very excited about the offer, I tried to take into account her point of view as well. So I tried to convince her. My arguments were: It is an excellent opportunity, it would be only for 2–3 years, when we returned she could take up her old job again with her father, etc.

She: I asked my father about this possibility, but my parents were very upset about the whole situation. My father reacted very strongly to the idea that I would leave/close the Barcelona office as an important part of the company. He made it very clear that if I would do that, I wouldn't be able to count on him anymore. He told me that I would not be able to enter the law firm again, I would lose all my clients, and to him it would be like losing a child. This put even more pressure on me, which was a horrible experience.

He: My parents were positive about the idea, but they were not aware what this would mean for her. Especially my mother, who never worked. They only thought about the idea that their son would be general director of a firm at 30 years old, with a big job and a big income.

She: Despite the heavy pressure of my father, I finally decided that my husband was more important than my father. My core argument was my husband. I was prepared to sacrifice myself for the excellent opportunity for my husband.

He: It was clear: although we went through difficult times, . . . that I would never leave her.

She: I experienced this as a moral pressure. If I refused to go, he would not have any choice. He would lose the chance of his lifetime; he would reproach me.

He: I was aware that it would mean a huge sacrifice for her, because one night we were dining with couples who went to Mexico. They told me that she could work as a secretary. This made me imagine the situation the other way around—that she would get a big offer to start up a law firm in Holland, and I had to work as carpenter. I never even considered separating from my wife.

She: I knew that it would be a sacrifice, but it was also an act of rebellion against my father, who reacted so strongly.

He: I also knew that for her it would be a sacrifice. We realized, whatever decision we would make, it would jeopardize one person's future. It was a real dilemma.

(Continued)

BOX 13.1.
(Continued)

She: The company also played an important role. He sort of planned to have his "lifetime career" there. If I asked him to refuse, I was afraid that he would reproach me for the rest of his life.

He: We finally made the decision to go to Mexico. Fortunately, because of unforeseen macroeconomic circumstances—the election of a new president and the brutal devaluation of the Mexican peso—the project was called off. Moreover, my supervisor—a comprehensive and good person—realized that, taking into account my family situation, he could not ask me to go to Mexico in this crisis period. Thus they proposed for me to go to Mexico frequently to build up the company in different stages. In this year, I was one month in Mexico, one month in Spain.

She: This still was a sacrifice to me, because I was alone, but relative to the previous situation, better.

He: Retrospectively, I realize that it would have been a serious mistake to go, because she would never have adapted to the situation. She would have suffered, because Mexicans are very "macho"; she would not have been able to do the kind of work she likes and that would have been terrible. She would have led the life of a housewife, and this would [have] depress[ed] her.

She: I also realize that we did not judge the risk that was involved in the decision.

He: Mexico City is a very aggressive city; I know different couples who separated after going there.

She: To me, this was certainly the most difficult period in my life. One also learns to put things into perspective—it would not have jeopardized his career not to go to Mexico.

He: We were less mature in that period.

She: The influence of this story on our later relationship is that it has enforced our relationship and I am less worried when he has to travel abroad. Recently, he got an attractive proposal to go and direct a bigger company in Seville. He considered the proposal. My reaction was the same as in the Mexico case, maybe even more extreme: Forget it.

He: Now, I would think it over more, certainly with the baby.

his wife's actual wage), and these weights obviously reflect certain values (in Spanish culture, he is supposed to take care of his family and carry the bulk of the responsibility for the family's income). I go beyond behavioral decision-making theory by assuming that through enactment (Daft & Weick, 1984), individual cognition and action create the environment within which further cognition and action take place.

I will refer to the concept of *resources*, or the conservation of resource theory (Hobfoll, 1989), in the significance of energy, time, money, or any other resource that can be invested (input), lost (cost), or obtained (reward) in the action. One important resource is an individual's level of physical and psychological health or strength that can be both an input (energy invested in an action) and an output (result of an action).

Early exchange theorists (Blau, 1964; Homans, 1958; Thibout & Kelly, 1961) assumed that people attempt to maximize their own utilities by weighing potential outcomes of their various courses of action. Analysis included both sides of the exchange, that is, the costs and benefits of both parties. Therefore, I will put individual decision making in the context of a *dyad*. If the actor is to maintain or protect his or her resources,[3] it will be the result of strengthening or weakening interactions with many others that he or she is tied to in multiple dyads. The choices the actor makes are simultaneously an output and an input of this complex set of interactions with others. The reason why I focus on the dyad as the context for my analysis is not because I consider joint decision making. Rather it is to allow for the dissection and analysis of the decision in detail, maintaining the lowest level of analysis without making the mistake of isolating work-family conflict from a social context. As I will explain later, it is only when we consider the interconnections between decisions made in multiple dyads that we can explain with sufficient detail the complex ongoing process of work-family conflict experienced by an actor. In sum, whereas some would study conflict as an outcome and a state experienced by an individual, I approach the same phenomenon differently, studying the deliberation process in an individual interacting with several involved parties.

Assumptions of the Decision Process Theory

I summarize the starting points in the following assumptions:

1. The situation the individual is confronted with is characterized by a minimum level of decision freedom, meaning that the actor has a choice between at least two alternative courses of action. A decision is a choice between alternative courses of action and its implications for the decision-maker and relevant others (e.g., supervisor, colleague, spouse, child).

2. For the analysis of work-family conflict, I put the decision maker first within the context of a single dyad and then within a set of multiple dyads. For each individual whose level of work-family conflict and specific decisions we want to predict, we need to specify the set of relevant dyads.[4]

3. Each individual has a certain set of resources, such as a person's temperament, physical and psychological strength or health, health behavior, social support network, financial resources, and coping capabilities. These resources condition the input of an individual. They may also be affected by an action. Hence, they will be evaluated when making a decision.

4. A human being is bounded in his or her rationality when making decisions. Although a person may have complete knowledge of his or her decision criteria (which is difficult, because very often we are not aware of all of them), the actor cannot possibly know all of the alternatives and the exact inputs, rewards, and costs associated with them.

5. Human beings have personal values and associated preferences. These

preferences are reflected in the relative weight of the decision criteria of an actor.

6. Choices may create an immanent result called learning, which can be defined as a reconfiguration of decision criteria or perceptions of what can be considered a reasonable level of inputs, rewards, and costs. This perception shifts as a function of time and experience.

7. Work-family conflict is an intermediate result in an ongoing sense-making and decision-making process in individuals. At each point in time, work-family conflict is a (temporary) result of decisions made in the past and a function of available resources. Choices individuals make in terms of giving priority to work or to family, or trying to combine both, are both a result of historical choices and an input for future choices.

A final and very fundamental assumption of the theory is that we need to make a distinction between different types of interaction between actors in a dyad: economic exchange and social exchange. For instance, the decision to discontinue a relationship will be processed quite differently in these two cases, using different decision rules. Because we need to draw on different theoretical frameworks, in following sections I will develop separate sets of hypotheses for these two cases.

8. Individuals use fundamentally different decision-making rules when engaged in a purely instrumental exchange or in a social exchange.

Economic Exchange

A first type of interaction context actors may be involved in is characterized by an economic exchange or transaction of mostly tangible rewards (labor for salary, food for shelter, and money for taking care of children). In this type of interaction actors are driven by extrinsic motivation, that is, the gratification of receiving an external reward. The exchange is elicited by the anticipation of a consequent reward or by some contractual agreement in which the reward is described. The actor interacts with the other in an instrumental way, that is, by using the other as a means to obtain certain rewards. In this case, I follow the premises of equity theory.

Equity theory (Adams, 1965; Greenberg, 1990) starts from the idea that one important cognitive process people use to determine their motivation is the observation and comparison of efforts and rewards. Driven by a concern of fairness or equity, we contrast our effort-reward ratio with similar people's ratios or with ratios we have previously experienced in other situations. In addition to inputs and rewards I distinguish costs associated with certain choices. Costs are not mentioned explicitly in equity theory but are conceptually distinct enough to be addressed explicitly and separately. Inputs precede and accompany an action whereas costs are the negative consequences of an action, as rewards are the positive outcomes of an action. With costs I mean losses in resources creating the need for resources above and beyond what one could reasonably expect as necessary input for a certain course of action. Examples are unwanted or unforeseen unfavorable outcomes and adverse consequences for health (Allen, Herst, Bruck, & Sutton, 2000), relationships, or reputation (Doby & Caplan, 1995). Probably because they are difficult to quantify or sometimes take a long time to be observed (e.g., heart attack, marital problems), these costs are seriously underestimated or even completely ignored. In keeping with equity theory I state:

Proposition 1: In each work-family decision, people evaluate inputs, costs, and rewards in both domains (work and family) against their decision criteria. More specifically, a decision maker compares the ratio of inputs, costs, and rewards with ratios of possible alternative choices within the same dyad or within alternative dyads.

If a person perceives a ratio of inputs (effort, qualification, skill, seniority) to outputs (pay, advancements, benefits, status) that is not equitable, he or she will sense a negative affective state of guilt (in the case of overpayment) or anger (in the case of underpayment). If a situation of equity is perceived, satisfaction will be experienced. We found many examples in our qualitative study. In one case, a married woman with a young son experienced frustration with her husband's promotion. Ever since that change, he drastically reduced his input to their relationship and to domestic tasks. The woman experienced this as an inequitable state because she could compare her situation with a possible alternative relationship that would offer her the prospect of a satisfying relationship and more respect for her role as a mother. This leads us to proposition 2:

Proposition 2: People try to maximize their own utilities by weighing the potential outcomes of various courses of action. An adverse ratio of inputs (high), costs (high), and rewards (low) will result in a perception of inequity and a negative emotional state (anger, disappointment).

Still according to equity theory, a negative state will motivate the person to modify his or her behavior, perceptions, or both:

Proposition 3: In the case of perceived inequity the individual will strive to restore a perceived state of equity. The action can be directed at changing perceptions, lowering inputs, demanding or searching higher rewards, or reducing costs.

Applied to work-family conflict, inputs would be time, energy, and skills invested in work-related tasks and family-related household chores, child care, and eldercare. Examples of rewards in the family context would be support and love received from family members or the satisfaction of the success and advancement of children in school and extracurricular activities. Here we should also mention positive spillover that can be considered as a reward coming from the other domain, such as the development of skills. Of special importance are the costs associated with the inputs, such as not being able to attend important events or parties or the loss of energy and enthusiasm after a day of hard work. Whereas the alternatives in a work context are specific (alternative jobs within the same firm that can be obtained through mutation, delocation, or promotion, or job offers in the labor market), the alternatives in a family context can range from anything as simple as a new washing machine or a better relationship with the spouse to something as drastic as moving to a new home or an alternative romantic relationship.

The next step is to see *how* individuals compute inputs, costs, and rewards to make work- and family-related decisions.

> Proposition 4: In determining his or her input, the actor will take into account the demands of the situation (needed or expected effort), available resources, and possible positive (rewards) and negative (costs) outcomes, striving for an equitable (input / [rewards − costs]) ratio (equitable compared with ratios of alternatives). Given the fact that decisions concerning inputs affect others, and that rewards are often granted by others, the decision makers while computing inputs, costs, and rewards will also take into account possible reactions of others, dyad per dyad, in terms of rewarding (rewards), nonreciprocating, or even punishing behavior (costs).

In one of the interviews I conducted, a respondent said he was forced to invest in company-specific skills, which, together with family-friendly policies, "hooked" him to his company. His explanation was that it would be difficult to change jobs without losing all the advantages the firm offered. This employee decided to stay with the company despite unfavorable working conditions (being paid less than the industry average, lack of managerial career track) because of the family-friendly arrangements he enjoyed. This case illustrates that employees may hesitate to leave a company (break a contact) because the overall (input / (rewards − costs]) ratio would be difficult to improve. Still, if it were not for these policies, the man testified, he would have left the company a long time ago, because he was disappointed in his career ambitions.

> Proposition 5: If the individual perceives a chronic state of inequity he or she will adjust his or her perceptions of equity or withdraw from the interaction. In a context of a purely economic exchange, an interaction will stop if the (input / (reward − cost]) ratio is unfavorable or if there is an alternative interaction that offers a more interesting ratio, taking into account the cost of breaking up the contact or contract. A person might hesitate to switch to an alternative even if the ratio is more interesting because the cost of breaking up the relationship is higher

than the difference in ratios justifies. But the relationship is fragile and is appreciated only in terms of extrinsic costs and rewards.

A single mother commented that because of her responsibility for her child, she could not take the risk of leaving her job, despite the fact that she had a bad relationship with her boss and was working below her level. Her inability to improve her situation was causing her sleep problems and irritability, and she admitted that her nervousness was affecting her baby. She wondered how long she could continue working in these circumstances. What kept her going, though, was the support of her parents, which made it possible for her to look for a new job.

Proposition 6: If neither an adjustment of equity perception nor withdrawal is possible, the individual will experience a lack of control and a strong negative emotional state that will affect his or her resources. The overall resourcefulness of a person is a function of the combined net outcomes of a set of inputs, costs, and rewards of interactions over multiple dyads (cf. infra). If this combined net outcome is adverse, it will result in a gradual depletion of the individual's energy with associated consequences for health (e.g., exhaustion, burnout, depression, or ill health). These health consequences are evaluated as costs of adverse interactions in subsequent periods.

Social Exchange

Let us now turn to another possible context in which actors can make work- and family-related decisions, that is, a situation characterized by a social exchange. Blau (1964) made the distinction between economic and social exchange. To Blau, economic exchange can be situated within strict contracts or agreements. Social exchange exists outside strict contracts. Rousseau and Wade-Benzoni (1995) also distinguished between "relational contracts," which implicitly depend on trust, loyalty, and job security, and "transactional contracts," within which employees do not expect a long-lasting relationship with their employer or organization but instead view their employment as a transaction in which, for example, long hours and extra work are provided in exchange for high pay and training and development (Rousseau & Wade-Benzoni, 1995; Smithson & Lewis, 2004). The exchange goes beyond enforceable, mostly tangible or quantifiable rewards to include exchanges of socially relevant rewards. Examples are intrinsic rewards (Deci, 1975; Deci & Ryan, 1985, 1987) and recognition in exchange for loyalty, commitment, and involvement. Moreover, according to Pérez-López (1991), social exchange may go beyond rewards. Through repeated interactions and the creation of mutual trust, individuals develop a social bond. In this type of relationship one or both persons have the feeling that they learn or develop through the relationship.

Interaction partners give each other a certain degree of leniency or trust. They do not expect an immediate or clear reciprocation in the exchange. The contract that binds the interacting actors is psychological in nature. Given that many of the rewards that are exchanged are intrinsic or intangible, the rational calculation of inputs, rewards, and costs becomes much more difficult. When individuals develop strong bonds with their organizations and/or spouses and families, they no longer rationally calculate inputs, rewards, and costs to maximize their utility. Individuals will not disengage from relationships simply because they perceive an inequitable ratio.

In the case mentioned earlier of the young woman frustrated with her husband's promotion, what initially kept her from leaving her husband was the fact that she was working for her husband's best friend. This job provided her with intrinsic motivation and a great sense of pride. To find an equally valuable alternative she would have to move from Spain to Italy, which implied a high cost because she did not want to separate her son from his father. This case clearly illustrates that significant others with whom we share important rewards are taken into account when weighing alternatives.

Proposition 7: In a context of a social exchange, an interaction will *not* be stopped if the (input / [reward − cost]) ratio is unfavorable. The individual will discontinue the relationship only:

(a) If the discrepancy between inputs (relatively high), costs (relatively high), and rewards (relatively low) becomes high enough and stays high for a sufficient period to reach the level of (perception of) insufficient reciprocation, prolonged imbalance, or abuse and/or:

(b) If there is an alternative relationship that offers an interesting enough alternative to offset the cost of breaking the relationship. This cost is very elevated though, and it includes the loss of many interdependent social ties and the loss of reputation.

A respondent in our study reflected on the impact of major restructuring in his firm. One of the production units was closed and over 200 jobs became redundant. The firm was widely known in the region for its progressive and family-friendly human resource policies. As a consequence of the restructuring, many years of effort to build trust among employees were destroyed, and the company did not lose just the employees who were laid off but also many talented people it wanted to retain, who preferred to switch to other employers because of the uncertain prospects in the firm: They could be the victims of a future downsizing operation. Suddenly, employees were evaluating in a very calculated way the existing inputs, costs, and rewards. This leads us to the next proposition:

Proposition 8: If loyalty, trust, or identification with the individual, organization, or family that was developed in the social exchange is abused or lost, the exchange will devaluate from a social to an economic exchange, and people will rationalize the utility of the exchange in terms of extrinsic inputs, costs, and rewards.

In the case of the young woman going through a crisis in her relationship, she did not separate from her husband even though she was receiving almost no rewards or inputs and despite an alternative relationship that promised a more favorable ratio of inputs, rewards, and costs. The costs of breaking with her husband (the suffering associated with the separation, the undesired consequences for her child, losing her job, and having to find a new job, probably abroad) were too high to justify the separation.

In addition to the high resistance against discontinuation, there is another reason why social exchange provides a whole different context that will influence individual decision making. If both the work and family domain offer a high level of autonomy and intrinsic motivation, serious conflicts can arise, because the individual will be inclined to spend a lot of time and energy in both. In this particular situation though, the satisfaction that results from these strong relationships will be a reward and increase the resources of the individual, which explains the capacity to endure long periods of imbalance and conflict.

Proposition 9: In the special case where actors are motivated intrinsically to engage in both work and family domains:

(a) Conflicts will intensify as a consequence of time and energy invested in both domains. Choices between the two will be especially difficult, translating in dilemmas that can affect the resources of the individual.

(b) At the same time, individuals are capable of enduring this conflict because of the surplus of rewards in both domains that may also spill over into the other domains. These positive spillovers can partially offset the conflicts and costs. Here, as a special case of proposition 4, the individual will regulate his or her inputs in the domains to maintain an acceptable level of (rewards − costs) in both domains.

Interdependency

Thibaut and Kelley's (1961) theory of interdependence adds an important concept to social exchange theory. They emphasize the dynamic aspects of dyadic interaction and point out the necessity of maximizing the satisfaction of both participants to maintain the interaction process. Thibaut and Kelley also introduce the idea of participants comparing the benefits of an interaction with the benefits of alternative interactions. This is an essential step, because it breaks open the dyad and allows for including the satisfaction experienced and information gathered in other, multiple dyads while making assessments. An example of how social exchange theory can be applied to the broader context of work and family is found in the study of Lambert (2000). She linked work-life benefits and organizational citizenship behavior, conceptualizing them as intangible currencies in an employer–employee exchange. According to Lambert, social exchange theory supports the possibility that, with work-family benefits, workers may feel obligated to exert "extra" effort in return for "extra" benefits.

This leads me to an important element in the decision process theory: the interdependence and interaction between inputs, costs, and rewards in multiple dyads. Given the scarcity of resources, an input in one dyad (e.g., working hours in the employee–supervisor dyad) may simultaneously be a cost in another dyad (e.g., reduced time in the spouse–spouse dyad). While making a decision, an individual will not simply evaluate his or her expected inputs, costs, and rewards of different decisions and/or interactions. Knowing that choices in one domain may have consequences in other domains, the individual will be aware of the costs and rewards a choice has for his or her "interaction partners." Interaction partners are others with whom an actor shares profits from his or her interactions with others. For instance, an important interaction partner is the spouse because he or she is generally a provider of important inputs and rewards. If the interaction partner's input in a relationship decreases as a result of choices made by the actor, it is only logical that the latter will take into account the effect of his or her choices on the former. In other words, the actor will take into account this interaction partner's costs and rewards while making choices. Consequently, given the process of close reciprocation decision makers have with their interaction partners, these interaction partners, when making decisions, will start taking into account the focal decision maker's costs and rewards as well. This is well illustrated by research on dual-career couples' coping strategies, such as scaling back their commitment to work to support their families (Becker & Moen, 1999). Translating this insight into a proposition I suggest:

Proposition 10: Decision makers make complex evaluations of:

  (a) ratios of multiple, interdependent dyads, appreciating the inputs, costs, rewards, and gains in resources in some interactions as inputs, costs, or rewards in other interactions; and

  (b) the costs and rewards of his or her decisions for "interaction partners." Interaction partners provide inputs and rewards to the actor regularly or share with the actor profits from interactions with others. Similarly these interaction partners take into account the costs and rewards of their decisions for the actor.

Another implication of the presence of multiple ties is that a decision maker may be reluctant to break a relationship, because it may imply the rupture with many other interaction partners as well. For instance, a person may stay in a job or marriage despite extremely unfavorable interactions with a supervisor or spouse. The reason is that breaking the relationship (resigning or divorcing) would imply elevated costs in terms of losing the multiple rewards one receives in interaction with colleagues, friends, or children who are tied to the supervisor or spouse. This idea has already been captured by proposition 7(b).

A final and very important implication of the existence of multiple dyads is that decision makers may use high rewards resulting from one set of interactions and the resultant resources to compensate or offset costs in another interaction. For instance, an individual may be able to invest a lot of energy in a relationship with a difficult colleague because of many rewarding relationships with others. This idea is a special case of proposition 10.

CONCLUSION

In sum, we can distinguish two clearly distinct contexts that dictate different decision rules in terms of giving priority to work or to family and withdrawing from work or family relationships: economic exchange and social exchange. Individuals will experience work-family conflict if, in their perception and based on their decision criteria, the actual situation is perceived as an unfavorable ratio of inputs, costs, and rewards that jeopardizes resources available for work and/ or family responsibilities. Work-family conflict is a result of a decision-making process involving multiple interdependent actors. The actor continuously compares the inputs, costs, and rewards of perceived options in alternative dyads and regulates his or her inputs to combine work and family. This decision making is bounded in its rationality and thus often will result in less-than-optimal solutions, because the individual cannot possibly know all options and anticipate correctly the required input and resulting costs and rewards. Moreover, the individual may not even question the less-than-optimal situation, given a certain level of motivation that limits the options because they may go against his or her loyalty toward a person or an organization.

Contributions of the Theory

An important contribution of the decision process theory is that it offers a complementary perspective on work and family. Whereas other theories focus on role expectations, borders between domains, or the antecedents and consequences of work-family conflict, decision process theory focuses on decision-making and learning in individuals. The theory is especially relevant in contexts where individuals have a sufficient control over the situation as to have a choice. Not only does the theory focus on individuals interpreting and reacting to a situation but it also focuses on individuals proactively shaping the situation (Watanabe, Takahashi, & Minami, 1998). The actor makes a decision on the basis of a unique set of decision criteria reflecting unique experiences and preferences or values. At the same time the theory does not deny that the person is a social actor engaged in—and continuously influenced by—different domains and associated roles. On the contrary, I have distinguished different types of relationships persons can be engaged in and the intimate association between the nature of the relationship and work/family decisions made.

A second contribution of the theory is that it offers a broad framework that can be used from an individual, family, or organizational perspective; it comprises both work and nonwork and both individual decision making and interindividual interaction. It offers the promise of a much-needed integrating framework to explain and link individual work-family conflict and organizational work-family policies. It has immediate utility for practitioners (human resource officers, career counselors, mentors, supervisors) who want to understand and prevent work-family conflict and create family-friendly workplaces. In line with Grandey and Cordeiro (2004) I confirm that equity theory is useful as an explanatory framework to look at both individual and organizational concerns for work-family conflict. Work-family policies can be considered as ways to increase rewards (e.g., by offering fringe benefits, such as medical insurance for family members), reduce costs (e.g., by offering flexible working hours so that employees do not have to miss important family events), reduce inputs (e.g., by offering child-care support so that the employees spend less time and money in finding and paying for public or private child care), or increase resources (e.g., by offering a health program or stress management training). As such, the theory can be used by practitioners as a framework to look for strategies to reduce work-family conflict. The theory can help these practitioners understand how a conflicting situation was created and how conflict can be reduced by analyzing the preferences and decision criteria; the inputs, rewards, and costs considered by the actor; and the (in)consistency of subsequent decisions. For instance, by mapping or making explicit preferences, decision-making criteria and rules, and rewards sought by employees, human resource officers may actually anticipate individuals refusing a promotion or expatriation assignment and/or withdrawal or resignation from their job.

A specific contribution of this theory is the distinction between two fundamentally different contexts in which work-family decision making can take place: economic exchange and social exchange. Theory on work and family has been in particular need of a theoretical explanation of extrarole behavior. First, because it is an undeniable reality in the workplace (e.g., organizational citizenship behavior). Second, because it is especially relevant to understand behavior in the family context (e.g., sacrifices people make for their family members). Third, because there may be crossover effects between extrarole behaviors displayed by organizations and employees (Lambert, 2000). Fourth, because it provides answers to questions that other theories do not address. For example, why are some people able to deal with extended periods of work-family conflict and not experience strain while others are not? How is it that people are able to make sacrifices for their work or families, jeopardizing their relationship or career?

Another contribution of the theory is that it elucidates the confusion around the precise role of work-family conflict as a stressor, a consequence of stress, or a moderator/mediator of the stressor-strain relationship. By considering work-family conflict as an intermediate state in a process in time, it can be understood as an *antecedent* (a debilitating factor undermining the resources of the individual; the cause of a reduced input in work and family relationships), a *moderator* (when people are debilitated by a loss in resources, stressors lead more easily to strain), a *mediator* (only if work stressors have collateral costs in the family will the individual experience a loss in resources), and a *consequence* (a cost in one domain as a consequence of overly investing in another domain).

Another way in which the decision process theory advances work and family linkage theories is the idea of interdependence between multiple dyads. This idea sheds new light on the distinction between—and at the same time, the connection between work-family and family-work conflict. Decision process theory points at feedback and interaction processes that, although they may be different constructs, link work-family and family-work conflict. For instance, work stress, a cost in the employee–organization dyad, may translate into reduced resources and spillover to the family in the form of a reduced input in the spouse–spouse and parent–child dyads. In turn, it may reduce the input of the spouse in the spouse–spouse dyad because—as some researchers have shown—the spillover of work stress reduces social support from the spouse (Adams, King, & King, 1996). The reduced social support of the spouse may in turn lower the input of the employee in the employee–organization dyad. The employee, bothered by worries about his or her spousal relationship, may also experience reduced resources (e.g., concentration problems, irritability at work), described as a negative spillover from family to work (Crouter, 1984).

Furthermore, decision process theory can account for a whole range of phenomena that previous theories can not or can only partially explain. First, it clarifies why multiple roles can be salutary instead of detrimental (Marks, 1977; Rothbard, 2001; Thoits, 1991), as proposed by role theory. In fact, decision process theory offers several explanations for the phenomenon. The input in a first domain does not create direct or indirect costs in the second domain. The rewards in the first domain can be used as valuable inputs in the second domain. The rewards in the first domain offset the costs created in the first domain for the second domain. The rewards of the first domain considerably increase the resources of the actor, which increases his or her input in the second domain.

Second, the theory offers a simple explanation for the existence of work-family enhancement or positive spillover and crossover effects of stress between spouses, two theoretical gaps identified by Parasuraman and Greenhaus (2002). Work-family enhancement occurs when rewards gained in one domain positively affect the other domain. Negative spillover can be reduced by preventing unwanted consequences or costs in one domain to affect the other domain. More specifically, decision makers can scrutinize the implications of their choices and mentors can help them in doing so. The close interdependence between interaction partners explains why they gain and/or suffer from the rewards and costs that result from actions of one partner. By taking into account each other's decision criteria, providing mutual support, and anticipating the potential costs of certain actions, resources can be boosted and costs for the other can be avoided. In other words, negative crossover can be prevented.

Third, decision process theory renders intelligible the existence of different interfaces between work and family that have been described (Edwards & Rothbard, 2000; Evans & Bartolomé, 1981), such as spillover, independence, conflict, and compensation. More important, the theory evinces how these can be linked with different outcomes. From a decision process perspective, people construe different ways to cope with spillover or loss of resources between work and family and with crossover effects between their own and their interaction partners' stress and work-family conflict. Some opt for flexibility, hoping that adapting their input in the function of demands will offset costs. Others prefer separation, reasoning that by putting a wall between the two domains they will be able to avoid the problem that inputs in one domain cause costs in the other. Still others perceive instrumentality, reasoning that the rewards in one domain are necessary as inputs in the other domain. Whatever justification or tactic is used, making actors conscious of the (lack of) rationality of their construction can help them see its limitations. For instance, separators are often unconscious that by separating work and family, they also deprive themselves of positive spillovers (rewards generated in one domain that function as inputs in another domain).

Limitations of the Theory and Suggestions for Future Research

As is often the case, within its very strength lies the weakness of a theory. The most important limitation of the theory is that it encompasses such a broad reality. Some critics may argue that the theory is too complex to meet one of the most crucial conditions of a theory: that it be falsifiable. But reality *is* complex and a simple theory would only be partial, leaving many questions unanswered. I have operationalized the theory in single propositions, making it possible to test the theory in parts. I understand that the type of research needed to make decision criteria, dyads, and the appreciation of alternatives explicit so as to make predictions of decisions and subsequent work-family conflict is more qualitative. I also acknowledge the need for in-depth analysis of decision-makers and the situations they are confronted with. The sophistication of the method should reflect the complexity of the reality. In terms of methodology, the theory summons case studies or experiments of decision making, ideally *ex ante* to test the predictive power of the theory or, if necessary, post hoc, because access to decision-making process prior to action may be troublesome. A possible alternative is to test part of the propositions with creative techniques that still allow some quantification, such as vignette studies as reported by Greenhaus and Powell (2003) and Peters and den Dulk (2003).

Another possible critique is that the decision process theory—by putting decision making in the center of the work/family issue—overemphasizes and overestimates the decision-making autonomy of a person. The fact that the theory was developed on the basis of qualitative research among white collar employees and managers may define my bias. I interviewed only relatively higher-educated people who obviously have more resources and decision autonomy. Some critics who follow a more deterministic model may argue that not all conflict is a result of a previous decision and that some phenomena cannot be explained without taking into account the vast impact of role expectations and social pressure. The most obvious example is in explaining why it is almost always the wife who will make the decision to sacrifice career for family. This theory may not be applicable in a context where individuals have no choice, but it can be useful to point out a lack of rationality and consideration of alternatives. This pertains to Simon's (1976) concept of bounded rationality, which means that decision makers have limited information-processing capacity and rationality. As noted in prospect theory (Tuchman, 1984; Tversky & Kahneman, 1981), losses may seem greater than gains (Kahneman & Tversky, 1979). Applied to the case of women sacrificing their career for family, the costs of possibly neglecting the education of their children may be overestimated in comparison with the potential gains of pursuing a career. Similarly, men sacrificing their family for their career may overestimate the loss of status and income in comparison with the quality of life and family relationships they can gain by scaling back. Confronting these men and women with their biases and helping them make choices coherent with their implicit decision criteria (values) may be a more productive approach than insisting on the importance of role expectations and gender stereotypes. By approaching work-family conflict as a decision-making problem, I invite scholars studying cognition in various disciplines (economy, statistics, social, and cognitive psychology) and practitioners to study biases and decision rules in work-family dilemmas in order to improve the quality of decision making in individuals, couples, and policy makers.

Another possible critique is that the decision process theory draws on many existing theories and is a patchwork of ideas taken from different theories. The reader may have noticed that I have referred especially to social cognitive theories such as equity theory and social exchange theory. I do not pretend to have invented the wheel. Rather, I have recombined ideas and drawn on the most relevant theories to explain the phenomenon at hand. I believe that social interaction and decision making are closely related yet still are fundamentally different in diverse situations, thus demanding different theoretical angles. My contribution consists in bringing these theories together in one overarching theory that may inspire future research to clarify this phenomenon of work-family and/or family-work conflict that concerns so many people in our contemporary society.

It is clear that with the gradual influx of women into the labor market over the past half-century double-income families have become the rule rather than the exception. In my view, individual decision making and choice offered by firms interact. On one hand, due to a lack of flexibility in organizations, many employees are forced into a conflicting situation (Shellenberger, 1992). On the other hand, there is an increasing trend of companies offering flexibility as a way to compete in increasingly tight labor markets. As alternatives arise, individuals more easily will switch organizations. Therefore I call for theories that link individual work-family conflict and workplace policies and practices, two literatures that have been virtually separated from each other. I would invite especially future research connecting individual decision making, choice, negotiation power, and scarcity in labor markets. Previous research has pointed out that companies operating in tight labor markets or low unemployment are more inclined to adopt work/family policies (Goodstein, 1994; Ingram & Simmons, 1995; Osterman, 1995; Poelmans, Chinchilla, & Cardona, 2003). In line with this research I would suggest that in those labor markets where power is limited because of a surplus in labor individuals' negotiation, government regulation is especially needed. If not, work/family policies will remain a privilege of higher educated employees who are in demand.

NOTES

1. I even suggest going beyond the S-O-R model, where the O represents the organism in the link between environmental conditions and responses. I follow the O-S-O-R model, suggesting that the nature of the environment to which the individual responds is at least partially constructed by the "cognizing organism" (Marcus & Zajonc, 1985), as is expressed in ideas like socially constructed realities, cause maps, and shared meaning (Ilgen & Klein, 1989).

2. To distinguish rational and bounded decision-making theories, one can refer to the distinction between classical and behavioral decision-making theory.

3. I do not assume that actors always strive to maintain their resources. Sometimes they consciously or unconsciously use or even abuse their resources to obtain certain rewards.

4. Depending on the specific person or situation, this may be the spouse/partner–spouse/partner dyad, the employee–supervisor dyad, the employee–employer dyad, or the parent–child dyads. In addition on can consider the dyads composed of the individual and (representatives of) his or her most salient in-group or reference groups (e.g., family, friends, work team, organization, religious group, political party).

REFERENCES

Adams, G. A., King, L. A., & King, D. W. (1996). Relationships of job and family involvement, family social support, and work-family conflict with job and life satisfaction. *Journal of Applied Psychology, 81*(4), 411–420.

Adams, J. S. (1965). Inequity in social exchange. *Advances in Experimental Psychology, 2*, 267–299.

Allen, T. D., Herst, D.E.L., Bruck, C. S., & Sutton, M. (2000). Consequences associated with work-to-family conflict: A review and agenda for future research. *Journal of Occupational Health Psychology, 5(2),* 278–308.

Barnett, R. C., & Baruch, G. K. (1985). Women's involvement in multiple roles and psychological distress. *Journal of Personality and Social Psychology, 49,* 135–145.

Barnett, R. C., & Hyde, J. S. (2001). Women, men, work, and family. An expansionist theory. *American Psychologist, 56*(10), 781–796.

Becker, P. E., & Moen, P. (1999). Scaling back: Dual-earner couples' work-family strategies. *Journal of Marriage and the Family, 61,* 995–1007.

Blau, P. (1964). *Exchange and power in social life.* New York: Wiley.

Carlson, D. S., & Kacmar, K. M. (2000). Work-family conflict in the organization: Do life role values make a difference? *Journal of Management, 26*(5), 1031–1054.

Carlson, D. S., & Perrewé, P. L. (1999). The role of social support in the stressor-strain relationship: An examination of work-family conflict. *Journal of Management, 25*(4), 513–540.

Clark, S. (2000). Work/family border theory: A new theory of work/family balance. *Human Relations, 53*(6), 747–770.

Cohen, S., & Wills, T. A. (1985). Stress, social support, and the buffering hypothesis. *Psychological Bulletin, 98,* 310–357.

Crouter, A. C. (1984). Spill-over from family to work: The neglected side of the work-family interface. *Human Relations, 37*(6), 425–442.

Cyert, R. M., & March, J. G. (1963). *A behavioral theory of the firm.* Englewood Cliffs, NJ: Prentice Hall.

Daft, R., & Weick, K. (1984). Toward a model of organizations as intreretation systems. *Academy of Management Review, 9,* 284–295.

Deci, E. L. (1975). *Intrinsic motivation.* New York: Plenum.

Deci, E. L., & Ryan, R. M. (1985). *Intrinsic motivation and self-determination in human behavior.* New York: Plenum.

Deci, E. L., & Ryan, R. M. (1987). The support of autonomy and the control of behavior. *Journal of Personality and Social Psychology, 53,* 1024–1037.

Doby, V. J., & Caplan, R. D. (1995). Organizational stress as a threat to reputation: Effects on anxiety at work and at home. *Academy of Management Journal, 38*(4), 1105–1123.

Edwards, J. R., & Rothbard, N. P. (2000). Mechanisms linking work and family: Clarifying the relationship between work and family constructs. *Academy of Management Review, 25,* 178–199.

Evans, P., & Bartolomé, F. (1981). *Must success cost so much? Avoiding the human toll of corporate life.* New York: Basic Books, Inc.

Goodstein, J. D. (1994). Institutional pressures and strategic responsiveness: employer involvement in work-family issues. *Academy of Management Journal, 37*(2), 350–382.

Grandey, A. A., & Cordeiro, B. L. (2004). Family-friendly policies and organizational Justice. Retrieved May 10, 2004, from http://www.bc.edu/bc_org/avp/winetwork/rft/wfpedia/index.html

Grandey, A. A., & Cropanzano, R. (1999). The Conservation of Resources model applied to work-family conflict and strain. *Journal of Vocational Behavior, 54,* 350–370.

Greenberg, J. (1990). Organizational justice: Yesterday, today, and tomorrow. *Journal of Management, 16*(2), p. 399–432.

Greenhaus, J. H., & Powell, G. N. (2003). When work and family collide: Deciding between competing role demands. *Organizational Behavior and Human Decision Processes, 90*(2), 291–303.

Gutek, B. A., Searle, S., & Klepa, L. (1991). Rational versus gender role explanations for Work-family conflict. *Journal of Applied Psychology, 76*(4), 560–568.

Higgins, E. T., Bond, R. N., Klein, R., & Strauman, T. (1986). Self-discrepancies and emotional vulnerability: How magnitude, accessibility, and type of discrepancy influence affect. *Journal of Personality and Social Psychology, 51,* 5–15.

Hobfoll, S. E. (1989). Conservation of resources: A new attempt at conceptualizing stress. *American Psychologist, 44,* 513–524.

Homans, G. C. (1958). Social behavior and exchange. *American Journal of Sociology, 63,* 597–606.

Homans, G. C. (1974). *Social behavior: Its elementary forms* (Rev. ed.). New York: Harcourt Brace Jovanovich.

Ilgen, D. R., & Klein, H. J. (1989). Organizational behavior. *Annual Review of Psychology, 40,* 327–351.

Ingram, P., & Simmons, T. (1995). Institutional and resource dependence determinants of responsiveness to work-family issues. *Academy of Management Journal, 38*(5), 1466–1482.

Janis, I. L., & Mann, L. (1977). *Decision making: A psychological analysis of conflict, choice, and commitment.* New York: Free Press.

Kahn, R. L., Wolfe, D. M., Quinn, R. P., Snoek, J. D., & Rosenthal, R. A. (1964). *Organizational stress: Studies in role conflict and ambiguity.* New York: Wiley.

Kahneman, D., & Tversky A. (1979). Prospect Theory: An analysis of choice under risk. *Econometrica, 47*(2), 263–291.

Katz, D., & Kahn, R. L. (1978). *The social psychology of organizations* (2nd ed.). New York: Wiley.

Kossek, E. E., Noe, R. A., & DeMarr, B. J. (1999). Work-family role synthesis: Individual and organizational determinants. *International Journal of Conflict Management, 10*(2), 102–129.

Lambert, S. J. (1990). Processes linking work and family: A critical review and research agenda. *Human Relations, 43,* 239–257.

Lambert, S. J. (2000). Added benefits: The link between work-life benefits and organizational citizenship behavior. *Academy of Management Journal, 43*(5), 801–815.

Lobel, S. A. (1991). Allocation of investment in work and family roles: Alternative theories and implications for research. *Academy of Management Review, 16,* 507–521.

Lobel, S. A. (1992). A value-laden approach to integrating work and family life. *Human Resource Management, 31*(3), 249–265.

Lobel, S. A., & St. Clair, L. (1992). Effects of family responsibilities, gender, and career identity salience on performance outcomes. *Academy of Management Journal, 35*(5), 1057–1069.

MacEwen, K. E., & Barling, J. (1994). Daily consequences of work interferences with family and family interference with work. *Work & Stress, 8,* 244–254.

March, J. (1994). *A primer on decision making. How decisions happen.* New York: Free Press.

March, J. G., & Simon, H. A. (1958). *Organizations.* New York: Wiley.

Marks, S. R. (1977). Multiple roles and role strain: Some notes on human energy, time and commitment. *American Sociological Review, 42,* 921–936.

Nippert-Eng, C. E. (1996). *Home and work: Negotiating boundaries through everyday life.* Chicago: University of Chicago Press.

Nisbett, R. E., & Wilson, T. D. (1977). Telling more than we know: Verbal reports and mental processes. *Psychological Review, 84,* 231–259.

O'Driscoll, M. P., Ilgen, D. R., & Hildreth, K. (1992). Time devoted to job and off-job activities, interrole conflict, and affective experiences. *Journal of Applied Psychology, 77,* 272–279.

Osterman, P. (1995). Work/family programs and the employment relationship. *Administrative Science Quarterly, 40,* 681–700.

Parasuraman, S., & Greenhaus, J. H. (2002). Toward reducing some critical gaps in work-family research. *Human Resource Management Review, 12,* 299–312.

Pérez-López, J. A. (1991). *The theory of human action.* Madrid: Ediciones Rialp.

Peters, P., & den Dulk, L. (2003) Cross-cultural differences in managers' support for home-based telework: a theoretical elaboration. *International Journal of Cross-Cultural Management, 3*(3), 329–346.

Piotrkowski, C. S. (1979). *Work and the family system.* New York: Free Press.

Poelmans, S. (2001). *A qualitative study of work-family conflicts in managerial couples. Are we overlooking some fundamental questions?* (Research paper no. 445). IESE Publishing, Barcelona, Spain.

Poelmans, S., Chinchilla, N., & Cardona, P. (2003). Family-friendly HRM policies and the employment relationship. *International Journal of Manpower, 24*(3), 128–147.

Polasky, L. J., & Holahan, C. K. (1998). Maternal self-discrepancies, interrole conflict, and negative affect among married professional women with children. *Journal of Family Psychology, 12*(3), 388–401.

Rosenbaum, M., & Cohen, E. (1999). Equalitarian marriages, spousal support, resourcefulness, and psychological distress among Israeli working women. *Journal of Vocational Behavior, 54,* 102–113.

Rothbard, N. P. (2001). Enriching or depleting? The dynamic of engagement in work and family roles. *Administrative Science Quarterly, 46,* 655–684.

Rousseau, D. M., & Wade-Benzoni, K. A. (1995). Changing individual-organizational attachments: A two-way street. In A. Howard (Ed.), *The changing nature of work.* San Francisco: Jossey-Bass.

Shellenberger, S. (1992). Lessons from the workplace: How corporate policies and attitudes lag behind workers' changing needs. *Human Resource Management, 31*(3), 157–169.

Simon, H. A. (1947). *Administrative behavior. A study of decision-making processes in administrative behavior.* Introduction. New York: Free Press.

Simon, H. A. (1976). *Administrative behavior: A study of decision-making processes in administrative behavior* (3rd. ed.). New York: Free Press.

Smithson, J., & Lewis, S. (2004). The psychological contract. Retrieved May 10, 2004, from http://www.bc.edu/bc_org/aup/wfnetwork/rft/wfpedia/index.htm

Staines, G. L. (1980). Spillover versus compensation: A review of the literature on the relationship between work and nonwork. *Human Relations, 33,* 111–129.

Tajfel, H. C., & Turner, J. C. (1985). The social identity theory of intergroup behavior. In S. Worchel & W. G. Austin (Eds.), *Psychology of intergroup relations* (2nd ed.), 7–24. Chicago: Nelson-Hall.

Thibaut, J. W., & Kelley, H. H. (1961). *The social psychology of groups.* New York: Wiley.

Thoits, P. A. (1983). Multiple identities and psychological wellbeing: A reformulation and test of the social isolation hypothesis. *American Sociological Review, 48,* 174–187.

Thoits, P. A. (1991). On merging identity theory and stress research. *Social Psychology Quarterly, 54,* 101–112.

Tuchman, B. W. (1984). *The march of folly.* New York: Knopf.

Tversky, A., & Kahneman, D. (1981). The framing of decisions and the psychology of choice. *Science, 221,* 453–458.

Watanabe, S., Takahashi, K., & Minami, T. (1998). The emerging role of diversity amd work-family values in a global context. In P. C. Earley & M. Earley (Eds.), *New perspectives on international industrial/organizational psychology* (pp. 319–332). San Francisco: New Lexington Press.

Westman, M., & Etzion, D. (1995). Crossover of stress, strain and resources from one spouse to another. *Journal of Organizational Behavior, 16*(2), 169–181.

Wiley, D. L. (1987). The relationship between work/nonwork role conflict and job-related outcomes: Some unanticipated findings. *Journal of Management, 13,* 467–472.

Zedeck, S. (Ed.) (1992). *Work, families, and organizations.* San Francisco: Jossey-Bass.

Zedeck, S., & Mosier, K. L. (1990). Work in the family and employing organization. *American Psychologist, 45*(2), 240–251.

14

Professionals Becoming Parents: Socialization, Adaptation, and Identity Transformation

Mary Dean Lee
McGill University

Pamela Lirio Dohring
McGill University

Shelley M. MacDermid
Purdue University

Ellen Ernst Kossek
Michigan State University

The focus of our research was to learn about the process of new identity construction and socialization into parenthood among career-oriented professionals voluntarily working less than full time for family reasons. Enhanced understanding of this process of identity transformation will potentially help employers respond to the changing demographics in the workforce—through offering different ways of working and design and delivery of more effective and more widely utilized work-life initiatives. Illumination of the process of professionals becoming parents will also benefit individuals and increase their capacity to continue to invest in their professional growth and development, while creating space for investing in children and family life. This study examined in depth the meaning behind reduced-load work arrangements among professionals, in order to explore changes in identity as these professionals-turned-parents adapted to their new life circumstances. Although professionals often invest years in training, preparing for a career, and developing a professional identity, little work has been done on how professionals adapt and are socialized to take on other significant life roles such as parent. The intent is to link state of the art theory and research from several disciplines (including sociology, social psychology, development psychology, management, and family studies) to enhance understanding of what happens when a professional becomes a parent.

The overall aim of this research was to gain insight into: (a) similarities and differences in the ways individuals describe their career and family orientations before and after arranging to work on a reduced-load basis, (b) the process of socialization into parenthood, (c) the process of adaptation of previous work and family routines to new realities, and (d) emergent identity changes and factors accounting for differences in the impact of parenthood on this group of professionals. The premise of this chapter is that we need to learn more about the transition to parenthood *in a career context* in order to increase understanding of individual development and identity transformation over time, as well as to provide employers with a more complete picture of the needs of employees for different ways of working and support structures as they try to make choices aligned with their changing work and personal contexts. Greater understanding of this process could lead to new theoretical insights as well as to practical ideas to help professionals cope with this major life transition.

Identity and Identity Change

We use the term *identity* to refer to the meanings attached to a person by self and others (Gecas, 1982). We assume that identities are socially constructed and negotiated in social interaction and that an individual's sense of self or identity is based both on personal traits as well as social roles and group memberships. Our investigation here seeks to examine carefully whether and how identity changes occur when career-oriented professionals become parents and also choose reduced-load work. The term *identity* has been used to refer to different phenomena in the fields of social psychology, sociology, and developmental psychology, for example self-esteem, personal identity, social identity. Here the focus is *not* on self-esteem, which involves an evaluation of self rather than self-concept; nor are we concerned with social identity, which has to do with the aspects of identity derived from group memberships or identification. Instead, we focus on self-concept or personal identity. Gecas (1982) points out that there are two different traditions in the study of conceptions of self in sociology. One approaches the study of identity through the roles people play, and identities are viewed as internalized roles (Desrochers, Andreassi, & Thompson, 2003). Identity theorists in this tradition (e.g., Stryker, 1968; Stryker & Burke, 2000) view roles as connecting persons to the social context. The structure of self-concept is considered a hierarchical organization of an individual's role-identities, and the more one is involved or enmeshed in relationships related to a particular role, the greater is one's commitment to that aspect of identity. This research stream within sociology has been called the structural interactionist perspective, or the Iowa school. Career theorist D. T. Hall (1976, 2002) has followed in this tradition in suggesting that people have different subidentities, or individual components of identity, based on different social roles a person occupies, for example father, church elder, soccer coach, manager, and so on. Many work-family scholars have also pursued this research tradition in proposing positive effects of multiple roles (Barnett, 1998; Marks & MacDermid, 1996).

The other research tradition on identity in sociology, commonly known as the Chicago school, is referred to as the processual interactionist approach. This school of thought has emphasized more of the ongoing process of negotiation of identity in a social context and the importance of individual social construction of reality. Gecas (1982, p. 11) suggests that indeed researchers in this tradition "view action and interaction as indeterminate, because of the unpredictable 'I' and the problem involved in aligning actions." This approach seems more compatible with learning from the sample of professionals being studied here, who can be viewed as actively negotiating identity and constructing their own reality through reduced-load work. But to understand identity transformation we need to focus not only on how these individuals act on their environments—their social situation both at work and at home—but also on how they are affected by these interactions. In short, identity is conceived as both cause and consequence in social interaction. *Identity transformation* is used here to mean a significant change in the way the individual views him- or herself in a social context, a shift in self-concept that goes beyond simply adding a role or subidentity.

Identity change or growth has been of great interest to adult development or life-span scholars, and one recurring theme in much of this literature has been the assertion that there are predictable, age-related transitions that shape identity over time (Erikson, 1963; Levinson, 1978). A contrasting developmental view is that of Robert Kegan (1982), who does not ascribe to the importance of age but sees individual growth and identity development as driven by how individuals cope with new situations that contain increasingly greater complexity. Kegan (1982) proposes a series of levels of identity, as individuals shift from being highly dependent and self-focused to being more autonomous and perhaps later to being capable of interdependence. He emphasizes the importance of individuals' interactions with others in a variety of environments, in determining the evolving self. Both of these developmental perspectives have more in common with the processual interactionist than with the structural interactionist perspective on identity. That is, the focus is more outward on how the individual continuously negotiates identity in a changing social context; whereas the structural interactionist takes a more inward, or intrapersonal perspective on different roles played and different subidentities and their interrelationships.

An abundant literature in management exists showing that changes in identity accompany career transitions, whether they occur in early career stages, as in job entry and socialization (Van Maanen & Schein, 1979), or later periods, as in transfers or promotions (Hill, 1992; Nicholson, 1984). At the same time theorists have suggested that there are continuities across individuals' careers resulting from somewhat stable configurations of motives, values, and interests as well as abilities. Schein (1978, 1996) calls these "career anchors." In family studies there is also a stream of theory and research focused on changes in identity that accompany the transition to parenthood (e.g., Antonucci & Mikus, 1988; Dion, 1989; Salmela-Aro, Nurmi, Saisto, & Halmesmaki, 2000; Strauss & Goldberg, 1999; Thompson & Walker, 1989). Both family and management scholars acknowledge the importance of identity and identity construction (e.g., Bielby & Bielby, 1989; Ibarra, 1999). But there has been little attention paid by scholars in either organizational studies or family studies to the *career* transition of parenthood, to the socialization into the new role of parent in the context of a professional career. The management literature has given little attention to the significance of parenthood in the overall development of a career. And the family literature has not integrated career continuity and discontinuity issues in its consideration of the transition to parenthood and associated adult development challenges that unfold over time.

Socialization

In a review chapter on adult socialization Dion (1985) defines *socialization* as "the process by which persons acquire the knowledge, skills, and dispositions that make them more or less able members of their society" (p. 3). She notes that the three main domains of adult socialization dealt with in the literature are work, marriage, and parenthood, but there has been more focus on socialization into work and occupational roles than into family roles. Socialization in the management literature has tended to be viewed as a process through which individuals learn the beliefs, values, orientations, behaviors, skills necessary to fulfill their new roles and function effectively within an organization (Ashforth & Saks, 1996; Hall, 2002; Van Maanen, 1976). Socialization can also refer to a process professionals go through when they experience major career transitions and need to acquire new skills and adapt to social norms and rules that govern conduct in the new context. Gecas (1982) notes that a major stream of research from the processual interactionist approach to the study of identity has focused on socialization. Ibarra (1999) recently linked socialization and identity in interpreting findings from a study of financial analysts promoted to management positions. She suggests these finance professionals developed "provisional selves" that allowed them to bridge the gap between their current capacities and self-concept and the representations they had about attitudes and behavior expected in their new roles.

Socialization into parenthood has not been investigated in the same way as socialization into occupational or work roles. The literature on becoming a parent tends to be framed as a transition, which suggests personal and/or marital adjustment; whereas socialization automatically conjures up the social context and situates parenthood in a broader social structure. The term *socialization* raises questions about *how* the transition plays out and what the influences are over time. The focus on transition reflects the clinical concern in the family literature about healthy adjustment to parenthood (Demo & Cox, 2000). Just as the socialization literature (e.g., Van Maanen & Schein, 1979) has maintained that identity changes accompany *work* role changes, family sociologists have asserted that the transition to parenthood has the potential to change the way parents think and feel about themselves and their environment (Daly, 1996; Strauss & Goldberg, 1999). Strauss and Goldberg (1999) suggest that this happens as a result of increased differentiation and reorganization of existing aspects of self, leading to a more coherent self across different roles. However, the framing of entry into parenthood as a transition, rather than a process of socialization, has perhaps limited the research focus and therefore the learning to be gained. In this time of the dual-earner family as the modal family structure and dramatically increased labor participation of mothers with young children, a socialization perspective on entry into parenthood could draw needed attention to emerging changes in how individuals learn the necessary skills to perform their new roles and subsequent implications for society, community, and organizations.

Process of Adaptation

Research on work and family in recent years has generated some interesting theorizing about how individuals and families are dealing with the high level of work and family demands (Barnett, 1998; Daly, 2002; Hall, 2002; Hall & Hall, 1979; Hertz, 1997; Hochschild, 1997; Kossek, Noe, & DeMarr, 1999; Moen & Wethington, 1992; Moen & Yu, 2000; Perlow, 1998; Sekaran & Hall, 1989). Moen and Wethington (1992, p. 234) coined the term *family adaptive strategies* to refer to "the actions families devise for coping with, if not overcoming, the challenges of living, and for achieving their goals in the face of structural barriers." Out of this framework a life course approach was developed to examine how couples make choices over time around engagement in work and family. In a subsequent study Moen and Yu (2000) plotted couple work-hour strategies at different life stages (e.g., one or both members of couple working under 39 hours per week, one or both over 45 hours, and both 39–45 hours). Using the same data set Becker and Moen (1999) found three "scaling back" work-family strategies, all of which involved the couple decreasing total work commitments. Kossek, Noe, and DeMarr (1999) proposed the term *work-family role synthesis* as a way of thinking about the strategies an individual uses to manage the enactment of work and caregiving roles. They identified two critical components to work-family role synthesis, boundary management and role embracement of multiple roles. Barnett (1998) has suggested that the concept of *fit* is critical to our enhanced understanding of effective management of work and personal life. She defines *fit* as "a dynamic process of adjustment between work conditions and the characteristics of workers and their strategies to meet their own needs"

(1998, p. 144). Hertz (1997) focuses on different approaches to child care as the centerpiece of organizing family life among dual-career couples.

Emotional Response

Emotion has not been a popular topic of study in organizational behavior until relatively recently, and its role in work motivation has been little explored (Seo, Barrett, & Bartunek, 2002). In fact, mainstream theories of work motivation place more emphasis on needs, external stimuli, and cognition (e.g., perceptions, goals). Emotion has not been considered a very important factor. Yet Seo et al. (in press) note that there is an extensive body of research that provides convincing evidence that human emotion influences human thought and behavior in all domains, whether at work or in other settings. In their paper they present preliminary evidence of how core affect has direct and indirect effects on work motivation. Furthermore, Rothbard (2001) recently proposed a model of engagement in work and family roles in which positive and negative affect help explain the dynamics of depletion and enrichment between roles. Certainly emotion would seem to be critical to our understanding professionals' socialization into parenthood and subsequent efforts to adapt work and family routines to the new demands of the situation, because fathers and mothers typically have affective responses to becoming parents (Oberman & Josselson, 1996; Strauss & Goldberg, 1999). In fact, individuals' variable emotional responses to parenthood could be a major force driving the process of identity transformation

Reduced-Load Work

Although there has been a proliferation of theoretical frameworks and typologies on approaches to effective engagement and enactment in the areas of career and family, there has been a tendency to focus on different types of strategies rather than the actual *process* of adaptation, and there has been little attention given to adaptation connected specifically to *new* parenthood. Yet a recent study of reduced-load work arrangements among professionals and managers (Lee, MacDermid, & Buck, 2002) indicated that the timing of requests for working less was strongly associated with the birth of a child. Working on a reduced-load basis, or part time, in a professional or managerial job, represents a relatively new alternative work arrangement that has been getting increasing attention in recent years (Barnett & Gareis, 2000; Corwin, Lawrence, & Frost, 2001; Epstein, Seron, Oglensky, & Saute, 1998; Lee, MacDermid, & Buck, 2000; Meiksins & Whalley, 2002). Lee, Engler, and Wright (2002) document increased percentages of doctors, lawyers, and accountants working less than full-time, and Corwin et al. (2001) estimates that 10% of corporate professionals work part time. Barnett and Gareis (2002) note that a number of studies show professional dissatisfaction with long work hours, and many scholars connect this trend with the increased number of dual-career and single-parent families and the struggle to balance the competing demands of work and family obligations (Spalter-Roth et al., 1997). Furthermore, there is evidence that working longer hours is clearly associated with *wanting* to work less in dual-career couples in which husband and wife are both working at least 35 hours (Clarkberg & Moen, 2001). It is also clear that more organizations are offering reduced-load work to professionals in an effort to retain talented employees (Barnett & Gareis, 2002).

Despite the growth in reduced-load work arrangements, little attention has been paid to the meanings behind this phenomenon and the implications for organizations that want to be responsive or even proactive in providing alternative ways of working for a changing workforce. What we explore here is the underlying function of reduced-load work in the context of professionals' lives and careers, as well as in the context of the organization. We view reduced-load work as a manifestation of the adaptation process professionals go through as they are socialized into a new role and experience identity transformation from career-oriented professional to professional *and* parent.

METHODOLOGY

Data for this chapter came from a subsample of a larger study of managers and professionals voluntarily working less than full time (.50–.90 of a full-time equivalent position) for family and/or lifestyle reasons and incurring commensurate reductions in compensation. Using a case study approach (Yin, 1994), we sought multiple perspectives on each work arrangement by interviewing not only the target managers and professionals but also four additional stakeholders per case. These included the worker's senior manager, a peer-level coworker, the spouse or partner (where applicable), and a human resource representative of the employing firm. The total sample consisted of 87 cases of reduced-load work in professional and managerial jobs in 45 different firms.[1] Because of equipment failure or lost audiotapes in four cases, the final sample was 83 cases from 43 firms. The study described here focused on 78 individuals in 75 cases (three were job share arrangements), where the target individual working reduced load was a parent with at least one child living at home. Seventy-four were women and four were men. Three were separated or divorced; one was a single parent; and 74 were married. The average age of the youngest child was 4.7. Participants were in a variety of kinds of professional and managerial positions (e.g., engineer, accountant, bank branch manager) in a variety of different kinds of companies (e.g., manufacturing, financial services, natural resources, telecommunications) in the United States and Canada. They had been working on a reduced-load basis an average of 4.2 years, and the average work load was 72% of full time, with the most typical reductions being three or four days, 60% or

80%. Participants were working an average of 32 hours a week at the time of the study, which represented an average of 17 hours less than they had been working when full time. Prorated to a full-time equivalent, salaries ranged from $31,111 to $175,000 U.S., with the mean salary $79,441 (at time of data collection 1996–1998).

The target respondents were all interviewed for one to two hours about the logistics of the reduced-load arrangement, how it came about, and how it was working out from a personal and family, as well as organizational perspective. Appendix A herein shows the entire interview protocol. The interviews were audiotaped and then transcribed verbatim. A grounded theory approach (Glaser & Strauss, 1967) was used in data analysis, with a focus on material specifically related to identity issues and socialization into parenthood. Keeping in mind themes in the work and family and socialization literatures, the authors read and reread transcripts and produced a reflective memo for each case, giving special attention to participant comments and responses related to the following topics or issues:

1. Career orientation:
   • *Prior* to becoming a parent.
   • Currently (while on reduced-load work).
   • Projecting into the future.
2. Family orientation.
3. Other aspects of identity or other roles.
4. Socialization into parenthood (learning about and entry into new role).
5. Adaptation.

In addition, the first author reviewed previously produced analytic memos that contained summary information on each case based on all stakeholder interviews. This was done to probe reasons given for pursuing reduced-load work and to review the process of negotiation with the employer as well as the overall story of previous and ongoing adjustments made over time in the actual enactment of the work arrangement.

The first author then reviewed the materials mentioned earlier, using the method of constant comparison advocated by Glaser and Strauss (1967) and produced the following building blocks for a tentative theoretical framework: a set of profiles that captured similarities and differences in respondents' descriptions of themselves before parenthood and at present; a catalog of the kinds of socialization into parenthood experiences that surfaced; and characterization of different dynamics that seemed to be operating in the adaptation process of making adjustments in work or home routines to accommodate new realities. Gradually, through multiple iterations of comparing and contrasting the experiences of respondents and integrating existing relevant theory, a tentative theoretical framework was developed to explain some of the dynamics in identity transformation and to guide future research on this issue.

OVERVIEW OF THEORETICAL FRAMEWORK

Out of this qualitative examination of how professionals enter into parenthood has emerged a tentative theoretical framework for understanding the socialization process, as well as the process of adaptation which together shape a new sense of self (see Fig. 14.1). Most professionals in their early career stages are consumed with developing the appropriate skills and knowledge, as well as acquiring the necessary repertoire of behaviors and conforming to organizational and/ or professional norms and regulations; and establishing and proving themselves by performing well and garnering recognition for staking out territory and promoting further career advancement. They are very committed to their careers and feel closely identified with their professions. We propose here that although most professionals share a great deal in common before they have children, there is variation in self-conceptions, which are represented in the model as five kinds of *Identity Before Parenthood*: Career Defined, Career Defined with Family Acquisition Plans, Career and Family: A Joint Venture, Alternating Career and Family, and Career Pursued in a Context. These are meant to capture some of the differences among professionals, before becoming parents, in the centrality of career and family to the self-concept and the goals and expectations about parenthood at a later point in time.

It is proposed here that once a professional becomes a parent, preparenthood identity is transformed through a complex and dynamic process of socialization into parenthood and concurrent adaptation of work and family routines. Meanwhile, the individual's emotional responses to becoming a parent, to the process of socialization, and to making changes or adjustments in work patterns play an important role in the evolution of identity. *Socialization* into parenthood consists of a process of learning about and entering into a new role. Of course, it begins in childhood through our own experiences with our own parents, and it continues through different stages of parents' lives when their children are different ages. But socialization into parenthood is especially intense around the time of first becoming a parent. It happens unconsciously and unintentionally through what individuals observe and experience. It happens as mothers and fathers have to begin to perform the new role in the particular circumstances of pregnancy and birth and early care of an infant, and in interaction with other important players. It unfolds as a function of the individual professional's work context, in terms of the kinds of parental leave policies and other work-life practices in place in the firm, as well as a result of the kinds of social norms and values that circumscribe the range of acceptable behaviors for employees who are parents. So-

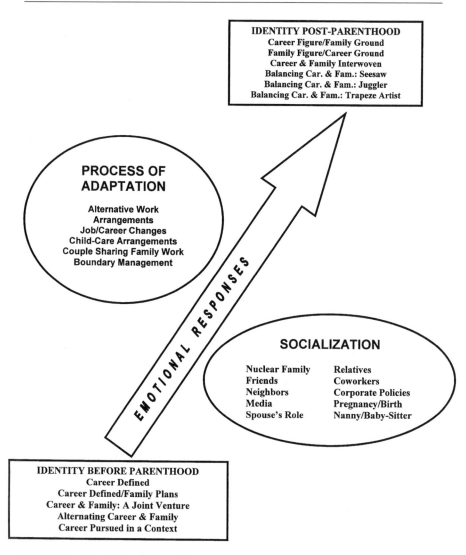

FIG. 14.1.   Identity transformation.

cialization is also going on when a person inquires or networks with colleagues about the possibilities for flexible or customized work arrangements within certain departments, or jobs, and so on.

So, individuals bring to the experience of having a child: their pre-existing identity as a professional, embedded in a complex network of relationships at work and at home (e.g., spouse and spouse's occupation, employer) and perhaps in the community; and a process of learning about parenthood. Then, as socialization continues—through the interaction of parents and child as well as family, friends, neighbors, coworkers, and so on, and through concomitant emotional responses—the individual begins a *Process of Adaptation* to the new parental role. Through experience and trial and error, the individual makes accommodations at work for the sake of family and accommodations in the family for the sake of work, in order to establish a new regime for satisfactory linking of parent and professional interfacing with the realities of negotiating career and family in daily life. Often some structural changes are initiated in work patterns, in order to lessen work time and burden. New arrangements around the family work also emerge.

Of course, as the socialization into parenthood continues and these professionals experiment with changes and adjustments in the work and family routines, they also have *Emotional Responses*, both positive and negative—to the new regimes, to being a parent, to trying to continue the fast-paced demanding career with a toddler or two at home, and so on. Those responses may also lead to further adaptations. And, of course, the kinds of changes and adjustments possible in the workplace are constrained by the type of position, work unit, and employer of the individual professional as well as his or her spouse.

So gradually what emerges then from this process of Identity Transformation is professionals whose sense of identity or self has changed from previously, to incorporate the new role of parent. The new kinds of Identity Postparenthood are proposed to include the following: Career Figure/Family Ground, Family Figure/Career Ground, Career and Family Interwoven, Balancing Career and Family: Seesaw, Balancing Career and Family: Juggler, Balancing Career and Family: Trapeze Artist. These new selves represent more than just adding of an additional role, because the overall essence of the individual is fundamentally altered as he or she continues to negotiate identity but in a new context and social structure that includes the workplace, family, and community. In this formulation of identity transformation the individual is not a static entity, and the interrelationships and dynamics among various roles the individual plays are viewed as meaningless outside of the context of the social situations where life is enacted. Identity is conceived of as more than the sum of its parts (e.g., roles), and the labels given to the new identities here are meant to allow comparing and contrasting how the individual is linked to the social context. These new identities can be thought of as representing provisional selves, and they express differences in the orienting force, or dominant orientation, or organizing principle in peoples' lives, as well as differences in the nature and stability of interlinking mechanisms joining professional and parent.

The emergent provisional self that comes out of the socialization into parenthood and the adaptation process of creating new work and family regimes is essentially highly variable. Individuals enter into parenthood with different self-images, expectations, experiences, emotions. And the socialization process is idiosyncratic. Furthermore, the adaptation process is strongly influenced by couple and relationship factors, as well as organizational factors that determine degrees of freedom the individual participant has to custom design a career work arrangement and a family work arrangement compatible with individual needs and desires.

FINDINGS

First, we examine similarities and differences in how the reduced-load professionals in our sample described themselves, conveyed their sense of self *before* having children. Second, we describe recurrent themes in respondents' accounts of their socialization into parenthood, that is, how they learned about and entered this new role. Third, we describe five of the most common kinds of changes or adjustments in work and family patterns that were enacted in the adaptation process. Fourth, we provide examples of the dynamic role of emotional responses in the overall process of identity transformation. Finally, we describe our sample's self-conceptions *after* becoming parents and propose a typology of different kinds of linking of parental and professional identity based on observed resolutions of the professional's journey involving incorporating parenthood into his or her sense of self.

Identity Before Parenthood

What we were looking for here was how these professionals thought about themselves *before* actually having a child. How did they talk about who they were and what they cared about, their dreams, and so on? What did their careers mean to them? Did they want a family and what were their expectations about how their careers might be affected if they did? Of course, given that all of the interviews occurred on average three to four years after the birth of the first child, this meant that respondents were looking back and reconstructing their sense of self, their identity from an earlier period. So the self-descriptions presented here are retrospective and likely tainted by their actual experiences with parenthood.

In examining the self-descriptions of the 78 individuals in the sample *before* parenthood, we found one striking similarity across all but a handful of the cases. They were all highly identified with their careers, and they had met with significant success and recognition and were proud of their career achievements. They also reported that the idea of abandoning their careers if they had children was never something they had considered. There were also some important differences in the ways these individuals represented who they were before parenthood, what role career played in their lives in general, what they wanted and expected in their careers and lives. For example, some had a more active and diverse set of activities and commitments in their lives apart from work. Some reported being more certain than others about wanting to have children, and they had a wide range of expectations about how having a family might affect their careers and how they would react or adapt to being a parent *and* a professional.

Career Defined. Those we labeled as career defined described themselves as very career-oriented, with ambitions to rise to the top and with little or no interest in having children. They presented an image of themselves as having been very successful and having been on an upwardly mobile career trajectory before having had children. They had not really planned to have a family or had given no real thought to whether they wanted children. They did not recall thinking ahead or anticipating any difficulties that might arise if they became parents. Ten of the 78 participants (12.8%) fit into this identity pattern.

Career Defined with Family Acquisition Plans. The second group identified was quite similar to the Career-Defined group in that these individuals were very ambitious and had been very successful so far in their careers. They were striving for the same high level jobs in their firms, and they did not anticipate any changes or difficulties in continuing their strong commitment to their careers after having children. The distinction between the two groups is that those in this second group said that they had always wanted to have a family and had assumed they would be able to "add on" family to their very career oriented lives, kind of like a planned business acquisition, with no significant problems. They had presumed that with lots of help from surrogate caregivers (e.g., nannies, day care, relatives) and hired help, the extra load would not be that great and they would be able to maintain their long work hours and involvement in key roles in their organizations unfazed. Thirty-two of 78 participants (41%) fit this pattern of preparental identity.

Career and Family: A Joint Venture. The third kind of self-description that surfaced came from a group of individuals with the same strong career orientation before children, the same ambition and success, recognition outlined in the previous patterns. Like those in the Career Defined with Family Acquisition Plans, they had always imagined that they would have a family as well as a career. However, these individuals said that they had known in advance that having children would change their lives, that it would involve a major expansion of responsibilities and perhaps some changes in their careers. In spite of this, they said they had looked forward to becoming a parent and considered it very important to their overall identity. They also expected to be able to move ahead and continue in their careers, just not quite in the same way or at the same pace. They described their expectations of "life after children" with images suggesting a kind of joint venture between career and family, assigning equal importance to the two in their lives. Twelve of 78, or 15.4%, fell into this pattern.

Alternating Career and Family.   This group was very committed to their work and saw themselves as giving their all to their careers as long as they did not have a family. Once they had children, they assumed they would put family first and continue their careers only as long as they could successfully orchestrate them around family as the priority. These individuals had high career goals before having children but were prepared to put them on hold for some period of time and concentrate more on family once they became parents. They assumed they would have to make compromises in their careers for the sake of family; and they were completely comfortable with such an eventuality, as it fit with their identity and sense of self, which was grounded in a clear commitment to family as the most important thing in life. Nine of 78, or 11.5%, fit this pattern.

Career Pursued in a Context.   The final kind of preparental self-conception presented was labeled to convey that these individuals claimed to have always pursued their careers in a context in which family or other life interests played a central role. Even before having children, they had never conceived of their careers as a key defining aspect of identity but rather as a pursuit in service of other goals in life. These individuals never made career the centerpiece in their lives, even before becoming parents, and they often had compelling interests or activities outside of their careers before having a family. They pursued their careers in the context of a life rather than as "the main show." They tended to talk more about the importance of sustained personal growth and development, making a contribution, or being able to pursue other interests in addition to their careers. Nevertheless, before becoming parents these individuals had achieved significant career success as professionals and felt proud of their accomplishments. Fifteen of 78, or 19.2%, of the sample fit this pattern of preparental identity.

Socialization into Parenthood

So the next question is: What brought these individuals from their sense of self before becoming a parent to their new identity afterward? Of course, we know already that they began with different self-conceptions and expectations of career and family even before becoming parents. In addition, they described different kinds of experiences, events, and associations in relation to their transition to parenthood. These different avenues of socialization included: (a) childhood and crossgenerational interaction, (b) peer and sibling same cohort models, (c) purposeful information seeking, and (d) self-learning during role entry.

Childhood and Crossgenerational Contact.   The concept of socialization as both learning as well as initiation into a new role means that it is a diffuse and extensive process that surely starts with an individual's experiences in childhood with their own parents, not to mention the ongoing relationships they have with parents into adulthood. Many participants talked explicitly about the model of parenting they had observed and experienced in their own nuclear family and the impact that it had had on them. Participants talked about their own (and/or their spouses') positive experiences with their own mothers or fathers—for example, being home when they came back from school, baking homemade cookies, being there to talk to them and give help with homework, or teaching them how to do things. But they also described mistakes they felt their parents had made and how they were attempting to avoid those pitfalls. Participants also frequently talked about ongoing, current dialogue (sometimes contentious) with their parents about how they were choosing to "parent." Of course, given the mean age of the sample, most were born around 1960, before the dramatic increase in number of mothers with young children in the labor force. So most of the study participants, though not all, had mothers who had not worked outside the home when their children were young.

Peer and Sibling Models. A second related kind of socialization experience was watching siblings, cousins, friends, and colleagues become parents and observing how they incorporated the new role, coped with the added demands, and so forth. Some participants gave accounts of what they had figured out they wanted to avoid; whereas others were inspired to try solutions they had observed among friends or relatives. In these kinds of socialization experiences, participants talked about just absorbing what was around them, for better or worse; they were not intentionally seeking out exposure to different models of parenting or learning about what parenting entails.

Purposeful Information Seeking. A third kind of socialization experience described was more intentional and involved seeking out specific information from coworkers or neighbors, friends of friends, and the like with young children to get their thoughts on what parenthood would involve and what kind of career adjustments were possible, helpful, and not too disruptive. This included talking to others who had tried various alternative work arrangements and gathering information from their employer and/or other employers about existing work-family policies and practices that might be useful to them once they became parents *and* professionals.

Self-Learning During Role Entry. A fourth kind of socialization experience that surfaced in participants' descriptions of the process of becoming parents had to do with the actual physical realities of pregnancy and birth, as well as the subsequent early weeks and months of intense learning about caring for an infant and getting to know a child. Prenatal experiences were mentioned, including fertility issues, multiple miscarriages, difficult pregnancies, twins, adoption. Participants who faced unexpected roadblocks or exceptional challenges in conceiving said that having had to face the possibility of *not* being able to be parents had made them more committed to being present and involved parents. They had been through a process of realizing how important parenthood was to them and they embraced the new role eagerly.

Many participants described specific aspects of the birth itself or the early weeks and months after the birth as important in their realization of how different their lives were going to be after parenthood. Some found these early experiences difficult and challenging and were eager to return to work after parental leave. Such sentiments often were associated with such things as a difficult birth, postpartum hormonal abnormalities, babies with feeding problems, incessant sleep deprivation, or depression about loss of autonomy. Others had more positive experiences; some even pinpointed events in this period as life-time high points or extraordinary, sublime, life-changing moments. They talked about such things as "falling in love" with their babies, about their own gradual development of a sense of mastery in the new role, or the joint couple experience of making room for a new member of the family.

Another important input that participants mentioned during this time right after the birth of a child was involvement of extended family, especially parents and siblings, who came to visit or help out in the early weeks or months. Participants talked about being more comfortable leaving their babies with relatives than with a paid caretaker whenever possible. Finally, there was often commentary about the degree of involvement of the father in the care of the baby in the early weeks and months. This represented learning about what parenting was going to be like in this particular family, whether more of a joint, shared enterprise, or one parent taking the main responsibility.

Participants also talked about learning from their own early experiences as parents, as well as from books and interaction with other parents with babies—in their neighborhoods, churches, play groups, and so on. For example, they mentioned learning from other mothers about things to do with a baby who will not stop crying; gradually getting to know their own baby and its peculiarities compared to other babies; figuring out when to take the baby to the doctor and when it is not worth it; learning ways to keep their baby physically close but still get things done (through the use of different carriers, etc.); or learning about things they could and could not control about sleep patterns, and so on.

Of course, socialization into parenthood can be viewed as ongoing and continuous in the sense that even after someone has made the transition to the new role of parent, the learning goes on as children grow and change and present new challenges at different stages of development. Some participants in fact talked about significant marker events, when their children were older, which led to major changes in the way they understood their roles as parent and ultimately the way they behaved in the family context. Ambert (2000) talks about the parent-child relationship being an integrated process of socialization in which children affect the parenting they get from their parents. Her perspective differs from traditional theories on childrearing which concentrate on the parents' in-dependent actions (or their actions alone) as shaping children's behavior and personality. Instead, she says that children themselves affect the way their parents raise them and also affect their parents' lives more than we would have previously thought. A story from one participant provides a good illustration of this point.

> I had a very interesting experience a couple of week ago, where my younger son was very upset on the way to school. And I'm sure there were other things going on at school, but anyway, he was not wanting to go into school. . . . So I sat down, I spent some time with him, and I said, "You're going to have to go in. I'll go in with you." So we walked in together and—and "You know, I really don't want to do this"—and he is not sick. And there is not much I was going to be able to do, because I really had to—work.
>
> So I said, "Gee, I'd really like to spend some time with you. How about let's not do it at lunchtime because that is not going to work for me. But I'll be at school at 2:30. You don't have to go to extended day today. And we'll spend the afternoon together." So I came in to work, I—I left work, I picked him up at 2:30, and he was so happy. . . . He just needed time with me, alone. He didn't ask me to buy him anything, which he often does. But what he wanted was just to spend time with me. We went home, we changed our clothes, we went and we had ice cream. And we then came home and we played a little bit of one-on-one basketball and kicked some soccer balls. Just whatever he wanted to do.

Socialization into parenthood necessarily includes the ongoing interaction be-tween parent and child and the parents' assimilation of the reality that their behavior and interaction with their child has, or can have, a powerful impact on the child's thriving or failure to thrive. It means figuring out how and when to act and not act to help children grow and develop, make friends and gradually become independent and spread their wings.

Adaptation Process

The third aspect of this inquiry was to look at different ways participants made adjustments or changes in their work patterns, both in the family and in their careers, as a result of becoming parents. In examining actual changes, of course, all those in the sample were working less than full time as one way to enable combining career and family successfully. There were also other aspects to their alternative work arrangements. Many participants experimented with working one or more days from home offices (completely equipped by the company) as part of their reduced-load work arrangement. And a few had no office other than the one at home and went into the workplace only sporadically for meet-ings. One manager even supervised from her home office a product development team of 15 who worked in four different locations across three different states.

The shifts in physical location of work were viewed partially as efforts at boundary management, as efforts to customize the boundaries between career and family in a way that worked best for all stakeholders in the situation. Another way participants made adjustments in their work arrangements was to match their own work schedules to the organization's peak demand seasons over a year. So, for example, a comptroller might work three days a week during most of the year but full-time for two weeks around each quarter end. Or an accountant might work full-time in tax season but three days a week the rest of the year.

A second kind of adaptation found was changing jobs or departments or even employers in order to find or create the desired work load and still be able to do interesting, challenging work. We also heard from many of the participants that they had adjusted in some way their career plans, goals, or expectations— short term and/or long term. However, a few insisted that even though they were working reduced load, they did not think it would affect their career advancement. And in fact a third of the sample had been promoted once or twice while working on a reduced-load basis. Among those who had altered their career plans or expectations, there was great variation in the degree of change in their thinking.

A third kind of adjustment or adaptation observed was in child care arrangements. Of course, all working parents must create a system for child care once the parental or maternal leave is over. And often the choices made differ for the first child and then with subsequent children. Our sample varied a great deal in their preferences here. For example, some insisted on extended family involvement, whereas others used on-site employer-sponsored or other institutional day care. Others hired nannies and dealt with a great deal of turnover, or alternatively found individuals who stayed five or ten years. In addition, once a professional changed his or her work arrangement, whether in terms of number of days of work, physical location of work, or a combination of the two, usually there was a need for change in child-care arrangements. For example, a software engineer cutting back to a three-day work week in the office wanted to then find a three-day-a-week nanny, because she would be at home alone with the baby on her two days off. On the other hand, a project manager working 80% of full time worked every day at her fully equipped home office, but she put in fewer hours per week overall. She wanted a five-day-a-week nanny so that she could spend significant time with her two year old more spontaneously throughout the days and the week, depending on her schedule as well as her son's schedule. But in most cases, child-care arrangements went through a number of changes over time, in response to number and ages of children, changes in work patterns of the professional and/or spouse, and changes with the hired help or services.

A fourth kind of adjustment in career/family routines found in the sample was shifts in the division of labor in the family. These professionals working less in the workplace often took on more of the family work at home, although a few insisted on keeping their increased time off strictly for themselves or for play time with children rather than for chores. However, an unexpected finding was that often the spouses got more involved in the family as a result of the reduced-load work arrangement. For example, if a reduced-load mother or father still maintained contact with the office on days off and was open to being called in on an emergency basis for meetings or client-related issues, the other member of the couple often undertook to be backup. This required the spouse to negotiate or create more flexibility in his or her own work schedule and arrangement.

So there were many different kinds of adjustments and changes made in work and family patterns as part of these professionals' process of adaptation to parenthood. And two clearly powerful constraints operating on this adaptation process were the organization context and the spouse or partner's career and employment situation. Employers offering less flexibility in terms of work load, work hours, work places, and the like restricted the range of accommodations available to the parent wanting to work less, both directly and indirectly, through the rigidity in the spouse or partner's work situation. The spouse or partner's actual occupation and interest in being involved significantly in the family work also has an impact on the kinds of adjustments possible. For example, if a father is a professional cellist in a symphony orchestra, a certain amount of travel per year is totally non-negotiable, as is being able to pick up a sick child from school if there is a rehearsal or performance in progress. However, if the cellist has periods of weeks off totally and refuses to share drop-off and pick-up of children, the shortfall is in his attitude not the constraints of the occupation.

The other common theme we found in the process of making changes and adjustments to accommodate career and family was a great deal of fluidity and transience in solutions found. In most cases this seemed to be a positive thing, for it allowed a kind of ongoing mutual accommodation process to go on. Something might work well for a few months, but then need to be modified because of family or work circumstances changing. As long as there was some flexibility on both the family and work sides, it was possible to engage in ongoing fine-tuning and recalibration or alignment. However, in some cases, individuals were looking for more permanence or stability, a more fixed arrangement because of lack of flexibility in one domain.

Emotional Responses

The transformation process for professionals from preparenthood to postparent-hood identity involves an iterative and idiosyncratic process of socialization into the new role of parent. Meanwhile these professionals are also learning by trial and error what kinds of changes or adjustments in work and family patterns allow for the way of life they want. To a great extent the socialization experiences are proposed to have a big effect on the adaptation process, albeit within the constraints of the workplace policies and culture and the career and workplace constraints of the spouse or partner. But there is a final important dynamic operating in the transformation of identity, and that is the individual's emotional reactions to the transition of becoming a parent in addition to a professional. These emotional responses then drive the spiraling effects of socialization on accommodation and change, and then the effects of those changes in work patterns on subsequent socialization and so on. Gradually over time a new post-parenthood identity emerges out of the individual's experiences with socializing influences, adaptation of work and family routines and concomitant emotional responses. Of course, we are not positing that emotional responses determine ultimate postparenthood identity patterns. However, they are considered critical to the identity transformation process, as they represent both cause and effect in relation to ongoing socialization into the new role of parenthood and attempts to accommodate new family commitments.

There was a wide range of emotions, both positive and negative, expressed and recounted in these interviews with professionals working on a reduced-load basis. In fact, in the process of stories being told and key events being recalled, it was not unusual for tears to be shed, or for anger and resentment to be close to the surface. On the other hand, enthusiasm, ebullience, and contentment were also in evidence. It should be noted that in the total overall sample of cases, 93% of the individuals working reduced load were very happy with their arrangements, and 66% of the cases were assessed as being highly successful from the point of view of the individual, the organization and the family. The most common emotions observed or described in the interviews can be divided into two categories, those related to family (e.g., being a parent, socialization into parenthood, division of labor in the family) and those related to career (e.g., job, reduced-load arrangement, career advancement).

Family

- Falling in love with baby or new role
- Exhilaration about expansion of self or self-discovery and exploration of new friends and activities apart from work
- Feelings of loss of self
- Feelings of failure or frustration in new role
- Anger or resentment about lack of support and family work load

Career

- Personal fulfillment about continued achievement, making a meaningful contribution, and future opportunity
- Thrilled and grateful to be able to have both a career and a family
- Comfortable with career trade-offs
- Anxious or ambivalent about career trade-offs

- Feelings of failure or frustration about work performance
- Anger or resentment about lack of support in the workplace

One observed emotional response that did not fall into either the family or career category:

- Feeling torn and fatigued by need for incessant strategic approach to making everything work

So these professionals experienced many of these emotional reactions, and sometimes they seemed paradoxical. For example, one might think that falling in love with one's baby could not be accompanied by a feeling of loss of self from becoming a mother. Yet the two sometimes did go hand-in-hand. Partly because of the mix of emotional responses, these professionals sometimes took action as a result of their reactions and sometimes they did not. And sometimes the action taken led to other emotional responses that were problematic. Or there were constraints in the situation, at work or at home, that made further change and adjustment of work or family regimes difficult. But the emotional responses to the new role, as well as to the processes of socialization and adaptation were integral to the gradual evolution of the new postparenthood identity. In the next section some examples of how the dynamics of emotional responses might link pre- and postparenthood identity patterns will be offered.

Identity as Professional and Parent

Participant self-conceptions after becoming parents suggested an array of different kinds of coupling of professional with parental identity. What we observed was variety in not only the nature of the interlinking of these different aspects of identity, but in the dominance or overall influence of one over the other, as well as the degree of fluidity in the interrelationship.

Career Figure/Family Ground.   There were some whose sense of self did not seem to change much after they became parents. Their predominant sense of self came from their professional identification and pursuit of their careers even with the addition of their new role as parent. For example, in the case of some Career-Defined individuals, becoming a parent represented a minor acquisition of a new role requiring a minor reconfiguration. Career remained the priority, and the rest of life was organized around professional goals and constraints. While family and family roles were perceived as an important part of life, the career remained front and center. Only 5 of 78 (5%) individuals fit into this pattern, which is not surprising given the nature of the sample and the fact that all had chosen to work less than full time.

Nevertheless, given that 10 of 78 described themselves as Career Defined *before* having children, and another 32 described themselves as Career Defined with Family Plans, which they did not expect to disrupt their careers in any way, the small number who fit this category of *post* parenthood identity is a testimonial to the power of identity transformation. Four of the five were in the preparental Career-Defined identity pattern, which is also not surprising. These individuals maintained a high level of commitment to their careers and were not prepared to alter the position of career in their overall life context. There was a sense of permanence and clarity about the source, the center of their life structure. Four of the five individuals in this postparenthood identity pattern were also either planning to terminate their reduced load arrangements in the near future or had just recently done so, either because they were not able to actually work less though they were being paid less, or because they had been offered a promotion that required them to be working full time.

The most predominant emotional reactions in this group were exhilaration with continued career achievement and opportunity, loss of self, and anger or resentment about lack of support. Because these professionals continued to invest heavily in their careers after becoming parents, they continued to do well in their careers and feel good about that. However, some of the professionals in this group clearly avoided spending time and home and yet expressed a sense of loss about their restricted ability to work as obsessively as before. Also, several of them expressed a great deal of resentment about their employers' unwillingness to actually allow them to carry a lower work load.

Research on the transition to motherhood has found that one of the key dimensions along which women differ when becoming parents is loss versus expansion of self (Oberman & Josselson, 1996). This issue has different significance for women and men who become parents in the context of a dynamic career and a professional identity independent of family. But we would still expect this issue to be front and center in terms of determining how these individuals seek to join, affix, or integrate their new role as parent to the preexisting professional identity. For example, the parent who experiences parenthood as involving a loss of self may be eager to reengage in the prior work context to reclaim and reaffirm the previous main source of identity. But as a result, that professional may short-circuit the socialization into parenthood and the potential for true embracement of the parental role and ultimately identity transformation. On the other hand, someone who experiences an expansion of self may feel inclined or compelled to completely drop out of his or her career, because his or her employer offers no options that allow for cutting back on work to make room for an expanded life as a professional and parent.

Family Figure/Career Ground.   In this postparenthood identity pattern these professionals also were very clear about their priorities, but family was clearly front and center. Their careers remained an important, even essential part of the picture, but they were orchestrated around family to a great extent. Twenty-two of 78 (28%) fit this pattern. Twelve of them were in the preparental identity pattern of Career Pursued in a Context. So they had known before having children that career would never be the "end-all and be-all" of their existence. Becoming a parent simply consolidated a prior commitment to a rich life beyond career and provided a new source of self-fulfillment. An additional four in this identity pattern had also been clear before having children that their careers would take a back seat to family once they became parents. They were in the Alternating Career and Family preparental identity pattern. However, four came to this postparenthood identity from Career Defined, and they told quite interesting stories about epiphany experiences that led them to a dramatic shift toward putting family, not career, first. The predominant emotional responses to parenthood among those in the Family Figure/Career Ground were quite positive. They experienced a sense of expansion of self, or blossoming and self-discovery, and they felt very comfortable about the career tradeoffs they were making.

Career and Family Interwoven. A third type of postparenthood identity found involved more of a merger or fusion of the two aspects of identity, professional and parent. Reduced-load professionals in this pattern used images or metaphors that suggested integration, synthesis or interweaving of career and family, as well as other important aspects of life. Their identity transformation was like a work of art in progress, an improvised dance, with shifting movement and rhythm through time and space. They talked about their involvement in different roles expanding and enriching their overall lives, rather than in terms of multiple roles competing for time in a finite universe. Their enactment of each role was enhanced by their experiences in other roles.

> Before it used to feel like I worked five days a week and I had a two-day weekend. Now it feels like I have a life. Even though I am in here every single day, I just can't believe the emotional difference it makes. I have an integrated life that all works. And I work here, I work there, I play here, I play there, and it is just a patchwork quilt that all fits together and makes sense.

There were 31, or 40%, of the sample in this pattern, and they started out for the most part with preparental identities of Career Defined with Family Plans or Career and Family: A Joint Venture. The predominant emotional responses were positive. These individuals experienced expansion of self and felt that their different roles were mutually enriching. They were very happy to be able to pursue both a career and a family, and they were comfortable with the career tradeoffs they were making. That is not to say that they did not experience disappointments and frustrations or resentment about lack of support. But they seemed to absorb these negative experiences into the overall fabric of their lives, which they were pretty happy with.

Balancing Career and Family: Seesaw, Juggler, and Trapeze Artist.   The final kinds of postparenthood identity that were observed among these professionals were labeled Balancing Career and Family: Seesaw; Balancing Career and Family: Juggler; and Balancing Career and Family: Trapeze Artist. In all three there was a focus on juggling, balancing, or otherwise orchestrating a way for the most important aspects of identity, the professional and the parent, two discrete even opposing aspects of identity, to coexist side-by-side. There was an ongoing sense of stress and strain around finding the balance, making the right connections, and there was an underlying assumption that unless one finds or creates the right balance, career and family will interfere with each other. These balancing act identity patterns also seemed quite fragile and tenuous, vulnerable to shifting circumstances in multiple life domains. In two of these kinds of interlinking of professional and parental roles (Seesaw and Juggler) the onus was clearly on the individual to find, create, craft, and sustain the balance, the symmetry among roles. In the third, Trapeze Artist, the balancing act involved a partner who was active in enabling the total process of orchestrating career and family. The challenge in all three balancing act identities was on how to establish a system for interlinking in which both the professional and parental aspects of identity had opportunities for expression and development, without their being at odds with one another.

The first kind of Balancing Career and Family identity was labeled Seesaw and was found among those who described career and family as all they had time for. They alternated between savoring the highs in one domain and then the other, but finding the point of equilibrium hard to arrive at and impossible to maintain. These individuals (10 out of 78, or 12.8%) seemed to be forever seeking a balanced alternation between favoring one role over the other depending upon the circumstances and how the wind was blowing. It was hard work, this balancing act, yet it did not seem to bother them, and in fact they liked the shifts, the movement, the occasional arrival at a place of temporary equilibrium, suspended in space. But the predominant emotional response among those in this pattern was feeling torn and fatigued by the continuous effort needed to monitor the ups and downs. They also tended to have experienced substantial frustration or strong feelings of dissatisfaction with their reduced-load work arrangements, and felt undersupported or valued at work. Yet it was not clear that changes could be accomplished, and so they were sticking with the status quo.

A second kind of balance-oriented new identity we labeled Juggler, because these individuals described themselves as needing to keep more than just two balls in the air. They had other significant involvements beyond career and family—like community volunteer work or playing in a competitive tennis league.

As with the Seesaw, the onus was on the individual to keep everything going, and the right height and pace for keeping the balls all coordinated was not easy to figure out. They often spoke in terms of figuring out how to be comfortable with trade-offs and to find the right equilibrium among different aspects of their lives. They also tended to express resentment about their doing the lion's share of the family work at home. There were four individuals (5% of the sample) in this balancing act group.

The final kind of new identity that involved a quest for balance or equilibrium we called Trapeze Artist, because there was less certainty, reliability, stability in the platform for interlinking of roles, partially because of the importance of the partner's role. These individuals had the most fragile and complex, carefully choreographed systems, which seemed to allow occasional amazing feats of coordination and peak achievements. Yet the risk of disaster and failure was high. Each day seemed to require a new highly orchestrated performance, moving like clockwork and executing perfectly timed coordination of bars and bodies. These individuals had lofty goals in both their careers and their family lives, and the kind of interlinking that should be possible; but there were many variables to figure out and control. Six of 78 (7.7%) fit this pattern.

DISCUSSION

This model is not intended to generate predictions about more successful or less successful identity transformation when professionals become parents. Nor is it laid out for the purpose of developing specific hypotheses about linkages between various elements in the model. Rather it represents an attempt to describe and elaborate on the process professionals go through when they become parents. Close examination of how individuals talk about this process and labeling and differentiating of their experiences with this process has provided some insights into the phenomenon of reduced load and other alternative work arrangements. For enactment of new work structures can be viewed as simply an expression of individuals' changing identities and their attempts to make adjustments to align their actual work regimes with internal shifts in provisional selves. Further development and refinement of this framework is needed, and more focused and timely questioning of professionals as they go through the transition of becoming a parent will allow greater elaboration of both the dynamics of the adaptation process and the contours of the new professional/parent identity.

The theoretical model of identity transformation developed from this data set makes explicit a different way of thinking about identity. Instead of thinking about professionals as adding a role when they become parents, the proposition here is that one's entire sense of self changes. Instead of focusing on whether multiple roles are enriching or depleting, the question becomes more how is an individual professional's overall identity affected when he or she becomes a parent. The career and organizational implications of this view of individual identity are profound, because the perspective challenges the predominant assumption of the separation of work roles and family roles and the organization's mandate being to help employees maintain boundaries or balance the two. If this view of professionals' identity changes over time is closer to actual reality, employers should be acknowledging, affirming and even adapting work structures more aggressively to suit a workforce with different motivation, priorities, and proclivities. A recent frontpage *Wall Street Journal* article (Chaker, 2003) indeed suggests some companies are already overhauling leave policies to "lure Moms back to work."

The contrasting types of postparenthood identity found among these professionals working on a reduced-load basis also suggest that this sort of alternative work arrangement is not a one-size-fits-all kind of phenomenon. The adjustment in work pattern is only a small piece of the overall puzzle, and it also works out better for some than others. It clearly allows some greater flexibility to orchestrate their lives in ways that are more satisfying and meaningful. But for others reduced-load work is just one of the many balls they have to continuously juggle or keep in some hypothetical balance. Reduced load work is not an automatic fix, a perfect solution. The model puts reduced-load work in a broader context, as just one element along with socialization and other work and family pattern adjustments, which lead to a new sense of self.

This model of evolving identity indirectly suggests that individual professionals cannot be assumed to stay the same, to be consistent over time—in their needs, desires, expectations, dreams. They change and evolve over time as their identities shift. Organizations that pay attention to their employees' changing circumstances and personal identities may be more likely to garner greater loyalty and commitment. However, the implication is then that organizations must be adaptable as well. Many of the reduced load work arrangements in the study were described as continuously evolving, being fine-tuned and renegotiated.

The powerful effects of socialization as seen in this model of identity transformation make it clear that organizations play an important role in identity transformation, not only through the kinds of alternative work arrangements or types of parental leaves offered, but also through the culture—the norms and values, coworker experiences, boss responses, and so on. From an individual's point of view, becoming more aware of different socializing influences could lead to individual professionals more actively and self-consciously seeking out specific kinds of influences when they feel the need to generate options, or even to alter their emotional responses to particular aspects of parenthood or dual-career family life. For example, if a professional is trying to decide whether and how to go back to work after maternity leave and speaks with colleagues who are not parents in the office, she will most likely be encouraged to return full time as soon as possible. But if she talks with another parent in her toddler's play group, then she might be more likely to raise the possibility of asking for a reduced-load arrangement or some kind of extended leave.

Two insights that have emerged from this study that need further exploration are related to the growth and development of the individual and to the increased capacity for integration or synthesis and resolution of emotional ups and downs, as a result of becoming a parent. Organizational career advancement systems should take into consideration the additional competencies and differentiated identity that parents bring to their positions. And more work should be done to explore how and why some people are able to interweave different elements in their lives, while others struggle with balancing, which involves a totally different kind of linking mechanism.

AUTHOR NOTE

We are deeply indebted to over 350 men and women who shared their time and insights with us. Other members of the research team were: Margaret L. Williams, Michelle L. Buck, Carol Schreiber, Leslie Borrelli, Sharon Leiba-O'Sullivan, Minda Bernstein, Stephen Smith. This research was made possible by financial support from the Alfred P. Sloan Foundation and the Social Sciences and Humanities Research Council of Canada.

NOTE

1. For more background on this study, see Lee, MacDermid, and Buck (2000) or Lee, MacDermid, Williams, and O'Sullivan (2002).

APPENDIX

Target Manager/Professional Interview Schedule

I. Career

Tell me about your reduced load work arrangement. (When it started, how and why it came about, how is it working out?)

Job Design

- Nature and scope of tasks
- What makes the load lower
- Work schedule (hours, days, evening, travel)

- Seasonal factors
- Special challenges of reduced load (being a manager with direct reports)
- Tools used to monitor, appraise, develop, support, and communicate with direct reports

Organizational Issues

- Pay and benefits
- Performance evaluation (yardsticks used)
- Career path

Negotiations

- Who is involved—at work/home?
- Formal/informal (policies in place or not)
- Options if request had been denied
- Concessions made

Success

- How successful and why?
- How satisfied and why?
- Strategies
- At working less and doing what you want with the extra time
- At performing job well
- At maintaining necessary support to continue—work and family
- Meaning of career success

Positives and Negatives

- Factors that make reduced-load work arrangement more difficult
- Factors that make reduced-load work arrangement easier

II. Family/Personal Life

Tell me about your family/personal life and how it has been affected by your reduced-load work arrangement.

Self

- Work load in family
- Health and overall psychological well-being
  (a) Before and after reduced load
  (b) What is necessary to maintain it

- Meaning of:
  - (a) Good wife/husband
  - (b) Good mother/father
  - (c) Healthy family life
  - (d) Good marriage
  - (e) Healthy children
- Unique personal qualities?

Partner

- Premarriage expectations of work and family arrangements
- Partner's occupation and work schedule
- Current satisfaction with partner relationship
- Partner's work load in family

Children/Others

- Ages and gender
- Child/eldercare arrangements
- Current well-being of children/others

Whole Family

- What is it like when all is well, not so well?
- What makes family life good/not so good?
- Peak experience

REFERENCES

Ambert, A. M. (2000). Children's role in the parent-child relationship: An interactive perspective on socialization. In N. Mandell & A. Duffy (Eds.), *Canadian families: Diversity, conflict and change* (pp. 48–77). Toronto: Harcourt Canada Ltd.

Antonucci, T. C., & Mikus, K. (1988). The power of parenthood: personality and attitudinal changes during the transition to parenthood. In G. Y. Michaels & W. A. Goldberg (Eds.), *The transition to parenthood: Current theory and research* (pp. 62–84). New York: Cambridge University Press.

Ashforth, B. E., & Saks, A. M. (1996). Socialization tactics: Longitudinal effects on newcomer adjustment. *Academy of Management Journal, 39,* 149–178.

Barnett, R. C. (1998). Toward a review and reconceptualization of the work/family literature. *Genetic, Social, and General Psychology Monographs, 124*(2), 125–182.

Barnett, R. C., & Gareis, K. C. (2000). Reduced-hours employment. *Work and Occupations, 27*(2), 168–187.

Barnett, R. C., & Gareis, K. C. (2002). Full-time and reduced-hours work schedules and marital quality. *Work and Occupations, 29*(3), 364–379.

Becker, P. E., & Moen, P. (1999). Scaling back: Dual-earner couples' work-family strategies. *Journal of Marriage and the Family, 61,* 995–1007.

Bielby, W. T., & Bielby, D. D. (1989, October). Family ties: Balancing commitments to work and family in dual-earner households. *American Sociological Review, 54,* 776–789.

Chaker, A. M. (2003, December 30). Luring moms back to work. *Wall Street Journal.* Retrieved January 15, 2004, from http:/online.wsj.com/article/05B107274614321797000,00.html

Clarkberg, M., & Moen, P. (2001). Understanding the time-squeeze: Married couples'preferred and actual work-hour strategies. *American Behavioral Scientist, 44*(7), 1115–1136.

Corwin, V., Lawrence, T. B., & Frost, P. J. (2001, July–August). Individual strategies of successful part-time work. *Harvard Business Review,* 120–127.

Daly, K. (1996). *Families and time: Keeping pace in a hurried culture.* Thousand Oaks, CA: Sage.

Demo, D. H., & Cox, M. J. (2000). Families with young children: A review of research in the 1990's. *Journal of Marriage and the Family, 62,* 876–895.

Desrochers, S., Andreassi, J., & Thompson, C. (2003). Identity theory. In *Work Family encyclopedia index,* (pp. 1–9). Retrieved January 15, 2004, from http://www.bc.edu/bc_org/avp/wfnetwork/rft/wfpedia/wfpIDTent.html

Dion, K. K. (1989). Socialization in adulthood. In G. Lindzey & E. Aronson (Eds.), *Handbook of social psychology* (vol. 2, pp. 123–148). New York: Random House.

Epstein, C. F., Seron, C., Oglensky, B., & Saute, R. (1998). *The part-time paradox.* New York: Routledge.

Erikson, E. H. (1963). *Childhood and society.* New York: Norton.

Gecas, V. (1982). The self-concept. *Annual Review of Sociology, 8,* 1–33.

Glaser, B. G., & Strauss, A. L. (1967). *The discovery of grounded theory: Strategies for qualitative research.* London: Wiedenfeld & Nicholson.

Hall, D. T. (1976). *Careers in organizations* Glenville IL: Scott, Foresman.

Hall, D. T. (2002). *Careers in and out of organizations.* Thousand Oaks, CA: Sage.

Hall, D. T., & Hall, F. S. (1979). *The two career couple.* Reading, MA: Addison-Wesley.

Hertz, R. (1997). A typology of approaches to child care. *Journal of Family Issues, 18*(4), 355–385.

Hill, L. A. (1992). *Becoming a manager: Mastery of a new identity.* Boston: Harvard Business School Press.

Hochschild, A. R. (1997). *The time bind: When work becomes home and home becomes work.* New York: Metropolitan Books.

Ibarra, H. (1999). Provisional selves: Experimenting with image and identity in professional adaptation. *Administrative Science Quarterly, 44*(4), 764–791.

Kegan, R. (1982). *The evolving self: Problems and process in human development.* Cambridge: Harvard University Press.

Kossek, E. E., Noe, R. A., & DeMarr, B. J. (1999). Work-family role synthesis: Individual and organizational determinants. *International Journal of Conflict Management, 10*(2), 102–129.

Lee, M. D., Engler, L., & Wright, L. (2002). Exploring the boundaries in professional careers: Reduced-load work arrangements in law, medicine, and accounting. In R. J. Burke & D. L. Nelson (Eds.), *Advancing women's careers* (pp. 174–205). London: Blackwell Press.

Lee, M. D., MacDermid, S. M., & Buck, M. L. (2000). Organizational paradigms of reduced-load work: Accommodation, elaboration, transformation. *Academy of Management Journal, 43*(6), 1211–1226.

Lee, M. D., MacDermid, S. M., & Buck, M. L. (2002). Reduced-load work arrangements: Response to stress or quest for integrity of functioning. In R. Burke & D. L. Nelson (Eds.), *Gender, Work, and Stress* (pp. 169–190). Washington, DC: American Psychological Association Press.

Lee, M. D., MacDermid, S. M., Williams, M. L., & O'Sullivan, S. L. (2002). Contextual factors in the success of reduced-load work arrangements among managers and professionals. *Human Resource Management, 41*(2), 209–223.

Levinson, D. J. (1978). *Seasons of a man's life.* New York: Knopf.

Marks, S. R., & MacDermid, S. M. (1996). Multiple roles and the self: A theory of role balance. *Journal of Marriage and the Family, 58,* 417–432.

Meiksins, P., & Whalley, P. (2002). *Putting work in its place: A quiet revolution.* Ithaca, NY: Cornell University Press.

Moen, P., & Wethington, E. (1992). The concept of family adaptive strategies. *Annual Review of Sociology, 18,* 233–251.

Moen, P., & Yu, Y. (2000). Effective work/life strategies: Working couples, work conditions, gender, and life quality. *Social Problems, 47*(3), 291–326.

Nicholson, N. (1984). A theory of work role transitions. *Administrative Science Quarterly, 29,* 172–191.

Oberman, Y., & Josselson, R. (1996). Matrix of tensions: A model of mothering. *Psychology of Women Quarterly, 20,* 341–359.

Perlow, L. (1998). Boundary control: The social ordering of work and family time in a high-tech corporation. *Administrative Science Quarterly, 43,* 328–357.

Rothbard, N. P. 2001. Enriching or depleting? The dynamics of engagement in work and family roles. *Administrative Science Quarterly, 46,* 655–684.

Salmela-Aro, K., Nurmi, J. E., Saisto, T., & Halmesmaki, E. (2000). Women's and men's personal goals during the transition to parenthood. *Journal of Family Psychology, 14*(2), 171–186.

Schein, E. H. (1978). *Career dynamics.* Reading, MA: Addison-Wesley.

Schein, E. H. (1996). Career anchors revisited: Implications for career development in the 21st century. *Academy of Management Executive, 10*(4), 80–88.

Seo, M., Barrett, L. F., & Bartunek, J. M. In press. The role of affective experience in work motivation. *Academy of Management Review.*

Spalter-Roth, R. M., Kalleberg, A. L., Rasell, E., Cassirer, N., Reskin, B. F., Hudson, K., Webster, D., Appelbaum, E., & Dooley, B. L. (1997). *Managing work and family: Nonstandard work arrangements among managers and professionals.* Washington, DC: Economic Policy Institute and Women's Research & Education Institute.

Strauss, R., & Goldberg, W. A. (1999). Self and possible selves during the transition to fatherhood. *Journal of Family Psychology, 13*(2), 244–259.

Stryker, S. (1968). Identity salience and role performance: The importance of symbolic interaction theory for family research. *Journal of Marriage and the Family, 30,* 558–564.

Stryker, S., & Burke, P. J. (2000). The past, present, and future of an identity theory. *Social Psychology Quarterly, 63*(4), 284–297.

Thompson, L., & Walker, A. J. (1989). Gender in families: Women and men in marriage, work, and parenthood. *Journal of Marriage and the Family, 51*(November), 845–871.

Van Maanen, J. (1976). Breaking in: Socialization to work. In R. Dubin (Ed.), *Handbook of work, organization, and society* (pp. 67–130). Chicago: Rand McNally.

Van Maanen, J., & Schein, E. H. (1979). Toward a theory of organizational socialization. In B. M. Staw & L. L. Cummings (Eds.), *Research in organizational behavior* (vol. 1, pp. 209–264). Greenwich, CT: JAI Press.

Yin, R. K. (1994). *Case Study research: Design and methods* (2nd ed.). Thousand Oaks, CA: Sage.

15

What Is Success?
Who Defines It?
Perspectives on the
Criterion Problem as It
Relates to Work and
Family

Jeanette N. Cleveland
Pennsylvania State University

Work psychologists have long recognized increasing diversity of the workplace. One of the most significant changes in the demographic characteristics of the workplace is the dramatic increase in the labor force participation of women— particularly married mothers (Smolensky & Gootman, 2003). Married mothers, even those with preschool children, are increasingly likely to remain in the workforce throughout their childbearing years. However, there is little discussion of the increasing proportion of *working families* among industrial and organizational psychologists or management scholars in the United States. In 1997, 68% of all children lived in a household in which all parents worked for pay (Bianchi, 2000). Although balancing work and family is not new for working women, what is new is that the pool of women who work outside the home when their children are young has expanded. Importantly, with more married mothers employed, there is evidence that the share of dual-earner couples working very long workweeks (over 100 hours for the husband and wife combined) has increased over the least three decades (Jacobs & Gerson, 2001).

Work psychologists have had a long-standing interest in the criterion problem, particularly with determining how to measure job performance and success at work. Many notable industrial and organizational psychologists have urged researchers to develop theories of employee performance (e.g., Campbell, 1990).

However, the approach to the problem followed by most researchers has been narrow and has tended to reinforce the status quo in terms of what is defined as success or successful behaviors in organizations. In particular, our definitions of what represents success in organizations at the individual level (e.g., job performance) and the organizational level (e.g., organizational effectiveness) have not changed over the decades in which the boundaries between the spheres of work and family have steadily eroded and increasingly overlapped. The definition and measures of success at work and the design of work continue to assume that all employees have an adult working at home in the role of the "caregiver" (Smolensky & Gootman, 2003). That is, our models for defining successful job performance, a successful career, and a successful organization (Murphy, 1998) continue to begin with the outmoded assumption that each worker can and should devote a great deal of time, attention, and loyalty to the organization, and that there is someone at home to take care of all of the other needs or demands of the nonwork side of life whenever the organization places demands on its members. The way psychologists and managers have defined and measured success, in general, and performance, in particular, may reflect institutional discrimination and set the stage for and perpetuate discrimination within organizations.

Why should we examine how success is measured in organizations? First, the content of criteria or performance (e.g., job task performance, citizenship behaviors) is narrowly defined, usually by a small and privileged subset of stakeholders, and definitions of performance and success often ignore the performance constraints and facilitators found in the larger context within which work is performed. Related to the narrow definition of the content of success, the sources of criterion information are usually limited (e.g., supervisory ratings of employee performance at work) and often restricted to only immediate workplace sources of information. Because the nonwork world increasingly is not buffered from the world of work (for lower-income families in which multiple jobs have long been a necessity, the spillover of work demands onto the family and other nonwork spheres is not a new phenomenon), defining *success* especially at organizational and societal levels strictly in terms of what happens at the workplace ignores the broader effects of work and work demands on the social systems that are central to our lives (e.g., families) (Presser, 2004). Second, current workplace measures of success largely reflect the values or the judgment of a subset of stakeholders (e.g., managers, investors) when, in fact, there are multiple stakeholders (e.g., working families, children) whose lives are affected by the way we structure work. Furthermore, there are multiple levels of success or performance, and success for the individual employee might not be beneficial for the family (including spouse and children), the organization (productivity), or society (an educated and healthy pipeline of future employees). Finally, the current workplace definitions and measures of success implicitly assume and advantage stakeholders or constituents with a specific family or marital structure and may disadvantage alternative and increasingly diverse family structures.

In this chapter, I argue that success is a much broader and encompassing construct that spills over from work to nonwork domains; that whoever defines success may receive undue advantage in both work and nonwork lives over those who have little or no voice in how success is defined; and that the criterion problem is one avenue of diversity research that may increase our understanding and handling of workplace discrimination and work-family interfaces. Furthermore, I draw on multiple literatures to address each of those points. Specifically, I begin the chapter with a discussion of the history of the criterion problem and single stakeholder bias associated with the criterion problem as reflected in the industrial and organizational (I-O) psychology literature. Next, drawing from the sociological literature, I present a discussion of pluralism, acculturation, and individual and institutional discrimination to make the case that there are realistically multiple stakeholders in not only the measures used to assess workplace performance but also in the boundaries and definition of the success construct.

THE CRITERION PROBLEM IN
INDUSTRIAL AND ORGANIZATIONAL
PSYCHOLOGY

According to Austin and Villanova (1992), the legacy of the 60 years of scientific research on criteria between 1917 and 1976 is the identification of the "criterion problem" (e.g., Flanagan, 1956). The term denotes the difficulty involved in the conceptualization and measurement of performance constructs, particularly when performance measures are multidimensional and are used for different purposes. There are many ways of defining a criterion (Austin, Villanova, Kane, & Bernardin, 1991). Bingham (1926) was perhaps the first to use the word *criterion* in one of the two ways that it is frequently used today: as "something which may be used as a measuring stick for gauging a worker's relative success or failure" (p. 1). Bechtoldt (1947) defined a criterion as a standard for evaluating other measures and as a means of describing individual performance on a success continuum (p. 357). Success is recognized as nearly always multidimensional in nature, suggesting that its sources of variability are complex. The choice of dimensions to represent or define success depends on how broadly or narrowly one interprets the meaning of performance or success (i.e., conceptual criterion; Nagle, 1953; Toops, 1944).

Defining criteria in organizations involves the conceptualization and measurement of success. The definition of what represents good job performance, a successful career, an effective organization, and so forth requires someone to make decisions about what will constitute facets of success and what will be considered not relevant. The most powerful stakeholders set the agenda and decide what will legitimately define success. In addition, the most powerful stakeholders influence how these dimensions of success are actually measured and by whom. In organizations, it is usually management who decides how to conceptually define and then measure success. This definition necessarily involves a value judgment, but few I-O psychologists or management researchers ask "Whose values?" The values of various stakeholders might lead to widely varying definitions of *performance* or *success*.

Traditionally, discussions of the criterion problem have started with the assumption that the conceptual or ultimate criterion of success is reasonably well defined and that the major problem involves the shift from conceptualizing or defining success to its actual measurement. When this shift is made, a gap is likely to develop between the ideal conceptualization of performance and success and its practical measurement. As shown in Fig. 15.1, the relationship between conceptual and practical measurement of success is depicted using two general notions: conceptual criterion and actual criteria. The term *conceptual, theoretical,* or *ultimate criterion* (Thorndike, 1949) as shown in Fig. 15.1 describes the full domain of performance and includes everything that ultimately defines success (Cascio, 2000). The ultimate criterion is strictly conceptual and therefore cannot be measured or directly observed. It embodies the notion of *true, total, long-term,* and *ultimate worth* to the employing organization (Cascio, 2000). Implicit in this model for analyzing criterion contamination, deficiency, and the like is the questionable assumption that we all know and agree about the conceptual definition of performance or success (i.e., the idea that the ultimate criterion is obvious and uncontroversial).

For example, the typical discussions of the ultimate criterion for defining success as a college professor includes the total number of articles, books, and chapters published throughout his or her tenure as a professor; the total number of students taught at the undergraduate and graduate levels or mentored throughout his or her career; the total amount of impact or influence on the careers of his or her students and colleagues and others in the discipline; and the total impact or influence on the thinking within his or her field and related fields and beyond. In short, an ultimate criterion is a construct that is conceptual in nature. Although it is stated in broad terms, the construct is important because the relevance or linkage of any operational or measurable criterion is better understood if the conceptual stage is clearly and thoroughly documented (Austin, 1964).

The conceptual (or ultimate or theoretical) criterion ideally is a collective measure of all relevant aspects of job performance (Guion, 1965; Landy & Conti, 2004) or a theoretical and ideal criterion that usually exists only the psychologist's mind (Blum & Naylor, 1968). The *actual criterion* as shown in Fig. 15.1 is the measure of success we (as academics and practitioners) have adopted, because we can never realistically, or with perfect reliability, validly

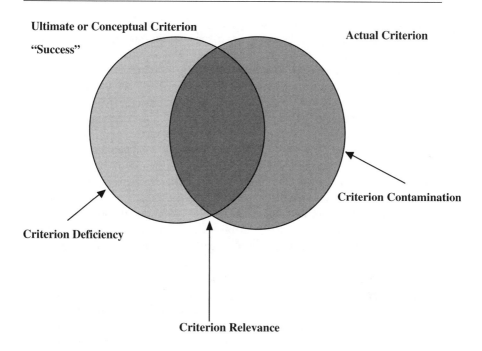

Ultimate or Conceptual Criterion

"Success"

Actual Criterion

Criterion Contamination

Criterion Deficiency

Criterion Relevance

Traditional Content of Ultimate Criterion - Success	Expanded Content of Ultimate Criterion-Success
Filing effficiency Written communication Oral communitcation	Written communication Oral communication Work-nonwork conflict Spousal stress Family Health & Well-being

FIG. 15.1   Hypothetical overlap between the actual measured criterion and the ultimate criterion resulting in three criterion constructs: deficiency, relevance, and contamination.

measure the ideal construct. The difference between the ultimate criterion and the actual criterion represents imperfections in measurement. In considering these two notions, there are three constructs of a measured criterion that emerge: criterion relevance, criterion contamination, and criterion deficiency.

Criterion relevance is the degree to which the actual criterion overlaps or corresponds to the true or conceptual criterion. *Criterion contamination* is that variance in the actual criterion that is unrelated to the ultimate or conceptual criterion. That is, it is bias and/or error associated with the actual measure of success (examples of bias may include gender or racial bias in the actual criterion measure whereas error is uncorrelated with anything). The criterion measure includes information unrelated to the behavior we are trying to assess. *Criterion deficiency* is the degree to which our actual criterion is lacking in certain variance necessary to the ultimate criterion. Unless there is perfect overlap between the actual and the ultimate criterion, there will be some portion of the ultimate criterion not represented in the actual criterion being used. It occurs when an actual criterion is missing information that is part of the behavior one is trying to measure (Landy & Conti, 2004). This area may be thought of as the degree to which our actual criterion is *deficient*.

There are many ways performance or success might be defined, particularly as one moves up the chain from describing what it means to perform well in a particular job over a quarter or a year to deciding what it means for an organization to be a success or a failure over a longer time frame. Various aspects of success are likely to differ in their value to multiple sets of potential users or constituents (e.g., researchers, managers, and members of organizations and individuals who evaluate social programs). A value orientation implies that the choice of criterion measures involves, at least, indirectly the interests of specific constituents over others (Cronbach, 1988; Fiske, 1951; Messick, 1995). For example, some stakeholders may value the accuracy of performance information while other constituents value how fairly an evaluation process is implemented. The failure to articulate the values involved in the decisions to include some aspects of performance in the conceptual definition of success while excluding others makes the criterion problem that much more subjective (cf. Fiske, 1951; Villanova, 1992).

Although early in the history of I-O psychology there was some recognition that the ways organizations measure success may reflect the values of some stakeholders while ignoring the values of others, psychologists and managers have devoted little time and effort to analyzing whose values common conceptions of the ultimate criterion reflect and how these value judgments connect with the criterion problem. This point is important because the dominant stakeholder decides which dimensions of success become part of the ultimate or conceptual criterion and which facets fall outside this definition (and therefore become part of criterion contamination). Who decides how success is defined and then measured and evaluated? Does this definition cover aspects of success important to multiple stakeholders? Do specific measures or models of success create advantages for one group over others? Little recent attention has been given to these questions; yet with the increasing diversity of the workplace and society more generally, these questions are becoming more important and need to be addressed.

What Is Success as Defined by I-O Psychologists?

I-O psychologists have had a long history of attempting to address the criterion problem by developing actual measures of performance that overlap theoretically with the ultimate or true criterion as much as possible without questioning the source or the adequacy of this ultimate criterion. For example, Campbell, Mc-Cloy, Oppler, and Sager's (1993) model of performance focuses on worker behavior in a given job. This model considers the extent to which the worker has control over work outcomes in order to protect against criterion contamination. By articulating eight of the most important aspects of performance in most jobs, this model is believed to give researchers and managers guidance on how to protect against criterion deficiency and reasonably cover the conceptual criterion. However, the specific performance components articulated by Campbell et al. (1993) and others address work success from what is arguably a very narrow perspective. There is an implicit assumption in this class of models of success that the performance demonstrated at work is independent from behavior associated with our nonwork lives, or at least that nonwork factors are not relevant for defining success at work. These models rarely recognize that outcomes measured on the job or in the workplace may be influenced by uncontrollable events that occur beyond the workplace; if they do recognize such nonwork effects, they are likely to be classified as *criterion contamination*.

I-O psychologists have thoroughly documented and developed very useful measures of workplace performance, productivity, or success. Organizations are moving toward models in which evaluative information of workplace performance is obtained from multiple sources including supervisors, peers, customers, and employees (Bracken, Timmreck, & Church, 2001; Waldman & Atwater, 1998). Yet these measures may still reflect the most powerful stakeholder's values, preferences, and definitions of success (e.g., management, white males with stay-at-home spouses) and not those of other important constituents both within the workplace and the larger society. The key points in considering the application of models that compare ultimate versus actual criteria are that the definition of ultimate criteria is always the outcome of a set of value judgments and that different stakeholders might reasonably have very different ideas about what an effective organization looks like, what represents a good and successful career, or even what good performance in a particular job really represents. For example, consider an organization that routinely turns a reasonable profit but in which employees work long hours for low pay and have high rates of occupational health problems, family dysfunction, and turnover. Is this a successful organization? It probably depends on whom you ask.

WHO ARE THE STAKEHOLDERS INVOLVED IN SOLVING THE CRITERION PROBLEM?

Employees and the Organization. Two key stakeholders are employees and management. The field of Industrial and Organizational or I-O Psychology has long recognized these two general stakeholders. In developing criterion measures, management calls on I-O psychology to develop and implement measures of assessing and evaluating employees in order to make personnel or administrative decisions including promotions, salary increase, or transfers (Murphy & Cleveland, 1995). Furthermore, I-O psychologists utilize multiple methods for tapping workers' perceptions of success as it has been defined by management. Work performance is often assessed in terms of individual behaviors and outcomes. However, employees of organizations are not the only persons who have a stake in determining how performance or success is defined. The definition of success chosen by an organization has important implications for spouses, families, and society in general. Suppose, for example, that an organization's definition of success or good performance requires its members to work long hours, to be on call during nonwork hours, and to relocate frequently. One result is that successful employees may be deeply dysfunctional in their roles as spouses, parents, or citizens.

Nonwork Relationships. Both working and nonworking (outside the home) spouses or partners of employees are also stakeholders in addressing the definitions of performance and success. The methods used to develop measures of success on the job have not traditionally included the participation of individuals who are critical in the nonwork lives of employees. However, the way success is defined or operationalized at work can influence nonwork behaviors (Kanter, 1977a, b); nonwork factors in turn may influence work performance either directly (via absenteeism or turnover) or indirectly. These nonwork influences are not likely to be identified when this constituent group is ignored.

Children. Other stakeholders in the way success is articulated are children. As the political, sociological, and family literatures all convey, children occupy one of the most powerless positions in our society. A large body of research on child development and family relationships indicates that specific characteristics of the workplace (e.g., spillover of work demands onto nonwork activities) can have significant impact on the successful development *and* the physical and mental health of children (Crouter, 1984; Smolensky & Gootman, 2003). The way we define success will have important effects on the behavior of workers (e.g., if face time is an important element of what is perceived to be successful, employees are likely to spend more time at work and less time with their families), and as a result children have a very direct interest in the way work roles and criteria are defined.

Society. Society (and our culture) is perhaps the most distal stakeholder in the criterion development process. As is true of our ultimate criterion, society's stakeholder interest are long-term focused. For example, there is evidence that the increased pace and hours spent at work and work or job insecurity have an effect on children's perceptions of and attitudes toward work (Barling, Dupre, & Hepburn, 1998; Eby, Allen, & Douthitt, 1999). It may be that the way organizations define and measure success at work today will yield short-term gains at the expense of long-term shortfalls. Organizations that succeed today by burning out their employees may "poison the well" in the sense that they will make it difficult for future employers to succeed. Similarly, organizations that monopolize the time, attention, and loyalty of their employees may interfere with the ability of those same employees to perform well in the role of parent or member of the community, all to the future detriment of society.

Power, Inequality, and the Criterion Problem

On the whole, men are assessed as more successful in organizations than are women, particularly when success is defined in terms of advancement, status, pay, and so forth (see Cleveland, Vescio, & Barnes-Farrell, in press). Literature on gender discrimination in the workplace usually has focused on the factors that limit women's achievement in these domains. However, research on power, inequality and gender suggests that the definition of success itself is a significant part of the problem. That is, definitions of what *good performance*, *career success*, and so forth represent are almost entirely the perspective of particular dominant groups (usually affluent, white males).

One way we can understand the criterion problem more broadly is to understand the values and political bases underlying the definitions of ultimate criteria. In particular, there are several streams of research that are concerned with the way those in power work to maintain their privileged position by defining what is good and valuable (e.g., deciding what represents good performance or organizational effectiveness) and by setting standards and criteria that maintain their position of dominance. First, studies of the way organizational leaders work to limit the scope and effectiveness of employee participation and decision making are discussed. Second, research on the way in which gender roles in the workplace and the home are structured to advantage males and disadvantage females is discussed. Both sections highlight the more general process that is the concern of this chapter—that is, the tendency for a small and privileged set of stakeholders to set the agenda by defining ultimate criteria (for evaluations of job performance or organizational effectiveness) in ways that help maintain their position of power and dominance.

Limiting Workers' Participation. Early writing on inequality (Marx & Engels, 1967) indicates that the most important source of inequality in society is control or ownership of the systems of economic production. That is, owners or controllers of production or organizations have power to set agenda for the working class. However, Weber (1968) cites limitations of the Marxist view, noting that a Marxist view of inequality was too narrow. While Marx claimed social class is wholly a matter of economic position or relationship to production, Weber noted that inequality involves more dimensions, including prestige or respect. Another feature of power includes the ability to influence others or to have an impact on the decision-making process of society in order to achieve one's goals. That is, one measure of power is a person's standing in politically active organizations and his or her access to the wealth or resources needed to promote specific causes.

According to Bachrach and Baratz (1970), pluralists believe that power means "participation in decision-making." If we examine the stakeholders who participate in the process of criterion development, then the measures used for assessing success should reflect both organizations and paid workers. However, the mere participation of employees in the development of performance measures *does not* ensure that workers are exercising their power and have the opportunity to include performance measures that reflect their values and interest. The pluralist model of power does not take into account the fact that power may be constrained by limiting the scope of decision making to relatively safe issues or domains (Bachrach & Baratz, 1970; Lasswell & Kaplan, 1950). Therefore, employees may be able to participate in the development of criterion measures against which they will be evaluated, but the scope of those measures may be defined for them by the more powerful controllers within the organization. In addition, there is no objective way to distinguish between *important* and *unimportant* issues that arise; so what is deemed important is assessed in relation to the scope and definition of the problem as determined by the more powerful group.

In the United States, business management has not welcomed unions and has often inhibited worker participation. The advancement of greater worker participation depends on a strong labor movement, which is more widespread in European countries than in the United States. During the 1960s and continuing today, employees have had opportunities to participate in Quality of Work Life programs, wherein employees meet in groups to solve problems. However, Bachrach and Botwinick (1992) note that management restricts participation by judging what constitutes admissible problems and acceptable solutions. That is, management has controlled participation in the problems that employee are allowed to solve.

During the participatory programs of the 1980s, job rotation, payment for increased skills and knowledge, and autonomous work teams emerged. However, in some cases, these programs created management-labor tensions because they were viewed as encroaching on areas of management prerogative (Bachrach & Botwinick, 1992). Initial stages of participation were sometimes successful, but this was usually followed by slower progress for solutions, in effect discouraging participation by workers. For example, at General Motors, top executives voiced concerns that allowing workers to participate in shop-floor decisions allowed them to question the prerogatives of management more generally. At Polaroid, the participatory program was stopped altogether because "it was too successful." These programs went so far as to question the necessity of supervisors. Management decided that it did not want operators who qualified. The employees' newly revealed ability to carry more responsibility was seen as a threat to the established way of doing things and to the established power patterns (Rooney, 1988).

Gendering Work.   Drawing from sociological and gender literatures, the structural perspectives on gender, power, and organizations focus on the ways the dominant social groups are able to control social and economic relations. The dominant groups control social and economic relations in order to secure their own privilege and maintain it, even at the expense of oppressing the less powerful groups. Within the structural perspective, two points are emphasized. First, there are coherent and systemic power relations that underlie all social relations and interactions. Power resides in dominant social groups who are then able to use their power to ensure their interests across a range of social arenas (Halford & Leonard, 2001). The focus of this perspective is not on individuals' uses of power but rather on the way society has come to work as a coherent system of power relations. Second, structural perspectives on power indicate that power relations can exist even in the absence of conflict. Individuals or groups may believe that they are choosing freely to behave in certain ways or to hold particular values. However, they may still be understood to be subject to the power of the more dominant interests.

According to Halford and Leonard (2001), belief in freedom from oppression and choice can be reinterpreted as the ultimate effect of power. For example, dominant social groups often promote value systems, comprised of beliefs and ways of understanding the world, which legitimate their dominance and offer a framework through which subordinated groups can accept their place. The power relations between dominant and subordinate groups are then obscured and the grounds for resistance to domination weakened or obliterated. A false consciousness is generated with the oppressed who come to understand their position as fair and equal. That is, the exercise of power in a specific situation does not have to occur in order for dominant groups to hold power.

Individual men do not have to take concerted action to maintain gender inequality in organizations. Structuralists suggest that the continuation of gender inequity can be explained in three ways. First, gendered power relations are taken for granted, or accepted even as reasonable and just (called *false consciousness*) (Halford & Leonard, 2001). Second, organizational forms are already a reflection of power, inherently privileging masculinity and male dominance. Third, even in situations where women see their real interests, direct conflict may not take place because the subordinated group knows that the powerful could exert influence if it wants to and this is enough to undermine opposition. For example, a woman may decide not to pursue a case of sexual harassment because she knows it might lead to still worse action on the part of her harasser (Crull, 1982).

Gendered power relations are reflected in organizational structures. According to this perspective (Kanter, 1977a) organizational structures are essentially gender-neutral, influencing both women and men in the same way. Organizational structures are gendered only in so much as men happen to populate the hierarchies at an earlier time than women. However, patterns of structural location become self-reinforcing. Once women and men occupy different positions, they tend to stay there (Kanter, 1977a). For example, men have historically occupied mid-and senior-level management. The fact that all managers were men in turn created a masculinized culture. Women were placed into dead-end and clerical jobs. Women in these jobs started to appear disinterested in their work, unmotivated, and more inclined to take care familial and domestic concerns.

Differences in men's and women's attachment to work are often interpreted as being caused by gender, but Kanter (1977a) suggests that women display these tendencies not because they are women but rather because they are stuck in dead-end jobs. Women's relative powerlessness is the result of their structural location and not their sex. The key point is that jobs shape behaviors and identities. It is not that men and women are intrinsically different but that organizational hierarchy exerts power by shaping male and female identities. Organizational structures, then, have come to sustain male privilege and power but Kanter (1977a) sees this as an unintended outcome and does not indicate that the structures are inherently gendered in any way.

A second argument is that organizational structures serve explicitly to keep women and men in their distinctive positions, taking the particular forms they do in order to maintain male power. This is a different argument about the relationship between gender and organizational structures that suggests that gendered organizational structures are actively sustained by men in their own interests. According to this perspective, organizational structures are in fact designed for the reproduction of male power. Ressner (1987), in studying Swedish government bureaucracies, concludes that bureaucratic hierarchies should be seen as patriarchal structures and that men dominate not only as managers but also as men. Ressner (1987) builds on Marixist interpretations of bureaucracy and scientific management, which emphasize the way bureaucracies allow the separation of control (by management) from execution (by workers, enabling managers to appropriate workers' knowledge and dominate workers more effectively) (Braverman, 1974; Thompson & McHugh, 1990). Ressner (1987) notes that organizational structures serve to constrain women's opportunities while at the same time enhance men's careers. Male power is understood to reside within bureaucratic rules and procedures.

There are also many informal processes through which gender relations are constructed and reproduced. These include attitudes, beliefs, and values as well as organizational symbols, language, and practices—organizational culture (Deal & Kennedy, 1982). Through these belief systems, power operates to construct understandings about gender performances, identities, and relationships within organizations. Culture can be an important method of power mobilization, the dominant voice of the organization, and reflects the structural conceptions of power. Men dominate the upper echelons of organizational structures where formal, hierarchical power is held and decisions are made. If a top-down view is taken, culture is set by managers and organizational culture is a means by which power is exercised by men over women to maintain the traditional shape of the organization.

It is white and largely male experiences and attitudes that shape the way in which organizations are defined. Research on organizational culture shows overwhelmingly how masculinity determines both the general culture and the gender cultures within organizations, with the result that women are subordinated not only at the structural level but also in terms of language and image (Hearn & Parkin, 1987) as well as interpersonal behavior (in both formal and informal contexts).

Some organizational theorists argue that the norms and values of modern organizations reflect only the man's world. Marshall (1984) suggests that organizations in Europe and the United States articulate primarily the male principle—that is, male forms of expression and achievement (of independence, focus, clarity, discrimination, competition, individualism, activity, control of the environment, and attention to parts). The female principle tends to be penalized (that of interdependence, patterns, being, acceptance, receptivity, and perception of wholes).

The language used in organizations typically includes numerous male metaphors drawing from sports and war that advantage males, not only in terms of what is communicated but also in terms of who communicates with whom and how it is communicated (the communication style that is viewed as appropriate). The structure of the language of organizations advantages men in at least three ways. First, men have more opportunities to communicate with each other when women are not present. Using the old boys' network as an example, Maddock and Parkin (1993) describe the "exclusion culture" where men build relationships with each other on the basis of common agreement and common assumptions. Davidson and Burke (1994) note that many studies indicate that women are largely excluded from such networks, which traditionally are composed of people who hold power in the organization (Fagenson, 1986; Hennig & Jardim, 1979; Kanter, 1977a). Second, Hearn and Parkin (1987) note how work organizations are havens of sexist language (e.g., chairman, manpower, statesman, spokesman). Job titles continue to be sexist. Supposedly gender neutral titles like *spokesperson* are often qualified with *female*; we rarely hear the phrase *male* spokesperson). From a structural perspective, the way language is used to represent and situate people is one of the most powerful mechanisms of legitimating and confirming power relations between groups such as men and women.

Power is not only disseminated through the static language of labeling and naming but is also perpetuated and maintained through language processes: Men and women talk differently. Men generally use a more competitive style of communicating while women use a more cooperative, inclusive style of communicating that may be viewed as less powerful (Coates, 1989). From this perspective (unlike Kanter's [1977a]), men actively maintain the structures that benefit them as men through rules, policies, hierarchies, culture, and language. This perspective suggests that challenging the gendered structure of organizations may not be good for everyone but would be good for women and families.

CRITERION DEFICIENT PERFORMANCE MEASURES: WHO DOES IT PLACE AT A DISADVANTAGE?

The closest the disembodied worker comes to a real worker is the male worker whose life centers on his full-time, life-long job, while his wife or another woman takes care of his personal needs and his children. . . . The woman worker, assumed to legitimate obligations other than those required by the job [does] not fit with the abstract job . . . hierarchies are gendered because they are . . . constructed on these underlying assumptions (Acker, 1990, p. 149).

Despite a general awareness that family structures have changed, most work in organizations is still structured with the implicit assumption that the prevailing family structure includes one earner and one stay-at-home person. Today's family structures are diverse, yet one fact is clear: Families with a single-earner and a stay-at-home wife are in the distinct *minority* (Smolensky & Gootman, 2003). In traditional, married families, often both adults work—not by choice but by economic necessity; dual earners frequently must juggle taking care of young children. In addition, a sizable proportion of families are permanent single parent families and an even larger segment are single parent families for some period of time (Smolensky & Gootman, 2003). The normative structures of work ignore the reality of these family structures.

Furthermore, the division of labor within households is not taken into consideration in typical work structures. Most women carry a disproportionate share of the domestic responsibilities. Men spend any average of 40 minutes each day on cooking and routine housework, compared to women for whom it occupies up to 2½ hours (Speakman & Marchington, 1999). Working women are more likely to find time during their business hours to take a sick member of the family to the doctor, visit the school, and so forth. Furthermore, women in paid employment continue to put greater number of hours in both childcare *and* household chores than men do (Crouter, Bumpus, Head, & McHale, 2001). In 2001, mothers of children under 18 years averaged about twice as much time as fathers in household chores (Smolensky & Gootman, 2003). In dual-earner families, men may increase their time with their children (compared to single-earner families) but their time spent on household chores is roughly the same as single-earner families. It is difficult to obtain an accurate picture of gender discrimination at work until we understand the tilted playing field that exists outside of work and within families.

Many organizations have cultures that ignore the fact that men and women participate in home life under different conditions (Allen, 2001). As a result, organizations that attempt to deal with discrimination by providing a level playing field within the organization may be pursuing an incomplete and futile strategy. If the playing field outside of work is tilted substantially in favor of men (e.g., in that most of the demands of the family and household fall upon women), providing a level playing field inside work is unlikely to provide equality of opportunity.

As a result of inequality in their nonwork demands, women operate at a competitive disadvantage compared to men. Not only do organizations fail to recognize that women carry more responsibility at home, but it is common for these facts to be turned around and used as the basis for prejudice against women. Thus, rather than being used as a basis for change and policy, the dominant (male) culture's set of values about home and work plays a key part in restricting the entry of women into the labor force (Mills, 1988). Young women may be disadvantaged because they are judged on their likelihood of getting married or having children, whereas older women will be judged, in part, on how sound their child-care arrangements are. Furthermore, women may enter only a restricted set of jobs. They may be recruited or selected only for lower level jobs and judged in terms of their private and domestic lives.

For example, Schneer and Reitman (1990) found that employment gaps in the career history of MBA were negatively associated with future income and career satisfaction. More women had gaps in their employment histories than did men (24% vs. 12%). Gaps were generally short, with 87% lasting a year or less. Women's gaps were evaluated as more voluntary, and the reason cited most frequently was childrearing. However, discontinuous employment histories were more negatively associated with future income and satisfaction for men than for women. Furthermore, there is partial support for the hypothesis that marriage hinders a women's career. Married women are more likely than unmarried women to hold low status and part-time work (Rosin & Korabik, 1990) and women in upper-level management positions are less likely to be married than men in similar positions (Parasuraman & Greenhaus, 1993). Married men experience a "family bonus" that has a positive effect on work-related achievement, especially financial rewards, if the spouse does not work. Children have a positive effect on fathers, but only those fathers whose wives are not in the workforce (Brett, 1997; Friedman & Greenhaus, 2000).

Women may feel pressure to hide or deny their personal or domestic lives, so as not to be judged on them. Hochschild (1989) terms this the "cultural cover up," and others (e.g., R. Drago, 2003, personal communication), "bias avoidance." The tendency to minimize or hide work-family conflicts may convey falsely the idea that it is perfectly feasible to combine easily a career with having children. There is reason to believe that stress is kept hidden and that family is not a reason for not getting work completed, even in cases where work-family conflicts are a significant factor in on-the-job performance (Leonard & Malinak, 1994).

The structure of work often starts with the assumption that all parents have full-time support at home—dichotomizing work and nonwork. Halford et al. (1997) found that women and men, when asked to evaluate the personal significance of a range of nonwork activities, revealed that gender differences are less marked than differences between sectors. For example, bank workers of both sexes appeared to be less work-oriented and more home-oriented than were local government workers and nurses. Contrary to the cultural assumptions, men in all sectors placed a slightly higher or similar emphasis to women on the value of spending time with their children, while women were equally as likely to place a high value on work.

IS WORK-FAMILY CONFLICT RELEVANT TO DEFINING SUCCESS?

Given I-O psychologists' interests in the work context, the work side of the work-family interface has been more focal in I-O research (Major & Cleveland, in press). Research in this field emphasizes the experiences of managers and professionals, as opposed to other types of workers (e.g., laborers), and it typically focuses on the individual employee and his or her performance at work. Although some I-O studies have examined outcomes for employed couples (e.g.,

Hammer, Allen, & Grigsby, 1997), these are few and research that includes or acknowledges children is sparse indeed.

I-O psychologists have been particularly interested in the effects of work-family conflict on employee job-related attitudes. It is important to note that work-family conflict has been treated by I-O psychologists not as a measure of success (or lack thereof) but rather as a criterion contaminant. However, by *not* considering work and family balance (or conflict) as part of our ultimate criterion, we are arguably deficient in our definition of success and likely are ignoring the values of a number of key stakeholders (e.g., families, children, society).

In this section, I argue that work-family conflict *should* be part of the definition of success, particularly at the organizational level. That is, an organization that frequently places demands on employees that interfere with their ability to function well as spouses, parents, caregivers, and so on *should* be considered as less successful than similar organizations that find a way to minimize their encroachment on the family roles of their employees. The decision not to include work-family balance in the scorecard used to evaluate organizations may make sense from the perspective of some stakeholders (e.g., investors, executives with stay-at-home spouses), but it is not likely to be in the interest of families, children, and perhaps even the society that provides the customers, infrastructure, employees, and support that is necessary for the organization's survival.

Two recent reviews of the literature concur that, as an outcome of work-family conflict, job satisfaction has received the most research attention in the I-O literature (Allen et al., 2000; Eby et al., in press) and that the links between work-family conflict and job satisfaction is decidedly negative (Allen et al, 2000; Kossek & Ozeki, 1998). Work-family conflict has likewise been linked to organizational commitment, turnover intentions (e.g., Lyness & Thompson, 1997; Netemeyer, Boles, & McMurrian, 1996), turnover (Greenhaus, Collins, Singh, & Parasuraman, 1997), and stress and health (Frone, 2000; Frone, Russell, & Cooper, 1997). Finally, some studies have found a negative relationship between work-family conflict and job performance (Aryee, 1992; Frone, 2003; Frone et al., 1997) as defined as task performance. By revealing links to outcomes that matter to business (e.g., turnover), this research illustrates that attending to work family is not simply a moral imperative, or the right thing to do, but also makes good business sense.

However, it has been consistently found that work-to-family conflict is more likely to occur than family-to-work conflict (Eagle, Miles, & Icenogle, 1997; Gutek, Searle, & Klepa, 1991; Netemeyer et al., 1996). Organizational demands on the time and energy of employees appear to be more compelling than those of the family because of the economic contribution of work to the well-being of the family (Gutek et al., 1991). Employees are often afraid to be away from the workplace and "presenteeism" takes its toll (Lewis & Cooper, 1999; Simpson, 1998). Workers are spending more time in the workplace in response to job insecurity, workplace demands, perceived career needs, and financial pressure.

Women and men in the United States increased their annual working hours by an average of 233 and 100 hours, respectively, between 1976 and 1993 (Bureau of Labor Statistics, 1997). In 1999, the average weekly full-time hours over all industries were 43.5 to 45.2 for certain professional and executives (Bureau of Labor Statistics, 1999). Many employees work longer hours, and dual-earner couples may work unusual hours or shifts. In both the United States and the UK workers feel they need to put in substantial face time to demonstrate their commitment (Bailyn, 1993; Lewis, 1997), and many in low wage occupations work in more than one job (Crouter & Booth, 2004). Measures of perceived job insecurity show a consistent increase in the United States (Reynolds, 1997). However, during the 1990s and currently, the consequences of the changing workplace involve anxieties and other problems associated with feelings of job insecurity (Burchell, Felstead, & Green, 1997).

Research in I-O psychology has examined the impact of employers' family-friendly initiatives on employees' work-family conflict, job attitudes, and outcomes. Yet the focus continues along narrowly defined lines. First, the unit of focus is often the individual employee. Second, the content of assessment involves work outcomes and ignores the impact of such policies on marital quality and family well-being. Third, the source of such information is based largely on the employee's own perceptions of work-family conflict and work outcomes; there is little research that also gathers information from spouses and children. In general, the research shows that employees appreciate family-friendly benefits, such as on-site child care (Kossek & Nichol, 1992; Rothausen, Gonzales, Clarke, & O'Dell, 1998), and are attracted to employers who offer them (e.g., Allen, 2001; Kossek & Ozeki, 1999).

Family-supportive policies are associated with reduced work-family conflict, enhanced organizational commitment, and organizational citizenship behavior (Lambert, 2000; Thomas & Ganster, 1995; Thompson, Beauvais, & Lyness, 1999). However, these positive results are achieved only when the workplace culture is supportive of such programs and employees are actually encouraged to utilize their benefits (Thompson et al., 1999). Furthermore, family-friendly policies become much less relevant in the face of significant job insecurity. Employees may believe that they cannot settle down and begin a family when there is little or no longer term contract or security with employers. Flexible work arrangements are undermined by job insecurity as well. Workplace policies such as parental leave are of limited value or benefit without a secure job, and there is evidence that many qualified employees decline opportunities to participate in these programs (Lewis et al., 1998).

Few of the studies examining the effects of family-friendly policies focus on the couple or the family as the unit of analysis. In addition, such factors as marital well-being and healthy family relations are rarely assessed. Finally, little research in I-O psychology or management taps spouses or children's perceptions of work-family conflict and employee or parental behaviors. As a result, we know little about how family-friendly policies actually affect families.

Though studied far less frequently than work-related outcomes, psychological research has not completely neglected outcomes in the family domain (Major & Cleveland, in press). Numerous empirical studies demonstrate a negative relationship between work-family conflict and life satisfaction (e.g., Adams, King, & King, 1996; Netemeyer, Boles, & McMurrian, 1996); the results of two recent meta-analyses (Allen et al., 2000; Kossek & Ozeki, 1998) lead to the same conclusion. The results are similar for work-family conflict and marital functioning and/or satisfaction (e.g., Duxbury, Higgins, & Thomas, 1996; Netemeyer et al., 1996) and family satisfaction (e.g., Parasuraman, Purohit, Godshalk, & Beutell, 1996). Yet again, often this research taps only the perceptions of the employed worker and does not collect information from spouses or children.

Children are virtually absent from I-O research on the work-family interface, and when they are included it is typically as demographic control variables (e.g., number of children, age of youngest child) in studies of an employed parent's family demands (see Rothausen, 1999, for a review). With few exceptions (e.g., Barling, Dupre, & Hepburn, 1998), children's outcomes are seldom considered in I-O work-family research. Moreover, I-O research lacks a rich treatment of the how children and other family variables influence employee behavior (cf. Eby et al., in press) or importantly, how workplace characteristics and the employment or parental behaviors of both working parents influence the well-being and work attitudes of their children. Furthermore, consistent with the discussion on the role of power and values, our current measures of success are deficient and lack consideration of our children's well-being.

In the traditional model, where the ultimate criterion is entirely workplace focused, including measures of work-family conflict in evaluations of careers, organizations, and so on would lead to criterion contamination. If we recognize that the worlds of work and nonwork are inextricably intertwined, we are likely to reach a very different conclusion—that is, that the failure to include variables such as work-family conflict in our definitions of success has led to conceptions of the ultimate criterion that are themselves deficient.

Closing in on Criterion Deficiency

In the last three to four decades, management and applied psychology operate as if family and nonwork life are separate and distinct from our work lives. Perhaps this is due to the relative homogeneity of the workplace in the late nineteenth and early twentieth centuries (a formative period for work organizations and for I-O psychology), when white males were the predominant members of the workforce, with nonpaid wives at home tending to children and nonwork needs. However, this characterization is certainly not accurate for workers—male or female, white or nonwhite—in the twenty-first century nor is it accurate for their families. Families are increasingly diverse in structure and it is increasing likely that all adult family members are paid employees working outside the home. With the changing demographic composition of the workforce, working families, and the changing demands and technology within organizations, the way success is defined and measured must undergo transformation as well. This transformation in evaluation at work needs to reflect the following. First, the domain of success must encompass a more varied content, including individual employee well-being and martial and family well-being, as well as traditional indicators of task and citizenship behaviors. Second, the domain of success must reflect multiple levels of analyses including individual employee, couples, families, teams, work units, organization productivity, and community quality. Furthermore, the multiple levels of analyses may include varying units of time—short term, including up to about one year, to longer term, including decades of time—for example, the time that a child often leaves home is 18 years and at this time, an employee may be either at the height of career performance or reentering a career. Third, the multiple stakeholders of work are not ones found only *at* work (e.g., employees, coworkers, customers); our definition of stakeholders must include nonworking and working spouses/partners and children. Finally, our nonwork lives should not be viewed as contaminants of job performance or success but rather as part of the ultimate criterion of success, and therefore very relevant and appropriate to assess.

I am not suggesting that organizations should now measure employee marital satisfaction or fire employees when they divorce or have problematic children. Rather, just as many organizations collect and monitor various safety criteria at the organizational level (e.g., accident rates), I am suggesting that an organization should monitor, at an aggregate level, the work and nonwork health of its organization. To ensure privacy for employees, information on nonwork issues can be collected at group or organization levels of analyses about marital health and family relationships, rather than from individual employees. However, information on work performance using task and citizenship behaviors can be collected at both individual and aggregated levels. Furthermore, it is important for organizations to tap not *only* perceptions of individual employees, coworkers, supervisors, and so forth but also the perceptions of their employees' partners/spouses and children. Just as 360-degree performance feedback programs have gained some popularity in management circles (Bracken et al., 2003), organizations should also receive feedback from nonwork sources (Shellenbarger, 2002). Using a type of "Family 360" may provide useful feedback to the employee.

Adopting a broader, more heteorogenous conceptualization of worker success would have important implications for the way we evaluate the validity and adequacy of our criteria. A broader concept of success may have greater face validity for employees and their families. Perhaps one basis for worker dissatisfaction with performance appraisal is that what employees value as success is not reflected in the organization evaluation process. Taking a broader perspective may also provide the organization with a strategic advantage within the public's eye. In addition, organizations could gain essential insight into potential human resource challenges facing working families, which can provide the basis for innovative and effective interventions. Not only would I-O psychologists and managers have more actual measures to tap success but they would also have more sources of performance information.

CONCLUSION

Much of research on job performance and organizational success is based on samples of white men and women in managerial and professional occupations (Powell, 1999). Relatively little research in the applied work psychology or management literatures has addressed the plight of women of color or the situations of older, poor, or rural women. The intersection of ethnicity and gender is not well understood, although there are good reasons to think that gender differences in the experience of work and family may be affected by ethnicity (cf. Mellor, Barnes-Farrell, & Stanton, 1999). Likewise, the dearth of research that examines how gender affects the experiences of men and women in low-income and non-career-oriented jobs leaves significant gaps in our knowledge of criterion deficiency issues and work-family discrimination.

In many cases, the working poor are single women with children or women and men in part-time or multiple part-time jobs paying minimum wages. The need to understand this growing segment of workers is increasingly critical as the welfare to work programs of the 1990s are now having an impact on the working poor and their children. The most blatant, serious forms of gender discrimination are likely to occur in part-time jobs occupied largely by women, where equal pay for full-time equal work is nonexistent, and where most women hold minimum wage jobs, and low skilled jobs. The children of working poor parents may be particularly at risk, and the case could be made that an organization with many poorly paid part-time employees is, regardless of its balance sheet, a failure.

We also need to address family interfaces with work cycles, careers, and work-nonwork balance. For example, one way that women have attempted to balance work and family needs is to take time off from work briefly when starting a family. Although this may not be an option for many women or men (for economic reasons), some dual-earner families make great sacrifices to make this possible. However, there is both sociological and economic evidence that once this brief gap occurs, a woman's income never catches up to her no-gap female peers (Budig & England, 2001; Waldfogel, 1998). It may be that while *some* women have employment gaps in order to adapt to incredibly rigid work structures for family care, women in general may need to continue to work longer and more productively than their male counterparts, with a greater likelihood of physical and mental health problems as a result.

Finally, I-O psychologists have yet to tap all we have to offer in terms of understanding discrimination at work. Historically, we have focused on examining gender or ethnic differences on predictor variables or comparing differences on job attitudes and a narrow range of work outcomes. Yet, we unquestioningly accept traditional definitions of job performance, promotions, salary, job title, organizational level, and so forth as encompassing the domain of success. Both implicitly and explicitly, the permeability of the boundaries between work and nonwork domains are ignored in our definitions of *success*. Instead we have rigidly held on to the belief that marital and family well-being does not fall within the purview of responsible organizations or our conceptual criterion. This flies in the face of evidence that many employees place family as their number one priority (Lewis & Cooper, 1999) and the wealth of evidence that employees' work demands regularly interfere with their ability to meet family demands and (to a lesser degree) employees' family demands interfere with their ability to carry out work demands (cf. Greenhaus & Parasuraman, 1999). Our current criteria for success (and theories of performance) are deficient because we ignore the facets and structures of work that affect nonwork areas of our lives. To rectify this situation, it is critical that I-O psychologists, experts in work psychology and behavior, address criterion deficiency by tapping previously ignored or taboo sources of work performance information. These include, for example, spousal ratings and children's reactions to the effects of parental work on family interactions. The ultimate success of organizations is not completely captured by examining profits and losses. A broader conception of a healthy, successful organization is also likely to include variables such as the marital health of employees, individual and family stress, children's physical health, educational development, and mental and social well-being.

In conclusion, in order to fully understand, predict, and address the criterion problem within organizations, it is necessary to appreciate the reciprocal relationships between work and nonwork and to recognize the larger developmental and cultural context in which work behaviors unfold. Furthermore, to provide a *level* playing field for all employees within organizations, it is critical to recognize that there may be a *tilted* playing field outside the workplace. Including nonwork factors in our evaluations of careers, jobs, and organizations is not a source of criterion contamination. Rather, failure to consider these factors in defining "success" is a source of criterion deficiency.

REFERENCES

Acker, J. (1990). Hierarchies, jobs, bodies: A theory of gendered organizations. *Gender and Society, 4,* 139–158.

Adams, G. A., King, L. A., & King, D. W. (1996). Relationships of job and family involvement, family social support, and work-family conflict with job and life satisfaction. *Journal of Applied Psychology, 81,* 411–420.

Allen, T. D. (2001). Family-supportive work environments: The role of organizational perceptions. *Journal of Vocational Behavior, 58,* 414–435.

Allen, T. D., Herst, D. E., Bruck, C. S., & Sutton, M. (2000). Consequences associated with work-to-family conflict: A review and agenda for future research. *Journal of Occupational Health Psychology, 5,* 278–308.

Aryee, S. (1992). Antecedents and outcomes of work-family conflict among married professional women: Evidence from Singapore. *Human Relations, 45,* 813–837.

Austin, A. W. (1964). Criterion-centered research. *Educational and Psychological Measurement, 24,* 807–822.

Austin, J. T., & Villanova, P. (1992). The criterion problem: 1917–1992. *Journal of Applied Psychology, 77,* 836–874.

Austin, J. T., Villanova, P., Kane, J. S., & Bernardin, H. J. (1991). Construct validation of performance measures: Issues, development, and evaluation of indicators. In G. R. Ferris & K. M. Rowland (Eds.), *Research in personnel and human resources management* (Vol. 9, pp. 159–233). Greenwich, CT: JAI Press.

Bachrach, P., & Baratz, M. S. (1970). *Power and poverty: Theory and practice.* New York: Oxford University Press.

Bachrach, P., & Botwinick, A. (1992). *Power and empowerment: A radical theory of participatory democracy.* Philadelphia: Temple University Press.

Bailyn, L. (1993). *Breaking the mold: women, men and time in the new corporate world.* New York: Free Press.

Barling, J., Dupre, K. E., & Hepburn, C. G. (1998). Effects of parents' job insecurity on children's work beliefs and attitudes. *Journal of Applied Psychology, 83,* 112–118.

Bechtoldt, H. (1947). Problems in establishing criterion measures. In D. B. Stuit (Ed.), *Personnel research and test development in the Bureau of Naval Personnel* (pp. 1237–1266). Princeton, NJ: Princeton University Press.

Bianchi, S. M. (2000). Maternal employment and time with children: Dramatic change or surprising continuity? *Demography, 37,* 401–414.

Bingham, W. V. (1926). Measures of occupational success. *Harvard Business Review, 5,* 1–10.

Blum, M. L., & Naylor, J. C. (1968). *Industrial psychology: Its theoretical and social foundations.* New York: Harper & Row.

Bracken, D., Timmreck, C., & Church, A. (2001). *The handbook of multisource feedback: The comprehensive resource for designing and implementing MSF processes.* San Francisco: Jossey-Bass.

Braverman, H. (1974). *Labor and monopoly capital: The degraduation of work in the twentieth century.* New York: Monthly Review Press.

Brett, J. M. (1997). Family, sex, and career advancement. In S. Parasuraman & J. H. Greenhaus (Eds.), *Integrating work and family* (pp. 143–153) Westport, CT: Quorum.

Budig, M. J., & England, P. (2001). The wage penalty for motherhood. *American Sociological Review, 66,* 204–225.

Burchell, B., Felstead, A., & Green, F. (1997, September). *The age of the worried work: Extent, pattern and determinants of insecurity in Britain over the last decade.* Paper presented at the 12th Annual Employment Research Unit Conference, Cardiff, Wales.

Bureau of Labor Statistics. (1997). *Workers are on the job more hours over the course of a year.* Issues in Labor Statistics, Summary 97–3. Washington, DC: U.S. Department of Labor.

Bureau of Labor Statistics. (1999, April). *Household data.* Washington, DC: U.S. Department of Labor.

Campbell, J. P. (1990). Modeling the performance prediction problem in industrial and organizational psychology. In M. D. Dunnette & L. M. Hough (Eds.), *Handbook of industrial and organizational psychology* (2nd ed., vol. 1, pp. 687–732). Palo Alto, CA: Consulting Psychologists Press, Inc.

Campbell, J. P., McCloy, R. A., Oppler, S. H., & Sager, C. E. (1993). A theory of performance. In N. Schmitt & W. C. Borman (Eds.), *Personnel selection in organizations* (pp. 35–70). San Francisco: Jossey-Bass.

Cascio, W. F. (2000). *Managing human resources: Productivity, quality of work life and profits.* New York: McGraw-Hill.

Cleveland, J. N., Vescio, T., & Barnes-Farrell, J. B. (in press). Gender discrimination in organizations. In R. Dipboye & A. Collela (Eds.), *Discrimination at work: The psychological and organizational bases.* Mahwah, NJ: Erlbaum.

Coates, J. (1989). Gossip revisited: Language in all-female groups. In J. Coates & D. Cameron (Eds.), *Women in their speech communities* (pp. 94–121). London: Long Man.

Cronbach, L. J. (1988). Five perspectives on validity argument. In H. Wainer & H. I. Braun (Eds). *Test validity* (pp. 3–17). Hillsdale, NJ: Erlbaum.

Crouter, A. C. (1984). Spillover from family to work: The neglected side of the work-family interface. *Human Relations, 37,* 425–442.

Crouter, A., Bumpus, M., Head, M., & McHale, S. (2001). Implications of overwork and overload for the quality of men's family relationships. *Journal of Marriage and Family, 63,* 404–416.

Crull, P. (1982). Stress effects of sexual harassment on the job: Implications for counseling. *American Journal of Orthopsychiatry, 52,* 539–544.

Davidson, M., & Burke, R. (1994). *Women in management: Current research issues.* London: Paul Chapman.

Deal, T. E., & Kennedy, A. (1982). Corporate cultures: The rites and rituals of corporate life. Reading, MA: Addison-Wesley.

Drago, R. (2003). Personal communication. Department of Industrial Labor Relations. The Pennsylvania State University.

Duxbury, L. E., Higgins, C. A., & Thomas, D. R. (1996). Work and family environments and the adoption of computer-supported supplemental work-at-home. *Journal of Vocational Behavior, 49,* 1–23.

Eagle, B. W., Miles, E. W., & Icenogle, M. L. (1997). Interrole conflicts and the permeability of work and family domains: Are there gender differences? *Journal of Vocational Behavior, 50,* 168–184.

Eby, L. T., Allen, T. D., & Douthitt, S. S. (1999). The role of nonperformance factors on job-related relocation opportunities: A field study and laboratory experiment. *Organizational Behavior and Human Decision Processes, 79,* 29–55.

Eby, L. T., Casper, W. J., Lockwood, A., Bordeaux, C., & Brinley, A. (in press). A twenty-year retrospective on work and family research in IO/OB: A content analysis and review of the literature. *Journal of Vocational Behavior.*

Fagenson, E. (1986). Women's work orientations: Something old, something new. *Group and Organization Studies, 11,* 75–100.

Fiske, D. W. (1951). Values, theory, and the criterion problem. *Personnel Psychology, 4,* 93–98.

Flanagan, J. C. (1956). The critical incidents technique. *Psychological Bulletin, 51,* 327–358.

Friedman, J. H., & Greenhaus, S. D. (2000). *Work and family—Allies or enemies?: What happens when business professionals confront life choices.* New York: Oxford University Press.

Frone, M. R. (2000). Work-family conflict and employee psychiatric disorders: The national co-morbidity survey. *Journal of Applied Psychology, 85,* 888–895.

Frone, M. R. (2003). Work-family balance. In J. C. Quick & L. E. Tetrick (Eds.), *Handbook of occupational health psychology* (pp. 143–162). Washington, DC: *American Psychological Association.*

Frone, M. R., Russell, M., & Cooper, M. L. (1997). Relation of work-family conflict to health outcomes: A four-year longitudinal study of employed parents. *Journal of Occupational and Organizational Psychology, 70,* 325–335.

Greenhaus, J. H., & Parasuraman, S. (1999). Research on work, family and gender: Current status and guture directions. In G. N. Powell (Ed.), *Handbook of gender and work* (pp. 391–412). Thousand Oaks, CA: Sage.

Greenhaus, J. H., Collins, K. M., Singh, R., & Parasuraman, S. (1997). Work and family influences on departure from public accounting. *Journal of Vocational Behavior, 50,* 249–270.

Guion, R. M. (1965). *Personnel Testing.* New York: McGraw-Hill.

Gutek, B. A., Searle, S., & Klepa, L. (1991). Rational versus gender role explanations for work-family conflict. *Journal of Applied Psychology, 76,* 560–568.

Halford, S., & Leonard, P. (2001). Gender, power, and organisations: An introduction. London: Palgrave, St. Martin's Press.

Halford, S., Savage, M., & Witz, A. (1997). *Gender, careers and organizations: Current development in banking, nursing and local government.* Basingstoke, England: Macmillan.

Hammer, L. B., Allen, E., & Grigsby, T. D. (1997). Work-family conflict in dual-earner couples: Within-individual and crossover effects of work and family. *Journal of Vocational Behavior, 50,* 185–203.

Hearn, J., & Parkin, W. (1987). *"Sex" at "work": The power and paradox of organization sexuality.* Brighton, England: Wheatsheaf Books.

Hennig, M., & Jardim, A. (1979). *The managerial woman.* London: Marian Boyars.

Hochschild, A. R. (1989). *The second shift: Working parents and the revolution at home.* London: Piatkus.

Jacobs, J. A., & Gerson, K. (2001). Overworked individuals or overworked families? Explaining trends in work, leisure, and family time. *Work and Family Occupations, 28,* 40–63.

Kanter, R. M. (1977a). *Men and women of the corporation.* New York: Basic Books.

Kanter, R. M. (1977b). *Work and family in the United States: A critical review and agenda for research and policy.* New York: Russell Sage Foundation.

Kossek, E. E., & Nichol, V. (1992). The effects of on-site child care on employee attitudes and performance. *Personnel Psychology, 45,* 485–509.

Kossek, E. E., & Ozeki, C. (1998). Work-family conflict, policies, and the job-life satisfaction relationship: A review and directions for organizational behavior/human resources research. *Journal of Applied Psychology, 83,* 139–149.

Kossek, E. E., & Ozeki, C. (1999). Bridging the work-family policy and productivity gap: A literature review. *Community, Work and Family, 2,* 7–32.

Lambert, S. J. (2000). Added benefits: The link between work-life benefits and organizational citizenship behavior. *Academy of Management Journal, 43,* 801–815.

Landy, F. J., & Conti, J. M. (2004). *Work in the 21st century: An introduction to industrial and organizational psychology.* New York: McGraw-Hill.

Lasswell, H. D., & Kaplan, A. (1950). *Power and society.* New Haven, CT: Yale University Press.

Leonard, P., & Malinak, D. (1994). Caught between two worlds: Mothers as academics. In S. Davies, C. Lubelska, & J. Quinn (Eds.), *Changing the subject: Women in higher education.* London: Taylor & Francis.

Lewis, S., & Cooper, C. L. (1999). The work-family research agenda in changing contexts. *Journal of Occupational Health Psychology, 4,* 382–393.

Lewis, S., Smithson, J., Brannen, J., Das Dores Guerreiro, M., Kugelberg, C., Nilsen, A., & O'Connor, P. (1998). *Futures on hold: Young Europeans talk about combining work and family.* London: Work-life Research Centre.

Lyness, K. S., & Thompson, D. E. (1997). Above the glass ceiling? A comparison of matched samples of female and male executives. *Journal of Applied Psychology, 82*, 359–375.

Maddock, S., & Parkin, D. (1993). Gender cultures: Women's choices and strategies at work. *Women in Management Review, 8*, 3–9.

Major, D. A., & Cleveland, J. N. (in press). Psychological perspectives on the work-family interface. In S. Bianchi, L. Casper & R. King (Eds.), *Work, family, health and well-being.* Mahwah, NJ: Erlbaum.

Marshall, J. (1984). *Women mangers: Travellers in a male world.* Chichester, England: John Wiley & Sons.

Marx, K., & Engels, F. (1967). *The communist manifesto.* Baltimore: Penguin Books.

Mellor, S., Barnes-Farrell, J., & Stanton, J. (1999). Unions as justice-promoting organizations: The interactive effect of ethnicity, gender, and perceived union effectiveness. *Sex Roles, 40*, 331–346.

Messick, D. (1995). Validity of psychological assessment: Validation of inferences from person responses and performances as scientific inquiry into score meaning. *American Psychologist, 50*, 745–749.

Mills, A. (1988). Organization, gender and culture. *Organization Studies, 9*, 351–369.

Murphy, K., & Cleveland, J. (1995). *Understanding performance appraisal: Social, organizational and goal-oriented perspectives.* Newbury Park, CA: Sage.

Murphy, K. R. (1998). *In search of success: Everyone's criterion problem.* SIOP Presidential Address at the Annual Conference for Industrial and Organizational Psychology, Dallas, TX.

Nagle, B. F. (1953). Criterion development. *Personnel Psycology, 6*, 271–289.

Netemeyer, R. G., Boles, J. S., & McMurrian, R. (1996). Development and validation of work-family conflict and family-work conflict scales. *Journal of Applied Psychology, 81*, 400–410.

Parasuraman, S., & Greenhaus, J. (1993). Personal portrait: The lifestyle of the woman manager. In E. A. Fagenson (Ed.), *Women in management: Trends, issues and challenges in managerial diversity* (pp. 186–211). Newbury Park, CA: Sage.

Parasuraman, S., Purohit, Y. S., Godshalk, V. M., & Beutell, N. J. (1996). Work and family variables, entrepreneurial career success and psychological well-being. *Journal of Vocational Behavior, 48*, 275–300.

Powell, G. N. (1999). Reflections on the glass ceiling: Recent trends and future prospects. In G. N. Powell (Ed.), *Handbook of gender and work* (pp. 325–346). Thousand Oaks, CA: Sage.

Presser, H. B. (2004). Employment in a 24–7 economy: Challenges for the family. In A. C. Crouter & A. Booth (Eds.), *Work-family challenges for low income parents and their children* (pp. 83–106) Mahwah, NJ: Erlbaum.

Ressner, U. (1987). *The hidden hierarchy: Democracy and equal opportunities.* Aldershot: Avebury, England.

Reynolds, J. R. (1997). The effects of industrial employment conditions on job related distress. *Journal of Health and Social Behavior, 38*, 105–116.

Rooney, P. M. (1988). Worker participation in employee-owned firms. *Journal of Economic Issues, 22*, 451–458.

Rosin, H. M., & Korabik, K. (1990). Marital and family correlates of women managers' attrition from organizations. *Journal of Vocational Behavior, 37*, 104–120.

Rothausen, T. J. (1999). "Family" in organizational research: A review and comparison of definitions and measures. *Journal of Organizational Behavior, 20*, 817–836.

Rothausen, T. Gonzaleg, S. A., Clarke, N. E., & O'Dell, L. L. (1998). Family-friendly backlash— Fact or fiction? The case of organizations' on-site child-care centers. *Personnel Psychology, 51*, 685–706.

Schneer, J. A., & Reitman, F. (1990). Effects of employment gaps on the careers of M.B.S.'s: More damaging for men than for women? *Academy of Management Journal, 33,* 391–406.

Shellenbarger, S. (2002). Executive dad asks family for a 360 review. *Wall Street Journal.* Retrieved June 12, 2002, from www.careerjournal.com

Smolensky, E., & Gootman, J. A. (2003). *Working families and growing kids: Caring for children and adolescents.* Washington, DC: The National Academies Press.

Speakman, S., & Marchington, M. (1999). Ambivalent patriarchs, shiftworkers, breadwinners, and housework. *Work, Employment and Society, 13,* 83–105.

Thomas, L. T., & Ganster, D. C. (1995). Impact of family-supportive work variables on work-family conflict and strain: A control perspective. *Journal of Applied Psychology, 80,* 6–15.

Thompson, C. A., Beauvais, L. L., & Lyness, K. S. (1999). When work-family benefits are not enough: The influence of work-family culture on benefit utilization, organizational attachment, and work-family conflict. *Journal of Vocational Behavior, 54,* 392–415.

Thompson, P., & McHugh, D. (1990). *Work organisation: A Critical introduction.* Houndmills, Basingstoke, Hampshire: Macmillan.

Thorndike, R. L. (1949). *Personnel selection: Test and measurement techniques.* New York: Wiley.

Toops, H. A. (1944). The criterion. *Educational and Psychological Measurement, 4,* 271–297.

Villanova, P. (1992). A customer-based model for developing job performance criteria. *Human Resource Management Review, 2,* 103–114.

Waldfogel, J. (1997). The effects on children on women's wages. *American Sociological Review, 62,* 209–217.

Waldman, D. A., & Atwater, L. E. (1998). *The power of 360-degree feedback: How to leverage performance evaluations for top productivity.* Houston, TX: Gulf.

Weber, M. (1968). *Economy and society.* Berkeley: University of California Press.

IV

Cultural and Social Perspectives

16

Work-Life Integration and Social Policy: A Social Justice Theory and Gender Equity Approach to Work and Family

Suzan Lewis
Manchester Metropolitan University, U.K.

Linda Haas
Indiana University—Indianapolis

Why is it accepted as fair, equitable, and just, in many contexts, that the pursuit of profit should be considered more important than people and families? Why is a gendered division of labor, rewards, and constraints at home and in the workplace often considered to be fair? Why is it sometimes considered unfair for new parents to take time off from work for family reasons? Under what circumstances do people contest working practices that disadvantage employees with family responsibilities? How can governments and organizations help challenge and change what are perceived to be fair allocations of work and family responsibilities and equitable working practices? In this chapter, we argue that social justice theory can be used effectively to answer important questions such as these, concerning progress toward the gender equitable integration of work and family in advanced industrialized societies.

Assumptions and perceptions of what is fair in relation to women's and men's work and family roles have changed over time. For example, in the United States, mothers' paid employment has become more acceptable, as has fathers' participation in early child care (Bianchi & Dye, 2001). However, research has documented the limited nature of employer responses to dramatic changes in labor force demographics, family patterns, and cultural expectations concerning appropriate roles for men and women in society. Some employers implement work-family or flexible working policies, but there is usually an *implementation gap*, that is, policies are not reflected in practice, particularly in the context of prevailing gendered organizational cultures (Blair-Loy & Wharton, 2002; Friedman & Johnson, 1997; Gerson & Jacobs, 2001; Haas & Hwang, 1995; S. Lewis, 1997, 2001; Perlow, 2002; Rapoport, Bailyn, Fletcher, & Pruitt, 2001).

Barnett (1999, p. 44) maintains that workplaces remain organized around a work-life model that reflects "dated and inaccurate understandings about women, men and the complex realities of work-life matters." She argues that a new model for work-life integration is needed, based on the beliefs that work and family are inextricably linked, that there are positive impacts of work-life integration, and that men as well as women are responsible for family caregiving. In addition to providing a full array of family-responsive supports and programs (like childcare subsidies, paid family leave, flextime), this new model challenges contemporary forms of work organization by focusing on productivity rather than face time, offering employees autonomy in how work is performed so they can adjust work to fit family needs. Collaborative interactive action research (Rapoport et al., 2001) in private corporations has been successful in revealing the gendered assumptions that underlie workplace practices and in demonstrating that it is possible to push a dual agenda promoting gender equity and workplace effectiveness when seeking to bring about fundamental change in working practices. However, this approach has not been widely adopted. The notion that working practices that are fair and equitable—in terms of gender justice—can also enhance workplace effectiveness appears to be counter intuitive in many contexts.

What might prompt corporations to move toward a *work-life systems model* with a focus on gender equitable win-win solutions? Pressure on corporations to change is increasing, from employees with family responsibilities, unions keen on recruiting a new generation of members, and human resource professionals attentive to the changing world outside the workplace and its implications for employee recruitment and retention (Godard, 2002; Goodstein, 1994). In this chapter, we draw attention to the fact that corporations exist within a wider social and political context, wherein particular cultural beliefs are reinforced about gender, other forms of social justice, and citizen entitlements to support for family caregiving. We are particularly interested in how governments may be able to move corporations toward supportive work-life practices and cultures that promote work-life integration for both women and men who exhibit a shared sense of responsibility for family care.

We focus in this chapter on government policy because this reflects a society's "political structures, policy traditions, social norms and power relations" (Godard, 2002, p. 252). We recognize that work organizations can affect governments, that multiple levels of government can be involved, and that it can be difficult for governments to alter the traditional rules, norms, practices, and beliefs that underlie most employer policies, especially when these are deeply embedded. Inevitably, employees will have to address some of these barriers as individuals and within families. But as long as the focus is on work-family policies that are organized at the employer level, especially in departments reserved for this purpose such as human resources, they are unlikely to be offered to workers at all levels and will remain marginalized with limited impact on the prevailing gendered model of work and separation of work and family spheres.

We propose that a greater understanding of the impact of government policy on corporate work-life practices and cultures, as well as on families and communities, can be achieved through adoption of the conceptual framework of social justice theory. This approach can be useful in understanding work-life integration at the family, workplace, societal, and international levels. We focus particularly on how government policies can affect individuals' sense of entitlement to support for integrating work and family and hence increase institutional pressures on employers to act in ways that are perceived as just in this respect. We emphasize the socially constructed nature of justice perceptions, and that ideas of what is fair and taken for granted as just in one context may be contested in another. Although our focus is on gender justice, we inevitably touch on some other justice issues as these cannot easily be disentangled.

The issue of how paid work and family caregiving responsibilities are to be combined is a central concern of a society's "gender contract," the "unspoken contract that regulates the gendered division of labor at different levels and in different contexts" (Tyrkkö, 2002, p. 110). According to O'Connor, Orloff, and Shaver (1999, p. 10), "Gender relations cannot be understood apart from the state, politics and policy; states influence gender relations, and are in turn influenced by gender relations." Consequently, explicit attention is paid to how government policies can influence men's as well as women's sense of entitlement to family supportive work policies and practices and to what extent state support for work-life integration reflects, contributes to, and/or undermines the cultural construction of gender contracts within specific policy contexts. Using Sweden as a case study, we demonstrate that social policy can influence sense of gender justice at a societal level, though this is not necessarily reflected in a simple way at the workplace level. The chapter ends with a discussion of directions for future research on gender equitable work-family integration and social policy, using social justice theory.

WHAT IS A SOCIAL JUSTICE PERSPECTIVE?

What is justice? This can be considered from a philosophical or a phenomenological perspective. The former, which searches for consensus, is primarily the concern of lawyers and policy makers, while social scientists take a phenomenological approach, asking why some acts are perceived to be just and others not, in given contexts. Perceived justice according to this approach is one means by which individuals make sense of their social world. A social justice approach is concerned with perceptions of fairness in the ways in which people are treated in different social institutions and contexts. It is recognized that there are no absolute definitions of what is fair and just but rather that definitions and perceptions of justice are socially constructed, usually by processes of social comparison, within specific contexts, and therefore differ across time and place, in families, workplaces, societies, and internationally. According to this approach, treatment is unfair when observers perceive it to be unfair. In this chapter we focus on gender justice, but a broader social justice perspective takes account of multiple forms of diversity and the ways in which diversity (including social class) affects perceptions of fairness (Colquitt, Conlon, Weeson, Porter, & Ng, 2001). Although perceptions of justice are subjective, they are developed within national contexts where norms about what is fair and just may be incorporated into social policy. A social justice perspective predicts that government policies can influence beliefs about what is fair and just by putting pressure on employers to consider work and family needs of men and women in their organizations.

It is useful here to draw on institutional theory that focuses our attention on the "institutional environments within which employers act" (Godard, 2002, p. 249) and what might be sources of pressure on institutionalized norms and practices in work organizations. These pressures include changing social expectations as reflected in laws and regulations, which are often associated "with a shift in interests and power that supports and legitimates existing arrangements" (Dacin, Goodstein, & Scott, 2002). Up to now, research based on institutional theory has focused on why workplaces introduce policies, while paying little attention to the implementation gap and actual working practice (Lewis, 2003). We use a social justice approach to focus on the (perceived) fairness of policies and practices as they are put into everyday use.

One reason why a social justice approach to work and family is important is that it illuminates the relationship between perceived equity or inequity and motivation for change. If a situation is perceived as fair and just, then there is little motivation to seek change, even though it may seem inequitable to actors not involved in that situation. Social action to effect change is more likely when actors feel unfairly treated or define a situation as inequitable. Arguably, some sense of inequity has fuelled the efforts of those calling for greater work-family integration. Insofar as government policies influence perceptions of what is fair and just, they have great potential to drive change. In the next section we discuss some of the principles of social justice and examine their applicability to issues of gender justice in the interdependent spheres of family and work and wider societal contexts.

CONCEPTUAL FRAMEWORK

Sense of Entitlement

A distinction can be made between supports that are expected and regarded as entitlements or rights, and those that are regarded as favors that have to be negotiated and/or reciprocated. An important element of social justice theory, and one that is central to our analysis, is the concept of *sense of entitlement*. This is used to denote a set of beliefs and feelings about rights and entitlements, or legitimate expectations, based on what is perceived to be fair and equitable (Bylsma & Major, 1994; Lewis, 1996; Major, 1993). It is different from, albeit influenced by, actual legal or other objective entitlements (Lewis & Lewis, 1997). Workers' limited subjective sense of entitlement to be able to work in ways that are compatible with family demands can create low expectations for employer and state policies, overgratitude for any support available, and a reluctance to demand further changes (Lewis, 1996; Lewis & Lewis, 1997), while a strong sense of entitlement to support contributes to actions for change.

Sense of entitlement is theorized as determined by social comparison processes (Lerner, 1987), influenced by social context, cultural ideology (Lewis, 1996), as well as social policy context (Lewis & Smithson, 2001). It is constructed on the basis of social, normative, and feasibility comparisons (Lewis & Lewis, 1996; Major, 1987, 1993). Judgments about what is fair or equitable are made on the basis of normative comparisons with others who are assumed to be similar to oneself (Bylsma & Major, 1994; Major, 1993). For example, women's reporting of relative satisfaction with an unequal division of family labor has been explained by their tendency to compare themselves with other women rather than with their male partners (Hochschild, 1989; Major, 1993; Thompson, 1991). Men's satisfaction with an unequal domestic division of domestic labor has also been explained by within-gender comparisons to other men rather than with their female partners (Ferree, 1990; LaRossa, 1988). Perceptions of what is feasible also influence sense of entitlement. If it is not constructed as feasible to have paid leave for new parents, for example, employees will not expect this, or they will be reluctant to take it up if it is available. If women think it is not feasible for their partners to reduce overtime work in order to participate more in family work, then they will not press for change.

Research on sense of entitlement has consistently shown that men and women feel entitled to different outcomes in employment, where, for example, women may feel less entitled to higher rates of pay and other rewards (Bylsma & Major, 1994; Desmaris & Curtis, 1997) and in family life, where women often express satisfaction with an unequal division of labor (Burgoyne & Lewis, 1994; Major, 1993; Reichle, 1996; Wilkie, Ferree, & Ratcliff, 1998). Thus, gender influences what is perceived as normative, appropriate, and feasible. When motherhood is constructed as a woman's primary role, employment is often constructed as something extra, which women take on for their own satisfaction and independence, even if their income is essential for the family (Lewis, Kagan, & Heaton, 1999). In this context, fathers' participation in family care is constructed as *help* rather than a shared responsibility, especially when breadwinning is considered their primary role (Hochschild, 1989). Hence, people with traditional gender expectations and/or who are living in more traditionally gendered societies will feel less entitled to support to enable them to work when they have family responsibilities, and men will feel less entitled to employer support for involvement in caring. Gender roles thus prescribe different entitlements for women and men in the home and in employment.

Justice Principles

Three principles have been identified that may be used to reach judgments about what is fair: equality, equity, and need (Deutsch, 1985). These principles may be invoked by different individuals and in different contexts at family, workplace, societal, or international levels. In this chapter, we focus on how these principles are related to gender justice and work-life integration, although they apply to other forms of justice, including the elimination of class privilege. The equality principle is the assumption that everybody should be treated the same regardless of performance or need (e.g., everyone should have equal access to flexible work). The equity principle relates outcomes to input, such that people should be treated according to merit (e.g., flexible working options should be available to those with a good performance record). The need principle argues that people should be treated according to needs (e.g., parents have greater need for flexibility—though often conceptualized in gendered terms).

Disagreements can occur when people use different justice principles to judge fairness (Young, 1999). The extent to which workplace policy focuses on equality, equity, and/or need may influence justice perceptions and sense of entitlement. For example, in some Swedish companies, only white-collar fathers have the right to determine their starting and stopping times at work, regardless of performance record or need, making it possible for them to share child-care responsibilities with their partners (Haas & Hwang, 1995). In this situation, blue-collar fathers in the same companies may perceive this situation to be unfair, using the equality and needs principles as justification.

Societies vary in terms of the extent to which government policy is based on the justice principles of equality, equity, and need. Only in a few societies, such as Sweden, is the equality principle a bedrock principle of social policy, going so far as to provide the same sort of welfare benefits (e.g., child allowances, paid parental leave, subsidized day care) to all, regardless of income level (Haas, 1996). Policy in the United Kingdom tends to be needs-based, although the needs (for example, of single parents) may be determined by government. Few societies have engaged in policy-making efforts prioritizing the needs of working parents and their children; however, this is beginning to receive attention in some international organizations.

Social and Organizational Justice Processes

Theories that focus on the processes whereby people make judgments about what is fair in specific contexts provide an additional framework for examining work-family issues. These processes are usually considered in workplace contexts but also have implications for gender justice in the family and at wider societal levels. Three major forms of justice processes are described in the literature: judgments about distributive justice, judgments about procedural justice, and judgments about interpersonal justice (Cropanzano, 1993; Folger & Cropanzano, 1998; Greenberg, 1990; Thibault & Walker, 1975; Young, 1999).

Perceptions of *distributive justice* are related to satisfaction with valued outcomes in relation to perceived input (e.g., related to hard work or financial input) (Folger & Konovsky, 1989; Major, 1987). To understand what seems fair, it is important to know what people desire as outcomes, the extent to which they feel they deserve these outcomes, and the extent to which they perceive that these desires have been met. For example, a male worker might say that it is very important to him that his job provides flexibility for him to combine work and family responsibilities. He may feel that he deserves this flexibility because of his loyalty and high-quality work that he perceives to be greater than other workers' input. He may judge that his own workplace does not actually provide flexibility and would therefore feel unfairly treated.

Procedural justice is perceived to occur when the decision-making methods for determining outcomes are perceived to be fair. One indication that the method is fair is that those concerned have an opportunity to convey their opinions (or have a "voice"). An unequal outcome can still be considered fair if the procedure that determined it appears to be fair. For example, we would predict that people who could voice their needs for parental leave to employers or government decision-making bodies and who are satisfied that their needs are heard and taken into account, might feel that the outcome regarding leave-taking entitlement is fair, even if the actual decision about the outcome went against their goal. The trouble with making leave-taking something that has to be negotiated with employers is that some employees are going to be in a better position to voice their concerns than others, for example, as valued or high-level employees, a shortcoming social policy change could solve.

Interpersonal justice refers to "social conduct with implications for other people's dignity" (Folger & Cropanzano, 1998, p. 29). For example, employees seeking the right to reduced work hours might feel they have been justly treated if the human resource director listened to their request politely and offered truthful information about the feasibility of such a work arrangement, even if the request was rejected.

Again, processes of social comparison are important. These judgments are made in relation to social referents. For example, based on equity theory (Adams, 1965), it is argued that notions of distributive justice are formulated by comparing perceptions of one's own ratio of inputs to outcomes with the ratio of inputs to outcomes of others. If people feel undervalued (or, to a lesser extent, overvalued) there is perceived inequity. People get less upset if they feel overvalued (Hegtvedt, 1993).

Much of the research on these processes of reaching justice judgments has been at the organizational level (Colquitt et al., 2001). In the next section we consider the applications of this conceptual framework at family, workplace, societal, and international levels.

LEVELS OF ANALYSIS

Individual employees' attitudes and behavior in regard to labor market participation and family caregiving are influenced by the cultures, policies, and practices of work organizations and by expectations and circumstances in the family. Work organizations and families in turn are embedded in a larger national context, where ideas about gender, family, and work are socially constructed and where social policy tends to support the society's existing gender contract and tendency to separate the social spheres of work and family. We argue that progress toward work-life integration for men and women will continue to be limited if we rely on individuals and families to negotiate this, even if individual exemplary companies establish supportive policies and programs. Therefore, we need to examine the impact of social policies designed to promote integration of work and family on families, organizations, and other social institutions and to recognize that progress toward enhanced equity will require changes at the interrelated levels of family, workplace, society, and international community.

Perceived Justice in the Family

Gender equity has been defined as a fair distribution of rewards and responsibilities among men and women (Rapoport & Rapoport, 1965). There is much evidence that despite women's increasing involvement in the world of paid work and decreasing involvement in unpaid domestic work, men's contribution to family work has not reached the level of women's (Bianchi, Milkie, Sayer, & Robinson, 2000; Ciscel, Sharp, & Heath, 2000; Gager, 1998; Hawkins, Marshall, & Meiners, 1995; Kluwer, Heesink, & Van de Vliert, 2002; Major, 1993; Mikula, 1998) and that women often express satisfaction with what might be regarded as inequitable and certainly unequal roles (Smith, Gager, & Morgan, 1998;

Wilkie et al., 1998). Women appear to have a lower sense of entitlement than men to equity in the family. Why should this be?

Discussion of fairness and justice perceptions at the family level tends to focus on distributive justice in terms of the division of domestic labor, caregiving, and income generation in two-parent families and to be based primarily on a subjective equity principle. That is, those who contribute more (input) in income terms are perceived as entitled to do less in terms of family work (Thompson, 1991). However, if work performed mainly by men, or if traditionally masculine skills are more highly valued and paid than female-dominated work or feminine skills, which is common in deeply gendered organizations and societies, then most men will earn more than their partners. This, in turn, influences perceptions of fairness concerning what each partner should be contributing to the distribution of labor.

Women tend to select referents for social comparison that support their lower sense of entitlement to equity in relation to family work (Kluwer et al., 2002; Major, 1993). For example, they often compare their situation with that of other heterosexual women rather than with male partners or with women living in lesbian households. A study of lesbian families found that these women found innovative ways to share care work with a greater fluidity between their employment and domestic responsibilities, as they were not constrained by gendered assumptions within their work and personal lives (Dunne, 2000).

If the principle of equality rather than equity is evoked (i.e., if both partners are working, family work should be distributed equally regardless of income) or if partners evoke different principles, this can contribute to family conflict (Frisco & Williams, 2003; Greenstein, 1996; Grote & Clark, 2001). The gender earnings gap can significantly affect perceptions of equity (or, in some cases, equality) in family work. Social policies have the potential to play a strong indirect role in shaping the family context for the distribution of work and family roles. These concern women's employment, such as antidiscrimination and equal pay for comparable work policies, tax policies that reward secondary earners in households, paid, flexible parental leave, and high-quality, affordable care for young children. Research on decision making and power relations within the family (Benjamin, 2001; Zimmerman, Haddock, Current, & Ziembe, 2003; Zvonkovic, Greaves, Schmierge, & Hall, 1996) focuses more on procedural and interpersonal justice perceptions, implicitly or explicitly. This research addresses questions of how each partner contributes to decisions about work and family responsibilities (procedural justice) and is respectful of his or her partner's views (interpersonal justice). However, wider societal values can obscure the need for explicit decision-making procedures. Because caregiving is socially constructed as women's primary responsibility, mothers are often perceived as having to make decisions about whether and how much to work outside the home and how to fit this in with child care, whereas male family roles as providers and the assumed secondary nature of their caregiving roles are taken for granted.

For change in roles and expectations to take place, it is important to articulate gender beliefs in order to challenge them, but this is not always easy to achieve, even among egalitarian families, in a context of little societal support for genuine equity (Zvonkovic et al., 1996). Research suggests that individuals with traditional gender attitudes engage less in crossgender comparisons and consequently are less likely to perceive unfairness in the division of labor or procedures whereby this is established (DeMaris & Longmore, 1996; Greenstein, 1996). In some national contexts, however, government policies can help to articulate and challenge traditional gender beliefs and norms, as Sweden has done by setting aside two months of paid parental leave for fathers (Haas & Hwang, 2000).

Perceived Justice in the Workplace

At the workplace level, perceptions of justice are also mediated by sense of entitlement and social comparison. This can be illustrated in relation to two examples: backlash against work-family benefits and the perceived equity of reduced-hours work.

Backlash

When work-family policies are implemented in organizations, they are often perceived to be targeted at parents of young children (mostly mothers). A U.S. study of parental leave shows that colleagues who are similar in terms of current needs or who view themselves as possibly having similar needs in the future are the most likely to be supportive of colleagues taking leave (Grover, 1991). Thus, coworkers' attitudes appear to be determined by social comparison processes and their ability to empathize with the person using informal or formal flexibility to fit in family demands. As mothers more often than fathers take up, or are expected to take up, such initiatives, this becomes an issue of gender justice as well as equity between parents and childfree employees. In contexts where coworkers do not have similar nonwork demands (either because they do not have children or other caring responsibilities or because they delegate them to partners, paid help, or others) nor plan to have children or take on other caregiving responsibilities, this can create resentment, or *backlash*, if it is felt that some parents are receiving special treatment (Young, 1999).

Judgments about whether work-family policies and practices are fair are likely to vary according to perceptions of outcomes (distributive justice), perceived fairness of processes (procedural justice—e.g., if work teams collaborated in their development), and management sensitivity and support in administering procedures (interpersonal justice). Employees without immediate caring responsibilities, and who feel they are expected to do more work to cover for others, are likely to perceive distributive injustice and this may be compounded by perceived procedural injustice if they are not consulted on benefit provision.

Perceived justice is also influenced by the justice principles invoked, that is, equity, equality, or need principles. If work-family policies are perceived to be targeted only at parents, the justice principle would be one of need; but colleagues are just as likely to use equality or equity principles in deciding what is fair. If they use equality principles, there will be an expectation that everyone should have access to the same or equivalent benefits, that is, flexible working opportunities should be available to all. Arguably, this is a fair expectation. However, these principles are not always clearly articulated and employees and their managers may not invoke the same principle, leading to perceptions of unfairness. Disputes about fairness can exacerbate work-family conflict for those with family responsibilities and have important implications for the use of employer policies and the ways in which they are introduced.

There is some debate about the extent of work-family backlash (Young, 1999). There have been few systematic studies of employees' sense of fairness about company-based work-family benefits, although Parker and Allen (2001) found that working parents of younger children are more likely to label company work-family benefits such as flextime, parental leave, and job-sharing as fair, compared to other workers, even those with older children, as did female employees in comparison to male employees. Their research also alerts us to the importance of considering race and ethnicity as factors influencing justice perceptions; in their study, minority employees were more likely than white employees to view work-family benefits as fair. Parker and Allen (2001) suggested that this might be due to minorities' greater acceptance of other human resource policies related to diversity, general sensitivity toward issues related to discrimination and greater feelings of obligation for family responsibilities. This illustrates the need for a social justice perspective to consider ways in which other forms of diversity, such as race and class, interact with gender to contribute to perceptions of what is fair in the workplace and elsewhere.

National diversity is also important. Significantly, most of the evidence regarding backlash comes from research in the United States and the United Kingdom, where family care is constructed as an individual rather than a collective responsibility. We know less about such processes in countries such as Sweden or Norway, where family care is constructed as a collective rather than an individual responsibility. In these contexts, governments can play an important role in developing a cultural discourse that prevents backlash, if, for example, policy makers portray policies for working parents as fair because these policies in fact support children, whom most agree are entitled to and need societal support.

Reduced Hours, Rewards, and Entitlements

Other possible issues of injustice in relation to work and family are not articulated because of low expectations and sense of entitlement, particularly among those who work less than the socially constructed norm of full time. Policies and practices related to working reduced hours illustrate this issue. In the United Kingdom, for example, some employers have introduced reduced hours schemes whereby employees, including those in senior management, work less than full time (e.g., four days a week or one hour a day less than the standard) in order to fulfill dependent care or other obligations. Pay is reduced accordingly, but benefits are retained proportionately (Lewis, 2001; Stamworth, 1999).

However, many senior people working reduced hours report accomplishing as much as they had when working full time (Lewis, 2001; Lewis, Cooper, Smithson, & Dyer, 2001; Raabe, 1998), albeit for less pay and with fewer opportunities for promotion. Thus a long hours culture, with the valuing of face time rather than output, reduces individuals' sense of entitlement to receive full rewards among those who complete work in a shorter time. Put another way, full-time working colleagues are rewarded for working inefficiently, based on a justice principle of equity, which measures input in terms of time rather than effort, or of equality, which idealizes standard hours, regardless of effort or need. Many employees working reduced hours perceive the irony of this, though not the injustice, and do not feel entitled to challenge it because of the pervasiveness of cultural assumptions about working time (Lewis, 2001).

Again, social policy context, particularly in relation to working time and family time, may influence sense of entitlement to reduce working time without being constructed as a second-class worker. This is apparent in Sweden, where the majority of mothers in the labor force work "long part time," around 30 hours a week, while receiving full benefits. This entitlement, codified in law applicable to parents of children under school age, appears to still be gendered, since only a small percentage of fathers work part time. The Netherlands provides an example of a society that is attempting to degender part-time work as an entitlement of working parents. Employees have considerable latitude in adjusting their work hours to suit individual needs without being overtly penalized through loss of income, pension rights, or career prospects. Parental leave can also be taken part time, helping to institutionalize part-time work. From 1985 to 1995, the percentage of Dutch men who worked part time more than doubled, from 8% to 17% (Yeandle, 2001).

Perceived Justice in Societal/National Contexts

Welfare State Regimes

Perceptions of what is just and fair in both the family and the workplace and their interface are constructed within wider societal contexts and influenced by normative assumptions about relative responsibilities for the integration of paid work and family. For example, in some countries the integration of paid work and personal life is perceived as an individual responsibility, with a role for employers if market forces permit; whereas elsewhere governments collectivize care by providing tax-funded child-care programs (e.g., paid parental leave and subsidized public child care).

Each government's approach to helping citizens integrate work and family is based on deeply embedded assumptions about gender, justice, families, and work. Indeed, Knijn and Kremer (1997, p. 330) argue: "[M]odern welfare states have shaped the needs and rights of caregivers and care receivers . . . in ways that contribute to gender inequality in citizenship rights." There can be disputes about what is fair, in terms of whether care is (1) a private or a public responsibility, (2) unpaid or paid, (3) structured to contribute to dependence or independence of caregivers and care receivers, and (4) prioritizing the rights of care receivers or caregivers.

Haas (2003) piloted a typology focusing on the caring dimension of welfare states in relation to parenthood (based on Appelbaum, Bailey, Berg, & Kalleberg, 2002). This distinguishes nations with regard to whether child care is considered a public responsibility and the extent to which policies and provisions—such as fathers' and mothers' access to flexibly scheduled work, high-quality, affordable public day care, and extended, flexible, and paid parental leave—aim to redistribute responsibility for child care between mothers and fathers. This approach seems congruent with J. Lewis' (1997, p. 160) call to evaluate the fairness of gender regimes in terms of the "two main questions for feminists concerning the provision of unpaid work: (i) how to value it and (ii) how to share it more equally between men and women."

According to Haas' (2003) typology, societies can fall into one of four types:

1. Privatized care model: Government policy makers consider it fair that caring is done primarily by mothers or extended family members; consequently, parents have little access to flexibly scheduled work, public day care, and paid parental leave (example: the United States).
2. Family-centered care model: Policy making is shaped by a traditional religious heritage, a strong commitment to preservation of the traditional family, or a concern about declining birth rates. Government policy makers believe it is fair to help women sequence care work and paid employment or to work part-time, for example by providing universal preschool for ages three and up (example: France).
3. Market-oriented care model: Strongly held values concerning the importance of mothers devoting themselves to home and children and the notion of individual rather than public responsibility for families have historically resulted in a lack of collective support for working parents (e.g., little publicly funded day care). Policy makers now recognize women's contri-

butions to labor market productivity and think it is fair to encourage employers to introduce support such as day care, based on a business-case argument (example: the Netherlands).

4. Valued care model: This is most evident in the Scandinavian nations, which have come a long way toward the goal of integrating women into the labor market and in providing comprehensive support systems for working parents, including publicly funded child care and well-developed parental leave systems that offer fathers incentives to take leave. Sweden has gone the furthest, and thus receives special attention here, particularly because it also demonstrates how there can be an implementation gap between social policy and workplace practices.

The Case of Sweden

Sweden is distinctive in the extent to which social policy has shaped individuals' sense of entitlement to equitable integration of work and family responsibilities. Care of young children is viewed as a shared responsibility of parents and the state. Parents feel entitled to time for care (e.g., through parental leave and part-time work) and to high-quality, low-cost public day care and afterschool care (Leira, 2002). Sufficient day care places now exist for all children whose parents desire them. Access to parental care and high quality day care are also seen as democratic rights of children (Haas, 1996). All parents have the right to paid parental leave consisting of 13 months of absence from work that can be taken on a part-time or full-time basis, with 80% compensation of usual pay and up to 60 days off per year per child with 70% pay, to care for a sick child. Two nontransferable months of parental leave are reserved for fathers and two for mothers to give families strong incentive for fathers to take leave.

There is interest in "transcending not just the gendered division of paid work but also of unpaid work and family care" (Leira, 2002, p. 23). Since Swedish men became entitled to take paid parental leave in 1974, a series of public campaigns and legislative changes have successfully increased men's use of parental leave and their sense of entitlement to involvement in early child care. Parental leave legislation "challenges conventional wisdom that has presumed the general 'right' of fathers to be exempted from prolonged periods as carers of children, and taken mothers as the 'natural' carers" (Leira, 2002, p. 84). Other nations have offered fathers paid parental leave as long as has Sweden, but none have tried so continuously to reeducate the population that children have rights to father care and that fathers should have the right to be absent from work to care for children.

Despite Swedish policy makers' commitment to gender equality, it has not been realized. Mothers still spend more hours in housework and child care than fathers do, work in a highly sex-segregated labor market at lower status jobs in the public sector, earn less than men, work part time more often than not, and take the vast majority of parental leave days available. The gendered usage of the most publicized instrument for gender equality, parental leave, makes a strong case, according to Parbring (2002, p. 8), that "women and men are [still] parents on different terms. . . . A father can choose to take parental leave while a mother is expected to do so." Moreover, Swedish men as well as women experience work-family conflict (Allard, Haas, & Hwang, 2001; Johansson, 2002).

Sweden therefore provides an interesting setting to understand the implementation gap, because there is an obvious disconnect between social policy and workplace practice. Advocates of gender equality have begun to realize that further progress depends on changing gendered workplace norms and practices. Although Swedish policy makers use the equality principle of social justice when developing equal employment opportunity and parental leave policy, it seems evident that Swedish work organizations do not yet all agree on this standard.

Nevertheless, institutional pressures from government can bring about change, albeit slowly, in some companies. In a study of six west coast Swedish companies employing mainly men in traditional occupations, Haas, Allard, and Hwang (2002) found that many more fathers were interested in taking paid parental leave and sharing child care than had in fact been able to do so. But this varied significantly by company; where organizational culture had been developed around the "caring ethic," fathers were more likely to take leave. Coworkers were reported as more supportive of fathers' leave taking than supervisors and top management, and when coworkers were supportive, fathers were more likely to take leave. However, it was within the workgroup that norms related to the long hours culture were most apparent, having the potential to affect perceptions of fairness in an organizational context. Fathers who reported that their work group operated on the basis of a long hours culture (where putting in hours was more important than performance and was the main route to advancement) were less likely to take parental leave than fathers whose groups were based on other work norms. If long hours are perceived as necessary, sense of entitlement to leave is reduced even in the Swedish ideological context. The need for face time reflects gendered organizational assumptions, overvaluing the capacity to be constantly available at the workplace and undervaluing skill such as relational skills, often associated with women, which may prevent the necessity to put in long hours, working in crisis mode (Rapoport et al., 2001).

Progress toward the goal of work-family integration has not been affected by economic concerns. However, fathers' reluctance and/or inability to take advantage of policies designed to promote work-family integration, like paid parental leave, suggests that there are important clashes between perceptions of justice in the family and in regard to the rights of mothers, fathers, and children and perceptions of justice in workplaces, including what it might take to be economically profitable in an increasing cutthroat economic environment.

National Variations in
Sense of Entitlement

Do different welfare state models and specific social policies affect what is perceived to be fair and just in the integration of paid work and family? A study of young adults in five European countries demonstrated that a sense of entitlement to support for reconciling work and family varies among the participants in different national contexts, reflecting the gender contracts underpinning welfare states and the gender-related values on which they are based (Lewis & Smithson, 2001). Participants in Sweden and Norway, where welfare states are based on an equality contract, demonstrated a higher sense of entitlement to support from the state and also for employer flexibility in terms of working hours. Conversely, most participants in Ireland, Portugal, and the United Kingdom, with more traditional gender contracts and social policy, expected less from both the state and employer, emphasizing instead family or self-reliance. Sense of entitlement to support for reconciling work and family was particularly low in Ireland, where public policy reflected the most traditional values in relation to work and family, especially motherhood. Consistent with previous research (e.g., Reichle, 1996), sense of entitlement to work and family support remained gendered among all these young adults, but less so in Sweden and Norway where there is strong state support for men as well as women to combine work and family roles.

Two salient factors affecting sense of entitlement within these national contexts were the ability to make comparisons with social policies in other European countries and the perception of economic benefits of workplace work-family arrangements to employers. Both can be explained by their impact on perceptions of feasibility of work-family supports, a crucial aspect of the social comparison process that underpins perceptions of social justice (Lerner, 1987). Awareness of supportive social policies in other countries permits social comparisons that demonstrate the feasibility of such provisions and also highlights the fact that such policies are normative in some contexts.

Perception of economic benefits to employers, or the business case for family friendly workplace policies (Bevan, Dench, Tamkin, & Cummings, 1999; Galinsky & Johnson, 1998), also enhances perceptions of feasibility and enables participants to construct employer supports as entitlements rather than favors. The impact of the business case on sense of entitlement in some contexts suggests that many of these young adults took the employer's perspective, even to the extent of privileging employers' assumed needs over their own. However, the sense of injustice expressed by women in Sweden and the United Kingdom when they felt that their maternity leave entitlements had been undermined by temporary employment contracts suggests that employer interests become less salient in the construction of what are rights or favors when sense of entitlement to statutory support is well established. Thus economic and labor market factors interact with social policy context to influence sense of entitlement to work-family support, indicating the importance of looking beyond immediate environments in examining and explaining sense of entitlement to support for work and family life.

These findings provide evidence that national social policies can indeed contribute to enhanced feelings of personal control in relation to the reconciliation of work and family and also suggest that communicating well-established policies such as child care provisions and progressive parental leave regulations to those in countries with fewer provisions may increase sense of entitlement. As violation of perceived entitlement can motivate changes in behavior, awareness of public policies elsewhere in Europe may lead to demands or campaigns for more state supports for work and family in countries with fewer state supports. For policy change to be effective, however, it must also address wider societal values, as state support both contributes to and is affected by the cultural construction of the gender contract.

SOCIAL JUSTICE AT THE INTERNATIONAL LEVEL

With increasing globalization, we need to be concerned about the wider international context that can both support and undermine social policies for integrating work and family in equitable ways. On the positive side, international organizations such as the United Nations (UN), the European Union (EU), and the International Labour Organization (ILO) can influence work-family policy development; whereas on the negative side, the globalization process, especially the hunt for cheap labor with minimal social protection, can undermine social policy or even render it irrelevant.

To begin with the positive, both the UN Beijing Platform for Action and the EU promote an active and visible policy of mainstreaming a gender perspective in all policies and programs so that before decisions are made, analysis is made of the effects on women and men respectively (Booth & Bennett, 2002; Woodward, 2003). Many governments and international organizations have assumed that mainstreaming simply means putting into place policies that will promote women's equal opportunity in the labor market, along the lines of the equality principle of justice (i.e., everybody should be treated the same) or the equity principle (i.e., people should be treated according to merit). However, this approach has been criticized with reasoning related to perceptions of distributive justice (it does not go far enough toward the valued outcome). According to mainstreaming advocates, mainstreaming should be much more radically transformative, involving all aspects of social policy making, including the work-family interface; the goal should be "a deliberate and systematic approach to integrating a gender perspective into analysis, procedures and policies" (Woodward, 2003, p. 68). Such integration requires that "gender issues escape the women's policy ghetto" (Woodward, 2003, p. 70), and relate to men as well as women. Calls for gender mainstreaming are also implicit calls for procedural justice, because it is assumed that those with a stake in bringing about gender equality should have a voice in policy making.

The UN and EU have established other policies designed to influence the direction of national policy involving working families. For example, the UN Declaration of the Rights of the Child emphasizes the importance of parental sharing of work and family responsibilities and society's responsibility for providing adequate child care, with article 18-3 that advises, "State parties shall take all appropriate measures to ensure that children of working parents have the right to benefit from child-care services and facilities" (Wolcott & Glezer, 1995, p. 145).

The ILO, founded in 1919 to promote social justice and national and international peace, has established a number of written conventions that member states are encouraged to adopt, designed mainly to promote employment opportunity, safe working conditions, and social security. For some time, the ILO has urged that governments continue to develop legislation supporting affirmative action, which is seen as an important strategy for achieving social justice for women and minorities in the labor market (Loutfi, 2001). More recently, the ILO has been concerned about how women's traditional responsibility for early childcare is an obstacle to equal employment opportunity for women. ILO Convention #156, titled "Workers with Family Responsibilities," urges nations to "make it an aim of national policy to enable persons with family responsibilities to exercise their right to obtain or engage in employment without being subject to discrimination, and to the extent possible, without conflict between their employment and family responsibilities" (Wolcott & Glezer, 1995, p. 139).

In the EU, the treaties that bind member states are largely concerned with creating a single economic market primarily for the benefit of employers, but it is acknowledged that economic and social progress must go hand in hand. Thus issues surrounding the rights of workers have been given serious consideration in the interests of social justice. The EU has implemented some forceful directives with which member states must comply, relating to the reconciliation of employment and family (a plank of its gender equality program).

EU directives are the result of agreements between member states, as well as negotiation between employer and employee representatives, to ensure perceptions of procedural justice and feasibility. They include, among others, a directive on the rights of part-time workers and a parental leave directive. The latter requires all member states to grant mothers and fathers in the labor force at least three months of unpaid parental leave as an individual nontransferable right. Men are included to encourage a more equal sharing of child-care responsibilities (Haas, 2003). While the parental leave directive did not dramatically challenge laws already in place in member states or substantially improve EU parents' access to parental leave, at least four nations (including Italy, Luxembourg, Portugal, and the United Kingdom) were put on notice that the EU would begin infringement proceedings in the Court of Justice for their failure to comply with the parental leave directive. This threat led to the establishment of parental leave policies in all four nations.

Crossnational variations in parental leave policy among EU member states reflect and contribute to national ideologies' concerns with gender justice and definitions of what constitutes *equality*, especially in regard to caring for family members. Membership in the EU puts institutional pressure on governments and employers and provides new social referents influencing perceptions of what is normative and feasible (Lewis & Smithson, 2001). It is especially noteworthy that until Finland and Sweden joined the community in 1995, progress toward mandating parental leave in the EU had stalled. As the EU has recently doubled with the admission of 15 more states, many of which had progressive parental leave policies under communism, albeit with little take up by men in practice, new social comparisons may develop.

On the negative front, there are supranational forces that affect perceptions of social justice and thereby undermine the efforts of individuals, corporations, and governments to promote gender equitable work-family integration. The most formidable is globalization, defined by Chow (2003, p. 444) as "the complex and multifaceted processes of worldwide economic, social, cultural and political expansion and integration which have enabled capital, production, finance, trade, ideas, images, people and organizations to flow transnationally across the boundaries of regions, nation-states and cultures."

While globalization can yield benefits, such as technological advancement, trade expansion, and economic development, it is also associated with costs, such as promotion of dependency of southern hemisphere countries on those in the north, repression of organized labor, and curtailment of workers' legal and social entitlements. Globalization can increase women's opportunities for employment and economic independence in developing countries. But the tendency of transnational firms to outsource their labor to nations with cheap labor and fewer regulations reduces women's employment opportunities in the West. Outsourcing also reinforces traditional gender hierarchies in developing societies by placing women in segregated and low-wage work, often in exploitative conditions where more liberal national policies concerning equal employment for women and reconciliation of work and family life are typically absent (Chow, 2003).

Viewed from the perspective of procedural justice, the voices of powerful investors drown out those of employees and communities in the developed and developing world. If this process continues, national social policies may well become irrelevant as employers find ways of transferring work to countries with minimal regulation. Interpersonal justice, as well as respect for human life and dignity, is consequently undermined, as the most vulnerable people in the global economy have few opportunities and no sense of entitlement to integrate work and family in the most basic of ways (Heymann, Earle, & Hanchate, 2004).

A social justice perspective suggests that some form of international solidarity and a new ideology concerning perceptions of what is fair and just on a global scale is needed to reduce globalization's negative impact on gender equality and work-family integration. These developments may depend on changing perceptions of distributive justice between the rich and poor countries of the world as well as accepted standards of social justice in the integration of work and family. This is likely to involve evoking a principle of need before equality or equity can be conceptualized at this level, but this is unlikely to happen while powerful stakeholders consider it fair to value profits above people in the developed and developing worlds.

DIRECTIONS FOR FUTURE RESEARCH

Theories help us understand what drives change. According to social justice theory, for fundamental change to occur there must be a thwarting of a goal and a belief that this is morally indefensible (Folger & Cropanzano, 1998). To take social action, that is, action at a social and not just individual level, there is a need to perceive social injustice and have sufficient power and resources for success (McCarthy & Zald, 1977). We have argued that social comparison plays a crucial role in perceptions of justice and that broadening the diversity of comparisons available may help highlight gender and other social injustices and the feasibility of social action. Social justice theory highlights the different possibilities offered by examining need, equality, and equity principles at family, workplace, societal, and global levels and the diverse interests that are served by competing perspectives. Most discussions of social justice focus on distributive justice, but we have argued that procedural and interpersonal justice perceptions are also important considerations in relation to work and family issues at the different levels.

This chapter illustrates how justice outcomes can result at one level of analysis from decisions made at another level. For example, public policy can impact gender equity in the family and employer policies, with implications for the integration of work and personal life. Crosslevel effects are rarely studied in empirical research, though such an approach is useful. For example, Kossek, Huber, and Lerner (2003) demonstrate that mandating labor market activity as a government public policy is not effective as an isolated strategy to uphold employability over time because of the need to take other levels of analysis into account, particularly poverty of residence. Our discussion also suggests that work-family linkages in industrialized societies should be examined within a broader social context and that governments may contribute in different ways to perceptions of equity and injustice and to sense of entitlement to support for the reconciliation of employment and family life.

In this chapter, we argued that social justice theory can be used effectively to develop and answer important questions concerning progress toward the integration of work and family in advanced industrialized societies. It promises to reveal important insights into the circumstances under which families come before profits, a gender equitable division of labor and rewards at home and in the workplace can be achieved, parents can feel entitled to take time off work for family reasons, and work organizations and governments are likely to change policies and practices to ensure a more fair allocation of work and family responsibilities.

Although space precludes a full exploration of the implications of this approach for practice, and much more research is needed, it is apparent that effective practice at each level of society needs to take account of what is perceived as fair at other levels. For example, policy at the national level, though important for changing sense of entitlement to gender equitable integration of paid work and personal life, is not sufficient without changes in workplace values and expectations, and the effectiveness of workplace initiatives in turn depend on perceptions of justice at the family and societal levels.

Research has scarcely been used to explore the potential of justice theory to understand progress toward work-family integration. Future research from a justice perspective could examine the following questions, at all levels of social life, including the family level, the workplace level, the national/societal level, and the international level:

1. What particular social policies, and what particular flexible working practices already in place, are perceived as fair, normative, and feasible in different societal contexts and why? For example, do people feel more entitled to support to deal with child-care responsibilities but not eldercare? The justice perceptions of policy makers and citizens in selected countries could be studied, including how fairness perceptions change over time.

2. Under what social circumstances do employees develop their own sense of justice and entitlement to work-family integration policies and practices; how can social comparisons with other countries, related to perceptions of feasibility and equality norms, affect individuals' sense of justice and entitlement? What are the relevant roles of social policy, national culture, and workplace socialization in shaping individuals' sense of entitlements to particular policies?

3. More research is needed on the impact of diversity. Who feels entitled to what and why? Does sense of entitlement vary crossnationally among different subgroups (race, ethnicity, social class), household type (single

parent, dual-earner, single-earner), and what helps to explain these variations? To what extent are equity, fairness, and justice possible for those who are not white, middle class, native-born heterosexual individuals living in dual-earner marriages (Parker & Almeida, 2001)?

4. How might a changing sense of entitlement toward workplace and government policies designed to promote work-family integration affect individual family members' sense of entitlement and equity in the family and the gender-based division of labor in the family?

5. What are the driving forces behind the development and effective implementation of work-family policies at the workplace and nation-state level? This is an issue related to procedural justice, likely to increase our understanding of the circumstances under which gender equitable work-life integration might actually be realized. What aspects of traditional organizational culture serve as barrier to the development of these policies and how might this change?

6. Why is there an implementation gap between policies and practices? If policies are considered fair, why are they not properly implemented and used—is there a mismatch between the equality, equity, and need principles? What are employers', supervisors', and coworkers' viewpoints about fairness, and how do these relate to the development and successful implementation of work-family policies, mandated by legislation or developed within organizations?

7. What would help companies achieve win-win solutions, whereby workforce productivity and work-life integration can both be achieved by changes in organizational cultures, policies, and practices that are perceived as fair by employers and employees in terms of distributive, procedural, and interpersonal justice? What are the circumstances under which awareness of possible inequities (changes in perceptions of justice and entitlement) promotes social change?

REFERENCES

Adams, J. S. (1965). Inequity in social exchange. In L. Berkowitz (Ed.), *Advances in experimental social psychology* (Vol. 2, pp. 267–299). New York: Academic Press.

Allard, K., Haas, L., & Hwang, P. (2001). Working fathers and work-family conflict in Sweden. Paper presented at the National Council on Family Relations, Rochester, NY.

Appelbaum, E., Bailey, T., Berg, P., & Kalleberg, A. L. (2002). *Shared work—Valued care.* Washington, DC: Economic Policy Institute. Retrieved January 3, 2003, from http://www.epnet.org

Barnett, R. C. (1999). A new work-life model for the 21st century. *Annals of the American Academy for Political and Social Sciences, 562,* 143–158.

Benjamin, O. (2001). Changing intimate relationships: An Israel-UK comparison. *Community, Work and Family, 4,* 173–194.

Bevan, S., Dench, S., Tamkin, P., & Cummings, J. (1999). *Family friendly employment. The business case.* Research report # 136. London, UK: DfEE.

Bianchi, S., & Dye, J. (2001). The participation of women and men in the U.S. labor force. In D. Vannoy (Ed.), *Gender mosaics* (pp. 460–472). Los Angeles: Roxbury.

Bianchi, S., Milkie, M., Sayer, L., & Robinson, J. (2000). Is anyone doing the housework? Trends in the gender division of household labor. *Social Forces, 70,* 191–229.

Blair-Loy, M., & Wharton, A. (2002). Employees' use of work-family policies and the workplace social context. *Social Forces, 80,* 813–845.

Booth, C., & Bennett, C. (2002). Gender mainstreaming in the European Union. *The European Journal of Women's Studies, 9,* 430–446.

Burgoyne, C., & Lewis, A. (1994). Distributive justice in marriage. *Journal of Community and Applied Social Psychology, 4,* 101–114.

Bylsma, W., & Major, B. (1994). Social comparisons and contentment: Exploring the psychological costs of the gender wage gap. *Psychology of Women Quarterly, 18,* 241–249.

Chow, E. (2003). Gender matters. *International Sociology, 18,* 443–460.

Ciscel, D., Sharp, D., & Heath, J. (2000). Family work trends and practices. *Journal of Family and Economic Issues, 21,* 23–36.

Colquitt, J., Conlon, D., Wesson, M., Porter, C., & Ng, K. (2001). Justice of the millennium: A meta-analytical review of 25 years of organizational justice research. *Journal of Applied Psychology 86,* 425–445.

Cropanzano, R. (1993). *Justice in the workplace.* Hillsdale, NJ: Erlbaum.

Dacin, M., Goodstein, J., & Scott, W. (2002). Institutional theory and institutional change. *Academy of Management Journal, 45,* 45–57.

DeMaris, A., & Longmore, M. (1996). Ideology, power, and equity: Testing competing explanations for the perception of fairness in household labor. *Social Forces, 74,* 1043–1071.

Desmaris, S., & Curtis, J. (1997). Gender and perceived pay entitlement. *Journal of Personality and Social Psychology, 72,* 141–150.

Deutsch, M. (1985). Equity, equality and need: What determines which value will be used as the basis for distributive justice? *Journal of Social Issues, 31,* 137–149.

Dunne, G. A. (2000). Opting into motherhood: Lesbians blurring the boundaries and transforming the meaning of parenthood and kinship. *Gender and Society, 14,* 11–35.

Ferree, M. (1990). Beyond separate spheres: Feminism and family research. *Journal of Marriage and the Family, 52,* 866–994.

Folger, R., & Cropanzano, R. (1998). *Organizational justice and human resource management.* Thousand Oaks, CA: Sage.

Folger, R., & Konovsky, M. (1989). Effects of procedural justice, distributive justice, and reactions to pay raise decisions. *Academy of Management Journal, 32,* 115–130.

Friedman, D., & Johnson, A. (1997). Moving from programs to culture change. In S. Parasuraman & J. H. Greenhaus (Eds.), *Integrating work and family: Challenges and choices for a changing world* (pp. 232–240). Westport, CT: Quorum.

Frisco, M., & Williams, K. (2003). Perceived housework equity, marital happiness, and divorce in dual-earner households. *Journal of Family Issues, 24,* 51–73.

Gager, C. (1998). The role of valued outcomes, justifications and comparison referents in perceptions of fairness among dual-earner couples. *Journal of Family Issues, 19,* 622–648.

Galinsky, E., & Johnson, A. (1998). *Reframing the business case for work-life initiatives.* New York: Families and Work Institute.

Gerson, K., & Jacobs, J. (2001). Changing the structure and culture of work. In R. Hertz & N. Marshall (Eds.), *Working families* (pp. 207–226). Berkeley: University of California Press.

Godard, J. (2002). Institutional environments, employer practices, and states in liberal market economies. *Industrial Relations, 41,* 249–285.

Goodstein, J. (1994). Institutional pressures and strategic responsiveness: Employer involvement in work-family issues. *Academy of Management Journal, 37,* 350–382.

Greenberg, J. (1990). Organizational justice. *Journal of Management, 16,* 399–432.

Greenstein, T. (1996). Gender ideology and perceptions of the fairness of the division of household labor. *Social Forces, 74,* 1029–1042.

Grote, N., & Clark, M. (2001). Perceived unfairness in the family: Cause or consequence of marital distress? *Journal of Personality and Social Psychology, 80,* 281–293.

Grover, S. (1991). Predicting the perceived fairness of parental leave policies. *Journal of Applied Psychology, 76,* 247–255.

Haas, L. (1996). Family Policy in Sweden. *Journal of Family and Economic Issues, 17,* 47–91.

Haas, L. (2003). Parental leave and gender equality: Lessons from the European Union. *Review of Policy Research, 20,* 89–114.

Haas, L., Allard, K., & Hwang, P. (2002). The impact of organizational culture on men's use of parental leave in Sweden. *Community, Work & Family, 5,* 319–342.

Haas, L., & Hwang, P. (1995). Company culture and men's usage of family leave benefits in Sweden. *Family Relations, 44,* 28–36.

Haas, L., & Hwang, P. (2000). Programs and policies promoting women's economic equality and men's sharing of child care in Sweden. In L. Haas, P. Hwang, & G. Russell (Eds.), *Organizational change and gender equity* (pp. 133–162). Thousand Oaks, CA: Sage.

Hawkins, A., Marshall, C., & Meiners, K. (1995). Exploring wives' sense of fairness about family work. *Journal of Family Issues, 16,* 693–721.

Hegtvedt, K. (1993). Approaching distributive and procedural justice—Are separate routes necessary? In J. Lawler, B. Markovesky, K. Heimer, & J. O'Brien (Eds.), *Advances in group processes,* (vol. 1, (pp. 195–221). Greenwich, CT: JAI.

Heymann, J., Earle, A., & Hanchate, A. (2004). Bringing a global perspective to community, work and family. *Community, Work & Family, 7,* 247–272.

Hochschild, A. R. (1989). *The second shift.* New York: Avon.

Johansson, G. (2002). Work-life balance: The case of Sweden in the 1990s. *Social Science Information, 41,* 303–317.

Kluwer, E., Heesink, J., & Van de Vliert, E. (2002). The division of labor across the transition to parenthood: A justice perspective. *Journal of Marriage and Family, 64,* 930–943.

Knijn, T., & Kremer, M. (1997). Gender and the caring dimension of welfare states. *Social Politics, 4,* 329–367.

Kossek, E., Huber, M., & Lerner, J. (2003). Sustaining economic and psychological well-being of mothers on public assistance. *Journal of Vocational Behavior, 62,* 155–175.

LaRossa, R. (1988). Fatherhood and social change. *Family Relations, 37,* 451–457.

Leira, A. (2002). *Working parents and the welfare state.* Cambridge, England: Cambridge University Press.

Lerner, M. (1987). Integrating societal and psychological rules of entitlement: Implications for comparable worth. *Social Justice Research, 1,* 107–125.

Lewis, J. (1997). Gender and welfare regimes. *Social Politics, 4,* 160–177.

Lewis, S. (1996). Sense of entitlement, family friendly policies and gender. In H. Holt & I. Thaulow (Eds.), *The role of companies in reconciling work and family life* (pp. 9–17). Copenhagen, Denmark: Danish National Institute of Social Research.

Lewis, S. (1997). "Family friendly" employment policies: A route to changing organizational culture or playing about at the margins? *Gender, Work and Organization, 4,* 13–23.

Lewis, S. (2001). Restructuring workplace cultures: The ultimate work-family challenge? *Women in Management Review, 16,* 21–29.

Lewis, S. (2003). Flexible working arrangements. In C. Cooper & I. Robertson (Eds.), *Annual Review of Industrial and Organisational Psychology* (pp. 1–28). New York: Wiley.

Lewis, S., Cooper, C., Smithson, J., & Dyer, J. (2001). *Flexible futures.* London: Institute of Chartered Accountants in England and Wales.

Lewis, S., Kagan, C., & Heaton, P. (1999). Economic and psychological benefits from employment. *Disability and Society, 14,* 561–575.

Lewis, S., & Lewis. J. (1997). Work family conflict. Can the law help? *Legal and Criminological Psychology, 2,* 155–167.

Lewis, S., & Smithson, J. (2001). Sense of entitlement to support for the reconciliation of employment and family life. *Human Relations, 54,* 1455–1482.

Loutfi, M. (2001). Women, gender and work—An overview. In M. Loutfi (Ed.), *Women, gender and work* (pp. 3–18). Geneva, Switzerland: International Labour Office.

Major, J. (1987). Gender, justice and the psychology of entitlement. In P. Shaver & C. Hendrick (Eds.), *Sex and gender* (pp. 124–148). Newbury Park, CA: Sage.

Major, J. (1993). Gender, entitlement and the distribution of family labor. *Journal of Social Issues, 49,* 141–159.

McCarthy, J., & Zald, M. (1977). Resource mobilization and social movement—A partial theory. *American Journal of Sociology, 82,* 1212–1241.

Mikula, G. (1998). Division of household labor and perceived justice. *Social Justice Research, 11,* 215–241.

O'Connor, J., Orloff, A., & Shaver, S. (1999). *States, markets, families.* Cambridge, England: Cambridge University Press.

Parbring, B. (2002, March). Föräldrar på olika villkor [Parents on different terms]. *Genus* [Publication of the Swedish Center for Gender Research], 8–13.

Parker, L., & Allen, T. (2001). Work/family benefits: Variables related to employees' fairness perceptions. *Journal of Vocational Behavior, 58,* 453–468.

Parker, L., & Almeida, R. (2001). Balance as fairness for whom? *Journal of Feminist Family Therapy, 13,* 153–168.

Perlow, L. A. (2002). Who's helping whom? Layers of culture and workplace behavior. *Journal of Organizational Behavior, 23,* 345–351.

Raabe, P. (1998). Being a part-time manager. In D. Vannoy & P. Dubeck (Eds.), *Challenges for work and family in the 21st century* (pp. 81–91). Hawthorne, NY: Aldine de Gruyter.

Rapoport, R., Bailyn, L., Fletcher, J. K., & Pruitt B. H., (2001). *Beyond work-family balance: Advancing Gender Equity and Workplace Performance.* San Francisco: Jossey-Bass.

Rapoport, R., & Rapoport, R. (1965). Work and family in contemporary society. *American Sociological Review, 30,* 381–394.

Reichle, B. (1996). From is to ought and the kitchen sink: On the justice of distributions in close relationships. In L. Montada & M. Lerner (Eds.), *Current societal concerns about justice* (pp. 103–135). New York: Plenum.

Smith, H., Gager, C., & Morgan, S. (1998). Identifying underlying dimensions in spouses' evaluation of fairness in the division of household labor. *Social Science Research, 27,* 305–327.

Stamworth, C. (1999). A best case scenario? Non-manual part-time work and job-sharing in UK local government in the 1990s. *Community, Work and Family 2,* 295–310.

Thibault, J., & Walker, L. (1975). *Procedural justice.* Hillsdale, NJ: Erlbaum.

Thompson, L. T. (1991). Family work—Women's sense of fairness. *Journal of Family Issues, 12,* 181–196.

Tyrkkö, A. (2002). The intersection between working life and parenthood. *Economic and Industrial Democracy, 23,* 107–123.

Wilkie, J., Ferree, M., & Ratcliff, K. (1998). Gender and fairness: Marital satisfaction in two-earner couples. *Journal of Marriage and the Family, 60,* 577–594.

Wolcott, I., & Glezer, H. (1995). *Work and family life—Achieving integration.* Melbourne: Australian Institute of Family Studies.

Woodward, A. (2003). European mainstreaming: Promises and pitfalls of transformative policy. *Review of Policy Research, 20,* 65–80.

Yeandle, S. (2001). Balancing employment and family lives. In V. Marshall, W. Heinz, H. Krüger, & A. Verma (Eds.), *Restructuring work and the life course* (pp. 142–158). Toronto, Canada: University of Toronto Press.

Young, M. (1999). Work-family backlash: Begging the question, what's fair? *Annals of the American Academy of Political and Social Science, 562,* 32–46.

Zimmerman, T., Haddock, S., Current, L., & Ziemba, S. (2003). Intimate partnership: Foundation to the successful balance of family and work. *American Journal of Family Therapy, 31,* 107–124.

Zvonkovic, A., Greaves, K., Schmierge, C., & Hall, L. (1996). The marital construction of gender through work and family decisions. *Journal of Marriage and the Family, 58,* 91–100.

17

Three Reasons for a Transnational Approach to Work-Life Policy

Winifred R. Poster
University of Illinois, Urbana-Champaign

This chapter makes the case for a transnational perspective on work-life issues. A transnational perspective is one that recognizes the increasing connectedness of social institutions on a global scale as a result of factors like advancing technology and communications, global capitalism, international governance bodies, and so on. I offer three reasons why this perspective is helpful and how it will advance work-life research.

The first reason is one of substance and scope. A transnational perspective fills a gap in the literature by *revealing a number of unexplored sources of work-family trends*. Most of the work-life research limits its view to local determinants of work-life trends (states, firms, labor markets, individuals, etc.) and neglects the fact that many work-life strains today are larger than organizations and their immediate environments. By reviewing recent transnational literature from the United States (where much of the work-life research is targeted and/or produced), I draw attention to several transnational trends affecting working families: globalizing work processes, a growing presence of foreign firms, and an internationalization of the workforce. If we link these globalization dynamics to current work-family trends (like increasing mandatory overtime, care deficits, and racial tension), we will be better able to explain why current remedies are inadequate and envision more effective solutions.

The second reason is one of methodology. Although there are many kinds of transnational methodologies, I discuss two here in particular. One is *global ethnography*, which sees particular sites (like workplaces) as prisms for viewing linkages between global and local forces (Burawoy et al., 2000). Global ethnography is also a way to see the "very production of the global" inside the local. These strategies can be helpful for identifying unexplored sources of work-life dynamics. The second transnational method I discuss is comparative case research, which contrasts organizational settings across different national locations. This is especially helpful for revealing hidden assumptions in work-family policy. Given that these unstated assumptions can be difficult to observe and recognize in single sites, a method that compares similar policies across sites—especially across *national* contexts—can help illuminate them. Theoretically, this method can also help move current research on work-life policies from what I see as an overemphasis on the back end of policies (i.e., their diffusion and their consequences) relative to the front end (i.e., their intent and design).

The third reason why a transnational perspective on work-life issues is helpful is one of theoretical orientation. A transnational perspective can enhance work-life research by exposing the power relations between firms and nations. For this purpose, I present a view of globalization that is informed by critical sociology (McMichael, 2000; Sassen, 1998). As I interpret it, this approach has several core premises (Poster, 2002). One is that organizational dynamics are not autonomous but embedded in social institutions that inherently involve power. This power takes many *local* forms (like the authority of employers over employees, institutional environments over organizations, etc.) but also many *transnational* forms (like the authority of parent firms over their subsidiary firms, Northern over Southern nations in the global economy, intergovernmental organizations over local organizations, etc.).

Another premise of the critical sociology approach is that transnational relations are inherently dynamic. This means that actors in the global economy (whether individuals, firms, nations, etc.) are not coexisting in a static way but rather are mutually influential on each other. (This also is the reason I use the term *trans*national rather than *multi-* or *inter*national; the latter tend to imply a neutrality across sites, ignoring both interactive relations and power.) A dynamic view of transnationalism is also important for recognizing the agency and resistance of actors in globally subordinate positions. Finally, this approach sees the sources and mechanisms of power within globalization as multiple and intersecting. Rather than limiting the analytical focus to global capital, economic institutions, and international markets, this approach examines the intersections of class dynamics with systems of race, gender, and nation. Taken as a whole, I argue that this approach can advance the work-life literature (and especially the popular framework of *culture*) by exposing the embeddedness of power in global work-life policies.

In making my case, I draw examples from the existing literature and from my own case studies of transnational corporations (TNCs) in the United States and India. This research was done in 1995–1996 on three firms—a U.S. high-tech firm in Silicon Valley (AmCo), its subsidiary in New Delhi, India (TransCo), and a comparable Indian-owned firm in New Delhi (IndCo). Research involved observations of work relations, examination of organizational materials, and 180 interviews with employees—both managers and workers, male and female, at professional and manufacturing levels.

My focus has been work-life policies in transnational workplaces, including three kinds of programs—work-family, gender, and diversity. For this reason, I define *work-life policy* broadly to be inclusive of all three. I link them together because, in a practical sense, they are often part of a package of benefits offered by organizations (Kossek & Lobel, 1996; Lobel, 1999). I also argue that they are fundamentally connected at the core on a theoretical level, because improving a person's work-family interface is dependent on understanding how his or her life is embedded in structures of gender, race, and class. By considering these policies as a unit, moreover, my intention is to avoid the bifurcations that often plague policy and scholarly discussions (Blankenship, 1993; Wexler, 1997); for instance, that "work-family" policy is for women and that "diversity" is for people of color.

The organization of this chapter loosely follows the three points listed earlier in terms of scope, method, and theoretical approach. In doing so, however, the substantive discussion moves from local to global. It starts with a local view, showing how research on U.S. work-life policy is enhanced by broadening the range of analysis to include global dynamics. The second vantage point is comparative. It contrasts work-family policy in two national sites to show how a transnational approach can benefit the local application of policies. The last section shifts the viewpoint and discussion outward. It looks at work-family policies for global settings like TNCs and intergovernmental organizations, and it explores common traps that can occur when practitioners avoid a transnational perspective. The conclusion of this chapter addresses drawbacks of a transnational perspective and offers suggestions for future work-family research.

A NEW LOOK AT FAMILIAR TERRAIN: EXPOSING THE *GLOBAL* IN LOCAL WORK-LIFE TRENDS

For much of the work-family literature, globalization is something that happens somewhere else—in the Third World perhaps, or at least "not here." One sign of this is that most of the theoretical and empirical models of work-life focus on local determinants alone—government and corporate policy, economic and labor market conditions, gender and family practices, individual choices, attitudes, and roles, and so on (Gerstel, Clawson, & Zussman, 2002; Hertz & Marshall, 2001; Parasuraman & Greenhaus, 1999; Parcel & Cornfield, 2000; Vannoy & Dubeck, 1998). However, a transnational perspective illuminates the way many of the current dilemmas of work-life are related to globalization (Haas, Hwang, & Russell, 2000; Lewis, 1997; Lewis & Lewis, 1996). Three examples demonstrate this: globalizing *work tasks*, transnational *firms*, and international *workforces*. The following is a review of recent studies in the United States that reveal how transnational forces are intensifying work and family linkages and putting strains on our current work-life programs.

Globalizing Jobs

Globalization is changing the very definition of what jobs are—their tasks, their locations, their meanings, their clientele, and so forth. The effect, very often, is an intensification of work and an erosion of supports for family in the United States. The form varies for workers at the upper and lower tiers of the occupational hierarchy, however.

For those at the top tier, globalization has lead to a speed-up of work and *care deficit*. One important source for this trend is advancing technology. With the development of the Internet and satellite communications, a great deal of professional work has moved online. Stockbrokers, for instance, are experiencing radical changes in their work loads and schedules as trading and communication networks have become accessible to clients in many countries and in many time zones (Blair-Loy & Jacobs, 2003). In turn, what used to be fixed or at least more controlled work hours are expanding, and some brokers report that they have little time for family except on weekends and short vacations.

Another reason for the care deficit in professional work is the implementation of *virtual teams*. Software engineers in a subcontracted firm in Ireland, for instance, find they have to communicate with *coworkers* (not just clients) in many different countries, and across eight different time zones (O'Riain, 2000). Moreover, their experiences contradict what media and popular culture figures are predicting about the ultimate impact of this work. Instead of ending time and space, globalization has produced the opposite trend: "Space is intensified by the necessity of local cooperation and the increased use of project teams in the face of the challenges posed by the global economy. Time becomes an ever more pressing reality in the deadline-driven workplace" (O'Riain, 2000, p. 278). One of the main implications is that workers are less able to negotiate for alternative work arrangements that support family time. In fact, the Irish engineers joke about proposals from the European Union (EU) that limit the workweek to 48 hours. In global settings like theirs, this would end up doubling the workload—one workweek for the U.S. firm and another for theirs.

Globalization of the upper tier also means more international travel for managers and professionals and new types of work-family tension (Adler, 2002). Because international travel is itself gendered, this transformation has had different implications for women and men. Traditionally, it was the male workers who went abroad, leaving their families behind. Wives typically faced strains like separation, isolation, and lack of support to manage the family. Other women have accompanied their husbands as "expatriate wives," generating feelings of alienation, lack of purpose, or being a third wheel. However, as corporations have become more global and women have gained a greater share of the workforce, the conditions for coordinating work and family have changed. For one thing, women are becoming global managers and professionals themselves. Their tensions are how to care for children and families while away for extended periods. In addition, there are increasing numbers of dual-job couples who have to manage global careers. This has generated unique work-life scenarios, like those of "trailing spouses" who need to find jobs and arrange work permits in their partner's new work site and "global commuters" who need to keep in contact with families over long distances through telephones and plane trips. Such circumstances are not addressed by traditional work-life policies.

At the bottom of the job hierarchy, globalization has not only intensified work but weakened previous work-life supports. To begin with, recent trends have undermined the foundation of working-families—the permanent (or least stable) job. Instead, workers are facing downsizing and layoffs, rising numbers of temporary, part-time, and contingent jobs, and a decline in the living wage (Carnoy, 2000; Wallace, 1998). In addition, access to formal work-life policies has dissipated, as fewer numbers of employers are willing to pay for health care and greater numbers are expanding overtime. The link of these dynamics to the bottom of the job hierarchy is evident in this volume: Susan Lambert and Elaine Waxman (chap. 6, this volume) show how low-wage workers in organizations often face the least job stability, income security, and access to benefits supporting work-life integration.

A transnational perspective suggests that these changes for low-income workers are related to global transformations. Of particular importance is the global restructuring of the nation's largest private firms. Because responsibility for work-life policies in the United States has been placed largely in the hands of the private sector, and because large corporations exert tremendous authority over smaller ones (where most people actually work), these firms hold a pivotal role in the outcome of work-life programs. Yet in the last few decades, there has been a significant change in the nature of these firms, involving an expansion of their geography, autonomy, and power (McMichael, 2000). In turn, these firms are retreating from their accountability to U.S. working families. This change has been triggered by several global events.

One is the consolidation of power in global financial institutions in the 1980s and 1990s. Banking groups like the World Trade Organization (WTO) and International Monetary Fund (IMF) have helped to keep the playing field of the global economy uneven—in the favor of large Northern firms. This happens through unfair trade laws and debt-relief programs, which perpetuate underdevelopment in Southern nations through structural adjustment policies attached to loan repayment (Cavanagh et al., 1996). By keeping the poor countries poor, institutions like the IMF ensure that firms from the South are unable to compete economically with those of the North, and ensure that labor forces in the South remain cheap for Northern firms.

It is no coincidence, then, that U.S. labor unions are now putting antiglobalization clauses in their mission statements and contracts with employers. The AFL-CIO, for instance, added a "Global Fairness" resolution to their convention in 2001, which calls for "changing the rules of the global economy, [and] building economic power for working families" among other things (AFL-CIO, 2001). Furthermore, their global focus is not merely directed at the immediate issues of corporate downsizing and layoffs. Rather, their statements call for *antipoverty programs for the Third World*, because these organizations are quite aware that it is the perpetuation of global economic imbalance that is driving U.S. firms overseas and undercutting work-life supports at home.

Another source of new globalizing strategies among large firms is the U.S. government. Through trade laws like the North American Free Trade Agreement (NAFTA) and the General Agrument on Tariffs and Trade (GATT), the state has granted U.S. corporations the freedom of international mobility. With the increased profits from exploiting new markets and cheaper labor forces abroad, these firms subsequently have more control over working families at home— especially in terms of developing new technology, cutting jobs, and driving down wages (Gross, 2001). In addition, the United States contributes to this process through another strategy as well—by reducing the financial accountability of firms to the government. From the 1950s to the 1990s, the share of corporate contributions to federal income tax (relative to each dollar paid by individuals and families) declined from 76 to 21 cents (Danaher, 1996). This means that as corporations go abroad, they take with them one of the largest sources of revenue that our state has for supporting social programs like work-life integration.

The impact of these global trends on working families is plain to see. Most obvious is the large-scale movement of employment overseas. The United States has lost 700,000 manufacturing jobs since 1970 (Carnoy, 2000). In the last few years, firms are beginning to outsource professional and lower white-collar jobs to Southern nations as well. While these trends have received much media attention, they mask less visible consequences of corporate mobility that are equally significant for work-life policy. An example is the loss of informal work-family benefits from large firms that are dispersed throughout local communities. The personalized impact of this is shown by the departure of firms like Kodak and Xerox from the Northeast. Aside from losing their own jobs, local employees have been equally distressed by the withdrawal of financial investments in neighborhood health centers and the withdrawal of broad-based employment opportunities that had enabled their extended families to remain together (Perrin, 1998).

Finally, the deterioration of work-life supports described earlier has exacerbated diversity strains in the workplace, especially racial tensions. Consider a case—albeit an extreme one—that occurred at a Lockheed Martin factory in Texas in 2003 (Halbfinger, 2003). Doug Williams, a disgruntled and bigoted white worker, had been making racist slurs and gestures in his multiracial work setting for several years. One day in 2003, he came to work with a shotgun and a rifle and opened fire on his colleagues. He wounded nine of them, killed five others, and then fatally shot himself. Although this incident is indicative of the wave of workplace shootings over the last decade (and the problematic role of guns in U.S. society), one part of this story stands out. The assault took place *right in the middle of a diversity seminar.*

A closer look shows how this event is connected to globalization. Lockheed Martin is a global company and has been laying off workers; by 2003, the number was in the tens of thousands. Many employees had been citing discriminatory practices in these layoffs (such as targeting workers who were age 40 and older), and in 1996, the firm settled a lawsuit filed by the Equal Employment Opportunity Commission. Personally, Williams was feeling the accumulating tensions of global downsizing and inequality within this context: He had been working more and more Sundays and overtime shifts, he had divorced his wife, and had left his kids. The day before the shooting, Williams had been asked to attend an ethics and sensitivity seminar, and this apparently became the focal point for his anxiety and aggression. While this analysis is not meant to excuse his behavior or displace the blame for a horrendous act, it merely suggests that racial tensions may be exacerbated in the context of globalization pressures. In turn, the very human resource (HR) programs that were originally designed to allay these strains can become their symbol or at least target in the twenty-first century.

Foreign Firms

A second important globalizing trend in the United States is the growing presence of foreign firms. More and more, the organizations for whom employees work in the United States are themselves global. In turn, work-life policies are being implemented through the filter of their foreign policies and management styles. This is making the experience of work-life policy *inseparable* from the nationality of corporate ownership. It also means that nationhood is increasingly the focal point for employee resistance in TNCs.

East Asian firms have taken center stage in this research. Japanese companies in the United States, for instance, are noted for their management techniques like cooperative work groups and teams. While these schemes promote a "culture of cooperation" on the surface, they are often embedded with other types of work-family inequities (Smith, 1997). Several case studies illustrate this: In a midwest Japanese automobile assembly plant, team structures were implemented along with arbitrary shift rotation and mandatory unscheduled overtime (Gott-fried & Graham, 1993); and in a rural Japanese garment factory, cultures of cooperation were accompanied by formalized communication channels, declin-ing wages, lack of union representation, and reduced control over work sched-ules (Feldman & Buechler, 1998). The key factor about these managerial strat-egies, however, is their intimate connection to national identity. TNC managers often introduce them explicitly as method of promoting their Japanese national identity, so that they can differentiate themselves from U.S. firms.

It is not surprising then, that workers' responses (and resistance) to these strategies are often directed at the nationhood of the management. The largely white and female workforce at the garment factory above reacted with "out-bursts" on the shopfloor, asserting themselves as "strong American women" in order to invoke, oppose, and deride a notion of weak Japanese identity among the mangers. Likewise, workers at the auto plant contested mandatory shift changes and overtime rules using the logic of Japanese management techniques, for example, that the decisions were made without the "participation of the team." Furthermore, there are gender hierarchies embedded in these nation and class hierarchies as well. Women workers contested the rules on the basis of family obligations and "their responsibilities as wives and mothers" (Feldman & Buechler, 1998, p. 621), in addition to abuses against the team. Moreover, they refused to work past normal hours (unlike the men) and tried to organize a work stoppage in protest. Thus, because work-family policies in TNCs are integrally related to issues of citizenship and gender, future policy strategies will need to address this as well.

Aside from these work-family dynamics, foreign firms are reshaping the meaning and experience of diversity. This is because TNCs are recasting tra-ditional workplace hierarchies: The presence of foreign managers often reverses conventional dichotomies of white managers and multicultural staff. An example is the auto plant in Feldman's case mentioned previously, where the workers are "white" and the managers are "of color." (This case also shows the complications of intersecting hierarchies, as the privilege of race among the operators is coun-teracted by their marginalization as women.)

Global ethnographies are exposing another diversity twist in these TNCs—subtle *intraethnic* hierarchies among the staff. Rather than being organized along "racial" or "color" lines, occupational strata are being formed along lines of *immigration status*. Kim (2002) provides a fascinating example of this with her study of Korean TNCs in the New York area. Here, "*race*" is homogenized in the sense that the Korean owners hire Korean workers. Yet, the managers still invoke a "differentiation of 'Korean-ness' based on immigrant generation . . . between the 'old Korea' and the Korean Americans. They interpret different work behaviors of Korean Americans and categorize them by their immigrant generation: 'first-generation,' '1.5-generation,' and 'second-generation.' " This has significant implications for diversity theory. While these policies have typically addressed tensions *between* racial/ethnic groups in the workplace (Jackson, 1992; Kossek & Lobel, 1996), these TNCs reveal how tensions are developing *among and within* racial/ethnic groups on the basis of nationality and citizenship status.

Finally, the changing nationality of managers raises issues for gender policy as well. Like the case just presented, immigration status is used as a means to exploit *women* workers, too. This is demonstrated by a recent case at Oracle corporation (one of the world's top software producers), in which a male manager was sued for coercing sexual favors out of his female subordinate (*Times of India*, 2003). The unique feature of this scenario is that both of these employees were born and educated in India. Furthermore, the manager—legitimizing his actions through national imagery—told his subordinate that her sexual acts were necessary to "learn the art of pleasing the American manager" (p. 1). In this way, nationality is manipulated in the context of gendered labor relationships; specifically American citizenship is reconstructed at the local level so that male managers can use it to their advantage against women in their own immigrant group. In addition, this case shows how the increasing globalization of management affects *professionals* rather than just blue-collar workers cited in the previous examples.

Moreover, international ownership poses new challenges for the practical issue of prosecuting offenders in these kinds of gender discrimination cases. For instance, there are rising numbers of sexual harassment claims in Japanese TNCs in the United States. The Japanese Ministry of Labor predicted that 57% of its 331 TNCs in the United States would face discrimination lawsuits in the 1990s (Efron, 1999). Indeed, the question of whom to hold accountable for gender discrimination in foreign firms (i.e., U.S. versus Japanese courts) is a new legal challenge. It reveals the limitations of current research on sexual harassment and discrimination, which will not be of much use for women working in U.S.-based foreign firms.

Immigrant Workforces

As the last case shows, there is yet another globalizing dynamic that affects work-life experiences in the United States—the transnationalism of the workforce itself. In fact, this recasts many of the work-life trends described in the first section. Many critical race scholars point out that the eroding quality of work and work-life benefits are also connected to the changing immigrant character of the workforce (Lowe, 1996).

This is apparent in electronics production, where managers prefer immigrant populations from countries as disparate as China, Mexico, the Phillippines, and

Ethiopia in order to make use of their pre-existing ethnic and community networks for recruitment (Chun, 2001; Hossfeld, 1990; Louie, 2001). They also take advantage of the vulnerability of this population by offering personal favors. In exchange, workers "agree to overtime, consent to unpredictable changes in work schedules, intensify their own working conditions, and monitor their co-workers" (Chun, 2001, p. 149). The same is true for Indian software engineers, who accept constant relocation and substandard wages as a consequence of their dependency on employers and the heavy restrictions embedded in H1-B visas (Ong, 2003; Saxenian, 2000; van der Veer, 2002). In this way, the intensification of work-family strain among both professional and production workers can be associated with the marginalization of immigrant workforces.

The magnification of work-life pressures for immigrant workers is probably best illustrated in the case of domestic, service, and other reproductive care workers. Indeed, the workers who are "doing the dirty work" in U.S. homes and offices are increasingly international (Anderson, 2000; Zarembka, 2003). During the last century at least, this work was dominated heavily by workers of local origin, in particular women of color—African Americans, Asian Americans, and Chicanas (Glenn, 2001). However, as these groups have moved hierarchically or vertically in the labor market, immigrants have taken their place.

The reasons are directly transnational. Sometimes these groups have come to the United States because the IMF structural adjustment programs (mentioned earlier) have depleted job opportunities in their home countries or because civil war, political unrest, and human rights abuses have made their homes unsafe. Other times, they come because of formal recruiting organizations, informal women's networks or personal contacts with U.S. foreign diplomats that have provided links between the North and South (Repak, 1995). In the end, 40% of the *legal* household workers are immigrant women (Hochschild, 2003), and most likely the figure is much larger among illegal workers. Given their alien status and lack of legal protections, such workers are especially vulnerable.

In turn, work-family strains are exacerbated for this group in ways that few other types of workers experience. Take nannies, for instance. Because their work *is* other people's homes, the boundary between work and home is completely obscured for these employees. Consequently, they often face conflicting expectations of being "part of the family" on one hand, but maintaining the "professional distance" of an employee on the other (Anderson, 2000; Hondagneu-Sotelo, 2003). More important, their own family lives are eclipsed and displaced. Not only do they face a "lack of time for family" (as in many of the cases described earlier), some also face a total separation from family. As they are unable to care for their own children abroad, this creates a "global nanny chain" of care deficit (Hochschild, 2000; Parrenas, 2001). The most egregious scenario is when the home/workplace literally becomes a prison. This happens to domestic workers who are trafficked from Southern countries and then held in near enslavement in their employers' homes in the United States

(Zarembka, 2003). For immigrant workers then, work-family tension takes an entirely different meaning.

Finally, immigration is casting a new spin on the dynamics of diversity. The reason is that immigrant workforces have become targets of global politics, and in turn, recipients of unique forms of discrimination. Historically, anti-immigrant backlash in the workplace has accompanied waves of labor immigration. However, in the contemporary era, this backlash is also connected to broader relations among nations in the global economy and, in particular, U.S. foreign policy.

An example is backlash against Asian American professionals. Even with the substantial contributions of Asian entrepreneurs and professionals to the development of U.S. industries like high-tech (Saxenian, 2000), they still experience forms of discrimination directed at their national identity. These incidences are often motivated by global politics, like the precarious orientation of the White House toward countries like China and Korea (as well as other Asian nations in the "axis of evil"). Such negative images are reproduced and strengthened in film and television with many sinister representations of Asians. Given this context, there have been suspicious campaigns against Asian professionals and scientists. This is illustrated in the case of Wen Ho Lee, a Taiwanese national and former U.S. government physicist, "who was detained in shackles and charged, without evidence, [for] giving classified nuclear secrets to China" (Ong, 2003, p. 258).

At the production level, global tensions of diversity are best exemplified by the recent experiences of Muslim workers. U.S. foreign policy has prompted everyday Americans to distrust Muslims in the post-9/11 era, through the mistreatment of U.S. Middle Easterners by public officials, and the media's equating of Arabs with terrorists. In turn, anti-Muslim incidents against U.S. citizens and residents have increased threefold in the year after the World Trade Center and Pentagon attacks. So, it is no surprise that reports of anti-Muslim discrimination have been increasing at corporations like Whirlpool (Washwani, 2002). In many ways, this company is symbolic of this broad trend of transnational workforces—more than half of its 60,000 workers worldwide are *not* of North American origin. In 2002, the *managers* at the Whirlpool factory in Tennessee were brought to suit for reportedly pulling off the head scarves of their Muslim female workers. Along with this, there were reports of managerial surveillance in the bathrooms and firings of workers who complained about these incidences. What is unique about Whirlpool, though, is that it has been applauded as a leader and symbol of diversity programs, including English as a second language, religious sensitivity training, "labor harmony," and so on. The extent of racial tension in the face of all this effort indicates how traditional strategies for diversity are strained in the face of globalization.

In sum, these accounts provided by global ethnographies urge scholars to look for the global in the local of the U.S. work-life nexus. While traditional work-family research looks at sources within individual roles or tastes, households or workplaces, and institutional contexts of unions, labor markets, state policies, and the like, I argue that many of these factors are themselves affected by transnational forces—such as globalizing firms, jobs, and workers. Furthermore, a transnational perspective reveals how globalization aggravates work-life tensions, especially for those marginalized by race, class, gender, and nation simultaneously.

THE COMPARATIVE VIEW: USING TRANSNATIONAL CASES TO INFORM LOCAL POLICY

A transnational perspective has potential benefits for improving work-life policy through its comparative methodology. This is especially relevant because the current literature tends to focus on the back end of policies—that is, how often the policies are adopted, how often workers use them, their impacts on family life, and so forth (for a review of this literature, see Glass & Estes, 1997). However, scholars are less concerned with the front end of work-family policies—that is, how and why they are designed to begin with. This is problematic in light of recent scholarship suggesting that the reasons firms adopt policies may have less to do with the needs of their workers as with other corporate interests—like alleviating pressures from their institutional environments, smoothing employee relations, or promoting careerist agendas of managers and HR professionals (Edelman et al., 2001; Kelly, 1999; Kelly & Dobbin, 1998). Furthermore, some studies are finding *negative* consequences of work-family policies, such as wage and promotion penalties for employees who use flextime and part-time work (Deitch, 2000; Weeden, 2000). These findings suggest that there are fundamental flaws in the design and/or implementation of these policies.

A transnational method of crosscase comparison across can address this problem by revealing the unstated assumptions within work-life policy that may undermine or derail their original aims. Such agendas may be difficult to observe and identify in a single work setting, especially when their practitioners may be unaware of them. For this reason, a methodology that compares similar policies across different sites—especially different national contexts—can help to illuminate these assumptions. My research on U.S. and Indian firms uses such an analysis and reveals how hidden agendas operate at both the institutional level of policy design and the local level of policy implementation.

What unifies the cases in my study is that both AmCo and IndCo are in the same industry, as leading firms in their countries, and with similar types of workers: managers, software engineers, computer sales, and manufacturing operators (Poster, 2000). One would think, therefore, that the work-family policies serving employees in such similar contexts would have many commonalities.

Instead, AmCo and IndCo design their policies in entirely different ways. At AmCo, the policies are almost entirely geared toward alternative work arrangements for accommodating family demands, like flextime, telecommuting, jobsharing, and part-time work. At IndCo, such policies are almost entirely geared toward material supports for workers' families, like paid maternity leave, on-site child care, rent subsidies, private school tuition for children, and shuttles for transporting workers between the home and office. In each case, managerial assumptions about what is good for employees or what is "normal" for the industry vary quite a bit. This can be problematic for employees. Even though workers in each site appreciate their benefits, they also express a desire for broader range of policies. Many AmCo workers lament the lack of child care, and some IndCo workers wish for more flexibility in scheduling. In this way, the comparative method illustrates how contextually based assumptions narrow the options for work-family policy.

Such assumptions not only guide the initial design of policies but the subsequent way they are interpreted and executed by local managers. We can see this when comparing AmCo to its own subsidiary in India, TransCo. Both firms have policies labeled "diversity," as directed by the home office in Silicon Valley. However, varying interpretations about the meaning of diversity generate entirely different applications the policy in each firm.

At AmCo, managers interpret diversity programs primarily in terms of gender. The HR vice president explains this in the department's hiring and promotion programs: "[Our] objective is, we clearly need to have in AmCo a better representation of women in higher level jobs. Our numbers aren't that great, so we need to accelerate the development of women, [and] increase the retention." In turn, the activities of the diversity office also center around women's issues, such as training seminars that teach respecting men's and women's styles of interpersonal relations and leadership. There is a silence on issues of class, however; and although race is acknowledged, few managers see it as a pressing issue. A male quality engineer in the corporate office explains: "I could cite some individual examples of racial discrimination, but as a whole, as a company policy, absolutely not."

At TransCo, managers interpret the policy in an opposite way—in terms of ethnicity and race. The president says: "The women thing I have not had. We have a correct ratio of women as exists in India in terms of the number of women working." An employee elaborates: "See, here the diversity issue which could be more important would be people belonging to one particular religious group or linguistic group or from a particular province—rather than the women and men ratio." Diversity programs, in turn, are directed at assessing the firm's representation of ethnic groups on the basis of categories like language, region, and religion.

In a separate analysis, I describe how these diverging notions have less to do with the kinds of tensions or discrimination that actually exist among the staff and more with the localized institutional contexts of India and the United States

(Poster, 2002, 2004; Poster & Prasad, 2005). Still, the broader point is the power of these assumptions in shaping work-life policy *outcomes*. Specifically, even when the same policy from a head office is intended for many units of the same firm, it can be mediated by the hidden agendas of managers at the local level, so that ultimately it is applied in narrow and conflicting ways.

In sum, a transnational perspective can illuminate the unstated assumptions of work-life policy that may go unacknowledged and even unobserved in single case studies. This advances the scholarly literature on work-life policy at the institutional level (by revealing the presence of such assumptions at the design stage) and the local level (by revealing their role during implementation). This analysis also challenges common explanations for the negative outcomes of work-policy. In both scholarly and corporate accounts, negative outcomes are typically dismissed as *"unintended consequences"*, or secondary effects. However, I argue that by using a transnational crosscase method like this, one can see how the problems of work-life policies may even be embedded in their initial design.

A GLOBAL VIEW: DEVELOPING WORK-LIFE POLICY FOR TRANSNATIONAL SETTINGS

A transnational perspective also has benefits for policy in global settings. This includes corporations that go abroad (TNCs), intergovernmental organizations (like the UN), and international legal agencies—all of which are charged with the task of designing and/or regulating policies for multiple nations simultaneously. Although much of the current research that informs these bodies is based on a *"cultural difference"* approach, I argue that a transnational approach directs scholarly attention toward overlooked tensions regarding the hierarchies among nations, firms, and employees. In turn, it is better able to address common traps in global work-life policy—like those of *"dominance"* and *"accommodation."*

Exposing Power

Much of the research on global firms (in both comparative social science and international management) is based on a *cultural* perspective (Hofstede, 1991). Frequently cited is the work of Geert Hofstede (1991), who conducted a study of IBM units in many countries. He argues that national cultures generate divergent forms of organizational and employee behavior, such as orientations toward individualism /collectivism, uncertainty acceptance/avoidance, masculinity/femininity (which Adler [2002] very appropriately relabels "career success/ quality of life"), and so on. This has become a standard framework for explaining the contrasts in employee policies across nations. The limitation of this approach is that *cultural behaviors* are extracted from their social embeddedness—and especially power relations. Most important, this approach presumes that *cultural differences are on equal footing*. In reality, the contexts in which these policies are designed or applied are rarely representative of equivalent authority relations. More often one organization's "cultural" behaviors have more institutional power than another's.

A transnational perspective can expose these power dynamics and their significance for work-life policy. This is illustrated in my research on diversity policy in AmCo and TransCo. Each firm's position in the global hierarchy informs its understanding of what diversity policy means and how to apply it. AmCo, to begin with, uses the rhetoric of global dominance in order to promote its status as an international firm. As the global HR vice president explains, the firm is striving to be "a truly global company," and the "the telltale sign" of this is having policies that are "transplantable" anywhere:

> Our corporate culture moves well with managers—they *want* to adopt the standard ways. Over time they move toward it. Employees embrace it too. *The words seem to translate into different languages. The meanings of the words seem to fit.* It fits with different religions, it fits with different cultures. The core values are very transplantable.

Diversity policies, in turn, are overinflated *global* scale—they are articulated as universal and "fitting with different cultures" without critical attention of how they are received in foreign settings. (Quite the contrary as we saw earlier, the reality is that the AmCo's interpretations of diversity *do not* coincide with those of TransCo.) Rather, this kind of rhetoric is socially constructed on and/or legitimized by AmCo's institutional power in relation to TransCo.

Global politics are equally salient in the rhetoric of diversity at the Indian subsidiary. TransCo managers respond to AmCo's overbearing and inflexible application of policies by taking an opposite (and equally inflexible) position—one that overemphasizes the localism of diversity experiences. A TransCo manager articulates this: "Frankly, in my opinion diversity is a more of an American issue than an issue here. But you know, it's been raised to the dimension of a global issue in this company, so we have to address it." With regard to gender in particular, a TransCo's HR vice president states: "You know, gender is a very live situation in the United States, but I don't think it is such a live situation in this organization over here." The dismissal of diversity as something that is "only American" reflects TransCo's marginalized position in the global hierarchy of the TNC. Managers use this rhetoric (at least in part) as a means to resist the overbearing and overuniversalizing policies from the head office. (Granted, this resistance is expressed in a highly inaccurate and derogatory manner.) In the end then, two sets of rhetoric are quite contradictory, and their underlying imbalance in structural authority becomes a barrier to communication between the firms.

This case shows how global power is endemic to the interpretations and meanings of work-life policy—even before it is even implemented. Moreover, this case challenges cultural explanations of corporate policies, by showing how orientations toward work-life policy are not on equal footing but rather embedded in the hierarchical relations of the TNC. Without explicit attention to these kinds of power dynamics in global settings (even in their rhetoric), work-family policy is likely to be ineffective or at least face considerable barriers.

Avoiding the Traps

There are many indications that these global power relations have derailed work-life policy. Here I describe two examples of this, which present cautionary tales of using a "cultural" rather than "transnational" approach.

Dominance   One policy trap from the cultural approach is when U.S. and other Northern TNCs use their position of power to enforce policies without the participation of, and/or consent by, locals. Names for this approach in the management literature have included "*cultural dominance*" (Adler, 2002) and "*ethnocentrism*" (Francesco & Gold, 1998). Sometimes this domineering orientation is unconscious, or results from managerial rationality (e.g., when TNCs export HR programs in conjunction with their other corporate programs). Other times, however, this approach reflects a deliberate global policy agenda in which Northern "culture" is superior is considered superior to that of the South.

Yet, there is a growing transnational research illustrating the limitations of this orientation for work-family policy. Studies of TNCs show that the same work-family programs used in parent firms are not necessarily ideal for, or well-received by, employees of the foreign subsidiaries. This happened in my study of AmCo and TransCo for instance (Poster & Prasad, 2005). Whereas flextime was generally welcomed at the parent company in the United States, it was not in India. TransCo employees were far less interested in policies that keep them in the office later at night and on weekends; in fact, many favored a standardization of hours into regular 9 to 5 schedules instead. The same thing was reported in an international finance firm (Wharton & Blair-Loy, 2002). Managers and professionals in the U.S. home office were accustomed to a "high-performance culture" of long hours and overtime. Yet their counterparts in a Hong Kong unit were more likely to resist this pressure and ask for part-time options. In these cases, the domination approach compromises productive working environments by neglecting the local needs of foreign workers.

Furthermore, another risk of the dominance approach is overriding the work-life policy gains of workers in other countries. This has happened with the maternity policies of U.S. TNCs in Europe (Kubal, 1999). On one hand, the local policies provide broad coverage for women workers who are pregnant. This originates from the European Union's (EU) Equal Pay Directive, which states that "the protection of women in their professional and family lives is an essential aspect of equality." Accordingly, EU employers are required to provide special privileges for pregnant women, like time off for breast-feeding, prenatal doctor visits, and 14 weeks' maternity leave. On the other hand, U.S. law (which regulates labor relations in U.S. TNCs) requires employers to treat pregnancy as a "*disability*." This means providing the same supports for pregnant workers as any other worker who has a disability and forbids special privileges like breast-feeding. The implication, therefore, is that applying this kind of work-family policy in TNCs would rollback recent gains for women under the EU and create an ironic situation in which their benefits would be far weaker than those of their fellow citizens working in neighboring firms.

Similarly, this dominance approach would undermine women's gains in other countries regarding sexual harassment. U.S. sexual harassment policy has certain kinds of benefits relative to other countries, such as a greater authority for employers to fire harassing offenders and, in some cases, larger cash awards for women who win lawsuits. However, many scholars and activists are concerned that applying this policy abroad in TNCs would mean a loss of power for victims in countries where labor and gender rights are more securely protected in national constitutions than in the United States (Ore-Aguilar, 2000; Saguy, 2000). In countries like France, Costa Rica, El Salvador, and Mexico, for instance, sexual harassment law has a different institutional base than in the United States—in criminal and/or labor codes, rather than antidiscrimination law. This means that sexual harassment is defined as an "act of violence" in the workplace and entitles victims to many kinds of rewards not offered in the United States, like back-pay compensation and employment reinstatement if victims were fired from their jobs. In addition, these legal systems provide harsher punishment for aggressors, like jail sentences and fines. Although neither the discrimination nor violence models are ideal, especially relative to the "gender model" of the UN (Ore-Aguilar, 2000), activists are already citing cases in which the imposition of U.S. law via TNCs in settings like Europe, Japan, and Latin America is having negative consequences for women workers (Efron, 1999; Friedman & Mertz, 1998).

Accommodation.   Another policy trap inherited from the cultural approach is the *under*utilization of authority in global contexts. This is when organizations from Northern nations (whether private, state, or nongovernmental) take a "hands-off" approach to work-family policy in Southern nations. This may be a function "*poly-*" or "*regio-*centric" management strategies, that is, leaving decisions up to the local management (Francesco & Gold, 1998) or deliberate strategies of "accommodation" or "compromise" to local practices

(Adler, 2002). It may be well intentioned but can have negative effects. This happens when the accommodation approach treats local norms as precious (because they are "*cultural*") and considers them best left undisturbed. In turn, it misses the possibility (and often reality) that local actors may abuse their authority and institute employee policy in discriminatory ways.

For this reason, the accommodation approach would clearly be a poor replacement for domination in my study. One example again is in diversity policy. As an indication of this abuse of power, TransCo managers were initially resistant to the diversity agenda altogether. HR managers had no plans at all to consider it when the firm first opened—despite the fact that their parent company had appointed a "diversity manager" in TransCo to do so. This manager explains:

> Diversity is one thing which was never on top agenda for the company, till about a year-and-a-half back. We as a company never looked at diversity as a concern to worry about in India. And the management team had heard about the concept of diversity, but we never worked on it consciously.

My observations indicate, however, that diversity programs are critically needed for many hiring and promotion deficiencies in the firm, such as a complete absence of women in higher management, and an overrecruitment of Hindu versus Muslims workers (Poster, 2004). Indeed, it was only when AmCo enforced specific requirements that TransCo managers set on a path of addressing diversity issues. This shows how pressure from parent organizations can be advantageous for counteracting negligent and sometimes discriminatory behaviors among local managers.

The accommodation approach also proves inadequate in light of recent work-life gains around the world. Many of these achievements have arisen through the intervention of international organizations rather than through the actions of local groups alone (Berkovitch, 1999). In fact, these international groups have been pivotal in work-life policy outcomes of many of the cases. The International Labour Office (ILO) was crucial in motivating countries like Australia to adopt work-family policy, through its Convention 156 concerning workers with family commitments. The EU inspired states like the UK to improve its parental leave policies (Lewis, 1997). And when it comes to diversity policy, the UN convention against discrimination by national and ethnic origin was influential for the establishment of the Russian Federation's affirmative action program (Konrad & Linnehan, 1999).

Finally, the UN's principle gender equality document—Convention for the Elimination of All Forms of Discrimination Against Women (CEDAW)—has been key in a number of women's grassroots struggles against corporations and other organizations. In 1995, Japanese women's groups used it against one of the nation's largest corporations, Sumitomo, to fight gender discrimination in wages and promotions (Lui & Boyle, 2001). CEDAW supplied these groups with crucial legal language and structural supports for winning the case. Likewise, a similar victory was won for women workers in India this way. In 1997, women's groups and nongovernmental organizations (NGOs) succeeded in one of the nation's most influential sexual harassment cases, by citing the government's ratification of CEDAW and its "binding accounts of women's rights in the workplace" (Nussbaum, 2001). Notwithstanding the challenges of enforcing these policies, international organizations and their interventions can be beneficial if not decisive in getting them adopted in the first place.

In these ways, a hands-off approach can be equally ineffective and/or harmful as a domineering one when it comes to work-life policy in global settings like TNCs. The reason is that power exists at both *higher* and *lower* levels of organizational relationships: from head offices as well as subsidiaries, from Northern nations as well as Southern nations, and so on. Given this, orientations like *"cultural sensitivity"*—often adopted by international corporate consultants addressing these issues in foreign firms—are just not enough. Without attention to transnational hierarchies as well, this approach will be unable to recognize and overcome the kinds of policy barriers endemic to global settings.

DISCUSSION

This chapter has attempted to show how a transnational perspective can advance the work-life research, particularly regarding work-family, gender, and diversity policy. A transnational perspective is one that recognizes how relations among global actors are dynamic, embedded in power, and reflective of intersecting systems of race, class, gender, and nation.

This perspective can broaden the *scope* of work-life research by drawing attention to the unexplored global sources of many pressing gender, diversity, and work-family strains. It reveals how jobs, firms, and workforces in the United States are internationalizing. As a result, analytical models that fail to address the connections between global and local forces will be increasingly ineffective in envisioning adequate policy solutions.

A transnational approach can also improve work-life policy through its *methodology*. For instance, a cross-case method within different national sites can help to expose the hidden assumptions in work-life policies and prevent them from acting as barriers to both policy design and implementation. Finally, a transnational perspective can advance *theoretical models* of work-life policy as well. It challenges the premise of social equivalence or neutrality embedded in *cultural* models of organizational behavior that dominate global work-life research. Instead, it reveals the significant role of *hierarchy* among nations, firms, and employees in work-life policies for global settings. In turn, a transnational approach illustrates how to avoid common policy shortcomings like *domination* and *accommodation*.

Limitations

There are several drawbacks or limitations of using a transnational approach. Methodologically, it can be more difficult to carry out than local or single-site analyses. It often requires more resources: more time (for arranging visas, doing fieldwork, etc.), larger budgets (for release time from teaching, international plane fare, local travel, hiring translators, etc.), and more complicated planning in terms of coordinating fieldwork in multiple sites. Transnational research may also involve more investigators than local analyses, as collaborating with local scholars can enhance the logistics and analytical perspective of the fieldwork.

Like any kind of empirical research, there are also theoretical or analytical compromises due to the constraints of the data. Case studies may offer a rich depth of analysis *within* organizations, but they may be less efficient at addressing the larger environment outside. Furthermore, although representativeness may not be the goal of this method, careful attention has to be made to the site selection to ensure that the case speaks for broader trends or has a relevant logic. There are also potential problems at the analysis stage. Because many levels of analysis are located within the same site, distinguishing what is local versus regional versus national, and so on, as the sources of work-life policy can be difficult. This is when scholars are prone to make broad claims about entire countries—when the findings actually reflect a specific site. Finally, case studies can pose obstacles to assessing variations in race, class, and gender. Given that nations are inherently diverse, capturing the full range of these pluralities in a single site may be hard to do.

CONCLUSION: FUTURE DIRECTIONS FOR TRANSNATIONAL WORK-LIFE RESEARCH

The themes of this chapter suggest several directions for future transnational research on work-life issues.

Local Policy.   One is how to make local work-life policies adaptable to globalization. Innovation is a necessity for work-life programs designed for white- and blue-collar workers alike. For instance, professional, technical, and managerial workers will increasingly need policies that enable the coordination of global clients and coworkers, while still preserving time for family life with some kind of bounded, consistent schedule. These workers also need supports for global careers, and managing households in the face of international assignments, expatriate families, and global commuting. Clearly, strategies like flextime or on-site child care will be insufficient for addressing these longer term and longer distance family responsibilities.

For low-income workers, the policy needs are more basic: strengthening the living wage, expanding access to stable jobs, broadening legal protections for immigrant workers like domestics, and so on. Future research should also address the attenuating responsibility of corporations for workers, especially given the globalization dynamics described in this chapter. For instance, one strategy is to increase the accountability of these large firms to U.S. workers—through more aggressive corporate taxes, curtailing free trade laws, broadening legal requirements for work-family policy (like corporate day care centers), and so forth.

Another strategy, however, is to shift the responsibility of work-life policies away from these TNCs altogether. This view questions whether private organizations should be the main providers of work-family programs, given that they are so insecure to begin with. With the large scale social changes posed by globalization, this instability is likely to increase. Yet, the policies that low-income workers need most are, by definition, ones that require stability—that is, child-care centers, dependent care for senior family members, health benefits, and so on (Gross, 2001). An alternative, therefore, is placing more responsibility on the state, or providing more resources for community groups, for administering work-life policy.

Globalization also urges diversity theory in new directions. One agenda is to develop a new vision of the workplace that takes advantage of national plurality rather than suppressing or ignoring it. While much of the literature reviewed here highlights the tensions of this process, there are optimistic accounts as well. For instance, studies of superplural regions like California show that the saturation of immigrant labor groups can potentially undo ethnic tensions (English-Lueck, 2002): "National origin and ethnic affiliation are only two of many foundations on which identity can be built. Work, the lodestone that has attracted so many Silicon Valley people, also provides an alternative basis for defining identity" (p. 125). Many elements of the work environment can be used to minimize differences or provide sources of cohesion: industry-based imageries (like the dominance of technology itself in a place like Silicon Valley), corporate-sponsored, panethnic events (like international festivals), or specific organizational campaigns (like Apple Corporation's former logo, re-applied to suggest that employees "bleed six different colors"). An even better idea is to search for this new *unifying theme* for plurality among the employees themselves.

Diversity strategy also needs to move in new directions regarding its activities. This analysis has shown how traditional diversity programs are increasingly inadequate in the face of globalization. This is illustrated in the cases of both Lockheed Martin and Whirlpool, where—even in the context of formal attempts to address racial tensions—activities like diversity seminars can become symbols for employee and managerial aggression. In less extreme cases, these seminars may be flawed in placing the responsibility of solving racial tensions on the workers rather than on management. In reality, employees at the bottom of organizational hierarchies—like production floor operators—have the least power to change the organization-wide cultures of discrimination. Instead, effective change must come from the top, through structural measures that provide punishments for racially discriminatory behavior, rewards for innovative forms of coworker unity, and steps for elevating immigrant workers in the occupational hierarchy.

Global Policy.   Finally, future research should address ways to improve global work-life policies. One task is clearly to define what is a global work-life policy, and what kinds of issues and programs can be universally representative of workers' needs in different locations. Intergovernmental organizations like the ILO are taking steps in this direction.

Furthermore, given the flaws of global dominance and accommodation as models for implementing policy, a logical alternative is to take a more intermediary position. Adler (2002) calls this "increasing cultural creativity," in reference to the practice of utilizing various talents of actors in global settings in a more balanced way, with more equal contributions. I agree that we need more two-way dialogue in the formation of policy—between parents and subsidiaries, between Northern and Southern nations, and between workers and managers. Indeed, if diverse participants and ideas can improve the efficiency of work groups at the organizational level (Ely & Thomas, 2001), the same may be true for work-life policy at the transnational level. The challenge posed by a transnational perspective, is how to engage in this discussion in ways that recognizes the power that global actors may enact in the process.

AUTHOR NOTE

Data collection was conducted with support from the National Science Foundation, the University of California at Berkeley Professional Studies Abroad in India Program, and a Stanford University McCoy Fellowship. I am grateful to Susan Lambert, Ellen Kossek, Anna Marshall, and an anonymous reviewer for their excellent comments and to the participants of the study for their generous offerings of time and knowledge. The opinions expressed herein are those of the author alone.

REFERENCES

Adler, N. J. (2002). *International dimensions of organizational behavior* (4th ed.). Cincinnati, OH: South-Western.

AFL-CIO. (2001). Convention resolution #3: Global fairness (pp. 15–22). Retrieved March 9, 2004, from www.aflcio.org

Anderson, B. (2000). *Doing the dirty work? The global politics of domestic labour*. London: Zed Books.

Berkovitch, N. (1999). *From motherhood to citizenship: Women's rights and international organizations*. Baltimore: Johns Hopkins University Press.

Blair-Loy, M., & Jacobs, J. A. (2003). Globalization, work hours, and the care deficit among stockbrokers. *Gender and Society, 17*(2), 230–249.

Blankenship, K. M. (1993). Bringing gender and race in: U.S. employment discrimination policy. *Gender and Society, 7*(2), 204–226.

Burawoy, M., Blum, J. A., George, S., Gille, Z., Gowan, T., Haney, L., Klawiter, M., Lopez, S. H., O'Riain, S., & Thayer, M. (2000). *Global ethnography: Forces, connections, and imaginations in a postmodern world*. Berkeley: University of California Press.

Carnoy, M. (2000). *Sustaining the new economy: Work, family, and community in the information age*. Cambridge: Harvard University Press.

Cavanagh, J., Anderson, S., & Pike, J. (1996). Behind the cloak of benevolence: World Bank/IMF policies hurt workers at home and abroad. In K. Danaher (Ed.), *Corporations are going to get your Mama: Globalization and downsizing of the American dream* (pp. 97–104). Monroe, ME: Common Courage Press.

Chun, J. J. (2001). Flexible despotism: The intensification of insecurity and uncertainty in the lives of Silicon Valley's high-tech assembly workers. In R. Baldoz, C. Koelser, & P. Kraft (Eds.), *The critical study of work: Labor, technology, and global production* (pp. 127–155). Philadelphia: Temple University Press.

Danaher, K. (1996). Introduction: Corporate power and the quality of life. In K. Danaher (Ed.), *Corporations are going to get your mama: Globalization and downsizing of the American dream* (pp. 15–32). Monroe, ME: Common Courage Press.

Deitch, C. (2000). "Family-friendly" employer policies, career ladders, glass ceilings and sticky floors. Paper presented at Work and Family: Expanding the Horizons, San Francisco.

Edelman, L. B., Riggs Fuller, S., & Mara-Drita, I. (2001). Diversity rhetoric and the managerialization of law. *American Journal of Sociology, 106*(6), 1589–1641.

Efron, J. M. (1999). The transnational application of sex harassment laws: A cultural barrier in Japan. *University of Pennsylvania Journal of International Economic Law, 20*(133), 1–33.

Ely, R. J., & Thomas, D. A. (2001). Cultural diversity at work: The effects of diversity perspectives on work group processes and outcomes. *Administrative Science Quarterly, 46*(2), 229–273.

English-Lueck, J. A. (2002). *Cultures@SiliconValley*. Stanford, CA: Stanford University Press.

Feldman, S., & Buechler, S. (1998). Negotiating difference: Constructing selves and others in a transnational apparel manufacturing firm. *Sociological Quartely, 39*(4), 623–644.

Francesco, A. M., & Gold, B. A. (Eds.). (1998). *International organizational behavior*. Upper Saddle River, NJ: Prentice Hall.

Friedman, K. H., & Mertz, C. R. (1998). "Borderline" Sexual Harassment. *Hofstra Labor & Employment Law Journal, 15*(569), 1–42.

Gerstel, N., Clawson, D., & Zussman, R. (Eds.) (2002). *Families at work*. Nashville, TN: Vanderbilt University Press.

Glass, J. L., & Estes, S. B. (1997). The family responsive workplace. *Annual Review of Sociology, 23*, 289–313.

Glenn, E. N. (2001). Gender, race, and organization of reproductive labor. In R. Baldoz, C.

Koerber, & P. Kraft (Eds.), *The critical study of work* (pp. 71–82). Philadelphia, PA: Temple University Press.

Gottfried, H., & Graham, L. (1993). Constructing difference: The making of gendered subcultures in a Japanese automobile assembly plant. *Sociology, 27*(4), 611–628.

Gross, H. E. (2001). Work, family, and globalization: Broadening the scope of policy analysis. In R. Hertz & N. L. Marshall (Eds.), *Working families: The transformation of the American home* (pp. 187–206). Berkeley: University of California Press.

Haas, L., Hwang, P., & Russell, G. (Eds.). (2000). *Organizational change and gender equity: International Perspectives on fathers and mothers at the workplace.* Thousand Oaks, CA: Sage.

Halbfinger, D. M. (2003 July 10). Factory killer had a known history of anger and racial taunts. *New York Times*, p. A14.

Hertz, R., & Marshall, N. L. (Eds.). (2001). *Working families.* Berkeley: University of California Press.

Hochschild, A. R. (2000). The nanny chain. *The American Prospect, 11*(4), 1–7.

Hochschild, A. R. (2003). Love and gold. In B. Ehrenreich & A. R. Hochschild (Eds.), *Global woman: Nannies, maids, and sex workers in the new economy* (pp. 15–30). New York: Metropolitan Books.

Hofstede, G. (1991). *Cultures and organizations: Software of the mind.* London: McGraw-Hill Book Company.

Hondagneu-Sotelo, P. (2003). Blowups and other unhappy endings. In B. Ehrenreich & A. R. Hochschild (Eds.). *Global woman: Nannies, maids, and sex workers in the new economy* (pp. 55–69). New York: Metropolitan Books.

Hossfeld, K. J. (1990). Their logic against them: Contradictions in sex, race, and class in Silicon Valley. In K. Ward (Ed.), *Women Workers and Global Restructuring* (pp. 149–178). Ithaca, NY: ILR Press.

Jackson, S. E. (Ed.). (1992). *Diversity in the workplace: Human resources initiatives.* New York: Guilford Press.

Kelly, E. (1999). Theorizing corporate family policies: How advocates built "the business case" for "family-friendly" programs. *Research in the Sociology of Work, 7,* 169–202.

Kelly, E., & Dobbin, F. (1998). How affirmative action became diversity management. *American Behavioral Scientist, 41*(7), 960–984.

Kim, J. (2002). *Experiencing globalization: Production of ethncity, gender, and identity in Korean transnational corporations in the United States.* Ann Arbor, MI: Dissertation Abstracts International.

Konrad, A. M., & Linnehan, F. (1999). Affirmative action: History, effects, and attitudes. In G. N. Powell (Ed.), *Handbook of gender and work* (pp. 429–452). Thousand Oaks, CA: Sage.

Kossek, E. E., & Lobel, S. A. (Eds.). (1996). *Managing diversity: Human resource strategies for transforming the workplace.* Cambridge, MA: Blackwell.

Kubal, U. R. (1999). U.S. multinational corporations abroad: A comparative perspective on sex discrimination law in the United States and the European Union. *North Carolina Journal of International Law & Commerical Regulation, 25*(207), pp. 1–44.

Lewis, S. (1997). An international perspective on work-family issues. In S. Parasuraman & J. H. Greenhaus (Eds.), *Integrating work and family: Challenges and choices for a changing world* (pp. 91–103). Westport, CT: Praeger.

Lewis, S., & Lewis, J. (Eds.). (1996). *The work-family challenge: Rethinking employment.* London: Sage.

Lobel, S. A. (1999). Impacts of diversity and work-life initiatives in organizations. In G. N. Powell (Ed.), *Handbook of gender and work* (pp. 453–476). Thousand Oaks, CA: Sage.

Louie, M.C.Y. (2001). *Sweatshop warriors: Immigrant women workers take on the global factory.* Cambridge, MA: South End Press.

Lowe, L. (1996). *Immigrant acts: On Asian American cultural politics.* Durham, NC: Duke University Press.

Lui, D., & Boyle, E. H. (2001). Making the case: The women's convention and equal employment opportunity in Japan. *International Journal of Comparative Sociology, 42*(4), 389–404.

McMichael, P. (2000). *Development and social change: A global perspective* (2nd ed). Thousand Oaks, CA: Pine Forge Press.

Nussbaum, M. C. (2001). International human rights law in practice—India: Implementing sex equality through law. *Chicago Journal of International Law, 2*(35), 1–18.

Ong, A. (2003). *Buddha is hiding: Refugees, citizenship, and new America.* Berkeley: University of California Press.

Ore-Aguilar, G. (2000). Sexual harassment and human rights in Latin America. In A. K. Wing (Ed.), *Global critical race feminism* (pp. 362–376). New York: New York University Press.

O'Riain, S. (2000). Net-working for a living: Software developers in a global workplace. In M. Burawoy (Ed.), *Global ethnography: Forces, connections, and imaginations in a postmodern world* (pp. 175–202). Berkeley: University of California Press.

Parasuraman, S., & Greenhaus, J. H. (Eds.). (1999). *Integrating work and family.* Wesport, CT: Praeger.

Parcel, T. L., & Cornfield, D. B. (Eds.). (2000). *Work and family: Research informing policy.* Thousand Oaks, CA: Sage.

Parrenas, R. S. (2001). *Servants of globalization.* Stanford, CA: Stanford University Press.

Perrin, A. J. (1998). Economic transition in a company town: The politics of work and possibility in postindustrial Rochester. In D. Vannoy & P. J. Dubeck (Eds.), *Challenges for work and family in the twenty-first century* (pp. 93–110). New York: Aldine de Gruyter.

Poster, W. R. (2000). Challenges for work-family policy in global corporations: Lessons from high-tech companies in India and the United States. Paper presented at Work and Family: Expanding the Horizons, San Francisco.

Poster, W. R. (2002). Racialism, sexuality, and masculinity: Gendering 'global ethnography' of the workplace. *Social Politics, 9*(1), 126–158.

Poster, W. R. (2004). Constructing "diversity": A global corporation struggles with race, class, and gender in employment policy. Unpublished Manuscript, Department of Sociology, University of Illinois, Urbana.

Poster, W. R., & Prasad, S. (2005; forthcoming). Work-family relations in transnational perspective: A view from high tech firms in India and the U.S. *Social Problems, 52*(1).

Repak, T. A. (1995). *Waiting on Washington: Central American workers in the nation's capital.* Philadelphia: Temple University Press.

Saguy, A. C. (2000). Employment discrimination or sexual violence? Definining sexual harassment in American and French law. *Law and Society Review, 34*(1091), 1–29.

Sassen, S. (1998). *Globalization and its discontents.* New York: The New Press.

Saxenian, A. (2000). Networks of immigrant entrepreneurs. In C.-M. Lee, W. F. Miller, M. G. Hanock, & H. S. Rowen, *The Silicon Valley edge* (pp. 248–275). Stanford, CA: Stanford University Press.

Smith, V. (1997). New forms of work organization. *Annual Review of Sociology, 23,* 315–339.

Times of India. (2003, July 27). Sex charge: Indian sues Indian boss in U.S., pp. 1–3. Retrieved July 27, 2003, from http://www.timesofindia.com

Van der Veer, P. (2002). Techno-coolies: Flexible citizenship and transnational networks. In *ICTs and Indian development.* Bangalore, India: Indo-Dutch Programme on Alternatives in Development.

Vannoy, D., & Dubeck, P. J. (Eds.). (1998). *Challenges for work and family in the twenty-first century.* New York: Walter de Gruyter.

Wallace, M. (1998). Downsizing the American dream: Work and family at century's end. In D.

Vannoy & P. J. Dubeck (Eds.), *Challenges for work and family in the twenty-first century* (pp. 23–47). New York: Aldine de Gruyter.

Washwani, A. (2002, May 3). Muslims charge discrimination at Whirlpool plant in La Vergne. Retrieved February 23, 2004, from www.tennessean.com/local/archives/02/15/17022232.shtml

Weeden, K. (2000). Is there a Flexiglass ceiling? The impact of family friendly work schedules on career outcomes. Paper presented at Work and Family: Expanding the Horizons, San Francisco.

Wexler, S. (1997). Work/family policy stratification: The examples of family support and family leave. *Qualitative Sociology, 20*(2), 311–323.

Wharton, A. S., & Blair-Loy, M. (2002). The "overtime culture" in a global corporation: A cross-national study of finance professionals' interest in working part-time. *Work and Occupations, 29*(1), 32–63.

Zarembka, J. M. (2003). America's dirty work: Migrant maids and modern-day slavery. In B. Ehrenreich & A. R. Hochschild (Eds.), *Global woman: Nannies, maids, and sex workers in the new economy* (pp. 142–153). New York: Metropolitan Books.

18

The Role of Speaking Up in Work-Life Balancing

Amy C. Edmondson
Harvard University

James R. Detert
Pennsylvania State University

INTRODUCTION

This chapter explores how working people—especially parents and others with meaningful time-consuming outside commitments—can engage in open and constructive conversations in the organizations in which they work to promote effective balancing of work and family lives. We conceptualize the work-life balance issue as an ongoing process rather than as a state to be achieved, and we explore the challenges of speaking up in this balancing process. Our rationale for focusing on process starts with a conviction that tensions between work and nonwork demands are inevitable in the life of an employee, such that examining means of resolving periodic conflicts and imbalances may be as important as developing policies and structures to reduce them.

Our aim in this chapter is to build a bridge between research on speaking up in the workplace and the research on the relationship between work and family life reviewed and expanded in this volume. In sum, we seek to apply what we have learned about speaking up at work more generally to the specific issue of achieving healthy work-life balancing.

Over the past few years we have been studying how people perceive the interpersonal climate in their workplaces and how this affects their willingness to speak up. In field studies in several organizational contexts, we have found substantial differences across individuals and groups in people's willingness to speak up, such as to express concerns, share views, ask questions, or request assistance with a work or personal issue. Furthermore, we have found that individuals working closely together typically hold common perceptions about how easy or difficult it is to speak up in their organization. These perceptions are based on shared firsthand experiences and on secondhand stories, myths, and "urban legends" circulated among colleagues and coworkers.

Our research, along with that of others, has identified a set of individual, group, and organizational factors as critical antecedents of these perceptions (Crant, 2000; LePine & Van Dyne, 1998; Milliken, Morrison, & Hewlin, 2003; Morrison & Milliken, 2000; Scott & Bruce, 1994). In this chapter, we suggest that the research on speaking up in organizations can be applied usefully to the specific issue of work-life balance. Because reluctance to speak up is often associated with concerns about negative consequences, this chapter emphasizes the conflicts and tensions associated with work-life balancing rather than the potential for positive spillovers between work and nonwork domains (e.g., Edwards & Rothbard, 2000; Greenhaus & Beutell, 1985).

Individuals in organizations constantly face subtle interpersonal risks related to being and expressing themselves at work. Among the more challenging of these risks is asking for time off—that is, asking for personal time that may be perceived by bosses or peers as a lack of commitment to the organization or as a request to do less than one's fair share. This is both practical (promotions and other valued rewards may be dependent on impressions held by bosses and others) and socioemotional (we value others' approval and regard). Another challenging task is communicating to a boss that one has underutilized ideas or skills—such that neither the individual nor the organization is getting the most from the employment experience.

One solution for minimizing the risks of speaking up about difficult issues is to avoid doing it. The problem with this solution is, of course, that it does little to help individuals resolve their role conflicts or perceived need deprivations. Individuals who feel they cannot discuss time- or strain-based work-life conflicts continue to be conflicted (Greenhaus & Beutell, 1985), and those who feel they cannot discuss the nature of their job with bosses continue to compensate for deficiencies in one domain by seeking them in another (Edwards & Rothbard, 2000). Another solution, one that we argue is ultimately more functional for both employees and employers, is to create conditions in which a constructive dialogue can take place among employees and their bosses and peers about effectively balancing work and life commitments. The rationale for this approach is explored in this chapter.

This chapter thus summarizes our research on speaking up in organizations ranging from huge corporations to small community hospitals, and it applies these findings to the particular challenge of achieving balance between work and life commitments. In this way, we seek to connect to and complement the work-life research reviewed briefly in a later section of this chapter and more extensively in other chapters in this book. We take the point of view that understanding how people perceive the informal, interpersonal, and cultural environment in which they work presents a critical underpinning for understanding work-life imbalances and for helping individuals and organizations create a healthy balancing process. We theorize the role of speaking up in this balancing process, with attention to three levels of analysis—organizational, group, and individual. We pay particular attention to how informal rather than formal control mechanisms affect work-life balancing, as well as to the effects of leadership chains—a concept that captures the interplay of multiple layers of management above most employees. We conclude by suggesting directions for future research and ways organizational leaders at all levels may contribute to effective work-life balancing.

SPEAKING UP AT WORK: FREQUENT OPPORTUNITIES, PERVASIVE BARRIERS

Imagine an employee with something on her mind that matters greatly to her, is profoundly relevant to her work experiences, and may have important implications for others with whom she works, as well as for the organization. Logically, in this situation, speaking up seems both necessary and natural. Yet, as everyone who has ever held a job knows, it is not that simple. Our research has investigated conditions under which employees do speak up with relevant thoughts, concerns, or questions, as well as those under which most employees will choose to remain silent (whether based on solid evidence about likely outcomes, on second-guessing others' reactions, or on cognitive biases that inflate perceived risk levels). What we have found in a series of studies is that people speak up when they feel it is interpersonally safe to do so and when they believe speaking up will make a difference.

Psychological Safety: Is It Safe to Speak Up?

Exploring factors promoting team and organizational learning, Edmondson (1996; 1999; 2002) showed that an interpersonal climate of psychological safety enables individuals to contribute observations, ideas, and knowledge to collective work. Hospital-based nurses were more willing to speak up about drug errors when they believed that physicians, colleagues, and managers would not automatically penalize them for being associated with an error (Edmondson, 1996). Similarly, team members of all types—from executives to production workers—

in a manufacturing company were more willing to engage in learning behaviors such as admitting error, asking questions, and seeking help when they experienced psychological safety. These teams were also better performers (Edmondson, 1999). The mechanism driving performance outcomes in both settings was the ability of individuals to speak up easily and naturally about what they knew—as well as about what they didn't know.

In another knowledge-driven organization—a large research-intensive multinational corporation—senior management was deeply concerned by survey results revealing that half of the employees were reluctant to speak up or challenge traditional ways of doing things (Detert, 2003). To explore the underlying reasons that informants were willing or unwilling to speak up, Detert (2003) conducted extensive interviews across functions, job types, and organizational levels in this company. His findings revealed the pervasiveness of fear in the speaking up process at the individual level and suggested, as did Edmondson (1999) and Morrison and Milliken (2000), that the organization was comprised of some units riddled with climates of fear and silence and others units in which psychological safety and openness were the norm.

Across our combined inquiries, analyses of qualitative data consistently reveal that people weigh the consequences of speaking up in an asymmetrical manner. Whereas anticipated gains from speaking up are analytically and rationally considered, anticipated losses are viewed emotionally. Informants speak of anticipated harm in dramatic and vivid ways, probably exaggerating the nature of this harm. For example, senior executives in one corporation reported a risk of being "purged" from the company for saying the wrong thing (Edmondson, 2002). Similarly, a sales representative in another large corporation found that it was extremely difficult to speak up about needing time even for work-related tasks. As he reported, "Someone [in the meeting] basically got up and said we need more time off to catch up on administrative things. And I said [to myself], 'Oh, that's going to hurt. And, I'm glad *I* didn't say that, even though I wanted to' " (Detert, 2003). In telling this story, the informant seems less aware of what the actual consequences ended up being for the speaker than of his own internal drama in imagining what they might have been had he spoken up. Other research similarly finds the cognitive processing associated with voice decisions to be heavily affect-laden (especially with the emotion of fear) (Milliken et al., 2003).

Anticipated Gains: Is It Worthwhile to Speak Up?

In some cases, employees may view the workplace as safe for speaking up yet not believe doing so is worth the effort. Psychological safety is thus necessary but not sufficient; speaking up is effortful, and employees must anticipate their effort will make a difference. Consistent with previous theory and research (e.g., Ashford, Rothbard, Piderit, & Dutton, 1998; Milliken et al., 2003; Morrison & Milliken, 2000; Ryan & Oestreich, 1998; Withey & Cooper, 1989), Detert (2003) found that people fail to speak up at work in part because they do not believe speaking up will make a difference. Across all levels and types of work, employees reported concluding, based on their own and their coworkers' attempts over time, that it was not worth the effort to speak up with their views. As the following example from a manufacturing operator illustrates, employees who feel consistently snubbed when speaking up eventually stop doing so:

> [I]t would help if you saw them take your suggestions back to whomever and actually consider it, rather than just throw it in the trash bucket as soon as you walk out the door. I think that's the way a lot of people feel—you can speak in a meeting, you can tell your manager. It doesn't go any further. It doesn't help resolve issues.

In a study of cardiac surgery operating room teams, Edmondson (2003) reported that nurses and technicians who believed their input mattered to patient outcomes were willing to speak up with observations, concerns, and questions while learning to use a new technology. In those teams in which this relationship had not been emphasized by the cardiac surgeons leading the team, nonsurgeons reported far less willingness to speak up.

Motivation for Speaking Up

We have built on our own and others' research on voice to suggest a motivational model in which the decision to speak up or remain silent is the result of an informal calculus individuals tacitly make when confronted with such an opportunity (Detert & Edmondson, 2003). In this model, issues of psychological safety and utility are framed as perceived gains and losses among a set of fundamental human needs (e.g., existence, relatedness, and growth [Alderfer, 1972]). We suggest that actual voice behavior occurs when an individual estimates his or her net state of need satisfaction will be increased by speaking up.

This model of cognitive and affective underpinnings of speaking up is consistent with research on risk perceptions. For example, research has found that individuals tend to assess quickly and effortlessly the interpersonal risk associated with a given behavior in their workplace before deciding what to say and do—and what not to say and do (Edmondson, 1999; Tetlock, 1999). That is, individuals weigh a potential action against the particular interpersonal costs, rhetorically asking, "If I say this, will I be hurt, embarrassed, or criticized?" A negative answer to this question allows one to speak. Although future research to understand better the cognitive and affective underpinnings of employee voice may take many directions, we focus in particular on understanding the role that fear plays in speaking up about sensitive topics. In our work and others (e.g., Milliken et al., 2003), fear emerges over and over as the most powerful emotion dictating whether an employee will speak up or remain silent. Whether such emotions lead to accurate or objective reads of a person's environment for speaking up is immaterial to their influence on behavior—when the emotion of fear takes over, organizational silence is a likely form of the psychological equivalent of the physiological "fight or flight" response (Frijda, 1986).

An individual's tacit estimation of the gains and losses that may follow an episode of speaking up, as well as the valence attached to these gains and losses, depend on individual differences (e.g., personality or previous work experiences) and on factors in the environment in which he or she is embedded. Habits of outspokenness, reticence, or conformity take shape over time—influenced in part by personal history, but as or more importantly, also by the behavior of colleagues and by other salient organizational signals. This explains why an action that might be unthinkable in one work group can be readily taken in another (e.g., announcing, "I am off to a Little League game; I'll be working late tomorrow to make up for it") (Detert, 2003; Edmondson, 2003).

One of the most ubiquitous—and potentially alterable—influences on anticipated gains and losses from speaking up is leadership behavior. Although it is difficult to alter individual personality traits or dispositions, leaders can take a number of steps to change factors that shape employee beliefs about outcomes of voice behavior.

Leadership Influences on Speaking Up

The behavior of leaders—a term we use to refer to anyone in a position of formal authority for one or more subordinates, whether a first level supervisor or the CEO—is a particularly salient force in shaping beliefs about speaking up. First, employees are particularly aware of leaders' behavior compared with that of peers (Tyler & Lind, 1992). They have regular firsthand experiences with their immediate supervisors. If a supervisor is supportive and coaching-oriented and has nondefensive responses to questions and challenges, members are likely to conclude that the workplace constitutes a safe environment for speaking up (Edmondson, 2003). In contrast, if leaders act in authoritarian or punitive ways, people are likely to fear the consequences of speaking up (Detert, 2003; Edmondson, 1996; Ryan & Oestreich, 1998).

Supervisor behavior also affects employee perceptions about the utility of speaking up: When supervisors regularly take action on concerns brought to their attention or serve as a link pin between the employee and higher levels of management when necessary (Likert, 1961), employees are more likely to view speaking up in positive terms. Conversely, when employees have direct supervisors whom they perceive not to take action on their concerns, they are likely to perceive the effort as futile.

Recent research suggests expanding theory beyond the effect of supervisors and team leaders to include the influence of *leadership chains* on speaking up (Detert, 2003). With support from qualitative and quantitative data, Detert (2003) shows that employees' speaking up beliefs and behaviors are affected not only by immediate supervisors but also by their supervisor's boss, and so on, to the top of the organization. Although the relative effects of different levels of management on employees varied from site to site depending on the nature of the work, the effects of a leadership chain of influence were unmistakable.

Leaders higher than direct supervisors have both direct effects on employees (e.g., a manufacturing employee may conclude that the plant manager is not genuinely interested in hearing workers' views in an all-employee forum) and indirect effects, such as when a leader's behavior (outspokenness, curiosity, directness, empathy) is taken as symbolic of what is appropriate within the organization. Leadership modeling, whether conscious or unconscious, leads others to act similarly, especially in interactions with subordinates and peers, which influences the climate at multiple organizational levels. For example, several years ago, the executive group of a prominent Japanese automotive manufacturer mandated that, going forward, senior managers would be required to take their total allotted vacation times. Realizing that manufacturing employees and engineers throughout the company were not taking vacations due to the power of the informal message sent by senior managers' behavior—that committed employees do not take vacations—the group sought to ameliorate the problem. Unless executives started to demonstrate that taking vacations was acceptable, lower level employees were not going to take theirs, whatever the formal policies.[1] The power of distal leadership influences on behavior is also captured in constructs such as "perceived organizational support" (Scott & Bruce, 1994; Zhou & George, 2001) and "context favorability" (Ashford et al., 1998).

Summary

A critical component of the work of managers is to create conditions in which people are able to contribute their skills and experiences to collective work. Our past research has focused on a particular aspect of this contribution–speaking up behavior. In the next section of this chapter, we examine factors affecting an employee's ability to nurture a healthy work-life relationship that stems from the premise that an ability to speak up at work plays a central role in this process. Our discussion focuses on the informal aspects of organizational life as impediments to successful balancing, because we find that the tacit forms of social control in organizations are more subtle and harder to address than the formal dimensions of control embedded in systems, policies, and procedures.

WORK-LIFE BALANCING

Looking Back: The Challenge and Past Research

In the past few decades, factors such as economic necessity and greater gender parity in the workforce have led to increasing numbers of dual-income families, in turn giving rise to more people attempting to balance the demands of work and family life. Incompatible conflicts that individuals experience between family and work roles run in two reciprocal directions: when work interferes with family life (work-to-family conflict) and when family obligations interfere with work (family-to-work conflict), (e.g., Greenhaus & Beutell, 1985). Most research has focused on work-to-family conflict and conceptualized these challenges as interrole conflicts. Other work has clarified the nature of these conflicts and identified "linking mechanisms" by which the two spheres of life are connected (Edwards & Rothbard, 2000).

Conceptualizing work-family interrelationships in terms of role conflicts has allowed researchers to hypothesize and test consequences (generally presumed to be negative) associated with the role strains associated with trying to juggle multiple demands simultaneously. In a recent review of 67 empirical work-family conflict articles published from 1982 to 1999, Allen, Herst, Bruck, and Sutton (2000) identified substantial work-related, nonwork-related, and stress-related outcomes of work-family conflict. Kossek and Ozeki (1998) conducted a meta-analysis of 50 studies focused on the relationship between work-family conflicts and job and life satisfaction. Despite the typical difficulties associated with such analyses (e.g., differences in sample demographics, measurement disparities), their results indicated that work-family conflict is significantly associated with lower levels of job and life satisfaction. In sum, it seems clear that higher work-family conflict is related to undesirable outcomes for both individuals and organizations.

To address these growing concerns, many organizations have implemented *formal* policies designed to reduce employee work-life conflicts and the associated negative outcomes. This has most commonly taken the form of new or extended benefits, such as the provision of on-site child care, support for education, and short-term leave policies for the care of ill or elderly family members. Ideally, such material supports and the existence of formal policies allow employees more flexibility in integrating across multiple roles and, indeed, Kossek and Ozeki (1998) found that job satisfaction is enhanced when individuals both have access to and are able to use a variety of work-family benefits. If judged in terms of formal policies and material supports, many organizations are clearly more supportive today than 10 or 20 years ago. Are employees therefore feeling better about their ability to manage competing demands? Recent research suggests not really.

As Lambert (1995, p. 136) reports, "There are growing concerns that family-responsive policies in the workplace . . . are under-utilized, inequitably distributed, and under-valued." Similarly, Kossek, Noe, and DeMarr (1999, p. 103) concluded, "Adoption of formal supports does not guarantee a family-friendly workplace." Citing work by Solomon (1994) and Blum, Fields, and Goodman (1994), Kossek and colleagues (1999) argue that work-family policy use generally lags potential value and that policies may have more public relations benefit for the company than actual benefit for workers. Lambert's (1995) research documents that workers with lower occupational status, lower income, and of minority descent are particularly likely to have used fewer benefits. A 2002 "workplace wellness survey" of over 1,400 Americans by Oxford Health Plans found that one in six employees said he or she "often miss[es] personal family activities due to [his or her] job" and that he or she is "unable to use up [his or her] vacation time due to demands at work." These findings were fairly consistent across the gender, age, and overall lifestyle characteristics of their random sample.

These findings suggest that corporate attention to formal policies is not enough to help employees achieve better work-life balance (Kofodimos, 1995; Kossek et al., 1999). Continued research focused narrowly on the provision and outcomes of formal policies also is unlikely to further the cause of employee work-life balance efforts. (Thompson, Beauris, & Lyness, 1999) have even argued that formal benefits and programs instituted without accompanying changes in workplace climate may negatively impact workers. We thus argue that greater attention to *informal* aspects of organizational life as influences on the use and perceived utility of *formal* work-life balance supports is likely to prove fruitful for the field. In the remainder of this chapter, we explore related possibilities, placing particular emphasis on the impact that informal control systems have on individuals' ability to speak up about work-life issues. First, we clarify our view of the work-life balance issue; then we call for integrated research that investigates relationships among work policies, reduced conflicts, and job and life satisfaction.

Looking Forward: From Balance to Balancing

Because the notion of *work-life balance* may obscure the dynamic nature of the ongoing balancing act carried out by an employee with substantial nonwork commitments, we conceptualize this important challenge as a *balancing process* rather than as a state to be realized. Like the tasks of *synthesizing* work-family roles or *managing* boundaries (Kossek et al., 1999), work-life *balancing* is an ongoing job, one that can be consciously managed by employees and employers. The process is necessarily—although rarely explicitly so—an ongoing negotiation between employee and employer. Both parties in this negotiation have needs and both have something to offer. Far too often, however, the negotiation is not explicit, such that potentially better solutions to the default balance (or imbalance) of work and life remain undiscovered. For example, an employing organization might benefit most from having high quality work accomplished, while an employee believes that what really matters is "face time." Explicit discussion could reveal exactly what constitutes the expected quality and/or quality of work and to what extent it matters when and where it is done.

Summary

Recent attention in work-life research to informal aspects of organizational life is likely to enhance our understanding of both the balancing process and how to improve it but the research is limited by a lack of specificity about what informal aspects of organizational life matter in this process.

To some extent, this is the nature of the phenomenon. Whereas *formal* control mechanisms in organizations are relatively explicit and easy to specify (e.g., organizational charts depicting the hierarchy of authority, formal job descriptions, formal contracts specifying hours or outputs owed, written policies on individual and family benefits), *informal* control mechanisms (e.g., culture, climate, group norms, shared cognitive maps) in organizations are by their very nature less explicit and visible (Barker, 1993; O'Reilly & Chatman, 1996). Many informal control mechanisms, such as group norms, arise naturally in social systems as a result of spontaneous interaction among people, such that people do not even realize their behavior is being guided by such forces under most circumstances (Berger & Luckmann, 1966; Bettenhausen & Murnighan, 1985; Gersick & Hackman, 1990; O'Reilly, Chatman, & Caldwell, 1991).

Even when organizational leaders deliberately introduce informal controls, such as by communicating shared values, it is not necessarily the case that people are aware of the influence this has on their subsequent behavior (Chatman & Jehn, 1994; O'Reilly, Chatman, & Caldwell, 1991). The influence of informal controls generally is seen as serving positive purposes (e.g., providing motivation, meaning, and community at work); however, research has also identified negative consequences of informal controls (e.g., excessive peer pressure [Barker, 1993] and unflattering interpersonal attributions [Cha & Edmondson, 2004; Isaacs, 1992]).

INFORMAL INFLUENCES ON SPEAKING UP IN WORK-LIFE BALANCING

We next examine three levels of analysis at which informal controls may affect work-life balancing. Some informal controls influence individuals throughout an organization whereas others apply only to smaller, embedded groups in an organization. We begin by describing informal factors at the *organization*-level, then move to *group*-level influences, followed by those embedded in *individual*-level cognition. We then discuss how these informal influences at multiple levels affect three specific tasks involved in employee work-life balancing (or lack thereof).

Organizational Influences

The *culture* or *climate* of the organization constitutes the most studied informal controls in the literature (James & Jones, 1974; Martin, 1992; Schein, 1992).[2] Consistent with Jepperson and Swidler (1994), we view culture as a metaconcept comprised of at least four major subconcepts or elements: *values* (choice statements that rank behavior or goals), *beliefs* (existential statements about how the world operates that often serve to justify values and norms), *norms* (specifications of values relating to interaction behavior), and *expressive symbols* (all material aspects of culture) (Hofstede, Neuijen, Ohayv, & Sanders, 1990; Peterson, 1979; Pettigrew, 1990; Schein, 1992). A view of culture comprised of these four elements takes into account the ideational (values and beliefs), behavioral (norms), and material (expressive symbols) aspects of culture (Hall & Neitz, 1993).

Although the relationship among these elements of culture, and the priority of each, continue to be debated and studied empirically, it is instructive to think of these aspects of culture as layered like an onion (Hofstede et al., 1990). That is, the material aspects of culture and the behavioral norms are the most visible and tangible part of culture but may not be the most accurate representation of the essence of the phenomenon. At the core of an organization's culture, we find values and basic assumptions (or taken-for-granted beliefs), which constitute the essence of the informal influences on behavior in the organization (Schein, 1992).

Values, beliefs, behaviors, and the meaning attached to symbols must be *shared* by an identifiable group of individuals to be considered informal social control mechanisms (Cooke & Rousseau, 1988; Gordon & DiTomaso, 1992). An individual's unique personal habits or fragmented, ambiguous views of what is or is not acceptable within an organization do not constitute informal control mechanisms because they are not a clear, external signal that individuals use to determine their own beliefs or behavior. To be the "social glue" that binds the organization (Smircich, 1983) and informally guides behavior within it, elements of the informal control system must be by definition those elements of organizational life that are shared by enough members to lead to relative homogeneity in beliefs and/or practices.

The literature on corporate culture presumes that key elements of the informal system are shared and internalized by members of the entire organization (Collins & Porras, 1994; Deal & Kennedy, 1982; Kotter & Heskett, 1992). This unitary view of culture places great emphasis on the role of top leaders, because it is their behavior that is taken as most symbolic of what the organization stands for when formal policies are insufficient for resolving day-to-day ambiguities about appropriate beliefs or behavior (Conger, 2000; Meindl, Ehrlich, & Dukerich, 1985; Schein, 1992). For example, many types of workers are not subject to formal policies about leaving work early to attend a child's occasional school activity. Thus, the example set by leaders creates an informal signal of what is possible and appropriate. For example, Detert (2003) noted the power of a leader in shaping employees' beliefs about work-life balancing. As one informant described it:

> A particular leader tried to share with us some things he does as far as work-life balance, and he gave an example of attending some event of his child's at 2:00 on a Friday afternoon. He said, "You know what? This was important to me, I walked out of work. I didn't tell anybody. I just went. And I felt good about doing that. But I also wanted to tell you that I worked Saturday and Sunday of that same weekend, eight hours each day." So here it was—this kind of work-life balance story—and the message that was perceived by the audience was that it's OK to do something personal during business hours, but make sure you make up that time, *and then some*, over the weekend.

Whether for description or prediction, culture can be analyzed in terms of both specific content and strength. Regarding content, cultures or climates can be described along generic dimensions—such as ideas about the basis of truth and rationality, about time, about human motivation, and about control and coordination of work (Detert, Schroeder, & Mauriel, 2000; Schein, 1992)—or along more specific dimensions seen as particularly relevant to a given organization (e.g., climate for voice or silence [Morrison & Milliken, 2000]; climate for service [Schneider, 1990]; climate for error management [Van Dyck, 2000]). When thinking about work-life balancing, deep beliefs about time, orientation to work, and responsibility are particularly salient, as are beliefs about collaboration, because interdependence affects the balancing effort. In a rare empirical study of relationships between specific dimensions of climate and work-family outcomes, Kossek, Colquitt, and Noe (2001) found that "work climate for sharing" and "work climate for sacrifice" predict (above all other independent variables) employee perceptions of work-family conflict, family-work conflict, and well-being.

Consistent with the view that a culture or climate represents that which is widely shared, the most commonly employed definitions of culture *strength* involve agreement (Collins & Porras, 1994; Gordon & DiTomaso, 1992; Koene, Boone, & Soeters, 1997; Zammuto & Krakower, 1991). Kotter and Heskett (1992, p. 15), for example, argue, "In a strong corporate culture, almost all managers share a set of relatively consistent values and methods of doing business." Likewise, Deal and Kennedy (1982, p. 14) assert that in strong culture companies values were shared by the employees, and managers "talked about these beliefs openly and without embarrassment; [and] they didn't tolerate deviance from the company standards." For Cooke and Szumal (1993), it is shared, highly crystallized behavioral norms that indicate a strong culture. But whatever component of culture is considered most important (e.g., values or behavioral norms), there is agreement among these authors that it is the degree of "shar-edness" that defines a strong organizational culture.

Many have argued that strong cultures characterize higher-performing orga-nizations. This link is explained by three mechanisms: *goal-alignment* (a strong culture helps employees march to the same drummer), *motivation* (strong cul-tures motivate effort because people want to belong), and *efficiency* (strong cul-tures provide needed structure and controls without having to rely on stifling and cumbersome formal bureaucracies) (Kotter & Heskett, 1992; Sorensen, 2002). Deal and Kennedy (1982) assert that lower level managers make "mar-ginally better decisions" as a result of a shared culture.

Strong cultures also may have a downside. Highly crystallized, shared infor-mal systems are likely to be hard to change. Thus, internalized norms about how nonwork demands are to be treated at work may be extremely resistant to change. Implementing change in a strong culture organization that has tradi-tionally not been focused on work-life balancing for employees is likely to be difficult. To illustrate, in ethnographic research in a high-technology corporation, Kunda (1992) described the intense corporate phenomenon of informal control over employees' beliefs about the company and about appropriate behavior. In this strong culture, wreckage from one's personal life (e.g., a divorce) was dis-cussed as a (positive) symbol of commitment to the organization and its goals. It is likely that efforts (even efforts of senior leaders) to create a more flexible or balanced company position on the boundaries between work and nonwork would be require more energy and persistence in such an organization than in one in which the informal systems are less strong, even if the weaker culture is similarly lacking in balance at the outset.

Group-Level Influences

By the mid-1980s, many researchers were beginning to question to notion that organizations were comprised of a single, unitary culture. Substantial evidence has since accrued to dispel the myth that all members of a large organization share similar values and beliefs or attach similar meanings to their behaviors or to symbols (see Martin, 1992, for a review). In short, organizations have sub-cultures, or "socially segregated sub-universes of meaning," because the com-plexity of organizational life leads to a "shared core universe" and "different partial universes coexisting in a state of mutual accommodation" (Berger & Luckmann, 1966). An organizational subculture exists when a subpopulation of an organization's membership shares a subset of similar beliefs about what is important and similar norms about appropriate attitudes and behaviors that differ in content from beliefs and norms regarding those issues held by other sub-populations. Thus, organizational subpopulations "often carve out of the same reality somewhat different islands of meaning" (Zerubavel, 1997), and different subpopulations within an organization actually experience different slices of objective reality.

Patterns of communication within an organization help explain the formation and perpetuation of subcultures. Structural and technological arrangements that result in frequent communication among certain groups of workers (Greenberg, 1999; Trice & Beyer, 1993) and infrequent communication between these and other groups of workers (Cooke & Rousseau, 1988; Hofstede, 1998; Martin, 1992; Wilkins & Ouchi, 1983) lead to distinct subcultures. The nature of technologies and the ways in which groups of workers are rewarded also give rise to subcultures. For example, when self-managed work teams are rewarded as a group for output and quality, it is likely that the teams will develop specific subcultural identities as they coordinate their efforts (Barker, 1993). Subcultures also form based on similar personal or background characteristics of members (Chatman, Polzer, Barsade, & Neale, 1998; Trice, 1993), similar levels or types of knowledge or training of workers (Hofstede, 1998; Trice & Beyer, 1993), similar occupational or professional orientation (Trice, 1993; Van Maanen & Barley, 1984), or other shared experiences (particularly anxieties) that lead certain members to joint coping (Trice & Beyer, 1993). Once formed, subcultures may become as difficult to change as the larger organizationwide culture, because the very "rightness" of local "habitual routines" means members often miscode or ignore information that indicates change is needed or consciously resist change based on its implied threat to a crucial part of their individual or collective identity (Bettenhausen & Murnighan, 1985; Gersick & Hackman, 1990).

Applied to understanding work-life balancing, this earlier research suggests that individuals will find themselves embedded at the most proximate level in a group setting with informal norms for behavior related to how much to work, where to work, and how to behave when conflicted by demands from multiple roles. Whether local subcultures enhance, are neutral to, or conflict with those of the broader organizational culture is an empirical question (Martin & Siehl, 1983) with important implications for work-life balancing efforts. For example, the negative impact of an organization culture that is not conducive to employee balancing may be partially or almost totally offset by membership in a local group with norms highly supportive of such efforts. For example, in one hospital setting—not known for work-life balance—a nurse reported that a critical reason she was happy in her job was that her own supervisor was exceptionally supportive of her and her coworkers' efforts to balance work and life: "[My supervisor] is very aware of our personal lives in a good way—she helps her staff balance the things they have going on in their life" (Tucker, 2003). Conversely, well-intentioned senior executives may fail to realize that their pronouncements (and even behaviors) regarding work-life balancing are being strongly diluted by team-level leaders who model or demand the opposite.[3]

Informal control mechanisms are powerful shaping forces in organizational behavior because they are rooted in the shared values and beliefs that constitute the core of organizational and group-level cultures. However, because work-life balancing is ultimately dependent on the actions of individuals, it is important to be clear about the link between organizational and group influences and individual cognition. In the following sections we discuss how values and beliefs come to be shared and internalized, in general, and propose three specific processes critical to understanding how informal control mechanisms influence whether an individual is more or less successful in balancing work and life concerns.

Individual Cognition

Over the course of a day, an individual is confronted with innumerable stimuli from the external world. The processing of these stimuli (including determining which to attend to and which to ignore) is accomplished using a "cognitive knowledge structure," which consists of interdependent schemas for particular concepts, entities, and events (Harris, 1994; Walsh, 1995). These knowledge structures allow individuals to orient themselves by comparing new stimuli to previously encountered stimuli. Under most circumstances, people employ such knowledge structures automatically, meaning they remain unaware of the cognitive processing as it occurs and shapes a behavioral response. Such processing is efficient (we would be paralyzed by stimuli overload if we were required to process all of it consciously), but it is also the reason why much behavior is habitual or routinized. Automatic processing is thus a double-edged sword— necessarily efficient and useful for handling well-known stimuli but potentially error-generating when used to process novel stimuli.

An individual's cognitive knowledge structure is partly unique and partly shared. Informal control mechanisms exist precisely because individuals who interact frequently develop over time large areas of convergence in knowledge structures. This similarity, or "cognitive consensuality" (Gioia & Sims, 1986), is the result of shared experiences and of emergent shared meaning of these experiences (Berger & Luckmann, 1966; Salancik & Pfeffer, 1978; Walsh, 1995). Thus, a cultural or subcultural belief becomes an informal *social* control mechanism as coworkers respond in a predictable way to a given stimulus.

A telling example is found in academia. In recent decades the percentage of women in tenure-track positions has risen dramatically. A growing number of administrators have adopted policies (e.g., extended tenure timetables) to accommodate the needs of women who are mothers. Evidence suggests that many of these women feel these formal policies are largely ineffective, because they continue to feel informally controlled by their male colleagues who judge them using an outdated set of schemas about what "real academics" should do (Bailyn,

2003). It is more likely that men are automatically and unconsciously using schemas that lead to continued inequitable treatment of women than consciously choosing to discriminate against their female colleagues (Bailyn, 2003). Understanding this cultural norm of academe, many women forgo having children (either during their tenure-track years or entirely) or in other ways act as much like the "male model" as they can (e.g., sticking to the same tenure clock as their male counterparts). Many who stay within the academic system feel continuously conflicted about their work-life balance, and many who might be outstanding contributors opt out because of its insidious informal controls over behavior.

To extend these ideas to work-life balancing more generally, we posit three processes by which informal control mechanisms in an organization affect individuals at the cognitive level. In each case, we provide illustrations drawn from various empirical contexts that demonstrate how an individual's beliefs and behaviors related to work-life issues are influenced by forces having little to do with the formal structures and policies of the organization.

Individual Sense Making. The process of forming knowledge structures involves "making sense" of the world in which one finds oneself (Weick, 1995). When faced with ambiguous situations, rather than ones in which formal rules or internal values provide clear guidance about how to behave, what cues do individuals attend to in their organizational sense-making activities? Clearly, individuals look for cues in informal channels—for example, in the behavior of leaders, who are likely to be seen as symbolizing the organization's desired response. In one strikingly hierarchical organization we studied, individuals looked to the words and actions of the most senior managers for guidance in how to think about time off from work:

> People can look at [Senior Manager A] and his position and say, "Wow, there he is, there he sits." So when he comes to a group of managers in a managers' meeting and says, "Let me show you how I achieved some things in my work-life balance blend. For example, if I'm taking the red-eye home, I'm playing golf the next day. I'm not going into the office." Then people go, "Wow, right." So if that's the environment and that's what's encouraged, if I'm working hard and I need to take time out for myself, then I'm going to do that too.

Untested Acceptance of Individual Sense Making. The influence of individual sense making on behavior is lasting, in part because we rarely test our privately derived interpretations. Particularly when social controls are pervasive, such as in strong culture organizations, initial impressions are internalized and remain unquestioned (O'Reilly & Chatman, 1996). Stated alternatively, informal controls lead quickly to automatic (largely unconscious, unreflective) processing. This is particularly true when the content conveyed includes the notion that the implicit interpretations or norms themselves are not discussable (Argyris, 1977).

The following example from the finance group in the large multinational firm we studied illustrates both how individual sense making is influenced by informal mechanisms and how an impression of expectations about working hours, once formed, is not tested for its accuracy:

> [Interviewer's question: Does your manager verbalize his expectations for you and others?] No, no. I mean, it's almost you get a sense. It's kind of like the corporate culture. It's like when you come in and you work from 8:00 to 5:00, but then it's almost like an eye looking if you get up—if you're the first one to get up at 5:00 to head to the door. So then you kind of out-compete each other and wait and see who is going to leave first. And it's 7:00, it's 8:00 at night and it's like . . .

The example suggests that this employee not only has internalized a view of what is expected within her work culture in regard to the length of the workday itself but also that she fails to envision a possibility of verbally questioning or challenging (e.g., getting up and leaving) the dysfunctional norm.

Other research suggests that the more established an organization or a work group within it, the more likely it is that informal norms are deeply internalized by members and therefore less open to testing. Gersick and Hackman (1990) argue that beyond the initial period of formation, groups are unlikely to discuss or test their norms with the exception of a small window during the midpoint of a specific task.

For ongoing groups, or for organizations as a whole, we question whether midcourse testing occurs unless explicitly built into the system. Barker (1993) found that early in the development of team self-management, team members openly discussed and resolved work-life balancing conflicts each time they emerged. Early on, these teams explicitly negotiated when to do overtime work and in which situations they would allow a worker to leave early (e.g., so one team member could forgo the overtime to attend a child's school play). Over time, however, these discussions resulted in solidified shared values and then behavioral norms, such that the norms became rigid (albeit still informal) rules about working overtime whenever necessary: "The blue team's agreement to work overtime to meet customer needs was not a one-time quick fix; it became a pattern that team members would follow as similar situations arose" (Barker, 1993, p. 422). Thus, what began as individual and collective sense making through active means became a passive process of following the rules about how to deal with work-life conflicts.

Proactive Influencing: Engaging in an Ongoing Dialogue. In conceptualizing work-life balancing as on ongoing process, we propose that a critical issue for both individuals and organizations is ensuring that informal norms (at group and organizational levels) allow and encourage the questioning and challenging of these norms. Employees are more likely to be satisfied with their balancing efforts if the culture of their organization allows them to describe their work-life conflicts openly (Kossek et al., 2001), seeking clarification if possible, and to describe any perceived inconsistency between formal policies or espoused values and enacted values (i.e., values-in-use) (Argyris & Schon, 1974). For example, the nurse mentioned earlier was able to raise the issue of nonwork commitments with her supervisor, facilitating her own balancing process.

In the organizations we studied, it was not uncommon for employees to say the organization "talks a good story" about work-life balance but actually has no process in place for working through or negotiating the difficult tensions between work and life roles. As the following example illustrates, hearing a senior manager espouse his support for work-life balance may be heartening but ultimately hollow if there are no mechanisms in place to translate general pronouncements into workable solutions:

> At the end of this meeting, [a senior vice president] said something about work-life balance that's an example of 'I have no clue what you're talking about.' I think he genuinely feels that that's what he wants for us—we're obviously stressing. Stressing and tired and scrambling. But I would like to know what he meant by work-life balance, especially when I have no control over my territory or what I do.

Given the pervasive level of fear we have identified related to speaking up in ways that might challenge leaders about how the organization is run, it is not surprising when employees do not initiate dialogue to help translate general pronouncements or formal policies into workable solutions. Neither testing one's perceptions nor engaging in constructive dialogue is made easier by the potential dominance of informal rather than formal influences on work-life balancing. In contrast, it may be especially difficult to create constructive dialogue about informal impediments to work-life balance because they are hard to pin down, often related to power differences and rarely amenable to quick, efficient fixes. Nonetheless, this dialogue is likely to be an essential part of achieving greater balancing.

Engaging in an ongoing dialogue about work-life balancing—including explicit testing of one's assumptions about what is and is not acceptable—is thus a strategy for dealing with the complexities of negotiating the multiple needs and offerings that together constitute a healthy work-life balancing act. At the same time, it is not an easy or simple solution but one that takes trial and error, practice, and considerable interpersonal skill and confidence.

IMPLICATIONS FOR RESEARCH
AND PRACTICE

Opportunities for Research

To advance and test the ideas put forward in this chapter, systematic research is needed to investigate cultural and other informal influences—organizational and group—on work-life balancing behavior. Field-based quasiexperiments (Cook & Campbell, 1979) seem an especially promising approach. In cases where organizations already have extensive formal work-life policies/benefits in place, research might begin with an investigation of usage patterns. This could include surveys of employees, with interviews or focus groups to supplement these data and find out what employees see as hindering them from using (or being satisfied with) existing policies or benefits. Our prediction is that numerous informal pressures, including leader behavior across multiple organizational levels, would be commonly identified as key barriers to employee use and satisfaction with the organization's formal mechanisms for assisting in work-life balancing.

With this information, the organization could undertake a quasiexperiment. In the most simple design, some units would undertake interventions specifically targeted toward reducing informal barriers, improving leader modeling and supportive behaviors, and helping all employees learn and practice new speaking up skills, while appropriately matched units would continue to have the same formal policies and benefits available to employees without interventions. A more complex design might have multiple treatment conditions, such that the effects of specific interventions (e.g., leadership coaching) could be assessed and compared. Given the overdetermined nature of employee silence, our intuition is that any single intervention will be less effective than a comprehensive program aimed at reducing the informal barriers to work-life balancing efforts.

In organizations lacking extensive formal policies, this research design could be modified to investigate the effects of adding new policies. Again, we would recommend qualitative research to understand not only which additional programs employees desire but also what they see as the barriers to using them. Using the logic of a quasiexperiment, new policies would be formally instituted across all units while the additional interventions on informal influences would be applied only to the treatment groups. Assessments in future periods would provide evidence of the effects of the organization's informal systems on the success of formal work-life programs.

This approach has the potential for new insights about causality and mechanisms through which effective balancing may occur. First, research into the implicit, subtle aspects of the work-life domain will require qualitative data. An *emic* design that uncovers employee beliefs can help shed light on how people view the challenges and conflicts they face in the work-life balancing process. Insights thus developed can inform interventions to address perceived barriers to balance. Second, quasiexperimental research is necessarily longitudinal, which may lead to a better understanding of causality than can the quantitative, cross-sectional research usually conducted in this domain.

We also suggest that research on the impact of informal influences on employees' balancing efforts should be multilevel. As the illustrations in this chapter have demonstrated, employees' beliefs and behaviors related to work-life concerns are affected by both immediate supervisors and distal leaders. Cultural and subcultural influences also reach across organizational levels. At a minimum, well-designed culture research should include a clear specification of the levels of analysis involved (Chao, 2000) and allow for the separation of the effects of individual dispositions/background/personality from higher level phenomena (e.g., a group's informal norms, a division-level culture, senior management culture) (Klein, Dansereau, & Hall, 1994). Hierarchical linear modeling (also known as multilevel or random coefficient modeling) (Bryk & Raudenbush, 1992; Kreft & deLeeuw, 1998) is a powerful technique for such analysis once the content (e.g., specific leadership behaviors, climate dimensions) of higher level influences has been identified and appropriate statistical evidence has demonstrated respondent agreement (i.e., sharing of beliefs, unstated assumptions, or meanings) at the desired level of aggregation (Bliese, 2000). This will require data from more than a small sample of executives or human resources personnel.

Finally, future research should incorporate moderating variables and mediating processes. A full discussion of these is beyond the present scope, but we hypothesize that the content or substance of the issue at hand (e.g., speaking up about *how much* to work versus *where* to work), the frequency of speaking up by the individual in question, and demographic characteristics of both parties (and perhaps of their unit as a whole) involved in a work-life balancing situation are among the potential moderators of relationships between informal influences and work-life balancing actions and outcomes. Similarly, the processes and mechanisms for speaking up may mediate such relationships.

Implications for Practice

A number of implications for management can be discussed briefly in advance of the completion of further research. First, training in communication skills may help employees and managers discuss work-life issues more constructively. Though leaders are responsible for setting the right tone, employees share responsibility for testing their sense making and their assumptions about the outcomes of speaking up. This does not imply that individuals should be required to take major risks to check their assumptions (e.g., retesting the safety of speaking up at a meeting where one repeatedly sees others crucified) without being met part way by leaders. It does imply that individuals should gather data on what happens when speaking up to a specific leader (e.g., testing the utility of speaking up even when one has heard that this leader never does anything anyway). A discussion of specific training programs are beyond the scope of this chapter, but stated generally most employees could probably benefit from training in constructive, persistent speaking up, and real-time opportunities to practice these skills in a safe environment (Argyris & Schon, 1974; Edmondson & Woolley, 2003).

Second, leaders must learn to "walk the talk" with regard to work-life issues. As noted throughout this chapter, leaders who say one thing and do another (e.g., espouse support for work-life balance but never take vacations themselves or unconsciously punish those who do) have a profound influence on subordinates' own beliefs and behaviors. Similarly, some leaders who do take steps to balance their work and nonwork commitments nonetheless fail to verbalize their actions in ways that make them seem acceptable or feasible for subordinates. In general, such leadership behaviors represent a misalignment between the espoused values of leaders (and the organization) and the values-in-use (Argyris & Schon, 1974; Schein, 1992). Interventions to help leaders get upward feedback about such misalignment and to act to eliminate such mixed signaling include internal processes and possibly external resources such as executive coaching.

Finally, formal organizational systems and policies (beyond work-life programs specifically) must support and enhance the desired informal norms. Expecting employees to speak up about work-life issues when formal and informal systems seem to reward quietly working out role conflicts or other problems alone exemplifies the "folly of rewarding A while hoping for B" (Kerr, 1975).

Organizations need systems to help leaders collect information on the types of policies/benefits sought by employees as well as the current barriers to employee use and satisfaction of existing policies/benefits. Formal systems also are needed to support upward feedback. Organizations also need systems to provide regular information about leader receptivity to employee voice. Employees must have regular opportunities to provide feedback formally and informally about their leaders' receptivity to their voice. Even if all leaders were intrinsically motivated to improve their openness to others' input, this system would still be valuable as a learning device due to the inevitability of blind spots, unconscious backtracking, and the general tendency for leaders and subordinates to have differing interpretations of leaders' behaviors (Kim & Yukl, 1998; Likert, 1961). Organizations need processes and forums for the discussion of employee work-life issues, including perceived informal barriers to satisfactory balancing efforts. As noted in one example in this chapter, it does little good for senior managers to espouse respect for work-life balancing efforts at infrequent large-group meetings if there are no processes in place to allow employees to work out the realities of such challenges when they return to their day-to-day demands.

In recommending all-employee training and a focus on managerial behavior and organizational system adjustments, we are not suggesting that individual differences are insignificant. On the contrary, it is precisely because individuals play unique roles and face unique demands on and desires for their work and nonwork time that we think no formal system can ever be designed to eliminate the need for individual employees to be able to speak up about mismatches between existing policies and personal needs. However, most employees are *not* likely to be courageous or proactive (Crant, 2000) or extraverted (LePine & Van Dyne, 2001) enough to speak up about such problems when working in organizations where informal cues strongly influence individual sense making and perceptions about the safety and utility of testing or engaging in dialogue about work-life conflicts.

CONCLUSION

This chapter discusses the importance of speaking up for employees seeking to balance work and family commitments. We develop linkages between speaking up research and work-family research to suggest a model of work-family balancing in which new and flexible—and inevitably fluid—compromises can be reached between employee and employer. Conceptualizing these compromises as a balancing process suggests that working people must negotiate the competing demands of jobs and lives in an ongoing way. We identified three essential processes underlying this balancing process: individual sense making, testing the assumptions and inferences thus developed, and engaging in a dialogue through which novel arrangements might be developed. This negotiation is shaped more by intrapersonal and interpersonal processes than by formal policies in organizations.

Our discussion emphasized the informal controls that shape expectations about behavior in the workplace. Few issues are more basic, yet potentially sensitive and personal, than how much time one feels one must put in at work. Clearly, it is possible for one to be wrong in one's assessment of this quantity, especially when it is not explicitly tested. There is thus enormous potential for unnecessary waste in work-life balancing if potentially better solutions (including alternative schedules or better definitions of what constitutes quality work) for both parties (employee and employer) remain undiscovered because of a collective inability to engage in the key cognitive and behavioral processes required for discovering them. With this in mind, we conceptualize work-life balancing as a challenge that centrally involves speaking up and, more important, engaging in a collaborative dialogue of discovery of needs and new possibilities.

NOTES

1. Personal communication with J. R. Detert, April, 2000.
2. Digging into the subtleties of differences between culture and climate is outside the scope

of this chapter, as are ontological debates about whether these phenomena represent something organizations have or are. For an excellent discussion of the former see Denison (1996); of the latter, see Smircich (1983).

  3. Although supervisory influences may differ from subordinate to subordinate as suggested by LMX research (see Schriesheim, Castro, & Cogliser [1999] for a review), team effectiveness research identifies leader effects at the group level, as does our own empirical work. In particular, in psychological safety research individual differences are swamped by group-level effects (e.g., Edmondson, 1996; Edmondson & Magelof forthcoming). We thus predict that informal, indirect supervisory influences will be consistent within groups (ranging from small local teams to larger units) even when formal, direct supervisory effects exist for dyads.

REFERENCES

Alderfer, C. P. (1972). *Existence, relatedness, and growth: Human needs in organizational settings.* New York: Free Press.

Allen, T. D., Herst, D.E.L., Bruck, C. S., & Sutton, M. (2000). Consequences associated with work-to-family conflict: A review and agenda for future research. *Journal of Occupational Health Psychology, 5*(2), 278–308.

Argyris, C. (1977). Double loop learning in organizations. *Harvard Business Review, 54,* 115–125.

Argyris, C., & Schon, D. A. (1974). *Theory in practice: Increasing professional effectiveness.* San Francisco: Jossey-Bass.

Ashford, S. J., Rothbard, N. P., Piderit, S. K., & Dutton, J. E. (1998). Out on a limb: The role of context and impression management in selling gender-equity issues. *Administrative Science Quarterly, 43,* 23–57.

Bailyn, L. (2003). Academic careers and gender equity: Lessons learned from MIT. *Gender, work, and organization, 10*(2), 137–153.

Barker, J. R. (1993). Tightening the iron cage: Concertive control in self-managing teams. *Administrative Science Quarterly, 38*(3), 408–437.

Berger, P. L., & Luckmann, T. (1966). *The social construction of reality: A treatise in the sociology of knowledge.* New York: Doubleday.

Bettenhausen, K., & Murnighan, J. K. (1985). The emergence of norms in competitive decision-making groups. *Administrative Science Quarterly, 30,* 350–372.

Bliese, P. D. (2000). Within-group agreement, non-independence, and reliability: Implications for data aggregation and analysis. In K. J. Klein & S.W.J. Kozlowski (Eds.), *Multilevel theory, research, and methods in organizations* (pp. 349–381). San Francisco: Jossey-Bass.

Blum, T. C., Fields, D. L., & Goodman, J. S. (1994). Organization-level determinants of women in management. *Academy of Management Journal, 37,* 241–268.

Bryk, A. S., & Raudenbush, S. W. (1992). *Hierarchical linear models: Applications and data analysis methods.* Thousand Oaks, CA: Sage.

Cha, S. E., & Edmondson, A. C. (2004). *How values backfire: Leadership, attribution, and disenchantment in a values-driven organization.* Working paper, Harvard Business School.

Chao, G. T. (2000). Multilevel issues and culture: An integrative view. In K. J. Klein & S.W.J. Kozlowski (Eds.), *Multilevel theory, research, and methods in organizations* (pp. 308–346). San Francisco: Jossey-Bass.

Chatman, J. A., & Jehn K. A. (1994). Assessing the relationship between industry characteristics and organizational culture: How different can you be? *Academy of Management Journal, 37,* 522–553.

Chatman, J. A., Polzer, J. T., Barsade, S. G., & Neale, M. A. (1998). Being different yet feeling similar: The influence of demographic composition and organizational culture on work processes and outcomes. *Administrative Science Quarterly, 43,* 749–780.

Collins, J. C., & Porras, J. I. (1994). *Built to last*. New York: HarperCollins.

Conger, J. A. (2000). Effective change begins at the top. In M. Beer & N. Nohria (Eds.), *Breaking the code of change* (pp. 99–112). Boston: Harvard Business School Press.

Cook, T. D., & Campbell, D. T. (1979). *Quasi-experimentation: Design and analysis choices for field settings*. Chicago: Rand McNally.

Cooke, R. A., & Rousseau, D. (1988). Behavioral norms and expectations: A quantitative approach to the assessment of organizational culture. *Group and Organizational Studies, 13*(3), 245–273.

Cooke, R. A., & Szumal, J. L. (1993). Measuring normative beliefs and shared behavioral expectations in organizations: The reliability and validity of the organizational culture inventory. *Psychological Reports, 72*, 1299–1330.

Crant, J. M. (2000). Proactive behavior in organizations. *Journal of Management, 26*(3), 435–462.

Deal, T., & Kennedy, A. A. (1982). *Corporate culture: Rites and rituals of organizational life*. Reading, MA: Addison-Wesley.

Denison, D. (1996). What is the difference between organizational culture and organizational climate? A native's point of view on a decade of paradigm wars. *Academy of Management Review, 21*(3), 619–654.

Detert, J. R. (2003). *To speak or not to speak: Multi-level leadership influences on organizational voice*. Unpublished doctoral dissertation, Harvard University.

Detert, J. R., & Edmondson, A. C. (2003, August). *Motivational bases of voice: Elaborating the relationship between leadership behaviors and employee needs*. Paper presented at the Annual Meeting of the Academy of Management, Seattle, WA.

Detert, J. R., Schroeder, R. G., & Mauriel, J. J. (2000). A framework for linking culture and improvement inititatives in organizations. *Academy of Management Review, 25*(4), 850–863.

Edmondson, A. C. (1996). Learning from mistakes is easier said than done: Group and organizational influences on the detection and correction of human error. *Journal of Applied Behavioral Science, 32*(1), 5–28.

Edmondson, A. C. (1999). Psychological safety and learning behavior in work teams. *Administrative Science Quarterly, 44*, 350–383.

Edmondson, A. C. (2002). The local and variegated nature of learning in organizations: A group-level perspective. *Organization Science, 13*(2), 128–146.

Edmondson, A. C. (2003). Speaking up in the operating room: How team leaders promote learning in interdisciplinary action teams. *Journal of Management Studies, 40*(6): 1419–1452.

Edmondson, A. C. & Magelof J. P. (forthcoming). Explaining psychological safety in innovation teams. In L. Thompson, & H. Chsi (Eds.), *Creativity and innovation in organizations*. Mahwah, NJ: Erlbaum.

Edmondson, A. C., & Woolley, A. W. (2003). Understanding outcomes of organizational learning interventions. In Easterby-Smith, M. & Lyles, M. (Eds.), *International handbook of organizational learning and knowledge management*. London: Blackwell, pp. 185–211.

Edwards, J. R., & Rothbard, N. P. (2000). Mechanisms linking work and family: Clarifying the relationship between work and family constructs. *Academy of Management Review, 25*, 178–199.

Frijda, N. H. (1986). *The emotions*. Cambridge, England: Cambridge University Press.

Gersick, C.J.G., & Hackman, J. R. (1990). Habitual routines in task-performing groups. *Organizational Behavior and Human Decision Processes, 47*, 65–97.

Gioia, D. A., & Sims, H. P., Jr. (1986). Introduction: Social cognition in organizations. In H. P. Sims, Jr. & D. A. Gioa (Eds.), *The thinking organization* (pp. 1–19). San Francisco: Jossey-Bass.

Gordon, G. G., & DiTomaso, N. (1992). Predicting corporate performance from organizational culture. *Journal of Management Studies, 29*(6), 783–798.

Greenberg, D. N. (1999, August 8–12). *Disentangling subcultures: The differentiated influence of societal and organizational factors*. Paper presented at the Annual Meeting of the Academy of Management, Chicago, IL.

Greenhaus, J. H., & Beutell, N. J. (1985). Sources of conflict between work and family roles. *Academy of Management Review, 10*, 76–88.

Hall, J. R., & Neitz, M. J. (1993). Sociology and culture. In J. R. Hall & M. J. Neitz (Eds.), *Culture: Sociological perspectives* (pp. 1–19). Englewood Cliffs, NJ: Prentice-Hall.

Harris, S. G. (1994). Organizational culture and individual sensemaking: A schema-based perspective. *Organization Science, 5*(3), 309–321.

Hofstede, G. (1998). Identifying organizational subcultures: An empirical approach. *Journal of Management Studies, 35*(1), 1–12.

Hofstede, G., Neuijen, B., Ohayv, D. D., & Sanders, G. (1990). Measuring organizational cultures: A qualitative and quantitative study across twenty cases. *Administrative Science Quarterly, 35*, 286–316.

Isaacs, W. N. (1992). *The perils of shared ideals.* Unpublished doctoral thesis, Oxford University, Oxford England.

James, L. R., & Jones, A. P. (1974). Organizational climate: A review of theory and research. *Psychological Bulletin, 81*(12), 1096–1112.

Jepperson, R., & Swidler, A. (1994). What properties of culture should we measure? *Poetics, 22*, 359–371.

Kerr, S. (1975). On the folly of rewarding A, while hoping for B. *Academy of Management Journal, 18*(4), 769–782.

Kim, H., & Yukl, G. (1998). Relationships of managerial effectiveness and advancement to self-reported and subordinate-reported leadership behaviors from the multiple-linkage model. In F. Dansereau & F. J. Yammarino (Eds.), *Leadership: The multiple-level approaches. Part A: Classical and new wave* (pp. 243–260). Stamford, CT: JAI Press

Klein, K. J., Dansereau, F., & Hall, R. J. (1994). Levels issues in theory development, data collection, and analysis. *Academy of Management Review, 19*(2), 195–229.

Koene, B. A., Boone, C.A.J.J., & Soeters, J. L. (1997). Organizational factors influencing homogeneity and heterogeneity of organizational cultures. In S. A. Sackmann (Ed.), *Cultural complexity in organizations* (pp. 273–293). Thousand Oaks, CA: Sage.

Kofodimos, J. (1995). *Beyond work-family programs: Confronting and resolving the underlying causes of work-personal life conflict.* Greensboro, NC: Center for Creative Leadership.

Kossek, E. E., Noe, R. A., & Colquitt, J. A., (2001). Caregiving decisions, well-being, and performance: The effects of place and provider as a function of dependent type and work-family climates. *Academy of Management Journal, 44*(1), 29–44.

Kossek, E. E., Noe, R. A., & DeMarr, B. J. (1999). Work-family role synthesis: Individual and organizational determinants. *International Journal of Conflict Management, 10*(2), 102–129.

Kossek, E. E., & Ozeki, C. (1998). Work-family conflict, policies, and the job-life satisfaction relationship: A review and directions for organizational behavior/human resources research. *Journal of Applied Psychology, 83*(2), 139–149.

Kotter, J. P., & Heskett, J. L. (1992). *Corporate culture and performance.* New York: Free Press.

Kreft, I., & deLeeuw, J. (1998). *Introducing multilevel modeling.* Thousand Oaks, CA: Sage.

Kunda, G. (1992). *Engineering culture: Control and commitment in a high-tech corporation.* Philadelphia: Temple University Press.

Lambert, S. J. (1995). An investigation of workers' use and appreciation of supportive workplace policies. In D. P. Moore (Ed.), *Best papers 1995: Proceedings of the Academy of Management.* Madison, WI: Omni Press.

LePine, J. A., & Van Dyne, L. (1998). Predicting voice behavior in work groups. *Journal of Applied Psychology, 83*(6), 853–868

LePine, J. A., & Van Dyne, L. (2001). Voice and cooperative behavior as contrasting forms of contextual performance: Evidence of differential relationships with Big Five personality characteristics and cognitive ability. *Journal of Applied Psychology, 86*(2), 326–336.

Likert, R. (1961). *New patterns of management.* New York: McGraw-Hill.

Martin, J. (1992). *Cultures in organizations: Three perspectives.* New York: Oxford University Press.

Martin, J., & Siehl, C. (1983). Organizational culture and counter culture: An uneasy symbiosis. *Organizational Dynamics, 12*(2), 52–64.

Meindl, J. R., Ehrlich, S. B., & Dukerich, J. M. (1985). The romance of leadership. *Administrative Science Quarterly, 30,* 78–102.

Milliken, F. J., Morrison, E. W., & Hewlin, P. F. (2003). An exploratory study of employee silence: Issues that employees don't communicate upward and why. *Journal of Management Studies,* (40), 1453–1476.

Morrison, E. W., & Milliken, F. J. (2000). Organizational silence: A barrier to change and development in a pluralistic world. *Academy of Management Review, 25*(4), 706–725.

O'Reilly, C. A., III & Chatman, J. A. (1996). Culture as social control: Corporations, cults, and commitment. In B. Staw & L. L. Cummings (Eds.), *Research in organizational behavior* (Vol. 18, pp. 157–200). Greenwich, CT: JAI Press.

O'Reilly, C. A., III., Chatman, J. A., & Caldwell, D. F. (1991). People and organizational culture: A profile comparison approach to assessing person-organization fit. *Academy of Management Journal, 34*(3), 487–516.

Oxford Health Plan, (2002). Workplace wellness survey. Retrieved May 25, 2004, from https://www.oxhp.com/press/index.html

Peterson, R. A. (1979). Revitalizing the cultural concept. *Annual Review of Sociology, 5,* 137–166.

Pettigrew, A. M. (1990). Conclusion: Organizational climate and culture: Two constructs in search of a role. In B. Schneider (Ed.), *Organizational climate and culture* (pp. 413–434). San Francisco: Jossey-Bass.

Ryan, K. D., & Oestreich, D. K. (1998). *Driving fear out of the workplace.* (2nd ed.). San Francisco: Jossey-Bass.

Salancik, G. R., & Pfeffer, J. (1978). A social information processing approach to job attitudes and task design. *Administrative Science Quarterly, 23,* 224–253.

Schein, E. H. (1992). *Organizational culture and leadership* (2nd ed.). San Francisco: Jossey-Bass.

Schneider, B. (1990). The climate for service. In B. Schneider (Ed.), *Organizational climate and culture* (pp. 383–412). San Francisco: Jossey-Bass.

Schriesheim, C. A., Castro, S. L., & Cogliser, C. C. (1999). Leader-member exchange (LMX) research: A comprehensive review of theory, measurement, and data-analytic practices. *Leadership Quarterly, 10*(1), 63–113.

Scott, S. G., & Bruce, R. A. (1994). Determinants of innovative behavior: A path model of individual innovation in the workplace. *Academy of Management Journal, 37,* 580–607.

Smircich, L. (1983). Concepts of culture and organizational analysis. *Administrative Science Quarterly, 28,* 339–358.

Solomon, C. M. (1994). Work/family's failing grade: Why today's initiatives aren't enough. *Personnel Journal, 73*(5), 72–87.

Sorensen, J. B. (2002). The strength of corporate culture and the reliability of firm performance. *Administrative Science Quarterly, 47,* 70–91.

Tetlock, P. E. (1999). Accountability theory: Mixing properties of human agents with properties of social systems. In D. M. Messick (Ed.), *Shared cognition in organizations: The management of knowledge* (pp. 117–138). Mahwah, NJ: Erlbaum.

Thompson, C. A., Beauvais, L. L., & Lyness, K. S. (1999). When work-family benefits are not enough: The influence of work-family culture on benefit utilization, organizational attachment, and work-family conflict. *Journal of Vocational Behavior, 54*(3), 392–415.

Trice, H. M. (1993). *Occupational subcultures in the workplace.* Ithaca, NY: ILR Press.

Trice, H. M., & Beyer, J. M. (1993). *The cultures of work organizations.* Englewood Cliffs, NJ: Prentice-Hall.

Tucker, A. L (2003). *Organizational learning from operational failures.* Unpublished DBA dissertation, Harvard University.

Tyler, T. R. and Lind, E. A. (1992). A relational model of authority in groups. In Advances in experimental psychology vol. 25, pp. 115–191). New York: Academic Press.

Van Dyck, C. V. (2000). *Putting errors to good use: Error management culture in organizations.* Unpublished doctoral dissertation, University of Amsterdam.

Van Maanen, J., & Barley, S. R. (1984). Occupational communities: Culture and control in organizations. In B. Staw & L. Cummings (Eds.), *Research in organizational behavior* (Vol. 6, pp. 287–365). Greenwich, CT: JAI Press.

Walsh, J. P. (1995). Managerial and organizational cognition: Notes from a trip down memory lane. *Organization Science, 6*(3), 280–321.

Weick, K. E. (1995). *Sensemaking in organizations*. Thousand Oaks, CA: Sage.

Wilkins, A. L., & Ouchi, W. G. (1983). Efficient cultures: Exploring the relationship between culture and organizational performance. *Administrative Science Quarterly, 28,* 468–481.

Withey, M. J., & Cooper, W. H. (1989). Predicting exit, voice, loyalty, and neglect. *Administrative Science Quarterly, 34,* 521–539.

Zammuto, R. F., & Krakower, J. Y. (1991). Quantitative and qualitative studies of organizational culture. *Research in Organizational Change and Development, 5,* 83–114.

Zerubavel, E. (1997). *Social mindscapes: An invitation to cognitive sociology*. Cambridge: Harvard University Press.

Zhou, J., & George, J. M. (2001). When job dissatisfaction leads to creativity: Encouraging the expression of voice. *Academy of Management Journal, 44*(4), 682–696.

19

The Development of Psychosocial Capital in Organizations: Implications for Work and Family Life

Sabir I. Giga
University of Manchester Institute of Science and Technology, U.K.

Cary L. Cooper
Lancaster University, U.K.

INTRODUCTION

In this chapter we discuss the theoretical underpinnings of employee psychological contracts and the impact of change on the implied employment relationship, with particular reference to individual employee expectations of the need to strike a healthier balance between employment commitments and their home lives. The concept of psychological contracts has gained a greater relevance as the relationship that individuals have with their organization changes ever rapidly. Closer examination of psychological contracts at any given moment in time may reveal how employees perceive changes and what issues they value highly. It is a framework around which we can develop strategy as well as gain an insight into other relevant subjects concerning employees, such as expectations of job security, career development, pay, and issues relating to the impact of their work on the quality of their home lives.

We refer to work-life balance as the flexibility for employees to have the benefit of spending time with family and friends and the opportunity to follow other leisure pursuits (Jones, 2003). Employers are making use of such incentives on an ever-increasing basis to attract and retain a satisfied and quality workforce.

However, raising employee expectations of work-life balance issues with little or no reference to overall organizational strategy and the ability to implement such measures may in the future give rise to job dissatisfaction and interpersonal conflict. For example, can every employee's options for the way they choose to work be accommodated? And what about individuals who want to work longer hours or those who have no family responsibilities—are they likely to be treated equitably?

Employers endeavor to fulfill individual employee expectations vis-à-vis their psychological contracts. However, problems could arise when encouraging teamwork and developing a cohesive working environment if individuals pursue their self-interests without being aware of or attempting to empathize with their fellow employee's circumstances. As a result, collective team goals and, indeed, organizational goals may be neglected.

Although human capital in the form of employees is an invaluable asset to organizations, sustained growth and long-term success is likely to be dependent on mutual understanding between individuals and the way that they bond together collectively as a team to develop social capital. Clearly, as each individual employee's circumstances are uniquely personified in his or her own psychological contract, a homogenous approach to the way employees work is unlikely to suit everyone. Moreover, any perceived unfairness—for example, giving one group priority over another, such as may be the case for working parents—may give rise to unfulfilled expectations and tension between fellow employees. In order for these individual expectations to crystallize in a manner that is conducive for teamwork and organizational development, we propose a framework within which organizations can create "psychosocial capital" as a bond between human and social capital.

PSYCHOLOGICAL CONTRACTS

[Psychological] contracts are created from what people do, not from what they say they will do or from what someone says they should do. For this reason the psychological contract is more a reality than are formal policies. In fact, it is the reality as opposed to what someone says reality should be. (Morrison, 1994)

In describing his understanding of the employee-management relationship, Argyris (1960) suggested the "psychological work contract" as mutually agreed expectations between employer and employee and an agreement equally significant to formal written employment contracts. He proposed that employers should maintain a fair remuneration system and provide adequate job security in order to sustain employee performance and job satisfaction. In 1962, Levinson et al. (cited in Thomas & Anderson, 1998) confirmed the obligatory nature of mutual expectations as the backbone of psychological contracts. This unwritten and implied reciprocal relationship between an individual and his or her employer enables both parties to develop expectations of each other (Schein, 1980). More recently, Rousseau (1995) discussed the relevance of this relationship with greater significance and regarded the psychological contract as promissory and mutual obligations, not just mutual expectations. In her view, psychological contracts refer to the perception of an implicit understanding between employers and employees, and can be defined as an individual's beliefs concerning the terms and conditions of a reciprocal agreement between two parties (Rousseau & Greller, 1994). This may be as a consequence of written contracts or may be implied in the expectations that each party has of the other. Consequently, both parties may have dissimilar perceptions of what their obligations are to one another (Herriot, Manning, & Kidd, 1997). Furthermore, as employee psychological contracts are influenced by many different sources, such as supervisors, directors, human resource professionals, and colleagues, not all sources may be valued equally (Turnley & Feldman, 1999).

According to Guest and Conway (1997), the determinants of a positive psychological contract are organizational culture, human resource policies and practices, previous employment experiences, expectations of future employment, and employment alternatives. Development of flexible employment opportunities may also increase employee loyalty toward the organization as a direct consequence of its portrayal of a caring image for the workforce (Scandura & Lankau, 1997).

Notwithstanding the subjective nature of the psychological contract, it contemplates confidence and fairness greatly. The strength of belief in the contract depends on how open, specific, and identifiable the promise is (McLean Parks & Schmedemann, 1994). Personnel activities such as recruitment and training influence the experiences of individuals in an organization. Each endeavor signifies a preference by the employer as to how he or she intends to deal with workers. Decisions about recruitment, conditions of employment, reward distribution, promotions and so on, all have an influence on individuals. This in turn affects the way employees choose to behave within the work environment. Questions on whether to take up employment, how much effort to exert, how to treat colleagues, and how long to stay with an organization are all raised during this phase (Rousseau & Greller, 1994).

From the moment a worker commences employment, a written contract stating details of the arrangement with his or her employer is produced. Both parties know exactly what is expected of the other for the arrangement to be successful. Furthermore, if either side fails to satisfy this agreement then the other party can take legal steps to resolve the matter. The employment contract explicitly states the job title, job description, salary, hours of work, notice period, holiday entitlement, pensions, and so on. In short, the employment contract is exchange of money for labor (Makin, Cooper, & Cox, 1996).

The psychological contract, however, does not involve any physical exchange. Here individuals understand their relationship with their organization with regard to the terms of the reciprocal exchange, what they perceive to be promised to them if they do what is asked or expected of them. They are useful in goal-setting by ensuring that the individual and organization make and keep commitments if they are followed strictly (Rousseau, 1995). Employees have a greater sense of security if they know that they have an established relationship with their employer (Shore & Tetrick, 1994). Whereas a legal contract establishes rights that can be acknowledged in a courtroom, psychological contracts establish emotions and attitudes that develop and regulate behavior (Spindler, 1994).

Employees observe their working relationships as a form of social exchange. Psychological contracts address many complicated employment issues that are saturated with emotions. Consequently, powerful sentiments are revealed when things go wrong with the contract (Morrison, 1994). Traditionally this parent-child relationship (see Table 19.1) also included limited scope for employee control in decision making, with the employer often restricting information communicated to employees (Kissler, 1994).

As employer and employee enter adult contracts focusing on mutual benefits, work-life balance issues may be brought to the forefront. Individuals have the opportunity of strengthening their relationships with managers and colleagues by adopting a practical approach to the issue and considering the implications of any proposed plans. Dependent on personal circumstances, employees may perceive implementation of work-life balance programs in their organization in a variety of ways, with some individuals even interpreting the situation as a reduction in their colleagues' commitment toward the organization. They, in turn, may make moves to change their obligations as well (Morishima, 1996). Following the rationality of equity theory, individuals may respond to a perceived inequitable employment relationship by making moves to change their obliga-

TABLE 19.1
Changes in the Employment Contract

Old Psychological Contract	New Psychological Contract
The employer and employee have a parent/child relationship.	The employer and employee enter adult contracts focusing on flexible/mutually beneficial work.
Employee's identity and worth are defined by the employer.	Employee's identity and worth are self-defined.
Employees who stay are good and loyal; others are disliked.	Regular flow of workers in and out is commonplace.
Loyal employees are guaranteed lifelong employment.	Lifelong employment is very unlikely; expect job/career changes.
The main route for advancement is through promotion.	The main route for advancement is a sense of personal accomplishment.

Note. Adapted from Kissler, 1994.

tions to their employer by developing noncompliant or deviant behavior in order to reestablish equity (Sparrow & Cooper, 1998).

It would be extremely difficult, if not impossible, to conduct an investigation into the content of individual psychological contracts, as the items that could be included are almost limitless. However, there is general agreement between researchers and practitioners that contract content has actually transformed in line with organizational changes (Anderson & Schalk, 1998).

ORGANIZATIONAL CHANGE

Streamlining and downsizing have enabled organizations to become more flexible and cut costs. They have also allowed organizations to compete more strongly by concentrating on key areas of their business and outsourcing other unavailable or limited resources to third parties (Harrison & Kelley, 1993). Flexible employment enables organizations to improve their performance by having the capability of adapting quickly to changing economic conditions (Schabracq & Cooper, 1997). However, the benefits are not all one-sided: There is significant demand from employees themselves, especially those who are unable to take up full-time or permanent work, for the opportunity to maintain an equilibrium between work and nonwork life through initiatives such as flexible work hours. Moreover, employers understand the need to amend their traditional role from developing the careers of inadequate employees to attracting experienced, high-calibre employees. In order to achieve this employer-of-choice status, organizations need to demonstrate competency in understanding and dealing with work-life issues.

De-layering has been a key theme in many restructuring programs. As a consequence, increasing numbers of highly qualified workers are competing for fewer managerial positions. In this situation, the changing psychological contract can be used as a tool for developing an understanding of the current relationship between employer and employee. It is evident that the employment relationship has changed dramatically over the last couple of decades, as traditional work contracts are replaced by contingent employment contracts. Simultaneously, within the employment environment there is a transfer from a paternalistic to a partnership relationship (Cavanaugh & Noe, 1999; Sparrow, 2000), and a change in psychological contracts from relational characteristics that imply long-term reciprocal obligations to more transactional principles that tend to be short term (Sparrow, 2000). As completely new industries develop supporting, innovative types of organizations maintained by innovative work processes and novel forms of employment, fresh demands are being made to support business pursuits alongside educational, housing, and social activities (Bradley & Woodling, 2000). Similarly, boundaries between organizations and personal lives have also been broken down further by organizations' expectations for employers to contribute to nonwork activities such as social events (Morishima, 1996).

It has been argued that change within an organizational context is one of the few certainties of contemporary living. Indeed, Kerr (1986) suggested that these changes liberate individuals and create what could be referred to as industrialism with a human face. However, the change process can be managed in a variety of ways, each resulting in different outcomes (Rousseau, 1995). The fact that the employer and employee do not have a traditional employment relationship in these circumstances may have consequences on their psychological contracts. Employers in the past were more interested in predictable performance than good performance, and employees were more concerned about getting promoted than about being effective (Hendry & Jenkins, 1997). In the modern organization both their attitudes have had to change. As organizations have become more flexible in their approach to the ways that employees can choose to fit work tasks into their daily lives, employees, too, have had to improve their job performance to demonstrate competence.

The new economy, in which opportunity, insecurity, flexibility, and uncertainty all coexist, is characterized by mutually dependent work functions and is influenced by changing technology. The boundaryless career is not typical of any particular career form but instead combines a variety of potential forms that challenge traditional employment concepts (Arthur & Rousseau, 1996). This enables employees to concentrate on various options available to them, making the most of their nonwork lives and overseeing the development of their own careers (Hendry & Jenkins, 1997).

As employees move between projects or organizations in an open labor market like Silicon Valley in the United States, they also break down boundaries between organizations and other societies in neighboring communities—integrating work and social life in the process. An organization's success can then relate to strengthening local communities and increasing social capital (Saxenian, 1996). The notion of boundaryless career suggests a return to the traditional meaning of *organization*—as a process rather than as a stable (static) group of people. This enables us to view organizations *dynamically* (Arthur & Rousseau, 1996). However, this term signifies the reduced significance of social structures contained within traditional organizations, deficiencies in social capital, and a potentially unhealthy increase in individualistic attitudes (Tolbert, 1996).

CHANGING EMPLOYEE EXPECTATIONS

Individuals in the workplace have different expectations of themselves and their colleagues throughout their careers. Psychological contracts are dynamic in nature, as they can be transformed without explicit agreement (Thomas & Anderson, 1998). They do not just change over time; change intrinsically shapes the contract. Furthermore, an employee can change an employer and simultaneously increase job satisfaction (Cavanaugh & Noe, 1999). In a balanced relationship both the employment parties are equally obligated in the exchange and therefore employees are likely to reciprocate their employers' actions by demonstrating, for example, a willingness to work extra hours when required during busy periods (Shore & Barksdale, 1998).

Although the psychological contract is subjective and individual experiences reported are likely to be unique and relevant to that particular employer/employee relationship, previous research suggests that many characteristics can be generalized (Rousseau & Tijoriwala, 1998). The psychological contract offers a useful framework for developing the motivation of and ease of communication with employees. As organizations aspire to provide superior and innovative products and services, they need people who are committed, effective, and proficient in their work. Such situations demand a positive psychological contract between an employer and employee based on trust, respect, and a sense of fairness.

The reported individual and societal costs of not achieving a healthy balance between work and nonwork pursuits include higher levels of stress, reduced job and life satisfaction, increasing levels of family breakdowns, and higher rates of substance abuse (Hobson, Delunas, & Kesic, 2001). As a result, a number of organizations are recognizing the benefits of including work-life balance issues as a central element of employee psychological contracts by implementing policies and programs that enable individuals to pursue nonwork interests.

WORKPLACE STRESS

Stress is concerned with appraisals of threat and/or loss and, therefore, may result when an individual's goals, anticipated or experienced, are not accomplished. One reason for diverse reactions to likely stressful situations is the goal that individuals pursue; the level of control they have over the situation and the level to which these goals are satisfied buffer stress (Semmer, 1996).

Many studies have identified a reduction in motivation and job satisfaction and an increase in stress due to insecurity and pressure at work. As organizations have become leaner and more flexible, they have failed to leave some scope for unpredicted change in human resources, either upward or downward. However, considerable projects are expected to be initiated instantaneously (Bradley & Woodling, 2000). One of the most significant causes of pressure at work is working long hours (Guest & Conway, 1997); this may be due to job insecurity, making employees feel a need to work longer hours in order to show commitment to their employer (Westman, 2000) or employees having too much work and not enough time to complete it (Jones, 2003).

It has been discussed that relationships with others, lack of control, and uncertainty are major causes of workplace stress. The psychological contract has traditionally enabled employees to develop a perception of their own expectations of their employer and of what they perceive are their employer's expectations of them (Morrison & Robinson, 1997). Employers endeavor to fulfill individual employee expectations vis-à-vis their psychological contracts. However, with little attention paid to building social capital, the consequences could be that the collective goals of teams and, indeed, the whole organization, are neglected as individuals pursue their self-interests and view themselves as "independent islands" who have no obligations to their colleagues (Cunningham, 2002).

SOCIAL CAPITAL

Although organisations are made up of individuals, they are successful to the extent that the collective action of these individuals is greater than the sum of its parts. (Cunningham, 2002)

Social relationships in organizations lead to the development of norms of trust and reciprocity that have spillover effects within neighborhoods, not just those individuals who have a vested interest in developing the relationship (McCulloch, 2001). Putnam (1995) described social capital as the features of social organizations such as networks, norms, and social trust that facilitate the coordination and cooperation of mutual trust. In this context, social capital is beneficial for individuals within a community as well as the whole of the community and is available to everyone (Kostova & Roth, 2003).

There are numerous benefits to be gained for organizations, the general economy, and society in general when implementing work-life strategies for employees, including improving productivity, recruitment, and retention levels; reducing absenteeism and stress; and promoting a caring image of which employees, potential employees, customers/clients, and shareholders can be proud (Daniels & McCarraher, 2000).

Although social capital has traditionally been applied within a political and sociological context, researchers have recently attempted to identify ways to improve economic performance based on social capital characteristics such as trust (Office for National Statistics, 2001). Social capital can also be applied to particular elements of an organization's community, such as teams and departments, in order to promote cohesion and a sense of belonging (McCulloch, 2001). In our opinion, one way this can be achieved is by building a bond that links social capital with individual psychological contracts.

PSYCHOSOCIAL CAPITAL

Much has been said of late on the advantages of creating social capital in geographical communities in an effort to create healthier, more prosperous nations.

Similarly, positive psychological contracts are a prerequisite of building healthier organizations. However, within an organizational context there are clear advantages for adopting strategies that combine both individual expectations and organizational citizenship concepts in an effort to create a more meaningful and effective bond between individual members.

We define *psychosocial capital* as the shared perceptions and emotions of individuals that create mutual understanding in terms of obligations, trust, and goals, and develop a cumulative organizational asset based on group (team) responsibility, identity, and bonding. Organizations that focus strictly on maximizing profits in the short term do so at the expense of sustaining growth and creating longer-term profitability by not paying attention to developing human resources and investing in psychosocial capital.

Changes in employment practices may affect employee identification with an organization, and thus cause a transformation in their psychological contract (Rousseau, 1998). The demise of the job-for-life is making employees think twice about commitment to their employer. According to Mowday, Porter, and Steers (1982), organizations have shown concern about the causes and remedies of reduced employee commitment, increased turnover, and absenteeism. Organizations that have introduced greater opportunities for employees to improve their work-life balance in order to attract and retain their services have found that this is not all that is required. Herriot and Pemberton (1997) suggested that innovation, which involves the rapid introduction of new or improved products or services to the marketplace, is also a necessary requirement. In order to innovate, individuals must have: (1) security so that risks can be taken, (2) agency to ensure that things occur, (3) autonomy to experiment with different ideas, (4) resources obtainable when appropriate, and (5) team working involving people with varied skills.

A recent comprehensive survey conducted in the United Kingdom identified Microsoft Corporation as the leading employer (McCall, 2003). Employees' views were canvassed on eight work-related factors, including:

Leadership: Feelings toward senior management.
My manager: Feelings of their immediate boss.
Personal growth: How challenged they are by their jobs.
Well-being: Feelings on work-life balance and stress.
My team: Feelings toward immediate colleagues.
Giving something back: Feelings about what the company puts back into society.
My company: Feelings toward the company.
Fair deal: Feelings about how equitable pay and benefits are.

According to the survey, 93% of Microsoft employees reported feeling proud to work for the company and believed that their work made a positive difference to their world. The cited factors, when pooled together, essentially look at the development of psychosocial capital in organizations (see Fig. 19.1). Human capital is arguably the most valuable asset that organizations can possess for the purpose of maintaining long-term profitability goals and increasing economic capital. Furthermore, in order to acquire and retain resourceful people, and in the process develop intellectual capital, organizations need to demonstrate a willingness to invest in psychosocial capital issues.

As evident from Fig. 19.1, the objective of building networks/teams is at the core of social capital principles. In contrast, although psychological contracts are a useful tool in developing an understanding of individual expectations and issues around job security and job satisfaction, tensions could arise when individual expectations take precedence over mutual team/organizational goals. Work-life strategies require individual team members to cooperate so that everyone is a potential beneficiary of the opportunities available—including the organization itself. In order to create the potential for this to succeed, we propose the conception of psychosocial capital in organizations.

DISCUSSION

Changes in people's careers need to be studied further. The traditional psychological contract implied employee job security and predictability with stable career paths with one employer (Hendry & Jenkins, 1997). Changes may be due to external pressures such as market conditions and competition, or they may be due to internal sources such as business development. Regardless of the motives for initiating change, repercussions of outcomes are likely to have an effect on individuals working in an organization. Furthermore, as substantial change within the workplace may necessitate revision of both the economic and psychological contracts, employees may require time and help to identify with the process.

Giving employees the opportunity to make the most of their home and work lives by increasing flexibility and devolving control is likely to improve the health of the organization in the long run. However, reference needs to be made to organizational strategy and the ability and willingness of individuals to develop a mutual understanding in an effort to establish a cohesive working environment.

It could be argued that the success of these practices is likely to be dependent on the level of control individuals have over work scheduling to effectively deal with potentially conflicting demands between their work and home lives (Wallace, 1999). Individuals should not be made to feel guilty or face retribution from supervisors and colleagues. Employees may not receive vital support from colleagues due to a variety of reasons, including "sour" social capital in organizations (Moerbeek & Need, 2003)—whereby certain individuals may not cooperate with their colleagues to help them maintain a balance between their

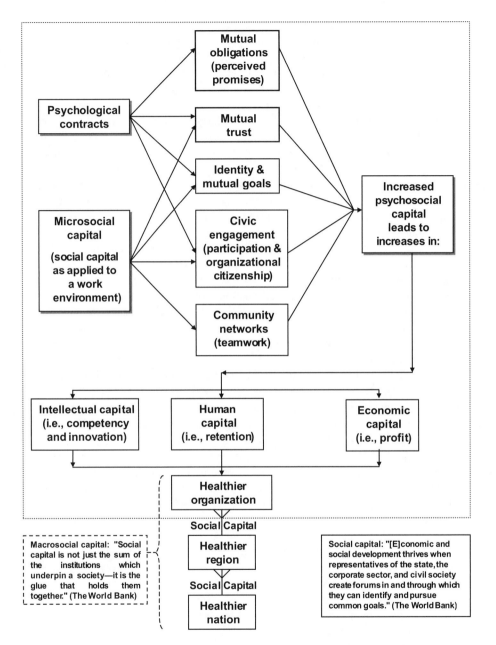

FIG. 19.1   The rationale for developing psychosocial capital organizations.

home and work lives. Colleagues may also feel aggrieved that certain individuals who lead a more balanced life are not pulling their weight and are less committed to the organization. In both cases, this lack of support could result in deviant and noncompliant behavior from fellow workers and may lead to conflict and tension. Organizations should encourage cultural change to support and respect employees who, for various reasons, opt to make use of such opportunities when offered by their employer. Similarly, individuals who are likely to adopt flexible working patterns should be made aware that they too have an obligation to accommodate organizational needs during busy periods or situations when there are staff shortages. Moreover, individuals who have no direct family responsibilities should not be used as scapegoats for ensuring that work is completed during these times, as they, too, should have the opportunity to enjoy nonwork interests and be treated equitably as far as work-life balance opportunity issues are concerned.

It is very important that employers recognize that as the significance of work in our lives has changed—in particular, a need for developing a sense of balance between our work and home lives—so has our psychological opposition to change. Individuals who are denied an opportunity to control how they plan their lives will become inefficient and eventually unwell. The predicament of many organizations is that although they have broken many aspects of the old psychological contract, they have failed to change characteristics of their culture that would enable development of new contracts. This is reflected in a lack of consistency in employment practices, particularly those concerning the development of family-friendly policies.

There is evidence that the traditional psychological contract is still alive and well. However, as the average employee now feels less loyalty toward his or her line manager and even less toward his or her employer (MacLachlan, 1996), one way of moving forward would be to develop psychosocial capital on the basis of the growing emotional attachment between colleagues (Rousseau & House, 1994). It has even been suggested that employee covenants be drawn up instead of contracts. These define the employment relationship as sharing commitment to ideas, issues, values, goals, and management processes to even a greater extent than the psychological contract (Kissler, 1994).

In order for organizations to stand out as "model employers of choice" and attract a highly skilled workforce, they need to offer more benefits and opportunities than their competitors (Rousseau, 1995). Organizations that understand the necessity of maintaining a diverse workforce to increase organizational strength can develop psychosocial capital to build cohesion and a sense of empathy between colleagues.

Although psychological contracts are a useful tool in developing an understanding of individual expectations, difficulties can arise, on the one hand, when individual aspirations take precedence over mutual team and organizational goals. It is also possible, on the other hand, that in certain circumstances team and organizational aspirations may not take into account individual circumstances. These issues are particularly significant for individuals concerned with advancing the work-life balance agenda within organizations. How do we create a working environment where people interact synchronously with one another when there are so many inconsistencies between individual expectations and organizational objectives?

We suggest that one way to move the agenda forward is to develop mutual trust. This trust should be not only between two people—that is, employer and employee, as is the case with psychological contracts—but also between groups and teams as encouraged by the notion of social capital. In our opinion, psychosocial capital can facilitate the formation of mutual understanding and develop a cumulative organizational asset based on group responsibility, identity, and bonding.

REFERENCES

Anderson, N., & Schalk, R. (1998). The psychological contract in retrospect and prospect. *Journal of Organizational Behavior, 19,* 637–647.

Argyris, C. (1960). *Understanding organizational behaviour.* London: Tavistock Publications.

Arthur, M. B., & Rousseau, D. M. (1996). The boundaryless career as a new employment principle. In M. B. Arthur & D. M. Rousseau (Eds.), *The boundaryless career* (pp. 3–20). Oxford, England: Oxford University Press.

Bradley, S., & Woodling, G. (2000). Accommodating future business intelligence: New work-space and work-time challenges for management and design. *Facilities, 18*(3/4), 162–167.

Cavanaugh, M. A., & Noe, R. A. (1999). Antecedents and consequences of relational components of the new psychological contract. *Journal of Organizational Behavior, 20,* 323–340.

Cunningham, I. (2002). Developing human capital in organisations. *Industrial and Commercial Training, 34*(3), 89–94.

Daniels, L., & McCarraher, L. (2000). *The work-life manual: Gaining a competitive edge by balancing the demands of employees' work and home lives.* London: The Industrial Society.

Guest, D. E., & Conway, N. (1997). Employee motivation and the psychological contract. In *Issues in people management.* London: Institute of Personnel Development.

Harrison, B., & Kelley, M. R. (1993). Outsourcing and the search for "flexibility." *Work, Employment and Society, 7*(2), 213–235.

Hendry, C., & Jenkins, R. (1997). Psychological contracts and new deals. *Human Resource Management Journal, 7*(1), 38–44.

Herriot, P., Manning, W.E.G., & Kidd, J. M. (1997). The content of the psychological contract. *British Journal of Management, 8,* 151–162.

Herriot, P., & Pemberton, C. (1997). Facilitating new deals. *Human Resource Management Journal, 7*(1), 45–56.

Hobson, C. J., Delunas, L., & Kesic, D. (2001). Compelling evidence of the need for corporate work/life balance initiatives: Results from a national survey of stressful life-events. *Journal of Employment Counseling, 38,* 29–44.

Jones, A. (2003). *About time for change.* London, England: The Work Foundation, in Association with Employers for Work-life Balance.

Kerr, C. (1986). Evolution of the workforce. In C. Kerr & P. D. Staudohar (Eds.), *Industrial relations in the new age* (pp. 38–42). San Francisco: Jossey-Bass.

Kissler, G. D. (1994, Fall). The new employment contract. *Human Resource Management, 33*(3), 335–352.

Kostova, T., & Roth, K. (2003). Social capital in mutinational corporations and a micro-macro model of its formation. *Academy of Management Review, 28*(2), 297–317.

MacLachlan, R. (1996, November). Employers urged to bridge credibility gap. *People Management, 7,* 7.

Makin, P., Cooper, C. L., & Cox, C. (1996). *Organizations and the psychological contract.* Leicester: The British Psychological Society.

McCall, A. (2003). 100 best companies to work for 2003. *Times Online.* Retrieved June 30, 2003, from www.timesonline.co.uk/article/0,,2096-587081,00.html

McCulloch, A. (2001, July 28). Social environments and health: Cross-sectional national survey. *British Medical Journal, 323,* 208–209.

McLean Parks, J., & Schmedemann, D. A. (1994, Fall). When promises become contracts: Implied contracts and handbook provisions on job security. *Human Resource Management, 33*(3), 403–423.

Moerbeek, H.H.S., & Need, A. (2003). Enemies at work: Can they hinder your career? *Social Networks, 25,* 67–82.

Morishima, M. (1996). Renegotiating psychological contracts: Japanese style. In C. L. Cooper & D. M. Rousseau (Eds.), *Trends in organizational behaviour* (Vol. 3, pp. 139–158). Chichester and New York: Wiley.

Morrison, D. E. (1994, Fall). Psychological contracts and change. *Human Resource Management, 33*(3), 353–372.

Morrison, E. W., & Robinson, S. A. (1997). When employees feel betrayed: A model of how psychological contract violation develops. *Academy of Management Review, 22*(1), 226–256.

Mowday, R. T., Porter, L. W., & Steers, R. M. (1982). *Employee-organization linkages.* New York: Academic Press.

Office for National Statistics. (2001). *Social capital: A review of the literature.* London, England: Social Analysis and Reporting Division, Office for National Statistics.

Putnam, R. (1995). Bowling alone: America's declining social capital. *Journal of Democracy, 6*(1), 65–78.

Rousseau, D. M. (1995). *Psychological contracts in organizations.* Thousand Oaks, CA: Sage.

Rousseau, D. M. (1998). The "problem" of the psychological contract considered. *Journal of Organizational Behavior, 19,* 665–671.

Rousseau, D. M., & Greller, M. M. (1994, Fall). Human resource practices: Administrative contract makers. *Human Resource Management, 33*(3), 385–401.

Rousseau, D. M., & House, R. J. (1994). Meso-organisational behaviour: Avoiding three fundamental biases. In C. L. Cooper & D. M. Rousseau (Eds.), *Trends in Organizational behaviour* (Vol. 1, pp. 13–30). Chichester and New York: Wiley.

Rousseau, D. M., & Tijoriwala, S. A. (1998). Assessing psychological contracts: Issues, alternatives and types of measures. *Journal of Organizational Behavior, 19,* 679–695.

Saxenian, A. (1996). Beyond boundaries: Open labour markets and learning in silicon valley. In M. B. Arthur & D. M. Rousseau (Eds.), *The boundaryless career* (pp. 23–39). Oxford: Oxford University Press.

Scandura, T. A., & Lankau, M. J. (1997). Relationships of gender, family responsibility and flexible work hours to organizational commitment and job satisfaction. *Journal of Organizational Behavior, 18,* 377–391.

Schabracq, M. J., & Cooper, C. L. (1997). Flexibility of labor, well-being and stress. *International Journal of Stress Medicine, 4*(4), 259–273.

Schein, E. H. (1980). *Organizational psychology.* Englewood Cliffs, NJ: Prentice-Hall.

Semmer, N. (1996). Individual differences, work stress and health. In M. J. Schabracq, C. L. Cooper,

& J.A.M. Winnubst (Eds.), *Handbook of work and health psychology* (pp. 51–86). Chichester and New York: Wiley.

Shore, L. M., & Barksdale, K. (1998). Examining degree of balance and level of obligation in the employment relationship: A social exchange approach. *Journal of Organizational Behavior, 19,* 731–744.

Shore, L. M., & Tetrick, L. E. (1994). The psychological contract as an explanatory framework in the employment relationship. In C. L. Cooper & D. M. Rousseau (Eds.), *Trends in organizational behaviour* (vol. 1, pp. 91–109). Chichester and New York: Wiley.

Sparrow, P. (2000). The new employment contract: Psychological implications of future work. In R. J. Burke & C. L. Cooper (Eds.), *The organization in crisis* (pp. 167–187). Oxford: Blackwell.

Sparrow, P., & Cooper, C. L. (1998). New organizational forms: The strategic relevance of future psychological contract scenarios. *Canadian Journal of Administrative Sciences, 15*(4), 356–371.

Spindler, G. S. (1994, Fall). Psychological contracts in the workplace: A lawyer's view. *Human Resource Management, 33*(3), 325–333.

Thomas, H.D.C., & Anderson, N. (1998). Changes in newcomers' psychological contracts during organizational socialization: A study of recruits entering the British army. *Journal of Organizational Behavior, 19,* 745–767.

Tolbert, P. S. (1996). Occupations, organizations, and boundaryless careers. In M. B. Arthur & D. M. Rousseau (Eds.), *The boundaryless career* (pp. 331–349). Oxford: Oxford University Press.

Turnley, W. H., & Feldman, D. C. (1999). A discrepancy model of psychological contract violations. *Human Resource Management Review, 9*(3), 367–386.

Wallace, J. E. (1999). Work-to-nonwork conflict among married male and female lawyers. *Journal of Organizational Behavior, 20,* 797–816.

Westman, M. (2000). Gender and job security. In R. J. Burke & C. L. Cooper (Eds.), *The organization in crisis* (pp. 119–131). Oxford: Blackwell.

20

Supervisor Support and Work-Life Integration: A Social Identity Perspective

Karen Hopkins
University of Maryland

INTRODUCTION

There is ample evidence that workers experience varying degrees of conflict, stress, and personal difficulties in trying to satisfy both career interests and life responsibilities. The successful integration of work and life requires different types of support: organizational support—family-responsive policies and practices, supportive superiors and coworkers; occupational support—flexible jobs, feedback, opportunities for socialization and interaction; and personal support—supportive and helpful family and friends (Barnett & Baruch, 1987; Bernas & Major, 2000; Friedman, Christensen, & DeGroot, 1999; Glass & Finley, 2002; Brough & Kelling, 2002; Kossek & Ozeki, 1998; Lechner, 1993; Ray, 1987; Ray & Miller, 1994; Scandura & Lankau, 1997; Thompson & Blau, 1994; Batt & Valcour, 2003; Voydanoff, 2002; Warren & Johnson, 1995). Although all of these types of support are important and facilitate work-life integration, the focus of this chapter is supervisor support.

Within the workplace, supervisors play an especially important role in providing workers both emotional support and work supports that mitigate work-life conflict and stress and facilitate work-life integration (Allen, 2000; Bowen, 1998; Dignam & West, 1988; Friedman, Christensen, & DeGroot, 1999; Lechner, 1993; Miller, Ellis, Zook, & Lyles, 1990; Moen, Harris-Abbott, Lee, & Roehling, 2000; Ray, 1987; Ray & Miller, 1994; Repetti, 1993; Rodgers & Rodgers, 1989; Rowley, Rosse, & Harvey, 1992; Warren & Johnson, 1995). The growing work-life literature identifies supervisors as critical in humanizing organizations by responding to employees' work and personal/family dilemmas and facilitating workers' use of family support policies and programs. Even if top management expresses concern for the personal welfare of employees, the immediate supervisor's response to work and family concerns is deemed more critical in setting the tone for a supportive environment (Galinsky, 1988; Ray & Miller, 1994).

The supervisor's role in supporting and helping workers has been examined within the context of the social support and work-life literatures and has been theoretically linked to social psychological theories of prosocial behavior, such as bystander-equity theory and leader-member exchange theory. These theories have focused on the personal and organizational characteristics that impact supervisors' supportive attitudes and behaviors. Social identity theory, although largely untested in this area of research, provides a promising context for broadening the personal and organizational influences on supervisor support for work-life integration by also examining supervisors' sense of personal identity and supervisors' identification with the organization and the work group.

This chapter bridges the domains of social support, social identity, and work-life to better understand supervisor support for work-life integration. First, the chapter provides an overview of the social support and social identity literatures as they relate to work-life integration. Second, the chapter identifies the factors that contribute to supervisors' supporting and helping workers with work-life integration and explores how gender and race shape workers' perceptions of supervisor support. Third, the chapter describes the myriad ways that supervisors can support and help workers with work-life challenges. The chapter concludes with implications and recommendations for supervisory practice and work-life integration and for future research related to supervisor support for work-life integration.

THEORETICAL FRAMEWORKS FOR SUPERVISOR SUPPORT FOR WORK-LIFE INTEGRATION

Over the last 50 years, the research on supervision has expanded beyond an emphasis on production to encompass personal support of workers. Researchers have drawn on a variety of theoretical perspectives in defining, explaining, and predicting supervisor support. The research on supervisor support has predominately come out of the social support and work-life literatures. Supervisor support for work-life integration has been primarily defined and measured by assessing workers' perceptions of:

1. Supervisors' concern and help—that is, show concern for workers, care about how workers think and feel, view each worker as an individual, respect each worker's confidentiality, help workers with personal problems (Cammann, Fichman, Jenkins, & Klesh, 1983).
2. Supervisors' sensitivity to work-life issues—that is, understand that workers have to meet family responsibilities as well as those related to the job (Warren & Johnson, 1995), accommodate workers when they have personal or family matters to attend to, and know about agency policies that impact personal or family needs or issues.
3. Supervisors' flexibility—that is, let workers come in late or leave early to accommodate family needs (Hugh & Galinsky, 1988).

Overall, workers want supportive supervisors who will be sensitive, flexible, and helpful with work-life issues and problems. The following summary of the social support literature related to supervisor support for work-life issues highlights theoretical perspectives and selected findings.

Supervisor Support

Likert (1967) first developed the *supportive model* of organizational behavior, which espoused supportive leadership and relationships that enhance the personal worth of employees and, ultimately, organizational effectiveness. Likert championed "psychological closeness" between supervisors and workers as one important component of the supportive model, a process through which supervisors strive to learn and understand workers' personal and work problems and psychologically support their performance. The supportive model extended beyond supervisor support to include organizational support. Organizations also needed to take responsibility for helping workers with personal and family problems that affected productivity. This notion gave birth to employee assistance programs (EAPs) and the expectation that supervisors would play one of the most important roles in helping troubled workers (Wright, 1984).

Bayer and Gerstein (1988) and Gerstein (1990) first adapted social-psychological theories of prosocial behavior to supervisory helping behavior, using models of bystander-emergency intervention and the equity theory of interpersonal relationships. The *bystander-emergency intervention perspective* (Gerstein, 1990) relies on the "dynamic combination" of the problem situation, personal characteristics of the victim and bystander, and the perceived costs of getting involved that determine the bystander's willingness to take action (p. 26).

This framework predicts that the more clear and severe the victim's (worker's) problem as perceived by the bystander (supervisor), the greater the similarities among them in personal characteristics and attitudes, and that the lower the personal or organizational costs to the bystander (supervisor) for helping, the more likely the bystander (supervisor) will engage in helping behavior.

The *equity model of prosocial behavior* suggests that "people strive to maximize their gains in relationships by balancing the relationship's rewards against its costs" Gerstein, 1990, p. 207). Supervisors therefore, according to this perspective, take some kind of action when a worker's behavior creates distress and inequitable relationships within the work group that result in production problems for the supervisor. Thus, Bayer and Gerstein argue that when the bystander-equity intervention models of prosocial behavior are applied to supervisory behavior, they help explain the supervisor-worker helping process. The bystander-equity model takes into account personal characteristics of supervisors, such as gender, race, and age; supervisors' attitudes and beliefs about workers' life problems; the type and seriousness of problems; and the costs involved in helping that may influence supervisors' support or intervention with workers.

Leader-member exchange theory is another theoretical perspective that has been used to examine the quality of the supervisor-worker relationship and its impact on work-family conflict. Leader-member exchange theory is a derivative of social exchange theory that proposes that gestures of goodwill are exchanged between employees and the organization, and subordinates and their superiors, when particular actions warrant reciprocity (Blau, 1964). Exchanges with supervisors or leaders are considered distinct from exchanges with organizations, although the nature of the supervisor-worker exchange may directly or indirectly influence workers' perceptions of organizational support (Thompson, Beauvais, & Lyness, 1999; Wayne, Shore, & Liden, 1997).

Quality supervisor-subordinate (leader-member) exchanges are based on trust, respect, loyalty, interaction and developmental, and interpersonal support (Dansereau, Graen, & Haga, 1975; Liden & Maslyn, 1993; Settoon, Bennett, & Liden, 1996; Wayne & Green, 1993; Wayne et. al., 1997). Supervisors tend to develop different exchange relationships with workers depending on the level of mutual trust, respect, loyalty, and support cultivated and experienced (Wayne & Green, 1993). When leader-member exchange theory was applied to women workers' work-family conflict and stress, it was discovered that women who had high-quality relationships with their supervisors (based on respect, trust, and support) experienced less work-family conflict and stress than women who had low-quality exchange relationships with supervisors (Bernas & Major, 2000). Like bystander-equity theory, the leader-member exchange theoretical perspective focuses on personal characteristics that affect supervisors' attitudes and actions, namely mutual respect, trust, and support between supervisor and worker.

Personal and Organizational Outcomes

The research also demonstrates that when supervisors are sensitive, flexible, and helpful with work-life issues, workers personally benefit and the organization benefits. Workers benefit by experiencing positive work-life outcomes, including lower levels of stress (Bernas & Major, 2000; Carlson & Perrewe, 1999; Galinsky & Stein, 1990; Lechner, 1993; Ray & Miller, 1994), reduced role conflict and role strain (Thompson et al., 1999; Warren & Johnson, 1995); and greater flexibility and autonomy in achieving work-life balance (Catalyst, 1997; Friedman et al., 1999; Scandura & Lankau, 1997).

Just as workers personally benefit from supervisor support for work-life integration, the organization also benefits through greater retention of employees, such as women following childbirth and parents with young children (Glass & Riley, 1998; Lyness, Thompson, Francesco, & Judiesch, 2000); stronger commitment (Lyness et al., 2000; Scandura & Lankau, 1997; Tombari & Spinks, 1999) and loyalty (Roehling, Roehling, & Moen, 2001) to the organization; increased efficiency and productivity (Friedman et al., 1999; Tombari & Spinks, 1999); and enhanced corporate image (Lee, MacDermid, & Buck, 2000).

As many organizations strive to develop more supportive cultures or climates through the implementation of family-friendly programs or family-responsive policies (Glass & Estes, 1997; Lambert & Hopkins, 1995; Lee et al., 2000; Warren & Johnson, 1995), it is the immediate supervisor's attitudes and behaviors that often determine workers' perceptions of organizational support (Bernas & Major, 2000; Galinsky, 1988; Ray & Miller, 1994). For example, just because family-friendly programs exist at the organizational level does not necessarily mean every supervisor will know about them, support them, or encourage using them at the line level. Conversely, in organizations without officially sanctioned work-life policies or programs, individual supervisors may help workers strike a work-life balance through supportive attitudes and management behaviors, such as recognizing workers' lives outside of the workplace and seeking creative approaches that benefit both the workers and the organization (Friedman et al., 1999).

Supportive Roles

The research also indicates that there may be some core roles that supervisors play that communicate supportive attitudes and behaviors, in general, whether the issue is training, performance management, or work-life balance. When supervisors are effective in these roles, workers perceive them as supportive for a variety of workplace issues. For example, supervisors play a key *gatekeeping* role in workers' knowledge and use of organizational benefits, resources, and programs that might help workers better manage work and life responsibilities (Gerstein & Bayer, 1988; Hopkins, 1997; Lambert & Hopkins, 1993). The research suggests that for workers who are struggling to balance work and personal life, supervisors are especially important as conduits to assistance. First, supervisors are key people that workers go to when they are experiencing both work and personal problems (Hopkins, 1997; Rodgers & Rodgers, 1989). Second, many workers rely on their supervisors to help them manage their work and family responsibilities by being knowledgeable about family-responsive policies or benefits (i.e., child or eldercare, flextime, job sharing, telecommuting) and by being accommodating for personal/family matters or emergencies (Galinsky, 1989; Lambert & Hopkins, 1993).

Other supportive roles that supervisors play are *coach* and *mentor*. The coaching supervisor initiates helpful dialogues with workers who are in need of assistance with problem solving. The goal of such a dialogue is for the supervisor and worker to explore together what needs to change, determine the goals that seem relevant for a change process, and specify how to follow-up in order to monitor and evaluate the change strategy (Hunt & Weintraub, 2002). The mentoring process relies heavily on the initiative of a supervisee or "mentee" to identify someone they respect, find approachable, and see as capable of providing useful advice and/or teaching. The goal of the mentoring relationship is to foster strength, mutual growth, and interdependence based on trust, openness, and authenticity (Bell, 1996). Mentoring can be especially beneficial for the development of women and minority workers (Scandura, 1998), and more positive mentee outcomes are related to mentoring by supervisors and coworkers rather than assigned formal mentors (Raabe & Beehr, 2003). One study showed that workers with mentors reported significantly less family-to-work conflict than workers without mentors, primarily due to mentors' support, advice, and role modeling (Nielson, Carlson, & Lankau, 2001).

Theoretical Gaps

Although the social support literature demonstrates the importance of the supervisor's role in work-life integration, much of the research has been based on identifying and cultivating best management practice. For the most part, these lines of inquiry tells us about different aspects of the supervisor-worker helping process and work-life outcomes but still leave some gaps. What appears to be lacking is a more comprehensive understanding of what helps explain and predict the circumstances under which supervisors support and help workers with work-life difficulties. One limitation in using theoretical perspectives such as bystander-equity theory or leader-member exchange theory to study supervisor support for work-life integration is that these theories appear to rely mostly on interpersonal attraction—how similar the supervisor is to the worker or how much the supervisor wishes to keep the work group interpersonally attracted or equitably balanced. However, this does not help explain those situations in which supervisors support and help workers who are unlike themselves or do so at some organizational or personal cost (i.e., when the intervention itself affects the interdependence of the rest of the work group, the worker leaves the organization, or the work group perceives the supervisor as unfairly helping one worker more than others). Additionally, a leader-member exchange or bystander-equity perspective would not necessarily address organizational factors (i.e., mandates, procedures, training) that might impact both the quality of the supervisor-worker relationship and supervisor support of work-life integration.

Another limitation in the existing research is that although it has focused on examining the personal characteristics that affect supervisors' behaviors, it has not addressed the influence that supervisors' own work-life experiences, problems, or help-seeking patterns may have on their response to workers' difficulties. It is unlikely that supervisors are problem-free and that their interactions with workers are not influenced or clouded by their own personal experiences. Finally, many studies have not sufficiently examined the real-life actions by supervisors in actual work settings, but rather what workers perceive or say supervisors do, and what supervisors report they would do in hypothetical situations.

Social identity theory may provide a theoretical framework that takes our understanding a step further by filling the holes in our ability to predict the circumstances under which supervisors will support and help workers who are struggling to manage work-life responsibilities. The next section describes the main assumptions of social identity theory and how it can be used to help explain supervisor support for work-life integration.

Social Identity Theory

The more progressive management models call for employees to "create relationships and conditions that allow both themselves and others to function competently" (Culbert, 1996, p. 82). Culbert proposes that a combination of self-interests and organizational agendas determine an employee's mind-set and perceptions that influence an employee's actions in a given situation. For example, it may be that the supervisors who are the most responsive and helpful to workers are those who have a vested interest in the success of their work group and who are strongly influenced by an organizational agenda that espouses employee well-being. When members of a work group function effectively, the organization benefits and the supervisor's own sense of personal accomplishment is bolstered. Supervisors in organizations that are primarily interested in productivity may likely respond to workers' problems by taking adverse disciplinary action or firing them.

Research indicates that employees who are identified with their employing organization are also identified with their work group and are more likely to engage in behaviors that benefit both the organization and the work group members, including helping out other members (Dutton, Dukerich, & Harquail, 1994; Van Dyne, Graham, & Dienesch, 1994). Thus, exploring supervisors' identification with both the organization and the work group appears to be important in understanding supervisor support for work-life integration.

Social identity theory has been gaining ground in organizational study and has been applied to research on work and family issues (Lobel, 1991; Posig, 1995; Wharton & Erickson, 1993). Social identity theory explains how individuals define themselves and others. It assumes that "people tend to classify themselves and others into various social categories" in order to define their "personal identity" and the extent to which they relate to and identify with others in their social environment (Ashforth & Mael, 1989, p. 20). In other words, people behave in ways that are consistent with what is important to them (Lobel, 1991). Social identity encompasses a person's total psychological identification with social groups and roles that are deemed meaningful and important in shaping attitudes, beliefs, and behaviors (Deaux, 1993; Hooper, 1985; Tajfel, 1978). How we see ourselves and how we interact with others is shaped strongly by our social identity (Garza & Borchert, 1990). People perceive themselves as having different roles in their daily personal and work life and some roles or identities are more important than others in how they define themselves and how much they are willing to invest themselves in a particular role (Bielby & Bielby, 1989; Krause, 1995). Supervisors who perceive their work roles as responsive and supportive with subordinates may be more apt to engage in helpful interactions with workers than supervisors who perceive their roles with subordinates as only task-centered.

Studies applying social identity theory to organizations and occupational groups have demonstrated high levels of work group identification, understanding, and salience of group membership (Alderfer & Smith, 1982; Allen & Stephenson, 1983; Ashforth & Mael, 1989; Kramer, 1991). In fact, at work, a person's self-concept derives from both the work group and the organization as a whole. The cognitive connections or identification that individual members have with their organization influences the kinds of interactions and behaviors that they engage in with other members of the organization (Dutton et al., 1994). Organizational identification can be described as the extent to which a person's self-concept "has many of the same characteristics he or she believes define the organization as a social group" (p. 239). Interpersonal consequences of employees' strong organizational identification include increased cooperation and effort toward coworkers and enhanced work group cohesion characterized by trust and a psychological attachment to work group members (Dutton et al., 1994). Research conducted on individuals, both alone and in groups, demonstrates that "behavior depends on the nature of the task and on the nature of the individual's perception of his relation to the group" (Olmstead, 1974, p. 150).

Social identity theory has the potential for providing a context for examining supportive supervisory attitudes and behaviors in work-life integration that addresses gaps in the research. There are several ways of examining supervisor support for work-life integration that capture the more personal aspects of helping, including supervisors' sense of personal identity, supervisors' identification with the organization, and supervisors' identification with the work group.

First, according to social identity theory, personal identity is based upon a combination of factors, including a set of values and beliefs and personal experiences (Ashforth & Mael, 1989). Supervisors' beliefs and attitudes about help-seeking and help-giving at work likely determine how supportive and helpful supervisors are with workers experiencing work-life conflict. For example, supervisors who believe that workers should talk to them about work-life problems and think that it is part of their job to help workers with personal problems may be more likely to intervene proactively with workers than supervisors who do not believe that workers should talk about their problems at work. Certain values and attitudes may predispose some supervisors to be supportive and helpful people in general, not just when there are performance problems. But supervisors' responses may also be affected by supervisors' own work-life experiences, and their experiences in seeking help for problems. For example, a supervisor who has experienced child-care problems and received support and assistance from a manager and the human resources department may be more likely to support workers in similar circumstances and refer them to human resources. Thus, a supervisor's sense of his or her own identity, which includes personal experiences, may help explain his or her behaviors with workers.

Second, Dubin (1974, p. 115) first stressed the need for "understanding the linkages between individual and organization" because the nature of the linkages may provide information as to why certain human resources policies may or may not be effective. Accepting this premise and applying it to supervisor support for work-life integration, it would be important to understand how supervisors are linked to the organization that employs them and how identified they are with the organization. If the organization has bought into the notion of work-life integration and the importance of supervisor support for workers, and establishes policies for helping workers, how does the supervisor envision him- or herself accepting and carrying out the policies? Additionally, the amount of support, training, and assistance from upper management in supervisors' identification and support for workers may influence what happens at the supervisor-worker level. For example, if supervisors feel supported by management, are provided appropriate training to do their job, and have opportunities for input into decision making, they may feel more identified and connected to the organization. Strong identification with the organization may lead managers and supervisors to act in more prosocial ways toward their subordinates for the overall good or benefit of organizational functioning. According to Dutton, Dukerich, and Harquail (1994), when individual members demonstrate behaviors that are inconsistent or interrupt the normal organizational routines or culture, it motivates other members to question and review what is happening.

Social identity theory expands the premises of bystander-equity theory and leader-member exchange theory by broadening the organizational context for supervisory action. Not only are the organizational mandates and perceived costs for monitoring and addressing work-life conflicts and problems important for explaining supervisor support and intervention, but also important are the roles supervisors perceive they play in the organization and their identification, commitment, and linkages to the organization as a whole. Context is also important to social identity; past context and changes in context can impact current identity (Deaux, 1993). Thus, shifts in organizational philosophy about supporting and helping employees, roles and expectations for supervisors, and changes in organizational directives can impact supervisors' identification with the organization, thereby affecting supportive behavior.

Third, the expanded view of supervision that has called for a new breed of supervisors to be supportive leaders and coaches may well have resulted in a stronger identification with the work group. Indeed, Barker and Tompkins (1994) found that employees' identification with their work group or team was stronger than their identification with the organization. A consequence of identification with the group is an emotional investment in how well the group performs and the success or failure of any one member in the group (Ashforth & Mael, 1989). Research also indicates that group cohesiveness comes about more from members being identified with the group than members liking each other or having similar characteristics (Hogg, 1987). In fact, group cohesiveness is a product of social identification, irrespective of interpersonal attraction. The more positive a member feels about his or her group, the more motivated the person is to promote in-group solidarity, cooperation, and support (Hogg & Abrams, 1990). The more cohesive a group is, the more likely its members will socially interact and influence each other (Turner, 1987).

Brown et al.'s (1986) research of factory workers revealed the strong interpersonal relationships and emotional attachment within work groups. Supervisors tend to have daily contact and interaction with the workers in their work group or unit. It would follow that in working together over time, supervisors develop a sense of identification, attachment, and investment in the work unit, just as workers do. Thus a psychological link develops between the supervisor and the work group. As supervisors become more psychologically close with workers, a common set of beliefs and values may develop over time, group norms will likely get established, and attitudes and behaviors are reinforced within the work group.

Overall, supervisors have a vested interest in managing the work group effectively. So it makes sense that the more psychologically identified they are with the work group, the more they will want the work group to be successful and its members psychologically healthy and focused on the work. Thus, this perspective also incorporates tenets of bystander-equity theory by which supervisors express their concern about individual worker well-being or distressed work group relations through emphasis on job performance and productivity. However, the extent to which supervisors are personally identified with the work group may well influence concern for worker well-being that goes beyond job performance. For example, if supervisors feel psychologically close to and a part of their work group, they may likely create an environment in which members of the work group feel free to talk over work-life problems and provide each other support. In the context of this supportive and responsive climate, supervisors may help workers based on workers' requests for help, supervisors' observations of workers' difficulties, and evidence of poor performance.

For many people, work is a fundamental aspect of life that helps give individuals a sense of purpose; thus, it makes sense for individuals to try to derive a sense of community at work, just as they strive to make their personal and family life richer and more meaningful. It may be that through this endeavor, supervisors become more identified with their "work family" and committed to the success of their work group, the individuals within it, and the organization that employs them.

Gender and Race

Social identity theory also provides a theoretical context for understanding how personal characteristics such as supervisors' gender and race combines with workers' gender and race to influence supervisor support for work-life integration. As more women, especially minority women, work outside the home (Blank, 1995; Duxbury & Higgins, 1994; Jackson, 1994; Seck, Finch, Mar-Barak, & Poverny, 1993), they are thought to be increasingly susceptible to personal and family difficulties that threaten their well-being and undermine satisfaction with both work and family life (Bailey, Wolfe, & Wolfe, 1996; Galinsky, Bond, & Friedman, 1993; Lambert, 1999; Roxburgh, 1996; Swanberg, 1997). Several studies have documented that women tend to have greater concerns than men around issues of work-family interference, marital satisfaction, emotional well-being, and depression (Bailey et al., 1996; Barnett & Baruch, 1987; Duxbury & Higgins, 1994; Jackson, 1994; Lambert & Hopkins, 1995; Raber, 1994). Women workers are more likely than men to be single parents managing family responsibilities on their own. Approximately 69% of working women are single parents; at least 54% of African American women workers are single parents (Casey & Pitt-Catsouphes, 1994).

Research also indicates that workers may have different patterns of help seeking for personal concerns depending on their gender and race. Two studies demonstrated that men appear to be more likely than women to approach a supervisor or coworker for help with a personal or family problem, whereas women are more likely to seek help from a family member or friend outside of work (Reed, 1994; Van Der Pompe & Heus, 1993). Galinsky, Ruopp, and Blum (1986) found that managers were more likely to hear about work-life problems from men than from women. Women and men tend to be supervised more often by men than women; perhaps women feel less comfortable than men discussing a work-life concern with a male supervisor. Lightner and McConatha (1995) found that female supervisors were more likely than male supervisors to identify behaviors indicative of work-life troubles even when workers did not disclose concerns. These findings suggest that female supervisors may be more attuned to workers' work-life issues.

The level of supervisor support and help that women workers, especially minority women, experience has not been sufficiently studied. Much of the research on supervisor support and intervention with workers has focused on Caucasian male workers and supervisors, with little emphasis on differences in experiences along gender and racial lines. In one study of Hispanic workers, both men and women were reluctant to talk about or seek help for work-life concerns, mostly because they tended to respond to cultural norms dictating that problems should stay within the family (Knouse, Rosenfeld, & Culbertson, 1992).

Only a few studies have explored how workers' gender and race may interact with their supervisor's gender and race to affect help seeking and help giving for work-life issues. Gerstein (1990), Greenhaus and Parasuraman (1993), Greenhaus, Parasuraman, and Wormley (1990), and Hopkins (2002) have explored both gender and race differences in various aspects of supportive supervisory behavior. Gerstein's bystander equity model of supervisory helping behavior suggested that when the supervisor and the worker were of the same gender or race, the supervisor was more likely to support and take action to help the worker. Greenhaus and Parasuraman's research, based on social identity theory, showed that how managers defined and perceived themselves influenced how they perceived and treated subordinates regarding job performance, career advancement, and supervisor support and mentoring. For example, supervisors felt personally distant from employees who differed from them in gender and race. Caucasian male supervisors perceived women and minority subordinates as "performing less effectively" than their Caucasian male peers, despite a lack of evidence to support those perceptions (Greenhaus & Parasuraman, 1993).

Hopkins found that the interaction of workers' gender and race and their supervisor's gender and race influenced the degree to which workers worried about losing their job due to personal/family problems, engaged in help-seeking, and perceived supervisory support. One cannot assume that women workers' experiences differ from men's or that minority workers' experiences differ from Caucasians without taking into account how those experiences may be altered when the supervisor is of the same or different gender or race than the worker. Women in this study were more likely than men to seek help for work-life problems, especially if their supervisor was a woman, but women workers found their male supervisors more understanding and flexible about work-life concerns than their female supervisors. The data in this study also indicated that African American women had less daily interaction with supervisors and they felt more isolated and alienated from their supervisors than did any other workers. In this organization, like many others, most of the supervisors were male and Caucasian, and Caucasian men supervised most of the African American women workers. Supervisors, especially Caucasian male supervisors, must be able to supportively interact and assist employees whose gender and race differs from their own.

Harrison, Price, and Bell (1998) distinguished between surface- and deep-level diversity in a study of their effects on work group cohesion. Surface-level diversity is characterized by differences in overt, biological characteristics, whereas deep-level diversity reflects differences in attitudes, beliefs, and values. Deep-level differences are ultimately more important than surface-level differences in determining the degree of social integration and cohesion. Beyond differences in demographics, there may be deep-level psychological differences between supervisors and workers that influence their interactions and workers' perceptions of support.

IMPLICATIONS FOR SUPERVISORY PRACTICE AND WORK-LIFE INTEGRATION

The research described previously has implications for organizations that increasingly are faced with managing a more diverse workforce, especially in lower-level jobs where welfare reform and a growing immigrant population have contributed to a more diverse group of employees (Bailey et al., 1996; Freidman & DiTomaso, 1996; Lambert, 1999). Furthermore, as employee demographics change and more employees bring lifestyle concerns into the workplace (Thomas, 1996), organizations are forced to develop a more supportive and responsive culture in order to both attract and retain a diverse, qualified workforce. Understanding how gender, race, and differing attitudes and beliefs influence supervisors' and workers' interactions and helping behaviors can be one important step toward creating an environment in which workers feel free to seek help for work-life issues and supervisors respond by being available, supportive, and helpful. There may be more that supervisors can do to support workers (especially women) experiencing work-life difficulties and more they can do to influence workers' use of helping resources.

It appears that one of the most important steps that supervisors can take toward being more responsive to women workers would be initiating more face-to-face contact and daily interaction, especially with African American women who are entering the workplace at an increasing rate. Being more available to minority women workers and offering increased opportunities for informal interaction may translate to being more supportive.

Several studies on work-family issues show that employees overwhelmingly desire more supportive and flexible supervisory responses to their work-family problems (Galinsky, Hughes, & Shinn, 1986; Hughes & Galinsky, 1994; Rothausen, 1994). More women than men and parents than nonparents rate flexibility of work schedule as important to their job satisfaction and organizational commitment (McGowan & Hart, 1992; Rothausen, 1994; Scandura & Lankau, 1997). Supervisors who are willing to be flexible are likely to be perceived by women as supportive (Hopkins, 2002). Indeed, research indicates that women in low-level clerical and technical jobs without flexibility report less supportive supervision (Hughes & Galinsky, 1994; Rothausen, 1994). In a study by Catalyst (1997), workers especially appreciated when supervisors were willing to entertain alternative work arrangements (e.g., part-time, teleworking, extended hours/shorter work week) and asked workers for their ideas and assistance in planning for how alternative arrangements could work.

At the organizational level, the more top executives or senior management perceive the need to adapt to changing demographics and to experiment with different ways of doing things, the more likely the organization will be to develop and institute a variety of alternative work arrangements (Lee et al., 2000). Indeed, one of the most effective organizational strategies for work-life integration appears to be work redesign (Batt & Valcour, 2003). Therefore, this is an area where supervisors can demonstrate concrete support for work-life integration by assisting workers in the redesign of work structures, experimenting with approaches that meet both the organization's needs and the worker's personal needs. Case studies of supervisors who help with work-life integration show that they clearly define work expectations in terms of results and simultaneously "ask employees to identify the important goals, concerns, and demands outside the office that require time and energy" (Friedman et al., 1999, p. 121). The supervisors use this information "to draw a road map" toward professional and personal success whereby "they give their employees specific goals but also great autonomy over how to achieve those goals" (p. 121).

Overall, there are a variety of other ways that supervisors can support and help workers with work-life challenges, including:

- Recognizing the pressures and demands of personal responsibilities on work life.
- Communicating genuine concern and understanding about employees' work-life problems.
- Being knowledgeable about work-life programs and policies.
- Disseminating information about organizational benefits, resources, policies, and programs to help workers better balance work and life responsibilities.
- Facilitating workers' use of work-life policies and programs and referring workers to helping resources.

- Planning for and managing maternity in collaboration with workers.
- Advocating for work-life policies and supports in the workplace.
- Engaging in coaching and mentoring workers.

Supervisor Development

Because the research indicates that attitudes, behaviors, and organizational and personal conditions could be enhanced or changed to facilitate supervisor support, there are also implications for how supervisors can be trained, mentored, and supported to appropriately respond to workers experiencing work-life conflict and problems. For example, work-life, organizational development (OD), or employee assistance (EAP) staff are often housed within the organization and can foster positive supervisor attitudes about intervening with employees having problems and help supervisors translate positive attitudes into more helpful and appropriate behaviors. These staff members can also help develop supervisors' ability to notice workers with work-life issues. There may be a need for increased and more comprehensive training for supervisors in identifying, supporting, and referring employees to helping resources. Work-life, OD, and EAP staff should consider utilizing assessment methods such as supervisor surveys, focus groups, or informal brown-bag lunch seminars to gain a better understanding of what supervisors need to help them support workers. These staffers can also help supervisors and workers develop peer support and assistance within work groups by encouraging supervisors to establish linkages to their programs. For example, a supervisory liaison could be appointed to the work-life or EAP programs from each department to educate and support other supervisors and work groups and provide feedback to work-life or EAP staff regarding training and consultation needs.

It is also important that work-life, OD, and EAP staffers assess how the organization supports supervisors in their role of helping workers with work-life integration. It is estimated that only about 10% of learned skills are transferred to the workplace (Curry, Caplan, & Knuppel, 1994). A contributing factor is management's failure to create a supportive task environment, including performance feedback, mentoring, modeling, and positive attitudes toward training (Gregoire, Propp, & Poertner, 1998, p. 9). Upper management should facilitate the transfer of learning to the work environment by following-up with workers after training in the following ways:

1. Ask supervisors to share what they learned in a department or staff meeting.
2. Discuss with supervisors how they plan to use the learning with their workers.
3. Make transfer to the job a work or department norm (Gregoire et al., 1998).

4. Provide opportunities for supervisors to practice what they learned.
5. Incorporate application of the new learning into job performance evaluations (Lombardo & Eichinger, 2000).
6. Provide reinforcement for the new behavior or demonstrated knowledge.
7. Create an environment for sharing new learning across the work group by helping staff to view themselves as a team delivering both formal and informal training to each other and by facilitating peer consultation processes (Garrett & Barretta-Herman, 1995).

Training, opportunities to interact with workers, and management support of supervisors' decisions all contribute to positive attitudes and supportive actions.

RECOMMENDATIONS FOR FUTURE RESEARCH: BUILDING ON SOCIAL IDENTITY THEORY

Social identity theory offers an appropriate theoretical perspective for examining and understanding supervisor support and help with workers who are trying to manage work-life conflict and problems. Just as social identity theory has gained value in examining organizational and work group dynamics and work and family issues, it can and should be used to study supervisory supportive behaviors in real-life work situations. Using a social identity perspective and a combination of observation, questionnaires, and qualitative interviews should provide a more complete picture of supervisor's supportive behavior.

Although there is significant research on the importance of supervisor support for work-life integration, there is relatively little information on the occupational, organizational, and personal characteristics that help explain the circumstances in which supervisors support and help workers with work-life difficulties. For example, do job stress and challenging responsibilities limit supervisors' ability to respond supportively with workers? Do upper management support and training enhance supervisors' helping behaviors with workers? To what extent does supervisors' awareness of workers' personal and family problems affect their supportive behaviors? Do supervisors' personal experiences in seeking help for their own work-life issues influence their attitudes and responses to workers? It is also necessary to take into account attitudinal and behavioral responses based on surface-level (e.g., gender and race) and deep-level (e.g., values and attitudes) differences between the supervisor and members of the work group. Thus, future research is needed to better understand, predict, and facilitate the circumstances in which supervisor support for work-life integration is likely to occur.

One study (Hopkins, 1997) suggested that personal factors do significantly influence supervisor support and help with workers with personal and family concerns, including:

1. Supervisors' positive attitudes about help giving and seeking (i.e., belief in the importance of supporting work-life integration and belief that helping workers with work-life concerns/problems is part of their job).
2. Their own experiences in seeking and receiving help for personal and family difficulties.
3. Their level of competence in identifying and helping workers with problems.
4. Their awareness of workers' personal and family issues.

Notably, the findings showed that supervisors' personal experiences in getting help for their own personal and family issues explained *how* they helped workers. Supervisors who used formal helping resources themselves through the company or in the community were more likely to refer workers to professional resources (i.e., EAP, human resource department, community agency). Supervisors who received informal help for their personal and family issues were more likely to just talk with workers about problems, support them, or suggest that workers talk over concerns with family or friends.

It may also be that supervisors' helping interactions with workers are influenced by more emotional, situation-specific factors and can only be explained by the situations or context in which they occur. As Skevington (1989) points out in her research of emotion in social identity theory, it is difficult to assess the more elusive affective aspects of behavior in a situation-specific context. This might be another aspect of supervisor support to be explored in future research.

It should also be noted that the theoretical perspectives discussed in this chapter, including social identity theory, do not address the underlying organizational structural factors such as job design and organizational culture that may also impact supervisor support. For example, jobs that overwhelm supervisors with work responsibilities can interfere with their ability to be supportive and responsive to workers. Jobs that are not challenging or do not provide supervisors with opportunities for advancement may detract from supervisors' identification and commitment to both the organization and the workers. An organizational culture that encourages covering up behaviors that indicate worker problems may keep supervisors from successfully identifying, supporting, and referring workers to helping resources. Therefore, it may be necessary to expand the application of social identity theory by also examining the structural aspects of supervisors' jobs and supervisors' commitment to the job itself.

A primary task in applying social identity theory to supervisor support for work-life integration is operationalizing and developing (or modifying) measures of supervisors' identification with the work group and the organization, the extent of supervisors' own work-life experiences and help-seeking, and their beliefs and attitudes about work-life integration. Additionally, it would be helpful to gauge the impact of supervisor support (attitudes and actions) on outcomes for workers' experiencing work-life difficulties. Does supervisor support and help ultimately lead to workers resolving their difficulties, or at least, experiencing less conflict and stress? We do not know enough about the effectiveness of supervisor support.

It is important to consider and test a variety of theories and frameworks for understanding and predicting human behavior, and no one theory should exclude the exploration of other theories in a particular area of study. However, using social identity theory to help explain supervisor support for work-life integration expands the breadth of what we examine and how we perceive the supportive interactions between supervisors and workers. Because supervisors, through their attitudes and behaviors, play a critical role in creating a responsive organizational culture for work-life integration, this information ultimately benefits organizations in their efforts to recruit and retain competent employees, improve productivity, adapt to change, and effectively compete in the marketplace.

REFERENCES

Alderfer, C., & Smith, K. (1982). Studying intergroup relations embedded in organizations. *Administrative Science Quarterly, 27,* 35–65.

Allen, P., & Stephenson, G. (1983). Intergroup understanding and size of organization. *British Journal of Industrial Relations, 21,* 312–329.

Allen, T. (2000). Family-supportive work environments: The role of organizational perceptions. *Journal of Vocational Behavior, 58*(3), 414–435.

Ashforth, B., & Mael, F. (1989). Social identity theory and the organization. *Academy of Management Review, 14*(1), 20–39.

Bailey, D., Wolfe, D., & Wolfe, C. (1996). The contextual impact of social support across race and gender: Implications for African American women in the workplace. *Journal of Black Studies, 26,* 287–307.

Barker, J., & Tompkins, P. (1994). Identification in the self-managing organization. *Human Communication Research, 21*(2), 223–240.

Barnett, R. C., & Baruch, G. K. (1987). Social roles, gender, and psychological distress. In R. C. Barnett, L. Biener, & G. K. Baruch (Eds.), *Gender and stress* (pp. 122–133). New York: Free Press.

Batt, R., & Valcour, P. (2003). Human resources practices as predictors or work-family outcomes and employee turnover. *Industrial Relations, 42*(2), 189–220.

Bayer, G., & Gerstein, L. (1988). Supervisory attitudes toward impaired workers: A factor analytic study of the behavioral index of troubled employees. *The Journal of Applied Behavioral Science, 24,* 413–422.

Bell, C. R. (1996). *Managers as mentors: Building partnerships for learning.* San Francisco: Berrett-Koehler.

Bernas, K., & Major, D. (2000). Contributors to stress resistance: Testing a model of women's work-family conflict. *Psychology of Women Quarterly, 24*(2), 170–178.

Bielby, W., & Bielby, D. (1989). Family ties: Balancing commitments to work and family in dual earner households. *American Sociological Review, 54,* 776–789.

Blank, R. (1995). Outlook for the U.S. labor market and prospects for low-wage entry jobs. In D. Nightingale & R. Haveman (Eds.), *The work alternative: Welfare reform and the realities of the job market* (pp. 174–190). Washington, DC: Urban Institute Press.

Blau, P. (1964). *Exchange and power in social life*. New York: Wiley.

Bowen, G. (1998). Effects of leader support in the work unit on the relationship between work spillover and family adaptation. *Journal of Family and Economic Issues, 19*(1), 25–52.

Brough, P., & Kelling, A. (2002). Women, work and well-being: The influence of of work-family and family-work conflict. *New Zealand Journal of Psychology, 31*(1), 29–38.

Brown, R., Condor, S., Mathews, A., Wade, G., & Williams, J. (1986). Explaining intergroup differentiation in an industrialist organization. *Journal of Occupational Psychology, 59*, 273–286.

Cammann, C., Fichman, M., Jenkins G., & Klesh, J. (1983). Assessing the attitudes and perceptions of organizational members. In S. Seashore (Ed.), *Assessing organizational change: A guide to methods, measures, and practices* (pp. 71–119). New York, Wiley.

Carlson, D., & Perrewe, P. (1999). The role of social support in the stressor-strain relationship: An examination of work-family conflict. *Journal of Management, 25*(4), 513–540.

Casey, J., & Pitt-Catsouphes, M. (1994). Employed single mothers: Balancing job and homelife. In M. Lundy & B. Younger (Eds.), *Empowering women in the workplace: Perspectives, innovations, and techniques for helping professionals* (pp. 37–53). New York: Haworth Press.

Catalyst. (1997). What individual and supervisor skills are critical for effective arrangements? In *A new approach to flexibility: Managing the work/time equation* (pp. 17–18). New York: Catalyst.

Culbert, S. (1996). *Mind-set management*. New York: Oxford University Press.

Curry, D., Caplan, P., & Knuppel, J. (1994). Transfer of training and adult learning (TOTAL). *Journal of Continuing Social Work Education, 6*(1), 8–14.

Dansereau, F., Graen, G., & Haga, W. (1975). A vertical dyad linkage approach to leadership within formal organizations: A longitudinal investigation of the role making process. *Organizational Behavior and Human Performance, 13*, 46–78.

Deaux, K. (1993). Reconstructing social identity. *Personality and Social Psychology Bulletin, 19*(1), 4–12.

Dignam, J., & West, S. (1988). Social support in the workplace: Tests of six theoretical models. *American Journal of Community Psychology, 16*, 701–724.

Dubin, R. (1974). *Human relations in administration* (4th ed.). Englewood Cliffs, NJ: Prentice-Hall.

Dutton, J., Dukerich, J., & Harquail, C. (1994). Organizational images and member identification. *Administrative Science Quarterly, 39*, 239–263.

Duxbury, L., & Higgins, C. (1994). Interference between work and family: A status report on dual-career and dual-earner mothers and fathers. In M. Lundy & B. Younger (Eds.), *Empowering women in the workplace: Perspectives, innovations, and techniques for helping professionals* (pp. 55–80). New York: Haworth Press.

Freidman, J., & DiTomaso, N. (1996). Myths about diversity: What managers need to know about changes in the U.S. labor force. *California Management Review, 38*, 54–77.

Friedman, S., Christensen, P., & DeGroot, J. (1999, November–December). Work and life: The end of the zero-sum game. *Harvard Business Review*, 119–127.

Galinsky, E. (1988). *The impact of supervisors' attitudes and company culture on work/family adjustment*. Paper presented at the Annual Convention of the American Psychological Association, Washington, DC.

Galinsky, E. (1989). Labor force participation of dual-earner couples and single parents. *Investing in People*. Background papers, Vol. 2, Commission on Workforce Quality and Labor Market Efficiency, U.S. Department of Labor, 1259–1312.

Galinsky, E., Bond, J., & Friedman, J. (1993). *The changing workforce: Highlights of the national study*. New York: Families and Work Institute.

Galinsky, E., Hughes, D., & Shinn, M. (1986). *The corporate work and family life study*. New York: Bank Street College of Education.

Galinsky, E., Ruopp, R., & Blum, K. (1986). *Corporate work and family life decision-maker study*. New York: Bank Street College of Education.

Galinsky, E., & Stein, P. (1990). The impact of human resource policies on employment: Balancing work-family Life. *Journal of Family Issues, 11,* 368–383.

Garrett, K., & Barretta-Herman, A. (1995). Moving from supervision to professional development. *The Clinical Supervisor, 13*(2), 97–110.

Garza, R., & Borchert, J. (1990). Maintaining social identity in a mixed-gender setting: Minority/majority status and cooperative/competitive feedback. *Sex Roles, 22*(11/12), 679–691.

Gerstein, L. (1990). The bystander-equity model of supervisory helping behavior: Past and future research on the prevention of employee problems. In P. M. Roman (Ed.), *Alcohol problem intervention in the work place: Employee assistance programs and strategic alternatives* (pp. 203–225). Westport, CT: Quorum.

Gerstein, L., & Bayer, G. (1988). Employee assistance programs: A systematic investigation of their use. *Journal of Counseling and Development, 66,* 294–297.

Glass, J., & Estes, S. (1996). Workplace support, child care, and turnover intentions among employed mothers of infants. *Journal of Family Issues, 17*(3), 317–335.

Glass, J., & Finley, A. (2002). Coverage and effectiveness of family-responsive workplace policies. *Human Resource Management Review, 12*(3), 313–337.

Glass, J. H., & Riley, L. (1998). Family responsive policies and employee retention following childbirth. *Social Forces, 76*(4), 1401–1435.

Greenhaus, J. H., & Parasuraman, S. (1993). Job performance attributions and career advancement prospects: An examination of gender and race effects. *Organizational Behavior and Human Decision Processes, 55,* 273–297.

Greenhaus, J. H., Parasuraman, S., & Wormley, W. (1990). Effects of race on organizational experiences, job performance evaluations, and career outcomes. *Academy of Management Journal, 33,* 64–86.

Gregoire, T., Propp, J., & Poertner, J. (1998). The supervisor's role in the transfer of training. *Administration in Social Work, 22*(1), 1–18.

Harrison, D., Price, K., & Bell, M. (1998). Beyond relational demography: Time and the effects of surface- and deep-level diversity on work group cohesion. *Academy of Management Journal, 41*(1), 96–108.

Hogg, M. (1987). Social identity and group cohesiveness. In J. Turner (Ed.), *Rediscovering the social group* (pp. 89–116). New York: Basil Blackwell.

Hogg, M., & Abrams, D. (1990). Social motivation, self-esteem and social identity. In D. Abrams & M. Hogg (Eds.), *Social identity theory: Constructive and critical advances* (pp. 28–47). New York: Harvester Wheatsheaf.

Hooper, M. (1985). A multivariate approach to the measurement and analysis of social identity. *Psychological Reports, 57,* 315–325.

Hopkins, K. (1997). Influences on formal and informal supervisor intervention with troubled workers. *Employee Assistance Quarterly, 13,* 33–54.

Hopkins, K. (2002). Interactions of gender and race in workers' help seeking for personal and family problems: Perceptions of supervisor support and intervention. *The Journal of Applied Behavioral Science, 38*(2), 156–176.

Hughes, D., & Galinsky, E. (1994). Gender, job and family conditions, and psychological symptoms. *Psychology of Women Quarterly, 18,* 251–270.

Hughes, D., & Galinsky, E. (1988). Balancing work and family life: Research and corporate application. New York: Bank Street College of Education.

Hunt, J., & Weintraub, J. (2002). *The coaching manager: Developing top talent in business.* Thousand Oaks, CA: Sage.

Jackson, B. (1994). African-American women in the workplace: A personal perspective from African-American female EAPs. In M. Lundy & B. Younger (Eds.), *Empowering women in the workplace: Perspectives, innovations, and techniques for helping professionals* (pp. 11–19). New York: Haworth Press.

Knouse, S., Rosenfeld, P., & Culbertson, A. (1992). *Hispanics in the workplace*. Newbury Park, CA: Sage Publications

Kossek, E. E., & Ozeki, C. (1998). Work-family conflict, policies, and the job-life satisfaction relationship: A review and directions for organizational behavior-human resources research. *Journal of Applied Psychology, 83*(2), 139–149.

Kramer, R. (1991). Intergroup relations and organizational dilemmas: The role of categorization processes. In L. L. Cummings & B. Staw (Eds.), *Research in Organizational Behavior* (pp. 191–228). Greenwich, CT: JAI.

Krause, N. (1995). Stress, alcohol use, and depressive symptoms in later life. *The Gerontologist, 35*(3), 296–307.

Lambert, S. J. (1999). Lower-wage workers and the new realities of work and family. *Annals, 562,* 174–190.

Lambert, S., & Hopkins, K. (1993). *Added benefits: The link between family-responsive policies and work performance at Fel-Pro Incorporated.* Research Report, Fel-Pro Project, School of Social Service Administration, University of Chicago.

Lambert, S. J., & Hopkins, K. (1995). Occupational conditions and workers' sense of community: Variations by gender and race. *American Journal of Community Psychology, 23,* 151–179.

Lechner, V. (1993). Support systems and stress reduction among workers caring for dependent parents. *Social Work, 38*(4), 461–469.

Lee, M., MacDermid, S. M., & Buck, M. (2000). Organizational paradigms of reduced-load work: Accommodation, elaboration, and transformation. *Academy of Management Journal, 43*(6), 1211–1226.

Liden, R., & Maslyn, J. (1993). Scale development for a multidimensional measure of leader-member exchange. Paper presented at the Annual Meeting of the Academy of Management, Atlanta, GA.

Lightner, E., & McConatha, J. (1995). Factors affecting supervisory referrals to employee assistance programs: The impact of race and gender. *Journal of Social Behavior and Personality, 10,* 179–188.

Likert, R. (1967). *The human organization.* New York: McGraw-Hill.

Lobel, S. (1991). Allocation of investment in work and family roles: Alternative theories and implications for research. *Academy of Management Review, 6*(3), 507–521.

Lombardo, M., & Eichinger, R. (2000). *For your improvement: A development and coaching guide.* Minneapolis, MN: Lominger Limited, Inc.

Lyness, K., Thompson, C., Francesco, A., & Judiesch, M. (2000). Work and pregnancy: Individual and organizational factors influencing organizational commitment, time of maternity leave and return to work. *Sex Roles, 41*(7–8), 485–508.

McGowan, K. R., & Hart, L. E. (1992). Exploring the contribution of gender identity to differences in career experiences. *Psychological Reports, 70,* 723–737.

Miller, K., Ellis, B., Zook, E., & Lyles, J. (1990). An integrated model of communication, stress, and burnout in the workplace. *Communication Research, 17,* 300–326.

Moen, P., Harris-Abbott, D., Lee, S., & Roehling, P. (2000). Promoting workforce effectiveness and life quality: Early evidence from the Cornell Couples and Careers study. In E. Applebaum (Ed.), *Balancing acts: Easing the burden and improving the options for working families* (pp. 291–326). Washington, DC: Economic Policy Institute.

Nielson, T., Carlson, D., & Lankau, M. (2001). The supportive mentor as a means of reducing work-family conflict. *Journal of Vocational Behavior, 59*(3), 364–381.

Olmstead, M. (1974). The effect of the group on the individual. In R. Dubin (Ed.), *Human relations in administration* (pp. 149–160). Englewood Cliffs, NJ: Prentice-Hall.

Posig, M. (1995). Work-family conflict clarified: Utilitarian versus social identity approach to role investment. *Dissertation Abstracts International, 55*(11–B), 5112.

Raabe, B., & Beehr, T. (2003). Formal mentoring versus supervisor and coworker relationships:

Differences in perceptions and impact. *Journal of Organizational Behavior, 24*(3), 271–293.

Raber, M. (1994). Women in the workplace: Implications for child care. In M. Lundy & B. Younger (Eds.), *Empowering women in the workplace: Perspectives, innovations, and techniques for helping professionals* (pp. 21–36). New York: Haworth Press.

Ray, E. (1987). Supportive relationships and occupational stress in the workplace. In T. Albrecht & M. Adelman (Eds.), *Communicating social support* (pp. 172–191). Newbury Park, CA: Sage.

Ray, E., & Miller, K. (1994). Social support, home/work stress, and burnout: Who can help? *Journal of Applied Behavioral Science, 30,* 357–373.

Reed, B. (1994). Women and alcohol, tobacco, and other drugs: The need to broaden the base within EAPs. In M. Lundy & B. Younger (Eds.), *Empowering women in the workplace: Perspectives, innovations, and techniques for helping professionals* (pp. 179–201). New York: Haworth Press.

Repetti, R. (1993). Short-term effects of occupational stressors on daily mood and health complaints. *Health Psychology, 12,* 125–131.

Rodgers, F., & Rodgers, C. (1989, November–December). Business and the facts of family life. *Harvard Business Review,* 320–327.

Roehling, P., Roehling, M., & Moen, P. (2001). The relationship between work-life policies and practices and employee loyalty: A life course perspective. *Journal of Family and Economic Issues, 22*(2), 141–170.

Rothausen, T. (1994). Job satisfaction and the parent worker: The role of flexibility and rewards. *Journal of Vocational Behavior, 44*(3), 317–336.

Rowley, D., Rosse, J., & Harvey, O. (1992). The effects of belief systems on the job-related satisfaction of managers and subordinates. *Journal of Applied Social Psycholgy, 22,* 212–231.

Roxburgh, S. (1996). Gender differences in work and well-being: Effects of exposure and vulnerability. *Journal of Health and Social Behavior, 37,* 265–277.

Scandura, T. (1998). Dysfunctional mentoring relationships and outcomes. *Journal of Management, 24*(3), 449–467.

Scandura, T. & Lankau, M. (1997). Relationships of gender, family responsibility and flexible work hours to organizational commitment and job satisfaction. *Journal of Organizational Behavior, 18*(4), 377–391.

Seck, E., Finch, W., Mor-Barak, M., & Poverny, L. (1993). Managing a diverse workforce. *Administration in Social Work, 17,* 67–79.

Settoon, R., Bennett, N., & Liden, R. (1996). Social exchange in organizations: Perceived organizational support, leader-member exchange, and employee reciprocity. *Journal of Applied Psychology, 81,* 219–227.

Skevington, S. (1989). A place for emotion in social identity theory. In S. Skevington & D. Baker (Eds.), *The social identity of women* (pp. 40–58). Newbury Park, CA: Sage.

Swanberg, J. (1997). *Work and family issues among lower-level workers.* Unpublished doctoral dissertation, Brandeis University, Waltham, MA.

Tajfel, H. (1978). *Differentiation between social groups: Studies in the social psychology of intergroup relations.* London: Academic Press.

Thomas, R., Jr. (1996). *Redefining diversity.* New York: Amacom.

Thompson, C., Beauvais, L., & Lyness, K. (1999). When work-family benefits are not enough: The influence of work-family culture on benefit utilization, organizational attachment, and work-family conflict. *Journal of Vocational Behavior, 54*(3), 392–415.

Thompson, C., & Blau, G. (1994). Moving beyond traditional predictors of job involvement: Exploring the impact of work-family conflict and overload. *Journal of Social Behavior & Personality, 8*(4), 635–646.

Tombari, N., & Spinks, N. (1999). The work/family interfave at Royal Bank Financial Group: Successful solutions—A retrospective look at lessons learned. *Women in Management Review, 14*(5), 186–193.

Turner, J. (1987). *Rediscovering the social group.* New York: Basil Blackwell.

Van Der Pompe, G., & Heus, P. (1993). Work stress, social support, and strains among male and female managers. *Anxiety, Stress and Coping, 6,* 215–229.

Van Dyne, L., Graham, J., & Dienesch, R. (1994). Organizational citizenship behavior: Construct redefinition, operationalization, and validation. *Academy of Management Journal, 37,* 765–802.

Voydanoff, P. (2002). Linkages between the work-family interface and work, family, and individual outcomes: An integrative model. *Journal of Family Issues, 23*(1), 138–164.

Warren, J., & Johnson, P. (1995). The impact of workplace support on work-family role strain. *Family Relations, 44,* 163–169.

Wayne, S., & Green, S. (1993). The effects of leader-member exchange on employee citizenship and impression management behavior. *Human Relations, 46,* 1431–1440.

Wayne, S., Shore, L., & Liden, R. (1997, February). Perceived organizational support and leader-member exchange: A social exchange perspective. *Academy of Management Journal,* 82–111.

Wharton, A., & Erickson, R. (1993). Managing emotions on the job and at home: Understanding the consequences of multiple emotional roles. *Academy of Managemnet Review, 18*(3), 457–486.

Wright, J. (1984). EAP: An important supervisory tool. *Supervisory Management, 29*(12), 15–23.

21

Recasting the Work-Family Agenda as a Corporate Social Responsibility

Marcie Pitt-Catsouphes
Bradley Googins
Boston College

INTRODUCTION

Who is responsible for the well-being of working families? Over the course of the past few decades, we have witnessed some subtle but important shifts in our thinking about this question. It was not too long ago that work-family issues were principally defined as "women's issues." However, as a larger percentage of men began to assume more responsibility for the care of children and elderly family members, work-family issues began to be framed as "family issues." It soon became apparent to many working families that it would be difficult—if not impossible—for them to fulfill their family and work responsibilities unless organizations and social institutions also recognized and responded to work-family priorities. In fact, 9 of every 10 (91%) of the nearly 12,000 employees who participated in the "1997 *BusinessWeek*'s Work and Family Corporate Ranking" indicated that they felt workplaces should address work-family issues, and nearly three fourths (73%) stated that they felt their communities should respond (Litchfield & Bankert, 1998).[1] This evolution in our thinking has been a significant transformation; while in the past, work-family issues may have been viewed primarily as private concerns, increasingly they are also identified business and societal issues (Googins, 1991).

There have been concerted efforts made by many individuals and groups to increase workplace responsiveness to employees' work-family priorities. Advocates have often presented employers with a business case argument for work-life initiatives.[2] This business case has been framed around strategic human resource (HR) objectives and contends that it is in employers' self-interest to understand and support employees' efforts to manage their work-family responsibilities (Galinsky & Johnson, 1998). The argument of the HR business case posits that employers could accrue benefits and reduce costs if they establish work-life initiatives that fit organizational needs and also address the needs of employees. During the 1990s—when there were labor market shortages and employers found it strategic to position their companies as *employers of choice*—the HR business case resonated with some managers who recognized that work-life initiatives could provide a competitive edge to their businesses as they attempted to address recruitment and retention challenges.

Unfortunately, there are indications that the HR business case for employer responsiveness may not have been sufficiently compelling to precipitate extensive organizational change or to stimulate the sustained commitment of workplaces to work-family issues. Survey research indicates that, despite the modest increase in employer-supported work-life initiatives, the number of employers that have developed comprehensive work-life initiatives is limited (see Hewitt and Associates, 1998; U.S. Department of Labor, 1999, 2000). For example, the 1998 Business Work-Life Study found that whereas a majority of U.S. workplaces with more than 100 employees offer some low cost work-life policies and programs—such as leaves to attend functions at their children's school—to their employees, only a small percentage of workplaces has established other types of work-life supports, such as subsidies that help defray the costs of child care (Galinsky & Bond, 1998).

If work-family advocates want to address the lag in workplace responsiveness to the needs of working families, it may be important to expand the framing of the business case. It is our contention that the HR business case for work-family initiatives may be necessary—but not sufficient—to engage business leaders in the development of a comprehensive work-family agenda. We suggest that work-family issues be seen not only as a HR imperative, but also be cast as a set of social issues that are relevant to sustainable business success. Once the quality of life of working families is recognized as a social issue that has strategic importance to businesses, it then becomes possible for business leaders to address these concerns from the perspective of corporate social responsibility (CSR). In this chapter, we discuss the advantages of pursuing the *corporate social responsibility argument* for business commitment to work-family issues. Furthermore, we suggest that business leaders become more accountable for the progress of their work-family agendas by openly discussing these issues in social reports, which are documents prepared for businesses' stakeholder groups.[3]

WORK-FAMILY AS A SOCIAL ISSUE AND A CORPORATE SOCIAL RESPONSIBILITY

Business leaders around the world have acknowledged the relevance of social issues, in part because experts in corporate citizenship have developed a strong business case for workplace response to social issues (see Rochlin, 2000; Weiser & Zadeck, 2001). There are many facets to this business case for CSR. It is often pragmatic for businesses to respond to certain social issues, such as the inadequacies of our education system or discriminatory practices, because these issues quickly cross over the threshold of the corporation and—if left unadressed—can impede business operations. Some business leaders become involved in social issues because they feel that corporate involvement is consistent with prominent organizational values. Oftentimes, business leaders respond to select social issues because they believe that the reputational capital of the firm could be enhanced if the members of key stakeholder groups, such as investors and customers, recognize that the business is attempting to give back to the society.

In the aftermath of a few widely publicized corporate scandals, corporate leaders are paying increasing attention to their businesses' reputations.[4] There are indications that a range of business stakeholders appear to have heightened expectations that businesses should respond to social issues. For example, the increase in public relations strategies such as cause-related marketing suggests that firms believe that *customers* (and potential customers) want businesses to align their business operation with social issues.[5] *Investors* are also expressing interest in the CSR behavior of companies by investing money in socially responsible investment (SRI) funds.[6] Business leaders have not overlooked the fact that these SRI funds often achieve the highest ratings by Morningstar and Lipper.[7] Finally, surveys have found that a substantial proportion of the *public-at-large* expects that businesses should respond to pressing social issues. According to a 1999 survey of 1,000 U.S. residents conducted by Conference Board, two of every five respondents (42%) feel that companies are responsible (partially or completely) for addressing a number of social issues, ranging from crime to poverty (Conference Board, 1999, cited in Weiser & Zadeck, 2001). In response to these new expectations, some business leaders have recognized the relevance of social issues and the importance of corporate citizenship strategies.

There are, of course, a range of social issues that could be identified as being important to a particular business. Sometimes business leaders focus on specific issues that are related to their firms' strategic interests (such as education, health care, social equity, diversity), whereas others focus on social issues connected to the externalities associated with a business's operations (including environmental impact, impact on the local economy, impact on the local rates of employment). It seems logical that work-family issues be one of the social issues that are perceived by business leaders as relevant (see Bailyn, Drago, & Kochan, 2001; Pitt-Catsouphes, Fassler, & Googins, 1998).

It is important to note that, in fact, some business leaders have already framed work-family concerns as priority social issues. The Conference Board recently reported the results of three corporate surveys conducted during the years 1999 to 2001 to which business representatives (CEOs, managers of corporate citizenship programs, board members) from more than 700 businesses responded (Muirhead, Bennett, Berenbeim, Kas, & Vidal, 2002). The respondents were asked to list issues that were perceived to be top priorities for the companies as corporate citizens. The greatest number of firms noted that the following issues were among the most important for their companies (from among a list of 19 possible issues): safety and health, sustainability, equal opportunities/global diversity, pollution control/air emissions, cash or product giving, professional development/employability, and *work-life balance*. These findings suggest that some businesses may be ready to view work-family issues as a corporate social responsibility as well as a HR strategy. The reframing of the work-family agenda as a corporate social responsibility for working families has several merits, such as the following:

Businesses might expand the spectrum of the concerns that are perceived as relevant to their work-family agenda. A social issue lens could help focus attention on important work-family outcomes, such as quality of life at work or at home and gender equity. As a consequence, as Lambert (1993) has noted, a wide range of business practices—including nondiscriminatory practices, access to health care, work hours, work conditions, work demands, and the predictability of work schedules—could become explicitly relevant to the work-family agenda (see also Lambert & Haley-Lock, 2004). In addition, businesses might no longer confine their work-family agendas to employees and their families, but might also respond to the priorities of other working families as well. With a broader framing of the work-family agenda, businesses might link their work-family agenda to corporate philanthropy, which provides resources to families in the communities where their workplaces are located (see Bailyn et al., 2001, pp. 8, 41–42). There are a number of notable examples of companies, such as IBM, AT&T, and Eli Lilly, that have developed community-based strategies for responding to work-family issues that reflect their concern for the quality of life of working families (Bailyn et al., 2001; Hammonds, 1997; WFD Consulting, 2003).

Businesses with a commitment to corporate citizenship might pay more attention to work-family issues if they were seen both as a CSR and a HR responsibility. Business leaders have, indeed, taken note of the new expectations for corporate social responsibility. Consequently, issues aligned with CSR might gain additional visibility at the workplace. In a classic investigation, Goodstein (1994) found that norms and expectations exert pressure on organizations and can affect firm responsiveness to work-family issues. Goodstein's study suggests that a social responsibility case for work-family issues is likely to have a particular influence on large corporations because our society expects that large businesses will be cognizant of and respond to important social concerns, such as the quality of life of working families. He states:

Advocates of employer adoption of work-family initiatives argue that employers who provide these benefits help address a critical societal concern and enhance their legitimacy and social fitness. . . . Consideration of legitimacy and social fitness are particularly salient for large organizations. By virtue of their size and visibility, large organizations are subject to attention from the state, media, and professional groups. . . . Because large organizations are visible and accountable to various constituencies, they have a strong incentive to take actions to ensure their legitimacy. . . ." (Goodstein, 1994, p. 356).[8]

As a corporate social responsibility, a work-family agenda could actively engage multiple stakeholder groups, which in turn could deepen and sustain business commitment to work-family issues. Most work-family initiatives concentrate on a single stakeholder group: employees (including managers—who are, of course, also employees). Because many work-life initiatives are delivered as "policies and programs" in a benefits model, the degree of employee active engagement in the development and implementation of work-life initiatives appears to be low.

Framed as a social issue, a work-family agenda could be of interest to a number of important business stakeholders, thereby expanding the base of support for work-family issues and creating opportunities for building alliances across the stakeholder groups (Bailyn et al., 2001; Pitt-Catsouphes et al., 1998). Even business leaders who might otherwise be reluctant to respond to work-family issues might be receptive to viewing them as priorities if multiple stakeholder groups expressed interest in these issues and expected that the organization should become more engaged in them.

Although some business analysts remain skeptical about the importance of the stakeholder perspective (see Vinten, 2000), there is evidence that many business leaders feel that organizational legitimacy—and potentially, performance—is affected by the quality of relationships between the organization and its stakeholder groups (Edwards, Birkin, & Halal, 2000; Woodward, 1996). The Conference Board reports that 59% of the manager respondents to a recent survey indicated that their companies have a "structured program for engaging stakeholders on a regular basis" (Muirhead, Bennett, Berenbeim, Kao, & Vidal, 2002, p. 52). Towers Perrin (cited in Weiser & Zadek, 2001) recently examined 25 companies that had been recognized as firms with strong relationships with five types of stakeholder groups: investors, customers, employees, suppliers, and communities where the businesses operate. Profitability during years of 1984 to 1999, as measured by changes in shareholder return, was compared to average of profits of all businesses in the S&P 500 over the course of those 15 years. The average increase for the S&P 500 was 19%; the average for the firms with strong stakeholder relationships was 43%. This analytic approach does not, of course, establish a cause-effect correlation between these two measures, and there could be many explanations for the statistical relationships between the management of stakeholder relationships and firm profitability. However, it is reasonable to note that well managed/high performance companies appear to consider stakeholder relationships to have some strategic importance to the business.

Business leaders who want to build strong relationships with stakeholder groups interested in a work-family agenda will need to develop communication processes about their businesses' agenda for working families (Hess, 1999, p. 5). Social reporting is a practice developed by the CSR field that promotes accountability for business operations and transparency in organizations' communications. Social reports provide a structure for discussing the firm's engagement in relevant social issues. If work-family priorities are identified by business leaders as being important social issues, it then becomes appropriate to discuss a work-family agenda in social reports.

SOCIAL REPORTING

In her classic monograph, *Work and Family in the United States: A Critical Review and Agenda for Research and Policy*, Kanter (1977) foresaw the importance of having businesses make public accounts for their commitments to work-family issues. She suggested, "If, as I suspect, the nature of the work world plays a dominant role in the possibilities for families and personal satisfaction in out-of-work life, then the organizations in which most Americans work might begin to take some responsibility for their effects on families and personal relations. Organizations could file a 'family responsibility' document in the same way as an affirmative action plan" (Kanter, 1977, p. 96). CSR specialists refer to documents such as those envisioned by Kanter as social reports. Social reporting, described as "a standard process for identifying, measuring, and reporting the ethical, social and environmental impact of an organization" (Johnson, 2001), provides opportunities for businesses to discuss their goals and accomplishments as socially responsible companies (Hess, 1999).[9] Increasingly, business leaders are preparing reports for their stakeholders that address either social and/or environmental concerns. At present, social reporting is voluntary. However, there are many reasons why business leaders prepare these reports. Social reporting practices may be adopted as communication strategies to:

1. Increase the organization's reputation and legitimacy among stakeholders.
2. Expand brand recognition, particularly among investors and customers.
3. Enhance relationships with stakeholder groups.[10]
4. Integrate social considerations into decision making.
5. Further engage the members of different stakeholder groups in the organization's vision with regard to social issues, such as work-family integration.
6. Document social impacts of business activities.

7. Sanction/legitimize stakeholder interest in corporate social behavior. (Clarke & Gibson-Sweet, 1999; Dierkes & Antal, 1986; see Swift, 2001).

The practice of social reporting increased during the 1990s (see, for example, Muirhead et al., 2002). CRSnetwork reports that the percent of Global 100 companies that produce some type of report on corporate citizenship, corporate social responsibility, or sustainability increased from 44% to nearly 50% from 2000 to 2002 (CSRnetwork, 2003). This trend could continue as information about business practices and externalities becomes more accessible and can more easily be scrutinized by different stakeholder groups. As Waddock observed, "Companies are increasingly being evaluated on social as well as financial performance criteria, whether they want to be or not" (Waddock, 2000, p. 324). Because managers are aware that the public is monitoring their business activities, they may adapt by adopting social reporting practices.

The art and science of social reporting are still in emergent stages.[11] At the present time, there is no consensus either about the content of social reports or the metrics used to measure business impact on key social issues (see Muirhead et al., 2002; p. 39). As summarized by Aronson and Reeves (2002, pp. 101–108), most of the standard formats used for social reporting assume that businesses will complete the reports voluntarily.[12] The voluntary nature of social reporting raises an important critique of the practice: Unless the reports are audited by a third party, they might evolve into publicity publications rather than documents that discuss organizational accountability in a transparent fashion.

There is significant variation in the type of issues discussed in businesses' environmental and social reports. In 2001, the Corporate Social Responsibility (CSR) Network (a consultant organization) conducted a survey of the 100 largest firms included in *Fortune*'s list of Global 500 businesses. This survey found that half of these firms had published global environmental reports. Slightly less than one of every five included information about health and safety, with similar percentages reporting on social equity (CSRnetwork, 2001). CSR notes that a minority of the businesses provided comprehensive, measurable data about environmental and social outcomes. Despite the limitations of social reports, the salience of work-family issues could be increased if they were discussed and examined in these documents.

A PRELIMINARY ANALYSIS OF SOCIAL REPORTS: THE WORK-FAMILY AGENDA

In an effort to explore the extent to which the firms discuss a work-family agenda as one of the social issues that they address in their social reports, we first analyzed the contents of a sample of social and environmental reports included in the CSRwire;[13] and we then reviewed the contents of the social and environmental reports available for the businesses included in *Working Mother Magazine*'s 1999–2002 Top 10 "Best Companies for Working Mothers."

CSRwire Database

CSRwire (available at www.csrwire.com) maintains a database of social and environment sustainability reports obtained from firms around the world.[14] The goal of the CSRwire reporting service is for companies to "communicate the positive social and environmental impacts in order to help enhance their reputation and minimize risk." (CSRnetwork, 2001). In 2003, the CSRwire database contained the reports from 350 firms. A list of these reports was retrieved on June 12, 2003, and a systematic sample was drawn to select reports from 35 different firms.[15] The years of publication ranged from 1999 to 2002. A majority of the companies (21 out of 35) whose reports were included in our sample are headquartered outside of the United States.[16] The firms are affiliated with a wide range of industry groups, with eight being in energy-related businesses (e.g., oil, gas) and three in the chemical industry. Twenty-seven of the 35 reports specify the standards that the companies have adopted as a way to structure the content of their reports and to gauge their progress. The standards adopted most often were either the ISO 14001 (environmental standards developed by the International Organization for Standardization [ISO]) and/or the GRI (social and environmental standards developed by the Global Reporting Initiative). More than half (22 of 35) of the reports sampled for our analysis mention that the companies had some type of external review/verification/auditing of their reports by firms such as PricewaterhouseCoopers, Ernst & Young, Det Norske Veritas, Environmental Assessment, and the Environmental Resource Management.[17]

Twenty-three of the 35 reports link corporate values to the content of their social and environmental reports. In the vision and leadership sections of the reports, CEOs often discuss their desire to demonstrate transparency, accountability, and ethical business practices to the public. Many of the reports referred to the companies' social policies, or "People Principles," as Royal Dutch Shell calls them (Royal Dutch Shell, 2001).[18]

Because we anticipate that different stakeholder groups might be able to influence business responsiveness to a work-family agenda, we scanned the reports for any mention of stakeholder groups. Nineteen of the reports specifically identify the stakeholder groups for whom the reports were written. Typically, the reports list a range of stakeholder groups, including investors, customers, and communities; however, only five of these reports mention employees as one of the important stakeholder groups.

We analyzed the content of the reports using the framework outlined by the *Sustainability Reporting Guidelines 2002* (GRI, Global Reporting Initiative 2002), which includes the following sections: Vision and Strategy, Profile, Governance and Management Systems, and Performance Indicators (economic, environmental, and social). Our analysis focused on the Social Indicators section, which is one of the three Performance Indicators. GRI subdivides the Social Indicators into four categories (see Table 21.1 for the GRI indicators for each of these four areas of corporate social responsibility):

1. Labor Practices and Decent Work;
2. Human Rights;
3. Society; and
4. Product Responsibility. (GRI, 2002)

It is our opinion that businesses' activities and practices related to a work-family agenda could be relevant to each of the four Social Indicators domains. For example, in the Society section of the report, GRI asks businesses to comment on their policies and on their monitoring practices that could have an impact on the community. Companies that have invested in a community-based carework infrastructure (such as the availability of after school programs) could certainly highlight their experiences in this portion of the report. Similarly, GRI asks businesses to list awards that they have received for social, ethical, and/or environmental performance. Workplaces that have been recognized on lists such as the annual list compiled by *Working Mother Magazine* could discuss the intended and unintended consequences of their work-life initiatives for working families. Although business leaders could decide to discuss their work-family agendas in each of these four sections of the report, the indicators associated with the first two categories, Labor Practices and Decent Work, and Human Rights, are most closely aligned with typical work-life initiatives and their outcomes.

Our analysis of the Social and Environmental Reports focused on three primary questions:

- What issues do companies address in their reports?
- Is there evidence that businesses consider the well-being of working families to be one aspect of their corporate social responsibilities?
- Are work-family issues mentioned in the reports?

Important Social Issues Addressed in the Reports

A majority (29) of the reports examined address both social and environmental issues; six reports discuss only environmental impacts of the business. Most of the reports devote extensive attention to environmental issues, concerns about employees' health and safety, and engagement in community partnerships (e.g., philanthropy, volunteerism). For instance, one report, ABB's 2000 Sus-

TABLE 21.1
GRI 2002 Social Indicators

		Core and Additional Indicators*
Labor Practices/ Decent Work	Employment	For example: **workforce demographics, turnover, employee benefits beyond those mandated**
	Labor/management relations	For example: % workforce organized labor, negotiation policies, provisions for worker representation
	Health and safety	For example: accidents, health/ safety committees; **absenteeism**, policies, ILO compliance indicators, health agreements
	Training and education	For example: training hours/year, **career development, policies for lifelong learning**
	Diversity and opportunity	For example: **equal opportunity policies/program, composition of management**
Human Rights	Strategy and management	For example: policies and monitoring structures with regard to standards such as ILO human rights standards, indicators of consideration of human rights as part of investment and selection of suppliers/contractors, **evaluation of human rights**, training with regard to human rights
	Nondiscrimination	For example: **policies and monitoring structures.**
	Freedom of association and collection bargaining	For example: freedom of association policy and monitoring
	Child labor	For example: policy excluding child labor and monitoring
	Forced and compulsory labor	For example: policy to prevent forced labor and monitoring
	Disciplinary practices	For example: description of appeal and grievance practices
	Security practices	For example: human rights training
	Indigenous rights	For example: policies to address needs of indigenous peoples, community grievance mechanisms
Society	Community	For example: policies and monitoring of community impact, **awards relevant to social/ethical/ environmental performance**
	Bribery and corruption	For example: policy and compliance related to bribery and corruption

(continued)

TABLE 21.1
(Continued)

		Core and Additional Indicators*
	Political contributions	For example: policy and procedures to manage lobbying and political contributions
	Competition and pricing	For example: description of policies to prevent anticompetitive behavior
Product Responsibility	Customer health and safety	For example: policies for safeguarding customer health and safety
	Products and services	For example: procedures for product information and labeling
	Advertising	For example: adherence to advertising codes
	Respect for privacy	For example: policies for consumer privacy

Source: Global Reporting Initiative, 2002.
*The bold font designates the indicators suggested by the GRI Guidelines that could readily be linked to a firm's work-family agenda.

tainability Report, notes that its social policy includes health and safety, employee consultation and communication, equality of opportunity, working hours, and business ethics (ABB Group, 2000, p. 8). Our review of the 35 reports found that among all the issues discussed, the information presented about environmental impacts tends to be the most detailed.

Statements of Corporate Social Responsibility for Employee Well-Being

As we anticipated, a majority of the reports (29 of 35) identify the businesses' role as *employers* as part of their corporate social responsibility. This finding was expected because a majority of the businesses use the GRI for their social report, which requests that companies assess their Labor Practices/Decent Work. Many of the businesses allude to their perceptions of the employer-employee relationship as being a social contract when discussing the following issues: competitive benefits, fair compensation, training, stock options, health and safety measures, management practices and training, and employee volunteer programs. Some of the firms mention that the company's vision or value statements address the importance of employee well-being. By implication, it would seem that these businesses feel it is important to discuss employee well-being in the social reports. Other social reports focus significant attention on company policies or practices. For example, Storebrand states, "Storebrand's human resources policies fully reflect the group's commitment to corporate social responsibility" (2002, p. 11) In the Social Highlights section of its Sustainability Report, Ericsson mentions that the company has adopted "a Code of Conduct defining employee rights and working conditions for Ericsson and our supply chain" (2001, p. 4).

Approximately one third of the businesses note that they use data from their employee surveys as metrics of the company's performance relative to employees' well-being.[19] ABB Group (2000, pp. 5, 9) notes that it has conducted case studies at a representative sample of its factories in seven different countries as a way to examine how the company's activities affect employees, families, and society at large.

One fourth (9) of the businesses specifically mention work-family issues in their reports. BASF links changes in its work processes with the implementation of its flexible work arrangements, stating, "We consider our employees to be a key to our success. We promote skills and training and have an open attitude toward flexible working hours and modern forms of work" (2002, p. 20). In the Diversity section of its report, Proctor & Gamble notes that the company offers "work/family balance benefits, including flextime, child care leave, and less-than-full-time schedules" (2001, p. 35). ABB comments that one of the shortcomings that emerged during the company's internal assessment process (conducted as part of its social reporting processes) was "long working hours for salaried staff"; the report states, "A mechanism will be needed to ensure improvement" (2000, p. 38). In the People section of its Sustainability Report, Carillion explains that as part of the assessments conducted in preparation of its social report, "We have reviewed our policies on Maternity, Parental Leave, Working Time, Stress and Alcohol and Drugs in order to support a healthy work/life balance for our people" (2001, p. 4).

The discussions about employers' responses to work-family issues were the most salient in five of the social reports: British Petroleum (BP), Bristol Myers Squibb, Royal Dutch Shell, Storebrand, and Vauxhall. For example:

- BP reports that is has a commitment to support employees as they attempt to balance their personal priorities. In addition, BP states that it supported the first "Global Women's Summit 2000: which addressed work-life issues" (2002, p. 17).
- Bristol-Myers Squibb, recognized internationally as a leader in the work-life area, focuses significant attention on the importance of work-life initiatives to the firm. The report states, "We affirm our commitment to foster a globally diverse workforce and a companywide culture that encourages excellence, leadership, innovation, and a balance between our personal and professional lives" (Bristol-Myers Squibb, 2001, p. ii). In the subsection on Flexible Work Arrangements, the company highlights its perspective of the strategic importance of its work/life initiatives and explains:

We know that a workforce committed to achieving the company's mission is our best competitive advantage. We also know that employees can bring to the workplace a host of personal issues that affect their ability to do their best. Conversely, employees take home many of the stresses they endure at work. These two worlds do not have to be at odds; through supportive management and innovative programs and services, the two spheres can work in concert to yield significant benefits for employees and the company (Bristol-Myers Squibb, 2001, p. 33).

- Royal Dutch Shell mentions different aspects of its work-life initiatives, including supports related to maternity and child care. The company focuses particular attention its flexible work arrangements policies, stating:

  Shell gives requests for flexible working serious consideration and wherever possible, without prejudicing the business, they are granted. Flexible work arrangements enabling employees to care for children are longstanding. However, increasingly consideration is given to career breaks and shorter work seeks to devote to other passions. . . . This flexibility is enabling employees to pursue interests as diverse as writing a novel, working with a community arts organization and honing equestrian skills. The feedback suggests that the employees concerned feel more refreshed and committed to the company (2001, p. 17).

- The social report of Storebrand claims that "Storebrand was the first financial institution to sign a collaboration agreement on 'more inclusive working life'; with the Norwegian social insurance priorities in 2002" (2002, p. 15) and comments on the company's commitment to work-family issues by explaining how its business leaders have addressed negative and unintended consequences associated with the use of alternative work arrangements. This report states, "Storebrand strives to ensure that employees enjoy a sound and healthy balance between their working life and private life. Incentive arrangements will be linked to individual performance, and not to additional time spent in the office (Human Resources Policy, Section 10—Social Responsibility)." This report further explains that the company recognizes the need for strong communications with employees who are an important stakeholder group: "Storebrand aims to maintain a close dialogue with its employees to identify specific areas where new or improved arrangements are wanted, so that measures can be implemented" (2002, p. 15).

- Vauxhall Motors positions itself as a company with a "family-friendly suite of policies . . . [that] set new standards in the area of maternity and paternity benefit for employees" (2001, p. 17). The firm also discusses the development of its social policy as part of its overall social responsibility. The report explains that "as part of an overarching company commitment to social responsibility," the company has begun to work with a steering group to "bring together under one umbrella policy Vauxhall's approach to social issues, including the global Sullivan Principles, and existing, more detailed policies covering equal opportunities, health and safety, family-friendly policies and employee development" (2001, p. 18).

Our review of these reports reaffirmed that social reports may offer a mechanism for broadening the discussion of workplace responsiveness to work-family issues. For example, two of the firms, Storebrand and ABB, state that their corporate social responsibility values make it necessary for them to consider the businesses' impact on employees *and on their families*. Four of the social reports discuss how layoffs affect employees, and outline the steps that the companies have taken to limit or avoid layoffs and to minimize their negative consequences.[20] These examples illustrate how a firm's work-family agenda could be expanded by using a CSR framework. Although a traditional HR perspective might not consider layoffs to be included under the rubric of a company's work-life initiatives, a CSR perspective of a work-family agenda might recognize the connections between layoffs and the impact on working families.

In summary, our analysis of the reports selected from the CSRwire database found that most businesses discuss some aspects of their employees' work experiences as a social responsibility. However, work-family issues are salient in only a minority of the social reports sampled.

Working Mothers Magazine List of Best Companies for Working Mothers

In an effort to consider whether companies recognized as work-life leaders might be more likely to comment on work-family issues in their social reports than other firms, we searched for social reports of companies selected as being among the "10 Best Companies for Working Mothers" by *Working Mothers Magazine* during the years 1999, 2000, and 2001. We searched CSRwire's database for these social reports and also reviewed the companies' Web sites to locate these reports. Unfortunately, we were able to access only two social reports for the ten companies nominated in 1999; no social reports for the companies nominated in 2000; and three social reports for those companies nominated in 2001. Given the small number of reports reviewed, our analysis did not result in findings per se, but rather helped to shed light on the potential for using social reports as a way for businesses to publicly examine the progress of their work-family agendas. Three of the companies address their work-family agendas in their reports.

Deutsche Bank

Deutsche Bank, which was among the Top 10 of the *Working Mothers* list in 1999, issued a "Corporate Cultural Affairs" report in 2002. The GRI guidelines were used to structure the report. The Bank's work-life initiatives were discussed in the report's human resources section. The company mentioned that it is striving to be an employer of choice and notes that policies, such as flexible work policies and job sharing, are among the steps that the Bank has taken to reach this goal.

Bristol-Myers Squibb and Citigroup

These companies were two of those in the Top 10 in 2001, and both mentioned their work-life initiatives in their social reports. Citigroup's 2002 "Citizenship Report" discusses its work-life initiatives as one of its "Major Corporate Citizenship Accomplishments in 2002." In the 2003 Sustainability Report, Bristol-Myers noted that it had devoted significant attention to the opening of child care centers. In addition, Bristol-Myers provides work-life metrics in the Measuring Social Progress section, where they highlight the number of employees who have used different work-life policies and programs.

Our attempt to locate and examine the social reports of companies that have been designated as among the best workplaces for working mothers suggests that most of these companies have not prepared social reports that are easily accessible. It is possible that there are opportunities for work-life managers in these businesses to work collaboratively with the CSR practitioners in their companies to consider how social reports that include transparent discussions about a work-family agenda could be prepared and disseminated.

CHALLENGES AND CONCLUSION

The work-family agenda may be approaching a crossroads. To date, many employers have framed their work-life initiatives around a HR business case that essentially positions work-family issues as HR challenges/opportunities for businesses that are primarily of interest to a single stakeholder group: employees. Of course, the work-family experiences of employees *are* important HR priorities for businesses, and work-life initiatives do offer creative tactics and strategies to managers and supervisors who want to thoughtfully respond to the needs of their employees as well as to the demands of the business. Although it is important to continue to articulate and refine the HR business case for work-family issues, this framing has not, to date, resulted in a sustained surge in the adoption of comprehensive work-family agenda by businesses.

Casting work-family issues as a social responsibility offers opportunities to redefine the horizons of the work-family agenda, to involve different stakeholders in the development and implementation of the agenda, and to increase businesses accountability for their actions. This approach could also enable business leaders to draw attention to their accomplishments in the work-family arena as one way to strengthen their firms' legitimacy in the eyes of their stakeholders.

To be sure, there are a number of challenges associated with an effort to integrate accounts of work-family in businesses' social reports. First, it will be necessary to develop strategies that can interest a greater number of business leaders in the social reporting practice itself. CEOs who recognize that social reporting practices can offer benefits to their businesses are likely to adopt these practices voluntarily. Hess suggests that some companies might respond to incentives, such as awarding a seal or other public recognition, that could indicate that particular companies have complied with some minimum standards established for social reporting (Hess, 1999, p. 9). Other firms may find that stakeholder groups, such as socially concerned investors or unions, might pressure them to use social reports as a way to increase the businesses' accountability for social issues, such as the quality of life of working families. Finally, some groups advocate legislative mandates that would require social reporting practices (see CSRnetwork, 2003; Hess, 1999).

A second significant challenge is associated with the content of social reports themselves. In particular, it will be important to evaluate the options for metrics that firms might use to measure their progress with regard to social issues, in general, and work-family issues, in particular (Bauer, Cauthorn, & Warner, 1974; Frederick & Myers, 1974; Muirhead et al., 2002, p. 34;). This debate is beyond the scope of this chapter, but it is important for practitioners and academics to continue a dialogue about measurable indicators.[21]

Finally, it is also important to anticipate that stakeholders are likely to raise legitimate concerns about the veracity of information that is included in social reports and about the absence (or softening) of discussions about the problems encountered by businesses as they attempt to make progress on their social agendas, such as promoting the quality of life of working families. We anticipate that stakeholders are particularly likely to scrutinize the reports of firms whose reputations have been compromised by past business practices that are perceived to have been questionable or unethical.

For work-family advocates, the biggest challenge may be the need to shift our thinking and to articulate an agenda for working families that is relevant to businesses in their roles as corporate citizens as well as employers.

AUTHOR NOTE

We would like to express our gratitude for the contributions made by Angela Comprone and Kathleen Witter of Boston College.

NOTES

1. The respondents to the *BusinessWeek* study were selected from a nonprobability sample.

2. Business leaders often refer to work-family concerns as *work-life* issues. In part, this reflects employers' desire to communicate their respect for the diversity of their employees' personal lives, whether or not employees identify themselves as part of a so-called traditional family. For the purposes of this chapter, we will use the term *work-family* when we discuss these issues as social issues and will restrict the use of the term *work-life* to designate the policies and programs established by employers to support their employees.

3. The referent "organizational stakeholders" includes individuals/groups that, directly or indirectly, affect or are affected by organizational decisions and actions. The stakeholders in business organizations often include investors/shareholders, customers, suppliers, employees, communities, the environment, and society-at-large.

Changes in the business environment may have contributed to an important paradigm shift among business leaders. In the past, business leaders tended to adhere to a *shareholder* perspective about business decision making, but today more corporate decision makers are articulating views about a broader *stakeholder* perspective. Whereas the traditional shareholder perspective concentrates businesses' attention primarily on their investors, the stakeholder perspective focuses the attention of business leaders on the priorities of different stakeholder groups and on the firm's relationships to/responsibilities for members of these different stakeholder groups. For discussions about stakeholder theory, see Andriof, Waddock, Husted, & Rahman, 2002; Clarkson, 1998; Friedman & Miles, 2002; Hill & Jones, 1992, Kennedy, 2000.

4. According to the Social Investment Forum (SIF), these scandals have precipitated responses, including: the adoption of business codes of conduct and ethics, the separation of audit and nonaudit services, and increased corporate disclosure on social and environmental issues (Social Investment Forum, 2003). Alisa Gravitz, executive director of Co-op America, a nonprofit investor education organization, has said: "Due to the recent wave of corporate scandals, we're seeing more and more investors concerned about the companies in which they invest. They're more active investors who demand that companies have ethical financial, social and environmental practices. Active involvement in shareholder advocacy has gone through the roof over the past few years. Socially responsible investing provides the best way for investors to demand better financial and ethical performance from companies" (Social Investment Forum, 2003).

5. The organization Business in the Community defines cause-related marketing as "a commercial activity by which businesses and charities or causes form a partnerships with each other to market an image, product or service for mutual benefit" (Business in the Community, 2002). According to Adkins, two-thirds (67%) of consumers feel that cause-related marketing should be a standard part of a company's business practice (Adkins, 1999, p. 3).

6. Waddock (2000) estimates that 9% of all investments in equities in the United States are screened for social criteria. According to the Social Investment Forum, assets in socially screened investment portfolios rose 35% from 1999 to 2001. The forum estimates that nearly 1 of every 8 investment dollars in the United States is managed by a socially responsible investment fund manager (Social Investment Forum, 2001). In 2001, there were 181 mutual funds in the United States that incorporated social screening into their assessment process. According to Calvert, an investment group that assesses corporations' socially responsible activities and outcomes, the screening by socially responsible investment funds typically "include enterprises with outstanding employer-employee relations, excellent environmental practices, products that are safe and useful, and operations that respect human rights around the world" (Social Investment Forum, 2001).

7. Between January and June 2002, Lipper data showed that socially responsible mutual funds had their assets increase by 3% while U.S. diversified funds decreased by 9.5%. Thirteen out of the 18 screened funds (72 %) with $100 million or more in assets tracked by the SIF achieved highest

ratings for performance from either or both Morningstar and Lipper for the one- and/or three-year periods ending June 2002 (Social Investment Forum, 2002, July 30). The socially responsible screened funds were more likely than all types of funds to earn top Morningstar Ratings for performance. Forty-three percent of funds tracked by the SIF received four or five stars from Morningstar, as opposed to 32.5% from the general mutual fund universe. In 2002, socially responsible mutual funds grew on a net basis, whereas the rest of the mutual fund industry contracted (Social Investment Forum, 2003).

8. Goodstein (1994) explored organizational adaptation to pressures in the environment. He considered five sets of pressures could affect employers' responsiveness to issues such as work-family experiences:

- cause (e.g., normative beliefs and societal expectations for the responsiveness of firms)
- constituents (e.g., employees with expressed work-family concerns and priorities)
- contents (e.g., congruence of work-family issues with organization's goals and existing policies)
- control (e.g., comparative responsiveness of other business in the same sector)
- context (e.g., including expectations of relevant professional associations, information about connection to business practices such as the return-on-investment of work-life policies and programs)

As anticipated, Goodstein found that structural factors, such as organizational size and the percentage of female employees, were related to organizational responsiveness to work-family issues. However, as noted earlier, the prevailing norms also exerted an influence on workplace responsiveness.

9. The key components of the social reporting practice often include:

- Development of processes to measure company impact on selected social issues.
- Collection of data at regular intervals, sometimes gathering information from members of stakeholder groups.
- Preparation of "transparent" reports that attempt to reflect the perspectives of different stakeholder groups.
- Dialogue with members of the stakeholder groups about results and action steps.
- Publication of reports.

Social reporting is sometimes distinguished from social accounting and auditing (Henriques, 2001). Social accounting usually suggests that the measures adopted as indicators of the firm's progress are translated into monetary equivalency terms, oftentimes expressed as the financial costs and benefits to the company. Social auditing suggests that the company obtains external verification of information, sometimes benchmarking with best practice standards, if available. In reality, a minority of social reports are submitted for any objective auditing by an outside organization; a recent survey found that fewer than one of every eight of the social reports published by *Fortune*'s Global 100 companies in 2001 were externally verified (CSRnetwork, 2001). Social reporting is sometimes connected to the balanced scorecard approach (see Arkin, 1996); however, it is important to note that business may adopt a balance scorecard review process for internal decision making without sharing the assessment information to so-called external stakeholder groups.

10. CSRnetwork reports that, during the years 2000 to 2003, increasing numbers of companies took steps to ensure that their stakeholders received information about sustainability reports (CSRnetwork, 2003).

11. There are at least three different social reporting models: the inventory model, the goals/objectives model, and the social indicators model.

Social Inventory Model—Business that adopt this model tend to list the various ways that they have addressed selected social issues through their philanthropy, volunteer activities/community involvement and employee relations initiatives. There is no single, systematic structure of social report inventories. Although businesses that adopt the inventory approach typically use a narrative and descriptive style, some businesses include measurable indicators of the positive and negative impacts of corporate activities. Firms that use the inventory model of social reports might describe the availability of different work-life policies and programs, provide utilization statistics, and/or highlight relevant outcome measures, such as indicators of employee stress, equity of earnings, or employees' commitment to the organization.

Social Goals/Objectives Model—The social reports developed according to the Goals/Objectives Model are structured as accountability practices. Businesses that use this approach adopt goals and measurable objectives that, presumably, reflect some of the priorities and expectations of the companies' stakeholder groups. Work-family measures could include indicators of input (such as the amount of money donated to a fund for the development of child-care resources), process (such as statistics related to the implementation of policies related to flexible work schedules), or impact (such as measures of employees' perception of work-family integration or conflict, measures of gender equity).

Social Indicator Model—Advocates of the Social Indicator Model recommend that different businesses report on the same outcome measures, making it possible to compare social impacts across firms (see Dierkes & Antal, 1986).

12. The social reporting formats used most frequently include: the 1997 Global Reporting Initiative, the 1999 Global Sullivan Principles, the 1986 Caux Principles, the 1998 Global Benchmarks, the SA 8000, the 1999 UN Global Compact, the 2000 UN Global Compact, the 1998 Ethical Trade Initiative, and the 1976 OECD Guidelines for Multinational Enterprises. In 2002, GRI published a list of 100 businesses that had notified GRI that they used the GRI Guidelines. Nineteen of these are headquartered in the United States. CSRnetwork's analysis of the Global 100 sustainability reports found that 39% of the reporting companies included in the 2003 Benchmark Survey used the GRI guidelines. The number of companies that have adopted the Global Sullivan Principles was approximately 130 in 2002 (CSRnetwork, 2003; Muirhead et al., 2002).

13. The text of this chapter refers at least once to the reports reviewed, with the exception of the reports prepared by the following three firms: AT&T (2000), Citigroup (2002), and Deutsche Bank (2002).

14. CSRwire contacts companies and requests permission to include social reports—if they are available—in the database. It is important to note that CSR does not purport that the database is exhaustive, and there are published social reports not included in the CSRwire database. The reports are sometimes labeled as *environmental and social reports* if they discuss both social and environmental issues.

15. The contents of the CSRwire report service list is subject to change as new reports are added and old reports deleted.

16. This reflects the fact that social reporting is a more common practice among businesses headquartered in Europe and Asia than in the United States. CSR comments, "The United States is home to the largest number of companies [among the Global 100](39%) but also hosts the largest number of non-reporting companies" (CSRnetwork, 2003, p. 19).

17. The rate of external verification among the reports sampled for this study appears to be higher than is typical. CSR reports that 17% of the Global 100 companies submit their reports for external verification/independent assurance (CSRnetwork, 2003, p. 6).

18. Royal Dutch Shell differentiates People Principles from Business Principles. As noted in its Sustainability Report 2001, "Business Principles describe the behaviors expected or every employee. They cover all aspects of our business operations including business integrity, politics, health safety and the environment and community. They also include our commitment to contribute to sustainable development" (Royal Dutch Shell, 2001). One of Shell's seven People Principles specifically focuses on work-family issues.

19. BP (2002, p. 4); Conoco (2002, p. 25); Ericsson (2001, p. 3); Flygt (2000, p. 21); ITT (p. 13); Mead (2001, p. 7); Petro/Canada (2002, p. 21); Ricoh Group (2001, p. 50); Royal Dutch Shell (2001, p. 16); Storebrand (2002, p. 15); and WMC Resources, Ltd. (2002, p. 42).

20. ABB Group (2000, p. 65); BP (2002, p. 4); Proctor & Gamble (2001, p. 35); and Vauxhall Motors (2001, p. 3).

21. Flygt/ITT, for example, refers to the measures it uses to gauge employee satisfaction with the company's psychosocial working conditions in its social report (p. 21). ABB notes that it is working with some of its sites to develop meaningful indicators (2000, p. 38).

REFERENCES

ABB Group. (2000). *ABB Group annual report 2000*. Sustainability report. Zurich, Switzerland: ABB.

Adkins, S. (1999). The ultimate win win win. Paper. London: Business in the Community, Retrieved June 10, 2004, from http://www.wnim.com/issue4/pages/crm.htm

Andriof, J., Waddock, S., Husted, B., & Rahman, S. S. (Eds.). (2002). *Unfolding stakeholder thinking: Theory, responsibility and engagement*. Sheffield, UK: Greenleaf Publishing.

Arkin, A. (1996). Open business is good for business. *People Management, 2*(1), 24+.

Aronson, S., & Reeves, J. (2002). *Corporate responsibility in the global village: The role of public policy*. Washington, DC: National Policy Association.

AT&T. (2000, July). *Sustainability: The triple bottom line*. EH&S report. Bedminster, NJ: AT&T. Retrieved July 23, 2003, from http://www.att.com/ehs/annual_report/triple_bottom_line.html

Bailyn, L., Drago, R., & Kochan, T. (2001, May). *Integrating work and family life: A holistic approach*. A report of the Sloan Work-Family Network. Cambridge, MA: MIT Sloan School of Management. Available online at: http://lsir.la.psu.edu/workfam

BASF. (2002). *Environment, health, & safety 2002*. Report. Ludwigshafen, Germany: BASF Aktiengesellschaft, Corporate Communications Department.

Bauer, R., Cauthorn, T., & Warner, R. (1974). Auditing the management process for social performance. *Business and Society Review, 15,* 39–46.

Bristol-Myers Squibb. (2001). *On the path towards sustainability—2001 sustainability progress report*. New York: Bristol-Myers Squibb.

British Petroleum (BP). (2002). *Performance for all our futures*. Report. Dorset, UK: British Petroleum.

Business in the Community. (2000). *Cause related marketing—profitable partnerships*. Paper. London: Business in the Community. Retrieved September 29, 2003, from http://www.bitc.org.uk/resources/research/research_publications/prof_pships.html

Business in the Community. (2002, September 2). Is there a revolution in 21st century giving? Paper. London: Business in the Community.

Carillion. (2001). *Sustainability report 2001*. West Midlands, UK: Carillion.

Citigroup. (2002). *Citigroup global citizenship report*. New York: Citigroup.

Clarke, J., & Gibson-Sweet, M. (1999). The use of corporate social disclosures in the management of reputation and legitimacy: A cross-sectoral analysis of UK top 100 companies. *Business Ethics: A European Review, 8*(1), 5–13.

Clarkson, M. (Ed.). (1998) *The corporation and its stakeholders: Classic and contemporary readings*. Toronto: University of Toronto Press.

Conoco. (2002). *Sustainable growth report*. Houston, TX: Conoco.

CSRnetwork. (2001). *The state of global environmental and social reporting: The 2001 Benchmark Survey. Executive summary*. Paper. Bath, UK: CSR Network, Limited. Retrieved August 6, 2003, from www.csrnetwork.com

CSRnetwork. (2003). *Material world: The 2003 benchmark survey of global reporting*. Report. Bath, UK: CSR Network, Limited.

Deutsche Bank. (2002). *Corporate cultural affairs report*. Frankfurt, Germany: Deutsche Bank.

Dierkes, M., & Antal, A. (1986). Whither corporate social reporting: Is it time to legislate? *California Management Review, 28*(3), 106–121.

Ericsson. (2001). *Sustainability report 2001.* Stockholm, Sweden: Ericsson.

Flygt. (2000). *Environmental report 2000.* ITT Flygt manufacturing plant. Stockholm, Sweden: Flygt, ITT Industries.

Frederick, W., & Myers, M. (1974). The hidden politics of social auditing. *Business and Society Review, 74*(11), 49–54.

Friedman, A., & Miles, S. (2002, January). Developing stakeholder theory. *Journal of Management Studies, 39*(1), 1–21.

Galinsky, E., & Bond, T. (1998). *The business work-life study.* Report. New York: Families and Work Institute.

Galinsky, E., & Johnson, A. (1998). *Reframing the business case for work-life initiatives.* Report. New York: Families and Work Institute.

Global Reporting Initiative (GRI). (2002). *Sustainability reporting guidelines.* Report. Amsterdam, The Netherlands: Global Reporting Initiative.

Goodstein, J. (1994). Institutional pressures and strategic responsiveness: Employer involvement in work-family issues. *Academy of Management Journal, 37*(2), 350–382.

Googins, B. (1991). *Work/family conflicts: Private lives—public responses.* New York: Auburn House.

Halal, W. (2000). Corporate community: A theory of the firm uniting profitability and responsibility. *Strategy & Leadership, 28*(2), 1–18.

Hammonds, K. (1997, May 26). Business gives caregivers a leg up. *BusinessWeek,* 3528, 88.

Henriques, A. (2001, January). Civil society and social auditing. *Business Ethics: A European Review, 10*(1), 40–44.

Hess, D. (1999, Fall). Social reporting: A reflexive law approach to corporate social responsiveness. *Journal of Corporation Law, 25*(1), 41–85.

Hewitt and Associates. (1998). *Work and family benefits provided by major U.S. employers in 1997.* Report. Lincolnshire, IL: Hewitt and Associates.

Hill, C. W., & Jones, T. M. (1992, March). Stakeholder-agency theory. *Journal of Management Studies, 29*(2), 131–154.

ITT. (2002). *Environmental, health and safety report.* White Plains, NY: ITT.

Johnson, H. (2001, May–June). Corporate social audits—This time around. *Business Horizons 44*(3), 29–36.

Kanter, R. (1977). *Work and family in the United States: A critical review and agenda for research and policy.* New York: Russell Sage Foundation.

Kennedy, A. (2000). The *end of shareholder value. Corporations at the crossroads.* Cambridge, MA: Perseus Publishing.

Lambert, S. J. (1993, June). Workplace policies as social policy. *Social Service Review,* (67), 237–260.

Lambert, S. J., & Haley-Lock, A. (2004). Theories of organizational stratification: Addressing issues of equity and social justice in work-life research. *Community, Work and Family, 7*(2), 179–196

Litchfield, L., & Bankert, E. (1998). Business Week's *work and family corporate ranking: An analysis of the data.* Report. Chestnut Hill, MA: Boston College Center for Work & Family.

Mead. (2001). *Sustainable development report.* Dayton, OH: Mead.

Muirhead, S. A., Bennett, C. J., Berenbeim R. E., Kao, A., & Vidal, D. J. (2002). *Corporate citizenship in the new century: Accountability, transparency, and global stakeholder engagement.* Report. New York: The Conference Board.

Petro-Canada. (2002). *Report to the community 2001.* Calgary, Alberta, Canada: Petro-Canada.

Pitt-Catsouphes, M., Fassler, I., & Googins, B. (1998). *Enhancing strategic value: Becoming a company of choice.* Work-Family Policy Paper Series. Chestnut Hill, MA: Boston College Center for Work & Family.

Proctor & Gamble. (2001). *2001 sustainability report.* Cincinnati, OH: Proctor & Gamble.

Ricoh Group. (2001). *Sustainability report.* Tokyo, Japan: Ricoh Group.

Rochlin, S. (2000). *Making the business case: Determining the value of corporate community involvement.* Report. Chestnut Hill, MA: Boston College Center for Corporate Citizenship.

Royal Dutch Shell. (2001). *Shell in the UK 2001.* Report. London, England: PXXC Publications.

Social Investment Forum. (2001, November 28). *2001 Report on socially responsible investing trends in the United States.* Paper. Washington, DC: Social Investment Forum, SIF Industry Research Forum.

Social Investment Forum. (2002, July 30). *Market slump providing unexpected boost to socially responsible mutual funds.* News release. Washington, DC: Social Investment Forum News. Retrieved August, 6, 2003, from http://www.socialinvest.org/areas/news/020730.htm

Social Investment Forum. (2003, January 29). *Fund performance update.* News release. Washington, DC: Social Investment Forum News. Retrieved August 20, 2003, from http://www.socialinvest.org/Areas/News/2002-Q4performance.htm

Storebrand. (2002). *Corporate social responsibility: Action plan 2003–2004.* Report. Oslo, Norway: Storebrand.

Swift, T. (2001, January). Trust, reputation and corporate accountability to stakeholders. *Business Ethics: A European Review, 10*(1), 16–26.

U.S. Department of Labor. (1999). *Employee benefits in medium and large private establishments, 1997.* Bulletin 2517. Washington, DC: Bureau of Labor Statistics. Retrieved August 12, 2003, from http://www.bls.gov/ncs/ebs/sp/ebbl0017.pdf

U.S. Department of Labor. (2000). *Employee benefits in medium and large private establishments, 1997.* Washington, DC: Bureau of Labor Statistics. Retrieved August 12, 2003 from http://data.bls.gov/servlet/SurveyOutputServlet

Vauxhall Motors. (2001, July). *The Vauxhall report for 2000: Annual sustainability report on economic, environmental, and social performance.* Luton, England: Vauxhall Motors.

Vinten, G. (2000). The stakeholder manager. *Management Decision, 28*(6), 377–383.

Waddock, S. (2000). The multiple bottom lines of corporate citizenship: Social investing, reputation, and responsibility audits. *Business and Society Review, 105*(3), 323–345.

Weiser, J., & Zadek, S. (2001, October). *Ongoing conversations with disbelievers. Persuading business to address social challenges.* Retrieved August 6, 2003, from www.conversations-with-disbeliever.net

WFD Consulting. *Community investment.* (2003). Retrieved August 24, 2003, from www.wfd.com/products/com_inv.html

WMC Resources, Ltd. (2002). *2002 sustainability report.* Southbank, Victoria, Australia: WMC Resources, Ltd.

Woodward, D., Edwards, P., & Birkin, F. (1996). Organizational legitimacy and stakeholder information provision. *British Journal of Management, 7,* 329–347.

V

Summary Chapters: Future Directions

22

Connecting Theory and Practice

Marian N. Ruderman
Center for Creative Leadership

How can theory on work-life integration be made more useful for practice? As we have seen in the previous chapters of this book, theoreticians have made great strides in promoting understanding of the dynamics of work-life interfaces. The various chapters in this book cover critical areas of content such as time usage, cross-cultural differences in approaches to work-life issues, conflict between work and family, and the impact of technology on work-life issues. Each chapter spirals back and forth between theory and data contributing to our theoretical understanding of work-life issues.

In contrast to the earlier chapters in this volume that focus on content, the present chapter looks at an issue of process—how do theories of work-life relationships connect to (or disconnect from) the real world of organizational practice? Despite the contribution of theory to building our knowledge base in a structured way, there is a disconnect between the theoretical world and the world of practice. The purpose of this chapter is to look at gaps between theory and practice and to suggest some ways of bridging the two. According to Lawler (1985), "It cannot simply be taken as a matter of faith that adhering to certain scientific research principles will lead to jointly useful research." It is important that research be designed in such a way that the knowledge gained will be put to practical use. Moreover, it is only through practice that we can actually test out the efficacy of a theory.

This chapter is organized into three sections: the different worlds of theorists and practitioners, theory-practice gaps, and suggestions for bridging theory and practice. It draws on a variety of sources of information including:

1. The literature on the adoption of human resource innovations.
2. Interviews with 7 work-life practitioners employed by corporations.
3. Discussions between researchers and practitioners at the conference developing this volume.
4. A survey of 27 leadership development specialists who work with individual managers focused on enhancing their leadership capabilities.

Together these various sources of information suggest that there are ways to tighten the links between theory and practice.

THE DIFFERENT WORLDS OF THEORISTS AND PRACTITIONERS

A starting point for understanding disconnects between theory and practice is to examine the different worlds of scholars and practitioners. Academia and business organizations are very different environments with different takes on issues relating to the relationship between work and family.

Both scholars and practitioners agree that priorities between work and personal goals compete, creating problems for both the individual and the organization; however, they differ in terms of the lens used to address the problem. Scholars are primarily interested in *why* these conflicts occur. They want to know what is the nature of the phenomena that drives conflicts between work and personal commitments. Scholars address the issue by developing a set of constructs to explain the issues. The constructs are related through propositions. Theoreticians then move back and forth between the propositions and empirical observations. Data collection is used to confirm, disconfirm, or extend the theory. Most scholars develop recommendations once there is evidence that a particular theory is empirically supported. Their recommendations take the form of generalities.

Organizational practitioners, on the other hand, are primarily focused on *how to fix* the problem of personal life interfering with work. They work with individuals or whole organizations. They specifically want to know *what to do* to address the issue of work-life conflict in a particular setting: what interventions prevent, fix, or ameliorate work-life conflict. For example, the leadership development specialists surveyed for this chapter work primarily with individual managers at the Center for Creative Leadership, a nonprofit leadership development institution. They were asked to report on the way managers describe work-life issues in a leadership development setting. Their responses (see Table 22.1) suggest that they interpret work-life issues in terms of what advice they can give to managers about how to handle work-life conflict. They perceive the data on work-life conflict in terms of techniques or approaches that make it less stressful for individuals, reflecting their focus on helping individuals. Practitioners in large corporations are also interested in an approach that focuses on how to fix the problem. However, their lens is embedded in an overall picture of how an organization can act. They want to know what the organization can do to address the problem—what policies, practices, and initiatives work to reduce the conflict in a way that ultimately benefits the organization. They are focused on how their organization can attract, develop, and retain top-notch personnel in light of the inherent challenges meeting the demands of work and personal priorities. They are interested in the specifics of what will work for their particular organization.

TABLE 22.1
Leadership Development Specialists' Views of the Work-Life Issues Managers Experience

Theme	Definition	Example
How to create balance in a nonstop business culture.	People want to know how to have greater work-life balance amid a company culture that encourages working 24/7.	Cell phones, PDAs, laptops, and so on are making it harder to get away from work when not physically on-site. Participants want to know how to manage this.
Fear of retribution.	Managers fear that taking advantage of work-life programs will hinder career advancement.	The fear that taking more time away from work for family might jeopardize their standing at work.
How to manage self-imposed standards.	Managers have self-imposed standards that make it difficult for them to engage in nonwork activities, although they would like to.	Managers who feel very pressured to succeed in the traditional way of moving up the ladder, usually meaning more time at the office and additional travel; they want to know how to successfully balance home and work given their drive to succeed.
How to manage conflicting priorities.	Participants want to know how to spend more time with family when they travel too much and work too hard.	Many participants feel that they are not there for loved ones and work to gain a different perspective on their priorities to change their behavior in this area.

Furthermore, human resource practitioners based in organizations have to be able to sell whatever recommendations they develop from a business perspective. Their focus is not just on findings that are true, but on findings that will convince others to implement their specific recommendations.

Combining the goals of scholars and practitioners provides a much broader view of the issue of work-life integration. The scholarly community addresses the fundamental question of why workers experience work-life challenges; the practitioner community pushes the immediate issue of how to address it. Together the different communities could create a multifaceted approach to the problem of the competing demands of work and private life. However, something happens on the way to more a comprehensive view. Ideally, answers to the "why" question should inform the answers to the "how to fix it" question and vice versa. Unfortunately the cycle of ideas into action and action into ideas falls short. The next section of this chapter looks at a variety of reasons why there is a gap between theory and practice. The final section provides suggestions for strengthening the connections between theoretical research and practice.

THEORY-PRACTICE GAPS

The term *theory-practice gap* is used here to convey a variety of disconnects between theory and practice. Despite the many years of research into the relationships between work and nonwork activities, the problem of how to handle competing demands of work and personal spheres remains significant.

There has been progress in identifying organizational practices to address work-life issues in organizations. On-site child-care centers, concierge services, summer hours, meals-to-go, eldercare referral services, sabbatical programs, flexible work options, job sharing, telecommuting, and on-site gyms receive a lot of attention in the media these days. The assumption is that these programs remove some of the friction between work and family obligations. However, according to a survey by the Bureau of Labor Statistics cited by Kossek (in press), the availability of such work-life benefits is quite low. Only 5% of employers provide flexible workplace policies and only 4% provide referrals for child care. A survey by the Alliance for Work-Life Progress (cited in Kossek, in press) reveals that even when these practices are implemented, the use of work-life practices is much lower than the availability of these programs.

Thus, it is important to look at the disconnects between theory and practice to see how theory and practice can combine to address work-life issues. There are several disconnects between theory and application that help to explain why, despite considerable knowledge about the work-family interface, the challenges of integrating work and family life still remain a key issue. These gaps include the underestimation of organizational context, individual reluctance to use programs, gaps in the knowledge base, communication differences, value differences, problems with research access, and a lack of feedback from practice to theory.

Underestimation of the Role of Organizational Context

The first barrier to the application of theory around work-life issues has to do with the difficulty of getting organizations to adopt recommended work-life practices. Researchers typically think of human resource innovations on their technical merit and forget that the context—economic, social, and political issues—needs to be taken into account in implementation (Johns, 1993). Researchers tend to justify practices on the basis of empirical data or theory; however, ideas should be sold in organizations in terms of what they can do for the organization given the particular organizational context.

The economy is an example of a contextual variable often overlooked in scholarly work on policies and practices. In these early years of the new millennium, with rising unemployment, business downturns, and a shaky stock market, the economy does not encourage organizations to embrace work-life innovations. In today's business world, with the limits on travel and financial issues, it is difficult to make the case for the adoption of work-life practices. In many cases, large companies are cutting back on available programs and the personnel responsible for implementing these programs. Companies are trying to become more productive, and one easy way to do this is to try to increase workloads by giving people more to do. Employers at the moment have their pick of the job market; it is easier to be an employer of choice in a tight economy. There is less motivation on the part of organizations to buy into work-life programs as a means of attracting and retaining top staff. However, this may be short-term thinking and ultimately could be problematic.

A long-term contextual argument bearing on work-life practices is that adoption of these innovations is advantageous in the war for talent. As the economy improves, organizations will start to compete again for the most talented individuals. It is likely that work-life innovations will again be seen as an important tool for attracting and retaining top talent. Moreover, this argument is likely to be strengthened as Generation X comes into play in the business world because Gen Xers are more likely to have a working spouse than members of previous generations (Bond, Galinsky, & Swanberg, 1998). Further, the longer-term view suggests it simply is not productive just to increase the workload. More work can create more personal problems, which in turn spill back over into the workplace (Bond et al., 1998). The advantages of doing more with fewer workers can be short-lived.

This long-term thinking influenced Eli Lilly's adoption of a variety of flexible work options to help workers have a life outside of work. Candi Lange of Eli Lilly explained that they have a culture that embraces flexible work options. Eli

Lilly has the typical programs such as flex weeks, job sharing, and working at home, which combine to create a culture that supports flexibility. They also have some less common programs such as a vacation school program that offers enrichment programs to school-age children of employees during school holidays. The goal behind these practices is to make Eli Lilly an employer of choice by coming up up with a number of ways to create flexibility to meet employees' needs. The company believes that it is important to take a holistic view of people in order to keep them attracted to Lilly over the long haul. These programs started years ago and were implemented in stages. They were designed to address the stated need of employees to have an employer who recognized the inherent conflicts of managing work and family life.

Other contextual factors that influence adoption of work-life innovations are globalization and technology. As the business world is moving to a 24/7 mentality, implementing work-life innovations becomes more complicated. Managers are now working longer hours to keep up with colleagues and competitors across the globe. Technology makes it possible to work anywhere and any time. Collaborating with colleagues in distant time zones can make it difficult to use some of the work-life practices: How do you decide who should be responsible for taking the conference call at 6:00 A.M.? How do geographically dispersed teams handle work on Monday mornings and Friday afternoons with weekend starting and ending times differing by location? Different work-life trade-offs may be necessary to accommodate the global work environment with its variety of time zones, languages, and cultural practices.

Another contextual factor has to do with the legal and social environment. One of the biggest stimulators of change in work-life practices was the Family Medical Leave Act of 1993. This legislation dramatically changed the types of family leave available in the United States. In the United Kingdom, the Employment Relations Act of 1999 spurred family-friendly policies. Throughout the European Union, there also has been a concentrated effort to improve the relationship between work and family (Lyness & Kropf, 2003); Sweden in particular is well-known for its subsidized child care and parental leave policies (Haas, Hwang, & Russell, 2000). Most of our research models do not take legal and social factors into account, yet these factors are vitally important when it comes to the adoption of innovations. Lewis and Haas (chap. 16, this volume) draw attention to the variety of ways government and societal actions can influence the relationship between work and other aspects of life.

Finally, a contextual factor that is often overlooked has to do with the power and influence of the parties recommending introduction of work-life practices. Typically such recommendations come out of human resource departments. Unfortunately, recommendations put forth by staff departments carry less weight than those from line departments. One human resource practitioner said that others in her company see the human resource function as "fluff." To counterbalance this perception, it is important to make a compelling case for work-life practices to top executives who must approve such proposals. The task is to sell these initiatives by showing executives that they can improve business by implementing these practices.

The danger of ignoring social context is that it is difficult to know when an innovation will work (Johns, 1993). Context can act as an unmeasured variable in many studies and as such has an influence on the adoption of innovation. In terms of the innovations stemming from theoretical research on work-life issues, this means that a large barrier to adoption of work-life practices is underestimating the power of organizational context.

Individual Reluctance to Use Work-Life Programs or Practices

Another disconnect between theory and practice has to do with the relatively low usage of corporate work-life practices. In the words of one of our corporate interviewees, "Implementing it is easy; utilization is hard." Individuals may not choose to use these programs because they simply do not value time away from work, their supervisors do not support them, or because they may be fearful of repercussions if they take advantage of the programs.

One reason why individuals may not use work-life practices is because they simply do not value having greater balance between their work and private life. Arlie Hochschild says in *The Time Bind* (1997) that for many people work can be refuge from home and they do not want to tamper with that. To many people the idea that work and personal life should complement one another is foreign; it is not a value they hold. Overidentification with career can be a potent force contributing to the underutilization of work-life practices (Edmondson & Deter, chap. 18, this volume).

Supervisory behavior plays a key role in understanding individual usage of organizational policies and programs for helping workers integrate work and personal spheres (Hopkins, chap. 20, this volume). The *1997 National Study of the Changing Workforce* points out how critical supervisory support is to the creation of a family-friendly environment and the ultimate use of work life practices (Bond et al., 1998). If managers feel that they cannot use these policies because their supervisors disapprove, this attitude gets transmitted down the hierarchy. It may be politically correct for organizations to offer work-life programs today but many senior executives implement them in a contradictory way.

Whether or not their supervisors support these programs, many individuals may chose not to use them because they work in an organizational culture that equates productivity with time spent on the job. Many workers today feel that in order to get ahead they must demonstrate an undivided focus on work. Individuals who feel very pressured to succeed in the traditional way of moving up the ladder are fearful of using work-life programs because they feel the programs could interfere with their success. Historically, the ideal worker (Williams, 1999) is someone who places work above all other priorities. They do not let family or private commitments interfere with work. People may avoid using work-life benefits because they fear being seen as less than the ideal worker. One of the human resource practitioners told us an interesting story about the use of fertility treatment benefits. In many cases, fertility treatments require frequent visits to a medical facility. Top employees were hesitant to use this benefit because they feared that taking the time off from work would make the fertility issue visible and would render them as a less-than-ideal employee in the eyes of their boss and coworkers. This fear is further compounded with the worry that coworkers would think they were working only for the fertility treatment coverage and subsequent maternity leave benefits.

Clearly, individual use of work-life practices is dependent on a variety of factors—the individual's own values, the supervisor, and the organizational climate. These variables have a tremendous impact on the usage of any particular practice.

The Knowledge Gap

Another cause for the divide between theory and practice has to do with gaps in our knowledge of work-life interfaces in organizations. Although there is a substantial amount of knowledge about work-family role conflict, we know less about the other mechanisms for explaining the linkages between work and family roles (Greenhaus & Singh, 2003). For example, these other linking mechanisms include segmentation and integration, both of which have received less attention in the literature than conflict. Segmentation, for example, refers to the separation of work and nonwork roles, time, and activities; in contrast, integration refers to the overlap of work and nonwork roles, time, and activities (Nippert-Eng, 1995). In practical terms, this means that segmentors are likely to keep the work-home boundary distinct and integrators are likely to bring work home and home to work. Some workers prefer the segmentation approach and others prefer the more integrated approach, with its blurred distinctions between work and home. As a research community we are just starting to understand the differential preferences for segmentation and integration and how they interact with human resource policies (Edwards & Rothbard, 2000; Nippert-Eng, 1995). Some human resource policies favor segmentors—for example, flexible work programs that allow for clear boundaries as to when work begins and ends—in contrast to other policies that favor integrators, such as telecommuting. Much remains to be learned about segmentation and integration and how they relate to employee usage of human resource policies and practices.

Another area that we need to explore has to do with the design of work. The research by Lotte Bailyn (1993) and others has demonstrated that the way work flows can exacerbate the conflicts between work and nonwork activities. Perlow (1997) has demonstrated that the redesign of work can improve efficiency and allow workers more time to attend to personal goals. However, this type of research, which experimentally adjusts the fundamental way work is carried out in organizations has only just begun. Organizations today design jobs without consideration of family needs—but how do we know this is the most effective way to design jobs? To have a better understanding of how work can be more effectively redesigned requires additional knowledge.

These gaps in our knowledge limit the ability to make accurate descriptions of work-life interfaces, let alone appropriate prescriptions for organizational practitioners. The shortage of research on these topics makes it difficult for practitioners to devise responsive human resource policies. Perhaps this volume's emphasis on understanding theory and accumulating knowledge will go a long way toward enhancing the level of knowledge available for application.

The Communication Gap

In addition to being limited by the available pool of knowledge, practice is also constrained by a communication gap between theoreticians and practitioners. Essentially the issue is that theoreticians and practitioners have different norms of communication, terminology, and language. Theoreticians put a premium on clear definitions and precise language. They label what they find, and use these labels as a means of advancing knowledge. However, different theoreticians use different terms depending on their discipline. Even at the conference that inspired this volume, theorists used different terms to discuss similar concepts. For example, *work-life conflict* was also called *work-life interference* and *negative spillover*. There is therefore a lack of a common language both across theoreticians from different disciplines and between theoreticians and practitioners. The result is a mix of languages that makes it difficult to discuss the results and implications of research the field has conducted.

Related to the notion of language differences is the problem that the results of research are not easily communicated to practitioners. Most research findings are disseminated via scientific journal articles; however, practitioners do not tend to read these. One practitioner interviewed said that the sharing of knowledge is "a 'face-to-face' process; we do not go to the library to look up results. We don't live with books and articles. We don't focus on statistics. We like to hear information from other people." However, the academic world in which most researchers reside offers its richest rewards for those who publish frequently in peer-reviewed journals. The different format of presentation desired by the different communities has an impact. To some extent the gap between theory and practice could be narrowed by a common manner of information presentation; however, mechanisms for presenting information in practitioner language are not well established. Academics are not rewarded for reaching out and publishing in practitioner outlets. Social scientists working in academia are in a publish-or-perish environment. The problem is that the publications that tend to carry the most weight are those geared for other academicians, not the ones for practitioners. One of the human resource practitioners interviewed told us that because of this dynamic, some academics come across as antipractice and as not wanting to reach out to the very people who supplied them with data.

The Value Gap

Researchers and practitioners also experience a disconnect because they value research differently. One of the key goals of the research community is to do research that has validity across situations. Good research in the academic world is material that produces findings that are generalizable and contribute to a body of knowledge. In the practice view, good research often leads to specific findings that apply to that setting at a particular point in time. Given all the complexities involved in any single organization, it is difficult for researchers striving for generalizability to come up with findings that are specific to a particular environment. The utilization of research-generated knowledge is constrained by the demands of the specific situation (Beyer, 1997). Therefore, some practitioners tend to view academic research as irrelevant because it is not tailored to specific organizational needs.

Similarly, academics and practitioners value different types of data in their work. Academics tend to value objective data that can be evaluated carefully and across many cases. Peer review of the results of a study is the ultimate test of quality. Practitioners, in contrast, often favor data that is subjective and is based on a recommendation from fellow practitioners. (Terpstra & Rozel, 1997). The test of quality is whether or not someone they know and trust experienced the intervention as favorable and saw it bring benefits to the organization. This preference for different types of data makes it difficult for scientists and practitioners to draw common conclusions from data.

Academic personnel and corporate practitioners also place different values on time frames associated with careful research. Human resource practitioners often want the answers quickly in response to a current set of challenges. However, methodology that will lead to a publication in a peer-reviewed journal often takes a substantial amount of time.

Research Access

Another reason for the divide between practice and theory is that it can be very difficult for theoreticians to access organizations that will allow structured studies of work-life practices. Inviting a group of researchers into an organization to collect data involves inherent risks: The study may result in unforeseen and undesirable results or it can create conditions for legal liability. Research also incurs a cost to organizations in terms of time and money and may be difficult to justify in an environment where all eyes are on profit. Rynes and McNatt

(2001) found that the typical organizational study involves 175 hours of the sponsoring organization's time.

Furthermore, the benefit to the sponsoring organization may be unclear. There appears to be something of a catch-22: Organizations say that they want research that demonstrates the benefits of work-life programs, yet there is a reluctance to allow researchers into organizations in such a way that costs and benefits can be demonstrated in a disciplined and structured way. Few organizations are wiling to allow studies that have the characteristics of sophisticated research design, such as control groups, repeated measures, and the control of extraneous variables. Experimental designs on issues of work-life practices are relatively rare. This conundrum makes it difficult to span the theory-practice divide. One technique that has been effective helping researchers obtain access is promising the organization input into the research design (Rynes & McNatt, 2001)—access is easier if the organization is invited to influence the materials, questions, and manipulations.

From Practice to Theory: The Other Side of the Feedback Loop

A final type of disconnect has to do with the loop back from practice to theory. Organizational practitioners are rewarded for doing a good job in reaching the goals of the organization. For work-life practitioners, this may entail identifying appropriate programs, justifying them, implementing the programs, and evaluating them. It does not include publishing those results with the larger work-life community. In fact, in many cases the work is considered proprietary and practitioners are restricted from sharing information publicly.

A drawback to this model is that it is difficult to improve theory development and to build on theory without adequate knowledge of how a given model works in the real world. Practical feedback is not readily given to theoreticians and there is a loss of important knowledge that comes from taking an action and seeing how it works. As a community interested in the work-life interface, we have no systematic mechanisms for transmitting practitioner knowledge to scholars.

Yet this sort of feedback can lead to developments in theory. A good example is some of the work done at the Center for Creative Leadership. For many years, we have run a leadership development program for women managers and executives. Several years ago, researchers were observing a module in the program intended to help women managers deal with role conflict in their lives. The module (now revised) was called "Total Life Issues." The goal of this training module was to identify and discuss the different stresses and strains women experienced in their attempts to manage both personal and professional roles. The women discussed their feeling of being overworked and its impact on other life roles. In many ways it was an application of role theory, in particular the role-scarcity perspective (Goode, 1960). The questions covered in the module were designed to elicit areas of conflict and to develop strategies for coping with the conflict. In addition, the module also asked participants to describe how different roles energized them. There were many answers. Participants mentioned learning from the various roles in their lives and carrying the learning from one role to another. In a research sense, this practice provided evidence of the role accumulation perspective (Marks, 1977; Sieber, 1974), which stands in contrast to the role-scarcity perspective. Briefly, the role-accumulation approach suggests that there are beneficial effects of commitment to multiple roles; role conflict is not the only and inevitable outcome of multiple roles (Rothbard, 2001). This observation of practice led to a structured study providing evidence in support of the role-accumulation perspective (Ruderman, Ohlott, Panzer, & King, 2002). This was a case in which practice influenced an empirical study that provided new evidence for a theoretical approach. Unfortunately, this type of feedback between practice and theory is rare.

Role accumulation as a theoretical perspective might lead to different interventions than role conflict. In fact, comparing the two theoretical perspectives suggests that practices that limit the amount of work to allow employees to have an outside life, in addition to the standard practices designed to reduce work-family conflict, might be highly beneficial. Practices that influence the design of work itself so there is more time for other aspects of life are a logical implication of the role-accumulation approach. Investigating such practices would shed light on our knowledge of role-accumulation dynamics. With the exception of the studies on work design conducted by Bailyn and her colleagues (see for example, Fletcher & Bailyn, chap. 9, this volume), little is known about how to modify work processes in order to enhance both work time and personal time.

SUGGESTIONS FOR BRIDGING THEORY AND RESEARCH

So what can the field do to bridge the gap between theory and practice? This can be a difficult question to answer. There are no easy remedies. Yet there are some steps that can be taken to point us in the right direction. They include enhancing the dissemination of knowledge to practitioner communities and conducting joint and multilevel research.

Enhancing the Dissemination of Knowledge

One of the most obvious ways to bridge the theory-practice gap is through the dissemination of knowledge about work-life interfaces and practices. All seven of the practitioners surveyed about their organizations' use of work-life innovations reported that available theory would be more useful if it was presented in a user-friendly format. The practitioners went on to explain that they do not have the time to read the research in the academic form; their culture is not one that is based on journals, books, or libraries. There is a gold mine of information available but it is not readily accessible.

So how can research be distilled for a lay audience? One way is through conference presentations. Practitioners mentioned that networking at professional conferences is one of the best ways to get research-based information. They attend conferences sponsored by the Conference Board, the Society for Human Resource Management, the Family and Work Institute, the Mid-West Work Family Association, the Association for Work-Life Progress, Boston College Center for Work and Family, and the Work and Family Roundtable sponsored by the Wharton school. The face-to-face medium allows for presentation of nuggets of findings and catches the practitioners' attention. Industry-academic conference-based alliances provide a helpful way to share information. For example, one human resource practitioner said:

> I know one of the things that I enjoy about the Boston College Center for Work and Family is the interaction that we have. I know every six months that I will have sessions with academics that are looking at the field of work-life, and they'll have the people who are doing the research come in and explain their research, but they'll also have sessions like an open session, where you can ask questions, or say what is going on in your company, and ask them if they can look at that in their research too.

Networking is also a way to discover what other organizations are doing and what they have learned. The conferences sponsored by the periodicals that do the "Best Companies to Work For" lists also provide a way for practitioners to find out what works and what does not. For example, *Fortune* puts out the 100 Best Companies to Work for List and *Working Mother Magazine* puts out the top 100 companies for working mothers. At events associated with these lists, practitioners get the opportunity to learn what is going on in the field. These conferences also provide the social and technical support practitioners need to launch new programs or revise existing ones.

Information and findings are also shared via the written word—but not via the periodicals that good theoreticians most commonly use. *BusinessWeek*, *Fortune*, the *Wall Street Journal*, *Harvard Business Review*, and *USA Today* are vehicles for transmitting information. Articles in these periodicals catch the attention of both human resource practitioners and line executives who might see something of value to suggest for their organization. Online newsletters with their "in your face" quality are also helpful. Web-based research about other companies' programs is another technique. The gist is to put information in a form that brings readers face-to-face with the findings. Although it may not seem a very "scholarly" thing to do, putting out a press release based on a research article may help to get knowledge in the hands of those of who need it most. The mention of a research finding in the *New York Times*, *Wall Street Journal*, or other key outlets goes a long way toward catching the eye of those who have the influence to make changes in the workplace. How a top manager interprets work-life issues is a key factor in adoption of practices (Milliken, Martins, & Morgan, 1998). Thus, presenting information in way that speaks to top decision makers is critical.

How do carefully conducted research studies get transformed into nuggets for practitioners or the media? The world of science and academia values carefully constructed studies that follow the structure of the discipline. The work is considered finished when it is put into a journal or a book. However, the practitioners interviewed for this chapter say that they want the knowledge in a different form than a journal article. They explain that research frameworks are quite valuable, but they are unlikely to be practitioner frameworks. Ambiguity about the specifics of when and where results apply is okay in academic frameworks, but in a corporate environment it is harder to embrace general concepts without supporting knowledge of techniques for applying the concepts. Creating a practitioner framework requires converting the knowledge into a more useable form that emphasizes distillation of the knowledge and specificity. Typically this process entails moving from generalities to the specific context, boiling information down to its essence, and using user-friendly language rather than academic jargon. One possible way to do this is to work with other disciplines. Editors and writers for the popular press may be helpful here, as well as instructional designers. Scientists are very good at using information specialists such as librarians for help at the front end of a research project but they are less skilled at using writers for the public at the back end. Perhaps using the expertise of other disciplines may help put knowledge in a form that is more accessible to organizational practitioners. The conference and meeting format is probably successful with practitioners because it allows for the opportunity to share ideas and brainstorm solutions to practical problems. Good research and theory development requires the skills of science; handing off knowledge requires writing and instructional skills. Specialists in communication can go a long way toward disseminating important findings.

We did notice a few ways that scholarly findings get into business organizations. One way is through new hires; recent MBAs bring with them the latest trends in human resources and the knowledge supporting these trends. In addition to MBAs some companies hire former academics, which serves as a way to introduce scholarly knowledge into human resource practices. This method may help infuse the knowledge shared in business school programs but it probably does little to introduce new research about families or child development into the corporate mix. Another way is through the use of university-based consultants who bring in their base of knowledge. The practitioners interviewed were unanimous in saying that scholarly findings are infused into organizations through people.

Joint Research

Another way to improve the suitability of research for application is through conducting joint research. Partnerships between researchers and organizations allow for the articulation of a joint agenda. Although there a few notable industry-academic alliances (e.g., Boston College Center on Work and Family), the current reality is that academicians and practitioners work separately. Academics are rewarded for publication in peer-reviewed journals; however, practitioners read the trade and popular press. Theoreticians in particular are noted for the careful development of concepts and understanding of relationships between variables. However, this type of work typically done in universities does not always get the theoretician out into organizations. Spending time on-site, working with organizations around work-life initiatives is an extremely important way to help theoreticians refine their insights. Coming face-to-face with a phenomenon helps to spur theoretical thinking. Dunnette (1990) explains that the most important way to advance the larger field of industrial and organizational psychology is by blending the skills of the practitioner and scientist. Greater collaboration between industry and academia will allow for research that is more useful. One way of supporting this is to foster networking opportunities between work-life practitioners and theoreticians. Rynes and McNatt (2001) found that research that is initiated by an organization often results in a high-quality project with adoptable findings. They found that organizations that recruit the researcher to join them are more likely to use the research findings. This suggests that methods of fostering contact between work-life practitioners and theoreticians are useful. Researchers and practitioners need to know one another. Both sides need to find a friend working in the other arena who could help to broaden their perspective. Perhaps visiting fellow opportunities for both practitioners and academics would help enhance the utilization of knowledge. Practitioners could teach at a university for a term and scholars could work with work-life practitioners for a term.

In terms of content, one particular type of research that is extremely helpful has to do with building the business case for work-life practices. Organizations are more inclined to adopt innovations if the economic or social payoff is clear (Kossek, 1987). Organizations do not make changes based solely on academic research. Each of the seven human resource practitioners interviewed stated that change is implemented on evidence that it will impact the business case and create value for the corporation.

Often this process starts with demonstrating the need for a particular practice. For example, Candi Lange of Eli Lilly described the push from employees for their flexible work options. The company conducted a survey in 1992 that provided compelling evidence that employees wanted greater control over their time and schedule. The data drove home the issue to senior management, many of whom had traditional family arrangements where dad worked and mom stayed home. The case was made that flexible work options fit with the company heritage of valuing people and would help them become the employer of choice. Joan Glubczynski of SC Johnson reported a similar experience with a task force gathering data from employees that was instrumental in convincing senior managers of the value of adopting particular practices.

Another type of research crucial to establishing the business case involves benchmarking in order to identify the competitive practices that are used by other major companies. It looks at leading employers and the positions they take regarding work-life issues. Currently many large corporations use consulting companies to do benchmarking research. The problem for knowledge management is that this knowledge tends to be proprietary and cannot be used to benefit the field in general. This makes it difficult for the field as a whole to learn from experience and accumulate a knowledge base. Also, consulting companies have no incentive to report their failures, so communal learning from mistakes is limited. Joan Glubczynski of SC Johnson argues that it would be very beneficial for companies and academics to partner around benchmarking research so that data from individual companies could be tied to outcomes across companies. For example, a good question might be, what is the impact of different types of work-life practices on health-care costs? This research would entail not only documenting what companies do—which is what typically is done—but also connecting it to the impact on health-care costs.

Research on the business case also involves demonstrating that a particular innovation makes financial sense. Practitioners would like to see researchers address cost-benefit tools to justify different programs. They would like to be able to say, "Here are the monetary advantages of implementing these programs, and here are the costs in terms of turnover and morale in terms of leaving things status quo." Data are extremely important to showing cost effectiveness. Obviously, this is not easy research to do; it requires complex longitudinal models, and there are many factors in implementation that violate the tenets of good research design. However, this messy kind of research could really help to evaluate the efficacy of a theoretically based intervention that contributes to the case for adopting a particular work-life practice.

Another topic for joint research is figuring out when and under what conditions various innovations are effective. In other words, what are the mediators and moderators of the effectiveness of particular practices? Our interviews with the human resource practitioners uncovered several practices that corporations tried to implement but were not able to make work. For example, in one company a child-care facility was cited as not working out and in another it was cited as an example of a great success. What causes the difference in response to this innovation? Did it have to do with the location of the child-care facility, the characteristics of the work force, the nature of the plan, or the other benefits available? Another research question of interest to the practitioners interviewed has to do with flexible work options and corporate culture. The basic question is how do these practices work in different types of organizational cultures? Also, how effective are the different techniques? Joint research could be conducted to understand the variables influencing usage of these practices.

Another possibility for joint research is to foster the publication of corporate research in this field. Many companies do their own research to justify a particular practice or to evaluate it, but they rarely tend to publish their findings because it is outside the parameter of their work. The most common ways by which company-specific findings are shared is through "Best Companies" awards that tend to be overlooked by academics as a peer-reviewed source of knowledge. Documentation of company-specific investigations via case studies can be particularly powerful in helping to make the business case of work-life innovations to other organizations. Alliances between industry and academia could be useful in developing these case studies and using their publication to contribute to furthering knowledge in the field at large. Retrospective case analyses may be a helpful strategy for developing grounded theory based on the knowledge gained through practice (Dunn & Swierczek, 1977).

Multilevel Research

An additional strategy for furthering ties between research and theory is conducting multilevel research. Often research is simply at one level of analysis—individual, familial, organizational or societal. The problem, though, is that work-life issues span these levels. Practice requires an understanding of how these different factors work in concert to influence work-life issues. Societal concerns such as legal issues, cultural values, and local history impact how work-life is viewed, as do organizational policies and norms. Family dynamics influence how individuals evaluate the impact of work on the family. Individual variables (e.g., age or personality) are obviously meaningful as well, but cannot be understood as purely an isolated phenomenon. Research integrating these different levels of factors helps to enrich our understanding of very complex work-life phenomena. This research can then be useful in figuring out whether to intervene at the individual, familial, organizational, or societal level, or at all four.

CONCLUSIONS

In an ideal world knowledge would flow from research to practice and back again with lessons learned from practice incorporated in knowledge development. There would be a continuous cycle of ideas into action and action into

ideas. In terms of work-life issues some of this cycle happens—problems identified in theory-based discussions have been addressed through a variety of innovative work-life practices. Laws have changed. A variety of work-life practices abound. There are academic industry alliances that foster the transmission
of knowledge.

However, have we gone far enough? The answer is clearly no. There is ample
room for a tighter coupling between theory and practice. This looseness comes
from a tendency to overlook organization context and individual decision-
making frameworks with regard to understanding adoption of research-based
innovations. There also is a communication gap evidenced by helpful studies
going unnoticed by the very practitioners who could use them. Furthermore, the
collaboration between researchers and corporations is limited, resulting in a hap-
hazard accumulation of knowledge across different organizations. The influence
of practice on theory is very weak, with there being relatively little opportunity
for practice issues to enrich the theoretical ones. The ties between theory and
practice are loose and could stand to be strengthened.

Is the gap growing with time? It is unfortunate to think that this disconnect
is expanding rather than contracting. However, there is no evidence that it is
shrinking. The leadership development specialists surveyed emphasize that managers increasingly are clamoring for help adjusting their work-life interface to
a more favorable relationship. Although we have knowledge about how to help
in this situation, it is hard to get individuals and organizations to use practices
resulting from the information. For example, certain work-life experiments such
as those involving the redesign of work or changing the norms around the ideal
worker are difficult to enact. Current economic pressures limit the effectiveness
of both researchers looking to find a better way of fashioning the world of work
and those practitioners who would like to use them. Until greater priority is put
on understanding the work-life interface, there is no reason to expect that this
gap will shrink. The current model of research studies using sophisticated analytic techniques to advance theory may be furthering the accumulation of
knowledge but it is not necessarily speaking to the very decision makers who
could make significant change.

Given the significance of work-life issues in workers' lives and the business
economy, it is imperative that our knowledge be of better quality and more
available to key organizational decision makers. There is helpful research that
is not being converted into enhanced organizational practices. Moreover, there
is considerable knowledge in the heads of practitioners that is not flowing to
theoreticians. Suggestions for strengthening the links between theory and practice include sharing information in a format friendly to practitioners, moving
from a research-based framework to a practitioner framework, conducting joint
research, and engaging in multilevel research that better captures the complexity
of the phenomenon.

All in all, there remains opportunity for great progress in this area. As a field we have made huge steps forward but it is time to increase the progress and bolster efforts to enhance the theory-practice linkages.

AUTHOR NOTE

The author thanks the conference attendees and supporters who took part in the interviews discussed in this chapter.

REFERENCES

Bailyn, L. (1993). *Breaking the mold: Women, men, and time in the new corporate world.* New York: Free Press.

Beyer, J. M. (1997). Research utilization: Bridging a cultural gap between communities. *Journal of Management Inquiry, 6,* 17–22.

Bond, J., Galinsky, E., & Swanberg, J. (1998). *The 1997 national study of the changing workforce.* New York: Families and Work Institute.

Dunn, W. N., & Swierczek, F. W. (1977). Planned organizational change—Toward grounded theory. *The Journal of Applied Behavioral Science, 13*(2), 135–157.

Dunnette, M. D. (1990). Blending the science and practice of industrial and organizational psychology: Where are we and where are we going? In M. D. Dunnette & L. M. Hough (Eds.), *Handbook of industrial & organizational psychology* (2nd. ed., vol. 1, pp. 1–28). Palo Alto, CA: Consulting Psychologists Press, Inc.

Edwards, J. R., & Rothbard, N. P. (2000). Mechanisms linking work and family: Clarifying the relationship between work and family constructs. *Academy of Management Review, 25,* 178–199.

Goode, W. J. (1960). A theory of role strain. *American Sociological Review, 25,* 483–496.

Greenhaus, J. H., & Singh, R. (2003). Work-family linkages. In M. Pitts-Catsouphes & E. E. Kossek (Eds.), *Work-family encyclopedia.* Retrieved February 25, 2003, from www.bc.edu/wfnetwork

Haas, L., Hwang, P., & Russell, G. (2000). *Organizational change and gender equity: International perspectives on the roles of fathers and mothers in the workplace.* Thousand Oaks, CA: Sage.

Hochschild, A. R. (1997). *The time bind: When work becomes home and home becomes work.* New York: Metropolitan Books.

Johns, G. (1993). Constraints on the adoption of psychology-based personnel practices: Lessons from organizational innovation. *Personnel Psychology, 46*(3), 569–592.

Kossek, E. E. (1987). Human resources management innovation. *Human Resource Management, 26*(1), 71–92.

Kossek, E. E. (in press). Workplace policies and practices to support work and families: Gaps in implementation and linkages to individual and organization effectives. In S. M. Bianchi, L. M. Casper, K. E. Christsensen, & R. B. King (Eds.) *Workforce/workplace mismatch? Work, family health, and well-being.* Mahwah, NJ: Erlbaum.

Lawler, E. E., III. (1985). Challenging traditional research assumptions. In E. E. Lawler III, A. M. Mohrman Jr., S. Mohrman, G. Ledford Jr., T. Cummings, & Associates (Eds.), *Doing research that is useful for theory and practice* (pp. 1–17). San Francisco: Jossey-Bass.

Lyness, K. S., & Kropf, M. B. (2003, August 4). *The relationships of national gender equality and organizational support with work-family balance: A study of European managers.* Paper presented at the Annual Meeting of the Academy of Management, Seattle, WA.

Marks, S. R. (1997). Multiple roles and role strain: Some notes on human energy, time and commitment. *American Sociological Review, 42,* 921–936.

Milliken, F. J., Martins, L. L., & Morgan, H. (1998). Explaining organizational responsiveness to work-family issues: The role of human resource executives as issue interpreters. *Academy of Management Journal, 41*(5), 580–592.

Nippert-Eng, C. E. (1995). *Home and work: Negotiating boundaries through everyday life.* Chicago: The University of Chicago Press.

Perlow, L. (1997). *Finding time: How corporations, individuals, and families can benefit from new work practices.* Ithaca, NY: Cornell University Press.

Rothbard, N. P. (2001). Enriching or depleting? The dynamics of engagement in work and family roles. *Administrative Science Quarterly, 46,* 655–684.

Ruderman, M. N., Ohlott, P. J., Panzer, K., & King, S. N. (2002). Benefits of multiple roles for managerial women. *Academy of Management Journal, 45,* 369–386.

Rynes, S. L., & McNatt, D. B. (2001). Bringing the organization into organizational research: An examination of academic research inside organizations. *Journal of Business and Psychology, 16*(1), 2–19.

Sieber, S. D. (1974). Toward a theory of role accumulation. *American Sociological Review, 39,* 567–578.

Terpstra, D. E., & Rozell, E. J. (1997). Psychology of the scientist: LXXI. Attitudes of practitioners in human resource management toward information from academic research. *Psychological Reports, 80,* 403–412.

Williams, J. (1999). *Unbending gender: Why work and family conflict and what to do about it.* New York: Oxford University Press.

23

Future Frontiers: Enduring Challenges and Established Assumptions in the Work-Life Field

Susan J. Lambert
The University of Chicago

Ellen Ernst Kossek
Michigan State University

Together, the chapters in this book paint a detailed portrait of the dramatic changes taking place at the beginning of the twenty-first century, both in the workplace and in the personal lives of workers. The structure, pace, and experience of work have intensified at the same time that family structures have weakened in terms of their ability to buffer workers from the stresses of the economy. Several authors note how the relationship between work and personal life is sure to be reciprocal, and we agree that attention should be paid to understanding how transformations in the family affect the workplace and work outcomes. However, this book's voice is focused on the workplace and to good effect. The chapters reveal the powerful roles organizational and job structures, policies, and processes play in mediating the relationship between workers and the economy, ultimately shaping the nature and quality of workers' personal and family lives.

In this chapter, we identify crosscutting themes of divergence and convergence from the organizational, individual, social, and cultural perspectives represented in this book. First, we consider themes that might be deemed points of contention, that is, enduring issues that are critical to the field of work-life scholarship and practice but for which there is limited consensus. This loosely coupled field must address some of these nagging issues if it is to advance to the next stage of knowledge development. We then contemplate themes that might be thought of as recognized knowledge, or at least established assumptions, in order to develop foundations for future research and practice. Our discussion draws primarily on the chapters included in this volume, although we also incorporate some of the issues raised by authors and practitioners during the Center for Creative Leadership conference that was held in May 2003 to support the book's development, as well as our general knowledge of the field. Our goal is to foster knowledge development by raising the level at which research on work-life issues can begin and to help practitioners understand the hidden issues undergirding current debates and research directions.

POINTS OF CONTENTION

The themes we explore in this section can be viewed as enduring issues that reflect concerns central to knowledge development in the work-life field. Some of these issues are addressed directly by scholars and practitioners, in this volume as well as in other scholarship. However, many of these issues are visible only by looking across chapters that adopt different perspectives, pursue different goals, or employ different methodologies.

What Are the Boundaries Defining the Work-Life Field? What Is Not a Work-Life Issue?

The work-life field has grown enormously over the past ten years, as evidenced by the number of academic centers focusing on work-life issues both in the United States and abroad, the range of journals across disciplines in which work-life topics are addressed, and the growth of membership organizations, such as the U.S.-based Alliance of Work-Life Progress (AWLP), that cater to what are now called *work-life professionals*. The range of topics at any conference or in any volume on work-life or work-family issues is vast: the quality of life in today's families, women's labor force participation, the allocation of household and paid labor, the quality and accessibility of child care, flexible work options, stress, and so forth. Basically, any research that examines aspects of work or personal life can, and probably has been, approached as a work-life issue. Clearly, the work-life field is no longer focused only on the effects of employer-sponsored child care, despite the fact that this is where the field began, and the problems of employer support for child care have yet to be fully solved. What does the field gain and lose by extending its parameters? Is there a work-life field of study? If so, how might we characterize it today?

The field has certainly gained enormously by expanding its focus beyond formal employer policies aimed at helping workers with visible caregiving demands (often women with young children) keep their personal lives from interfering with their work performance. In terms of knowledge development, the literature now holds a wealth of information on how work conditions affect personal life and vice versa. This literature is increasingly nuanced, focusing on the specific conditions in the workplace and in the home that are most important in explaining the ability of workers to combine effectively work and personal life. Moreover, this expansion has resulted in knowledge that tackles work-life issues at different levels—societal, organizational, job, interpersonal, and individual. Thus, one of the primary contributions we think has come with this expansion is that scholars are bringing new conceptualizations to the study of work-life issues. Indeed, we purposively invited scholars who write primarily outside the work-life literature to contribute to this volume because we wanted to introduce other work-life scholars and practitioners to perspectives we have found useful in our own research. Thus, overall, we see the broadening of the field as an essential step in knowledge development.

However, the more broadly the work-life field is defined, the harder it is to distinguish its core. If the field is about everything, it runs the risk of being about nothing. Moreover, at the developmental conference for this volume, practitioners voiced their concern when the possibility was raised of redefining the field in terms of "quality of life" issues rather than work-family or work-life issues. They argued that initiatives would be even harder to sell to managers; bearing responsibility for workers' whole quality of life seemed a stretch for managers who have a hard enough time concluding that companies bear some responsibility for creating and solving caregiving problems. Participants at the conference also expressed concern that if viewed too broadly, corporations' efforts may become mere window-dressing as they promote any program in terms of bettering workers' lives. Thus, we think there is merit in continuing to define the core of the field in terms of a focus on the relationship between work and personal life, necessitating research and practice that cross, and reconstruct, the boundaries between them.

Accepting that it is this relationship that is central to the field suggests at least one parameter: Theory and research needs to encompass relationships across work and personal life boundaries or needs to be focused on their nexus. For example, studies of families relevant to work-life issues would consider how certain qualities of family life can be linked to workplace conditions or employment outcomes. It would not be enough, for example, to examine the distribution of household labor between husbands and wives; the link to workplace conditions or employment outcomes also would need to be made. And studies of work relevant to the work-life field should consider how the effects of particular occupational conditions extend into workers' personal lives, into communities, and into society—perhaps in addition to their effects on performance. Studies at the community and societal level would be relevant to the extent they incorporate both work and family conditions as explanatory, mediating, or moderating factors or as outcomes, for example, by investigating how the effect of government policy on family well-being depends on employer practices.

This cross-sphere parameter seems basic, and one may think we should include it in our discussion of established assumptions in the next main section of this chapter. However, studies seem still to focus predominately on one sphere or another, often shorting the other domain. Examples include cases when scholars focusing on work only measure those family influences that can detract from individuals' ability to fulfill work demands, or when scholars focusing on the family frame and measure work in terms of how it detracts from family life. Another example of scholars' tendency to preference one sphere over another is their use of limited, even single-item, measures to capture the "other" domain when they would not dream of employing such inadequate measures to capture concepts relevant to their own sphere of interest.

Several contributions in this volume serve as examples of the contributions scholars outside the work-life field can make to knowledge development when encouraged to look across the boundaries of work and personal life. For example, the chapter by Roberts, Desai, and Madsen (chap. 5) breaks new ground by bringing understandings of high-reliability organizations to the work-life field, highlighting both the benefits and costs of organizational policies that require workers to separate their personal life from their work life. Valcour and Hunter's chapter (chap. 4) brings established knowledge on technology to the work-life field, examining how variations in the implementation of technology can affect workers' ability to establish a high-quality personal life. Edmondson and Detert (chap. 18) shed new light on how work-life issues are articulated and acted on in the workplace, drawing on exciting developments in research on the organizational conditions that allow workers to speak up about sensitive issues. Moss, Salzman, and Tilly (chap. 7) bring theories of labor markets to bear on work-life issues, helping us understand how larger economic conditions shape the ability of workers to maintain work schedules that facilitate caregiving. At the individual level, Friede and Ryan (chap. 10) employ nuanced understandings of personality to reveal how core self-evaluations are likely to matter in explaining variation in how workers manage boundaries between work and personal life.

These chapters, and several others in the volume, contribute to the work-life field by offering new and developing frameworks useful for conceptualizing certain features of work or personal life and then tracing—in some cases empirically, in other cases conceptually—the implications of these features across boundaries. Thus, although the chapters in this volume do not reveal a consensus in answering the question "What isn't a work-life issue?" they demonstrate that there remains an enormous advantage to a sustained focus on the intersection of and reciprocal relationship between work and personal life. Employees neither show up at work as tabula rasa nor return home ready and able to simply turn off that day's events.

Do We Need a Consensus on How to Conceptualize and Measure the Relationship Between Work and Personal Life?

How the relationship between work and personal life is characterized is of ongoing and central concern in work-life scholarship. The chapters in this volume reveal little consensus in terms of the language and core concepts used to capture the relationship between work and personal life, invoking different images of that relationship. For example, Edwards and Rothbard (chap. 11) focus on work-life fit, arguing that one size does not fit all; this brings to mind a relativistic standard that a good fit for one person may be a matter of being more involved in work than family, but may be the opposite for another. Fletcher and Bailyn (chap. 9) argue that the goal of workplace interventions and social policy should be to promote work-life integration, which slackens the separation between work life and personal life allowing involvement and satisfaction with both. Poelmans (chap. 13) views the relationship between work and personal life as a set of interlocking decisions that can be understood by examining the negotiations among actors at home and at work. Several chapters conceptualize the relationship between work and personal life in terms of managing their boundaries, depicting a great deal of potential fluidity between the two. At the prebook conference, attendees even debated whether there should be a hyphen between work and life when talking about the work-life field.

Obviously, we did not force a consensus among the authors contributing to this volume—but should we have? The field's struggle with terminology is more than just that. It is a struggle to find the best conceptualization of the relationship between work and personal life. It is also an effort to develop a shared disciplinary history of core concepts. Our view is that researchers should employ the conceptualization that is best suited to furthering the knowledge they are seeking to develop. However, this assessment can be made, only when the theoretical underpinnings of the terms are taken into consideration. On the one hand, MacDermid's chapter (chap. 2) is a wonderful example of the importance of understanding the theoretical traditions out of which common conceptualizations have evolved. She explains how work-family conflict, and ultimately work-family enhancement, developed out of structural-functionalist traditions, especially out of role theories that differentiated intra- and interrole conflict. On the other hand, notions of work-family spillover derive from Melvin Kohn's (1977) classic research on how occupational structure shapes life off the job; the original focus was on the link between occupational structure and the quality of men's leisure activities.

In past research, scholars might choose to focus on *spillover* if seeking to identify the workplace conditions that matter for personal life, whereas they might focus on *conflict* or *enhancement* if approaching the relationship in terms of role theory. However, in practice scholars have tended to adopt the most commonly used terms, which currently seem to be notions of work-life *integration* and work-family *conflict*. Unlike many of the authors in this volume, researchers oftentimes do not explain the basis of their selection of terminology, and one wonders how much thought is typically given to choosing among different possible conceptualizations.

Scholars today can advance the work-life field by carefully considering, and explaining, the theoretical origins of the terminology they employ to depict the relationship between work and personal life. Kanter's (1977) research on the separate spheres of work and family helped to develop the notions of boundary management. The focus on work-life integration continues the development of role theory by moving beyond conflict and enhancement to the possibility of merging life roles, undercutting the tenets of structural-functionalism as put forth by Parsons (1982). Like work-family fit, work-life *balance* comes out of theories of role stress but is less relativistic.

The terms scholars adopt paint an image of the relationship between work and personal life, thus opening or closing possibilities for intervention. As MacDermid (chap. 2) points out, viewing work and family roles as primarily conflicting has helped to fuel workplace policies aimed at ensuring that workers' personal issues do not interfere with their work performance. Alternatively, by framing work-life issues in terms of support for the reconciliation of work and life responsibilities, Lewis and Haas (chap. 16) point out how Europeans have begun to carve out a larger role for government policy and intervention.

Although the terminology may vary, the chapters in this volume suggest growing agreement on certain basic qualities of the relationship between work and personal life. Many authors argue that the relationship between work and personal life is not a fixed point but a process that evolves with changing circumstances and choices and certainly over the life course. Moreover, any particular point in this process is not considered an end in itself; that is, it could be good or bad, depending on personal characteristics and preferences. For example, Edwards and Rothbard (chap. 11) make the point that configurations that fit at one stage of life may not fit at another stage. Similarly, Lee, MacDermid, Dohring, and Kossek (chap. 14) describe how overinvolvement in work may enhance well-being before parenthood but may detract from quality of life afterward. However, there remains little consensus, in terms of the outcomes that should be considered at different points in the process of combining work and personal life and whether and when the focus should extend beyond the individual to other "stakeholders" such as spouses, children, and communities.

Moreover, methods are not keeping up with changing conceptualizations. From a reading of the larger work-life literature, one is struck by the fact that despite problems of common-method variance and the recognition that work-life relationships may wax and wane over the life span, most work-life research is cross-sectional and employs self-report data gathered largely via surveys. Longitudinal research measuring change over time and qualitative research investigating the processes linking work and personal life are less well represented.

Kossek and Ozeki (1998) document how researchers vary in the measures they use to capture similar concepts, such as work-family conflict, and highlight the need for measures that differentiate among types of nonwork roles and work roles. It must also be remembered that traditional theories and their associated measures were developed mostly from research on two-parent, male-headed, Caucasian American households. This fact alone should be an incentive for scholars to think carefully about both our conceptualizations and our measures. Yet, current research often employs—with little explanation—the same measures to samples of dual-earners, single-parents, gays/lesbians, single parents, and so forth.

In sum, there is limited consensus on the terminology and even some of the variables used to capture the relationship between work and personal life, both in this volume and in the larger literature. This lack of consensus is fitting—if it is the result of scholars carefully choosing particular conceptualizations on the basis of theory and their goals for knowledge development. Regardless of the conceptualization adopted, there is growing consensus that the relationship between work and personal life is best conceived as a process rather than a static state and that scholars need to assess, rather than simply assume, how varying relationships between work and personal life (be they defined in terms of boundary management, work-life integration, work-life balancing, or work-family fit) are related to the well-being of individuals, families, communities, and societies.

How Do We Create Knowledge That Crosses Disciplinary Boundaries and Levels of Analysis? What Are the Methodological and Conceptual Challenges of Doing So?

The level of analysis at which research is targeted is important to clarify perhaps primarily because it subsequently may dictate the level of intervention. For example, research focused at the individual level offers the possibility of identifying practical skills for work-life management; workers can effect change themselves rather than depending solely on their employer. Research focused at the work group level can reveal ways to improve social dynamics, support, and norms. Research at the organizational level can uncover needed improvements in organizational policies, practices, and cultures. Societal-level research can foster changes to national culture and government policies that reduce the mismatch between personal demands and workplace realities.

Although research at each level has a great deal to offer in terms of advancing both theory and practice, we suspect that crosslevel research may be extremely valuable for advancing the field in new ways. With few exceptions, most of the chapters in this volume raise, and some address, multilevel questions. From an organizational perspective, for example, Moss, Salzman, and Tilly (chap. 7) raise concerns about the effects of changing opportunity structures on the ability of workers to manage caregiving. Friede and Ryan (chap. 10) consider how individuals' responses to organizational policies and practices depend on their core self-evaluations. The chapters (Lewis & Haas, chap. 16; Pitt-Catsouphes & Googins, chap 21) adopting cultural perspectives are concerned with the effects of social policy on both institutions and individuals. Yet, in each chapter it is clear which level is foreground and which levels are background; we had a fairly easy time placing most of the chapters in a particular section of the book. What, then, are the conceptual and methodological challenges that must be overcome to do crosslevel research—that is, research that not only gives equal weight to multiple levels of analysis but that examines their intersection?

The conceptual and methodological challenges of doing crosslevel research take at least two forms. One is conceptualizing and studying multiple levels within perspectives; for example, tackling work-life issues from multiple organizational levels—firm, job, worker—or from the individual, couple, or family levels. Several of the chapters in this volume do this. For example, Lambert and Waxman (chap. 6) look at how opportunities for balancing work and personal life are adopted in policy at the firm level, implemented in practice at the job level, and then experienced by workers at the individual level. Similarly, Poster (chap. 17) examines diversity policies at the corporate level, as implemented at specific work sites, and as experienced by workers. Poelmans (chap. 13) presents a framework for looking at work-life decisions at the individual, couple, and family levels. Thus, progress has been made in conceptualizing crosslevel examinations within a particular context. Moreover, given the historic focus of the field, it is not surprising that there are ample examples of research that cross boundaries. However, most of this research is at the individual level, examining the relationship between individuals' experiences at work and their experiences at home.

What is largely missing from the literature is research that looks across levels *and* boundaries, that examines, for example, how employer policies affect family life. The conceptual challenges to this type of research are daunting. Few individuals can master all the theories that might be needed to conceptualize adequately different contexts *and* levels. The methodological challenges are as great. Doing research across levels means gathering data at multiple levels. For example, asking workers about their employers' policies and practices creates data at the individual level. From individual level data we can learn whether individuals have access to employer-sponsored child care, for example, but we cannot learn how their employer structures access to care; the worker may be the exception rather than the rule. Gathering data at the organizational level requires a direct assessment of employers' policies and practices, perhaps through interviews with managers and reviews of corporate documents. Similarly, gathering data at the family level requires more than simply asking individuals about their own family experiences. Thus, often different methodologies are required to gain information at different levels of analysis—perhaps mapping community programs and parameters, surveys of workers, interviews with managers, observations of jobs, ethnographies of families, and so forth.

The work-life field has advanced in terms of crosslevel analysis within boundaries and in terms of within-level analysis across boundaries. Without research that crosses boundaries and levels of analysis, however, assessments of the relative efficacy of potential interventions to support workers' efforts to effectively manage work and family life will be based primarily on assumptions of unmeasured effects at other levels, tenable though they may be.

What Is Today's Business Case for Employer Support of Work-Life Integration? Do We Still Need to Make One?

The issue of how to make the business case for supporting workers' personal lives seems as old as the field. In fact, one could argue that work-life research began to gel as a field when it started to study the effects of formal work-family supports on employee performance, entering public discussion through the news media. Traditionally, making the business case has meant convincing corporate executives that work-life policies are a win-win solution for both employers and employees. Selling work-life issues to corporate executives still tends to take the form of showing how employer supports for work-life issues benefit the bottom line either by reducing employment costs (such as the costs of recruitment, absenteeism, and training) or by improving worker performance (such as workers' willingness to help their coworkers and to contribute new ideas). Such arguments have been useful for dissipating assumptions that supporting workers' personal lives is beyond the purview and responsibility of employers.

However, the field's quest to make a business case may have come at a cost. Many formal employer supports largely operate as work supports; that is, they were designed to help workers keep their personal responsibilities from interfering with their job involvement and performance. It is more difficult to sell supports that strengthen involvement in personal life, notably more active caregiving, in terms of enhancing worker performance and ultimately firm profitability. The more time you spend with your children, the less time you are likely to have for your work. Although several chapters in this volume make it clear that work hours are related only loosely to performance, the case for supports that facilitate involvement in family and community is on shaky ground if it is pitched primarily in terms of convincing employers that it will pay off on their bottom-line. As Kossek, Lobel, and Brown (in press) point out, if employers' only motivation for investing in work-life supports is for business reasons, then they may be prone to drop supports during economic downturns. Moreover, they argue that making a business case for work-life supports emphasizes a shareholder perspective that supports the interests of employers, as compared to a stakeholder perspective that also takes into account the interests of employees, their families, the community, and society.

Fortunately, progress has been made in changing the nature of the business case. Over the past two years, a group of non-profit organizations (e.g., the Families and Work Institute, the Work Life Leadership Council, Boston College Roundtable, the Alliance of Work Life Progress, and the Conference Board) have led an effort to fashion a new business case that shifts the focus from the individual to the family and community and that moves the debate from a narrow focus on short-term profitability to a longer-term strategy of investing in employee and community well-being.[1] Two chapters in this volume extend these developments further. Lewis and Haas (chap. 16) argue that the case the work-life field should be making is a societal one, that important social rights should not be left to the discretion of employers and instead should be ensured by government. Pitt-Catsouphes and Googins (chap. 21) redefine work-life issues in terms of social issues, reframing the business case in terms of corporate social responsibility; corporations would be encouraged, if not required, to demonstrate their support for work-family issues to shareholders and the citizenry.

We concur that treating work-life issues as social issues is an important direction for the field and that it is essential if all workers are to have access to the supports they need to develop fulfilling personal lives. Nonetheless, we think it is still important to make a business case. Laws cannot ensure that supervisors will be supportive of workers or that workers will be evaluated on outcomes rather than face time. Moreover, social policies aimed at changing workplace practices necessarily involve employers in their implementation; history has taught us that employers can come up with creative ways to undermine employment laws if they are so motivated. Thus, the prospects of workers accessing the supports they need—whether from government, their employer, or their community—are improved greatly when employers are willing participants in the transformation of work, in the life of the larger community, and in the implementation of social policy.

If there is a business case to be made, what should it look like today? Ruderman's chapter (chap. 22) points out how differences in the goals and approaches of academics and practitioners create barriers to research that furthers both theory and practice. Discussion at the prebook conference highlighted the disconnect between how academics and practitioners view the business case. Practitioners discussed their need for pragmatic information on how specific programs and policies have resulted in specific outcomes in specific industries—information they think would help them sell particular initiatives within their particular firms. Scholars talked about the business case in terms of explaining variance in outcomes that have implications for performance. They also discussed the limitations of case study research for building more generalizable knowledge, preferring representative samples that can be generalized across employers rather than firm- or industry-specific ones.

As Ruderman points out, practitioners tend to pay the closest attention to individual-level analyses that offer ways that employers might ease workers' stress or increase supervisors' supportiveness. By contrast, less attention is given to ideas of how to restructure fundamentally the way firms conduct business, design jobs, implement new technologies, or distribute benefits. It is not that the practitioners are uninterested in these ideas, but they do not readily see how they can make a case for such sweeping changes in their settings. This is probably the reality. Making a business case for supports for work-life integration will only get us so far in transforming the workplace, let alone the home.

A key challenge for the field, then, is to craft a new business case that is consistent with a broader social agenda that spans the boundaries of work and personal life, one that lays the foundation for employers' willing involvement in implementing this agenda. A case that focuses primarily on maximizing corporate profits is likely to be at odds with a progressive social agenda, such as one that incorporates expanded access to paid leave and well-designed reduced-hour jobs.

An underlying issue in building a new business case is the extent to which firms value workers and see their performance as essential to firm profitability. Work-life policies need to be seen as a bundle with other human resource (HR) strategies that invest in workers (Perry-Smith & Blum, 2000). If they are viewed as such, then firms are more likely to invest in their workforce—including supports for their personal life (Osterman, 1995). Moreover, research within firms demonstrates that workers in jobs deemed valuable to company success are better compensated and supported and have greater access to work-life supports (Konrad & Mangel, 2000). Thus, a first step in making a new business case is to reframe the logic for work-life supports. Instead of beginning articles with information on how the demographics of the workforce have changed, the field might also supply information on the extent to which firms gain a competitive advantage when they pursue profits primarily through quality enhancement rather than cost containment, discussing the ways in which workers—men and women—add value to service and production.

Work-life scholars and practitioners could make a unique contribution to building this new business case by explicating the contributions lower-level workers can make to firm success when their jobs are designed to allow them to do so. The chapters by Valcour and Hunter (chap. 4), Moss, Salzman, and Tilly (chap. 7), and Lambert and Waxman (chap. 6) highlight how the same work can be accomplished through jobs that allow workers to make unique and important contributions, rather than rendering their labor easily replaceable. Part of making the case of the importance of workers' contributions to firm success would be to demonstrate how lower-level workers are on the front lines of customer service and technological innovation, and to point out the competitive advantage firms reap when they design jobs that allow these workers to add value to their product or service. Thus, a first step in making a new business case would be to focus on how workers—at all levels—are key to firm performance and profitability. Litchfield, Swanberg, and Sigworth's (2004) recent report that identifies corporations "best practices" for supporting lower-wage workers begins with a discussion of the value of lower-wage employees to corporations, providing an excellent example of how to construct a more inclusive business case.

The next step in creating a business case that lays the foundation for a broader social agenda would be to address problems in the implementation of current workplace and social policies. Were the United States to expand rights for workers, employers would play a key role in implementing any rights that are linked to employment status. Are they prepared to distribute these rights? The U.S. experience with the Family and Medical Leave Act (FMLA) suggests not. According to the most complete study of the FMLA since its adoption (U.S. Department of Labor, 1995), only 10.8% of private-sector workplaces are even covered by the FMLA; altogether, 55% of workers meet the eligibility requirements outlined by the act. Workers' "right" to parental leave is limited by employment factors that have little to do with workers' need for time at home: specifically, employer size ($\geq$ 50 employees), hours worked (1,250 in past 12 months), and length of service with current employer ($\geq$ 1 year). Moreover, as Lambert and Waxman (chap. 6) point out, workers in lower-level jobs often cannot access sick or vacation time or employer-sponsored health insurance. Thus, the second step in a new business case would be to focus on barriers to distributing supports that are available in many workplaces today, at least on the books. This may require changing employment laws to limit the ability of employers to define access to benefits in terms of employment status (temporary, nonstandard, part-time) or to identify barriers to access created by job design. Increasing the distribution of supports currently available would help to lay a foundation for the implementation of new social policies that expand the rights of workers to supports for work-life integration.

Recognizing the value of workers to firm performance and tackling issues in the distribution of work-life supports should facilitate greatly the next step, which is to explicate the need to support workers' personal life per se. In this step, the challenge is to broaden the case to encompass family supports as well as work supports, and changes in corporate culture as well as in formal policy. One might argue that the field has already made the case to employers that they benefit when they attend to workers' personal lives; but, as argued before, this case has resulted in a focus on supports that allow workers to continue their (over)involvement in work. The key now is to demonstrate how supports for personal life are part of an enlightened, long-term corporate self-interest or, preferably, to move the discussion beyond self-interest toward notions of corporate social responsibility as suggested in the chapter by Pitt-Catsouphes and Googins (chap. 21). Perhaps the biggest challenge for the field is to change the very nature of the business case, to enable arguments for supporting workers' personal life to be put forth without selling them in terms of enhancing firm profitability.

The final step in making a new business case is to assess more systematically the merits and limitations of different avenues for intervention. Practitioners are clear that one size does not fit all; both resources and good will are wasted when initiatives fall short of intended consequences. Practitioners' preferences for knowledge that is industry-focused might be interpreted as a quest for in-depth information on the conditions under which certain initiatives have their intended effects. Studies that examine the effects of specific interventions using rigorous experimental methods are needed to rule out possible competing explanations for findings that support the efficacy of work-life supports; improved workplaces may be better in terms of not only their work-life policies but also their culture and their ability to attract and retain good employees (Kossek, in press).

The field has to take responsibility for more than simply documenting the carnage when workers do not have the supports they need to effectively manage work and personal responsibilities. Part of making the business case for work-life supports is demonstrating that business can make a difference—and how to make the difference—within the constraints and opportunities that operate in today's global economy. Clearly, partnerships between scholars and practitioners are needed in order to advance this agenda. Right now, it has been our experience that few employers systematically collect data to quantitatively or qualitatively evaluate the effectiveness of their work-life policies. This could involve collecting baseline data before an initiative is introduced and then follow-up data from several perspectives to capture the effects on work, workers, and their families. Administrative data, personnel records, bio-data, and productivity measures may all be essential.

In sum, today's business case for work-life efforts should lay the foundation for a broader social agenda aimed at improving the quality of life for workers and their families. The new case cannot be completely made on the basis that supports for workers' personal life always pay off with regard to the bottom line. Sometimes this may not be true, especially in the short run. Although it is important to identify the circumstances under which supports for work-life integration are a win-win solution for employees and employers, the field must own up to the possibility that supports may be needed even though they do not contribute to, and may even detract from, firms' profitability. The field can help change the nature of the case, and the debate, by keeping the focus on the reasons for investing in workers more generally, by explaining how investment in workers today necessitates attention to their personal lives, and by generating pragmatic information on how businesses can deliver needed supports to workers. Moreover, tackling problems in the distribution of supports already available in many workplaces has the potential to put into place the mechanisms needed for distributing new supports to workers.

ESTABLISHED ASSUMPTIONS

The themes we identify in this section are ones that seem to have become part of the fabric of social inquiry into work-life issues, at least as reflected in this volume. Certain approaches to knowledge development are common across the chapters, even if not articulated formally by the authors. Recognizing the often unspoken rules of the work-life "trade" seems useful for identifying the parameters of the field and may propel scholars toward an active consideration of the kinds of approaches the field may be taking for granted. Moreover, articulating what may be newly developing standards for work-life research may prove useful clues for those outside the field who wish to contribute to the work-life literature.

Research Should Examine the Practical Implementation of Work-Life Policies and Programs

One theme that cuts across chapters, perspectives, and levels of analysis is the importance of looking closely at the implementation of work-life policies and other practices aimed at improving the ability of workers to manage work and personal responsibilities. At the international level, for example, Poster's chapter (chap. 17) focuses on how the implementation of the same diversity policy in the same company varies between work sites in different countries, depending on local workplace customs and the ways in which discourses around gender and ethnicity are constructed in that society. Similarly, Lewis and Haas (chap. 16) observe how the potential of social policies to support workers' ability to balance work and family life depends on gender differentials in wages and on the extent to which interpersonal relationships in the family continue to define family work as women's work. They describe in depth what they call "the implementation problem"—that is, the disconnect between social policy intentions and workplace realities.

At the organizational level, Valcour and Hunter (chap. 4) offer a contextualized approach to technology. They consider how the relationship between technological change and work-life integration depends on how new technologies are implemented in particular organizational, individual, and family contexts. The same technology can expand or constrict workers' ability to access flexibility, for example, depending on how it is implemented by the organization and by workers in their own lives. Lambert and Waxman (chap. 6) reveal how opportunities available to all workers as a matter of employer policy are, in practice, often implemented unevenly across organizational levels and jobs.

At the individual level of analysis, chapters highlight how understanding the effects of workplace conditions necessitates a close examination of variations in how individuals enact and experience formal job structures and policies. Notably, Kossek, Lautsch, and Eaton (chap. 12) discuss how individuals vary in their use of flexible work options, creating different challenges for managing personal responsibilities. They argue, for example, that flexibility may actually increase work hours among individuals who allow porous boundaries between work and personal life, and that control over how the job is conducted is more strongly related to employee well being than use of or access to flexibility. Friede and Ryan (chap. 10) specify core dimensions of personality that play a role in how individuals select, appraise, and cope with job stress shaping the way that formal job structures and policies are implemented in everyday life. Giga and Cooper (chap. 19) explain how the strength of a person's psychological contract with an employer depends on what the company and its representatives actually do, rather than what they say they will do.

In sum, the field no longer limits itself to examinations of what policies and programs companies have adopted. It is now common for researchers to look beyond what organizations *say* they do to examine what organizations actually do to support workers' efforts to meet work and personal demands. Moreover, fuller consideration now is given to understanding how individual qualities and interpersonal relationships temper or exacerbate problems in the implementation of workplace supports. Further crosslevel research that traces the relationships among organizational policy, employer practice, and ultimately worker experience, is needed if we are to identify the conditions under which employers' policies and practices enhance the ability of workers to combine effectively work and personal life.

Research Should Look Beyond Formal Work-Life Policies

Much of the early organizational research on work-life issues concentrated on workers' access to and use of formal organizational supports, such as employer supports for child care, flextime programs, and parental leave policies. Sutton and Noe's chapter (chap. 8) makes clear the importance of continuing to investigate how formal supports are implemented by employers and used by employees. Although formal policies can make it easier for workers to remain productive while fulfilling caregiving responsibilities, this is not always the case. Many so-called work-life policies still do a better job of supporting work life than personal life. And as Pitt-Catsouphes and Googins (chap. 21) point out, although the proportion of firms reporting formal work-life initiatives has increased over the past two decades, they remain only a small minority. Fortunately, perhaps, research has revealed that other aspects of the workplace may be as, or more, important than formal policies in promoting workers' efforts at balancing work and personal life.

The chapters in this book reflect a growing consensus that researchers and practitioners must look beyond formal organizational policies to identify the key conditions of work that shape the ways in which workers combine work and personal life. For example, Hopkins' chapter (chap. 20) focuses on the central role supervisors play in setting the tone for how personal issues are dealt with in the workplace, in linking workers to available services and supports, and for directly intervening to support workers through difficult times. Her work breaks new ground by identifying the behaviors that characterize supervisors whom workers deem supportive. Moss, Salzman, and Tilly (chap. 7) consider how workers' access to work hours that fit family routines can be improved or diminished through industry restructuring. Fletcher and Bailyn (chap. 9) examine how particular aspects of job design, such as how interdependencies among workers are handled, shape the extent to which professionals are able to avoid overwork. Edmondson and Detert (chap. 18) analyze how the interpersonal climate in a workplace sends messages to workers concerning the extent to which it is safe to speak up about work-life issues.

An ongoing challenge for the field is to bring to the foreground a broad set of employment conditions for examination and to distinguish which of these either have the biggest effect on or can be managed most effectively to improve workers' prospects of balancing work with personal life. Formal work-life policies need to be one, but cannot be the only, component of a research agenda aimed at enhancing employer responsiveness.

More Effective Collaboration Between Researchers and Practitioners Is Needed

A recurring theme both in the book and at the prebook conference is that more work needs to be done to translate the lessons from work-life research into work-life practice. There is genuine interest on the part of many researchers in this volume to help identify the stages needed to move from research to practice. Although working with HR professionals continues to be key to advancing the field, scholars and practitioners note the need to widen the audience beyond HR—to go deeper into the organization. On the one hand, authors believe that practitioners could use help in understanding and selling more structural changes in the workplace and in countering arguments about the nature of our business. On the other hand, practitioners indicate that academics need to be more attuned to pragmatic business realities. As noted earlier, practitioners and academics often define the "business case" very differently.

Ruderman (chap. 22) argues that crosslevel research holds promise because problems with work-life integration can be traced from the societal level down to the worker level. For example, Ruderman notes that when there are strong situations due to job design or culture, it makes little sense for research to focus on individual differences or propensities. However under more flexible situations researchers and practitioners can help individuals take advantage of available choices. Collaboration between scholars and practitioners is most likely to take place when each has something to gain. Intervention research, or other types of change-oriented work-life studies, are likely to hold such a common ground; researchers are able to employ rigorous research methods to test theory and practitioners are able to get hard data on the effects of specific changes in their workplace.

Expand Definitions and Measures of Good Performance and Success

As noted in several chapters throughout the volume, notions of what makes for a good performer and ultimately a successful worker have been based on traditional models that no longer fit the realities or preferences of many of today's workers—male or female. From an organizational perspective, Fletcher and Bailyn (chap. 9) explain how assessments of worker performance are often based on face time, which helps to create a long-hours culture among technical and professional workers. They advocate an increased focus on neglected aspects of performance essential to the work performed in today's organizations, such as integrative functions vital to team work, and, as much as possible, basing performance appraisals on measurable results. Cleveland's chapter (chap. 15) focuses squarely on new definitions of performance that recognize the permeability of boundaries between work and family, calling for definitions of performance that incorporate the perspectives of multiple stakeholders, including spouses, partners, and children.

Chapters adopting individual perspectives on work-life issues are especially helpful in explaining why in today's world individual success should not be defined in terms of traditional notions of advancement up an organizational hierarchy. Lee, MacDermid, Dohring, and Kossek (chap. 14), for example, develop a framework of how parenthood often redefines professionals' orientation toward work, leading those individuals to base their assessments of success as much on their development as a parent as on their development as a professional.

The chapter by Pitt-Catsouphes and Googins (chap. 21) adopts a crosscultural perspective to consider how firms can be held more accountable for their responsiveness to work-life issues, advocating that firms' success at addressing these issues be systematically examined and communicated to investors and the public. Lewis and Haas (chap. 16) argue that we must look at the performance of societies, assessing the extent to which they foster supportive employer practices and deliver supports directly to workers and their families.

In sum, the work-life field is adopting new and expanded definitions of performance and success that take into consideration workers' preferences across the life course and their desire to contribute to their work group, to their community, and to society. Moreover, the field is also devising ways to incorporate responsiveness to work-life issues into definitions and measures of corporate and societal performance and success. Careful conceptual work is needed to specify which aspects of performance and success are most likely to show the effects of different types of work-life supports, be they formal or informal. Kossek, Lautsch, and Eaton (chap. 12) report that workers' use of formal flextime options is positively related to supervisors' appraisals of performance, suggesting that the best workers pay no cost for using formal supports (if this finding is the result of supervisor bias limiting those using formal supports) or that employers pay little cost for allowing workers this access (if worker performance is actually better). They also find that women managers and professionals are more likely to blend boundaries and that individuals who blend rather than segment work roles are more likely to receive lower ratings. More research is needed to distinguish the circumstances under which supports for work and personal life have different costs and benefits for workers and firms.

Attention to Gender Is Critical (Still)

The chapters in this book reflect a growing consensus that men, as well as women, face significant challenges in combining work with personal life, especially when it involves caregiving responsibilities. Work-life issues are no longer considered solely a women's issue. However, the consensus that both men and women face difficulties balancing work and family responsibilities does not mean that gender is no longer relevant to the field. To the contrary, the chapters in this volume make clear that gender issues must be addressed if we are to improve men's and women's prospects for effectively combining work and personal life.

The research in this volume, and elsewhere, demonstrates how inequalities in the workplace and in the home create very different circumstances for men and women and thus present men and women with different challenges for managing work and personal life. For example, Cleveland (chap. 15) points out that as long as definitions of good performance focus on behaviors and skills that favor men, men will be propelled toward overinvolvement in work and women will be discouraged from full participation. Fletcher and Bailyn (chap. 9) argue that redesigning jobs to promote work-life integration necessitates tackling gender disparities in the types of skills that are valued and in the ways in which performance is assessed. Indeed, in the perspective they put forth, issues of job design are inextricable from those of gender disparities.

Lewis and Haas (chap. 16) consider gender issues at the societal level, noting how countries vary in the extent to which workers' rights to work-life supports are mediated by employer discretion and thus vary in the extent to which they reinforce rather than reduce, gender inequality in the workplace and in the home. Poster (chap. 17) argues that understanding a country's discourse of gender and ethnicity is critical to understanding cultural differences in the implementation of employer diversity policies.

In sum, regardless of the extent to which gender equity is a stated goal, there seems to be substantial consensus that the field must continue to address issues of gender in both research and practice. Differences and similarities in the life courses and life circumstances of men and women need to be investigated and acknowledged in order to develop an understanding of the factors that shape the ways in which individuals construct their work and personal lives, and in order to develop interventions that hold the potential of helping both men and women succeed as workers, partners, parents, and citizens.

CONCLUSION

The themes discussed in this chapter highlight a number of the advances in the work-life field that have taken place over the decade since Zedeck's book *Work, Families, and Organizations* (1992) was published. Scholars have continued to approach work-life issues from a broad set of theories and frameworks, bringing individual, organizational, social, and cultural perspectives to bear on the work-life nexus. The field poses and addresses increasingly nuanced questions. Clearly, the field has moved beyond a narrow focus on traditional roles in traditional families to pursue a broader range of issues and populations. Current conceptualizations of the relationship between work and personal life allow for the possibility that the two can be mutually beneficial rather than at odds.

The themes of divergence highlight some of the challenges the field must tackle if we are to continue to develop knowledge in useful ways over the next decade. Methods have not quite kept up with theoretical advances. Like much research in other fields, common-method variance and cross-sectional designs limit our ability to trace relationships across levels of analysis and to tease out causal pathways. Longitudinal studies are required to investigate the processes linking work and personal life, multimethod studies to trace relationships across levels of analysis, and intervention research to build causal knowledge that rules out competing explanations. Partnerships between scholars and practitioners are a must if the rigor of workplace-based research in particular is to be enhanced and if findings are to be of practical use.

What remains as true today as a decade ago is the importance of recognizing that *work* is central to understanding work-life issues. The chapters of this book help direct attention to the ways in which conditions of employment are critical to worker and family well-being, revealing multifaceted and reciprocal relationships. By building on the contributions in this book, and on the work of other scholars for whom work is of central concern, 10 years from now we should be in the position to celebrate rather than lament the field's attention to the work side of work-life.

NOTES

1. Ellen Galinsky, personal communication, May 29, 2004.

REFERENCES

Kanter, R. (1977). *Work and family in the United States: A critical review and agenda for research and policy.* New York: Russell Sage Foundation.

Kohn, M. (1977). *Class and conformity: A study in values.* 2nd ed. Chicago: University of Chicago Press.

Konrad, A., & Mangel, R. (2000). The impact of work-life programs on firm productivity. *Strategic Management Journal, 21,* 1225–1237.

Kossek, E. E. (in press). Workplace policies and practices to support work and families: Gaps in implementation and linkages to individual and organizational effectiveness. In S. Bianchi, L. Casper, & R. King (Eds.), *Workforce/workplace mismatch? Work, family, health, and well-being.* Mahwah, NJ: Erlbaum.

Kossek, E. E., Lobel, S., & Brown, J. (in press). Human resource strategies to manage work force diversity: Examining "the business case." In A. M. Conrad, P. Prasad, & J. K. Pringle (Eds.), *Handbook of workplace diversity.* Thousand Oaks, CA: Sage.

Kossek, E. E., & Ozeki, C. (1998). Work-family conflict, policies, and the job-life satisfaction relationship: A review and directions for organizational behavior/human resources research. *Journal of Applied Psychology, 83,* 139–149.

Litchfield, L., Swanberg, J. & Sigworth, C. (2004). Increasing the visibility of the invisible workforce: Model programs and policies for hourly and lower wage employees. Report 31 of the Boston College Center for Work & Family, Carroll School of Management, Boston College.

Osterman, P. (1995). Work/family programs and the employment relationship. *Administrative Science Quarterly, 40,* 681–700.

Parsons, T. (1982). *On institutions and social evolution: Selected writings.* Chicago: University of Chicago Press.

Perry-Smith, J. E., & Blum, T. C. (2000). Work-family human resource bundles and perceived organizational performance. *Academy of Management Journal, 43*(6), 1107–1117.

U.S. Department of Labor. (1995). *A workable balance: Report to Congress on family and medical leave policies.* Washington, DC: Commission on Leave (Christopher Dodd, chairman).

Zedeck, S. (1992). *Work, families, and organizations.* San Francisco: Jossey-Bass.

Author Index

T

U

V

Subject Index

Page references followed by b indicate boxed material.
Page references followed by f indicate a figure.
Page references followed by t indicate a table.